Frommer's®

Sweden

6th Edition

by Darwin Porter & Danforth Prince

Here's what the critics say about Frommer's:

"Amazingly easy to use. Very portable, very complete."
—**BOOKLIST**

"Detailed, accurate, and easy-to-read information
for all price ranges."
—**GLAMOUR MAGAZINE**

"Hotel information is close to encyclopedic."
—**DES MOINES SUNDAY REGISTER**

"Frommer's Guides have a way of giving you a real feel
for a place."
—**KNIGHT RIDDER NEWSPAPERS**

WILEY

Wiley Publishing, Inc.

Published by:

WILEY PUBLISHING, INC.

111 River St.
Hoboken, NJ 07030-5774

ISBN 978-0-470-43214-3

Editor: Emil J. Ross
Production Editor: Heather Wilcox
Cartographer: Andrew Dolan
Photo Editor: Richard Fox
Production by Wiley Indianapolis Composition Services

Front cover photo: Boat huts in Smögen, on the Bohuslän Coast
Back cover photo: Reindeer in Abisko National Park, Swedish Lapland

For information on our other products and services or to obtain technical support, please contact our Customer Care Department within the U.S. at 877/762-2974, outside the U.S. at 317/572-3993 or fax 317/572-4002.

Wiley also publishes its books in a variety of electronic formats. Some content that appears in print may not be available in electronic formats.

Manufactured in the United States of America

5 4 3 2 1

CONTENTS

4 SUGGESTED SWEDEN ITINERARIES 57

5 SETTLING INTO STOCKHOLM 68

6 DISCOVERING STOCKHOLM 114

7 GOTHENBURG & BEYOND 166

8 SKÅNE (INCLUDING HELSINGBORG & MALMÖ) 211

vi

SWEDEN

CONTENTS

LIST OF MAPS

AN INVITATION TO THE READER

In researching this book, we discovered many wonderful places—hotels, restaurants, shops, and more. We're sure you'll find others. Please tell us about them, so we can share the information with your fellow travelers in upcoming editions. If you were disappointed with a recommendation, we'd love to know that, too. Please write to:

Frommer's Sweden, 6th Edition
Wiley Publishing, Inc. • 111 River St. • Hoboken, NJ 07030-5774

AN ADDITIONAL NOTE

Please be advised that travel information is subject to change at any time—and this is especially true of prices. We therefore suggest that you write or call ahead for confirmation when making your travel plans. The authors, editors, and publisher cannot be held responsible for the experiences of readers while traveling. Your safety is important to us, however, so we encourage you to stay alert and be aware of your surroundings. Keep a close eye on cameras, purses, and wallets, all favorite targets of thieves and pickpockets.

ABOUT THE AUTHORS

As a team of veteran travel writers, **Darwin Porter** and **Danforth Prince** have produced titles for Frommer's including guides to Italy, France, the Caribbean, England, and Germany. A film critic, columnist, and broadcaster, Porter is also a Hollywood biographer. His recent releases include *Brando Unzipped,* documenting the private life of Marlon Brando, and *Jacko: His Rise and Fall,* the first complete biography ever written on the tumultuous life of Michael Jackson. Prince was formerly employed by the Paris bureau of the *New York Times* and is today the president of Blood Moon Productions and other media-related firms. Porter and Prince's latest non-travel-related venture, jointly co-authored and published in 2008 by Blood Moon, is *Hollywood Babylon—It's Back!,* which one critic described as "the hottest compilation of intergenerational scandal in the history of Hollywood."

FROMMER'S STAR RATINGS, ICONS & ABBREVIATIONS

Every hotel, restaurant, and attraction listing in this guide has been ranked for quality, value, service, amenities, and special features using a **star-rating system.** In country, state, and regional guides, we also rate towns and regions to help you narrow down your choices and budget your time accordingly. Hotels and restaurants are rated on a scale of zero (recommended) to three stars (exceptional). Attractions, shopping, nightlife, towns, and regions are rated according to the following scale: zero stars (recommended), one star (highly recommended), two stars (very highly recommended), and three stars (must-see).

In addition to the star-rating system, we also use **seven feature icons** that point you to the great deals, in-the-know advice, and unique experiences that separate travelers from tourists. Throughout the book, look for:

Finds	Special finds—those places only insiders know about
Fun Facts	Fun facts—details that make travelers more informed and their trips more fun
Kids	Best bets for kids and advice for the whole family
Moments	Special moments—those experiences that memories are made of
Overrated	Places or experiences not worth your time or money
Tips	Insider tips—great ways to save time and money
Value	Great values—where to get the best deals

The following **abbreviations** are used for credit cards:

AE	American Express	DISC	Discover	V	Visa
DC	Diners Club	MC	MasterCard		

FROMMERS.COM

Now that you have this guidebook to help you plan a great trip, visit our website at **www. frommers.com** for additional travel information on more than 4,000 destinations. We update features regularly to give you instant access to the most current trip-planning information available. At Frommers.com, you'll find scoops on the best airfares, lodging rates, and car rental bargains. You can even book your travel online through our reliable travel booking partners. Other popular features include:

- Online updates to our most popular guidebooks
- Vacation sweepstakes and contest giveaways
- Newsletters highlighting the hottest travel trends
- Podcasts, interactive maps, and up-to-the-minute events listings
- Opinionated blog entries by Arthur Frommer himself
- Online travel message boards with featured travel discussions

What's New in Sweden

Now that it's linked by the Øresund Bridge with Denmark, Sweden is becoming more closely allied with the Continent. It's a trend that began when it entered the European Union and one that has continued aggressively postmillennium. Stockholm in particular no longer seems isolated in the remote north—it's become a cosmopolitan city in its own right.

Immigrants are also changing the face of Sweden. Interspersed among all those light-skinned blond and blonde locals are newly arrived visitors from such places as Turkey, Eastern Europe, and even the Sahara. Immigrants are spreading out and settling not just in Stockholm and Gothenburg but also in some of the country's smaller villages and towns.

As it moves deeper into the millennium, Sweden still clings to its krona as a mode of currency, although more and more commercial concerns are lobbying for Sweden to fall under the euro umbrella. Who knows what results will be revealed whenever the currency issue is put to a vote again?

STOCKHOLM Hotels Reopening after 2 years of a major restoration, **Scandic Anglais,** Humlegardsgatan 23 (© 08/517-340-11; www.scandichotels.com), has been given a new lease on life. The highlight of the hotel is now the seventh-floor terrace bar overlooking a panoramic view of Stockholm, which is especially dramatic at night. Rooms are decorated in warm earth tones and wood-laminated floors have been installed throughout.

The top furniture designers of Scandinavia, both past and living today, are represented in the decor of the **Clarion Hotel Sign,** Östra Järnvägsgatan 35 (© 08/676-98-00), a chic bastion of taste. Bedrooms are showcases—yet also imbued with grand comfort—and on the eighth floor is one of the finest spas in the city.

Pärlan, Skepparegatan 27 (© 08/663-70-70), in the Östermalm district, may have been a girls' school in the 1950s, but now it's a boutique hotel on the second floor of a restored building that dates from the 19th century. Furnishings are a bit funky, a mishmash of antiques or flea-market specials, and bedrooms are furnished in a homelike and comfortable way.

Just 5 minutes from the Central Station, the **Hilton Hotel Slussen,** Guldgränd 8 (© 08/517-353-00), has many luxurious touches in spite of the fact that it was built over a traffic tunnel. On the island of Södermalm, it is easily accessible from the center of Stockholm. Most of the rooms are spacious, and all of them are attractively and comfortably furnished.

Restaurants Media attention has focused on the opening of **Mathias Dahlgren,** in the Grand Hotel at Södra Blasieholmshammen 8 (© 08/679-35-84). Two different dining experiences await you here, in the formal dining room or at the bar. Chef Dahlgren has on several occasions been named chef of the year in Sweden. His six-course tasting menu is perhaps the finest in Stockholm.

A famed New York restaurant, Aquavit, has opened **Aquavit Raw Bar & Grill** in the Clarion Hotel Sign, at Östra Järnvägsgatan 35 (© **08/676-98-50**), near the Central Station. Its Swedish fare is refined and made with some of the finest of regional produce. The raw bar is the best in town, and you can order a platter of "seven tastes" in seafood.

A hip new address for dining is **East Restaurant & Bar,** Stureplan 13 (© **08/611-49-59**), with its Asian-inspired menu and sophisticated young clientele. Recipes from all over Asia are used in the imaginative dishes prepared with quality ingredients and robust flavors.

Inferno, Drottninggatan 85 (© **08/20-16-50**), is a bar, restaurant, and club patronized by an artsy crowd. Many of the recipes are modern versions of those served at the time of August Strindberg, the writer, who used to live in this restored building. The place is patronized by a hip scene of actors and artists, who stay late at night listening to some of the best DJs in the city.

After Dark Fashionistas go to **Laroy,** Biblioteksgatan 23 (© **08/545-076-50**), in the Arnoldshuset. A skilled DJ sets the mood for the young and beautiful who show up here to be entertained until 3am. A comparable club on the hot list is the **White Room,** Jakobsbergsgatanm 29 (© **08/545-076-00**), with its all-white interior and theatrical lighting. In the early morning hours, this club becomes the wildest party in Stockholm.

GOTHENBURG Hotels In 2008, **Hotel Flora,** Grönsakstorget 2 (© **031/13-86-16**), burst onto the scene and became one of the most desirable addresses in town, with a modern design and much comfort. The staff is friendly and welcoming, and the entertainment street of Avenyn lies only a stone's throw away.

Restaurants One of the best restaurants in Sweden has opened, and it's unpretentiously called the **Basement Restaurant &** **Bar,** at Gotabergsgatan 28 (© **031/28-27-29**). The continental cuisine is creative and wonderfully delicate, the ingredients market fresh. The staff serves the best tasting menu in Gothenburg, and it is changed daily.

HELSINGBORG The old Grand, the finest hotel in the city, is now the **Clarion Hotel Grand,** Stortorget 8–12 (© **042/38-04-00**), following a recent takeover by the multinational chain. The new managers have made many improvements in their update of this classic. The golden oldie is still old, but not so creaky anymore.

A chain has also taken over management of another classic, now called the **Best Western Hotel Helsingborg,** Stortorget 20 (© **800/780-7234** or 042/37-18-00). It still has much of its antique appeal, though modern amenities have been installed and rooms updated.

MALMÖ Best Western has also taken over one of the top hotels of Sweden's "third city." The **Best Western Mäster Johan Hotel,** Mäster Johansgatan 13 (© **800/780-7234** or 040/664-64-00), still remains our favorite hotel. It still has the same beautifully furnished rooms, although it seems more modern and up to date following a recent renovation.

In an expansive mood, Best Western has bought Noble House, another Malmö landmark. It is now the **Best Western Noble House,** Gustav Adolfs Torg 47 (© **800/780-7234** or 040/664-30-00). Recent improvements and refurbishing have kept it at the top of the list of the best hotels in Malmö.

LUND In this university city, **Oskar,** Bytaregatan 3 (© **046/18-80-85**), is expensive but worth it for those who want the intimacy of a small boutique hotel. It was created by restoring two town houses from the 19th century in the heart of Lund. A sophisticated sense of Scandinavian design prevails here.

KALMAR In this historic port city in Eastern Sweden, the Best Western chain has continued its takeover of Swedish hotels. The **Best Western Kalmarsund Hotell,** Fiskaregatan 5 (© **800/780-7234** or 0480/ 48-03-80), has been subtly improved and refurbished; it continues to offer affordably priced and quite decent rooms that are standard rather than exciting.

KARLSTAD In the heart of Värmland, the **Clarion Hotel Plaza,** Västra Torggatan 2 (© **054/10-02-00**), is now running the former Radisson SAS Plaza Hotel, one of the finest of the province's hotels. Modern comforts and chain-hotel efficiency rule today, and the dining facilities, including the new Plaza Restaurant, have been considerably upgraded.

The Best of Sweden

Sweden presents visitors with an embarrassment of riches, everything from sophisticated cities to medieval towns to Europe's last untamed wilderness. To help you decide how best to spend your time in Sweden, we've compiled a list of our favorite experiences and discoveries. In the following pages, you'll find the kind of candid advice we'd give our close friends.

1 THE BEST TRAVEL EXPERIENCES

- **Shopping in the "Kingdom of Crystal":** Many visitors come to Sweden just to shop for glass. In the "Kingdom of Crystal," which stretches some 112km (70 miles) between the port city of Kalmar and the town of Växjö in Småland province, some of the world's most prestigious glassmakers, including Kosta Boda and Orrefors, showcase their wares. At least 16 major glassworks welcome visitors to this area and offer cut-rate discounts in the form of "seconds"— goods containing flaws hardly noticeable except to the most carefully trained eye. Visitors can see glass being blown and crystal being etched by the land's most skilled craftspeople. See section 2, "Växjö," in chapter 9.
- **Viewing the Awe-Inspiring Northern Lights:** In the darkest of winter in the north of Sweden (called Lapland or Norrbotten), you can view the shimmering phenomenon of the northern lights on many clear nights, usually from early evening until around midnight. The sun and solar winds create this amazing light show when electrons from the sun collide with atmospheric atoms and molecules. See chapter 13.
- **Touring the Land of the Midnight Sun:** Above the Arctic Circle, where the summer sun never dips below the horizon, you have endless hours to enjoy the beauty of the region and the activities that go with it—from hiking to whitewater rafting. After shopping for distinctive wooden and silver handicrafts, you can dine on filet of reindeer served with cloudberries. You can even pan for gold with real-life pioneers in Lannavaara, or climb rocks and glaciers in Sarek's National Park. See chapter 13.

2 THE BEST ACTIVE VACATIONS

- **Fishing:** Sweden offers some of the world's best fishing for fresh- and saltwater fish—its pristine lakes and streams are crystal clear, and many of them are extremely well stocked. See especially chapters 7 and 13.
- **Golfing:** Many Swedes are obsessed with golf. Most courses, from the periphery of Stockholm to Björkliden (above the Arctic Circle), are open to the public, and enthusiasts can play under the midnight sun. Halland, south

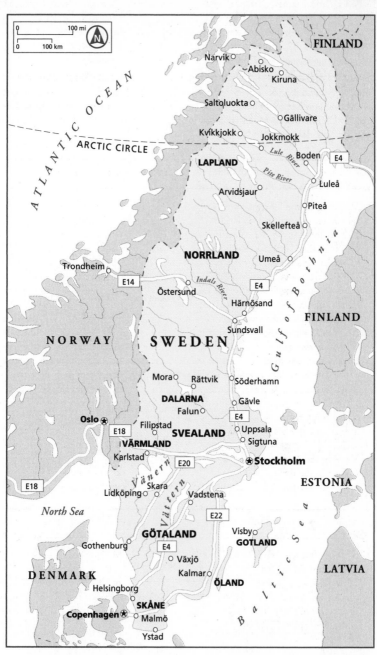

of Gothenburg, is called the Swedish Riviera, and it's the golf capital of the country. Båstad is the most fashionable resort in Halland, and you can play a game of golf here at two prestigious courses: the **Båstad Golf Club** at Boarp (© **0431/783-70**) and the **Bjäre Golf Club** at Solomonhög (© **0431/36-10-53**), both located right outside the center of Båstad. See section 8, "The Bohuslän Coast & Halland," in chapter 7.

- **White-Water Rafting:** Sweden has some of Europe's best white-water rafting. Trips run the gamut from short and comfortable rides through peaceful landscapes to heart-stopping races on fast-running rivers. In Dalarna, the best white-water rafting is on the Väster-dalälven River rapids, which are rated moderately difficult. In northern Värmland, 5km (3 miles) south of Höljes, you can take easy white-water trips in paddle boats. See chapter 12.

- **Hiking:** The Kungsleden (Royal Trail) provides the hike of a lifetime as it takes you through the mountains of Lapland, including Kebnekaise, the highest mountain in Sweden (2,090m/6,857 ft.). This 500km (311-mile) trail cuts through the mountains of Abisko National Park to Riksgränsen on the Norwegian frontier. See section 4, "Tärnaby & Hemavan," in chapter 13.

- **Skiing:** In Lapland, you can enjoy both downhill and cross-country skiing year-round. In Kiruna, serious skiers head for the Kebnekaise mountain station, where skiing can be combined with dog-sledding and other winter sports. South of the city of Gällivare, you arrive at Dundret, or "Thunder Mountain," for some of the finest skiing in the north. The hotel to stay at here also is called **Dundret** (© **0970/145-60**), and its staff possesses all the expertise needed to link you up with cross-country and downhill skiing alike. Inaugurated in 1955, its chairlift to the top of the slopes was the first of its kind in Sweden. For Dundret, see section 7, "Gällivare," in chapter 13.

3 THE BEST MARINE VACATIONS

- **Exploring the "Garden of Skerries" Around Stockholm:** Few cities enjoy a marinescape as dramatic as Stockholm's. The city is surrounded by some 24,000 islands and islets (some no more than skerries or rocks jutting out of the water), and the water is dotted with colorful yachts. You can easily explore the archipelago in summer, using the car ferries and bridges that connect it. The highlight of the journey is taking a boat trip from the center of Stockholm to the town of Sandhamn, a ride that will introduce you to the scenic highlights of a place many Stockholmers call home in summer. See section 7, "Side Trips from Stockholm," in chapter 6.

- **Riding Along the Göta Canal:** This canal, known as Sweden's "blue ribbon," links Stockholm in the east with Gothenburg in the west, and is one of Scandinavia's major tourist attractions. As boats travel along the canal, some of the most beautiful panoramas in Sweden unfold. The canal dates from 1810 and covers 565km (351 miles) of beautiful scenery. Artificial canals, lakes, and rivers are linked by a series of 65 locks, some of them rising 90m (295 ft.) above sea level. Any travel agent can book you on this trip. See section 1, "The Göta Canal," in chapter 11.

- **Angling on the Göta Älv:** The southwestern sector of Lake Vänern, which is part of the Göta Canal (see above), has been called an angler's El Dorado, especially in the valley of the River Göta. The Göta Älv's well-stocked trout waters make for some of Scandinavia's finest spinning and fly-fishing. More than 30 different species of fish live in Lake Vänern, especially perch, pike, and different types of carp. Some 35,000 young salmon and trout are released annually to keep the waters well stocked.

- **Sailing the *Gustaf Wasa*:** The best way to go between the lakeside resorts of Mora and Leksand in Dalarna—the province most steeped in Swedish folklore—is by boat. This way you can see and experience this most traditional of Swedish provinces from a seascape, as the scenery along the shoreline unfolds before you. Leksand itself is the doorway to the province's most scenic lake, Siljan. No less an authority than Hans Christian Andersen pronounced this trip idyllic. After a panoramic journey, you'll arrive in Mora, a provincial town in Upper Dalarna, where passengers disembark to see the Santa complex (Santa's house and factory). See section 5, "Leksand," in chapter 12.

4 THE MOST SCENIC TOWNS & VILLAGES

- **Sigtuna:** Sweden's oldest town, founded at the beginning of the 11th century, stands on the shores of Lake Mälaren, northwest of Stockholm. High Street, with its low-timbered buildings, is believed to be the oldest street in Sweden. Traces of Sigtuna's Viking and early Christian heritage can be seen throughout the town. See section 7, "Side Trips from Stockholm," in chapter 6.

- **Uppsala:** Located northwest of Stockholm, Uppsala is Sweden's major university city and boasts a celebrated 15th-century cathedral. Nearby Gamla Uppsala (see below) also is intriguing, built on the site of Viking burial grounds where animals and humans were both sacrificed. See section 7, "Side Trips from Stockholm," in chapter 6.

- **Lund:** This town, situated 18km (11 miles) northeast of Malmö, rivals Uppsala as a university town. It, too, is ancient, having been founded by Canute the Great in 1020. The town is filled with centuries-old buildings, winding passages, and cobblestone streets; a major attraction is its ancient cathedral, one of the finest expressions of Romanesque architecture in northern Europe. See section 3, "Lund," in chapter 8.

- **Visby:** On the island of Gotland, this once was a great medieval European city and former Viking stronghold. For 8 days in August, this sleepy Hanseatic town awakens for the annual Medieval Week, which features fire eaters, belly dancers, and tournaments. Visby's ruins of 13th- and 14th-century churches and memories of a more prosperous period are intriguing in any season. See section 2, "Gotland & Visby," in chapter 10.

- **Rättvik:** This is a great resort bordering Lake Siljan in the heart of Dalarna, a province known for its regional painting, handicrafts, and folk dancing. Timbered houses reflect Dalarna's old-style architecture, and on summer nights, fiddle music evokes the long-ago past. See section 7, "Rättvik," in chapter 12.

- **Jokkmokk:** Located just north of the Arctic Circle, this is the best center for absorbing Lapp (or Sami) culture. The Lapps hold their famous "Great Winter Market" here in early February, a tradition that is centuries old. You can visit a museum devoted to Sami culture in the center of town and then go salmon fishing in the town's central lake. See section 5, "Jokkmokk," in chapter 13.

5 THE BEST PLACES TO GO BACK IN TIME

- **Gamla Uppsala** (Uppsala): Some 1,500 years ago, the Kingdom of the Svea (Swedes) was ruled from a spot outside the modern university city of Uppsala, north of Stockholm. Gamla Uppsala, 5km (3 miles) north of the city center, is now one of the most revered historic spots in Sweden. Here Viking life dominated, and animals and humans were sacrificed to pagan gods. It is suspected, although not authenticated, that three Swedish kings dating from the 6th century were entombed here. See section 7, "Side Trips from Stockholm," in chapter 6.

- **Skansen** (Djurgården, Stockholm): Called "Old Sweden in a Nutshell," this is the best open-air museum in all of Sweden in terms of numbers of dwellings and authenticity. Some 150 structures were moved from places ranging from the château country in southwest Sweden to as far north as Lapland. From manor houses to windmills, they're all here, giving visitors an idea of how Sweden used to look. This is an especially valuable stop for visitors who see only Stockholm and don't have time to visit the rest of the country. Folk dancing and concerts enliven the atmosphere, and young Swedes demonstrate the creation of handicrafts from the 17th and 18th centuries. See p. 120.

- **Kivik Tomb** (Bredaror): The Kivik Tomb was discovered in 1748 in the château country of Sweden, north of the coastal town of Simrishamn. It immediately became the most important Bronze Age discovery in the country. One of the former members of the discovery team compared it to being "invited into the living room of a Bronze Age family." Not only the usual bronze fragments were uncovered but also some grave carvings and, most notably, tomb furniture. A total of eight runic slabs depict scenes from everyday life, including horse-drawn sleigh-riding, plus a bit of prehistoric humor in what appears to be a troupe of dancing seals. See p. 251.

- **Eketorp Ring-Fort** (Öland): This fortified village, built inside of a ring-shaped enclosure for defensive purposes, is the most important of more than a dozen prehistoric forts known to have existed on Öland in prerecorded times. It appears that the heavily protected village was inhabited by various settlers from A.D. 300 to 1300. Swedish archaeologists have filled the settlement with the Iron Age–style houses that once existed here, and they have reconstructed a massive wall along its edges. Although it is a reconstruction, it is believed to be an authentic replica of what the ring fort and village once looked like, giving amazing insight into life in the Sweden of ages ago, when prehistoric people fought to survive in an inhospitable terrain. See p. 294.

6 THE BEST MUSEUMS

- **Millesgården** (Lidingö, outside Stockholm): Sweden's foremost sculptor, Carl Milles (1875–1955), lived here and created a sculpture garden by the sea that now has been turned into a museum. Milles relied heavily on mythological themes in his work, and many of his best-known pieces are displayed here. See p. 124.

- **Nationalmuseum (National Museum of Art;** Stockholm): One of the oldest museums in the world (it celebrates its

217th birthday in 2009), the National Museum houses Sweden's treasure-trove of rare paintings and sculpture. From Rembrandt to Rubens, and from Bellini to van Gogh, a panoply of European art unfolds before your eyes. In addition to paintings, you'll find antique porcelain, furniture, and clocks. See p. 119.

- **Vasamuseet (Royal Warship *Vasa*;** Stockholm): In the Djurgården, this 17th-century man-of-war, which is now a museum, is a popular tourist attraction. The *Vasa* is the world's oldest known complete ship. It capsized and sank on its maiden voyage in 1628 before horrified onlookers. The ship was salvaged in 1961 and has been carefully restored; 97% of its 700 original sculptured decorative motifs were retrieved. See p. 121.

- **Göteborgs Konstmuseum** (Gothenburg): This is the city's leading art museum, a repository of modern paintings that's strong on French Impressionists, including van Gogh and Bonnard. Modern artists, such as Picasso and Edvard Munch, also are represented, as are sculptures by Milles. See p. 186.

- **Ájtte** (Jokkmokk): In true Lapp country, this is the best repository of artifacts of the Sami culture. Integrating nature with culture, the museum is the largest of its kind in the world. It depicts how the Lapps lived and struggled for survival in a harsh terrain, and features the houses they lived in as well as the animals and weapons needed for their livelihood. See p. 372.

7 THE BEST CASTLES & PALACES

- **Drottningholm Palace and Theater** (Drottningholm): Lying 11km (6³/₄ miles) from Stockholm on an island in Lake Mälaren, Drottningholm, or "Queen's Island," has been dubbed the Versailles of Sweden. It is a magnificent royal residence, a gem of baroque architecture with a palace, gardens, a Chinese pavilion, and one of the most remarkable court theaters in Europe. Since 1981, Sweden's royal family has occupied the south wing. See p. 123.

- **Kungliga Slottet** (Stockholm): One of the few official residences of the royal family that is open to the public, this palace in Gamla Stan (Stockholm's Old Town) dates back 700 years. Encompassing 608 rooms, it is used today by the Swedish king and his family mainly for ceremonial occasions. The 18th-century Royal Apartments, with their painted ceilings, glittering chandeliers, and heirloom tapestries, are the highlight of any visit. See p. 114.

- **Castle of Bosjökloster** (Lund): The origins of this former Benedictine convent date from 1080. Closed in the 1500s, at the time of the Reformation, it fell into disrepair but has since been restored to some of its former glory. Situated on the shores of Lake Ringsjö, today the castle is surrounded by a recreation area with beautiful gardens. The great courtyard here is one of high drama, with thousands of flowers and exotic shrubs. You can bring along a picnic lunch to enjoy on the grounds. See p. 245.

- **Kalmar Slott** (Kalmar): Once called "the key to Sweden," this historic castle was the setting for the Kalmar Union that temporarily united the thrones of Denmark, Norway, and Sweden in 1397. The original structure dates from the 12th century, but in the 16th century, King Gustav Vasa rebuilt it, and his sons eventually transformed it into a Renaissance palace. The castle is the major site in this port city in southern Sweden, which also makes a good base for exploring the "Kingdom of Crystal," the bargain-filled area of glassworks manufacturers (see above). See p. 269.

- **Läckö Slott** (Lidköping): Lying in the vicinity of the pleasant little town of Lidköping, this castle on the waters of Lake Vänern is straight from a fairy tale. Between 1298 and 1681, 250 rooms were built, many quite large; only the royal palace in Stockholm is larger than Läckö. As you approach from a distance, its distinctive white walls, towers, and turrets seem to rise out of the water. The palace furnishings eventually were carted off and the rooms left bare, but over the years many of the original furnishings have been reclaimed and returned. A visit here and a walk through the once-royal grounds is a highlight of any trip to the waters of Lake Vänern. See p. 315.

8 THE BEST CATHEDRALS & ABBEYS

- **Riddarholm Church** (Stockholm): Evoking pre-Reformation Sweden, this is one of the best-preserved Franciscan churches left in northern Europe. After being consecrated at the turn of the 14th century, it served for centuries as the mausoleum for Swedish royalty. The church's cast-iron steeple, which dates from 1841, remains one of the most distinctive landmarks of the Stockholm skyline. The interior is especially impressive; coats of arms of knights of the Order of Seraphim, founded in 1336, cover the walls. The floor is paved with gravestones. After you visit the church, you can walk through Stockholm's Old Town, Gamla Stan. See p. 125.

- **Uppsala Domkyrka** (Uppsala): This twin-spired Gothic structure, nearly 120m (394 ft.) tall, was constructed in the 13th century. Today the silhouette of this largest cathedral in Scandinavia dominates the landscape, affording Uppsala the status of ecclesiastical capital of Sweden. Its layout is simple compared with other major European cathedrals, yet its high Gothic aura is nevertheless impressive. In one of the chapels on the south aisle, you can visit the tomb of the philosopher Emanuel Swedenborg (1688–1772). See p. 156.

- **Domkyrkan** (**Cathedral of Lund;** Lund): The apex of Romanesque architecture in Sweden, this imposing twin-towered gray sandstone cathedral is one of the most ancient in Sweden. Building on it started sometime in the 1080s by King Canute II, though it wasn't consecrated until 1145. Some of the sculptural details of its architecture evoke Lombardy or other parts of Italy. This is especially evident in its apse, which dates from the 1130s. See p. 240.

- **Vadstena Abbey** (Vadstena): Sweden's greatest abbey, on the shores of Lake Vättern, is dedicated to its patron saint, St. Birgitta. In the Middle Ages, the abbey was at the center of a pilgrimage, which earned it the appellation of "Rome of the North." One of the most important stopovers for those taking the Göta Canal trip, Vadstena is dominated by its Klosterkyrkan, or Abbey Church, built between the mid–14th and 15th centuries to the specifications of its founder, St. Birgitta herself. This Gothic church is rich in art and relics from the Middle Ages. See p. 285.

- **Kiruna Kyrka** (Kiruna): This church in the far north of Sweden, in the midst of Lapland, would hardly make it in the grand cathedral circuit of northern Europe. It is, however, one of the most unusual churches in the world and raises a lot of eyebrows at first sight. It was constructed in 1912 like a stylized Sami tent, with an origami design of rafters and wood beams. In Lapland, it is hailed as "the Shrine of the Nomadic people." A free-standing bell tower in front is supported by props and the tombstone of the founder of Kiruna. The altarpiece scene representing Paradise as a Tuscan, not Lappish, landscape is the only incongruous note. See section 8, "Kiruna," in chapter 13.

---

9 THE BEST HOTELS

- **Grand Hotel** (Stockholm; ✆ **08/679-35-00;** www.grandhotel.se): Opposite the Royal Palace, this is the most prestigious hotel in Sweden; many well-known people have stayed here, including Nobel Prize winners. Set on the waterfront, it dates from 1874 but is continuously renovated to keep it in state-of-the-art condition. The rooms have been luxuriously redecorated, and the bathrooms are made of Italian marble with underfloor heating. In 2006, the Grand was vastly improved and enlarged with 72 additional bedrooms and a luxurious new penthouse. See p. 77.
- **Nordic Hotel** (Stockholm; ✆ **800/337-4685** or 08/505-630-00; www.nordic hotel.se): Unique for the Swedish capital, this hotel is as modern and dramatic as the 21st century itself. Turning to the cold Arctic waters of the north and the northern lights for its architectural inspiration, the hotel creates an "only in Sweden" aura that definitely makes you feel like you're in the far north of Europe. See p. 80.
- **Victory Hotel** (Stockholm; ✆ **08/506-400-00;** www.victory-hotel.se): In the Old Town, this small but stylish hotel ranks among the top in Sweden. Originally built in 1642, the hotel is famous for treasure once buried here (part of which can be seen at the Stockholm City Museum). The well-furnished bedrooms, with modern beds, typically have exposed beams and pine floors.

On a small rooftop terrace, tables are arranged around a fountain. See p. 88.
- **Radisson SAS Scandinavia Hotel** (Gothenburg; ✆ **800/333-3333** in the U.S., or 031/758-50-00; www.radissons as.com): Since its opening in 1950, Gothenburg's premier hotel has hosted everybody who's anybody, including the Beatles. Located on Gothenburg's attractive main boulevard, near the cultural center, it's a cosmopolitan hotel with a fresh and contemporary ambience. The best double rooms are quite spacious and decorated in a semimodern, sleek style; about a quarter of the guest rooms are equipped with balconies. See p. 174.
- **Elite Plaza** (Gothenburg; ✆ **031/720-40-00;** www.elite.se): This is not only the newest but also one of the very best hotels to open in Gothenburg in recent years. A 19th-century insurance company was gutted and recycled into a superior first-class hotel with many of its original architectural features intact. The building got a new lease on life, and visitors to Gothenburg today have a place to stay that's as good as some of the most superior lodgings in Stockholm. See p. 172.
- **Elite Hotel Marina Plaza** (Helsingborg; ✆ **042/19-21-00;** www.marina plaza.elite.se): This innovative hotel faces out from the port city of Helsingborg over the Öresund and toward the eastern coast of Denmark, across from

"Hamlet's Castle." A nautical decor prevails, and large glass windows are typical of the sleek, contemporary architecture of Sweden. With its rock gardens, abundant flowers, and fountains, it is a lovely place to spend the night in grand comfort and style. See p. 218.

- **Stadshotell** (Kalmar; ✆ 0480/49-69-00; www.profilhotels.se): With very reasonably priced rooms (at times less than 900SEK/$180/£90 a night for a double), this is an exceptional choice for lodgings in this historic port city in southeastern Sweden. A landmark hotel—constructed in 1906 but completely modernized in 1999—it still retains its look of romanticized architecture, with gables and a bell tower. Many Art Nouveau embellishments remain, including cut-glass chandeliers and an Edwardian-style library. Its bedrooms are the largest and most comfortable in town. See p. 270.

- **Halltorps Gästgiveri** (Borgholm; ✆ 0485/850-00; www.halltorpsgast giveri.se): It has been a restaurant longer than it has been a hotel, but this inn on the Baltic Island of Öland still dates from 1850. Bedrooms are light and airy and frequently renovated, ensuring a good night's sleep in comfort and style. Its restaurant, Bakfickan, or "hip pocket" in English, is one of Öland's best. See p. 301.

- **Ronnums Herrgård** (Vargön; ✆ 0521/26-00-00): One of the most idyllic stopovers along the Göta Canal is in Vargön, which a poet once labeled "Little Paris." In this charming setting, you can enjoy life in a restored 18th-century manor house with yellow clapboards and a red roof, nestled amid its own parklike grounds. Even better, this taste of how life was lived in old Sweden comes at a very reasonable price. See p. 323.

- **Elite Stadshotellet Karlstad** (Karlstad; ✆ 054/29-30-00; www.elite.se): In the heart of the folkloric province of Värmland, this hotel, with its neo-baroque facade, is one of the most impressive of the 19th-century hotels remaining in Sweden. If you like old-fashioned style but modern comfort, this is for you. From its British-inspired pub to the gourmet restaurant, it's a winner. See p. 334.

- **The Ice Hotel** (Jukkasjärvi; ✆ 0980/668-00; www.icehotel.com): Surely there is no hotel in all of Europe as curious as this one deep in the heart of Swedish Lapland. Every winter, the hotel is carved out of the ice at a point 200km (124 miles) north of the Arctic Circle. Come spring, the igloo-shaped hotel literally melts away. In its glacial setting, guests can check in for an icy night—hopefully with a good bed partner. If you've ever dreamed of living like an Eskimo, here is your chance. See p. 382.

- **Scandic Hotel Kramer** (Malmö; ✆ 040/693-54-00; www.scandic-hotels.com/kramer): A wholesale redesign has given this old favorite a new lease on life for its postmillennium reincarnation. Increasingly, the Kramer is becoming *the* place to stay in Malmö for many discerning visitors, although the hotel competition is rough here. See p. 229.

10 THE BEST RESTAURANTS

- **Operakällaren** (Stockholm; ✆ 08/676-58-00): Opposite the Royal Palace, this deluxe restaurant has long been the standard by which the competition is judged. Still going strong after all these years, it is deservedly the most famous restaurant in Sweden—and the best. Its French-inspired cuisine with Swedish overtones is world-class. See p. 93.

- **Paul & Norbert** (Stockholm; ✆ 08/663-81-83): With only eight tables on the fashionable Strandvägen, this exclusive and innovative restaurant is set in a patrician residence dating from 1873. It's the creation of German owner Norbert Lang. In winter, the Swedish game served here is without equal in the entire country—just try the pigeon with Calvados sauce. And you can always count on something tempting and unusual; sautéed sweetbreads in nettle sauce, anyone? See p. 93.

- **Gripsholms Värdshus Restaurant** (Mariefred; ✆ 0159/347-50): If you're seeking traditional Swedish food with French overtones, this is the best dining choice on the periphery of the capital. Local game dishes, including wild grouse, are featured in autumn, and marinated salmon with a mild mustard sauce is a year-round favorite. Tastings also can be arranged in the wine cellar. See p. 161.

- **Sjömagasinet** (Gothenburg; ✆ 031/775-59-20): By far the most intriguing restaurant in town, this is one of the finest places to go for seafood on the west coast of Sweden. In the western suburb of Klippan, the converted 1775 warehouse serves an array of fresh fish whose flavor never diminishes, regardless of the sauce or preparation. The fish and shellfish *pot-au-feu*, with a chive-flavored crème fraîche, is worth the trek. See p. 180.

- **Årstiderna I Kockska Huset** (Malmö; ✆ 040/23-09-10): In a North German–style building from 1523, the leading restaurant of Sweden's "third city" is a bastion of good eating—its dishes are fresh, handled with skill, and served with flair. You'll be as impressed as we were by the exceedingly good cuisine, which attracts a crowd of prime ministers, artists, and theater people alike. See p. 231.

- **Gastro** (Helsingborg; ✆ 042/24-34-70): The kitchens of Sweden and France come together at this restaurant that has emerged as the best in town. Lots of fresh fish, from the straits of Helsingborg and the Baltic, appear on the menu. Many Danes cross the strait for dinner here. See p. 220.

- **Kalmar Hamn Krog** (Kalmar; ✆ 0480/41-10-20): Since it opened in 1988, this international restaurant has quickly moved to the front of the line. Hailed as the best in this historic port city, it prepares reasonably priced food with flair, using only market-fresh ingredients, deftly handled by the staff. The chefs borrow freely from the world's larders, using spices or ingredients from any country where their culinary imaginations wander. See p. 272.

- **Halltorps Gästgiveri** (Borgholm; ✆ 0485/850-00): On the historic Baltic island of Öland, this dining room serving Swedish food takes you back to the good old days. You can feast on the dishes beloved by your great-grandparents—provided they came from Sweden. Herbs and vegetables come from suppliers who grow them right on the island, and the local fishers bring in their catch of the day. The place is charming and a bit stylish, and it occupies one of the oldest manor houses on the island. See p. 301.

2

Sweden in Depth

Roughly the size of California, Sweden has some 280,000 sq. km (108,109 sq. miles) of landmass, bordering Finland to its northeast and Norway to its west. As the northern end creeps over the Arctic Circle, the southern third of Sweden juts into the Baltic Sea. This southern tier is the site of most of the population; much of the north is uninhabited and occupies one of the last great wildernesses of Europe.

Known for its warm summers and bitterly cold winters, Sweden is a land of lakes and forests, mountains and meadows. Because of generally poor soil and a rocky landscape, Swedes have turned to mining, steel production, and forestry to spur their economy.

Swedes are known for their almost mystical love of nature. Although they travel abroad in winter to escape the cold, Swedes are their own greatest tourists when the all-too-brief summer arrives. Many Swedes have second homes in remote parts of the country.

Many visitors heading for history- and monument-rich France or Italy mistakenly think Sweden lacks attractions. This is not the case: Sweden possesses 1,140 historic fortresses, 2,500 open-air runic stones, and 25,000 protected Iron Age graveyards, and the Stockholm area alone has 10 royal castles. As in parts of the American West, you'll encounter one thing in Sweden that is not always available in other parts of Europe: the wide-open yonder. Space characterizes Sweden's vast forests, mountains, and national parks. Sometimes you can travel for miles without encountering another soul.

Stockholm is, of course, the major target of nearly all visitors. More than 7 centuries old, it is a regal place, filled with everything from the winding cobbled streets of the medieval district to the marble, glass, and granite of its high-rises in the commercial center. While many other world capitals may have passed their prime, Stockholm grows better with age. No longer as provincial as it was even 15 years ago, today it's lively, vibrant, and filled with nightlife, great restaurants, and countless shopping opportunities, along with a sophisticated, savvy population enjoying one of the world's highest standards of living. And no other European capital has such a dramatic landscape as the surrounding 24,000 islands, skerries, and islets.

But Sweden only begins in Stockholm. At least two other major cities merit exploration: Gothenburg and Malmö. Gothenberg, a major seaport, is filled with tree-lined boulevards, restaurants, museums, endless shopping, elegant buildings, and nightclubs. And it enjoys striking scenery along Sweden's craggy western coastline. North of Gothenburg lie sleepy fishing harbors in rocky coves and offshore islands where city folk come in summer to retreat.

Southwestern Malmö boasts one of northern Europe's most attractive medieval centers, and also is a good base for exploring the ancient university city of Lund, with its mass of students, a revered 12th-century Romanesque cathedral, medieval streets, and numerous museums.

However grand the cities may be, any native Swede will tell you that the countryside is the chief reason to visit. Our favorite destinations, the folkloric provinces of Dalarna and Värmland, form Sweden's heartland. Filled with forests and vast lakes, this is the landscape described in the country's greatest literature. Some towns, especially around

Lake Siljan, still look as they did in the Middle Ages. Folk dances and music festivals keep the summer lively.

The ancient province of Skåne in the southwest is called the château country, for the French-like castles that still dot its landscape of undulating fields and curving, rocky coastline. In spring, black windmills and white churches pose against a background of yellow rape, crimson poppies, and lush green meadows.

For sheer scenic drama, nothing equals Lapland, that remote and isolated region of Europe in the north, home to the Lapps (or Sami) and their reindeer herds. It's a domain of truly awesome proportions. Birch-clad valleys and sprawling woodlands of pine give way to waterfalls, roaring river rapids, mountain plateaus, and fens covered with moss. The numerous rivers of the region snake down from the mountains to spill out into the Gulf of Bothnia, and the locals have long ago accepted and adapted to the harsh lifestyle imposed on them by the weather. Unspoiled nature under the midnight sun is a potent attraction.

Finally, there is the island of Gotland in the Baltic, which knew its heyday in Viking times. This land of beaches, spas, and sailing has a warmer climate than the rest of Sweden. Some 100 churches and chapels still remain on the island, and its capital, Visby, is one of the oldest cities of Sweden. Its Old Town wall stretches for over 3km (1³/₄ miles) and is capped by 44 towers. Crenellated turrets and long, thin, arched windows evoke the Middle Ages.

Sweden is a country where you can enjoy history and urban pleasures, but the nation's heart and soul can be found in its vast landscapes. From a summer wilderness fragrant with fields of orchids and traversed by wild elk to the dark wintry landscape dotted by husky sleds and paraskiing, Sweden provides a stunning vacation experience.

1 SWEDEN TODAY

Sweden is one of the most paradoxical nations on earth. An essentially conservative country, it is nonetheless a leader in social welfare, prison reform, and equal opportunity for women.

Despite trouble maintaining its once-bustling economy, Sweden has long enjoyed some of the highest wages and the best standard of living in Europe. There may be trouble in paradise, but compared with the rest of the world, Sweden is better off than most other nations.

This is a land where the urbane and the untamed are said to live harmoniously. With a population density of only 18 people per square kilometer (48 per square mile), there's ample space for all of Sweden's nine million residents. About 85% of Sweden's citizens live in the southern half of the country. The north is populated by Sweden's two chief minority groups: the Sami (Lapp) and the Finnish-speaking people of the northeast. Among the cities, Stockholm is the political capital, with a population of 1,435,000; Gothenburg, the automobile-manufacturing center, has 705,000; and Malmö, the port city, has around 500,000.

Once home to an ethnically homogenous society, Sweden has experienced a vast wave of immigration in the past several years. Today more than 10% of Sweden's residents are immigrants or children of immigrants. Much of this influx is from other Scandinavian countries. Because of Sweden's strong stance on human rights, it also has become a major destination for political and social refugees from Africa and the Middle East. A vast number of immigrants seeking asylum come from the former Yugoslavia.

Sweden's government is a constitutional monarchy supported by a parliamentary government. The royal family functions primarily in a ceremonial capacity. The actual ruling body is a one-chamber parliament, whose members are popularly elected for 3-year terms. The present government is headed by a Social Democrat, Goeran Persson. Because of Sweden's location in the Baltic, it has been active in promoting peace among the warring Baltic states. The country is an active member of the United Nations and was admitted as a full member to the European Union in 1995.

Like other European countries, Sweden's policy of cradle-to-grave welfare has been threatened in recent years. The main topic of debate in the parliament is how to sustain Sweden's generous welfare system while putting a halt to ever-increasing taxes, currently at 59%. At this time, the state provides health insurance as well as many generous family benefits, including an allowance for care providers, 15 months paid parental leave after the birth of a child (divided between both parents), tax-free child allowances, and education stipends for children. When a Swede reaches retirement at age 65, he or she is entitled to a hefty pension that rises with inflation.

Education plays an important role in Sweden. Schools are run by various municipalities, providing free tuition, books, and lunches. Although attendance is mandatory for only 9 years, 90% of Swedes pursue some form of higher education. Adult education and university study are funded by the state.

Sweden's advanced level of education coincides with its high-tech industrial economy. Although in years past Sweden's economy was based on agriculture, in the latter half of the 20th century and post-millennium, industry has become predominant, employing nearly 80% of all Swedish workers. More than 50% of Sweden's exports are composed of heavy machinery, including cars, trucks, and telecommunications equipment. Companies such as Saab and Volvo (bought by Ford Motor Co.) produce vehicles familiar throughout the world. Despite Sweden's industrial milieu, the country manages to produce some 80% of its own food.

Although such a highly industrialized nation depends on its factories, Sweden has enacted stringent environmental policies. The task of monitoring the country's environment is the responsibility of local governments. Each of Sweden's 286 municipalities has the right to limit pollutant emissions in its own sector.

The environment has always played an integral role in the lives of Swedes. Sweden has 20 national parks; although these wilderness areas are not regulated by law, Sweden's policy of free access entitles citizens to unlimited admission at no charge.

Another important element is Sweden's strong focus on culture. Over the past 25 years or so, Swedes have turned their attention to music. Today young people are purchasing more recorded music and attending more live concerts than they were even a decade ago. Book reading is on the rise (more than 10,000 titles are published in Sweden every year, and Swedes traditionally have had a literacy rate of more than 99%), museum attendance has increased, and there's greater interest in the media. Swedes spend an average of 6 hours per day immersed in some form of mass media (newspapers, magazines, television, radio, and so forth).

Increasingly, Sweden is being pressed to drop its neutrality and to join an expanding NATO. The country continues to resist that pressure. Although Sweden has been a member of the European Union since 1995, polls today indicate that it would reject membership if a new election were held.

There is a certain nostalgia sweeping Sweden today, a desire to return to the way life used to be when Sweden was one of the three or four richest countries in the world.

As Sweden moves even deeper into the 21st century, its problems continue. For example, businesses can't grow because it's too expensive to hire people. Observers have noted that young Swedes are starting to think internationally, and some of them are leaving Sweden to take positions elsewhere in the global economy. "The people leaving are the very people that Sweden needs the most," one Swedish businessman lamented to the press.

2 LOOKING BACK AT SWEDEN

THE VIKINGS Although documented by little other than legend, the Viking age (roughly A.D. 700–1000) is the Swedish epoch that has most captured the attention of the world. Before this period, Sweden had been relatively isolated, although travelers from the south brought some artifacts from different civilizations.

The base of Viking power at the time was the coastal regions around and to the north of what is now Stockholm. Either as plunderers, merchants, or slave traders—perhaps a combination of all three—Swedish Vikings maintained contact with the East, both Russia and Constantinople, and with parts of western Europe, including Britain and Ireland. Swedish Vikings joined their brother Vikings in Norway and Denmark in pillaging, trading with, or conquering parts of Ireland and the British Isles, their favorite targets.

CHRISTIANITY & THE MIDDLE AGES With the aid of missions sent from Britain and northern Germany, Christianity gradually made headway, having been introduced in 829 by St. Anskar, a Frankish missionary. It did not become widespread, however, until the 11th century. In 1008, Olaf Skottkonung, the ruler of a powerful kingdom in northern Sweden, converted to Christianity, but later in the century, the religion experienced hardships, with civil wars and a pagan reaction against the converting missionaries.

Ruling from 1130 to 1156, King Sverker united the lands of Svear and Gotar, which later became the heart of modern Sweden. A strong centralized government developed under this king.

Christianity finally became almost universally accepted under Eric IX, who ruled until 1160. He led a crusade to Finland

A BRIEF HISTORY

- A.D. **829** Christianity is introduced by St. Anskar.
- **1008** Pagan Viking king Olaf Skottkonung converts to Christianity.
- **1130–56** King Sverker unites the lands of Svear and Gotar, the heart of today's modern nation.
- **1160** King Eric IX presides over a Christian country and becomes patron saint of Sweden.
- **1248** Birger Jarl abolishes serfdom and founds Stockholm.
- **1319** Magnus VII of Norway unites Sweden with Norway.
- **1350** Black Death sweeps across Sweden.
- **1389** Margaretha rules Sweden, Norway, and Denmark by the Union of Kalmar.
- **1523** Gustavus Vasa founds the Vasa Dynasty.
- **1598** King Sigismund is deposed after a brief union of the thrones of Sweden and Poland.
- **1600–11** Karl IX leads Sweden into ill-fated wars with Denmark, Russia, and Poland.
- **1611** Gustavus II Adolphus ascends to the throne; presides over ascension of

continues

and later became the patron saint of Sweden. By 1164, his son, Charles VII, had founded the first archbishopric at Uppsala. The increasing influence of this new religion led to the death of the Viking slave trade, and many Vikings turned to agriculture as the basis of their economy. A landowning aristocracy eventually arose.

Sweden's ties with the Hanseatic ports of Germany grew stronger, and trade with other Baltic ports flourished at the city of Visby, on the island of Gotland. Sweden traded in copper, pelts, iron, and butter, among other products.

Sweden's greatest medieval statesman was Birger Jarl, who ruled from 1248 to 1266; during his reign, he abolished serfdom and founded Stockholm. When his son, Magnus Ladulås, became king in 1275, he granted extensive power to the Catholic Church and founded a hereditary aristocracy.

AN INTRA-NORDIC UNION Magnus VII of Norway (1316–74) was only 3 years old when he was elected to the Swedish throne, but his election signaled a recognition of the benefits of increased cooperation within the Nordic world. During his reign, there emerged distinct social classes, including the aristocracy; the Catholic clergy (which owned more than 20% of the land); peasant farmers and laborers; and a commercial class of landowners, foresters, mine

owners, and merchants. The fortunes and power of this last group were based on trade links with a well-organized handful of trading cities (the Hanseatic League) scattered throughout Germany and along the Baltic coastline. As trade increased, these cities (especially Visby, on the island of Gotland) and their residents flourished, and the power of the Hanseatic League grew.

In 1350, the Black Death arrived in Sweden, decimating the population. This proved to be the greatest catastrophe experienced by the Western world up to that time. Imported from Asia, after wreaking havoc in China and Turkistan, it is thought to have spread to Sweden through trade with Britain. The plague seriously hindered Sweden's development, although the country didn't suffer as much as nations such as England.

In 1389, the Swedish aristocracy, fearing the growing power of the Germans within the Hanseatic League, negotiated for an intra-Nordic union with Denmark and the remaining medieval fiefdoms in Norway and Finland. The birth process of this experimental union began in the Swedish city of Kalmar, which gave its name in 1397 to the brief but farsighted Union of Kalmar. A leading figure in its development was the Danish queen Margaretha, who was already queen of Denmark and Norway when the aristocracy of Sweden offered her the throne in 1389.

Sweden as a great European power.

- **1648** Treaty of Westphalia grants Sweden the possessions of Stettin, Bremen, and West Pomerania.
- **1654** Queen Christina abdicates the Swedish throne.
- **1655–97** Long reign of Charles XI renews Sweden's strength.
- **1718** Demise of the Swedish empire after Charles XII,

leader of the Swedish army in the Great Northern War, is killed in battle.
- **1746–92** Gustavus III revives the absolute power of the monarchy.
- **1809** Napoleon names Jean Bernadotte as heir to the throne of Sweden.
- **1889** The Social Democratic Party is formed.
- **1905** Sweden grants independence to Norway.

- **1909** Suffrage for all men is achieved.
- **1921** Suffrage for women and an 8-hour workday are established.
- **1940** Sweden declares its neutrality in World War II.
- **1946** Sweden joins the United Nations.
- **1953** Dag Hammarskjöld becomes secretary-general of the United Nations.

Despite the ideals of the union, it collapsed after about 40 years because of a revolt by merchants, miners, and peasants in defense of Sweden's trade links with the Hanseatic League, coupled with power struggles between Danish and Swedish nobles.

Although the union was a failure, one of its legacies was the establishment—partly as a compromise among different political factions—of a Riksdag (parliament) made up of representatives from various towns and regions; the peasant classes also had some limited representation.

Queen Margaretha's heir (her nephew, Eric of Pomerania; 1382–1459) became the crowned head of three countries (Norway, Denmark, and Sweden). He spent most of his reign fighting with the Hanseatic League. Deposed in 1439, he was replaced by Christopher of Bavaria, whose early death in 1448 led to a major conflict and the eventual dissolution of the Kalmar Union. The Danish king, Christian II, invaded Stockholm in 1520, massacred the leaders who opposed him, and established an unpopular reign; there was much civil disobedience until the emergence of the Vasa dynasty, which expelled the Danes.

THE VASA DYNASTY In May 1520, a Swedish nobleman, Gustavus Vasa, returned from captivity in Denmark and immediately began to plan for the military expulsion of the Danes from Sweden. In 1523, he captured Stockholm from its Danish rulers, won official recognition for Swedish independence, and was elected king of Sweden.

In a power struggle with the Catholic Church, he confiscated most Church-held lands (vastly increasing the power of the state overnight) and established Lutheranism as the national religion. He commissioned a complete translation of the Bible and other religious works into Swedish, and forcefully put down local uprisings in the Swedish provinces. He established the right of succession for his offspring and decreed that his son, Eric XIV, would follow him as king (which he did, in 1543).

Although, at first, Eric was a wise ruler, his eventual downfall was due, in part, to his growing conflicts with Swedish noblemen and a marriage to his unpopular mistress, Karin Mansdotter. (Previously, he had unsuccessfully negotiated marriage with the English queen, Elizabeth I.) Eric eventually went insane before he was replaced by Johan III.

The next 50 years were marked by Danish plots to regain control of Sweden and Swedish plots to conquer Poland, Estonia, and the Baltic trade routes leading to Russia. A dynastic link to the royal families of Poland led to the ascension of Sigismund (son of the Swedish king Johan III) in Warsaw. When his father died, Sigismund

- 1973 Karl XVI Gustaf ascends the throne.
- 1986 Olof Palme, prime minister and leader of the Social Democrats, is assassinated.
- 1992 Sweden faces currency crisis.
- 1994 Refugees and the welfare system strain Sweden's budget.
- 1995 Along with Finland and Austria, Sweden is granted full membership in the European Union.
- 1996 Social Democrat Goeran Persson, Sweden's finance minister, is elected prime minister.
- 1997 World headlines link Sweden to past sterilization programs and Nazi gold.
- 1998 Social Democrats remain in power on pledge to continue huge welfare programs.
- 2000 The 24-billion SEK ($3-billion) Øresund bridge links Denmark and Sweden for the first time.
- 2002 Sweden okays same-sex adoption.
- 2006 Sweden's governing party voted out after 12 years.

became king of both Sweden and Poland simultaneously. His Catholicism, however, was opposed by Sweden, which expelled him in 1598. He was followed by Karl (Charles) IX (1566–1632), who led Sweden into a dangerous and expensive series of wars with Denmark, Russia, and its former ally, Poland.

By 1611, as Sweden was fighting simply to survive, Gustavus II Adolphus (1594–1632) ascended the throne. Viewed today as a brilliant politician and military leader, he was one of the century's most stalwart Protestants at a time when political alliances often were formed along religious lines. After organizing an army composed mainly of farmers and field hands (financed by money from the Falun copper mines), he secured Sweden's safety and, with his armies, penetrated as far south as Bavaria. He died fighting against the Hapsburg emperor's Catholic army near the city of Lützen in 1632.

When he died, his heir and only child, Christina (1626–89), was 6 years old. During her childhood, power was held by the respected Swedish statesman Axel Oxenstierna, who continued the Thirty Years' War in Germany for another 16 years. It finally concluded with the Treaty of Westphalia in 1648. Christina, who did not want to pursue war and had converted to Catholicism (against the advice of her counselors), abdicated the throne in 1654 in favor of her cousin, Charles X Gustav (1622–60).

After his rise to power, Charles X expelled the Danes from many of Sweden's southern provinces, establishing the Swedish borders along the approximate lines of today. He also invaded and conquered Poland (1655–56), but his territorial ambitions were thwarted by a national uprising. He later defeated the Danes (1657–58), and at the time of his death, Sweden was ringed by enemies. Charles X was succeeded by Charles XI (1655–97), whose reign was fiscally traumatic. The endless wars with Denmark (and other kingdoms in northern

Germany) continued. However, an even greater problem was the growing power of wealthy Swedish nobles, who had amassed (usually through outright purchase from the cash-poor monarchy) an estimated 72% of Sweden's land. In a bitter and acrimonious process, Charles redistributed the land into approximately equal shares held by the monarchy, the nobles, and Sweden's independent farmers. The position of small landowners has remained secure in Sweden ever since, although the absolute monarch gained increased power. With Charles's newfound wealth, he greatly strengthened the country's military power.

Charles XII (1682–1718) came to the throne at the age of 4 with his mother, the queen, as regent. Denmark, Poland, and Russia allied themselves against Sweden in the Great Northern War, which broke out in 1700. Charles invaded Russia but was defeated; he escaped to Turkey, where he remained a prisoner for 4 years. In 1714, he returned to Sweden to continue fighting but was killed in 1718. Charles XII presided over the collapse of the Swedish empire.

Under Frederick I (1676–1751)—though chancellor Count Arvid Horn (1664–1742) had the real power—Sweden regained some of its former prestige. Horn formed an alliance with England, Prussia, and France against Russia. The *Hattar* (Hats) and *Mossorna* (Caps) were the two opposing parties in the Riksdag then, and the Hats began a war with Russia in 1741. The conflict continued through the reign of the next king, Adolphus Frederick (1710–71).

Although he initiated many reforms, encouraged the arts, and transformed the architectural landscape of Stockholm, Gustavus III (1746–92) revived the absolute power of the monarchy, perhaps as a reaction against the changes effected by the French Revolution. He was assassinated by a group of fanatical noblemen while attending a ball at the opera.

THE 19TH CENTURY The next king was Gustavus IV (1778–1837). Because he hated Napoleon, Gustavus IV led Sweden into the Third Coalition against France (1805–07). For his efforts, he lost Stralsund and Swedish Pomerania; in the wars against Russia and Denmark, Sweden lost Finland in 1808. The next year, following an uprising, Gustavus IV was overthrown and died in exile.

A new constitution was written in 1808, granting the Riksdag equal power with the king. Under these provisions, Charles XIII (1748–1818), the uncle of the deposed king, became the new monarch.

Napoleon arranged for his aide, Jean Bernadotte (1763–1844), to become heir to the Swedish throne. Bernadotte won a war with Denmark, forcing that country to cede Norway to Sweden (1814). Upon the death of Charles, Bernadotte became king of Sweden and Norway, ruling as Charles XIV. During his reign, Sweden adopted a policy of neutrality, and the royal line that he established is still on the throne today. Charles XIV was succeeded by his son, Oscar I (1799–1859), who introduced many reforms, including freedom of worship and of the press.

The Industrial Revolution of the 19th century changed the face of Sweden. The Social Democratic Party was launched in 1889, leading to a universal suffrage movement. All males acquired the right to vote in 1909.

THE 20TH CENTURY Norway declared its independence in 1905, and Sweden accepted the secession. Sweden adhered to a policy of neutrality during World War I, although many Swedes were sympathetic to the German cause. Many Swedish volunteers enlisted in the White Army during the Russian Revolution of 1917.

In 1921, women gained the right to vote, and an 8-hour workday was established. The Social Democratic Party continued to grow in power, and, after 1932, a welfare state was instituted.

Although Sweden offered weapons and volunteers to Finland during its Winter War against the Soviet Union in 1939, it declared its neutrality during World War II. Sweden evoked long-lived resentment from its neighbor, Norway, whose cities were leveled by the Nazi troops that had been granted free passage across Swedish territory. Under heavy Allied threats against Sweden in 1943 and 1944, Nazi troop transports through the country eventually were halted. Throughout the war, Sweden accepted many impoverished and homeless refugees. The rescue attempts of Hungarian Jews, led by Swedish businessman and diplomat Raoul Wallenberg, have been recounted in books and films.

Sweden joined the United Nations in 1946 but refused to join NATO in 1949. Rather more disturbing was Sweden's decision to return to the Soviet Union many German and Baltic refugees who had opposed Russia during the war. They were presumably killed on Stalin's orders.

Dag Hammarskjöld, as secretary-general of the United Nations in 1953, did much to help Sweden regain the international respect that it had lost because of its wartime policies. In 1961, toward the end of his second 5-year term, he was killed in an airplane crash.

Sweden continued to institute social reforms in the 1950s and 1960s, including the establishment of a national health service.

At only 27 years old, Karl XVI Gustaf became king of Sweden in 1973, following the death of his grandfather, Gustaf VI Adolf. (The king's father had been killed in an airplane crash when the king was still a child.) In 1976, he married Silvia Sommerlath, who was born in Germany. King Karl XVI Gustaf and Queen Silvia have three children.

The Social Democrats ruled until 1976, when they were toppled by a Center/Liberal/Moderate coalition. The Social Democrats returned in 1982 but lost their majority in 1985 and had to rely on Communist support to enact legislation.

The leader of their party since 1969, Olof Palme was prime minister until his assassination outside a movie theater in Stockholm in 1986. A pacifist, he was a staunch critic of the United States, especially during the Vietnam War. In spite of an arrest, the murder has not been satisfactorily resolved.

Following the assassination of Olof Palme, vice prime minister Ingvar Carlsson was shoehorned into power, in accordance with provisions within the Social Democratic Party's bylaws. There he remained as an honest but dull caretaker until the end of Palme's elected term, devoted to promoting the party platforms of bountiful social benefits coupled with staggeringly high taxes.

In the early 1990s, Sweden faced some of the most troubling economic problems in recent memory, foremost of which was slow economic growth. Inflation was severe. In 1992, the government, then led by Conservative prime minister Carl Bildt, experienced a currency crisis that made headlines around the world. In September 1994, the Social Democrats, again spearheaded by Ingvar Carlsson, were returned to office after a brief interim of Conservative rule. The election brought the proportion of women in the Swedish Parliament to 41%, the highest in the world.

In 1995, Sweden, along with Finland and Austria, was granted full membership in the European Union, thereby providing a context for much-needed economic growth. In 1996, Prime Minister Carlsson, citing advanced age and a growing distaste for public life (in which he was the butt of many jokes that compared his appearance to that of an old shoe), retired midway through the elected term of his party.

Following well-established parliamentary procedures, fellow Social Democrat Goeran Persson took his place. A highly capable former finance minister, Persson appealed to Swedes with a platform that advocated cutting taxes and curtailing government spending. Despite personal talent, Persson has been judged as a capable but remote administrator whose most visible drawback is a chilly, somewhat arrogant personal style that has provoked murmurs of discontent among some members of the Swedish electorate.

Just as its own image as one of the most progressive nations on earth was being questioned, a chilling chapter from Sweden's past was revealed in 1997. Sweden had as many as 60,000 of its citizens sterilized, some involuntarily, from 1935 to 1976. The ideas behind the sterilization program had similarities to Nazi ideas of racial superiority. Singled out were those judged to be inferior, flawed by bad eyesight, mental retardation, and otherwise "undesirable" racial characteristics. The state wanted to prevent these genetic characteristics from being passed on. This law wasn't overturned until 1976. The respected newspaper *Dagens Nyheter* stirred national debate and worldwide headlines when it ran a series of articles about the former program.

(Fun Facts) There's Something About the Swedes

The Swedes are responsible for inventing much that has changed modern life all over the world, including the safety match, alternating current, the milk separator, the refrigerator, the vacuum cleaner, and the ball bearing. And, of course, there's the zipper (which has led to all sorts of interesting situations).

Swedish Yankees

The Swedes first settled in North America in 1638, when the colony of New Sweden was established at the mouth of the Delaware River. The settlement was captured by the Dutch 17 years later, and the settlers evacuated to New Amsterdam, the town that became New York. Fascination with the New World overcame Sweden's population in earnest in 1846, and waves of Swedes set out to seek health, wealth, religious freedom, and a land of their own. During a 5-year period beginning in 1868, five annual crops failed in Sweden, leading to the migration of at least 100,000 people. Between 1846 and 1873, a total of 1.5 million Swedes emigrated to North America—a figure that's especially impressive considering that Sweden's entire population was only around 4 million. The drain on the country's human resources was disastrous. Of all European countries, only Ireland lost a larger proportion of its population to emigration.

The first, and among the best-publicized, group of Swedish immigrants was a 1,500-member religious sect known as Jansonists (Erikjansare), whose leader, Erik Jansson, founded a colony in Illinois known as Bishop's Hill. Conceived as a utopia, where all goods and property would be shared in common, it attracted national journalistic attention until an enraged disciple, furious at Jannson's refusal to allow his wife to leave the community, shot Jansson. Jansson's disciples, who believed he was immortal and would soon be resurrected, scattered throughout the Midwest and eventually established their own farms.

As if this weren't bad enough, Sweden's once-lustrous reputation received more battering in 1997 with revelations of wartime iron exports that fed Hitler's military machine and of postwar Swedish hoarding of German gold, much of it looted from Nazi victims, which it received in payment for the metal.

In an election in September 1998, Social Democrats, still led by Goeran Persson, remained in power on a pledge to increase spending on the country's huge welfare program. The party secretary of the Moderates, Gunner Hokmark, found little comfort in the election, claiming, "It puts Swedes in a left lock that is stronger than any other country of Europe."

POSTMILLENIUM The government presently spends 46% of the gross national product on welfare, more than any other industrialized country. The income taxes required to support this public outlay take 59% of the pay of people. Employers pay up to 41% of employee remuneration into social security and pension plans. The former Communist Party now is called the Left Party, and it has steadily been growing in approval with voters.

In May 2000, Sweden, for the first time in its history, became physically linked with the Continent by the Øresund Bridge. Construction on the 16km (10-mile) motor and railway link began in 1995. Both Queen Margrethe of Denmark and King Carl Gustaf of Sweden inaugurated the span that links the Scandinavian peninsula with Europe.

The bridge gives the island of Zealand (the eastern part of Denmark) and Scania (the southern part of Sweden) a shared bridge, serving some 3.5 million inhabitants in the area.

The Øresund region, which encompasses parts of both Sweden and Denmark, is the largest domestic market in northern Europe—larger than Stockholm and equal in size to Berlin, Hamburg, and Amsterdam combined. Built at a cost of 24 billion SEK ($3 billion), it is the largest combined rail and road tunnel in the world.

In theory, a vehicle now can travel in roughly a straight line from the Arctic coast of Norway to the Mediterranean shores of Spain. For centuries, it has been a dream to link the Continent from its northern tip to its southern toe. The "Øresund Fixed Link" spans the icy Øresund Sound between the cities of Copenhagen and Malmö.

In 2002, Sweden again became one of the world leaders in advanced social legislation when parliament voted to let same-sex couples adopt children. Under the new bill, gays registered in a legal partnership, allowed in Sweden since 1995, can be considered joint adoptive parents. One of the partners will also be able to adopt the child of another.

While Sweden is hardly viewed as a Banana Republic, where its leaders are routinely assassinated, violence against public officials has come to Scandinavia: One of the attacks in modern Sweden occurred on September 11, 2003, when Ann Lindh, Sweden's minister for foreign affairs, was stabbed and mortally wounded while on a personal errand. She stood as a role model for many younger women and a representative of a modern, outward-looking Swede.

In a surprise political move, Sweden in September of 2006 swept away 12 years of center-left government, voting to reject its longtime prime minister, Goran Persson, in favor of a conservative candidate who has pledged to revise the welfare state. A right-of-center coalition, led by the leader of the Moderate Party, Fredrik Reinfeldt, beat the Social Democrats. Because most Swedes prize political stability, Reinfeldt took pains to cast his plan as a "fine-tuning" rather than a full-scale overhaul of Sweden's economic model.

Unlike residents of some countries of the world, most Swedes, according to surveys, seem content with their big-government, high-tax system. However, joblessness remains an issue with many young Swedes, who have begun migrating to oil-rich Norway for better jobs with more pay.

3 SWEDEN'S ART & ARCHITECTURE

PRE-CHRISTIAN ART Swedish art began in the Stone Age with rock carvings by cavemen, which depicted hunters and the beasts they pursued. With the coming of the Bronze Age, carvings began to depict more human figures, such as armed men plowing and hunting. From the 5th to the 9th centuries, during the Iron Age and the time of the Vikings, the human figure was mainly ignored in favor of lions, monsters, birds, and fantastic dragons.

Zoomorphic shapes were also used as decorative elements on the runic stones of the era. One of the best examples of this was found in Gotland, depicting the epic journey of a slain warrior's ship to the land of the dead. It dates from the 8th century.

THE MIDDLE AGES Beginning in the 11th century, the earliest churches were constructed on the sites of pagan temples and were rectangular timber structures. None have survived. By the 12th century, stone became the building material of choice for the construction of Romanesque monasteries and churches. Notable examples of this style include the Lund Cathedral and the Sigtuna Monastery.

Appearing in the 13th century, the Gothic style brought in brick as a building material. The most outstanding example of this style was the Cathedral at Uppsala, north of Stockholm.

About 1,500 Swedish churches, plus a few burghers' houses in Stockholm and Visby, date from the Middle Ages. The 13th-century city walls enveloping Visby are some of the best preserved of their type in Europe, and the layout of Stockholm's Gamla Stan, or Old Town, still follows its medieval routes from the Middle Ages.

Painting in this period consisted mainly of mural paintings in the medieval churches: Storybook illustrations explaining biblical stories were needed as most of the population was illiterate. Wooden altarpieces were also imported into Sweden from Germany.

THE RENAISSANCE The coming of the Renaissance and the acceptance of the Protestant religion in Sweden in the 16th century brought changes in architectural styles imported from Italy via Belgium and Holland. The castles of Gripsholm were erected, for example, in 1537 during the reign of Gustavus I; the castle at Vadstena was built in 1545. Kalmar Castle, with its massive walls and fusion of medieval and Renaissance features, also was constructed during this period of upheaval.

Painters and sculptors during the 16th and 17th centuries took a back seat. Most art came from European masters imported to the royal courts.

BAROQUE Sweden rose to become a world power in the 17th century, and noblemen built palaces to reflect their newly acquired wealth. Most of these were based on French models. French influences were also in evidence throughout most of the architecture of the 18th century.

Many Swedish artists went abroad, including the sculptor Johan Tobias von Sergel (1740–1814), who spent 12 years in Rome, where he came under a heavy baroque influence. But the baroque never took hold in Sweden the way it did in Germany to the south. Emerging in 1750 and lasting for a century, folk art flourished instead in Sweden, and was used to decorate farmsteads and homes with representations of biblical figures depicted in modern dress. Floral motifs dominated most of this provincial art.

Gustavus III, who reigned until 1792, favored both the Rococo and Neoclassical styles. A fusion of these two styles can be seen in the Opera House in Stockholm and the Royal Exchange.

CLASSICISM & EMPIRE Using classical precedents, architects were inspired by Italy in the second half of the 1700s; the 1773 School of the Academy of Arts, in Stockholm, is one such example, as is th Palace Theater in Gripsholm. After the loss of Finland in the Napoleonic Wars, Swedish architects concentrated on the military, erecting the Karlsborg Fortress and the Göta Canal.

REVIVALISM During industrialization in the 19th century, the Art Nouveau movement produced no building of note in Sweden. Rather, architects pursued whatever fantasy suited them: Fredrik Wilhelm Scholander, for example, was inspired by Assyrian motifs for Stockholm's Synagogue, while Friedrich August Stüler looked to the Renaissance for his National Museum of Fine Arts in Sweden.

NATIONAL ROMANTIC STYLE As the 1800s ended and the 20th century burst onto the scene, the architects of the day turned from classicism. They preferred a more National Romantic and Jugenstil style, designing often in brick and wood. The crowning achievement of this period is the Stockholm City Hall designed by Ragnar Östberg and built between 1903 and 1923.

MODERN & POSTMODERN Massive building projects were undertaken after

World War II to accommodate a burgeoning population. Entire dormitory suburbs were constructed, often in a dull, bland style. The emphasis was on functionalism and modernity. Many architecturally sensitive Swedes cited the negative social consequences of these peas-in-a-pod communities enveloping Sweden's cities.

Postmodernism then emerged in the 1950s, encompassing a variety of different trends, even some used during the National Romantic period. Designers of 20th-century buildings used such terms as "minimalism" or "neofunctionalism."

Sculpture in this time was dominated by Carl Milles (1875–1955); a major work of his, the *Gustavus Vasa* wood carving, is in the Nordiska Museum in Stockholm.

Art in the 21st century has brought a return in some quarters to the narrative, especially as expressed in fantastic stories. A Swedish critic wrote that much of modern art in Stockholm "derails with both moral and ethical problems." Specifically cited was Jonas Dahlberg's surveillance cameras in toilets, which test the boundaries of privacy. The critic suggested, "Do we dare enter a toilet any more?"

4 THE LAY OF THE LAND

Sweden stretches about 1,600km (994 miles) from north to south and is one of the farthest countries from the equator. From north to south, Sweden lies at roughly the same latitude as Alaska.

Sweden can be divided into three main regions: the mountainous northern zone of Norrland; Svealand, the lake-filled, hilly region of central Sweden; and Götaland, the broad plateau in southern Sweden, home of most of the country's agricultural enterprises.

Much of the land is pristine: Forests cover more than half of Sweden, and less than 10% of the land is used for agriculture. Sweden has more than 100,000 lakes, including Vänern, the largest in western Europe. About 9% of the countryside is covered by lakes, which play an important role in transporting goods from the Baltic ports to cities throughout Sweden and the rest of Scandinavia. Canals link many of these lakes to the sea. The most important of these is the Göta Canal. Constructed in the 19th century, this 600km-long (373-mile) canal links Gothenburg in the west to Stockholm in the east. Some 195km (121 miles) of canals were constructed to connect the various lakes and rivers that make up this waterway.

Sweden's rivers tend to be short and to empty into its numerous lakes. They're used for short-haul transportation, linking the network of lakes, but especially for providing hydroelectric power to fuel the many factories scattered throughout the countryside. The most important rivers are the Pite, the Lule, and the Indal.

Sweden's expansive seacoast is more than 2,500km (1,553 miles) long. The west is bounded by the Kattegat and the Skagerrak, and the east by the Gulf of Bothnia and the Baltic Sea. Numerous small islands and reefs dot the eastern and southwestern coasts. If all the inlets and islands were included, the coastline of Sweden would measure 7,500km (4,660 miles). Öland and Gotland, Sweden's largest, most populated islands, are situated in the Baltic Sea, off the eastern coast.

Sweden is a center for alpine activities, including skiing, hiking, and glacier walking—most of which take place in the mountainous regions of Norrland. This far-northern area is home to many of the country's highest peaks, including its highest mountain, Kebnekaise, at 2,080m (6,824 ft.).

The flora of Sweden varies with the region. There are five rather disparate zones,

> **Fun Facts** **Did You Know?**
>
> - Sweden ranks second after Finland in coffee consumption per capita worldwide. In 2003, the Swedes consumed an average of roughly three to five cups per person per day.
> - Counting all the inlets, promontories, and islands, Sweden has a coastal strip 7,500km (4,660 miles) long—a fifth of the Earth's circumference.
> - More than half the couples living together in Sweden are unmarried.
> - Sweden has contributed two words to international gastronomy: *smörgåsbord* (smorgasbord in English) and *Absolut*.
> - In 2003, the world's longest smorgasbord was prepared in Sweden, stretching for 718m (2,356 ft.).
> - Sweden is one of the five nations that established colonies in North America.

each supporting a distinct array of plant life: the tundra in the north, coniferous forests below the timber line, central Sweden's birch forests, coniferous forests in the south, and the beech and oak zones found in the southern regions.

Animal life also differs depending on the region. The countryside teems with bears, elk, reindeer, fox, wolves, and otters. Numerous game birds also make their home in Sweden's expansive forests.

5 SWEDEN IN POPULAR CULTURE

BOOKS

ART & ARCHITECTURE The most comprehensive survey of Swedish art is found in *A History of Swedish Art,* by Mereth Lindgren, published in 1987. For architecture buffs, *Sweden: 20th Century* was published in 1998, so it's current almost to the dawn of the 21st century. You can see the emergence of Swedish modernism in this opus.

HISTORY & MYTHOLOGY *The Early Vasas: A History of Sweden, 1523–1611,* by Michael Roberts, covers one of the most dramatic and action-filled eras in Sweden's long history. *Scandinavian Folk & Fairy Tales,* edited by Claire Booss, is an extraordinary collection filled with elves, dwarfs, trolls, goblins, and other spirits of the house and barnyard.

BIOGRAPHY *Sweden in North America (1638–1988),* by Sten Carlsson, follows the lives of some of the 2% of the North American population that has some sort of Swedish background—from Greta Garbo to Charles Lindbergh.

Alfred Nobel and the Nobel Prizes, by Nils K. Ståhle, traces the life of the 19th-century Swedish industrialist and creator of the coveted awards that bear his name.

Garbo: Her Story, by Antoni Gronowicz, is a controversial, unauthorized memoir based on a long and intimate friendship; it goes beyond the fabulous face, with many candid details of this most reluctant of movie legends.

LITERATURE & THEATER *A History of Swedish Literature,* by Ingemar Algulin, is the best overview on the subject—from the runic inscriptions of the Viking age up to modern fiction.

The Story of Gösta Berling, by Selma Lagerlöf, is the acclaimed work—originally published in 1891—that Garbo filmed.

Three Plays: Father, Miss Julie, Easter, by August Strindberg, provides an insight into the world of this strange Swedish genius who wrote a number of highly arresting dramas; these are some of his best known.

PIPPI LONGSTOCKING The world was saddened to learn of the death in 2002 of Astrid Lindgren, the Swedish writer of the Pippi Longstocking tales, who died at the age of 94 at her home in Stockholm. One of the world's most widely translated authors, Lindgren horrified parents but captivated millions of children around the globe with her whimsical, rollicking stories about a carrot-haired *enfant terrible.* In 1999, she was voted the most popular Swede of the century, having produced more than 70 books for young people. The best known is *Pippi Longstocking,* first published in 1945.

FILM *Ingmar Bergman: The Cinema as Mistress,* by Philip Mosley, is a critical study of Bergman's *oeuvre* dating from his earliest work as a writer-director in the late 1940s up to *Autumn Sonata.*

Swedish Cinema, from Ingeborg Holm to Fanny and Alexander, by Peter Cowie, covers the complete history of Swedish films, from the emergence of the silent era to the rise of Ingmar Bergman, up to the most recent wave.

FILM

Ingmar Bergman is easily the country's most famous director. Born in Uppsala in 1918, he made his debut in 1938 as an amateur director at a theater in Stockholm, but didn't release his first feature film, *Crisis,* until 1946. It wasn't until the 1950s that he attracted world attention with such critically acclaimed films as *The Seventh Seal* (1957) and *Wild Strawberries* (1957). In the decades to come, he went on to score one success after another, including *Fanny and Alexander* (1982). Each Bergman film deals with a universal theme, such as human isolation. In his own words, his films look "deep into the twilight room of the human soul."

One Swedish celebrity who's perhaps even more famous than Ingmar Bergman is the similarly named Swedish actress **Ingrid Bergman** (1916–82). She appeared in some of the finest Hollywood movies of the 1940s, such films as *Notorious, The Bells of St. Mary's,* and *Casablanca.*

Another internationally known Swedish director is **Lasse Hallström,** born in 1946 and known for directing actors in Oscar-nominated pictures, including Michael Caine in *The Cider House Rules* (1999) and Leonardo DiCaprio in *What's Eating Gilbert Grape* (1993).

MUSIC

After the United States and Britain, Sweden is practically the third-biggest exporter of music in the world. Sweden also dominates the music scene in Scandinavia, producing the songs most often heard in Denmark and Norway. The biggest success story is accorded to **ABBA,** one of our all-time favorite groups, active from 1972 until 1982. One of the best-selling acts in the history of music, the quartet topped worldwide charts and continues to sell albums to this day—more than 300 million records so far. That means a lot of people like "Dancing Queen" and "Fernando."

Another popular band (but not half as successful as ABBA) is **Ace of Base,** a dance pop band from Gothenburg that released its debut album in 1992, scoring major success throughout the '90s with such hits as "Don't Turn Around" and "Cruel Summer." Two of the group's albums, *The Sign* and *The Bridge,* went platinum in the United States.

The **Cardigans** have also enjoyed international success. Formed in the town of Jönköping in 1992, the group has had hits in various genres, including alternative rock and early indie leanings that evoke '60s-inspired pop. After their breakthrough second album, *Life,* in 1995, the band scored their biggest international hit single with "Lovefool."

The rock band the **Hives** rose to prominence at the turn of the millennium as a leading part of a worldwide garage rock revival. In their matching black-and-white suits, The Hives scored their biggest hit with the song "Hate to Say I Told You So."

A more recent group, the **Concretes,** have also burst onto the scene. Despite generating some excitement with their recording *In Colour,* The Concretes seem unlikely to take the world by storm unless they can come up with a really big hit. But they're still busy writing and recording songs, so it's too early to write them off.

6 EATING & DRINKING IN SWEDEN

The fame of the *smörgåsbord* (smorgasbord)—a buffet-style feast—is justly deserved. Using a vast array of dishes—everything from Baltic herring to smoked reindeer—the smorgasbord can be eaten either as hors d'oeuvres or as a meal in itself.

One cardinal rule of the smorgasbord: Don't mix fish and meat dishes. It is customary to begin with *sill* (herring), prepared in many ways. Herring usually is followed by other treats from the sea (jellied eel, smoked fish, and raw pickled salmon); then diners proceed to the cold meat dishes, such as baked ham or liver paste, which are accompanied by vegetable salads. Hot dishes, often Swedish meatballs, come next and are backed up by cheese and crackers and sometimes a fresh fruit salad.

The smorgasbord is not served as often in Sweden as many visitors seem to believe, as it requires time-consuming preparation. Many Swedish families reserve it for special occasions. In lieu of the 40-dish smorgasbord, some restaurants have taken to serving a plate of *assietter* (hors d'oeuvres). One of the tricks for enjoying smorgasbord is timing. It's best to go early, when dishes are fresh. Late arrivals may be more fashionable, but the food often is stale.

The average times for meals in Sweden are generally from 8 to 11am for the standard continental breakfast, noon to 2:30pm for lunch, and as early as 5:30pm for dinner to around 8 or 8:30pm. (Many restaurants in Stockholm are open to midnight—but don't count on this in the small villages.)

A Swedish breakfast at your hotel might consist of cheese, ham, sausage, egg, bread, and perhaps *filmjölk,* a kind of sour-milk yogurt. **Smörgas,** the famous Swedish open-faced sandwich, like the Danish *smørrebrød* and Norwegian *smørbrød,* is a slice of buttered bread with something on top. It is eaten for breakfast or anytime during the day, and you'll find it at varying prices, depending on what you order and where you order it.

Unless you decide to have smorgasbord (never served in the evening) at lunch, you'll find that the Swedes do not go in for lavish spreads in the middle of the day. The usual luncheon order consists of one course, as you'll observe on menus, especially in larger towns. Dinner menus are for complete meals, with appetizer, main course and side dishes, and dessert included.

Generally, Swedish chefs tend to be far more expert with **fish dishes** (freshwater pike and salmon are star choices) than with meat courses. The Swedes go stark raving mad at the sight of *kraftor* (crayfish), in

Ikea Style

One of the most famous manufacturers of household furniture and housewares in the world is Ikea, founded after World War II. Ikea's stores are sprawling warehouses filled with a cornucopia of inexpensive modern furniture and household accessories in clean lines. Their trademark style involves ample amounts of birch trim and birch veneer, sometimes accented with black, always presented in a "less is more" format that shows the virtues of simplicity and efficiency. From the core of two megastores set to the north and south of Stockholm, a series of other outlets have sprung up around the world. Vital to the organization's self-image is the presence of a cafeteria serving all-Swedish food. It provides cost-conscious refreshments and pick-me-ups that fortify shoppers (and those who merely crave *frikadeller* [meatballs]) at budget prices.

season from mid-August to mid-September. This succulent, dill-flavored delicacy is eaten with the fingers, and much of the fun is the elaborate ritual surrounding its consumption.

A platter of thin **pancakes,** served with lingonberries (comparable to cranberries), is the traditional Thursday-night dinner in Sweden. It often is preceded by yellow split-pea soup seasoned with pork. It's good any night of the week—but somehow better on Thursday.

Swedish cuisine used to be deficient in fresh vegetables and fruits, and relied heavily on canned goods, but this is no longer true. Potatoes are the staff of life, but fresh salads also pepper the cuisine landscape, especially in big cities.

The calorie-laden Swedish pastry—the mainstay of the *konditori* (cafeteria)—is tempting and fatal to weight-watchers.

DRINKS *Kaffe* (coffee) is the universal drink in Sweden, although tea (taken straight) and milk also are popular. The water is perfectly safe to drink all over Sweden. Those who want a reprieve from alcohol might find the fruit-flavored **Pommac** a good soft-drink beverage, but Coca-Cola is ubiquitous.

The state monopoly, Systembolaget, controls the sale of alcoholic beverages. Licensed restaurants may sell alcohol after noon only (1pm on Sun).

Schnapps, or aquavit, served icy cold, is a superb Swedish drink, often used to accompany smorgasbord. The run-of-the-mill Swedish **beer** (pilsner) has only a small amount of alcohol. All restaurants serve *lättol* (light beer) and *folköl,* a somewhat stronger brew. Swedish vodka, or **brännvin,** is made from corn and potatoes and flavored with different spices. All *brännvin* is served ice-cold in schnapps glasses. Keep in mind that aquavit is much stronger than it looks, and Sweden has strictly enforced rules about drinking and driving. Most Swedes seem to drink their liquor straight. But mixed drinks, especially in urban areas, are now more commonplace. Either way, the drink prices are sky-high.

3

Planning Your Trip to Sweden

In the pages that follow, we've compiled everything you need to know about how to handle the practical details of planning your trip in advance—from airlines to a calendar of events to details on currency and more.

1 VISITOR INFORMATION

In the **United States,** contact the **Scandinavian Tourist Board,** 655 Third Ave., 18th Floor, New York, NY 10017 (℃ **212/885-9700;** www.goscandinavia.com or www.visitsweden.com), at least 3 months in advance for maps, sightseeing information, ferry schedules, and other advice and tips.

In the **United Kingdom,** contact the **Swedish Travel & Tourism Council,** 11 Montague Place, London W1H 2AL (℃ **020/7108-6168**).

You also can try the website **www.visitsweden.com**.

MAPS Many tourist offices supply maps of their districts free, and you also can contact one of the Swedish automobile clubs. Bookstores throughout Sweden also sell detailed maps of the country and of such major cities as Gothenburg and Stockholm. If you plan to tour Sweden, consider the best Road Atlas published: *Vägatlas over Sverige,* published by Mötormännens Riksförbund. It's detailed and very reliable and is available at most bookstores.

2 ENTRY REQUIREMENTS

U.S., Canadian, U.K., Irish, Australian, and New Zealand citizens with a **valid passport** don't need a visa to enter Sweden if they don't expect to stay more than 90 days and don't expect to work there. If, after entering Sweden, you want to stay more than 90 days, you can apply for a permit for an extra 90 days, which as a rule is granted immediately. Go to the nearest police headquarters or to your home country's consulate. If your passport is lost or stolen, head to your consulate as soon as possible for a replacement.

For information on how to get a passport, go to "Passports" in the appendix—the websites listed provide downloadable passport applications as well as the current fees for processing passport applications. For an up-to-date country-by-country listing of passport requirements around the world, go to the "Foreign Entry Requirement" Web page of the U.S. Department of State at **http://travel.state.gov.**

CUSTOMS

WHAT YOU CAN BRING INTO SWEDEN Foreign visitors can bring along most items for personal use duty-free, including fishing tackle, a pair of skis, two tennis rackets, a baby carriage, two hand-held cameras with 10 rolls of film, and 400 cigarettes or a quantity of cigars or

Destination: Sweden—Predeparture Checklist

- Citizens of European Union countries can cross into Sweden for as long as they wish. Citizens of other countries must have a passport.
- If you purchased traveler's checks, have you recorded the check numbers and stored the documentation separately from the checks?
- Did you pack your camera and an extra set of camera batteries, and purchase enough film? If you packed film in your checked baggage, did you invest in protective pouches to shield film from airport X-rays?
- Do you have a safe, accessible place to store money?
- Did you bring identification cards that could entitle you to discounts, such as AAA and AARP cards, student IDs, and so on?
- Did you bring emergency drug prescriptions and extra glasses and/or contact lenses?
- Do you have your credit card PIN numbers?
- If you have an e-ticket for your flight, do you have documentation?
- Did you leave a copy of your itinerary with someone at home?
- Do you have the address and phone number of your country's embassy with you?

pipe tobacco not exceeding 500 grams. Strict limits exist on importing alcoholic beverages. However, for alcohol bought tax-paid, limits are much more liberal than in other countries of the European Union.

WHAT YOU CAN TAKE HOME Rules governing what you can bring back duty-free vary from country to country and are subject to change, but they're generally posted on the Web.

Returning **U.S. citizens** who have been away for at least 48 hours are allowed to bring back, once every 30 days, $800 worth of merchandise duty-free. You'll be charged a flat rate of duty on the next $1,000 worth of purchases. Be sure to have your receipts handy. On mailed gifts, the duty-free limit is $200 or less. You cannot bring fresh foodstuffs into the United States; tinned foods, however, are allowed. For more specific guidance, contact the **Customs & Border Protection (CBP),**

1300 Pennsylvania Ave., Washington, DC 20229 (© **877/287-8667;** www.cbp.gov), and request the free pamphlet *Know Before You Go.* For a clear summary of Canadian rules, request the book *I Declare* from the **Canada Border Services Agency,** 1730 St. Laurent Blvd., Ottawa K1G 4KE (© **800/461-9999** in Canada, or 204/ 983-3500; www.cbsa-asfc.gc.ca). If you're a citizen of the United Kingdom, contact **HM's Customs and Excise Office,** National Advise Service, Dorset House, Stamford Street, London SE1 9PY (© **0845/010-9000;** www.hmce.gov.uk). Australian citizens should contact the **Australian Customs Service,** GPO Box 8, Sydney NSW 2001 (© **1300/363-263** in Australia; www.customs.gov.au). New Zealanders should contact **New Zealand Customs,** 17–21 Whitmore St., Box 2218, Wellington, NZ (© **04/473-6099;** www.customs.govt.nz).

3 WHEN TO GO

THE CLIMATE Sweden's climate is hard to classify because temperatures, influenced by the Gulf Stream, vary considerably from the fields of Skåne to the Arctic Circle wilderness of Lapland.

The country as a whole has many sunny days in summer, but it's not super hot. July is the warmest month, with temperatures in both Stockholm and Gothenburg averaging around 64°F (18°C). February is the coldest month, when the temperature in Stockholm averages around 26°F (–3°C). Gothenburg is a few degrees warmer.

It's not always true that the farther north you go, the cooler it becomes. During summer, the northern parts of the country—from Halsingland to northern Lapland—may suddenly have the warmest weather and the bluest skies. Check the weather forecasts on television and in the newspapers. (Swedes claim these forecasts are 99% reliable.)

SUMMER When it comes to weather, the ideal time to visit Sweden is from June to August. At this time, all its cafes and most attractions, including open-air museums, are open, and thousands flock to the north of Sweden to enjoy the midnight sun. (However, except for special festivals and folkloric presentations, the major cultural venues in Sweden, including opera, dance, ballet, and theater, shut down in summer.) Summer also is the most expensive time to fly to Sweden, as this is peak season. To compensate, hotels sometimes grant summer discounts. (It pays to ask.)

SPRING & FALL The months of spring and autumn, notably May through June and the month of September, are almost prettier than the Swedish summers. When spring comes to the Swedish countryside, wildflowers burst into bloom after a long dark winter.

WINTER Scandinavia's off season is winter (about Nov 1–Mar 21). Many visitors, except those on business, prefer to avoid Sweden in winter. The cold weather sets in by October, and you'll need to keep bundled up heavily until long past April. However, other more adventurous tourists go to Sweden in spite of, or even because of, the winter. Students have returned to such university cities as Stockholm and Lund, and life seems more vibrant then. Cultural activities also abound. Skiers also go to Sweden in winter, but we don't recommend it. It is pitch dark in winter in the north of Sweden, and the slopes have to be artificially lit. You'd be better off soaking up the alpine sun in Germany, Switzerland, or Austria.

Of course, one of the most eerie and fascinating things you can experience in Sweden is to see the shimmering northern lights, and they can be viewed only in the winter.

Sweden's Average Daytime Temperatures (°F/°C)

	Jan	Feb	Mar	Apr	May	June	July	Aug	Sept	Oct	Nov	Dec
Stockholm	27/–3	26/–3	31/–1	40/4	50/10	59/15	64/18	62/17	54/12	45/7	37/3	32/0
Karesuando	6/–14	5/–15	12/–11	23/–5	39/4	54/12	59/15	51/11	44/7	31/–1	9/–13	5/–15
Karlstad	33/1	30/–1	28/–2	37/3	53/12	63/17	62/17	59/15	54/12	41/5	29/–2	26/–3
Lund	38/3	36/2	34/1	43/6	57/14	63/17	64/18	61/16	57/14	47/8	37/3	37/3

Fun Facts The Midnight Sun

In summer, the sun never fully sets in northern Sweden; even in the south, daylight can last until 11pm, and then the sun rises around 3am. The best vantage points and dates when you can see the thrilling spectacle of the midnight sun are as follows: **Bjoürkliden,** from May 26 to July 19; **Abisko,** from June 12 to July 4; **Kiruna,** from May 31 to July 14; and **Gällivare,** from June 2 to July 12. All these places can be reached by public transportation.

Remember that although the sun may be shining brightly at midnight, it's not as strong as at midday. Bring along a warm jacket or sweater.

SWEDEN CALENDAR OF EVENTS

The dates given here may in some cases be only approximations. Be sure to check with the tourist office before you make plans to attend a specific event. For information on Walpurgis night and midsummer celebrations, call the local tourist offices in the town where you plan to stay. (See individual chapters for the phone numbers.)

JANUARY

Kiruna Snow Festival, Kiruna. The biggest snow festival in Europe takes place in this far northern city under the northern lights, featuring dog-sledding and reindeer racing. Call the Kiruna Lapland Tourist Bureau for more information at ✆ **0980/188-80** (www.snow festival.se). January 27 to February 1.

Gothenburg Film Festival, Gothenburg. Entering its fourth decade, this festival attracts film buffs from all over Europe, showing 400 movies, often months before their official release. For more information, call the Gothenburg Film Festival at ✆ **0303/339-30-00** (www.filmfestival.org). January 23 to February 2.

APRIL

Walpurgis Night, nationwide. Celebrations with bonfires, songs, and speeches welcome the advent of spring. These are especially lively celebrations among university students at Uppsala, Lund, Stockholm, Gothenburg, and Umeå.

Visit **www.scandinavica.com/culture/ tradition/walpurgis.htm** for info. April 30.

MAY

Drottningholm Court Theater, Drottningholm. Some 30 opera and ballet performances, from baroque to early romantic, are presented in the unique 1766 Drottningholm Court Theater in Drottningholm, with original decorative paintings and stage mechanisms. Call ✆ **08/660-82-25** (www.dtm.se) for tickets or ✆ **08/587-140-00** for information. Late May to late September.

JUNE

Midsummer, nationwide. Swedes celebrate Midsummer Eve all over the country. Maypole dances to the sound of the fiddle and accordion are the typical festive events of the day. Dalarna observes the most traditional celebrations. Check **www.sweden.se**. Mid-June.

JULY

Around Gotland Race, Sandhamn. The biggest and most exciting openwater Scandinavian sailing race starts and finishes at Sandhamn, in the Stockholm archipelago. About 450 boats, mainly from Nordic countries, take part. Call ℂ **08/571-530-68,** in Stockholm, for information (www.gotlandrunt.se). Two days in mid-July.

Rättviksdansen (International Festival of Folk Dance and Music), Rättvik. Every other year, for some 20 years, around 1,000 folk dancers and musicians from all over the world have gathered to participate in this folkloric tradition. Check **http://goscandinavia. about.com**. Last week in July.

Stockholm Jazz Festival, Stockholm. This is a big summer event occurring on the grounds and inside the Modern Art Museum on the island of Skeppsholmen. An outdoor band shell is erected, and members of the audience sit on the lawn to hear top jazz artists from Europe and America. Tickets cost 350SEK to 450SEK ($48–$62/£24–£31) per person. For more information, search **www.stockholm jazz.com**. Last week in July for 7 days.

Gay Pride, Tantolunden at Liljeholmsbron, Stockholm. The largest gay pride festival in the Nordic countries features workshops, concerts, theater, and attractions for 1 week. There's even a local parade where Vikings go gay and/or in drag. For more information, call Stockholm Pride at ℂ **08/33-59-55** (www. stockholmpride.org). July 31 to August 6 (dates can vary).

AUGUST

Medieval Week, Gotland. Numerous events are held throughout the island of Gotland—including medieval tours, concerts, plays, festivities, and shows. For more information, contact the Office of Medieval Week, Hästgatan 4, S-621

56 Visby (ℂ **0498/29-10-70;** www. gotland.net). Early August.

Minnesota Day, Utvandra Hus, Växjöu (Småland). Swedish-American relations are celebrated at the House of Emigrants with speeches, music, singing, and dancing; the climax is the election of the Swedish-American of the year. Call ℂ **0470/201-20** for information. Second Sunday in August.

DECEMBER

Nobel Day, Stockholm. The king, members of the royal family, and invited guests attend the Nobel Prize ceremony for literature, physics, chemistry, medicine, physiology, and economics. Attendance is by invitation only. The ceremony is held at the concert hall and followed by a banquet at City Hall. Visit **http://nobelprize.org** for info. December 10.

Lucia, the Festival of Lights, nationwide. To celebrate the shortest day and longest night of the year, young girls, called "Lucias," appear in restaurants, offices, schools, and factories, wearing floor-length white gowns and special headdresses, each holding a lighted candle. They are accompanied by "star boys"—young men in white, with wizard hats covered with gold stars, each holding a wand with a large golden star at the top. One of the "Lucias" is eventually crowned queen. In olden days, Lucia was known as "Little Christmas." This celebration is observed nationwide. Actual planned events change from year to year and vary from community to community. The best place for tourists to observe this event is at the open-air museum at Skansen in Stockholm. December 13.

4 GETTING THERE & GETTING AROUND

GETTING THERE
By Plane

Flying in winter—Scandinavia's off season—is cheapest; summer is the most expensive season. Spring and fall are in between. In any season, midweek fares (Mon–Thurs) are the lowest.

The Major Airlines

Travelers from the U.S. East Coast usually choose **SAS** (© **800/221-2350** in the U.S.; www.flysas.com). Another major competitor is **American Airlines** (© **800/ 433-7300** in the U.S.; www.aa.com), which offers daily flights to Stockholm from Chicago, and excellent connections through Chicago from American's vast North American network. Travelers from Seattle usually fly SAS to Copenhagen, then connect to one of the airline's frequent shuttle flights into Stockholm.

Other airlines fly to gateway European cities and then connect to other flights into Stockholm. **British Airways** (© **800/ AIRWAYS** [247-9297] in the U.S. and Canada; www.britishairways.com), for example, flies from more than 25 North American cities to London/Heathrow, and then connects with onward flights to Stockholm. **Northwest** (© **800/225-2525** in the U.S.; www.nwa.com) also flies at frequent intervals to London, from which ongoing flights to Stockholm are available on either SAS or British Airways. Finally, **Icelandair** (© **800/223-5500** in the U.S.; www.icelandair.com) has proved to be an excellent choice for travel to Stockholm, thanks to connections through its home port of Reykjavik.

People traveling from Britain can fly **SAS** (© **0870/6072-77-27** in London; www.flysas.com) from London's Heathrow to Stockholm on any of five daily nonstop flights. Flying time is about 2¹/₂ hours

each way. Likewise, SAS flies daily to Stockholm from Manchester, making a brief stop in Copenhagen en route. Flight time from Manchester to Stockholm is about 3¹/₂ hours each way.

Flying for Less: Tips for Getting the Best Airfare

Passengers sharing the same airplane cabin rarely pay the same fare. Travelers who need to purchase tickets at the last minute, change their itinerary at a moment's notice, or fly one-way often get stuck paying the premium rate. Here are some ways to keep your airfare costs down.

- Passengers who can book their tickets long in advance, who can stay over Saturday night, or who fly midweek or at less-trafficked hours may pay a fraction of the full fare. If your schedule is flexible, say so, and ask if you can secure a cheaper fare by changing your flight plans.

- You can also save on airfares by keeping an eye out in local newspapers for promotional specials or fare wars, when airlines lower prices on their most popular routes. You rarely see fare wars offered for peak travel times, but if you can travel in the off-months, you may snag a bargain.

- Search the Internet for cheap fares at such sites as **Travelocity, Expedia,** and **Orbitz.**

- Consolidators, also known as bucket shops, are great sources for international tickets, although they usually can't beat the Internet on fares within North America. Start by looking in Sunday newspaper travel sections; U.S. travelers should focus on the *New York Times, Los Angeles Times,* and *Miami Herald. Beware:* Bucket shop tickets are usually nonrefundable or rigged with

Baggage Weight Allowance

Effective September 2006, **SAS** imposed a maximum weight allowance of 70 pounds (32kg) per bag. If any piece of baggage exceeds this weight, it must be repacked or sent as cargo.

stiff cancellation penalties, often as high as 50% to 75% of the ticket price, and some put you on charter airlines, which may leave at inconvenient times and experience delays. Several reliable consolidators are worldwide and available online. **STA Travel** (© **800/781-4040;** www.statravel.com) has been the world's lead consolidator for students since purchasing Council Travel, but their fares are competitive for travelers of all ages. **ELTExpress** (www.flights.com) has excellent fares worldwide, particularly to Europe. They also have "local" websites in 12 countries. **FlyCheap** (© **800/FLY-CHEAP** [359-2432]; www. 1800flycheap.com), owned by package-holiday megalith MyTravel, has especially good fares to sunny destinations. **Air Tickets Direct** (© **888/858-8884;** www.airticketsdirect.com) is based in Montreal and leverages the currently weak Canadian dollar for low fares.

By Car from Continental Europe

FROM GERMANY   You can drive to the northern German port of Travemuünde and catch the 7¹/₂-hour ferry (www.direct ferries.co.uk) to the Swedish port of Trelleborg, a short drive south of Malmö. This route saves many hours by avoiding transit through Denmark. If you want to visit Denmark before Sweden, you can take the 3-hour car ferry from Travemuünde to Gedser in southern Denmark. From Gedser, the E64 and the E4 express highways head north to Copenhagen. After a visit here, you can take the Øresund Bridge from Copenhagen to Malmö.

FROM NORWAY   From Oslo, E18 goes east through Karlstad all the way to Stockholm. This is a long but scenic drive.

By Train from Copenhagen or Oslo

Copenhagen is the main rail hub between the other Scandinavian countries and the rest of Europe. Seven daily trains run between Copenhagen and Stockholm, six between Copenhagen and Gothenburg. All connect with the Danish ferries that operate to Sweden via Helsingør or Frederikshavn.

At least three trains a day depart from Oslo to Stockholm (travel time: about 6¹/₂ hr.). One of the trains leaves Oslo around 11pm. Three trains run from Oslo to Gothenburg daily (travel time: about 4 hr.).

Rail Passes for North American Travelers

If you plan to travel extensively on the European and/or British railroads, it would be worthwhile for you to get a copy of the latest edition of the *Thomas Cook European Timetable of Railroads*. It's available online at **www.thomascooktime tables.com**.

EURAILPASS   If you plan to travel extensively in Europe, the **Eurailpass** might be a good bet. It's valid for first-class rail travel in 18 European countries. With one ticket, you travel whenever and wherever you please; more than 100,000 rail miles are at your disposal. Here's how it works: The pass is sold only in North America. A Eurailpass good for 15 days costs $796, a pass for 21 days is $1,032, a 1-month pass costs $1,281, a 2-month pass is $1,808, and a 3-month pass goes for $2,232. Children under 4 travel free if they don't occupy a seat; all children under 12 who take up a seat are charged half-price. If you're under 26, you can buy a **Eurail Select Pass Youth.** For three countries, a Youth Pass costs $328 for 5 days in 2 months; $365 for 6 days in 2 months; $428 for 8 days in 2 months, and $495 for 10 days in 2 months. Travelers considering buying a 15-day or 1-month pass should estimate rail distance before deciding whether a pass is worthwhile. To take full advantage of the tickets for 15 days or a month, you'd have to spend a great deal of time on the train. Eurailpass holders are entitled to substantial discounts on certain buses and ferries as well. Travel agents in all towns and railway agents in such major cities as New York, Montreal, and Los Angeles sell all of these tickets. For information on Eurailpasses and other European train data, call **RailEurope** at ℭ **877/ 272-RAIL** [7245], or visit it on the Web at **www.raileurope.com**.

Eurail Select Saver Pass offers a 15% discount to each person in a group of three or more people traveling together between April and September, or two people traveling together between October and March. The Saver Pass is valid all over Europe for first class only. One adult can travel in three countries at the following prices: $428 for 5 days in 2 months, $474 for 6 days in 2 months, $564 for 8 days in 2 months, and $647 for 10 days in 2 months. Even more freedom is offered by the **Saver Flexipass,** which is similar to the Eurail Saverpass, except that you are not confined to consecutive-day travel. For travel over any 10 days within 2 months, the fare is $939; for any 15 days over 2 months, the fare is $1,234.

Eurail Flexipass allows even greater flexibility. It's valid in first class and offers the same privileges as the Eurailpass. However, it provides a number of individual travel days over a much longer period of consecutive days. Using this pass makes it possible to stay longer in one city and not lose a single day of travel. There are two Flexipasses: 10 days of travel within 2 months for $797, and 15 days of travel within 2 months for $1,049.

With many of the same qualifications and restrictions as the Eurail Flexipass, the **Eurail Youth Flexipass** is sold only to travelers under age 25. It allows 10 days of travel within 2 months for $609 and 15 days of travel within 2 months for $803.

EURAIL SWEDEN PASS If you're traveling just in Sweden, this pass allows you unlimited travel on the national rail system of Sweden from 3 to 8 days in 1 month. You have a choice of first- or second-class travel, with discounts for youths and seniors. Prices are as follows: First class for adults is $389 to $589; youth $262 to $407; seniors $299 to $455. Second class for adults is $299 to $455; youth $229 to $339; seniors $197 to $319.

SCANRAIL PASS If your visit to Europe will be primarily in Scandinavia, the Scanrail pass may be better and cheaper than the Eurailpass. This pass allows its owner a designated number of days of free rail travel within a larger time block. (Presumably, this allows for days devoted to sightseeing scattered among days of rail transfers between cities or sites of interest.) You can choose a total of any 5 days of unlimited rail travel during a 2-month period, 8 days of rail travel within a 2-month period, 10 days of rail travel within a 2-month period, or 21 days of unlimited rail travel. The pass, which is valid on all lines of the state railways of Denmark, Finland, Norway, and Sweden, offers discounts or free travel on some (but not all) of the region's ferry lines as well. The pass can be purchased only in North America. It's available from any office of **RailEurope** (ℭ **800/848-7245**) or **ScanAm World Tours,** 108 N. Main St., Cranbury, NJ 08512 (ℭ **800/545-2204;** www.scandinaviantravel.com).

You can choose only second-class rail transport: 5 days out of 2 months costs $173 to $346, 8 days out of 2 months costs $219 to $437, 10 days out of 2 months costs $243 to $485, and 21 consecutive days of unlimited travel costs $232 to $463. Seniors get an 11% discount, and students receive a 30% discount. Check **www. scanrail.com**.

Rail Passes for British Travelers

If you plan to do a lot of exploring, you might prefer one of the three rail passes designed for unlimited train travel within a designated region during a predetermined number of days. These passes are sold in Britain and several other European countries and can be used only by European residents.

An **InterRail Global Pass** (www.inter rail.com) allows unlimited travel through Europe, except Albania and the republics of the former Soviet Union.

Adults purchasing an InterRail global Pass can travel first or second class. In first class, prices are $329 for 5 days in 10 days; $489 for 10 days in 22 days; $629 for 22 days continuous; or $809 for 1 month. In second class, the cost is $249 for 5 days in 10 days; $359 for 10 days in 22 days; $469 for 22 days continuous; and $599 for 1 month continuous.

An **InterRail Global Youth Pass** is also sold and is available only in second class. Youth are defined as those travelers ranging from age 12 up to and including 25 years of age. The cost is $159 for 5 days in 10 days, $239 for 10 days in 22 days, $309 for 22 days continuous, and $399 for 1 month continuous.

For information on buying individual rail tickets or any of the just-mentioned passes, contact **National Rail Inquiries,** Victoria Station, London (© **0845/748-4950;** www.nationalrail.co.uk). Tickets and passes are also available at any of the larger railway stations as well as selected travel agencies throughout Britain and the rest of Europe.

By Ship & Ferry

FROM DENMARK Ferries ply the waters for the brief run from Helsingør, a short drive north of Copenhagen, and Helsingborg, Sweden, just across the narrow channel that separates the countries. The 25-minute trip on a conventional ferry (not a catamaran) runs at 10- to 40-minute intervals, 24 hours a day. Operated by **Scandlines** (© **33/15-15-15** in Copenhagen; www.scandlines.dk), it's one of the most popular ferry routes in Europe. Round-trip passage costs 74€ ($118/£59) for a car with up to nine passengers; the ticket is valid for up to 12 months.

FROM ENGLAND Two English ports, Harwich (year-round) and Newcastle-upon-Tyne (summer only), offer ferry service to Sweden. Harwich to Gothenburg takes 23 to 25 hours, Newcastle to Gothenburg 27 hours. Boats on both routes offer overnight accommodations and the option of transporting cars. Prices are lower for passengers who book in advance through the company's U.S. agent. For details, call **Sea Europe Holidays,** 6801 Lake Worth Rd., Ste. 107, Lake Worth, FL 33467 (© **800/533-3755** in the U.S.; www.seaeurope.com).

FROM GERMANY **Stena Line Ferries** (© **031/85-80-00;** www.stenaline.com) sails daily from Kiel to Gothenburg. The trip takes 14 hours and costs £124 ($248) for a one-way passage.

GETTING AROUND SWEDEN
By Plane

WITHIN SWEDEN Stockholm is Sweden's major gateway for Scandinavia's best-known airline, **SAS** (Scandinavian Airlines System), while the airport at Gothenburg supplements Stockholm by funneling traffic into the Swedish heartland. In the mid-1990s, SAS acquired **LIN Airlines (Linjeflyg);** thus, it now has access to small and medium-size airports throughout Sweden, including such remote but scenic outposts as Kiruna in Swedish Lapland. Among the larger Swedish cities serviced by SAS are Malmö, Karlstad, and Kalmar.

During the summer, SAS offers a number of promotional "minifares," which enable one to travel round-trip between two destinations for just slightly more than the price of a conventional one-way ticket on the same route. Children under 12 travel free during the summer, and up to two children 12 to 17 can travel with a parent at significantly reduced rates. Airfares tend to be most reduced during July, with promotions almost as attractive during most of June and August. A minimum 3-night stopover at the destination is required for these minifares, and it must include a Friday or a Saturday night. When buying your tickets, always ask the airline or travel agency about special promotions and corresponding restrictions.

Those under 26 can take advantage of SAS's special **standby fares,** and seniors over 65 can apply for additional discounts, depending on the destination.

WITHIN SCANDINAVIA The best way to get around the whole of Scandinavia is to take advantage of the air passes that apply to the entire region or, if you're traveling extensively in Europe, to use the special European passes. The vast distances of Scandinavia encourage air travel between some of its most far-flung points. One of the most worthwhile promotions is SAS's **Visit Scandinavia Airpass.** This pass, available only to travelers who fly SAS across the Atlantic, includes up to eight coupons, each of which is valid for any SAS flight within or between Denmark, Norway, and Sweden. Each coupon costs $96, $128, or $160, a price that's especially appealing when you consider that an economy-class ticket between Copenhagen and Stockholm can cost as much as 1,250SEK ($250/£125) each way. The pass is especially valuable if you plan to travel to the far northern frontiers of Sweden; in that case, the savings over the price of a regular economy-class ticket may be substantial. For information on purchasing the pass, call **SAS** (✆ **800/221-2350**).

By Train

The Swedish word for train is *tåg,* and the national system is the Statens Järnvägar, the Swedish State Railways.

Swedish trains follow tight schedules. Trains leave Malmö, Helsingborg, and Gothenburg for Stockholm every hour throughout the day, Monday through Friday. Trains depart every hour, or every other hour, to and from most big Swedish towns. On *expresståg* runs, seats must be reserved.

Children under 12 travel free when accompanied by an adult, and those up to age 18 are eligible for discounts.

By Bus

Rail lines cover only some of Sweden's vast distances. Where the train tracks end, buses usually serve as the link to remote villages. Buses are often equipped with toilets, adjustable seats, reading lights, and a telephone. Fares depend on the distance traveled. The one-way fare for the 525km (326-mile) trip from Stockholm to Gothenburg is 170SEK to 270SEK ($34–$53/£17–£27). **Swebus** (✆ **036/290-80-00;** www.swebusexpress. se), the country's largest bus company, provides information at the bus or railway stations in most cities. For travelers who don't buy a special rail pass (such as Eurail or ScanRail), bus travel can sometimes be cheaper than traveling the same distances by rail. It's a lot less convenient, however— except in the far north, where there isn't any alternative.

By Car Ferry

Considering that Sweden has some 100,000 lakes and one of the world's longest coastlines, ferries play a surprisingly small part in its transportation network.

After the car ferry crossings from northern Germany and Denmark, the most popular route is from the mainland to the island of Gotland, in the Baltic. Service is available from **Oskarshamn and Nynäshamn** (℗ **0771/22-33-00** for information). The famous "white boats" of the **Waxholm Steamship Company** (℗ **08/679-58-30;** www.waxholmsbolaget.se) also serve many destinations in the Stockholm archipelago.

By Car

Sweden maintains an excellent network of roads and highways, particularly in the southern provinces and in the central lake district. Major highways in the far north are kept clear of snow by heavy equipment that's in place virtually year-round. If you rent a car at any bona fide rental agency, you'll be given the appropriate legal documents, including proof of adequate insurance (in the form of a "Green Card"), as specified by your car-rental agreement. Current driver's licenses from Canada, the United Kingdom, New Zealand, Australia, and the United States are acceptable in Sweden.

RENTALS The major U.S.-based car-rental firms are represented throughout Sweden, both at airports and in urban centers. The companies' rates are aggressively competitive, although promotional sales will favor one company over the others from time to time. Prior to your departure from North America, it will be advantageous to shop around to find the lowest available rates. Membership in AAA or another auto club may enable you to get a moderate discount. Be aware that you may avoid a supplemental airport tax by picking up your car at a central location rather than at the airport.

Avis (℗ **800/331-1212;** www.avis. com) offers a wide variety of cars and has offices in all major cities in Sweden. **Hertz** (℗ **800/654-3131;** www.hertz.com) has offices located in all major cities, as well as major airports.

One auto supplier that might not automatically come to mind is **Kemwel** (℗ **800/ 678-0678;** www.kemwel.com), a broker that accumulates into one database the availability of rental cars in markets across Europe, including Sweden. Originally established in 1908, and now operating in close conjunction with its sister company, **Auto Europe** (℗ **800/223-5555;** www. autoeurope.com), it offers convenient and prepaid access to thousands of cars from a variety of reputable car-rental outfits throughout Europe, sometimes at rates a bit more favorable than those you might have gotten if you had gone through the hassle of contacting those companies directly. Car rentals are prereserved and prepaid, in dollars, prior to your departure for Europe, thereby avoiding the confusion about unfavorable currency conversions and government tax add-ons that you might have discovered after your return home. You're given the option, at the time of your booking, whether you want to include collision damage and other forms of insurance. Most car rentals can be picked up at the airport or in the downtown offices of cities throughout Sweden, and there's usually no penalty for one-way rentals.

For a list of car-rental agency telephone numbers and websites, see p. 392.

---

5 MONEY & COSTS

THE SWEDISH KRONA Sweden's basic unit of currency is the **krona** (or **SEK**). Note that the Swedes spell the plural kronor with an *o* instead of an *e* as in the kroner of Denmark and Norway. One krona is divided into 100 **oüre.** Bank notes are issued in denominations of 20, 50, 100, 500, 1,000, and 10,000 SEK.

The Swedish Kronor

At presstime for this edition, faced with some of the greatest fiscal instability since before World War II, U.S. and Swedish currency experts held widely varying opinions about the 2-year outlook for the interrelated values of the kronor, the dollar, the pound, and the euro. With that in mind, the following is a very rough guide for how the Swedish kronor might stack up against other international currencies during the lifetime of this edition.

For American readers: At the time of this writing, $1 U.S. = approximately 5SEK. (Stated differently, 1 krona = approximately 20 U.S. cents.) This was the rate of exchange used to calculate the simplified dollar values provided throughout this edition.

For British readers: At this writing, £1 U.K. = approximately 10SEK (or one krona = approximately 10 U.K. pence). This was the rate of exchange used to calculate the pound-designated values throughout this edition.

Regarding the euro: At the time of this writing, 1€ = approximately 10SEK, or, stated differently, 1SEK = approximately 10 eurocents.

These monetary relationships can and probably will change during the lifetime of this edition. For more on exact ratios between these and other currencies, check an up-to-date source at the time of your arrival in Sweden.

Silver coins are issued in denominations of 50 oüre and 1SEK and 5SEK.

ATMS PLUS, Cirrus, and other networks connect with automated teller machines throughout Scandinavia. Always determine the frequency limits for withdrawals and check to see if your PIN code must be reprogrammed for usage on your trip abroad. For **Cirrus** locations abroad, call © **800/424-7787** or visit **www.mastercard.com**. For PLUS usage abroad, check the PLUS site on the Web at **www.visa.com** or call © **800/843-7587**. *Note:* Remember that many banks impose a fee every time you use a card at another bank's ATM, and that fee can be higher for international transactions (up to $5 or more) than for domestic ones (where they're rarely more than $2). In addition, the bank from which you withdraw cash may charge its own fee. For international withdrawal fees, ask your bank.

CREDIT & CHARGE CARDS American Express, Diners Club, and Visa are widely recognized throughout Sweden. Discover cards are not accepted. If you see a Eurocard or Access sign, it means that the establishment accepts MasterCard. With an American Express, MasterCard, or Visa card, you also can withdraw currency from cash machines (ATMs) at various locations. Always check with your credit or charge card company about this before leaving home. Also, note that many banks now assess a 1% to 3% transaction fee on **all** charges you incur abroad (whether you're using the local currency or your native currency).

TRAVELER'S CHECKS You can buy traveler's checks at most banks. They are offered in denominations of $20, $50, $100, $500, and sometimes $1,000. Generally, you'll pay a service charge ranging from 1% to 4%.

The most popular traveler's checks are offered by **American Express** (© **800/528-4800;** http://home.americanexpress.com—this number accepts collect calls, offers service in several foreign languages, and

What Things Cost in Stockholm	SEK	US$	UK£
Taxi from the airport to the city center	220	44	22
Basic bus or subway fare	20	4	2
Double room at Berns Hotel (very expensive)	2,650	530	265
Double room at the Adlon Hotel (moderate)	1,350	270	135
Double room at the Bema (inexpensive)	950	190	95
Dinner for one, without wine, at Operakällaren (very expensive)	990	198	99
Dinner for one, without wine, at Prinsen (moderate)	340	68	34
Dinner for one, without wine, at Tennstopet (inexpensive)	224	45	22
Pint of beer (draft Pilsener) in a bar	45–60	9–12	4.50–6
Coca-cola in a cafe	20–30	4–6	2–3
Cup of coffee in a cafe	25	5	2.50
Movie ticket	85	17	8.50

exempts Amex gold and platinum card-holders from the 1% fee); **Visa** (© **800/732-1322**), from which AAA members can obtain Visa checks for a $9.95 fee (for checks up to $1,500) at most AAA offices or by calling © **866/339-3378**; and **MasterCard** (© **800/223-9920**).

American Express, Thomas Cook, Visa, and **MasterCard** offer **foreign currency traveler's checks,** which are useful in Sweden, as they're accepted at locations where dollar checks may not be.

If you carry traveler's checks, keep a record of their serial numbers separate from your checks, in the event that they are stolen or lost. You'll get a refund faster if you know the numbers.

6 HEALTH & SAFETY

STAYING HEALTHY

Sweden is viewed as a "safe" destination, although problems, of course, can and do occur anywhere. You don't need to get shots, most food is safe, and the water in cities and towns is potable. If you're concerned, order bottled water. It's easy to get a prescription filled in towns and cities, and nearly all hospitals in Sweden have English-speaking doctors and well-trained medical staffs.

What to Do If You Get Sick away from Home

Nearly all doctors in Sweden speak English. If you get sick, consider asking your hotel concierge to recommend a local doctor—even his or her own. You can also try the emergency room at a local hospital. Many hospitals also have walk-in clinics for emergency cases that are not life-threatening; you may not get immediate attention, but you won't pay the high price of an emergency room visit. We list hospitals and emergency numbers under "Fast Facts," in the various city chapters.

If you worry about getting sick away from home, consider purchasing **medical travel insurance** and carry your ID card in your purse or wallet. In most cases, your existing health plan will provide the coverage you need.

If you suffer from a chronic illness, consult your doctor before you depart. For conditions such as epilepsy, diabetes, or heart problems, wear a **MedicAlert identification tag** (✆ **888/633-4298;** www. medicalert.org), which will immediately alert doctors to your condition and give them access to your records through Med-icAlert's 24-hour hot line.

Contact the **International Association for Medical Assistance to Travelers** (IAMAT; ✆ **716/754-4883** or 416/652-0137; www.iamat.org) for tips on travel and health concerns in the countries you're visiting and lists of local, English-speaking doctors. The U.S. **Centers for Disease Control and Prevention** (✆ **800/311-3435** or 404/498-1515; www.cdc.gov) provides up-to-date information on necessary vaccines and health hazards by region or country. In Canada, contact **Health Canada** (✆ **613/957-2991;** www.hc-sc.gc.ca).

Travel Health Online (www.tripprep. com), sponsored by a consortium of travel medicine practitioners, may also offer helpful advice on traveling abroad. You can find listings of reliable clinics overseas at the **International Society of Travel Medicine** (www.istm.org).

U.K. nationals will need a **European Health Insurance Card** (EHIC; ✆ **0845/606-2030;** www.ehic.org.uk) to receive free or reduced-cost health benefits during a visit to a European Economic Area (EEA) country (European Union countries, plus Iceland, Liechtenstein, and Norway) or Switzerland.

We list **hospitals** and **emergency numbers** under "Fast Facts: Sweden" on p. 387.

STAYING SAFE

Sweden has a relatively low crime rate, with rare but increasing instances of violent crime. Most crimes involve the theft of personal property from cars or residences. Pickpockets might be a problem in public areas. Beware of pickpockets and purse snatchers who often work in pairs or groups, with one distracting the victim while another grabs valuables. They often operate in or near major tourist attractions, such as Stockholm's Old Town, restaurants, amusement parks, museums, bars, buses, and subway trains. Hotel breakfast rooms and lobbies attract professional, well-dressed thieves who blend in with guests and target unsuspecting tourists and business travelers. Valuables should not be left unguarded in these places, or in parked vehicles.

The loss or theft abroad of a U.S. passport should be reported immediately to the local police and the nearest U.S. embassy or consulate. The embassy/consulate staff can, for example, assist you by finding appropriate medical care, contacting family members or friends, and explaining how funds can be transferred. Although the investigation and prosecution of the crime is solely the responsibility of local authorities, consular officers can help you to understand the local criminal justice process and to find an attorney, if needed.

U.S. citizens may refer to the Department of State's pamphlet, *A Safe Trip Abroad,* for ways to promote a trouble-free journey. The pamphlet is available by mail from the **Superintendent of Documents, U.S. Government Printing Office,** Washington, DC 20402, or via the U.S. Department of State website at **http://travel. state.gov/travel/tips/safety/safety_1747. html.**

A number of resources and organizations in both North America and Britain exist to assist travelers with special needs in planning their trips to Sweden.

TRAVELERS WITH DISABILITIES

About two million people in Sweden have a disability; as a result, Sweden is especially conscious of their special needs. In general, trains, airlines, ferries, and department stores and malls are wheelchair accessible. Always call ahead to check on accessibility in hotels, restaurants, and sights you want to visit.

For information about wheelchair access, ferry and air travel, parking, and other matters, your best bet is to contact the Scandinavian Tourist Board (see "Visitor Information," earlier in this chapter). For information on youth hostels with special rooms for those with disabilities, contact **Svenska Turistföreningen,** P.O. Box 25, S-101 20 Stockholm (✆ **08/463-21-00;** www.stfturist.se).

Organizations that offer assistance to travelers with disabilities include **Moss Rehab** (✆ **800/CALL-MOSS** [225-5667]; www.mossresourcenet.org), which provides a library of accessible-travel resources online; **SATH** (Society for Accessible Travel and Hospitality; ✆ **212/447-7284;** www.sath.org), which offers a wealth of travel resources for people with all types of disabilities and informed recommendations on destinations, access guides, travel agents, tour operators, vehicle rentals, and companion services; and the **American Foundation for the Blind** (AFB; ✆ **800/232-5463** or 212/502-7600; www.afb. org), a referral resource for the blind or visually impaired that provides information on traveling with Seeing Eye dogs.

AirAmbulanceCard.com (✆ **877/424-7633**) is now partnered with SATH and allows you to preselect top-notch hospitals in case of an emergency.

Access-Able Travel Source (✆ **303/232-2979;** www.access-able.com) offers a comprehensive database on travel agents from around the world with experience in accessible travel; destination-specific access information; and links to such resources as service animals, equipment rentals, and access guides.

Many travel agencies offer customized tours and itineraries for travelers with disabilities. Among them are **Flying Wheels Travel** (✆ **507/451-5005;** www.flying wheelstravel.com) and **Accessible Journeys** (✆ 800/846-4537 or 610/521-0339; www.disabilitytravel.com).

Flying with Disability (www.flying-with-disability.org) is a comprehensive information source on airplane travel.

Also check out the quarterly magazine *Emerging Horizons* (www.emerging horizons.com), available by subscription.

The "Accessible Travel" link at **Mobility-Advisor.com** offers a variety of travel resources to persons with disabilities.

British travelers should contact **Holiday Care** (✆ **0845-124-9971** in the U.K. only; www.holidaycare.org.uk) to access a wide range of travel information and resources for elderly people and people with disabilities.

For more on organizations that offer resources to travelers with disabilities, go to Frommers.com.

GAY & LESBIAN TRAVELERS

Stockholm is the gay capital of Scandinavia, and Sweden ranks along with Norway, Denmark, and The Netherlands as among the most tolerant and gay-friendly nations on earth. Even gay marriage is now legal in this enlightened, sophisticated country. The age of consent is almost uniformly the same as for heterosexuals, usually 15 or 16. However, outside Stockholm and Gothenburg, you'll find few gay bars.

Many gay and lesbian organizations in Stockholm welcome visitors from abroad. Foremost among these is the **Federation for Gay and Lesbian Rights (RFSL),** Sveavägen 57 (Box 350), S-10126 Stockholm (© 08/501-62-900; www.rfsl.se), open Monday through Friday from 9am to 5pm. Established in 1950, the group has headquarters on the upper floors of the biggest gay nightlife center in Stockholm. Meetings are held weekly—a Wednesday 3pm meeting for gay men over 60 and a twice-monthly meeting of "Golden Ladies" (yes, they use the English expression) for lesbians over 50, plus a Monday-night youth session for those 18 to 21. They also operate a **Gay Switchboard** (© 08/501-62-970), staffed with volunteers; call daily from 8am to 11pm for information. The biggest event of the year is **Gay Pride Week,** usually held the first week in August. Call or write the RFSL for information.

The **International Gay and Lesbian Travel Association (IGLTA;** © **954/776-2626;** www.iglta.org) is the trade association for the gay and lesbian travel industry, and offers an online directory of gay- and lesbian-friendly travel businesses; go to their website and click on "Members." In Canada, contact **Travel Gay Canada** (© 416/761-5151; www.travelgaycanada.com).

Many agencies offer tours and travel itineraries specifically for gay and lesbian travelers. **Above and Beyond Tours** (© 800/397-2681; www.abovebeyond tours.com) is the exclusive gay and lesbian tour operator for United Airlines. **Now, Voyager** (© 800/255-6951; www.now voyager.com) is a well-known San Francisco–based gay-owned and -operated travel service. **Olivia Cruises & Resorts** (© 800/631-6277; www.olivia.com) charters entire resorts and ships for exclusive lesbian vacations and offers smaller group experiences

for gay and lesbian travelers. **Gay.com Travel** (© **415/834-6500;** www.gay.com/travel or www.outandabout.com) is an excellent online successor to the popular *Out & About* print magazine. It provides regularly updated information about gay-owned, gay-oriented, and gay-friendly lodging, dining, sightseeing, nightlife, and shopping establishments in every important destination worldwide. It also offers trip-planning information for gay and lesbian travelers for more than 50 destinations along various themes, ranging from Sex & Travel to Vacations for Couples.

The following travel guides are available at many bookstores, or you can order them from any online bookseller: *Spartacus International Gay Guide* (www.spartacusworld.com/gayguide) and *Odysseus: The International Gay Travel Planner,* both good, annual, English-language guidebooks focused on gay men; and the *Damron* guides (www.damron.com), with separate, annual books for gay men and lesbians. For more gay and lesbian travel resources, visit Frommers.com.

SENIOR TRAVEL

Mention the fact that you're a senior when you first make your travel reservations. Many Swedish hotels offer discounts for seniors. Visitors over age 65 can also obtain 30% off first- and second-class train travel (except Fri and Sun) on the Swedish State Railways. Seniors get discounts on the ferries crossing from Denmark to Sweden, and on certain attractions and performances. However, you may have to belong to a seniors' organization to qualify for certain discounts. In Stockholm, there are discounts on transportation, concert, theater, and opera tickets.

Members of **AARP** (formerly known as the American Association of Retired Persons), 601 E St. NW, Washington, DC 20049 (© **888/687-2277;** www.aarp.org), get discounts on hotels, airfares, and car rentals. AARP offers members a wide range of benefits, including *AARP The Magazine* and a monthly newsletter. Anyone over 50 can join.

Many reliable agencies and organizations target the 50-plus market. **Elderhostel** (② 800/454-5768; www.elderhostel.org) arranges study programs for those ages 55 and older (and a spouse or companion of any age) in the U.S. and in more than 80 countries around the world, including Austria. Most courses last 2 to 4 weeks and many include airfare, accommodations in university dormitories or modest inns, meals, and tuition.

Recommended publications offering travel resources and discounts for seniors include: the quarterly magazine *Travel 50 & Beyond; Travel Unlimited: Uncommon Adventures for the Mature Traveler;* and *Unbelievably Good Deals and Great Adventures That You Absolutely Can't Get Unless You're Over 50,* by Joann Rattner Heilman.

Frommers.com offers more information and resources on travel for seniors.

FAMILY TRAVEL

Most Swedish hoteliers will let children under 13 stay in a room with their parents free, although some do not. Sometimes this requires a little negotiation at the reception desk. **Babysitting** services are also available through most hotel desks or by applying at the Tourist Information Office in the town where you're staying. Many hotels have children's game rooms and playgrounds.

Swedes like kids but don't offer a lot of special amenities for them. For example, a kiddies' menu in a restaurant is a rarity. You can, however, order a half-portion, and most waiters will oblige.

At attractions—even if it isn't specifically posted—inquire whether a kids' discount is available. European Community citizens under 18 are admitted free to all state-run museums.

To locate accommodations, restaurants, and attractions that are particularly kid-friendly, refer to the "Kids" icon throughout this guide.

Recommended family travel Internet sites include **Family Travel Forum** (www.familytravelforum.com), a comprehensive site that offers customized trip planning; **Family Travel Network** (www.familytravelnetwork.com), an award-winning site that offers travel features, deals, and tips; **Traveling Internationally with Your Kids** (www.travelwithyourkids.com), a comprehensive site offering sound advice for long-distance and international travel with children; and **Family Travel Files** (www.thefamilytravelfiles.com), which offers an online magazine and a directory of off-the-beaten-path tours and tour operators for families.

For a list of more family-friendly travel resources, turn to the experts at Frommers.com.

STUDENT TRAVEL

If you're planning to travel outside the U.S., you'd be wise to arm yourself with an **International Student Identity Card** (ISIC; www.istc.org), which offers substantial savings on rail passes, plane tickets, and entrance fees. It also provides you with basic health and life insurance and a 24-hour help line. The card is available for $22 from **STA Travel** (② 800/781-4040 in North America; www.sta.com or www.statravel.com), the biggest student travel agency in the world. If you're no longer a student but are still under 26, you can get an **International Youth Travel Card** (IYTC) for the same price from the same people, which entitles you to some discounts. **Travel CUTS** (② 800/667-2887 or 888/359-2887; www.travelcuts.com) offers similar services for both Canadians and U.S. residents. Irish students may prefer to turn to USIT (② 01/602-1906; www.usitnow.ie), an Ireland-based specialist in student, youth, and independent travel.

Single travelers are often hit with a "single supplement" to the base price. To avoid it, you can agree to room with other single travelers on the trip, or you can find a compatible roommate before you go from one of the many roommate-locator agencies.

Travel Buddies Singles Travel Club (© 800/998-9099; www.travelbuddies worldwide.com), based in Canada, runs small, intimate, single-friendly group trips and will match you with a roommate free of charge and save you the cost of single supplements. **TravelChums** (© 212/787-2621; www.travelchums.com) is an Internet-only travel companion matching service with elements of an online personals-type site, hosted by the respected New York–based Shaw Guides travel service.

For more information, check out Eleanor Berman's latest edition of *Traveling Solo: Advice and Ideas for More Than 250 Great Vacations,* a guide with advice on traveling alone, whether you're on your own or on a group tour.

8 SUSTAINABLE TOURISM

Sustainable tourism is conscientious travel. It means being careful with the environments you explore and respecting the communities you visit. Two overlapping components of sustainable travel are ecotourism and ethical tourism. **The International Ecotourism Society (TIES)** defines **ecotourism** as responsible travel to natural areas that conserves the environment and improves the well-being of local people. TIES suggests that ecotourists follow these principles:

- Minimize environmental impact.
- Build environmental and cultural awareness and respect.
- Provide positive experiences for visitors and hosts.
- Provide direct financial benefits for conservation and for local people.
- Raise sensitivity to host countries' political, environmental, and social climates.
- Support international human rights and labor agreements.

You can find some eco-friendly travel tips and statistics, as well as touring companies and associations—listed by destination under "Travel Choice"—at the **TIES** website, **www.ecotourism.org**. Also check out **Ecotravel.com**, which lets you search for sustainable touring companies in several categories (water-based, land-based, spiritually oriented, and so on).

While much of the focus of ecotourism is about reducing impacts on the natural environment, **ethical tourism** concentrates on ways to preserve and enhance local economies and communities, regardless of location. You can embrace ethical tourism by staying at a locally owned hotel or shopping at a store that employs local workers and sells locally produced goods.

Responsible Travel (www.responsible travel.com) is a great source of sustainable travel ideas; the site is run by a spokesperson for ethical tourism in the travel industry. **Sustainable Travel International** (www.sustainabletravelinternational.org) promotes ethical tourism practices, and manages an extensive directory of sustainable properties and tour operators around the world.

In the U.K., **Tourism Concern** (www.tourismconcern.org.uk) works to reduce social and environmental problems connected to tourism. The **Association of Independent Tour Operators** (AITO; www.aito.co.uk) is a group of specialist operators leading the field in making holidays sustainable.

Volunteer travel has become popular among those who want to venture beyond

It's Easy Being Green

Here are a few simple ways you can help conserve fuel and energy when you travel:

- Each time you take a flight or drive a car, greenhouse gases release into the atmosphere. You can help neutralize this danger to the planet through "carbon offsetting"—paying someone to invest your money in programs that reduce your greenhouse gas emissions by the same amount you've added. Before buying carbon offset credits, just make sure that you're using a reputable company, one with a proven program that invests in renewable energy. Reliable carbon offset companies include **Carbonfund** (www.carbonfund.org), **Terra-Pass** (www.terrapass.org), and **Carbon Neutral** (www.carbonneutral.org).

- Whenever possible, choose nonstop flights; they generally require less fuel than indirect flights that stop and take off again. Try to fly during the day—some scientists estimate that nighttime flights are twice as harmful to the environment. And pack light—each 15 pounds of luggage on a 5,000-mile flight adds up to 50 pounds of carbon dioxide emitted.

- Where you stay during your travels can have a major environmental impact. To determine the green credentials of a property, ask about trash disposal and recycling, water conservation, and energy use; also question if sustainable materials were used in the construction of the property. The website **www.greenhotels.com** recommends green-rated member hotels around the world that fulfill the company's stringent environmental requirements. Also consult **www.environmentallyfriendlyhotels.com** for more green accommodations ratings.

- At hotels, request that your sheets and towels not be changed daily. (Many hotels already have programs like this in place.) Turn off the lights and air-conditioner (or heater) when you leave your room.

- Use public transport where possible—trains, buses, and even taxis are more energy-efficient forms of transport than driving. Even better is to walk or cycle; you'll produce zero emissions and stay fit and healthy on your travels.

- If renting a car is necessary, ask the rental agent for a hybrid, or rent the most fuel-efficient car available. You'll use less gas and save money at the tank.

- Eat at locally owned and operated restaurants that use produce grown in the area. This contributes to the local economy and cuts down on greenhouse gas emissions by supporting restaurants where the food is not flown or trucked in across long distances.

the standard group-tour experience to learn languages, interact with locals, and make a positive difference while on vacation. Volunteer travel usually doesn't require special skills—just a willingness to work hard—and programs vary in length from a few days to a number of weeks. Some programs provide free housing and food, but many require volunteers to pay for travel expenses, which can add up quickly.

For general info on volunteer travel, visit **www.volunteerabroad.org** and **www. idealist.org**.

Before you commit to a volunteer program, it's important to make sure any money you're giving is truly going back to the local community, and that the work you'll be doing will be a good fit for you. **Volunteer International** (www.volunteer international.org) has a helpful list of questions to ask to determine the intentions and the nature of a volunteer program.

9 THE ACTIVE VACATION PLANNER

BIKING Much of Sweden is flat, which makes it ideal for cycling tours. Bicycles can be rented all over the country, and country hotels sometimes make them available free of charge. A typical rental is 125SEK ($25/£13) per day. For more detailed information, contact the local tourist board.

FISHING In Stockholm, within view of the king's palace, you can cast a line for what are some of the finest salmon in the world. Ever since Queen Christina issued a decree in 1636, Swedes have had the right to fish in waters adjoining the palace. Throughout the country, fishing is an everyday affair; it's estimated that one of every three Swedes is an angler.

If you'd like to fish elsewhere in Sweden, you'll need a license; the cost varies from region to region. Local tourist offices in any district can give you information about this. Pike, pikeperch, eel, and perch are found in the heartland and the southern parts of the country.

GOLFING With about 400 rarely crowded courses, Sweden may have more golf enthusiasts than any other country in Europe after Scotland. Visitors are often granted local membership cards, and greens fees vary, depending on the club. Many golfers fly from Stockholm to Boden in the far north in the summer months to play by the light of the midnight sun at the **Björkliden Arctic Golf Course,** which opened in 1989 some 240km (149 miles) north of the Arctic Circle. It's not only the world's northernmost golf course—it's one of the most panoramic, set against a backdrop of snow-capped peaks, green valleys, and crystal lakes. The narrow fairways and small greens of this 9-hole, par-36 course offer multiple challenges. For details, contact the **Björkliden Arctic Golf Club,** Kvarnbacksvägen 28, Bromma S-168 74 (✆ **08/564-88-840;** www.bjorklidengolf klubb.se). For general information on courses in Sweden, contact the **Svenska Golffoür-bundet,** P.O. Box 84, Daneered S-182 11 (✆ **08/622-15-00;** www.golf.se).

HIKING Sarek, in the far north, is one of Europe's last real wilderness areas; Swedes come here to hike in the mountains, pick mushrooms, gather berries, and fish. The **Svenska Turistfoürening (Swedish Touring Club),** P.O. Box 25, Amiralitetshuset 1, Flaggmansvägen 8, S101 20 Stockholm (✆ **08/463-21-00;** www.stfturist.se), provides accommodations in the area in mountain huts with 10 to 30 beds. The staff knows the northern part of Sweden well and can advise you about marked tracks, rowboats, the best excursions, the problems you're likely to encounter, communications, and transportation. The company also sells trail and mountain maps.

HORSEBACK RIDING Many opportunities for overnight horseback pack trips exist in such wilderness areas as the forests of Värmland or Norrbotten, where reindeer, musk oxen, and other creatures roam. The most popular overnight horseback trips start just north of the city of Karlstad in Värmland. A typical horseback trip begins in the lakeside village of Torsby and follows a forested trail up a mountain. An average of 4 hours a day is spent on the horse, with meals cooked over an open fire.

In northern Sweden, two popular starting points are Funäsdalen, close to the Norwegian border, and Ammarnäs, not far from the Arctic Circle and the midnight sun. These trips begin in June. Local tourist offices can provide further information.

Sweden also has many riding stables and riding schools. Ask about them at local tourist offices. One of the most popular excursions is a pony trek through the region surrounding Sweden's highest mountain, Kebnekaise.

If you're in Stockholm, you might try a ride or two around the rinks at nearby **Djurgårdens ridskola,** Kaknäs, Djurgården (② 08/660-21-11), or a bit farther afield at **Boügs Gård AB,** in Sollentuna (② 08/96-79-71), which maintains Icelandic ponies, as they thrive throughout the region's frigid winters. Both sites can help arrange overnight treks through the surrounding fields and forests, even though most of their business derives from rink-riding and equestrian lessons.

One more unusual choice is exploring the *Orsa* (outback) by horse and covered wagon. In the province of Dalarna, you can rent a horse and wagon with space for up to five people. The outback is an almost unpopulated area of wild beauty, and the route goes past beautiful summer pastures, small lakes in the midst of forests, and panoramic views. Rides are available June through August. Clients cover about 16km (10 miles) a day, sleeping in or beside the covered wagon, following a preselected itinerary, and usually overnighting beside lakes or rivers. For more information, contact **Häst och Vagn,** Torsmo 1646, S-794 91 Orsa (② 0481/531-00).

If you prefer to make your horseback riding arrangements before you depart the United States, perhaps as part of an organized bus, rail, or self-drive tour, **Passage Tours of Scandinavia,** 235 Commercial Blvd., Fort Lauderdale, FL 33308 (② 800/548-5960 or 954/776-7070; www.passage tours.com), can custom-design a suitable tour for you, usually configured with visits to Sweden's cultural, architectural, or historical highlights en route.

RAFTING White-water rafting and river rafting are both popular here. Visitors have the option to take either short or weeklong trips. In Värmland, contact **Branäs Sport AB,** Branäs Fritidsanläggin, Gondolvägem 1, S-680 60 Sysslebäck (② 054/13-26-00; www.branas.se). River rafting is the tamer option because it involves rafting a slow-moving river, versus white-water rafting on rapids. For information about the best river rafting in Sweden, contact **Kukkolaforsen-Turist & Konferens,** P.O. Box 184, S-953 91 Haparanda (② 922/310-00; www.kukkola forsen.se).

If you want to try log rafting, we recommend a lazy trip down the Klarälven River, winding through beautiful and unspoiled valleys between high mountains, with sandy beaches where you can swim, if temperatures and river conditions allow. There also is excellent fishing for pike and grayling. You will travel through northern Värmland at a speed of 2kmph (1¼ mph) from the mouth of the Vinguümngssjoün Lake in the north to Ekshärad in the south, a distance of 110km (68 miles) in 6 days. Overnight accommodations are arranged either on the moored raft or ashore. Each raft can accommodate between two and five people, and the trips are available from May to August. Participants supply their own food and fishing equipment. Contact **Branäs Sverigeflotten,** Klara Strand 66, S-680 63 Likenäs (② 564/402-27; www. sverigeflotten.com).

SAILING & CANOEING Canoes and sailing boats can be rented all over the country; you can obtain information about this from the local tourist office. Often hotels situated near watersports areas have canoes for rent.

SWIMMING If you don't mind swimming in cool water, Sweden has one of the world's longest coastlines—plus some 100,000 lakes—in which you can take the plunge. The best bathing beaches are on the west coast. The islands of both Oüland and Gotland have popular summer seaside resorts. Beaches in Sweden are generally open to the public, and nude bathing is allowed on certain designated beaches. Topless bathing for women is prevalent everywhere. If a Swedish lake is suitable for swimming, it's always signposted.

WALKING & JOGGING Local tourist offices can provide details and sometimes even supply you with free maps of the best trails or jogging paths. In Stockholm, hotel reception desks often can tell you the best places to go jogging nearby.

10 PACKAGES FOR INDEPENDENT TRAVELERS

Package tours are simply a way to buy the airfare, accommodations, and other elements of your trip (such as car rentals, airport transfers, and sometimes even activities) at the same time and often at discounted prices.

One good source of package deals is the airlines themselves. Most major airlines offer air/land packages, including **American Airlines Vacations** (© 800/321-2121; www.aavacations.com), **Delta Vacations** (© 800/221-6666; www.deltavacations. com), **Continental Airlines Vacations** (© 800/301-3800; www.covacations.com), and **United Vacations** (© 888/854-3899; www.unitedvacations.com). Several big **online travel agencies**—Expedia, Travelocity, Orbitz, Site59, and Lastminute.com—also do a brisk business in packages.

11 ESCORTED GENERAL-INTEREST TOURS

Sweden's various regions, especially Dalarna and Lapland, offer such a variety of sights and activities that you may want to take an organized tour. The following tours are just a small sample of what's available. Contact your travel agent to learn about tours of interest to you or to design a special one with you in mind.

ScanAm World Tours (© 800/545-2204; www.scanamtours.com) offers some of the country's best tours, taking you on Göta Canal cruises or along lakes, on waterways, and into the folkloric district of Dalarna. Minimum tours for 2 nights, including hotels, cost 2,550SEK to 3,100SEK ($510–$620/£255–£310) per person. From here, tours range upward to 7 nights, including hotels, costing 12,930SEK ($2,586/£1,293) per person.

"Gotland Island and the City of Roses" is a cruise on the Gotland Line from Stockholm to Nynäshamn or from Oskarshamn to Visby, including 2 nights at the Visby Hotel or Hotel Solhem. The 3-day tour is available May through September.

Scantours (© 800/223-7226; www.scantours.com) offers the most widely diverse tours of Sweden, ranging from Göta Canal cruises to a combined Stockholm and Helsinki jaunt, lasting 5 days and 4 nights.

Passage Tours (© 800/548-5960; www. passagetours.com) offers trips to both Stockholm and the "Kingdom of Crystal," with stopovers in such glass factories as Kosta Boda and Orrefors. Trips to the port of Kalmar on the Baltic Sea are also included, as well as visits to the island of Oland.

12 SPECIAL-INTEREST TOURS

ADVENTURE TOURS In the U.S. For overall adventure travel, including skiing, hiking, and biking, the best bet is **Borton Overseas,** 5412 Lyndale Ave. S., Minneapolis, MN 55419 (© 800/843-0602 or 612/822-4640; www.borton overseas.com), which offers sea kayaking and backpacking expeditions in Sweden. Tours should be arranged before you go.

In the U.K. The oldest travel agency in Britain, **Cox & Kings,** Gordon House 10, Greencoat Place, London SW1P 1PH (© 020/7873-5000; www.coxandkings. co.uk), was established in 1758; at that time, the company served as the paymasters and transport directors for the British armed forces in India. Today the company sends large numbers of travelers from Britain throughout the rest of the world and specializes in unusual—if pricey— holidays. Scandinavian tours include cruises through the region's spectacular fjords, bus and rail tours through sites of historic and aesthetic interest, and visits to the best-known handicraft centers, Viking burial sites, and historic churches. The company's staff focuses on tours of ecological and environmental interest.

Those who would like to cycle their way through the splendors of Scandinavia should join Britain's oldest and largest association of bicycle riders, the **Cyclists' Touring Club,** Cotterell House, 69 Meadrow, Godalming, Surrey GU7 3HS (© 0844/736-84-51; www.ctc.org.uk). Founded in 1878, it charges £35 ($70) a year for membership, which includes information, maps, and a subscription to a newsletter packed with practical information and morale boosters, plus recommended cycling routes through virtually every country in Europe. The organization's information bank on scenic routes through Scandinavia is especially comprehensive. Membership can be arranged over the phone with an appropriate credit card (such as Master-Card, Visa, Access, or Barclaycard).

See the Active Vacation Planner info, on p. 50, for tips on arranging adventure travel without tour companies.

LEARNING VACATIONS One good source of information about courses in Sweden is the **American Institute for Foreign Study (AIFS),** River Plaza, 9 W. Broad St., Stamford, CT 06902 (© 866/906-2437; www.aifs.org). This organization can set up transportation and arrange for summer courses, with room and board included.

The biggest organization dealing with higher education in Europe is the **Institute of International Education (IIE),** 809 United Nations Plaza, New York, NY 10017 (© 212/883-8200; www.iie.org). A few of its booklets are free, but for $47 (£24), plus $6 (£3) for postage, you can purchase the more definitive *Short Term Study Abroad.* Visitors to New York can use the resources of its Information Center, which is open to the public Tuesday through Thursday from 11am to 4pm. The institute is closed on major holidays.

One recommended clearinghouse for academic programs throughout the world is the **National Registration Center for Study Abroad (NRCSA),** 823 N. Second St., P.O. Box 1393, Milwaukee, WI 53201 (© 414/278-0631; www.nrcsa.com). The organization maintains language-study programs throughout Europe.

HOME STAYS   **Friendship Force International (FFI),** 34 Peachtree St., Suite 900, Atlanta, GA 30303 (© **404/522-9490;** www.friendshipforce.org), is a non-profit organization that fosters and encourages friendships among people worldwide. Dozens of branch offices throughout North America arrange en masse visits, usually once a year. Because of group bookings, the airfare to the host country usually is less than the cost of individual tickets. Each participant spends 2 weeks in the host country—one as a guest in the home of a family, and another traveling throughout the country.

Servas, 1125 16th St., Ste. 201, Arcata, CA 95521 (© **707/825-1714;** www.usservas.org), is an international, nonprofit, non-governmental, interfaith network of travelers and hosts whose goal is to help promote world peace, goodwill, and under-standing. (Its name means "to serve" in Esperanto.) Servas hosts offer travelers hospitality for 2 days. Travelers pay an $85 (£43) annual fee and a $25 (£13) list deposit after filling out an application and being approved by an interviewer. (Inter-viewers are located across the United States.) They then receive Servas directories listing the names and addresses of Servas hosts.

HOME EXCHANGES   One of the most exciting breakthroughs in modern tourism is the home exchange. Home exchanges cut costs: You don't pay hotel bills, and you also can save money by shopping in markets and eating in. Sometimes even the family car is included. Of course, you must be comfortable with the idea of hav-ing strangers in your home, and you must be content to spend your vacation in one place. Also, you may not get a home in the area you request.

Intervac, U.S. & International, 30 Corte San Fernando, Tiburon, CA 94920 (© **800/756-HOME** [4663] or 415/435-3497; www.intervacus.com), is part of the largest worldwide exchange network. It publishes four catalogs a year, containing more than 10,000 homes in more than 50 countries. Members contact each other directly. The cost is $65 to $195 (£33–£98) plus postage, which includes the purchase of three of the company's cata-logs (which will be mailed to you), plus the inclusion of your own listing in which-ever one of the three catalogs you select.

Home Link International (© **800/638-3841;** www.homelink.org) will send you five directories per year—one of which contains your listing—for $80 (£40).

---

13 STAYING CONNECTED

TELEPHONES

The country code for Sweden is **46.** To call Sweden from the United States, dial the international access code 011, then 46, then the city code, then the regular phone number. *Note:* The Swedish phone num-bers listed in this book are to be used within Sweden; when calling from abroad, omit the initial 0 in the city code.

For directory assistance: Dial © **118118.**

For operator assistance: If you need operator assistance in making a call, dial © **90200.**

Local and long-distance calls may be placed from all post offices and from most public telephone booths, about half of which operate with phone cards, the others with coins. Phone cards are sold at post offices and newsstands in denominations of 35SEK ($7/£3.50), 60SEK ($12/£6), and 100SEK ($20/£10). Rates are measured in units rather than minutes. The farther the distance, the more units are consumed. Telephone calls made through hotel switchboards can double, triple, or even quadruple the base charges at the post office, so be alert to this before you dial. In some instances, post offices can send faxes for you, and many hotels offer Internet access—for free or for a small charge—to their guests.

Swedish phone numbers are not standard. In some places, numbers have as few as four digits. In cities, one number may have five digits, whereas the phone next door might have nine. Swedes also often hyphenate their numbers differently. But since all the area codes are the same, these various configurations should have little effect on your phone usage once you get used to the fact that numbers vary from place to place.

Numbers beginning with 08 and followed by 00 are **toll-free numbers.** But be careful: Numbers that begin with 08 followed by 36 carry a 3.50SEK (70¢/35p) surcharge per minute. Also, many companies maintain a service line beginning with 0180. These lines might appear to be toll free but really aren't, costing 1.20SEK (24¢/12p) per minute. Other numbers that begin with 0190 carry a surcharge of 19SEK ($4/£1.90) per minute—or even more. Don't be misled by calling an 800 number in the United States from Sweden. This is not a toll-free call but costs about the same as an overseas call.

Alternatively, you can dial the various telecommunication companies in the States for cheaper rates. From Sweden, the access number for **AT&T** is ☏ **0800/888-0010,** for MCI ☏ **0800/888-8000. U.S.A. Direct** can be used with all telephone cards and for collect calls. The number from Sweden is ☏ **013/000-10. Canada Direct** can be used with Bell Telephone Cards and for collect calls. This number from Sweden is ☏ **013/000-14.**

If you're calling from a public pay phone, you must deposit the basic local rate.

CELLPHONES

The three letters that define much of the world's wireless capabilities are **GSM** (Global System for Mobiles), a big, seamless network that makes for easy cross-border cellphone use. In general, reception is good. But you'll need a Scriber Identity Module Card (SIM). This is a small chip that gives you a local phone number and plugs you into a regional network. In the U.S., T-Mobile, AT&T Wireless, and Cingular use this quasi-universal system; in Canada, Microcell and some Rogers customers are GSM; and all Europeans and most Australians use GSM. Unfortunately, per-minute charges can be high—usually 5SEK to 7.50SEK ($1–$1.50/50p–75p) in western Europe.

For many, **renting** a phone is a good idea. While you can rent a phone from any number of overseas sites, including kiosks at airports and at car-rental agencies, we suggest renting the phone before you leave home. North Americans can rent one before leaving home from **InTouch U.S.A.** (☏ **800/872-7626** or 703/222-7161; www.intouchglobal.com) or **RoadPost** (☏ **888/290-1616** or 905/272-5665; www.roadpost.com). InTouch will also, for free, advise you on whether your existing phone will work overseas.

Buying a phone can be economically attractive, as many nations have cheap prepaid phone systems. Once you arrive at your destination, stop by a local cellphone shop and get the cheapest package; you'll probably pay less than 500SEK ($100/£50) for a phone and a starter calling card. Local calls may be as low as .50SEK (10¢/5p) per minute, and in many countries incoming calls are free.

INTERNET & E-MAIL
With Your Own Computer

More and more hotels, cafes, and retailers are signing on as Wi-Fi (wireless fidelity) "hot spots." Mac owners have their own networking technology: Apple AirPort. **T-Mobile Hotspot** (www.t-mobile.com/hotspot or www.t-mobile.co.uk) serves up wireless connections at coffee shops nationwide. **Boingo** (www.boingo.com) and **Wayport** (www.wayport.com) have set up networks in airports and high-class hotel lobbies. IPass providers (see below) also give you access to a few hundred wireless hotel lobby setups. To locate other hot spots that provide **free wireless networks** in cities in Sweden, go to **www.jiwire.com**.

For dial-up access, most business-class hotels offer dataports for laptop modems, and a few thousand hotels in Sweden now offer free high-speed Internet access. In addition, major Internet service providers (ISPs) have **local access numbers** around the world, allowing you to go online by placing a local call. The **iPass** network also has dial-up numbers around the world. You'll have to sign up with an iPass provider, who will then tell you how to set up your computer for your destination(s). For a list of iPass providers, go to **www.ipass.com** and click on

"Individuals Buy Now." One solid provider is **i2roam** (© **866/811-6209** or 920/233-5863; www.i2roam.com).

Wherever you go, bring a **connection kit** of the right power and phone adapters, a spare phone cord, and a spare Ethernet network cable—or find out whether your hotel supplies them to guests.

Without Your Own Computer

To find cybercafes, check **www.cyber captive.com** and **www.cybercafe.com**. Cybercafes are found in all large Swedish cities, especially Stockholm and Gothenburg. But they do not tend to cluster in any particular neighborhoods because of competition. They are spread out, but can be found on almost every business street in large cities.

Aside from formal cybercafes, most **youth hostels** and **public libraries** have Internet access. Avoid **hotel business centers** unless you're willing to pay exorbitant rates.

Most major airports now have **Internet kiosks** scattered throughout their gates. These give you basic Web access for a per-minute fee that's usually higher than cybercafe prices.

Suggested Sweden Itineraries

Vacations are getting shorter, and a "lean-and-mean" schedule is called for if you want to experience the best of Sweden in a relatively small amount of time. If you're a time-pressed traveler, as most of us are, with only 1 week to spend in Sweden, you may find the "Sweden in 1 Week" itinerary the most helpful. If you'd like to see the best of the provinces, follow the 1-week itineraries for southern Sweden or Dalarna and Värmland.

1 THE REGIONS IN BRIEF

GÖTALAND The southern part of Sweden takes its name from the ancient Goths. Some historians believe they settled in this region, which is similar in climate and architecture to parts of northern Europe, especially Germany. This is the most populated part of Sweden and includes eight provinces—Östergötland, Småland (the "Kingdom of Crystal"), Västergötland, Skåne, Dalsland, Bohuslän, Halland, and Blekinge—plus the islands of Oüland and Gotland. The Göta Canal cuts through this district. **Gothenburg** is the most important port in the west, and **Stockholm,** the capital, is the chief port in the east. Aside from Stockholm, **Skåne,** the château district, is the most heavily visited area. Its dunes, moors, and pastures are often compared to the Danish countryside. Many seaside resorts line the west and east coasts.

SVEALAND The central region encompasses the folkloric province of **Dalarna** (**Dalecarlia** in English) and **Värmland** (immortalized in the novels of Selma Lagerloüf). These districts are the ones most frequented by visitors. Other provinces include Våstmanland, Uppland, Soüdermanland, and Nårke. Ancient Svealand often is called the cultural heart of Sweden. Some 20,000 islands lie along its eastern coast.

NORRLAND Northern Sweden makes up Norrland, which lies above the 61st parallel and includes about 50% of the landmass. It's inhabited by only about 15% of the population, including Lapps and Finns. Norrland consists of 24 provinces, of which **Lapland** is the most popular with tourists. It's a land of thick forests, fast-flowing (and cold) rivers, and towering mountain peaks. Lapland, the home of the Lapp reindeer herds, consists of tundra. **Kiruna** is one of Norrland's most important cities because of its iron-ore deposits.

2 SWEDEN IN 1 WEEK

One week provides just enough time to skim the surface of Sweden. If you move fast enough, you'll be able to see the highlights of **Stockholm** in just 2 days and take a 1-day trip to visit two ancient cities—**Uppsala,** the site of one of Scandinavia's greatest universities, and **Sigtuna.** The itinerary also calls for 2 days on the island of **Gotland,** highlighted by the medieval walled city of **Visby.** Back on the mainland you will still have 2 days left to explore the old port of **Kalmar** to see its famous castle and to go shopping in the **glassworks district** of Sweden.

Days ❶ & ❷: Stockholm ★★★: Gateway to Sweden

On **Day 1,** arrive in **Stockholm** as early as you can so you will have more time for sightseeing. After checking into a hotel for 2 or 3 nights (see Day 3, below), set out to explore the capital of Sweden.

There is no better introduction to the city than our 3-hour walking tour of **Gamla Stan** or Old Town (coverage begins on p. 130). After lunch in an Old Town tavern, head for the **Royal Palace** (p. 114), which is the official address of the King and Queen of Sweden.

In the afternoon, explore Scandinavia's top attraction, the **Royal Warship** *Vasa* (p. 121), a 17th-century man-of-war pulled from the bottom of the sea. For a night of fun, go to **Skansen** on Djurgården (p. 120), which is an open-air museum with a vast array of attractions. It stays open until 10pm in summer.

On the morning of **Day 2,** set out to see all the highlights you missed on Day 1. The two greatest attractions that remain are both outside the city. If you work out the transportation details, you can see the first sight, **Drottningholm Palace and Theater** (p. 123), in the late morning and the second attraction, **Millesgården** (p. 124), by the end of the afternoon. For your final evening in Stockholm, head to **Gröna Lunds Tivoli** (p. 148), an amusement park. It's not as great as the original Tivoli in Copenhagen, but it's still fun.

Day ❸: Sigtuna ★ & Uppsala ★★★

On the morning of **Day 3,** you can still use Stockholm as your base, returning that evening, or you can stay in Uppsala.

Head northwest of Stockholm for 48km (30 miles) to visit the ancient town of

Sigtuna on a north arm of Lake Mälaren. This is Sweden's oldest town, founded at the beginning of the 11th century. To reach it, drive north on the express highway, E4, until you reach the turnoff leading west into the center of Sigtuna. Spend 2 hours wandering its old streets before returning to the E4 for the final lap to **Uppsala,** a distance of 68km (42 miles) northwest of Stockholm.

Have lunch in this old university city. In the afternoon visit **Uppsala Domkyrka** (p. 156), the largest cathedral in Scandinavia; continue with the **Linnaeus Garden & Museum** (p. 156), founded by the world-famous botanist; and end the day at **Gamla Uppsala** (p. 158) to see what remains of Old Uppsala, founded 15 centuries ago as the capital of the Svea kingdom.

Days ❹ & ❺: Gotland ★★ & Visby ★★★

On the morning of **Day 4,** leave Stockholm, or Uppsala as the case may be, and drive 219km (136 miles) south of Stockholm to catch the car ferry at Nynäshamn heading for the island of Visby, taking 3 hours and 15 minutes.

After disembarking, visit the medieval walled city of **Visby** for a 2-night stopover. Spend the rest of the afternoon exploring its medieval streets (p. 306).

On the morning of **Day 5,** while still checked into a hotel in Visby, set out to discover the island on your own set of wheels, having armed yourself with a detailed map from the tourist office. (See **"Exploring Gotland by Car"** in chapter 10.) Return to Visby by nightfall.

Day ⑥: Kalmar ★,
the Key to Sweden

On the morning of **Day 6,** check out of your hotel in Visby and drive to the embarkation point for the mainland. Take a ferry that goes from Visby to the eastern coast port of Oskarshamn. Once here, follow E66 south to the port of **Kalmar,** a distance of 409km (254 miles) from Stockholm. You can arrive in Kalmar in time for a late lunch.

In the afternoon, visit **Kalmar Slott** (p. 269), a castle founded in the 12th century and once called "the key to Sweden" because of its strategic position. In the fading afternoon, wander Kalmar's warren of cobblestone streets and market squares, most of them a holdover from the 17th century. Check into a hotel in Kalmar for the night.

Day ⑦: Växjö & the Kingdom of Crystal ★★★

On the morning of **Day 7,** your final day in Sweden, leave Kalmar in the morning and drive 110km (68 miles) to **Växjö,** the capital of the so-called "Kingdom of Crystal," or glassworks district. From Kalmar head west on Route 25.

Once in Växjö, check into a hotel for the night. If your ancestors came from this district, you'll want to visit the **House of Emigrants** (p. 274). If not, you can spend the rest of the day visiting the glass factories, the best of which are **Boda Glasbruk, Orrefors Glasbruk,** and **Kosta Glasbruk** (see p. 276).

After an overnight at Växjö, you can head back to Stockholm for transportation links to where you're going next—possibly back home.

3 SOUTHERN SWEDEN IN 1 WEEK

Most foreign visitors, certainly those touring Sweden by car, head to the south after they leave Stockholm. If you follow the 1-week tour outlined above, you'll actually reach three of the south's highlights: **Visby** on the island of Gotland, the port of **Kalmar,** and the **Kingdom of Crystal,** centered on Växjö. On this tour we extend those 4 days by 3, allowing you to take in the medieval town of **Ystad,** the university city of **Lund,** with a final stop at the port city of **Malmö,** the third largest in Sweden.

Days ❶ to ❹:

Follow the same itineraries as outlined under Days 4, 5, 6, and 7 of "Sweden in 1 Week" (see above).

Day ❺: Simrishamn & Ystad ★★

On the morning of **Day 5,** leave Växjö following Route 30 southeast to the coast, which will put you on a larger highway, E66, heading west to the city of Karlshamn. Continue west on this road until you come to the junction with a secondary coastal road, Route 10, heading to the village of **Kivik.** Here you can stop to see a remarkable find, the **Kivik Tomb** (p. 251), discovered in 1748. This site contains Sweden's most amazing Bronze Age relic. After a visit, continue on Route 10 southeast along the coast into **Simrishamn,** a distance of 192km (119 miles) from Växjö. After wandering its ancient streets for an hour or so, continue on Route 501 southwest to Ystad for the night, a distance of 40km (25 miles).

En route to Ystad, there are two major attractions along the way, including **Glimmingehus** (p. 251), lying 10km (6¹/₄ miles) southwest of Simrishamn. This castle from 1499 contains the best-preserved medieval keep in Sweden. Once back on Route 501, stop next at **Backakra** (p. 251), the farm of Dag Hammarskjöld,

the former United Nations secretary-general. The site is found 31km (19 miles) southwest of Simrishamn. After driving on to **Ystad** and checking into a hotel there, you can wander its medieval core at night, taking in some 300 half-timbered houses in its maze of narrow streets.

Day ❻: The University City of Lund ★★

Leave Ystad on the morning of **Day 6,** cutting across the southern tip of Sweden along an express highway (E65). At the approach to Malmö, avoid the city for the moment, and head northeast along E22 into Lund. Mileage between Ystad in the east and Lund in the west is 73km (45 miles).

After checking into a hotel in Lund for the night, visit its major attraction, **Domkyrkan** (p. 240), the Lund Cathedral, the finest manifestation of Romanesque architecture in Sweden. There are many treasures to view here, and you should allow at least 1¹/₂ hours for a visit. Afterward, you can visit the **Historiska Museet** (p. 240), the second largest museum of archaeology in Sweden. In town, secure the makings of a picnic lunch to be enjoyed in the **Botaniska Trädgården** (p. 238), Lund's botanical gardens. In the afternoon, plan a visit to the **Kulturen**

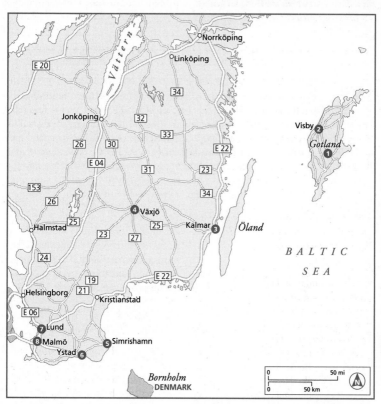

(p. 240), the Museum of Cultural History, one of the finest open-air museums in the south. The rest of the day can be spent browsing through local shops and wandering Lund's medieval streets.

Day ❼: Malmö ★★, Sweden's "Third City"

On the morning of **Day 7,** head southwest for only 18km (11 miles) to **Malmö,** following the E22 express highway. After checking into a hotel, set out to see the city's attractions in 1 day, which is possible if you move fast enough.

Start out by visiting the city's two most historic squares, **Stortorget** and **Lilla Torg**

(p. 223), before descending on **Malmöhus Castle** (p. 223), with its array of museums. You should be out of this vast compound in time for a 1pm lunch.

In the afternoon, call at the **Malmö Konsthall/Art Gallery** (p. 226), one of the best art museums in the country, and visit **St. Petri** (p. 226), or St. Peter's Church, a Gothic edifice from the 14th century. Between May and September, you can wind up the evening by going to **Folkets Park** (p. 237), the People's Park, which boasts a vast array of gardens and dancing pavilions.

Malmö is a major transportation hub for Sweden, so you can fly or take the bus easily from here. Many international flights also leave from Copenhagen in Denmark, which is now within easy reach of Malmö across the spectacular bridge over Öresund Sound.

4 FOLKLORIC DALARNA & VÄRMLAND

This tour takes us west from Stockholm into the folkloric provinces of Dalarna and Värmland, the heart of Sweden. In American terms, it's equivalent to leaving New York and heading for the Midwest. This land of lakes and inland seas—often called Sweden in miniature—features mountains and rich agricultural plains. We think **Lake Siljan** is the most beautiful lake in Europe, although there are many who might dispute our claim. In just 1 week, you can hit all the highlights of these two provinces, including **Karlstad,** the capital of Värmland. You can also vary the scenery by descending into copper mines at **Falun.** Then it's back to nature again, as you visit four of the most scenic and idyllic resorts in the country, including **Leksand** and **Mora,** and our two favorites, **Tällberg** and **Rättvik.**

Day ❶: Karlstad, Gateway to Värmland

On the morning of **Day 1,** leave Stockholm and head west for 248km (154 miles) on an express highway, E18. Once you check into a hotel for the night, we suggest a lake cruise aboard the *Vestrag* (p. 331), which lasts an hour. The beauty of Sweden's lakes is reason enough to go to Värmland and especially Dalarna.

Back in town, you can visit the **Värmlands Museum** (p. 333). If you have the time and inclination, you can also drive to the town of Karlskoga, 56km (35 miles) east of Karlstad, to visit **Alfred Nobel's Björkborn** on the edge of Lake Möckeln. For more details, see p. 332. This was the former home of the dynamite king who created the Nobel Prizes. If it's summer, you can cap off the evening at **Mariebergsskogen,** a park complete with rides (p. 332), back in Karlstad.

Day ❷: Sunne, Selma Lagerlöf Country

On the morning of **Day 2,** leave Karlstad and drive 61km (38 miles) northwest to **Sunne,** following Route 61 west to the junction with Route 234, which you take northwest into Sunne itself.

On Lake Fryken, Sunne offers boat trips, a golf course, and an old manor house (see **Sundsbergs Gård,** p. 337). In the afternoon you can drive 10km (6¹⁄₄ miles) to the southeast to visit **Mårbacka Minnesgård** (p. 337), the former home of Selma Lagerlöf, who won the Nobel Prize for literature. Return to Sunne for overnighting.

Day ❸: Filipstad, Land of John Ericsson

On the morning of **Day 3,** leave Sunne and do some cross-country travel for an overnight in our next stopover at **Filipstad,** a distance of 128km (80 miles) east. The simplest way to reach Filipstad is to return from Sunne to Karlstad on Route 234. Follow the signs east along Route 61, bypassing the northern rim of Karlstad until you reach the junction of Route 63 heading northeast into Filipstad. You can also head east along Route 241 out of Sunne, taking a series of small country roads until you reach (we hope) Filipstad; you'll need a very detailed map to do that.

Once in Filipstad, you can visit **Långbans Gruvby,** the home of the Swedish-American inventor John Ericsson, who

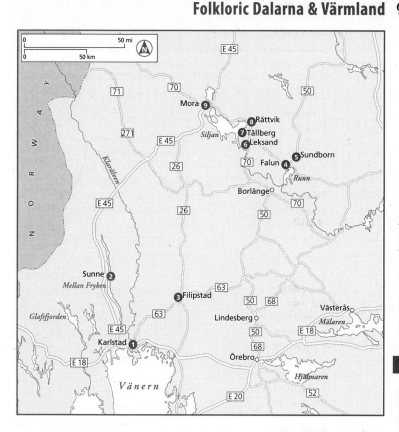

helped the Yankees defeat the Confederacy by creating the warship the *Yankee Monitor*. His house is found in a well-preserved mining village. You can also visit **Lesjöfors Museum** (p. 340), which illustrates 3 centuries of Värmland history.

Day ❹: The Copper Mines of Falun ★

On the morning of **Day 4,** leave Filipstad heading north to **Falun,** following Route 63, which merges with Route 60 before it reaches our goal. The distance is 173km (107 miles). The copper mines here are preserved under the guidance of UNESCO's World Heritage Sites. In the old capital of Dalarna, check into a hotel for the night. Later, explore **Falu Koppargruva** (p. 344), the world's largest producer of copper during the 17th century, where you can take an elevator to deep within the bowels of the earth. Yet there's a lot more to Falun than copper mines, as a visit to the **Dalarnas Museum** (p. 343) proves. With its folk costumes and exhibits, this is the richest folkloric museum in Dalarna province. Visits are also possible to the **Carl Larsson-gården** (p. 342), the former home of one of Sweden's greatest artists, lying a 20-minute drive from Falun in the small village of Sundborn.

Day ❺: Leksand, Doorway to Lake Siljan

Leave Falun on the morning of **Day 5,** heading for the lakeside resort of **Leksand,** 48km (30 miles) to the west. From Falun, head south on Route 60 to the junction with Route 70 going northwest into Leksand. At Leksand you can take **boat rides along Siljan,** Sweden's most beautiful lake, and see such attractions as **Fräsgården** (p. 348), one of the best open-air museums in the province. You can also visit **Munthes Hildasholm** (p. 348), the former home of Axel Munthe (1857–1949), the world-famous Swedish author and doctor. Overnight in Leksand.

Day ❻: Tällberg ★★★ & Rättvik ★★

Even more enchanting than Leksand itself are the twin lakeside villages of **Tällberg** (our favorite) and **Rättvik.** If Tällberg's hotels are full in summer, you can try Rättvik, which is almost, but not quite, as charming. Tällberg lies 13km (8 miles) north of Leksand. Continue north on Route 70; the distance between Tällberg and Rättvik is only 3.1km (2 miles), and it too lies along Route 70.

Regardless of your choice for overnighting, both of these resorts are worth exploring. Their obvious allure is in swimming and boating on the lake. At Tällberg, you can visit **Holen Gustaf Ancarcronas** at Holen (p. 350), a collection of restored wooden-framed buildings. The chief attraction of Rättvik is **Gammelgården** (p. 353), an antique Dalarna farmstead.

Day ❼: Mora ★★ of Anders Zorn Fame

On the morning of **Day 7,** leave either Rättvik or Tällberg and continue along Route 70 into the resort of **Mora,** which lies 45km (28 miles) west of Rättvik. Overnight here. Mora lies between Lake Orsa and Lake Siljan, so most visitors come here to have fun on the lake.

You can also visit the **Zorn Museum** (p. 355), the former home of Anders Zorn (1860–1920), who competes with Carl Larsson for the title of Sweden's greatest painter. Since it adjoins the museum, you can visit the **Zornsgården** (p. 356) next.

From Mora, you can return to Stockholm if you're using that city as your transportation hub. The driving distance between Stockholm and Mora is 328km (204 miles).

5 SWEDEN FOR FAMILIES

Sweden offers many kid-friendly attractions. Your biggest concern with having children along here is pacing yourself with enough museum time. Our suggestion is to limit **Stockholm** to a couple days, **Gothenburg** to a single day, and combine a visit to the "third city" of **Malmö** and the university city of **Lund** on your final day. The entire family can then enjoy a drive across Sweden, bypassing the **Göta Canal** and spending the night in the ancient town of **Mariestad.**

Days ❶ & ❷: Family Fun in the Capital ★★★

On the morning of **Day 1,** set out to explore **Stockholm** by taking our 3-hour walking tour of **Gamla Stan** (Old Town; p. 130). Your kids will think it's a movie set created by Disney. Have lunch in the Old Town and follow that with a visit to

the **Kungliga Slottet** (p. 114), the royal palace. Kids also enjoy seeing the **Changing of the Royal Guard** (p. 115), but that can be difficult to schedule. The palace is such a vast complex that children always find lots of attractions here to interest them, though. After a stroll through, head for the **Vasamuseet** (Royal Warship *Vasa;*

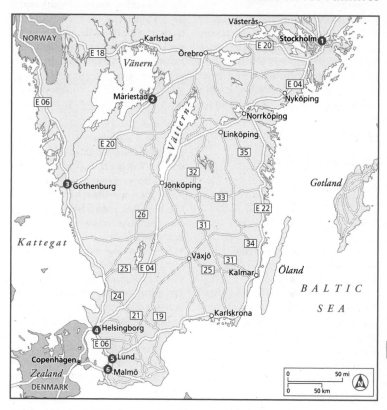

p. 121), the 17th-century man-of-war that sank on its maiden voyage. Spend your first night in Stockholm at **Gröna Lunds Tivoli** (p. 148), a vast amusement park that many kids will likely think of as the highlight of the Swedish capital.

On the morning of **Day 2,** set out to see the Stockholm attractions you didn't have time for on Day 1. Begin the day by taking in the vast compound of **Skansen** (p. 120), Sweden's greatest open-air museum. This vast parkland with old workshops and some 150 antique buildings is like a time warp for kids. Skansen will absorb your entire morning. To cap your afternoon, hop on one of the **canal cruises** offered by Stockholm Sightseeing

(p. 135). Afterward, no doubt your kids will demand to be taken back to **Gröna Lunds Tivoli** (p. 148) for their final night in Stockholm.

Day ❸: Mariestad ★ & the Göta Canal ★★★

The **Göta Canal** is the most scenic water route in Sweden, linking Stockholm in the east with the "second city" of Gothenburg in the west. In all, it's a journey of 560km (348 miles), which can be comfortably broken up into 2 days of driving. Leave Stockholm on the morning of **Day 3,** taking the E3 expressway west all the way to the town of **Mariestad** (p. 324). In the first day you'll need to cover 318km

(198 miles). Mariestad is the best center for taking cruises on **Lake Vänern,** which, with its 20,000 small islands and islets, is the world's largest freshwater archipelago. Try to get as early a start in Stockholm as you can so you'll arrive in Mariestad in time to take one of the cruises of this vast inland lake. Check with the tourist office as soon as you arrive in Mariestad to see what's available.

Days ❹ & ❺: Arrival in Gothenburg ★★★

On the morning of **Day 4,** leave Mariestad and continue in a southwest direction along E3 to the capital of the west coast of Sweden, the maritime city of **Gothenburg,** a distance of 180km (112 miles). Some kids we've encountered traveling in Sweden with their families have told us they like Gothenburg more than Stockholm.

On your first day, take the classic **Paddan boat ride** (see "Paddan Sightseeing Boats," p. 190), traveling through the moat and canal out to the harbor and the giant dockland. Return for a stroll along the **Avenyn,** the main street of Gothenburg.

As the afternoon fades, head for **Liseberg Park** (p. 187), the largest amusement park in Scandinavia. You can spend the evening here, because it's open until 10 or 11pm in summer. Dozens of restaurants, including fast-food joints, await you. Return to your hotel, where you'll stay for 2 nights as you take in Gothenburg's sights.

On the morning of **Day 5,** get up early to visit the **fish auction** at the harbor, beginning at 7am (p. 186). After seeing **Feskekörka** (p. 186), the "fish church," take tram 6 to the **Guldhedens Vattentorn** (p. 185), a water tower, for the most panoramic view of Gothenburg. Later, go to the **Götaplatsen** (p. 185), in the center of Gothenburg, to gaze upon the **Poseidon Fountain,** sculpted by Carl Milles, Sweden's greatest sculptor. This is a great place for a photo op for the entire family.

Later in the afternoon, explore **Botaniska Trädgården** (p. 188), with its array of natural amusements. In the late afternoon or early evening, nearly all families will want to return to **Liseberg Park** (p. 187) for another night of fun.

Day ❻: Helsingborg, Gateway to Denmark

On the morning of **Day 6,** leave Gothenburg and drive south for 230km (143 miles) to **Helsingborg** at the narrowest point of the Öresund, a body of water that separates Sweden and Denmark. At this point the two countries are only 5km (3 miles) apart, and Denmark lies a 25-minute ferry ride from Helsingborg. From Gothenburg, drive south on the E6 to reach Helsingborg.

After checking into a hotel for the night, set about to explore the attractions of Helsingborg, including the **Fredriksdal Open-Air Museum and Botanical Garden** (p. 214), and the **Kårnan Slott** (p. 214), a former royal residence lying 5km (3 miles) north of Helsingborg.

In the midafternoon you can—for a lark—cross over on the ferry to **Helsingør** in Denmark to visit the so-called "Hamlet's Castle." Return to Helsingborg for the night.

Day ❼: Lund ★★ & Malmö ★★

On the morning of **Day 7,** your final day in Sweden, leave Helsingborg in the morning and drive along E6 in the direction of **Malmö.** At the junction with Route 66, make a detour north to the university and cathedral city of **Lund.** Lund is a distance of 56km (35 miles) from Helsingborg.

At Lund, entice your child to accompany you to the **Domkyrkan** (p. 240), or Cathedral of Lund. The 14th-century astronomical clock here is sure to enchant with its Middle Ages–styled clashing knights marking the hours and the blare of trumpets. Before the morning fades, you can also visit the **Kulturen** (p. 240), an open-air museum of old houses, complete with a kid-pleasing carriage museum. After lunch in Lund, head on to Malmö for the night, where you can check into a hotel. Malmö lies only 18km (11 miles) south of Lund; take Route 66.

With time remaining in the afternoon, you can visit **Malmöhus Slott** (p. 223), the old Malmö castle that has so many museums and galleries that all members of a family are likely to find *something* of interest. After dinner, reward your kids with a visit to **Folkets Park** (p. 237), or People's Park, filled with Tivoli-like amusements, including a playhouse just for kids.

The following morning it's just a short drive over Öresund Bridge into **Copenhagen,** where transportation arrangements can be made for most parts of the world.

Settling into Stockholm

Stockholm is the most regal, elegant, and intriguing city in Scandinavia, although don't tell our Danish and Norwegian friends that we said that. Stockholm presides over a country the size of California (without the massive population) and believes in high taxes and big government. Although the city was founded more than 7 centuries ago, it did not become the official capital of Sweden until the mid–17th century. Today Stockholm reigns over a modern welfare state, and it is one of the world's most liberal, progressive, and democratic societies, a devotee of such issues as same-sex unions and gender equality.

Because of Sweden's neutrality, Stockholm was saved from aerial bombardment during World War II, so much of what you see today is antique, especially the historical heart, Gamla Stan (the Old Town). Yet Sweden is one of the world's leading exponents of modern architecture,

specifically *funkis* (functionalist) architecture and design, and you will find it here as well. Swedish fashion and Swedish design in glassware, furnishings, and industrial products remain at the cutting edge.

In our opinion, Stockholm also enjoys the most dramatic setting of any small capital city in Europe, with a population of 1.9 million people. The city was built on 14 islands in Lake Mälaren, which marks the beginning of an archipelago of 24,000 islands, skerries, and islets stretching all the way to the Baltic Sea. A city of bridges and islands, towers and steeples, cobblestone squares and broad boulevards, Renaissance splendor and steel-and-glass skyscrapers, Stockholm also has access to nature just a short distance away. You can even go fishing in the downtown waterways, thanks to a long-standing decree signed by Queen Christina.

1 ORIENTATION

GETTING THERE

BY PLANE   You'll arrive at **Stockholm Arlanda Airport** (© **08/797-60-00;** www.arlanda.se for information on flights), about 45km (28 miles) north of the city on the E4 highway. A long, covered walkway connects the international and domestic terminals.

Depending on traffic, the fastest, but not necessarily the cheapest, way to go from the airport to the Central Station within Stockholm is on the **Arlanda Express** train (www.arlandaexpress.com), which takes only 20 minutes and is covered by the Eurailpass. This high-speed line is the finest option for the rail traveler. Trains run every 15 to 20 minutes daily from 5am to midnight. If you don't have a rail pass, the cost of a one-way ticket is 220SEK ($44/£22) for adults and 110SEK ($22/£11) for seniors and students 8 to 25 (those under 8 ride free). For more information, call © **771/72-02-00.**

A slower (about 40 min.) but cheaper option involves taking a bus from outside the airport terminal building. It will take you to the **City Terminal** (www.flygbussarna.com), on Klarabergsviadukten, for 99SEK ($20/£10).

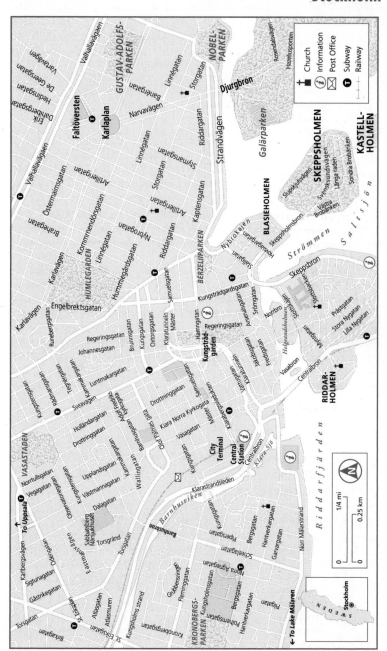

A taxi (www.flygtaxi.se) to or from the airport is expensive, costing 435SEK to 600SEK ($87–$120/£44–£60) or more. (See "Getting Around," below, for the name of a reputable taxi company.)

BY TRAIN Trains arrive at Stockholm's **Centralstationen (Central Station;** ☎ 07/ 717-57-575 in Sweden) on Vasagatan, in the city center where connections can be made to Stockholm's subway, the T-bana. Follow the TUNNELBANA sign, which is sometimes abbreviated to merely the capital letter "T" in blue ink on a white background, enclosed in a blue circle.

Only large towns and cities can be reached by rail from Stockholm's Centralstationen.

BY BUS Buses also arrive at the Centralstationen city terminal, and from here you can catch the T-bana (subway) to your final Stockholm destination. For bus information or reservations, check with the bus system's **ticket offices** at the station (☎ 08/600-10-00; www.flygbussarna.se). Offices in the station labeled BUS STOP sell bus tickets. For travel beyond Sweden, call **Euroline** (☎ 08/762-59-60; www.eurolines.com).

BY CAR Getting into Stockholm by car is relatively easy because the major national expressway from the south, E4, joins with the national expressway, E3, coming in from the west, and leads right into the heart of the city. Stay on the highway until you see the turnoff for Central Stockholm (or Centrum).

Parking in Stockholm is extremely difficult unless your hotel has a garage. Call your hotel in advance and find out what the parking situation is, as most hotels do not offer parking. However, if you're driving into the city, you can often park long enough to unload your luggage; a member of the hotel staff will then direct you to the nearest parking garage.

BY FERRY Large ships, including those of the **Silja Line,** Kungsgatan 2 (☎ 08/22-21-40), and the **Viking Line,** Centralstationen (☎ 08/452-40-00), arrive at specially constructed berths jutting seaward from a point near the junction of Södermalm and Gamla Stan. This neighborhood is called Stadsgården, and the avenue that runs along the adjacent waterfront is known as Stadsgårdshamnen. The nearest T-bana stop is Slussen, a 3-minute walk from the Old Town. Holders of a valid Eurailpass can ride the Silja ferries to Helsinki and Turku at a reduced rate.

Other ferries arrive from Gotland (whose capital is Visby), but these boats dock at Nynäshamn, south of Stockholm. Take a Nynäshamn-bound bus from the Central Station in Stockholm or the SL commuter train to reach the ferry terminal at Nynäshamn.

VISITOR INFORMATION

The **Stockholm Tourist Center,** Sweden House, Hamngatan 27, off Kungsträdgården (Box 16282), S-10325 Stockholm (☎ 08/508-285-08; www.stockholmtown.com), is open year-round June to August Monday to Friday from 9am to 7pm, Saturday 10am to 5pm, and Sunday 10am to 4pm. Maps, brochures, and advice are available for free, and tickets to sporting and cultural events, tourist cards, the Stockholm Card, and books are for sale. The staff will also reserve rooms for you, on-site, at hotels and youth hostels.

The largest organization of its kind in all of Sweden is the **Kulturhuset,** Sergels Torg 3 (☎ 08/508-315-08; www.kulturhuset.stockholm.se). It was built in 1974 by the city of Stockholm as a showcase for Swedish and international art and theater. There are no permanent exhibits; instead, the various spaces inside are allocated to a changing array of paintings, sculpture, photographs, and live performance groups. Kulturhuset also serves as the focal point for information about other cultural activities and organizations throughout Sweden and the rest of Europe. Inside are a snack bar, a library (which has newspapers in several languages), a reading room, a collection of recordings, and a somewhat bureaucratic openness to new art forms. Open Tuesday to Friday 11am to 7pm, Saturday and Sunday 11am to 5pm. No admission is charged.

CITY LAYOUT

MAIN STREETS & ARTERIES Stockholm's major streets—**Kungsgatan** (the main shopping street), **Birger Jarlsgatan, Drottningsgata,** and **Strandvägen** (which leads to Djurgården)—are on Norrmalm (north of the Old Town), and are reserved (with some exceptions) mainly for pedestrians. **Stureplan,** which lies at the junction of the major avenues Kungsgatan and Birger Jarlsgatan, is the commercial hub of the city.

About 4 blocks east of Stureplan rises **Hötorget City,** a landmark of modern urban planning that includes five 18-story skyscrapers. Its main traffic-free artery is **Sergelgatan,** a 3-block shopper's promenade that eventually leads to the modern sculptures at the center of Sergels Torg.

About 9 blocks south of Stureplan, at **Gustav Adolfs Torg,** are both the Royal Dramatic Theater and the Royal Opera House.

A block east of the flaming torches of the opera house is the verdant north–south stretch of **Kungsträdgården**—part avenue, part public park—which serves as a popular gathering place for students and a resting spot for shoppers.

Three blocks to the southeast, on a famous promontory, are the landmark Grand Hotel and the National Museum.

Most visitors to Stockholm arrive at the SAS Airport Bus Terminal, the Central Station, or Stockholm's Central (Public) Bus Station. Each of these is in the heart of the city, on the harborfront, about 7 blocks due west of the opera house. **Kungsholmen (King's Island)** lies across a narrow canal from the rest of the city, a short walk west from the Central Station. It's visited chiefly by those who want to tour Stockholm's elegant Stadshuset (City Hall).

South of **Gamla Stan (Old Town),** and separated from it by a narrow but much-navigated stretch of water, is **Södermalm,** the southern district of Stockholm. Quieter than its northern counterpart, it's an important residential area with a distinctive flavor of its own and a nostalgic reputation for housing, sometimes in overcrowded squalor, the factory workers of the 19th century's industrial revolution. Fast-growing, with a higher density of new, counterculture bars, stores, and nightclubs than any other district of Stockholm, it emerged around the turn of the millennium as one of the most talked-about districts in the capital. Greta Garbo claimed this island as the site of her childhood home.

To the east of Gamla Stan, on a large and forested island completely surrounded by the complicated waterways of Stockholm, is **Djurgården (Deer Park).** The summer pleasure ground of Stockholm is the site of many of its most popular attractions: the open-air museums of Skansen, the *Vasa* man-of-war, Gröna Lund's Tivoli, the Waldemarsudde estate of the "painting prince" Eugen, and the Nordic Museum.

FINDING AN ADDRESS All even numbers are on one side of the street, and all odd numbers are on the opposite side. Buildings are listed in numerical order but often have an *A, B,* or *C* after the number. In the very center of town, numbered addresses start from Sergels Torg.

MAPS Free maps of Stockholm are available at the tourist office, but if you want to explore the narrow old streets of Gamla Stan, you'll need a more detailed map. Pocket-size maps, with a street index that can be opened and folded like a wallet, are sold at most newsstands in central Stockholm and at major bookstores, including **Akademibokhandeln,** Mäster Samuelsgatan 28 (© **08/402-11-00**).

NEIGHBORHOODS IN BRIEF

As you'd expect of a city spread across 14 major islands in an archipelago, Stockholm has many neighborhoods, but those of concern to the ordinary visitor lie in central Stockholm. We'll begin with the most nostalgic and evocative—and our longtime favorite for sleeping or dining—the Old Town.

Gamla Stan (Old Town) The "cradle" of Stockholm, Gamla Stan lies at the entrance to Lake Mälaren on the Baltic and, along with the excavated wreck of the *Vasa,* is the most popular attraction in Stockholm. The buildings here, in general, are most evocative of 18th-century Stockholm, built in romantic architectural styles, and there are many options for eating and drinking. The area's downside is that there are few hotels, and they tend to be expensive. Gamla Stan's major shopping street is the narrow Västerlånggatan, reserved almost exclusively for pedestrians, but many artisans' galleries, souvenir shops, and antiques stores abound on its small lanes. Its main square, and the heart of the ancient city, is Stortorget.

Norrmalm North of Gamla Stan, what was once a city suburb is now the cultural and commercial heart of modern Stockholm. Chances are that your hotel will be in this district, as the area is generously endowed with hotels in all price ranges. This is also the most convenient location for most visits, as it encompasses the City Terminal and the Central Station. Hotels here are not the most romantic in town, but they're generally modern, up-to-date, and well run.

The most famous park in Stockholm, Kungsträdgården (King's Garden), is in Norrmalm. In summer, this park is a major rendezvous point. Norrmalm also embraces the important squares of Sergels Torg and Hötorget, the latter a modern shopping complex. Norrmalm's major pedestrian shopping street is Drottninggatan, which starts at the bridge to the Old Town.

Vasastaden As Norrmalm expanded northward, the new district of Vasastaden was created. It's split by a trio of main arteries: St. Eriksgatan, Sveavägen, and Odengatan. The area around St. Eriksplan is called "the Off-Broadway of Stockholm" because it has so many theaters. Increasingly, this district has attracted fashionable restaurants and bars and has become a popular residential area for young Stockholmers who work in fields such as journalism, television, and advertising.

Vasastaden is slightly more removed from the action, but it's still a good bet for hotels. In international terms, Norrmalm would be like staying in New York's Times Square or London's Leicester Square, whereas Vasastaden would be equivalent to staying on the Upper East Side or Notting Hill. Hotels in Vasastaden come in a wide range of price categories.

Kungsholmen Once known as "Grey Friars Farm," Kungsholmen (King's Island), to the west of Gamla Stan, is the site of City Hall. One of its major arteries is Fleminggatan. Established by Charles XI in the 17th century as a zone for industry and artisans, the island is now gentrified with bars and restaurants. Some industry remains, though: Along Norrmälarstand, old Baltic cutters tie up to the banks, and Stockholm's newspapers have their headquarters at Marieberg on the southwestern tip of the island.

Södermalm South of Gamla Stan, Södermalm (where Greta Garbo was born) is the largest and most populated district in Stockholm. Once synonymous with poverty, this working-class area today is becoming more fashionable, especially with artists, writers, and young people. If you don't come here to stay in one of the moderately priced hotels or to dine in one of its restaurants, you should come to take the Katarina elevator, at Södermalmstorg, Slussen, for a good view of Stockholm and its harbor.

Östermalm In central Stockholm, east of the main artery Birger Jarlsgatan, lies Östermalm. In the Middle Ages, the royal family used to keep its horses, and even its armies, here. Today it's the site of the Army Museum. The area boasts wide straight streets and is home to one of the city's biggest parks, Humlegården, dating from the 17th century.

This is another of the city's hotel districts. While not as conveniently located as Norrmalm and Vasastaden, it's often easier to get rooms here.

Djurgården To the east of Gamla Stan (Old Town) is Djurgården (Deer Park), a forested island in a lake that's the summer recreation area of Stockholm. Here you can visit the open-air folk museums of Skansen, the *Vasa* man-of-war ship, Gröna Lund's Tivoli (Stockholm's own version of the Tivoli), the Waldemarsudde estate and gardens of the "painting prince" Eugen, and the Nordic Museum. The fastest way to get here is over the bridge at Strandvägen/Narvavägen.

Skeppsholmen On its own little island, which can be reached by crossing the Skeppsholmsbron bridge from the Blasieholmen district, Skeppsholmen is like a world apart from the rest of bustling Stockholm. Most people visit it to see the exhibits at the Moderna Museet (see chapter 6, "Discovering Stockholm"). Skeppsholmen also is home to *af Chapman,* Sweden's most famous youth hostel, a gallant, tall ship that is a Stockholm landmark.

2 GETTING AROUND

BY PUBLIC TRANSPORTATION

You can travel throughout Stockholm county by bus, local train, subway (T-bana), and trams, going from Singö in the north to Nynäshamn in the south. The routes are divided into zones, and one ticket is valid for all types of public transportation in the same zone within 1 hour of the time the ticket is stamped.

REGULAR FARES The basic fare for public transportation (in Stockholm this means subway, tram/streetcar, or bus) requires tickets purchased from the agent in the tollbooth on the subway platform, not from a vending machine. Each ticket costs 20SEK ($4/£2), and allows travel to points within most of urban Stockholm, all the way to the borders of the inner city. You can transfer (or double back and return to your starting point) within 1 hour of your departure for free. For more information, search **www.sl.se/ English**.

SPECIAL DISCOUNT TICKETS   Your best transportation bet is to purchase a **tourist season ticket.** A 1-day card, costing 100SEK ($20/£10) for adults and 60SEK ($12/£6) for ages 7 to 20 and seniors, is valid for 24 hours of unlimited travel by T-bana, bus, and commuter train within Stockholm. It also includes passage on the ferry to Djurgården. Most visitors will prefer the 3-day card for 200SEK ($40/£20) for adults and 120SEK ($24/£12) for ages 7 to 20 and seniors, valid for 72 hours in both Stockholm and the adjacent county. The 3-day card also is valid for admission to Skansen, Kaknästornet, and Gröna Lund. Kids up to 7 years of age can travel free with an adult. These tickets are available at tourist information offices, in subway stations, and at most news vendors. Call ℂ **08/600-10-00** for more information.

Stockholmskortet (**Stockholm Card;** www.stockholmtown.com) is a personal discount card that allows unlimited travel by bus, subway, and local trains throughout the city and county of Stockholm (except on airport buses). You can take a sightseeing tour with City Sightseeing, where you can get on and off as often as you please. These tours are available daily from mid-June to mid-August. In addition, the card enables you to take a boat trip to the Royal Palace of Drottningholm for half-price. Admission to 75 museums and attractions is also included in the package.

You can purchase the card at several places in the city, including the Tourist Center in Sweden House, Hotell Centralen, the Central Station, the tourist information desk in City Hall (in summer), the Kaknäs TV tower, SL-Center Sergels Torg (subway entrance level), and Pressbyrån newsstands. The cards are stamped with the date and time at the first point of usage. A 24-hour card costs 330SEK ($66/£33) for adults and 160SEK ($32/£16) for ages 7 to 20 and seniors; a 48-hour card is 460SEK ($92/£46) for adults and 190SEK ($38/£19) for children and seniors; and a 72-hour card is 580SEK ($116/£58) for adults and 220SEK ($44/£22) for children and seniors.

BY T-BANA (SUBWAY)   Before entering the subway, passengers tell the ticket seller the destination, and then purchase tickets. Subway entrances are marked with a blue "T" on a white background. For information about schedules, routes, and fares, phone ℂ **08/600-10-00.**

BY BUS   Where the subway line ends, the bus begins; therefore, if a subway connection doesn't conveniently cover a particular area of Stockholm, a bus will. The two systems have been coordinated to complement each other. Many visitors use a bus to reach Djurgården (although you can walk) because the T-bana doesn't go here.

BY CAR

If you're driving around the Swedish capital, you'll find several parking garages in the city center as well as on the outskirts. In general, you can park at marked spaces Monday through Friday from 8am to 6pm. Exceptions or rules for specific areas are indicated on signs in the area.

BY TAXI

Taxis are expensive—in fact, the most expensive in the world. The meter starts at 45SEK ($9/£4.50), and costs can range upwards from 307SEK ($61/£31) per hour. Those that display an illuminated dome light can be hailed directly on the street, or you can order one by phone. **Taxi Stockholm** (ℂ **08/15-00-00;** www.taxistockholm.se) is one of the city's larger, more reputable companies. Unlike other Nordic nations, Sweden has not been successful at regulating its taxi industry. More than any other nation in Scandinavia, in Sweden, it's best to inquire before you get in whether the taxi is metered or—if the driver is proposing a set price—what the price will be.

Fun Facts Subway Art in the World's Longest Gallery

In 1950, two women came up with the idea of commissioning artists to decorate the subway stations of Stockholm. Some of the country's finest artists were asked to participate; their work is displayed in "the longest and deepest art gallery in the world," some 100 stations stretching all the way from the center of Stockholm to the suburbs.

BY FERRY

Ferries from Skeppsbron on Gamla Stan (near the bridge to Södermalm) will take you to Djurgården if you don't want to walk or go by bus. They leave every 20 minutes Monday to Friday from 7:40am to midnight, and about every 15 minutes on Saturday to Sunday, 9am to midnight, charging 30SEK ($6/£3) for adults and seniors and children 7 to 12; passage is free for children under 7.

BY BICYCLE

The best place to go cycling is on Djurgården. You can rent bicycles from **Djurgårdsbrons Skepp o Hoj,** Djurgårdsbron (© 08/660-57-57), for about 250SEK ($50/£25) per day. It's open May to August daily from 9am to 9pm.

Fast Facts Stockholm

American Express For local 24-hour customer service, call © **08/429-56-00.**

Area Code The international country code for Sweden is **46;** the city code for Stockholm is **08.** (If you're calling Stockholm from abroad, drop the 0.) You do not need to dial 8 within Stockholm; do so only if you're outside the city.

Babysitters Stockholm hotels maintain lists of competent babysitters, nearly all of whom speak English. There is no official agency; rather, it's a word-of-mouth system. Your hotel reception desk can assist you.

Bookstores For a good selection of English-language books, including maps and touring guides, try **Akademibokhandeln,** Mäster Samuelsgatan 28 (© **08/402-11-00**), open Monday to Friday from 10am to 7pm, Saturday from 10am to 4pm, and Sunday from noon to 4pm.

Car Rentals See the appendix, "Fast Facts, Toll-Free Numbers & Websites," for a list of car-rental agencies. In Stockholm, some of the big car-rental companies include **Avis,** Ringvägen 90 (© **08/644-99-80**), and **Hertz,** Vasagatan 24 (© **08/24-07-20**).

Currency Exchange There's a currency exchange office, **Forex,** at the Central Station (© **08/411-67-34**), open daily from 7am to 9pm. It's fully approved by both the Bank of Sweden and the Swedish tourist authorities, offers some of the best exchange rates in town, and takes some of the lowest commissions for cashing traveler's checks. Several other offices are scattered throughout the city.

Dentists Emergency dental treatment is offered at **St. Eriks Hospital,** Flemminggatan 22 (*C* **08/545-512-20**), open daily from 8am to 5pm.

Doctors If you need 24-hour emergency medical care, check with **Medical Care Information** (*C* **08/320-100**). There's also a private clinic, **City Akuten,** at Apelberg Sq. 48, 1st floor (*C* **08/545-291-85**).

Drugstores **C. W. Scheele,** Klarabergsviadukten 64 (*C* **08/454-81-30**), remains open 24 hours a day.

Embassies & Consulates See "Fast Facts: Sweden," in the appendix.

Emergencies Call *C* **112** for the police, ambulance service, or the fire department.

Eyeglasses **The Nordiska Kompaniet,** Hamngatan 18–20 (*C* **08/762-80-00**), a leading Stockholm department store, has a registered optician on duty at its ground-floor service center. The optician performs vision tests, stocks a large selection of frames, and makes emergency repairs.

Hospitals Call **Medical Care Information** at *C* **08/32-01-00** and an English-speaking operator will inform you of the hospital closest to you; operators are available 24 hours daily.

Internet Cafe A convenient cybercafe is **Dome House,** Sveavägen 108 (*C* **08/612-61-10**), open daily 11am to 3am, charging 19SEK ($4/£2) per hour.

Lost Property If you've lost something on the train, go to the Lost and Found office in the Central Station, lower concourse (*C* **08/762-25-50**). The police also have such an office at the police station at Kungsholmsgatan 37 (*C* **08/401-01-00**). The Stockholm Transit Company (SL) keeps its recovered articles at the Klaraostra Kyrkogata 6 (*C* **08/600-10-00**).

Luggage Storage & Lockers Facilities are available at the Central Station on Vasagatan, lower concourse (*C* **08/762-25-95**). Depending on the size of your baggage, the cost of storage ranges from 30SEK to 80SEK ($6–$16/£3–£8) per day. Lockers also can be rented at the ferry stations at Värtan and Tegelvikshamnnen, at the Viking Line terminal, and at the Central Station.

Police Call *C* **112** in an emergency.

Post Office The main post office is at Centralstationen 10126 (*C* **08/781-24-25**), open Monday to Friday 7am to 10pm, and Saturday and Sunday 9am to 6pm. If you want to pick up letters while you're abroad, they should be addressed to your name, c/o Post Restante, Post Center, Central Station 11120, Stockholm, Sweden.

Shoe Repair In the basement of **Nordiska Kompaniet,** Hamngatan 18–20 (*C* **08/762-80-00**), a leading Stockholm department store, there is a shoe-repair place, which also may be able to repair broken luggage.

Taxis See "Getting Around," above.

Telephone, Telex & Fax Instructions in English are posted in public phone boxes, which can be found on street corners. Very few phones in Sweden are coin-operated; most require a phone card, which can be purchased at most newspaper stands and tobacco shops.

Post offices throughout Stockholm now offer phone, fax, and telegram services. Of course, most guests can ask their hotels to send a fax. All but the smallest boarding houses in Stockholm today have fax services.

Toilets Public facilities can be found in the Central Station, in all subway stations, and in department stores, as well as along some of the major streets, parks, and squares. In an emergency, you can use the toilets in most hotels and restaurants, although generally they're reserved for patrons.

3 WHERE TO STAY

By the standards of many U.S. or Canadian cities, hotels in Stockholm are very expensive. If the high prices make you want to cancel your trip, read on. Dozens of hotels in Stockholm offer reduced rates on weekends all year, and daily from around mid-June to mid-August. For further information, inquire at a travel agency or the tourist center (see "Orientation," earlier in this chapter). In summer, it's best to make reservations in advance, just to be on the safe side.

Most of the city's medium-priced hotels are in Norrmalm, north of the Old Town, and many of the least-expensive lodgings are near the Central Station. There are comparably priced inexpensive accommodations within 10 to 20 minutes of the city, easily reached by subway, streetcar, or bus. We'll suggest a few hotels in the Old Town, but these choices are limited and more expensive.

Note: In most cases, a service charge ranging from 10% to 15% is added to the bill, plus the inevitable 21% MOMS (value-added tax). Unless otherwise indicated, all of our recommended accommodations come with a private bathroom.

BOOKING SERVICES **Hotell Centralen,** Vasagatan (© **08/508-285-08;** www.stockholmtown.com), on the street level of the Central Station, is the city's official housing bureau; it can arrange accommodations in hotels, pensions (boarding houses), and youth hostels—but not in private homes. There is no booking fee. It's open Monday to Friday 9am to 6pm, Saturday 9am to 5pm, and Sunday 10am to 4pm.

IN NORRMALM (THE CENTER)
Very Expensive
Grand Hotel ★★★ Opposite the Royal Palace, this hotel—a bastion of elite hospitality since 1874—is the finest in Scandinavia. The most recent restoration was in 2006, which retained the grand and conservatively modern styling of the lobby, but added 72 additional bedrooms and made major changes to the bar and to the grander of the hotel's two restaurants. Despite major alterations at roughly 10-year intervals throughout this hotel's life, its old-world style and sense of luxury has always been maintained. Guest rooms come in all shapes and sizes, all elegantly appointed in any of seven different decorative styles. The priciest rooms overlook the water, and we'd recommend that you go for these first, although they are invariably sought after. The hotel's ballroom is an exact copy of Louis XIV's Hall of Mirrors at Versailles. Almost as a matter of national pride, the hotel retains an allegiance to the daily presentation, at lunchtime, of a lavish smorgasbord—one of the very few establishments in Scandinavia that does so. It's a daunting challenge, considering the hard work and expense involved for the hotel's food

SETTLING INTO STOCKHOLM

5

WHERE TO STAY

To Uppsala

VASASTADEN

KRONOBERGS-
PARKEN

City
Terminal

Central
Station

← To Lake Mälaren

Riddarfjärden

RIDDAR-
HOLMEN

Kungsträd-
garden

To Södertälje

SÖDERMALM

Söder Mälarstrand

SWEDEN

Stockholm

Adlon Hotell **11**
Berns Hotel **24**
Clarion Hotel Sign **1**
Clas på Hörnet **4**
Comfort Hotel Wellington **28**
Crystal Plaza Hotel **8**
Elite Hotel Stockholm Plaza **7**

Esplanade Hotel **25**
First Hotel Reisen **21**
Grand Hotel **22**
Hilton Hotel Slussen **19**
Hotel Bema **2**
Hotel Diplomat **26**
Hotel Hellsten **5**

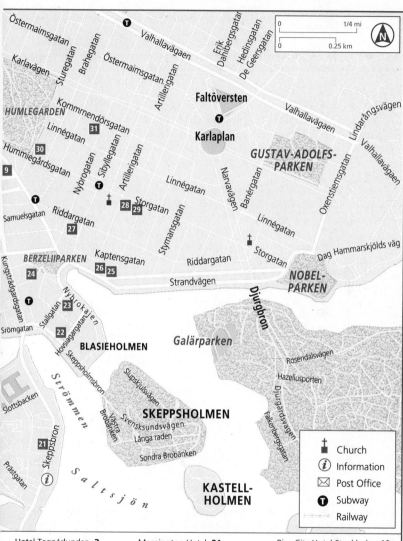

Östermaimsgatan
Valhallavägaen
Karlavägen
Sturegatan
Brahegatan
Erik Dahlbergsgatan
Hedinsgatan
De Geersgatan
Östermaimsgatan
Artillerigatan

Faltöversten

Valhallavägaen

HUMLEGARDEN
Kommrnendörsgatan
Linnégatan
31
Nybrogatan
Sibyllegatan
Artillerigatan

Karlaplan

Lindarångsvägen
Valhallavägaen

GUSTAV-ADOLFS-
PARKEN

Hummiegårdsgatan
30
9

Linnégatan
Narvavägen
Banérgatan
Oxenstiernsgatan

Samuelsgatan
Riddargatan
28 **29** Storgatan
Stymansgatan
Linnégatan

27

BERZELIIPARKEN
24
Kaptensgatan
26 **25**
Riddargatan
Storgatan
Dag Hammarskjölds väg

Kungsträdgårdsgatan
Nybrokaien
23
Strandvägen
NOBEL-
PARKEN

Stallgatan
22
Hovslagaregatan
BLASIEHOLMEN
Djurgbron

Strömgatan
Skeppsholmsbron

Strömmen
Slupskjulsvägen
Västra
Brobänken
Svensksundsvägen
Långa raden
Sondra Brobänken

SKEPPSHOLMEN

Galärparken

Rosendalsvägen
Hazeliusporten
Djurgårdsvägen
Falkenbergsgatan

Slottsbacken
21
Skeppsbron
Prästgatan
Skeppsbron
(i)

Saltsjön

KASTELL-
HOLMEN

✝	Church
(i)	Information
✉	Post Office
T	Subway
⊢⊢⊢⊢	Railway

0 ——— 1/4 mi
0 ——— 0.25 km
N

Hotel Tegnérlunden **3**
Hotell Kom **6**
Hotell Kung Carl **9**
Hotell Örnsköld **27**
Lady Hamilton Hotel **16**
Lord Nelson Hotel **20**
Mälardrottningen **17**

Mornington Hotel **31**
Nordic Hotel **12**
Pärlan **29**
Radisson SAS Royal
  Viking Hotel **13**
Radisson SAS Strand Hotel **23**
Rex Hotel **5**

Rica City Hotel Stockholm **10**
Scandic Anglais **30**
Scandic Sergel Plaza **14**
Sheraton Stockholm Hotel
  & Towers **15**
Victory Hotel **18**

and beverage team, but the smorgasbord, the superb service, and a sense of imperial charm remain distinguishing characteristics of this monumental hotel landmark.

Södra Blasieholmshamnen 8, S-103 27 Stockholm. ✆ **08/679-35-00.** Fax 08/611-86-86. www.grand hotel.se. 380 units. 1,490–6,490SEK ($298–$1,298/£149–£649) double; from 6,500SEK ($1,300/£650) suite. AE, DC, MC, V. Parking 395SEK ($79/£40). T-bana: Kungsträdgården. Bus: 46, 55, 62, or 76. **Amenities:** 2 restaurants; bar; fitness center; sauna; room service; laundry service; dry cleaning; nonsmoking rooms; rooms for those w/limited mobility. *In room:* TV, minibar, hair dryer, safe, Wi-Fi.

Expensive

Berns Hotel ★★   This is the hotel of choice for many celebrities visiting Stockholm. That can be either good or bad for you. When Axl Rose, from the rock group Guns N' Roses, stayed here in 2006, he bit one of the doormen—and the hotel was then mentioned in tabloids around the world. But, chances are, you won't get to witness something as exciting as that. When not hosting rock stars, the Berns can actually be rather subdued.

During its 19th-century heyday, beginning in 1863, this was the most elegant hotel in Sweden, with an ornate Gilded Age interior that was the setting for many a legendary rendezvous. In 1989, following years of neglect, it was rebuilt in the original style, and the restaurant facilities were upgraded. Although the dining and drinking areas are usually crowded with sometimes-raucous club kids and bar patrons, the guest rooms are soundproof and comfortably isolated from the activity downstairs. The Red Room is the setting and namesake of Strindberg's novel *Röda Rummet*.

Näckströmsgatan 8, S-111 47 Stockholm. ✆ **08/566-322-00.** Fax 08/566-322-01. www.berns.se. 65 units. 2,650SEK–4,800SEK ($530–$960/£265–£480) double; 3,375SEK–10,500SEK ($675–$2,100/£338–£1,050) suite. Rates include buffet breakfast. AE, DC, MC, V. Parking 425SEK ($85/£43). T-bana: Östermalmstorg. **Amenities:** Restaurant; bar; sauna; room service; babysitting; laundry service; dry cleaning; nonsmoking rooms. *In room:* TV, minibar, hair dryer, Wi-Fi.

Hotel Diplomat ★   This hotel is a bit stuffy, but that's what its guests prefer. Well-managed, discreet, and solid, the Diplomat is a conservative operation that knows how to handle business clients and corporate conventions. Built in 1911, it retains hints of its original Art Nouveau styling. Public areas are more streamlined. The individually conceived guest rooms are decorated with well-crafted furniture. Many rooms contain bay windows overlooking the harbor; most of the less expensive accommodations face a quiet inner courtyard. Rooms range in size from cramped singles to spacious doubles with sitting areas, high ceilings, and hints of their original Art Nouveau styling. At least once, take the circular stairs for views of the hotel's antique stained-glass windows.

Strandvagen 7C, Östermalm, S-104-40 Stockholm. ✆ **08/459-68-00.** Fax 08/459-68-20. www.diplomat hotel.com. 128 units. 1,530SEK–3,295SEK ($306–$659/£153–£330) double; 2,695SEK–4,995SEK ($539–$999/£270–£500) suite. Rates include breakfast on weekends. AE, DC, MC, V. Parking 390SEK ($78/£39). T-bana: Storeplan. **Amenities:** Restaurant; 2 bars; room service; babysitting; laundry service; dry cleaning; nonsmoking rooms; rooms for those w/limited mobility. *In room:* TV, minibar, hair dryer, Wi-Fi.

Nordic Hotel ★★ (Finds)   Madonna might find the Diplomat staid, but she could check in here bare-breasted and no one would raise an eyebrow. There's nothing in Scandinavia quite like this hotel, which was voted "The World's Sexiest Hotel" by *Elle* magazine. It definitely has a split personality—its astrological sign is Gemini. Lying on either side of a new square, Vasaplan, the hotel stands adjacent to the express rail link with the airport, or the central rail station. You're given a choice of a room of "watery calm" in the

367-room Nordic Sea or "post-minimalist luminescence" in the 175-room Nordic
Light.

Nordic Sea, which tends to welcome members of large groups and bus tours, turns to the ocean for its inspiration and features a 2,400-gallon aquarium and steel walls constructed from ship hulls. The comfortable rooms have a certain elegant simplicity, along with beautiful bathrooms. These accommodations range in size from extra small to extra large. Nordic Light, equally modern, equally angular, and positioned just across the boulevard from its more conservative twin, is the more intriguing of the two hotels, and the one that tends to be filled with individual clients, often from the media industry. The suggestive light patterns projected onto the bleach-walls of both the bedrooms and the public areas of the Nordic Light re-create the ever-changing patterns of the lights of the north.

4–7 Vasaplan. ⓒ **800/337-4685** in the U.S., or 08/505-630-00. Fax 08/505-630–40. www.nordichotels.se. 367 units in Nordic Sea, 175 units in Nordic Light. 1,630SEK–4,000SEK ($326–$800/£163–£400) double Nordic Sea; 1,120SEK–4,000SEK ($224–$800/£112–£400) double Nordic Light. AE, DC, MC, V. T-bana: Centralen. **Amenities:** Restaurant; 2 bars; minigym; some spa treatments; steam bath; sauna; room service; laundry service; dry cleaning; nonsmoking rooms; rooms for those w/limited mobility. *In room:* TV, minibar, coffeemaker, iron, safe, Wi-Fi.

Radisson SAS Strand Hotel ★

We often bypass Radisson SAS hotels, as we prefer Scandinavia's more evocative and atmospheric hotels. But this place has much to recommend it and doesn't suffer from the curse of bandbox modern. In stark contrast to the angular modernity of many other SAS hotels in Scandinavia, the Strand has a traditional and charming *Jugendstil* (Art Nouveau) exterior. Originally built in 1912, but with a comfortable and stylish interior that doesn't retain a shred of its original turn-of-the-20th-century embellishment, it lies amid a complicated network of canals and waterways. The bedrooms are outfitted with solid furniture and light pastel colors. Rooms are available in a wide range of sizes; the ones at the lowest end of the spectrum are rather small and have less-than-comfortable bathrooms. The more expensive rooms are considerably larger and plusher, and come with large beds more suited to North American tastes. Overall, you'll get the feeling that, although comfortable and more than adequate, the hotel won't appeal to the more socially ambitious—especially because the Grand Hotel is just a short walk away.

Nybrokajen 9, S-103 27 Stockholm. ⓒ **800/333-3333** in the U.S., or 08/50-66-40-00. Fax 08/50-66-40-01. www.radisson.com. 152 units. 1,795SEK–3,495SEK ($359–$699/£180–£350) double; 3,700SEK–4,900SEK ($740–$980/£370–£490) suite. AE, DC, MC, V. Parking 290SEK ($58/£29) per night. T-bana: Kungsträdgården. **Amenities:** Restaurant; bar; sauna; room service; babysitting; laundry service; dry cleaning. *In room:* A/C, TV, minibar, coffeemaker, hair dryer, trouser press, safe, Wi-Fi.

Scandic Anglais

This hotel was shut down for 2 years while its restorers renovated it and added technology to bring it up to 21st-century standards. They have succeeded admirably. Rooms are decorated in warm earth tones and are cozy and contemporary, with wood laminate flooring throughout. Its highlight is a 7th-floor terrace bar overlooking Stockholm. In the heart of the city's business and entertainment district, the hotel is convenient, well run, and efficient in its service personnel.

Humlegardsgatan 23, S-102 44 Stockholm. ⓒ **08/517-340-00.** Fax 08/517-340-11. www.scandichotels. com. 230 units. 1,490SEK–3,600SEK ($298–$720/£149–£360) double, 4,420SEK–4,590SEK ($884–$918/£442–£459) suite. Rates include buffet breakfast. AE, DC, MC, V. T-bana: Östermalmstorg. Parking: 300SEK ($60/£30). **Amenities:** Restaurant; bar; fitness center; room service; laundry service; dry cleaning; nonsmoking rooms; rooms for those w/limited mobility. *In room:* A/C, TV, minibar, hair dryer, safe, Wi-Fi.

Moderate

Adlon Hotell   Some hotels can be bit dull while still reliable, comfortable, affordably priced, and serviceable in every way. Such is the case with the Adlon. This 1884 building was redesigned by brothers Axel and Hjalmar Jumlin in the 1920s. Upgraded and improved many times since, it lies near the Central Station (and the subway) and is convenient to buses to and from Arlanda Airport. All the rather small rooms have been renovated and are comfortably furnished.

Vasagatan 42, S-111 20 Stockholm. ✆ **08/402-65-00.** Fax 08/20-86-10. www.adlon.se. 83 units. 1,350SEK–2,595SEK ($270–$519/£135–£260) double. Rates include breakfast. AE, DC, MC, V. Parking 260SEK ($52/£26) in garage 1 block away. T-bana: Centralen. **Amenities:** Bar; lounge; laundry service; dry cleaning; nonsmoking rooms. *In room:* TV, minibar, beverage maker (in most), hair dryer.

Clas på Hörnet ★★ (Finds)   To escape the blandness that infuses certain Swedish hotels, we like to check in here if only for nostalgic reasons. Built in the 1730s as a private house, this small, upscale, and very charming inn is less than a kilometer (about ²/₃ mile) north of the commercial heart of Stockholm. Its attention to period detail—supervised by the curators of the Stockholm City Museum—lends a distinctive country-inn ambience that's enhanced with bedrooms outfitted in the late-18th-century style of Gustavus III. Each of the bedrooms is outfitted in a different color scheme and motif, usually with cheerful colors, wide floorboards, antiques, and all the amenities you'd expect from a well-managed and intimate hotel. Many have four-poster beds. The in-house restaurant, Clas på Hornet (Clas on the Corner), is recommended separately under "Where to Dine," later in this chapter.

Surbrunnsgatan 20, S-113 48 Stockholm. ✆ **08/16-51-36.** Fax 08/612-53-15. www.claspahornet.se. 10 units. Sun–Thurs 1,695SEK ($339/£170) double, 2,395SEK ($479/£240) suite; Fri–Sat 1,395SEK ($279/£140) double, 1,995SEK ($399/£200) suite. Rates include breakfast. AE, DC, MC, V. Parking 225SEK ($44/£23). Bus: 46 or 53. **Amenities:** Breakfast room; lounge; nonsmoking rooms. *In room:* TV, minibar, Wi-Fi.

Clarion Hotel Sign ★★   The epitome of Nordic taste and design, this hotel is a showcase for some of the top furniture designers of the 20th century, including legends Hans Wegner, Bruno Mathsson, Arne Jacobsen, and the Finn, Alvar Aalto. Even the architect of the mammoth building of granite and glass by the Central Station facing Norra Bantorget Square was the celebrated Gert Wingårdh. The eighth floor of the hotel features one of the finest spas in the city. The hotel is also the site of one of the city's best restaurants, the Aquavit Grill & Raw Bar.

Östra Järnvägsgatan 35, S-101 26 Stockholm. ✆ **08/676-98-00.** Fax 08/676-98-99. www.clarionsign. com. 558 units. 1,325SEK–1,995SEK ($265–$399/£133–£200) double; 7,150SEK ($1,430/£715) suite. AE, DC, MC, V. Parking: 240SEK–395SEK ($48–$79/£24–£40). T-bana: Any train to Central Station. **Amenities:** Restaurant; bar; room service; health club; laundry service/dry cleaning; nonsmoking rooms. *In room:* A/C, TV, minibar, hair dryer, safe, Wi-Fi.

Comfort Hotel Wellington ★   This is a good, safe address—the type of place your great aunt wants you to stay in Stockholm. A longtime favorite with British travelers, the nine-story Wellington sounds like something you'd find in London. Built in the late 1950s, it maintains some English decorative touches and lies in a quiet but convenient neighborhood less than a kilometer (about ²/₃ mile) east of Stockholm's commercial core. The public rooms are filled with engravings of English hunting scenes and leather-covered chairs. Some of the small but stylish guest rooms overlook a flower-filled courtyard, and units on higher floors have panoramic views.

Storgatan 6, S-11451 Stockholm. ℂ **08/667-09-10.** Fax 08/667-12-54. www.wellington.se. 60 units. Summer and Fri–Sat year-round 1,495SEK–1,895SEK ($299–$379/£150–£190) double; rest of year 2,595SEK–2,895SEK ($519–$579/£260–£290) double. Rates include breakfast. AE, DC, MC, V. Parking 250SEK ($50/£25). T-bana: Östermalmstorg. **Amenities:** Breakfast room; bar; sauna; laundry service; dry cleaning; nonsmoking rooms; rooms for those w/limited mobility. *In room:* TV, hair dryer, iron (in some), trouser press (in some), Wi-Fi.

Crystal Plaza Hotel   This hotel is rich in atmosphere, but doesn't have as much style as the previously recommended Clas på Hornet. Even so, it's a reliable and fine choice in every way. A charming, richly detailed, turn-of-the-20th-century hotel, the Karelia was transformed after several large-scale renovations in the 1990s. Many aspects of the building's original grandeur were retained, including the soaring Romanesque entranceway, the decorative double staircase, and the copper-capped tower. Trying to stay abreast of the times and changing Swedish tastes, the hotel has installed a rather good Thai restaurant.

Birger Jarlsgatan 35, S0111 45 Stockholm. ℂ **08/406-88-00.** Fax 08/24-15-11. www.crystalplazahotel.se. 111 units. Sun–Thurs 1,600–1,835SEK ($320–$367/£160–£184) double; Fri–Sat 1,000–1,835SEK ($200–$367/£100–£184) double; 2,635SEK ($527/£264) suite. Rates include breakfast. AE, DC, MC, V. Parking 300SEK ($60/£30). T-bana: Östermalmstorg. Bus: 46. **Amenities:** Restaurant; bar; laundry service; dry cleaning; nonsmoking rooms. *In room:* TV, minibar, coffeemaker, hair dryer, trouser press, safe (in most), Wi-Fi.

Elite Hotel Stockholm Plaza ★   This would not be our first choice for a hotel in Stockholm. But it certainly came in handy one night when we flew into Stockholm unexpectedly and nearly all hotels were full. It's a bit pricey for what you get, but the first-class hotel is well run. And it's built on a triangular lot that might remind some visitors of New York's Flatiron Building. From the time of its construction in 1884 until its complete makeover in 1984, the building had many uses—as a run-down rooming house, private apartments, and offices. The light, fresh guest rooms have tiled bathrooms. We found the staff most hospitable.

Birger Jarlsgatan 29, S-103 95 Stockholm. ℂ **08/566-220-00.** Fax 08/566-22-020. www.elite.se. 151 units. 893SEK–2,500SEK ($179–$500/£89–£250) double; 1,658–4,800SEK ($332–$960/£166–£480) suite. Rates include breakfast. AE, DC, MC, V. Parking 250SEK ($50/£25). T-bana: Hötorget or Östermalmstorg. **Amenities:** Restaurant; bar; dance club; sauna; room service; laundry service; dry cleaning; nonsmoking rooms; 1 room for those w/limited mobility. *In room:* TV, minibar (in some), hair dryer, Wi-Fi.

Esplanade Hotel ★   This informal hotel, where the only meal served is breakfast, lies immediately adjacent to the more expensive and more richly accessorized Diplomat. Respectable and discreet, it attracts representatives from the neighboring embassies and others who like its comfortable charm and traditional atmosphere. Constructed as part of the same beaux-arts architectural complex—at the time, a boarding house—as the Diplomat in 1910, it was transformed into a hotel in 1954, occupying two floors of a six-story building, the remainder of which are devoted to offices. Many of the rooms are furnished in old-fashioned style. Single rooms are minuscule. Most doubles have double-glazed windows, extra-long beds, and well-kept, decent-size tile bathrooms. Four rooms open onto a view of the water, and the high-ceilinged lounge features a balcony with a view of Djurgården.

Strandvägen 7A, S-114 56 Stockholm. ℂ **08/663-07-40.** Fax 08/662-59-92. www.hotelesplanade.se. 34 units. Mon–Thurs 2,095SEK–2,295SEK ($419–$459/£210–£230) double; Fri–Sun 1,495SEK–1,695SEK ($299–$339/£150–£170) double. Rates include breakfast. AE, DC, MC, V. Parking nearby 275SEK ($55/£28). T-bana: Östermalmstorg. Bus: 47 or 69. **Amenities:** Breakfast room; lounge; sauna; room service; laundry service; dry cleaning; nonsmoking rooms. *In room:* TV, minibar, hair dryer, Wi-Fi.

Hotell Kung Carl ★ "The staff is kindly and caring," a Swedish habitué of this place told us, "and the hotel is always reliable, tastefully furnished, and fairly priced." What more could you ask for? Excitement? (No way.) Discreet, tasteful, and quietly glamorous, this hotel in the heart of Stockholm was built in the mid-1800s by a religious group that offered lodgings to women newly arrived in Stockholm from the countryside. It's one of the longest-operating hotels in the city, and despite being elevated to four-star government status thanks to many improvements, it retains an old-fashioned charm. The midsize-to-spacious bedrooms are furnished in a comfortable but slightly dated style. There's no restaurant on the premises, but the lobby bar sells pizza and sandwiches.

Birger Jarlsgatan 21, S-111 87 Stockholm. ℂ **08/463-50-00.** Fax 08/463-50-50. www.hkchotels.se. 121 units. 1,211SEK–3,040SEK ($242–$608/£121–£304) double; 2,095SEK–5,000SEK ($419–$1,000/£210–£500) suite. Rates include breakfast. AE, DC, MC, V. Parking 220SEK ($44/£22). T-bana: Östermalmstorg. **Amenities:** Restaurant; bar; lounge; room service; laundry service; dry cleaning; nonsmoking rooms; rooms for those w/limited mobility. *In room:* A/C (in some), TV, minibar, hair dryer, iron (in some), safe, sauna (in some), Jacuzzi (in some), Wi-Fi.

Radisson SAS Royal Viking Hotel ★ We infinitely prefer the grace of the Radisson SAS Strand (see above). But if you're in Stockholm to attend a convention or want to catch an early-morning train for a quick getaway, this hotel has convenience going for it. This airline-affiliated nine-story tower is in a commercial neighborhood near the railway station and the Stockholm World Trade Center. It has a soaring, plant-filled atrium, its most winning feature. Especially popular in summer with organized tours and conventioneers, it offers rooms with stylized modern furniture and good, firm beds. Many units are minisuites, well accessorized with electronic extras.

Vasagatan 1, S-101 24 Stockholm. ℂ **800/333-3333** in the U.S., or 08/506-540-00. Fax 08/506-540-01. www.radissonsas.com. 459 units. 1,295SEK–2,790SEK ($259–$558/£130–£279) double; 1,195SEK–5,000SEK ($239–$1,000/£120–£500) suite. Children under 17 stay free in parent's room. Rates include breakfast. AE, DC, MC, V. Parking 390SEK ($78/£39). T-bana: Centralen. **Amenities:** Restaurant; 2 bars; heated indoor pool; fitness center; Jacuzzi; sauna; room service; laundry service; dry cleaning; nonsmoking rooms; rooms for those w/limited mobility. *In room:* TV, minibar, hair dryer, trouser press, Wi-Fi.

Scandic Sergel Plaza ★★ (Kids) We sat up one night here with a woman member of the Swedish Parliament talking about politics. Before 2am, she'd convinced us that the government of Sweden was "superior" to all other democracies. If you stay here, chances are you'll have your own encounters with parliamentary Sweden, as this classic hotel was designed in 1984 as living quarters for parliament members who come into Stockholm from the provinces. Of course, today, its rooms are open to all, and it is an especially inviting choice for families (see the info on "Family-Friendly Hotels," below). The hotel lies at the entrance to Drottninggatan, the main shopping street. The elegant public decor includes 18th-century artwork and antiques. The beautifully decorated guest rooms are done up in a tasteful but traditional modern style, using reproductions. The best rooms are on the executive floors, with enhanced luxury and services.

Brunkebergstorg 9, S-103 27 Stockholm. ℂ **08/517-263-00.** Fax 08/517-263-11. www.scandic-hotels.com. 403 units. 1,020SEK–2,790SEK ($204–$558/£102–£279) double; 3,580SEK–5,000SEK ($716–$1,000/£358–£500) suite. Rates include breakfast. AE, DC, MC, V. Parking 295SEK ($59/£30). T-bana: Centralen. Bus: 47, 52, or 69. **Amenities:** Restaurant; bar; children's playroom; room service; laundry service; dry cleaning; nonsmoking rooms; rooms for those w/limited mobility. *In room:* TV, minibar, hair dryer, trouser press (in some), Wi-Fi.

Sheraton Stockholm Hotel & Towers ★ (Kids) We've already gone on record as shying away from impersonal chain hotels, but for many visitors this is one of the best in its category. Sure, it's short on Swedish charm but excellent by other hotel standards,

Family-Friendly Hotels

Scandic Sergel Plaza (p. 84)   At "Siggie's Castle," kids can play with toy cars, construct brick buildings, watch videos, and even read books.

Hotel Tegnérlunden (p. 86)   Twenty big, airy rooms are ideal for families on a budget.

Sheraton Stockholm Hotel & Towers (p. 84)   This well-run chain has always pampered children. The spacious rooms are comfortably shared with parents.

attracting many business travelers and even families, both foreign and domestic. Sheathed with Swedish granite, the eight-story hostelry is within view of Stockholm's City Hall (Rådhuset). The guest rooms are the largest in the city, with one king or two double beds with bedside controls and closets with mirrored doors. A family of three or four can fit comfortably into most of them. Most units offer sweeping views of the city, many over Gamla Stan. The restaurants serve market-fresh ingredients deftly handled by a skilled kitchen staff.

Tegelbacken 6, S-101 23 Stockholm. © **800/325-3535** in the U.S. and Canada, or 08/412-34-00. Fax 08/412-34-09. www.sheratonstockholm.com. 462 units. 1,345SEK–2,900SEK ($269–$580/£135–£290) double; from 4,000SEK ($800/£400) suite. AE, DC, MC, V. Parking 300SEK ($60/£30). T-bana: Centralen. **Amenities:** 2 restaurants; bar; indoor heated pool; fitness center; sauna; room service; babysitting; laundry service; dry cleaning; nonsmoking rooms; rooms for those w/limited mobility. *In room:* TV, minibar (in some), beverage maker (in suites), hair dryer, safe, Wi-Fi.

Inexpensive

Inexpensive is a relative term when applied to Stockholm hotels. What might be considered inexpensive in Stockholm would be superpricey in western Kansas.

Hotel Bema   Backpackers, students, and cyclists appreciate the youthful ambience and the good-natured reception here. You will too, given that the place is functional with a few frills and a fair price (for Stockholm). When it was constructed in 1905, this building was an apartment house, lying within a 10-minute walk of Stockholm's railway station. Today it's been converted into a small and intimate hotel, just battered enough to relieve the inhibitions of anyone who fears formality. The decor and amenities date from 1987, when the owners radically upgraded the place in a contemporary style. The rooms are not exactly plush, but the bathrooms are neatly maintained and come with tub/shower combinations.

Upplandsgatan 13, S-11123 Stockholm. © **08/23-26-75.** Fax 08/20-53-38. www.hotelbema.se. 12 units. Mon–Thurs 950SEK–1,050SEK ($190–$210/£95–£105) double; Fri–Sun 750SEK–850SEK ($150–$170/£75–£85) double. Rates include breakfast. AE, DC, MC, V. Parking 150SEK ($30/£15) in nearby garage. Bus: 69. **Amenities:** Breakfast service in rooms; nonsmoking rooms. *In room:* TV, Wi-Fi.

Hotell Kom (Value)   When we first checked into this establishment, it was a youth hostel. Those days are long gone. Although still owned by the Swedish version of the YWCA and YMCA, the hotel is vastly improved and upgraded, and that's reflected in its prices. It's no longer 125SEK ($25/£13) a night, but you still get good value and a warm welcome here. Rooms, although small, are tastefully and comfortably furnished in the latest Swedish modern style. The building itself is well maintained and up-to-date, and many of the rooms open onto good views of the cityscape—it's in a residential neighborhood scattered with stores and private apartments. A number of simple and rather small budget rooms are also rented on the ground floor, each with two bunk beds. These bargains can accommodate up to four guests.

Döbelnsgatan 17, S-11140 Stockholm. © **800/780-7234** or 08/412-23-00. Fax 08/412-23-10. www.komhotel.se. 128 units. Mon–Thurs 1,470SEK–2,140SEK ($294–$428/£147–£214) double; Fri–Sun 1,025SEK–1,470SEK ($205–$294/£103–£147) double; budget rooms 650SEK ($130/£65) double, 850SEK ($170/£85) quad. Rates include breakfast. AE, DC, MC, V. Parking 190SEK ($38/£19). T-bana: Rådmansgatan. **Amenities:** Breakfast room; lounge; fitness center; sauna; laundry service; dry cleaning; nonsmoking rooms; rooms for those w/limited mobility. *In room:* TV, minibar, hair dryer, trouser press, safe, Wi-Fi.

Hotell Örnsköld   Years ago when we were checking out this hotel, we spotted the great Swedish director Ingmar Bergman passing through. Only later did we learn that he wasn't calling on a mistress but was checking prop storage and staff housing, which even today are partial functions of this establishment near the Royal Dramatic Theatre. The five-story building was built in 1910, and the hotel is situated on the second floor. High-ceilinged rooms have simple, contemporary furnishings, and more expensive units are big enough to hold extra beds, if necessary. All units contain well-kept bathrooms with shower units. A few cubicle rooms—called "cabins"—have no windows.

Nybrogatan 6, S-11434 Stockholm. © **08/667-02-85.** Fax 08/667-69-91. www.hotelornskold.se. 27 units. 1,295SEK–2,195SEK ($259–$439/£130–£220) double; 495SEK ($99/£50) "cabin." Rates include breakfast. AE, MC, V. T-bana: Östermalmstorg. **Amenities:** Lounge; laundry service; dry cleaning. *In room:* TV, minibar, hair dryer, iron, Wi-Fi.

Hotel Tegnérlunden ★ (Kids)   Stay here if you want comfort but not a lot of style. Like a London townhouse hotel, this hidden hotel lies next to a leafy park, unusual for Stockholm, and its best feature is its airy rooftop breakfast room. The famous playwright August Strindberg used to walk by the door, allegedly working up quotations. In spite of a big expansion, the hotel still retains a personal atmosphere. Many of the tasteful, functionally furnished rooms are suitable for families because of their size. They're also blissfully quiet, especially those opening onto the rear. The rooms vary in size and shape and are well maintained.

Tegnrlunden 8, S-113 59 Stockholm. © **08/54-54-55-50.** Fax 08/54-54-55-51. www.hoteltegnerlunden.se. 102 units. 990SEK–1,850SEK ($198–$370/£99–£185) double; 1,600SEK–3,000SEK ($320–$600/£160–£300) suite. Rates include buffet breakfast. AE, DC, MC, V. Parking 250SEK ($50/£25) in nearby garage. Bus: 47, 53, or 69. **Amenities:** Breakfast room; bar; sauna; laundry service; dry cleaning; nonsmoking rooms; rooms for those w/limited mobility. *In room:* TV, hair dryer, iron (in some), Wi-Fi.

Mornington Hotel ★   With more than 200 rooms, this hotel is just too big to live up to its slogan, "a home away from home." But it does try to conjure up that image with its friendly and helpful staff, among the finest we've discovered in chilly Stockholm. There are grace notes such as a library with more than 4,000 volumes and a small rock garden. To play up its image as an English-inspired hotel, they've even added rows of flower boxes to brighten up the concrete exterior. Mornington was built in 1956 and has been renovated several times, including a big expansion in 2005 that added dozens of rooms. Most rooms still have standard decor, and many are quite small.

Nybrogatan 53, S-102 44 Stockholm. © **08/507-33-000.** Fax 08/507-33-039. www.mornington.se. 215 units. 1,103SEK–2,298SEK ($221–$460/£110–£230) double; 2,500SEK–3,300SEK ($500–$660/£250–£330) suite. Rates include buffet breakfast. AE, DC, MC, V. Parking 180SEK ($36/£18). T-bana: Östermalmstorg. Bus: 49, 54, or 62. **Amenities:** Restaurant; bar; sauna; room service; laundry service; dry cleaning; nonsmoking rooms; rooms for those w/limited mobility. *In room:* TV, hair dryer, iron, Wi-Fi.

Pärlan "Pearl" (its English name) lies in the Östermalm district, immediately east of the center. On a tranquil street, it stands near the landmark Östermalmtorg, with its market and theaters. It's also convenient to the ferries taking you through the Stockholm archipelago. Once a girls' school in the early 1950s, the building was later transformed into one of the more charming of the boutique hotels of Stockholm. Pärlan lies on the second floor of a restored building from the 1800s. It's furnished in a funky style, a fusion of legitimate antiques with other trappings perhaps bought at a flea market. Bedrooms are medium in size and well kept, furnished in a homelike, comfortable way. Breakfast is served on a balcony overlooking the central courtyard. Pärlan is a slightly offbeat but endearing choice and has a lot of fans, so reserve in advance.

Skepparegatan 27, S-114 52 Stockholm. ✆ 08/663-50-70. Fax 08/667-71-45. www.parlanhotell.com. 9 units. 1,150SEK–1,395SEK ($230–$279/£115–£140) double. Rates include breakfast. AE, MC, V. T-bana: Storeplan. **Amenities:** Breakfast room. *In room:* TV, Wi-Fi.

Rica City Hotel Stockholm An efficient chain hotel, the Rica City lacks a lot of soul, but boasts a fine address—the location is perhaps the most central in Stockholm. "If the hotel doesn't warm your heart, the flower market is next door," one of the staff members told us. The hotel is also sandwiched between two of Stockholm's biggest department stores (PUB and Åhléns City). Inside, the hotel has small but comfortable guest rooms, each in a modern Scandinavian design and decked out with mirrors, hardwood trim, carpeting, and tiles. Although the hotel doesn't serve alcohol, it maintains a restaurant that's open Monday to Friday 6:30am to 3pm, and Saturday and Sunday 7:30am to 3pm. In the Wintergarden, you can enjoy breakfast under the open sky—but only in summer when the weather's fair.

Slöjdgatan 7 (at Hötorget), S-111 81 Stockholm. ✆ 08/723-72-00. Fax 08/723-72-09. www.rica-hotels. com. 292 units. 1,195SEK–1,995SEK ($239–$399/£120–£200) double; 1,995SEK–2,195SEK ($399–$439/£200–£220) suite. Rates include breakfast. AE, DC, MC, V. Parking 225SEK ($45/£23). T-bana: Hötorget. **Amenities:** Restaurant; lounge; sauna; nonsmoking rooms; rooms for those w/limited mobility. *In room:* TV, minibar, hair dryer, Wi-Fi.

ON GAMLA STAN (OLD TOWN)
Expensive

First Hotel Reisen ★★ In the 18th century, this hotel facing the water was the most famous coffeehouse in the Old Town, lying just a few alleys from the Royal Palace. Sea captains, sailors, and tradesmen frequented the place. In 1819, the Merchant Society took it over and turned it into nautical-style lodgings. Today it's a comfortable and stylish hotel, decked out with dark wood, brick walls, and beautiful fabrics, although it doesn't quite match the charm and atmosphere generated by its two competitors nearby, the Lady Hamilton and Victory (see below). The three-building structure attractively combines the old and the new; rooms are furnished with a mix of modern and traditional designs. Beds are frequently renewed, and the bathrooms are excellent, with deep tubs, massaging showerheads, scales, marble floors, heated towel racks, and phones. Some suites have Jacuzzis, and top-floor accommodations open onto small balconies.

Skeppsbron 12, S-111 30 Stockholm. ✆ 08/22-32-60. Fax 08/20-15-59. www.firsthotels.com/reisen. 144 units. 1,350SEK–2,550SEK ($270–$510/£135–£255) double; 3,050SEK–5,000SEK ($610–$1,000/£305–£500) suite. Rates include breakfast. AE, DC, MC, V. Parking 425SEK ($85/£43). Bus: 43, 46, 55, 59, or 76. **Amenities:** Restaurant; bar; indoor pool; sauna; room service; laundry service; dry cleaning; nonsmoking rooms. *In room:* TV, minibar, hair dryer, iron, trouser press, Jacuzzi (in some), Wi-Fi.

Lady Hamilton Hotel ★★ (Finds) Is it a hotel or a museum? Named after Lord Nelson's beloved mistress, this inn combines both Swedish and English history in a building dating from 1470. It is one of the most atmospheric choices in the Old Town. In 1975, Majlis and Gunnar Bengtsson transformed it into Old Town's most romantic stopover. During restoration, they found a well from 1300 where former residents used to fetch water; guests can now use it for a cool dip. This hotel lies on a quiet street on Gamla Stan, surrounded by souvenir shops and restaurants. Dozens of antiques are scattered among the well-furnished guest rooms, and most rooms have beamed ceilings. The beds (queen or double) are of high quality. Top-floor rooms have skylights and memorable views over the Old Town. You'll get a sense of the origins of this hotel when you use the luxurious sauna, which encompasses the stone-rimmed well that formerly supplied the building's water. The ornate staircase wraps around a large model of a clipper ship suspended from the ceiling.

Storkyrkobrinken 5, S-111 28 Stockholm. (*C*) **08/506-401-00.** Fax 08/506-40-110. www.ladyhamilton hotel.se. 34 units (some with shower only). 2,050SEK–3,050SEK ($410–$610/£205–£305) double. AE, DC, MC, V. Parking: 395SEK ($79/£40). T-bana: Gamla Stan. Bus: 48. **Amenities:** Bistro; bar; sauna; room service; babysitting; laundry service; dry cleaning; nonsmoking rooms. *In room:* TV, minibar, hair dryer, Wi-Fi.

Victory Hotel ★★★ We didn't think we'd find a better hotel than Lady Hamilton until we spent our first night here. It's our favorite place in Old Town. Named after the naval hero Lord Nelson's flagship, it is an exclusive boutique hotel, and also the flagship of the Bengtsson family's private hotel chain in Old Town. Small but stylish, the Victory offers warm, inviting rooms, each named after a prominent sea captain. They sport a pleasing combination of exposed wood, antiques, and 19th-century memorabilia. The hotel rests on the foundations of a 1382 fortified tower. In the 1700s, the building's owners buried a massive silver treasure under the basement floor—you can see it in the Stockholm City Museum. There's a shiny brass elevator, but from the stairs you'll see one of Sweden's largest collections of 18th-century nautical needlepoint, much of it created by sailors during their long voyages. The inn is filled with all other sorts of nautical antiques, and, in the lobby, you can read one of Lord Nelson's heart-rending letters to Lady Hamilton, dating from 1801.

Lilla Nygatan 5, S-111 28 Stockholm. (*C*) **08/506-400-00.** Fax 08/506-400-10. www.victory-hotel.se. 45 units (some with shower only). 2,150SEK–3,658SEK ($430–$732/£215–£366) double; 6,600SEK–7,500SEK ($1,320–$1,500/£660–£750) suite. AE, DC, MC, V. Valet parking 395SEK ($79/£40). T-bana: Gamla Stan. Bus: 48. **Amenities:** Restaurant; bar; plunge pool; sauna; 24-hr. room service; babysitting; laundry service; dry cleaning; nonsmoking rooms; rooms for those w/limited mobility. *In room:* TV, minibar, hair dryer, safe, Wi-Fi.

Moderate

Lord Nelson Hotel Set astride the most congested street of Gamla Stan, "the narrowest hotel in Sweden" is the less expensive and slightly more claustrophobic clone of the somewhat more plush and better accessorized Lady Hamilton and Victory Hotels, two also-recommended nearby hotels which are members of the same chain. You'll get the same intensity of nautical charm, the same plethora of varnished mahogany, and the same polished brass and copper here, though. You'll also discover a higher-than-usual percentage of cabin-size single rooms, as the hotel caters to business travelers. "Cabins" are genuinely tiny—the kind a merchant marine might feel completely at home in—but each is charmingly macho, with expensively crafted mahogany trim and/or paneling and a sense of shipshape efficiency. Don't even think of checking in here if you travel with steamer trunks and a ton of paraphernalia—you simply won't fit into your room. But if you do opt for this place, know in advance that you'll be in the heart of the Old City, close to everything, and you can while away some very happy time on the rooftop terrace (they call it "the poop deck"), high above the grimy rooftops of Old Stockholm.

Västerlånggatan 22, S-111 29 Stockholm. © **08/506-401-20.** Fax 08/506-401-30. www.lordnelsonhotel. se. 29 units. 1,490SEK–1,935SEK ($298–$387/£149–£194) double; from 890SEK ($178/£89) cabin room. AE, DC, MC, V. Valet parking 390SEK ($78/£39). Bus: 48. **Amenities:** Basement-level sauna; laundry service; dry cleaning; free Internet access from library computer. *In room:* TV, hair dryer.

Mälardrottningen ★ (**Finds**)　　During its heyday, this was the most famous motor yacht in the world, the subject of gossip columns everywhere, thanks to the complicated friendships that developed among the passengers and, in some cases, the crew. Built in 1924 by millionaire C. K. G. Billings (and later acquired by Barbara Hutton), it was the largest motor yacht in the world (72m/236 ft.). The below-deck space originally contained only seven suites. The yacht was converted into a hotel in the early 1980s and permanently moored beside a satellite island of Stockholm's Old Town. The cabins are now cramped and somewhat claustrophobic, but being Hollywood buffs, we love to stay here and pay our respects to the stars of the Golden Age who sailed aboard the vessel. Most units have bunk-style twin beds, and all have neatly kept bathrooms. Considering the hotel's conversation-piece status and its location close to everything in the Old Town, it might be worth an overnight stay, just for the adventure.

Riddarholmen, S-11128 Stockholm. © **08/545-187-80.** Fax 08/24-36-76. www.malardrottningen.se. 60 units. Mon–Thurs 1,300SEK–2,350SEK ($260–$470/£130–£235) double; Fri–Sun 1,080SEK–2,330SEK ($216–$466/£108–£233) double. Rates include buffet breakfast. AE, DC, MC, V. Parking 220SEK ($44/£22) per hour. T-bana: Gamla Stan. **Amenities:** Restaurant; bar; sauna; laundry service; dry cleaning; nonsmoking rooms. *In room:* TV, hair dryer, Wi-Fi.

ON LÅNGHOLMEN

Långholmen Hotel　　If you've ever fantasized about living in a women's prison cell, your dreams can come true here. Beginning in 1724, on the little island of Långholmen, this structure was a state penitentiary for women charged with "loose living." The last prisoner was released in 1972, and today it's a restored and reasonably priced hotel, which, in addition to comfortable but small rooms, also houses a museum of Sweden's prison history and a good restaurant. Instead of a prison induction area, you get the hotel's reception area and a 24-hour snack bar. Accommodations were carved from some 200 cells, creating cramped but serviceable rooms equipped with small showers and toilets. This is one of the best hotels in Stockholm for single visitors on a budget, as 89 rooms are rented only to solo travelers. Just 13 rooms are large enough to accommodate two people.

Långholmsmuren 20, S-102 72 Stockholm. © **08/720-85-00.** Fax 08/720-85-75. www.langholmen.com. 102 units. Sun–Thurs 1,740SEK ($348/£174) double; Fri–Sat 1,370SEK ($274/£137) double; extra bed 250SEK ($50/£25) per person. AE, MC, V. Rates include breakfast. T-bana: Hornstul. Bus: 4, 40, or 66. Free parking with permit. **Amenities:** Restaurant; bar; laundry service; dry cleaning; nonsmoking rooms; rooms for those w/limited mobility. *In room:* TV, hair dryer, Wi-Fi.

ON SÖDERMALM
Expensive

Hotel Rival ★★★ (**Finds**)　　This is the leading hotel, and by far the most intriguing place to stay, on the rapidly gentrifying island of Södermalm. In many ways, it's our favorite hotel in Stockholm. Originally opened in 1937, this hotel-cafe-bakery-cinema received a new lease on life in 2002, via funding by former ABBA member Benny Andersson. It was conceived in direct contrast to the Grand Hotel, a grande dame that clings to the haute bourgeoisie of imperial Sweden. The Rival might almost be defined as a sprawling series of nightclubs, bistros, and entertainment lounges, on top of which a network of bedrooms is available for whatever rock star or rock-star wannabe happens to be in residence in Stockholm. Partially wood-sheathed bedrooms are loaded with the electronic equipment you'd need to play CDs or DVDs, and because of the tie-in with ABBA, you'll find a CD of the group's favorite hits in every room. Breakfast buffets, served in a sun-flooded, second-floor room that doubles as the hotel's bistro at lunch and dinner, are appealingly lavish, with wide choices of traditional Swedish food. The more animated, close-to-the-action bedrooms open onto the Mariatorget—one of Stockholm's loveliest squares. Quieter ones front a rather uninspired courtyard.

Mariatorget 3, S-11891 Stockholm. ℰ **08/545-789-00.** Fax 08/545-789-24. www.rival.se. 99 units. 1,390SEK–3,090SEK ($278–$618/£139–£309) double; 3,690SEK–5,790SEK ($738–$1,158/£369–£579) suite. AE, DC, MC, V. T-bana: Mariatorget. **Amenities:** 2 restaurants; 3 bars; gym; room service; laundry service; dry cleaning; nonsmoking rooms; rooms for those w/limited mobility. *In room:* A/C, TV, minibar, hair dryer, iron, safe, Wi-Fi.

Moderate

Hilton Hotel Slussen ★   This Hilton's location is a turn-off: It stands atop a tunnel above a six-lane highway with rushing traffic. The good news is that its architects wisely planned for it to be built on shock-and-noise absorbing "cushions," so you won't be disturbed by the traffic as you relax in your whirlpool, sit by the fire in the lounge, or work out in the gym. Just 5 minutes from the Central Station, the hotel is first class in service, amenities, and comfort. The best units—spacious, attractively furnished and filled with luxurious touches—are the deluxe rooms or the executive units. Standard rooms are also good, with modern Swedish decor, such as ergonomic chairs or marble bathrooms, many opening onto views of the waters of Riddarfjärden. The location is at Slussen, on the island of Södermalm, easily accessible from the center of Stockholm.

Guldgränd 8, Södermalm, S-104 65 Stockholm. ℰ **08/517-35-300.** Fax 08/517-35-311. www.hilton.com. 292 units. 1,590SEK–2,290SEK ($318–$458/£159–£229) double, 3,090SEK ($618/£309) junior suite; 3,890SEK ($778/£389) suite. AE, DC, MC, V. **Amenities:** 2 restaurants; bar; piano bar; indoor pool; gym; sauna; business center; room service; laundry service; dry cleaning; nonsmoking rooms. *In room:* A/C, TV, minibar, hair dryer, safe, Wi-Fi.

Inexpensive

Acapulco Hotell Ⓚⓘⓓⓢ   In Södermalm, this is an apartment hotel rented at an affordable price in tab-happy Stockholm. It's a good choice for a group or families, as accommodations range from a studio that can comfortably accommodate only two up to an apartment housing five. Most units are spacious, although the bathrooms are small, as are the kitchenettes. Rooms on the top floor open onto balconies overlooking a square, where locals sunbathe or have picnics in summer. Guests can do their own cooking, and there's a market nearby. Hotel services such as cleaning and bed linens are provided.

Bjurholmsplan 23, S-116 94 Stockholm. ℰ **08/702-33-00.** Fax 08/702-33-01. www.acapulco-hotell.se. 37 units. 1,195SEK–1,345SEK ($239–$269/£120–£135) double; 1,345SEK–1,595SEK ($269–$319/£135–£160) triple; 1,585SEK–1,995SEK ($317–$399/£159–£200) quad; 1,795SEK–2,195SEK ($359–$439/£180–£220) quintet. AE, DC, MC, V. T-bana: Skanstull. **Amenities:** Breakfast room; kitchenette. *In room:* W-Fi.

Columbus Hotel Ⓥⓐⓛⓤⓔ   In the fast-rising district of Södermalm lies one of the best deals in Stockholm. The small and personally run Columbus is found near Katarina Church and 2 blocks from the Medborgarplatsen, the most frequented square of the district, with its bars, nightlife, and live music. Renovated bedrooms, some quite small, were installed in a house built in 1780 by the local brewer; the ground floor was his brewery. In 1812, it was turned into the headquarters of the city guards, who were called (for some reason) "sausages." The least expensive doubles are located on the third floor in a so-called annex. Sparse furnishings, some of which are antiques, and hardwood floors grace the bedrooms. There are some luxurious suites, however. Hard-boiled eggs, cold cuts, fresh milk, yogurts, and jams grace the breakfast buffet, which also contains black currant juice and cod roe.

Tjärhovsgatan 11, S116 21 Stockholm. (℃ **08/503-112-00.** Fax 08/503-112-01. www.columbus.se. 70 units. 1,295SEK–2,295SEK ($259–$459/£130–£230) double; from 2,495SEK ($499/£250) suite; annex 925SEK ($185/£93) double, 1,150SEK ($230/£115) triple. MC, V. Parking: 150SEK ($30/£15). Bus: 59 or 66. **Amenities:** Breakfast room; nonsmoking rooms; Wi-Fi in lobby. *In room:* TV.

NORTH OF THE CENTER

Hotel Arcadia Believe it or not, this five-story, angular hotel, today a first-class choice, was once a featured place to stay in our now-defunct *Scandinavia on $10 a Day* guide. During the school year it was a dormitory, but in summer, the rooms were rented to visitors. In 1995, it was renamed the Arcadia and restored as a first-class hotel. Students of yesterday wouldn't recognize the place today, although it still carries some of the aura of its 1950s-style architecture (no great compliment). It's located on a tree-lined boulevard on a hillside with a good view, a 5-minute walk from the railway station. The hotel has a restaurant, Babylon, serving Swedish and international food, and there is an outdoor terrace for sunbathing and reading. Be warned in advance that bedrooms here are not particularly plush or large, but they are well maintained, with good beds and small but adequate bathrooms.

Körsbärsvägen 1, S-114 23 Stockholm. (℃ **08/566-21-500.** Fax 08/566-21-501. www.elite.se. 91 units. Sun–Thurs 1,700SEK–2,200SEK ($340–$440/£170–£220) double; Fri–Sat 1,530SEK–2,000SEK ($306–$400/£153–£200) double. Rates include breakfast. AE, DC, MC, V. Parking 230SEK ($46/£23). T-bana: Tekniska Högskolan. **Amenities:** Restaurant; bar; lounge; laundry service; dry cleaning; nonsmoking rooms. *In room:* TV, minibar, hair dryer, Wi-Fi.

NEAR THE AIRPORT

Radisson SAS SkyCity Hotel ★ For quick getaways on a jet plane in the morning, this is your most serviceable choice at the airport. This three-story hotel lies at Arlanda Airport, 39km (24 miles) north of Stockholm. Built in 1993, it's a part of the sprawling SkyCity airport complex that includes banks, travel agencies, restaurants, cafes, souvenir shops, and the busiest of the airport's terminals (nos. 4 and 5). Bedrooms are outfitted in one of three distinct styles: Scandinavian modern, Asian, and business-class units with slightly upgraded extras. The hotel's SkyCity Bar and Restaurant is the best for food and drink within the airport complex.

SkyCity, P.O. Box 82, S-19045 Stockholm–Arlanda. (℃ **800/333-3333** or 08/50-67-40-00. Fax 08/50-67-40-01. www.radissonsas.com. 230 units. 1,095SEK–2,190SEK ($219–$438/£110–£219) double; 1,495SEK–3,100SEK ($299–$620/£150–£310) suite. Rates include breakfast. Children under 17 stay free in parent's room. AE, DC, MC, V. Parking 280SEK ($56/£28). Airport bus departs at 10-min. intervals for the city center, 89SEK ($18/£9) each way. **Amenities:** Restaurant; bar; fitness center; Jacuzzi; sauna; room service; massage; laundry service; dry cleaning; nonsmoking rooms; rooms for those w/limited mobility. *In room:* A/C, TV, minibar, coffeemaker (in some), hair dryer, trouser press (in some), safe (in some), Wi-Fi.

IN VASASTADEN

Hellsten and Rex Hotels ★ Set immediately across the same street from one another, and owned and developed by the same charming and somewhat eccentric entrepreneur (Per Hellsten, an ongoing player in Sweden's music industry), these hotels share some of the same staff members and a lot of similar artistic aspirations. The residential neighborhood they occupy is the fashionable Vasastaden, a short walk northwest of the close-to-everything Stureplan. The more intriguingly furnished and more expensive of the two is the (four-star) Hellsten Hotel, which maintains a commercial recording studio in its cellar. Originally built in 1898, it was conceived as a red-brick textile mill. Amid the skylights, the sheets of glass, and the unusual Asian and African furniture and art, you'll still see traces of the original decor, including old-fashioned linen closets in unexpected cubbyholes and white-ceramic wood-burning stoves. Bedrooms (except for those on the uppermost floor, which have sloping ceilings and, in some cases, exposed wooden beams) have lavish plaster detailing on their ceilings and many hints of their original 19th-century grace. About a dozen of the rooms contain four-poster beds and original-to-the-building white-tile ceramic stoves.

The government-rated three-star Rex is the less opulent of the two hotels, without the exotic sense of decorative fantasy that's the norm at the Hellsten—it's comfortable, though. The building that contains it once functioned as the headquarters of the Swedish Lutheran Church. Rooms throughout the hotel are efficiently but not plushly decorated, in stark contrast to the more lavish digs at the Hellsten. Accommodations on the topmost floor are among the smallest in the hotel.

Hellsten Hotel: Luntmakargatan 68, SE-113 51 Stockholm. © **08/661-86-00.** Fax 08/661-86-01. www. hellsten.se. Rex Hotel: Luntmakargatan 73, SE-113 51 Stockholm. © **08/16-00-40.** Fax 08/661-86-01. www.rexhotel.se. In Hellsten Hotel, 1,490SEK–2,690SEK ($298–$538/£149–£269) double; 1,890SEK–3,090SEK ($378–$618/£189–£309) suite. In Rex Hotel, 1,190SEK–2,290SEK ($238–$458/£119–£229) double. Rates include breakfast. AE, DC, MC, V. T-bana: Rådmansgatan. **Amenities:** Restaurant; bar; indoor pool and exercise area (in the Hellsten but also open to residents of the Rex); laundry service; dry cleaning. *In room:* TV, minibar, hair dryer, Wi-Fi.

4 WHERE TO DINE

Split-pea soup, sausages, and boiled potatoes are still around, but in the past decade Stockholm has emerged as a citadel of fine dining. Its improved reputation is due partly to the legendary freshness of Swedish game and produce and partly to the success of Sweden's culinary teams at cooking contests throughout the world. Some social pundits claim that Sweden's chefs are now practically as famous as its national hockey-team players.

Food is expensive in Stockholm, but those on a budget can stick to self-service cafeterias. There are an estimated 1,500 restaurants and bars in Stockholm alone, so you'll have plenty of choices. At all restaurants other than cafeterias, a 12% to 15% service charge is added to the bill to cover tipping, and the 21% value-added tax also is included in the bill. Wine and beer can be lethal to your final check, so proceed carefully. For good value, try ordering the *dagens ratt* (daily special), also referred to as dagens lunch or dagens menu, if available.

IN NORRMALM (THE CENTER)
Very Expensive
Mathias Dahlgren ★★★ SWEDISH/INTERNATIONAL   At this exclusive restaurant, two different dining experiences complement each other: the *Matsalen* ("Dining Room") and *Matbaren* ("Food Bar"). The chef, for whom the restaurant is named, has been named chef of the year in Sweden twice since 2000. He is known for his surprising combinations of taste, his contrasting textures, and his highly evolved sauces. Meals start

with a marble-size ball of bread that was a staple of his childhood. Main courses can be humble and regional, as evoked by Dahlgren's pig's cheek paired with sausage, Jerusalem artichokes, and black trumpet mushrooms. Or they can be grand, with more elaborate dishes such as a six-course tasting menu, saddle of roe deer, or a fusion of cauliflower and lobster. Desserts can be daringly modern, such as pumpkin vanilla licorice. Guests pass through a sea-blue bar on the way to the Food Bar, which has simpler Swedish dishes, such as bricket of lamb with potatoes and truffles, salmon tartare with apples and horse-radish cream, or the classic raw and smoked reindeer with whitefish roe.

In the Grand Hotel, Södra Blasieholmshammen 8. ℂ **08/679-35-84.** Reservations required. Main courses *Matsalen* 325SEK–455SEK ($65–$91/£33–£46); tasting menu 1,300SEK ($260/£130); *Matbaren* meal 1,000SEK ($200/£100). AE, DC, MC, V. *Matsalen* Mon–Sat 7pm–midnight; *Matbaren* Mon–Fri noon–2pm, Mon–Sat 6pm–midnight. Bus: 45, 55, 62, or 76.

Operakällaren ★★★ FRENCH/SWEDISH   Opposite the Royal Palace, this is the most famous and unashamedly luxurious restaurant in Sweden. Its lavishly elegant decor, style, and service are reminiscent of a royal court banquet at the turn of the 20th century. Its other claim to fame: It turned Stockholmers into serious foodies. Its promise of a world-class French-inspired cuisine has lured us back time and time again, although we dread facing the final bill. The house specialties are impeccable. Many come here for the elaborate fixed-price menus; others prefer the classic Swedish dishes or the modern French ones. A house specialty that's worth the trip is the platter of northern delicacies, with everything from smoked eel to reindeer, along with Swedish red caviar. Salmon and game, including grouse from the northern forests, are prepared in various ways. There's a cigar room too. If you attend, dress as if you were facing Joan Rivers on the red carpet—and it's Oscar night.

Operahuset, Kungsträdgården. ℂ **08/676-58-00.** www.eng.operakallaren.se. Reservations required. Main courses 260SEK–470SEK ($52–$94/£26–£47); 8-course degustation 990SEK ($198/£99) or 1,900SEK ($380/£190) with wine. AE, DC, MC, V. Tues–Sat 6–10pm. Closed Dec 25–Jan 8. T-bana: Kungsträdgården.

Paul & Norbert ★★★ CONTINENTAL   A Swedish actress who is a frequent visitor told us (somewhat enigmatically), "The food here is better than it should be." And so it is. In a patrician residence dating from 1873, adjacent to the Hotell Diplomat, this is the finest and most innovative restaurant in Stockholm. Seating only 30 people, it has a vaguely Art Deco decor, beamed ceilings, and dark paneling. Perfectly prepared main dishes include sautéed medallion of fjord salmon, scallops, and scampi in lobster sauce; crisp breast of duck with caramelized orange sauce; and juniper-stuffed noisettes of reindeer immersed in caraway sauce with portabella. Chef Norbert Lang also prepares a tantalizing terrine of scallops in saffron sauce. The foie gras is the finest in town.

Strandvägen 9. ℂ **08/663-81-83.** www.paulochnorbert.se. Reservations required. Main courses 185SEK–320SEK ($37–$64/£19–£32); 4-course menu with wine 950SEK ($190/£95); 5-course fixed-price menu 850SEK ($170/£85); 7-course fixed-price menu 1,000SEK ($200/£100); 3-course lunch menu 350SEK ($70/£35). AE, DC, MC, V. Tues–Fri noon–2pm; Mon–Sat 6–11pm. Closed Dec 24–Jan 6. T-bana: Östermalmstorg.

Expensive

Aquavit Raw Bar & Grill ★★ SWEDISH   Contemporary elegance and a certain culinary daring combine at this outpost of the famed New York restaurant. The chefs here use prime regional produce to turn out a highly refined cuisine that never over-reaches and invariably satisfies. The kitchen's prowess is exemplified by a series of starters that range from duck rillette with lingonberries and chantarelles to a corn soup with

SETTLING INTO STOCKHOLM

5

WHERE TO DINE

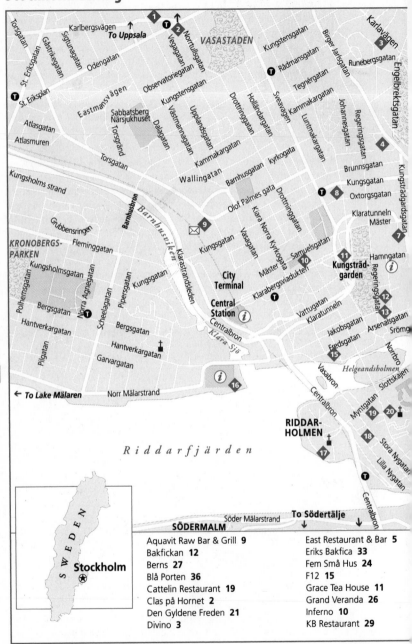

SÖDERMALM

Aquavit Raw Bar & Grill **9**
Bakfickan **12**
Berns **27**
Blå Porten **36**
Cattelin Restaurant **19**
Clas på Hornet **2**
Den Gyldene Freden **21**
Divino **3**

East Restaurant & Bar **5**
Eriks Bakfica **33**
Fem Små Hus **24**
F12 **15**
Grace Tea House **11**
Grand Veranda **26**
Inferno **10**
KB Restaurant **29**

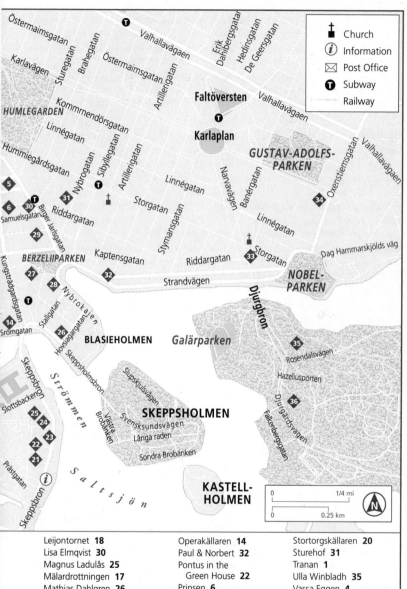

Leijontornet **18**
Lisa Elmqvist **30**
Magnus Ladulås **25**
Mälardrottningen **17**
Mathias Dahlgren **26**
Melanders Skeppsbron **23**
Naglo **13**
NK Saluhall **7**

Operakällaren **14**
Paul & Norbert **32**
Pontus in the
  Green House **22**
Prinsen **6**
Restaurangen **8**
Spring **34**
Stadshuskällaren **16**

Stortorgskällaren **20**
Sturehof **31**
Tranan **1**
Ulla Winbladh **35**
Vassa Eggen **4**
Wedholms Fisk **28**

chorizo and watercress. The raw bar is also the best in town, and includes those divine Swedish belon oysters. Tasty main courses include halibut poached in almond milk or, from the grill, dry-age Swedish rib-eye with onion rings or even a mixed seafood grill with aioli. If you want to be a bit more lavish, order the platter of "seven tastes" in seafood. For dessert, try the "Arctic Circle," a combination of fresh blueberries and goat-cheese ice cream.

In the Clarion Hotel Sign, Östra Järnvägsgatam 35. ℂ **08/676-98-50.** www.aquavitgrillrawbar.com. Reservations recommended. Main courses 195SEK–325SEK ($39–$65/£20–£33). AE, DC, MC, V. Mon–Fri 11:30am–2pm, 5–11pm; Sat noon–11pm; Sun noon–4pm, 5–11pm. T-bana: Any train to the Central Station.

Berns ★ SWEDISH/INTERNATIONAL/ASIAN   This classic restaurant might have opened in 1860 as a "pleasure palace," but it's definitely keeping up with the times—even looking forward to Asia for new inspiration. Each day a different Swedish specialty is featured, including fried filet of suckling pig with fresh asparagus, calves' liver with garlic and bacon, or grilled *tournedos,* those classic dishes that thrilled Sweden back when Eisenhower was running for reelection and Elvis appeared for the first time on TV. More innovative main dishes include cuttlefish with black pasta and tomato sauce, and filet of ostrich with mushroom cannelloni and Marsala sauce. Then there are those more exotic dishes that have been appearing on the menu—for instance, salt-grilled char with white radish and cucumber salad with wasabi dressing or Japanese broth with teriyaki-fried salmon. While eating, look up: Three monumental chandeliers light the main hall. Or check out the Red Room (*Röda Rummet),* which August Strindberg frequented and described in his novel of the same name. It's still there—plush furniture and all—and is used by guests at Berns' Hotel.

Näckströmsgatan 8. ℂ **08/566-322-22.** www.berns.se. Reservations recommended. Breakfast buffet 175SEK ($35/£18); lunch main courses 95SEK–220SEK ($19–$44/£9.50–£22); dinner main courses 195SEK–375SEK ($39–$75/£20–£38). AE, DC, MC, V. Daily 7am–11pm. T-bana: Östermalmstorg.

Divino ★★ ITALIAN   When we can't face another platter of boiled halibut, we head here for an Italian fix. It's a long way from sunny Italy to this far-northern capital city, but the aptly named Divino manages to travel the distance with its Mediterranean flavors intact. Many local food critics hail Divino as Stockholm's finest Italian restaurant, and we have to agree. The chefs work overtime here to come up with unusual variations of the classics, including sweetbreads flavored with lemon and fresh thyme, or a tantalizing foie gras with almond foam and figs. A starter of scallops is perfectly cooked and flavored with fresh tomatoes and basil. Monkfish and lobster are served on one platter and flavored with vanilla bean along with fresh fennel. Among the meat and poultry courses, we highly endorse the guinea fowl with morels, duck liver, and green asparagus, or else the veal entrecôte with prosciutto, sage, and a flavoring of Marsala. The restaurant's elegant decor, from white-clothed formal table settings to antiques scattered about, and mammoth wine cellar, filled with some of Italy's best vintages, seals the deal.

Karlavägen 28. ℂ **08/611-02-69.** www.divino.se. Reservations required. Main courses 305SEK–330SEK ($61–$66/£31–£33). AE, MC, V. Mon–Sat 6–11pm. Closed Mon in July. T-bana: Östra Station or Rädmansgatan.

East Restaurant & Bar ★ ASIAN   An Asian-inspired menu and a very hip bar scene draw a sophisticated young clientele to what is hailed as the premier Far Eastern restaurant of Sweden. Recipes from different food cultures of Asia are combined with a blend of Japanese and Scandinavian design. The chefs sail eastward with the skill of a practiced and imaginative navigator. Dishes are packed with robust flavors, as evoked by the selection of sushi for appetizers, followed by duck tamarind or fresh tuna in a cognac and teriyaki sauce for a main dish. Ever had salmon passion salsa? You can here. One of the best dishes is a lemon-flavored chicken with chili.

Stureplan 13. (08-611-49-59. Reservations recommended. Main courses 195SEK–296SEK ($39–$59/. £20–£30). AE, MC, V. Mon–Fri 11:30am–1pm; Sat–Sun 5pm–1am. T-bana: Östermalmstorg.

F12 ★★★ SWEDISH/INTERNATIONAL Set within the high-ceilinged interior of the Royal Academy of Arts, this is one of Stockholm's premier restaurants. The decor is ultrasophisticated and hip, even nightclubish, with its apple-green and lime-colored walls; long, shimmering curtains; and the kind of uncluttered minimalism you'd expect at a fashionable venue in Milan. Because it's near the Swedish parliament and various government ministries, it tends to attract government officials at lunch, but a classier and far trendier clientele in the evening—you'd expect to see a visiting rock star or an entertainment-industry icon there. One local food critic described the food as "confident, generous, and brilliantly handled," and we concur. The menu divides your choices into either "innovative" or "traditional" cuisine. The best traditional choices might include beef carpaccio with Parmesan; seafood bouillabaisse with saffron; codfish bacalao with white onions; or a navarin of suckling lamb with chanterelles. "Innovative" choices feature tuna tataki with mango slices and cream; caviar served with cauliflower and white chocolate (you heard right); or veal with tuna sauce, grapefruit, and licorice (you heard right again).

Fredsgatan 12. (08/24-80-52. www.f12.se. Reservations required. Lunch main courses 265SEK–295SEK ($53–$59/£27–£30); dinner main courses 305SEK–495SEK ($61–$99/£31–£50); 2-course set menu 315SEK ($63/£32); 3-course set menu 350SEK ($70/£35). AE, DC, MC, V. Mon–Fri 11:30am–2pm; Mon–Sat 5pm–1am. T-bana: Kungsträdgården.

Inferno ★ SWEDISH This bar, restaurant, and club is a favorite haunt of artists and actors, including Andreas Wilson, who's appeared in such movies as the Oscar-nominated Swedish flick *Evil.* The food is good, or else you can drop in to listen to some of the best DJs in the city . . . and to drink. The writer August Strindberg used to live in this building, which is named after one of his books. Surprisingly, many of the recipes that are used to create the dishes date from the lifetime of Strindberg, including some of his favorite foods. Of course, for modern tastes these recipes have been updated. For starters, try juniper berry–cured filet of deer with lingonberries or a warm beet salad with plums and blue cheese. Main-dish delights range from a seafood casserole flavored with saffron and tarragon butter to orange- and carnation-glazed breast of duck with red wine jus. The milk-chocolate soup with boiled pears and roasted almonds comes as a surprise and delight.

Drottninggatan 85. (08/20-16-50. Reservations required. Main courses 150SEK–200SEK ($30–$40/£15–£20). AE, DC, MC, V. Tues–Wed 7pm–midnight; Thurs 5pm–1am; Fri–Sat 4pm–1am. T-bana: Centralen.

Restaurangen ★★ INTERNATIONAL It will be a black day indeed for us if we ever have a bad meal here. Come not for the high-ceilinged decor (whose angularity might remind you of an SAS airport lounge), but for combinations of cuisine that many cosmopolitan Swedes find absolutely fascinating. Owner and chef Malker Andersson divides his menu into "fields of flavor," as defined by unexpected categories. These include, among others, lemon or coriander themes. If you want a taste of lemon, try the lemon-flavored fresh asparagus and potatoes; for coriander, coriander-infused shellfish ceviche. The chef roams the world and doesn't try to duplicate classical international dishes but to combine the traditional dishes of one country with the time-honored dishes of another country. See, for example, the amazing and very tasty Mexican tacos combined with French foie gras and Russian caviar. Because none of the portions are overly large, some diners interpret a meal here as something akin to a series of high-end tapas.

Oxtorgsgatan 14. ✆ **08/22-09-52.** www.restaurangentm.com. Reservations recommended. 3-course fixed-price menu 300SEK ($60/£30); 5-course fixed-price menu 400SEK ($80/£40); 7-course fixed-price menu 475SEK ($95/£48). AE, DC, MC, V. Mon–Fri 11:30am–2pm; Mon–Sat 5pm–midnight. T-bana: Hörtorget.

Spring ★ ASIAN/SCANDINAVIAN The trendiness of this place never plays second fiddle to the Eastern and Western fusion cuisine. The key is not only Chef Johan Lindqvist's skill in the kitchen, but a carefully chosen list of high-quality and fresh ingredients. During your lunch (no dinner), dishes such as steamed chicken dumplings appear, all in delicate hues and brimming with flavor, followed by Japanese eel with foie gras and a maki tempura. There is more to come, including an amazing poached cod in ginger bouillon with shiitake mushrooms and bok choy; grilled veal entrecôte with sea urchin butter and sweetbreads seasoned with five spices; and confit of turbot with a crab and radish terrine. The minimalist decor of blond ash wood from northern Sweden is livened up by the bold-colored furniture from Asia. Mostly upwardly mobile young people have made Spring a hit since the day it opened. "We view it as 'in' to eat here," one of the young Stockholmer patrons told us. We have to agree.

Karlavägen 110. ✆ **08/783-15-00.** Reservations required. Main courses 150SEK–195SEK ($30–$39/£15–£20). AE, MC, V. Mon–Fri 11:30am–2pm. T-bana: Östra Station or Rädmansgatna.

Vassa Eggen ★ ⬭Finds⬭ INTERNATIONAL Follow the gourmands to one of the most cutting-edge restaurants in Stockholm. This fashionable eatery lies in the center of the city, but gastronomic influences from all over the world are revealed in the light, airy dining room, accented by a beautiful glass dome. Using only the finest products, the young chefs here concoct a cuisine pleasing to both the eye and the palate. The Swedish version of *Gourmet* magazine put Vassa Eggen on the culinary map by proclaiming its oxtail tortellini with mascarpone cheese served in a consommé "a masterful balance of acidity, salt, sweetness, and spices." Other raves were to follow, including our own. The melon soup with Serrano ham will win you over, or else the fried herring with a potato purée. A duck terrine with a truffle polenta flavored with sherry shows a masterful touch, as does the main course of char in a creamy lobster juice. A perfectly prepared brill is cooked in brown butter and flavored with horseradish.

Birger Jarlsgatan 29. ✆ **08/21-61-69.** www.vassaeggen.com. Reservations required. Main dinner courses 275SEK–355SEK ($55–$71/£28–£36); lunch main courses 185SEK–265SEK ($37–$53/£19–£27); tasting menu 895SEK ($179/£90). AE, DC, MC, V. Mon–Fri 11:30am–2pm and 6–11pm; Sat 6–11pm. Closed in July. T-bana: Östermalmstorg.

Wedholms Fisk ★ SWEDISH/FRENCH The trendy gourmet guides of Europe have passed this one by, but we still cling to it for the memories. It may no longer be cutting edge, but it still remains the leader of the pack among classic Swedish restaurants. (At least Greta Garbo thought so. Disguised as "Harriet Brown," she always came here for at least one meal during her secret visits to her hometown.) It has no curtains in the windows and no carpets, but the display of modern paintings by Swedish artists is riveting. The cuisine can be both innovative and traditional—ranging from an innovative chèvre mousse accompanied a simple tomato salad to grandmother's favorites, such as

Tips   **Bar Food**

Don't rush into a bar in Stockholm for a pick-me-up martini. "Bars" in Stockholm are self-service cafeterias, and the strongest drink that many of them offer is apple cider.

cream-stewed potatoes. Or you might begin with marinated herring with garlic and bleak (a freshwater fish) roe, or tartare of salmon with salmon roe. The chef has reason to be proud of such dishes as perch poached with clams and saffron sauce, prawns marinated in herbs and served with Dijon hollandaise, and grilled filet of sole with Beaujolais sauce. For dessert, try the homemade vanilla ice cream with cloudberries.

Nybrokajen 17. ✆ **08/611-78-74.** www.wedholmsfisk.se. Reservations required. Lunch main courses 185SEK–230SEK ($37–$46/£19–£23); dinner main courses 285SEK–545SEK ($57–$109/£29–£55); 5-course tasting menu 795SEK ($159/£80). AE, DC, MC, V. Mon 11:30am–2pm and 6–11pm; Tues–Fri 11:30am–11pm; Sat 5–11pm. Closed for lunch in July. T-bana: Östermalmstorg.

Moderate

Bakfickan ★★ (Finds) SWEDISH   "The Hip Pocket" (its English name) is, at least for now, a secret address that mainly local foodies know about and want to keep to themselves. It actually shares the same kitchen with its glamorous neighbor, Operakällaren (see "Very Expensive," above, in this section), which means that you get the same food but at only a fraction of the price. When they're in season, we like to come here for Swedish specialties from the far north, such as reindeer and elk. For a starter, dig into the French oysters with a vinaigrette sauce and black bread. That can be followed with a plate of assorted North Sea herring combined with herring from the Baltic. It's a good choice, though you might look longingly at the grilled roast rib of beef with béarnaise sauce being served at the next table. For dessert, try the moist and delectable French chocolate cake with freshly whipped cream for dessert.

Jakobs Torg 12. ✆ **08/676-58-00.** www.operakallaren.se. Reservations not accepted. Main courses 120SEK–271SEK ($24–$54/£12–£27). AE, DC, MC, V. Mon–Fri 11:30am–11pm; Sat noon–10pm. T-bana: Kungsträdgården.

Clas på Hornet ★ SWEDISH/CONTINENTAL   Swedes come here to celebrate their nautical heritage in cuisine, and for some of the most authentic seafood flavors in town. If you want to imitate the locals, you might begin your meal with an "archipelago platter," a selection of fish caught in the islands near Stockholm, and finish with a medley of Swedish cheese and homemade bread. Another choice we find delectable, although it may be an acquired taste, is the blini stuffed with bleak roe, trout roe, and onions. The menu offers options other than seafood, too. Take the cream of wild mushroom soup served with strips of reindeer—your local diner back home isn't likely to have that. In autumn, diners can be seen ordering roast venison with a timbale of chanterelles. This place is part of the previously recommended hotel of the same name. Decorative touches evocative of the late 1700s adorn the five cream-colored dining rooms. Homage to the place has even appeared in the poetic verse of one of Sweden's most valued poets, Carl Michael Bellman.

Surbrunnsgatan 20. ✆ **08/16-51-30.** www.claspahornet.se. Reservations recommended. Main courses 265SEK–295SEK ($53–$59/£27–£30). AE, DC, MC, V. Mon–Fri noon–midnight; Sat 5pm–midnight. Bus: 46.

Eriks Bakfica ★ (**Value**) SWEDISH   Today you can get food from around the world in Stockholm, ranging from Mexican to Thai. Yet Swedes still cherish the tradition of *husmanskost* (wholesome home cooking), and, since 1979, this has been the cherished address where they find it. We always check out the array of herring appetizers that are changed daily, but what really attracts us to this place is the tantalizing "archipelago stew," a ragout of fresh fish (it varies daily) prepared with tomatoes and served with garlic mayonnaise. "It's my version of the Riviera's bouillabaisse," the chef told us. We don't know where the chef gets his marinated salmon, but we wish our deli around the corner stocked it. If you drop in for lunch, you might ask for Erik's cheeseburger with a special "secret sauce." You have to ask for it, because it isn't on the menu—savvy locals know it's one of the town's best burgers.

Fredrikshovsgatan 4. (**℃**) **08/660-15-99.** Reservations recommended. Main courses 150SEK–300SEK ($30–$60/£15–£30). AE, DC, MC, V. Mon–Fri 11:30am–3pm; Sat 5–11pm. Bus: 47.

Grand Veranda ★★ (**Kids**) SWEDISH   We'll go out on a limb here and proclaim that this restaurant serves the best smorgasbord in Sweden today. Of course, we haven't tasted all the smorgasbords in Sweden, but it's fun to make bold statements. On the ground floor of Stockholm's most prestigious hotel, and fronted with enormous sheets of glass, this restaurant opens onto a wide-angled view of the harbor and the Royal Palace. The Veranda is famous for its daily buffets, which are artfully (exquisitely, even) laid out in a satellite room off the main dining room. Scads of local business clients, assisted by a top-notch and smartly uniformed service staff, come here for a nostalgic reminder of a gentrified and very upscale Swedish tradition. If you happen to be at a table with a Swedish purist, or a Swede who remembers his or her manners, you're likely to get a quick lesson in smorgasbord etiquette, the cardinal rules of which are as follows: Don't mix fish and meat courses on the same plate, don't mix hot and cold food on the same plate, and keep your visit(s) to the dessert table separate from your trips to the tables containing the other food items. If the buffet doesn't appeal to you, there's a selection of a la carte dishes as well, including filet of reindeer marinated in red wine, pasta with lamb, or braised wild duck and deep-fried root vegetables served with an apple-cider sauce. This is your chance to sample the offerings of the most famous hotel in Sweden, to enjoy wonderful food, and to have one of the best views in town—all for a reasonable price.

In the Grand Hotel, Södra Blasieholmshamnen 8. (**℃**) **08/679-35-86.** Reservations required. Lunch main courses 145SEK–295SEK ($29–$59/£15–£30); dinner main courses 155SEK–395SEK ($31–$79/£16–£40); Swedish buffet 425SEK ($85/£43). AE, DC, MC, V. Daily noon–3pm and 6–11pm. T-bana: Kungsträdgården. Bus: 46, 55, 62, or 76.

KB Restaurant SWEDISH/CONTINENTAL   This is a traditional artists' rendezvous in the center of town, and we've been patronizing it for years. It's not exciting in any way, but it provides what a patron calls "comfort food." He's got a point. The dishes are always beautifully prepared, and we could almost make a meal out of their freshly baked sourdough bread with Swedish butter. We like to begin with salmon trout roe and Russian caviar. The kitchen turns out an enticing roasted lamb, which, at least on one occasion, was stuffed with zucchini in a thyme-flavored bouillon. In summer, our favorite desserts are the sorbets made with fresh fruits and berries picked in the countryside. One of our most memorable desserts here—and hopefully it'll be on the menu for you—is a lime soufflé with orange-blossom honey. After dinner, head to the informal bar for some often-animated conversation.

Lisa Elmqvist ★ (Kids) SEAFOOD   It may not boast refined cuisine, but this is an authentic taste of Sweden done exceedingly well. It's our favorite spot for eating amid the food stalls of Stockholm's produce market (Östermalms Saluhall). Resembling a bistro under the tent at a country fair, the likable cafe and oyster bar bears the name of one of Sweden's leading culinary matriarchs. Because of its good, affordable food, and its take-charge, no-nonsense format, it's an appropriate choice for families. Owned by one of the city's largest fish distributors, its menu varies with the catch. Some patrons come here for shrimp with bread and butter for 112SEK to 165SEK ($22–$34/£11–£17). A smoked salmon tartar is served with red onion and sour cream, or else you can order it marinated with a sweet mustard sauce. Fresh boiled lobster also appears on the menu, but at lethal prices. In such a fishy atmosphere, you don't expect tempting desserts, but get them anyway, including a tantalizing butterscotch tart and an even better chocolate tart made with white and dark truffles and served with fresh raspberries.

Östermalms Saluhall, Nybrogatan 31. ℂ **08/553-404-10.** www.lisaelmqvist.se. Reservations recommended. Main courses 135SEK–210SEK ($27–$42/£14–£21). AE, DC, MC, V. Mon–Thurs 9:30am–6pm; Fri 9:30am–6:30pm; Sat 9:30am–4pm (9:30am–2pm July–Aug). T-bana: Östermalmstorg.

Naglo SWEDISH   We've seen chefs come and go here, yet the food remains reliable and tasty regardless of who's in charge. The location is one of the most convenient in Stockholm, right on a landmark square at the opera and overlooking the Royal Palace. Some restaurants in such a position might be mere tourist traps, but this one stays honest, offering a rustic, old-fashioned charm to satisfy different tastes and pocketbooks. Local patrons begin their meal with a plate of herring washed down with a glass of aquavit, or else the smoked salmon with Swedish red caviar. Perfectly executed main dishes include one of our favorites, filet of pikeperch with basil, fresh asparagus, and a lobster sauce. This is also a place that knows how to make potato hash, most often accompanying a filet of beef.

Gustav Adolfs Torg 20. ℂ **08/10-27-57.** www.naglo.com. Reservations recommended. Main courses 200SEK–300SEK ($40–$60/£20–£30); fixed-price lunch 275SEK ($55/£28). AE, DC, MC, V. Mon–Fri 11:30am–2pm, 5pm–midnight; Sat 5pm–midnight. T-bana: Kungsträdgården.

Prinsen ★ SWEDISH   Since 1897, this restaurant, a 2-minute walk from Stureplan, has been a favorite haunt of artists. Because some of them were struggling and unable to pay their bills, the walls of the restaurant are hung with many of their artworks, presented in lieu of payment. Some will tell you that "The Prince" (its English name) is riding on its rich bohemian past, but artists still come here for the satisfying *husmanskost*. Seating is on two levels, and in summer tables are placed outside. The cuisine remains fresh and flavorful, a mostly Swedish repertoire with some French inspiration. The sautéed salmon tastes like it was just hauled in from the fjords, and the staff continues to serve old-fashioned favorites such as veal patties with homemade lingonberry preserves. Resisting trends, the cooks serve such grandmotherly favorites as a herring platter or *biff rydberg* (beef with fried potatoes and an egg). Lately, more contemporary dishes have been creeping onto the menu—nontraditionalist fare like licorice soup or snails in chocolate sauce. If you come later in the evening, you'll see that Prinsen morphs into a sort of local drinking club.

Mäster Samuelsgatan 4. ℂ **08/611-13-31.** www.restaurangprinsen.com. Reservations recommended. Main courses 169SEK–355SEK ($34–$71/£17–£36). AE, DC, MC, V. Mon–Fri 11:30am–11:30pm; Sat 1–11:30pm; Sun 5–10:30pm. T-bana: Östermalmstorg.

Sturehof ★ SWEDISH   This is the most classic French-style brasserie in all of Stockholm, and it's been going strong since the day it opened back in 1897, thanks to a reinvention for the millennium. It remains the best spot in central Stockholm for dining at almost any time of the day or night. In summer you can sit out on the terrace and watch Stockholmers pass by. Or else you can chill out in the upper lounge, with the sweet young things. The dining room is more formal and elegant with uniformed waiters and stiffly pressed white linen tablecloths. Seafood and shellfish have been a century-long tradition here, and so it continues to this day. Expect a daily changing menu of *husmanskost*. Herring is king here, be it tomato herring, curry herring, or the locally famous *sotare* (small grilled Baltic herring). The smoked Baltic herring appetizer couldn't be better if we'd smoked it ourselves. This is also one of the few places around still serving boiled salt veal tongue, a local delicacy. After dinner, if the mood suits, you can drop in to check out **O-baren,** a backroom den with a bar and a dance floor playing rock music along with hip-hop and soul.

Stureplan 2. ℂ **08/440-57-30.** www.sturehof.com. Main courses 135SEK–545SEK ($27–$109/£14–£55). AE, DC, MC, V. Mon–Fri 11am–2am; Sat noon–2am; Sun 1pm–2am. T-bana: Östermalmstorg.

Tranan Ⓥalue SWEDISH   Now that the section of Stockholm known as Vasastaden is growing chic, this working-class pub has gone more upmarket, attracting young professionals of all sexual persuasions from the neighborhood. Always a real local favorite, the 1915 tavern serves very good food and draws a friendly crowd attracted by affordable prices and the kitchen's deft handling of fresh ingredients. The menu offers an array of traditional Swedish dishes that often have French overtones, such as filet of beef served with fried potatoes, egg yolk, and horseradish. Other menu items are conservative and flavorful, in many cases virtually unchanged since the day the restaurant was founded. Such examples include Swedish pork and lard sausage (actually tastier than it sounds) served with mashed potatoes and pickled beets, herring platters, toast Skagen piled high with shrimp, and *biff rydberg* (cubes of sautéed filet steak served with braised onions, sautéed potatoes, egg yolk, cream, and horseradish). One Swede told us he comes here at least twice a week to order the Swedish meatballs and mashed potatoes. Later you can go downstairs to enjoy an authentic local bar, where DJs spin the latest hits on Friday and Saturday nights. Patrons must be 23 or older to enter the bar.

Karlbergvagen 14. ℂ **08/527-281-00.** www.tranan.se. Reservations recommended. Main courses 95SEK–280SEK ($19–$56/£10–£28). AE, DC, MC, V. Mon–Fri 11:30am–11:45pm, Sat–Sun 5–11:45pm; cellar bar until 1am. T-bana: Odenplan.

Inexpensive
Grace Tea House ★ Ⓕinds CHINESE   By anyone's standards, this is a cultural oddity, representing the marriage of its owner and founder, Grace Guo, who met her Swedish husband in her hometown south of Shanghai. She wisely used her subsequent move to Stockholm as a forum for the promotion of China's most esoteric and desirable teas. Within a meticulously crafted environment of polished paneling and Chinese brush paintings, you'll find a shop selling the most sophisticated array of teas we've ever seen, including tea made from the rare grey leaves of a species that grows only on one side of one mountain in central China. We also recommend dropping in here for a delicious, authentically Chinese, and very health-conscious lunch. Forget chow mein—this is the

Family-Friendly Restaurants

Grand Veranda (p. 100)   Many foreign families like to patronize this landmark because of the lavishness of its buffets. You should find something to please everyone.

Lisa Elmqvist (p. 101)   Because this restaurant is found in the produce market, Östermalms Saluhall, having lunch here is a colorful adventure. One favorite dish to try is a portion of shrimp with bread and butter. Families can dine under a tent, which evokes a county-fair setting.

Solliden   Near the top of the Skansen compound, a Williamsburg-type park dating from 1891, Solliden (✆ **08/566-370-00**) is a cluster of restaurants set in a sprawling building. This all-purpose dining emporium has an array of eating facilities, which makes it attractive to families. Solliden offers a lunch smorgasbord. It's open only from June to August daily noon to 4pm.

kind of food you won't see much of outside China. The set-price menu begins with a soup made from dried forest mushrooms imported from western China, dim sum (dumplings) with fish-based dipping sauce, and spring rolls. If you're interested, your meal can include a presentation from Grace or one of her assistants on tea—how to brew it, how to serve it, and how to recognize the degree of its rarity.

Beridarebanan 1 (next to Drottninggatan 32). ✆ **08/56-84-88-98.** www.exclusivetea.se. Set-price 3-course "healthy lunch" 80SEK ($16/£8); pots of tea 70SEK–150SEK ($14–$30/£7–£15) per person. AE, DC, MC, V. Mon–Sat 11am–7pm. T-bana: Central Station or Sergels Torg.

ON GAMLA STAN (OLD TOWN)
Very Expensive

Pontus in the Green House ★★★ FRENCH/SWEDISH   Budding Aristotle Onassis types take young Jackie wannabes here to impress with the most expensive ingredients in Sweden—we're talking Iranian caviar of the type enjoyed by the deposed Shah himself, as well as foie gras and truffles imported from Umbria. Set within a building whose foundations date back to the 16th century, on the western edge of Gamla Stan, this is a well-orchestrated and elegant restaurant. Just don't confuse it with a nearby clone, **Pontus by the Sea** (✆ **08/20-20-95**), where the dining experience is roughly equivalent but less popular than this, the original and still the more sought-after of the two venues. Your dining experience might begin with a drink or aperitif in the ground-floor Greenhouse Bar, one side of which contains tables which are less grand than those of the main restaurant and a "bar menu" that's a lot less elaborate than the one that's featured upstairs. In the formal restaurant, you'll find a plush-looking late Victorian decor characterized by elaborately crafted banquettes, a monumental and highly ornate bar, touches of scarlet, and a somewhat unresponsive staff. Chef Pontus Frithiof was inspired by two of the most newsworthy chefs of England, Marco Pierre White and Gordon Ramsay. Their influence is seen in dishes that include barbecued pikeperch with smoked herbs, crayfish terrine, and clams with aioli and fennel; a spectacular version of lamb with two sauces; or crayfish with a potato-based paella, saffron, mussels, and a shellfish sausage.

Österlånggatan 17. ℭ **08/23-85-00.** Reservations required. Main courses in the street-level bar 75SEK–145SEK ($15–$29/£7.50–£15). Main courses in the upstairs restaurant 120SEK–795SEK ($24–$159/£12–£80). AE, DC, MC, V. Mon–Fri 11:30am–1am; Sat 1pm–1am. T-bana: Gamla Stan.

Expensive

Den Gyldene Freden ★ SWEDISH "Golden Peace" is said to be Stockholm's oldest tavern. The restaurant opened in 1722 in a structure built the year before. The Swedish Academy owns the building, and members frequent the place on Thursday nights. You may never have heard of them, but towering cultural figures in Sweden, including the singer-poet Carl Michael Bellman and the singer-composer Evert Taube, have dined here over the years. The cozy dining rooms are named for Swedish historical figures who were patrons. Today it's popular with artists, lawyers, and writers. You'll get good traditional Swedish cooking, especially fresh Baltic fish and local game, along with more modern dishes like sautéed duck breast with pickled pumpkin (a first for us), baked char with wasabi flavoring, and beef carpaccio on goat-cheese toast with a citrus salsa. Want something different for dessert? How about warm rose-hip soup with vanilla ice cream? Of course, if you order that, you'd be denying yourself the "symphony" of lingonberries or the longtime favorite: Stockholm's best dark chocolate cake, served with fresh raspberries and coffee ice cream.

Österlånggatan 51. ℭ **08/24-97-60.** www.gyldenefreden.se. Reservations recommended. Lunch main courses 155SEK–255SEK ($31–$51/£16–£26); dinner main courses 145SEK–325SEK ($29–$65/£15–£33). AE, DC, MC, V. Mon–Fri 11:30am–2:30pm and 5–11pm; Sat 1–11pm. T-bana: Gamla Stan.

Fem Små Hus ★ SWEDISH/FRENCH This historic restaurant, with cellars that date from the 17th century and a history of serving fine food and ale to visitors since 1698, is furnished like a private castle, complete with European antiques and oil paintings. Its name, which translates as "Five Small Houses," derives from the way an entrepreneur combined the cellars of five once-separate houses into a coherent, well-accessorized series of nine candlelit dining rooms. The result somehow manages to be both rustic and baronial at the same time. This atmospheric restaurant draws a *belle clientele* glad to savor the master chef's creations and his flair for marrying market-fresh ingredients. The best ingredients from Sweden's forests and shores are incorporated into the dishes. Beautifully prepared dishes include platters of assorted herring; filets of fried reindeer with cranberries and port-wine sauce; oven-baked salmon with white-wine sauce, summer vegetables, and new potatoes; and filets of veal with morel sauce and a "touch of Gorgonzola." The cuisine and staff are worthy of the restaurant's hallowed reputation, among the best we've encountered in Stockholm.

Nygränd 10. ℭ **08/10-87-75.** www.femsmahus.se. Reservations required. Main courses 195SEK–450SEK ($39–$90/£20–£45); set menus 450SEK–575SEK ($90–$115/£45–£58). AE, DC, MC, V. Sun–Tues 5–11pm; Wed–Sat 5pm–midnight. T-bana: Gamla Stan.

Leijontornet ★★ SWEDISH/INTERNATIONAL Each time we cross the threshold of this deluxe restaurant, it's a pleasure. This is one of the Old Town's most stylish and fashionable restaurants, noted for its fine cuisine and the quality of its service. From the small, street-level bar where you can order a before-dinner drink, patrons descend into the intimately lit cellar (the restaurant was built around a medieval defense tower). To reach this restaurant, you need to negotiate a labyrinth of brick passageways through the Victory Hotel. Dishes often arrive at your table looking like works of art, and some of the country's finest produce appears on the menus. We recommend that you start with langoustines on pearl barley with a warm shellfish jelly and juniper-smoked parsnips; the

terrine of Swedish duck liver in apple jelly with hazelnuts in plum marmalade; or the
Seville orange salad, which surprisingly comes with crisps of a pig's ear. All the main
dishes are models of elegance and flavor, especially the seaweed-fried cod with a pea and
oyster purée, spider crab, and a smoked shrimp foam, which probably took hours to
prepare. For dessert, opt for the dewberry pudding with molasses and a cream cheese
mousse, delectably set off with a saffron croustade with buttermilk foam.

In the Victory Hotel, Lilla Nygatan 5. (C) **08/506-400-80.** www.leijontornet.se. Reservations required.
Lunch main courses 135SEK–250SEK ($27–$50/£14–£25); fixed-price dinner 795SEK ($159/£80). AE, DC,
MC, V. Mon–Fri 11:30am–2pm; Mon–Sat 6–10pm. Closed July and bank holidays. T-bana: Gamla Stan.

Moderate

Mälardrottningen ★ (Finds) SEAFOOD/INTERNATIONAL The novelty of dining aboard the former yacht of Barbara Hutton—she was once called the richest woman
on the planet—has a certain appeal. This upscale floating restaurant is set on the deck of
a boat built by industrialist C. K. G. Billings in 1924; it's now a hotel (see "Where to
Stay," earlier in this chapter). Though a lot of the allure here is its novelty, the food is well
prepared, with some of the flair associated with the ship's heyday. Menu items change
with the seasons but might include imaginative offerings such as salmon-filet spring roll
with pepper-garlic vinaigrette, pear-and-goat-cheese salad with thyme-flavored honey,
and skewered scampi served with Parmesan cheese and chutney made from pesto and
bananas. One of the least expensive main courses—appropriate for foggy days beside the
harbor—is a heaping portion of marinated mussels in white wine and butter sauce,
served with french fries. More formal dishes include a parfait of chicken livers with an
apricot and oregano brioche; cream of chanterelle soup with a pumpkin- and sage-fla-
vored gnocchi; prosciutto-wrapped tiger prawns; grilled Dublin Bay prawns with a fennel-flavored butter sauce; and fried filets of pikeperch with crisp-fried paella, red peppers,
and lobster sauce.

Riddarholmen. (C) **08/545-187-80.** Reservations recommended. Main courses 115SEK–175SEK ($23–
$35/£12–£18). AE, DC, MC, V. Mon–Sat 6pm–midnight. T-bana: Gamla Stan.

Melanders Skeppsbron SWEDISH Set directly on the waterfront a very short
walk from the southern edge of Gamla Stan, this is a cozy, classy, well-managed brasserie
with a minimalist but well-designed interior and a wide-open terrace that's extremely
alluring on a warm summer's day. There's even more to recommend it: The setting is
well-scrubbed, immaculate even, and the open kitchens provide plenty to look at during
the course of your meal. Traffic flows by on at least two sides of the restaurant, giving
diners the impression of occupying a calm oasis in the middle of the busy city. The restaurant prides itself on a wider collection of Swedish aquavits (at least 30) than virtually
any other establishment. The cuisine reminds many Swedes of the food their parents
served them as children, but with newfangled (and delicious) permutations. You might
start with a platter of herring, either pickled or fried or both, smoked shrimp with aioli,
bleak roe, or smoked salmon. Locals favor Swedish meatballs with lingonberries, pickled
cucumber, and mashed potatoes. One of the cooks told us that his mother served that
same dish every day of the week except Sunday. We prefer the whole fried lemon sole
with capers, tomatoes, blackened butter, and new potatoes. Dessert might be panna cotta
(crème brûlée with cloudberries) or perhaps a selection of Scandinavian cheeses.

Skeppsbrokajen. (C) **08/22-57-55.** www.melanders.se/Skeppsbron.htm. Reservations not needed. Main
courses 125SEK–155SEK ($25–$31/£13–£16). AE, DC, MC, V. Mon–Fri 11am–10pm; Sat noon–10pm.
T-bana: Gamla Stan.

Tips **Cheap Dining in a Food Boutique**

You'll find some of the widest and best selections of cost-conscious food within Stockholm's most lavish delicatessen: **NK Saluhall** ("Food Emporium") in the cellar of the NK (Nordiska Kompaniet) Department Store, Hamngatan 18–20 (℅ **08/762-80-00**).

It serves up to 10 kinds of wine by the glass, priced at 65SEK to 95SEK ($13–$19/£6.50–£9.50). At the cheese bar, select the ingredients for a platter of cheese, accompanied by bream, jam, marmalade, and pickles, which to us represents one of the high points of the civilized world. A few years ago, the organizers of this cheese bar won third prize in a pan-European contest for the best selection of cheese in Europe. Platters with one kind of cheese cost 65SEK ($13/£6.50); platters with three cheeses, 125SEK ($25/£13); platters with five kinds of cheese, 165SEK ($33/£17).

Main courses here cost from 115SEK to 250SEK ($23–$50/£12–£25). Fish is grilled, smoked, or pickled. The best examples include grilled tuna filets on a salade niçoise, smoked halibut with aioli sauce, or lobster bisque with mussels and a garlic-based rouille sauce.

Both NK and its food court are open Monday to Friday 10am to 7pm, Saturday 10am to 6pm, and Sunday noon to 5pm (T-bana: Kungsträdgården).

Stortorgskällaren SWEDISH   You won't get culinary fireworks here, but you will get a solid, reliable menu, a cheerful atmosphere, and lots of robust flavor. In the winter, this restaurant occupies medieval wine cellars whose vaulted ceilings date from the 15th century and whose old walls and chandeliers complement the plush carpeting and subtle lighting. In summer, seating is on the outdoor terrace, beside a charming square opposite the baroque facade of the Swedish Academy. In bad weather, you can dine in the street-level dining room. The menu changes often: You might begin with pâté of wild game with blackberry chutney and pickled carrots, or cured salmon and white bleak roe served with crème fraîche and onions. There's also grilled filet of pikeperch served with lime sauce and deep-fried potatoes, and chanterelle mushrooms on toast, served with strips of smoked reindeer. Another specialty is a casserole of Baltic fish seasoned with saffron.

Stortorget 7. ℅ **08/10-55-33.** Reservations required. Main courses 185SEK–285SEK ($37–$57/£19–£29); fixed-price menu 295SEK–465SEK ($59–$93/£30–£47). AE, DC, MC, V. Daily 11am–11pm. T-bana: Gamla Stan.

Inexpensive

Cattelin Restaurant ★ **Value** SWEDISH   Time and food fads have passed it by since its opening in 1897, but we still view this as one of the best and most reasonably priced restaurants in Stockholm. It has survived wars, disasters, and changing tastes, and still manages to pack 'em in, so it must be doing something right. For one thing, in a city where diners have been known to faint when presented with their tabs, it keeps its prices sane, and the food is still good and fresh. Don't expect genteel service—the clattering of china can sometimes be almost deafening, but few of the regular patrons seem to mind. First-rate menu choices include various preparations of beef, salmon, trout, veal, and chicken, which frequently make up the daily specials that often are preferred by

lunch patrons. The fixed-price lunch is served only Monday to Friday 11am to 2pm. On
certain Friday nights, after meal service ends, the place is reconfigured into a gay bar and
dance club, a sign of the changing times.

Storkyrkobrinken 9. ✆ **08/20-18-18.** www.cattelin.com. Reservations recommended. Main courses
159SEK–238SEK ($32–$48/£16–£24); set-lunch menu 174SEK ($35/£17). AE, DC, MC, V. Mon–Fri 11am–
11pm; Sat 11am–3pm; Sun noon–11pm. T-bana: Gamla Stan.

Magnus Ladulås SWEDISH/INTERNATIONAL This is a local favorite, and
deservedly so, because the cookery is first-rate and the ingredients are market fresh and
carefully chosen. We've been here when it was a little dull, and we've been here at its most
raucous—packed with visiting Uppsala students celebrating their graduation. Although
the patrons on any given night are unpredictable, the food is not. We often go for the
steak specialty, which is cooked as you like on a hot stone placed at your table; the mixed
seafood plate with lobster sauce; or the fresh salmon flown in from Lapland. The restaurant was converted from a vaulted inner room of a 12th-century weaving factory, and it
includes a bar that's worth a stop for a drink before your meal.

Österlånggatan 26. ✆ **08/21-19-57.** Reservations recommended. Main courses 159SEK–239SEK ($32–
$48/£16–£24). AE, DC, MC, V. Mon–Thurs 5–10pm; Fri–Sat 5pm–1am. Closed for lunch July 15–Aug 15.
T-bana: Gamla Stan.

ON KUNGSHOLMEN
Expensive

Kungsholmen Restaurant ★ INTERNATIONAL This is a restaurant with a
theme, and the theme involves dining as theater, where celebrities and beautiful people
pop in with regularity, and where seven different "food stations" are open to view around
the perimeter of the restaurant. In addition to a parade of stylish and shapely blonds of
both genders, all the members of rock group Depeche Mode arrived, with fanfare, on the
night of our visit, adding even more drama to the firecracker decor of black and matador
red. Food items emerge, steaming, from separate kitchens that management defines as
"bars," each devoted separately to sushi, salads (six different meal-size choices), soups
(our favorites included the bouillabaisse and the Thai chicken soup), bread (burgers,
barbecued pork-based "pig sandwiches," pita stuffed with roasted lamb and goat cheese),
bistro items (*osso buco* with risotto, seafood pasta), grilled items (shrimp with chili and
lime, Moroccan-style lamb chops, steak with Béarnaise), or ice cream (try the strawberry
milkshake with ginger).

Expect a Swedish version of a large, raucous restaurant in Paris, replete with *frissons* of
recognition associated with various entrances and exits, and a hip, attractive, and somewhat harried staff. If you're hungry and an insomniac, this restaurant is open later than
most of the other places in Stockholm. Seating, especially around happy hour, is supplemented with tables set up on a floating platform anchored immediately offshore: Known
as the Pontonen Restaurant, it's open daily from 5pm to 1am and it has its own (floating)
kitchen and bar, serving main courses priced at 65SEK to 310SEK ($13–$62/£6.50–
£31). It's a self-contained social entity all its own—where clients seem to drink a lot, have
a lot of fun, and remain more or less oblivious to the goings-on within its more stylish,
and more trend-conscious, sibling.

Norr Mälarstrand, Kajplats 464. ✆ **08/505-244-50.** Reservations recommended. Main courses 160SEK–
310SEK ($32–$62/£16–£31). AE, DC, MC, V. Sun–Wed 5pm–1am; Thurs–Sat 5pm–2am. T-bana: Rådhuset.
Bus: 3 or 62.

Stadshuskällaren ★ SWEDISH/INTERNATIONAL Near the harbor in the basement of City Hall, this two-in-one restaurant—after passing through a beautiful carved wooden doorway, you'll enter an interior that is divided into the Skänken, which serves lunch only, and the Stora Matsalen—offers an opportunity to sample food enjoyed by Nobel Prize winners. (The chefs here prepare the annual Nobel Prize banquet.) Out comes a mountain grouse breast baked in black trumpet mushrooms with caramelized apples, poached onions, and broad beans, served with a Norman Calvados sauce and potato cake. You can opt, of course, for other main-course delights, including a confit of salmon filet with roasted Jerusalem artichokes, marinated beets, and a lemon emulsion; or else grilled turbot with smoked almonds. And to top it all off, how many times do you see a Roquefort cheesecake on the menu? This surprise dessert came with a fig and cherry compote.

Stadshuset. ✆ **08/506-322-00.** Reservations required. Main courses 255SEK–325SEK ($51–$65/£26–£33); 3-course fixed-price dinner 545SEK–645SEK ($109–$129/£55–£65); Swedish tasting menu 975SEK ($195/£98); fixed-price lunch (Aug–May only) 175SEK–325SEK ($35–$65/£18–£33). AE, DC, MC, V. Skänken: Mon–Fri 11:30am–2pm. Stora Matsalen: Mon–Fri 11:30am–11pm; Sat 2–11pm. No lunch July–Aug. T-bana: Rådhuset. Bus: 3 or 62.

ON DJURGÅRDEN

Expensive

Ulla Winbladh ★ SWEDISH More than most of Stockholm's restaurants, this is a highly reliable and sought-after staple, thanks to its origins in 1897 as part of Stockholm's World Fair, and thanks to a name that conjures up images of passionate love for most Swedes. (Was she a hooker or was she a madonna? Only Sweden's most famous 18th-c. poet, Bellman, knew for sure, as Ulla was his mistress, to whom he dedicated some of his most evocative poetry.) Because it was acquired by its present management in 1994, this restaurant has impressed even the most jaded of Stockholm's foodies. It occupies a sprawling, stone-built, white-sided pavilion set in an isolated position on the Djurgården. Inside, a series of dining rooms is outfitted like a 19th-century manor house, with unusual paintings and a sense of graceful prosperity. There's also an outdoor terrace lined with flowering plants. The menu focuses on time-tested, somewhat conservative Swedish cuisine, always impeccably prepared. (Patrons who agree with this assessment include members of the Swedish royal family and a bevy of well-known TV, theater, and art-world personalities.) Menu items include at least three different preparations of the inevitable herring; marinated salmon with a terrine of watercress, bleak roe, and asparagus; fish casserole with potatoes and shellfish sauce; Swedish meatballs in cream sauce with lingonberries and pickled cucumbers; and a beautiful version of poached halibut with hard-boiled egg, shrimp, and melted butter.

Rosendalsvägen 8. ✆ **08/534-89-710.** www.ullawinbladh.se. Reservations required. Main courses 110SEK–365SEK ($22–$73/£11–£37). AE, DC, MC, V. Mon 11:30am–10pm; Tues–Fri 11:30am–11pm; Sat noon–11pm; Sun noon–10pm. Bus: 47.

Moderate

Villa Kallhagen ★ SWEDISH This place is best in summer, when you'll feel like you're dining in the Swedish countryside, although it lies only a 5-minute ride from the heart of the city. Do as we do, and precede dinner with a stroll along the nearby park's canal, Djurgårdkanalen. At least you'll work up an appetite, and you'll want one for the

Fast-food eateries and fresh food markets abound in Stockholm, especially in the center of the city, around Hötorget. Here you can visit **Hötorgs Hallen,** a fresh food market where you can buy the makings of an elegant picnic. Recently arrived immigrants sell many Turkish food products here, including stuffed pita bread.

For the most elegant fare of all, however, go to **Östermalms Hallen,** at the corner of Humlegårdsgatan and Nybrogatan, east of the city center. Stall after stall sells picnic fare, including fresh shrimp and precooked items that will be wrapped carefully for you.

With your picnic fixings in hand, head for **Skansen** or the wooded peninsula of **Djurgården.** See p. 120 for info.

crowd-pleasing fare, which is both market fresh and well prepared. The chef's culinary technique never fails him, and his inventiveness and precision with local ingredients always impress us. For an appetizer, try the creamy crayfish and a fresh chanterelle salad with bleak roe served on fennel bread. The most traditional dish on the menu, and an old favorite of ours, is fried Baltic herring with Dijon mustard sauce and drawn butter. You'll also enjoy the oven-baked chicken with port-wine sauce or the lemon-fried veal (moist and tender) with mashed potatoes and a Parmesan terrine (a delightful accompaniment).

Djurgårdsbrunnsvägen 10. (C) **08/665-03-00.** Reservations required. Lunch main courses 138SEK–249SEK ($28–$50/£14–£25); dinner main courses 165SEK–290SEK ($33–$58/£17–£29); tasting menu 290SEK ($58/£29); Sun brunch 275SEK ($55/£28). AE, DC, MC, V. Mon–Fri 11:30am–2pm and 5–11pm; Sat 11:30am–4pm, 5–11pm; Sun brunch 11:30am–5pm. Closed July. Bus: 69 from Central Station.

Inexpensive

Blå Porten★ (Finds) SWEDISH   Positioned close to the entrances of both Skansen and the Vasa Museum, on the sparsely populated island of Djurgården, the "Blue Door" is a well-kept secret that's at its most quaint and country-ish in summertime, when the flowers in its courtyard bloom and its fountains complement the idyllic setting. Technically, this is the food and beverage outlet of an arts exhibition space known as the Liljevalchs Konsthalle, and yes, you'll recognize its understated entrance by its blue-painted door. Don't expect the staff to run around servicing your order; everything is very low-key and unfussy, and the only staff member you're likely to see is the cashier who rings up your order after you select it from an assortment of old-fashioned plank-topped tables. Each of them is piled high with pastries (the lemon tart is divine, as are the heart-shaped cookies layered with vanilla custard), as well as such rib-sticking dishes as oven-baked, herb-crusted herring with potatoes; quiche with feta cheese and spinach; beet salad with goat cheese and honey-lime dressing; and an array of open-faced sandwiches.

In the Liljevalchs Konsthalle, Djurgårdensvägen 64. (C) **08/663-87-59.** www.blaporten.com. Reservations not accepted. Sandwiches 60SEK–80SEK ($12–$16/£6–£8); pastries 35SEK–50SEK ($7–$10/£3.50–£5); platters 80SEK–165SEK ($16–$33/£8–£17); fixed-price menus 475SEK–525SEK ($95–$105/£48–£53). AE, MC, V. Mon–Fri 11am–10pm; Sat–Sun 11am–7pm. Bus: 47.

SETTLING INTO STOCKHOLM

5

WHERE TO DINE

Inexpensive

Tennstopet SWEDISH   One rainy, windswept night we stumbled onto this place by accident, and we've been showing up ever since to share a genuine English pint with the locals. (The name means "pewter tankard.") You can toss some darts and hear stevedores complain about Swedish taxes cutting into their beer allowance. The food is the type that accompanies heavy drinking—good, hearty, filling, and as reasonable in price as anything is in "unreasonably" priced Stockholm. If you visit for lunch, you might face a big platter of pork chops, fresh vegetables, bread, butter, and coffee—what the typical Swedish workman eats. At night, dishes are a bit more elaborate, including a fairly decent plank steak, salmon schnitzel, or else a ragout of fish and shellfish. This old pub and restaurant lies in the northern part of the city near Hotel Oden.

Dalagatan 50. ✆ **08/32-25-18.** www.tennstopet.se. Reservations recommended. Main courses 112SEK–296SEK ($22–$59/£11–£30). AE, DC, MC, V. Mon–Fri 4pm–1am; Sat–Sun 1pm–1am. T-bana: Odenplan. Bus: 54.

ON SÖDERMALM

Expensive

Bistro Rival ★★ (Finds) INTERNATIONAL   This hip bistro is the focal point for a series of lesser bars, lounges, and entertainment venues that all flourish, in a congenially cooperative way, within the same (also recommended) hotel. The guiding light here (or at least the *éminence grise*) is ABBA member Benny Andersson, whose reflected glory permeates the spirit of much of this place. As the bistro is on the hotel's second floor, and because there's a long and narrow balcony on which tables are situated during clement weather, diners can also look down on one of the most popular and animated series of boccie ball games in Sweden. The menu presents a toss-up between one of the freshest and most tantalizing Caesar salads made in Stockholm and toast Skagen, which isn't really toast at all, but a piled-high mound of shrimp flavored with dill. Other tempting options: The grilled chicken is so tasty and perfectly flavored that it doesn't need to be gussied up with sauce, and goes well with Swedish herring and endless rounds of aquavit. More adventurous palates may opt for the carpaccio of beef or seasonal filet of reindeer with fresh chanterelles and blackberries.

In the Hotel Rival, Mariatorget 3. ✆ **08/545-789-00** Reservations recommended. Main courses 178SEK–260SEK ($36–$52/£18–£26). AE, DC, MC, V. Daily 4–11:30pm (restaurant), with bar remaining open until till midnight–2am, depending on business. T-bana: Mariatorget.

Eriks Gondolen ★★ (Finds) INTERNATIONAL/FRENCH   We like everything about this restaurant except what it costs to dine here. Partially suspended beneath a pedestrian footbridge that connects the island of Gamla Stan with the island of Söder-malm, it requires access through a (free) private elevator from the Stadsgården. Once hauled up the equivalent of 11 stories, you'll enter to see a restaurant with a decor that hasn't changed much since it was built as an engineering oddity in 1935—but you'll also get great panoramic views. The bar is cozy, and the dining room is well managed and very popular; men usually wear jackets and ties. Menu items reflect a mixture of French and Swedish cuisine. The starter salad, composed of fresh shellfish—including succulent shrimp and lobster, but also smoked salmon with lime yogurt and sesame flavoring, is one of the best we've enjoyed in Old Town. You might also delight in the terrine of duck with artichokes, mushrooms, apple compote, and hazelnuts; and the velvety cream-of-langoustine soup with pan-fried crayfish. For a main course, try the filet of veal, zestily flavored with lemon and freshly ground black pepper, with a honey-glazed salsify on the side. A mushroom bruschetta with beets, a truffle aioli, and a lentil vinaigrette shows off the chef's imagination, as does his classic Dover sole, dressed up with smoked salmon and scallops and sprinkled with fresh lime sauce.

Stadtsgården 6. ✆ **08/641-70-90**. Reservations required. Lunch main courses 105SEK–375SEK ($21–$75/£11–£38); dinner main courses 195SEK–425SEK ($39–$85/£20–£43); fixed-price menu 495SEK ($99/£50). AE, DC, MC, V. Mon–Fri 11:30am–1am; Sat 4pm–1am. T-bana: Slussen.

Inexpensive

Garlic & Shots MEDITERRANEAN/INTERNATIONAL   We once said we could go for garlic in anything but ice cream, only to be proven wrong by a dessert served here. This theme restaurant follows two strong, overriding ideas: Everyone needs a shot of garlic every day, and everything tastes better if it's doctored with a dose of the Mediterranean's most potent ingredient. The no-frills setting is artfully spartan, with bare wooden tables that have hosted an unexpectedly large number of rock stars. Expect garlic in just about everything, from soup (try the garlic-ginger with clam) to such main courses as beefsteak covered with fried minced garlic; and Transylvania-style vampire steak, drenched in horseradish, tomato, and garlic sauce. And then there's the garlic ice cream, which tastes a hell of a lot better than it sounds: The garlic is mixed in with honey ice cream and sweetened with green peppercorn strawberries and chocolate-dipped garlic cloves. Now, what to drink to wash down all these flavors? Garlic ale or garlic beer, of course.

Folkungagatan 84. ✆ **08/640-84-46**. www.garlicandshots.com. Reservations recommended. Main courses 105SEK–345SEK ($21–$69/£11–£35). MC, V. Daily 5pm–1am. T-bana: Medborgarplatsen.

ON LÅNGHOLMEN
Moderate

Långholmen Restaurant ★ (Finds) INTERNATIONAL   We realize you wouldn't normally think of heading to an old prison dining room for food, but don't rule out this offbeat choice yet. This premier dining venue is housed within the Långholmen Hotel, the former state penitentiary turned hotel. From the windows of the old-fashioned dining room, you can still see the high brick walls and other decor that caused a lot of inmates a great deal of mental distress—from small doors with heavy bolts to bars on the

---

(Tips) **Cheap Eats**

While touring Djurgårdsvägen, you can enjoy lunch at **Café Blå Porten,** Djurgårdsvägen 64 (✆ **08/663-87-59**), a cafe/cafeteria that often draws patrons of the Lilijevalch art gallery next door. Soups, salads, sandwiches, and hot meals are served.

Also at Östermalmstorg is the well-known **Örtagården,** Nybrogatan 31 (✆ **08/662-17-28;** www.ortagarden.gastrogate.com), on the second floor of the Östermalms food hall. It allows you to help yourself to a small smorgasbord of both hot and cold Swedish fare costing 85SEK to 125SEK ($17–$25/£8.50–£13). It is increasingly rare to find the typical Swedish smorgasbord in Stockholm these days, and Örtagården is a holdout of the old culinary tradition.

windows. Ironically, within the establishment's restored venue, these mementos are show-cased rather than concealed—even the paintings, many in gentle pastels, reflect the workhouse drudgery that used to prevail here. Diners come today for an unusual insight into the hardships of the 19th century, and menu items that change with the seasons. Examples include a carpaccio of shellfish, smoked breast of duck with a walnut-cranberry vinaigrette, a combination of lobster and turbot stewed with vegetables in a shellfish bouillon, and *tournedos* of venison with juniper berries, smoked ham, pepper sauce, and Swedish potatoes. This is hardly prison food—in fact, only market-fresh ingredients are used, and the staff here is clearly dedicated to pleasing your palate.

Kronohäktet. © **08/720-85-50.** Reservations recommended. Lunch main courses 106SEK–188SEK ($21–$38/£11–£19); dinner main courses 215SEK–230SEK ($43–$46/£22–£23); 3-course fixed-price dinner 450SEK–520SEK ($90–$104/£45–£52). AE, DC, MC, V. Mon–Fri 11:30am–10pm; Sat noon–10pm; Sun noon–4pm. T-bana: Hornstul. Bus: 4, 40, or 66.

AT SOLNA

Ulriksdals Wärdshus ★ (Finds SWEDISH   This out-of-town establishment loaded with atmosphere serves one of the best smorgasbords in Sweden, and almost rivals the lavish spread at the Grand Hotel. On the grounds of Ulriksdals Royal Palace on Edviken Bay, you can dine in the all-glass Queen Silvia Pavilion, which opens onto gardens owned by the king and queen. The smorgasbord, featuring 86 delicacies (both shellfish and meat), is accompanied by beer or aquavit. Most people eat in five courses, beginning with herring that comes in 20 varieties. They follow with salmon and then meat dishes, including *frikadeller* (meatballs) or perhaps reindeer, then a choice of cheese, and finally dessert. Some dishes are based on old farm-style recipes, including "Lansson's Temptation," which blends anchovies, heavy-cream potatoes, and onions. Over the Christmas season, the almost-doubled buffet is lavishly decorated in a seasonal theme and costs 600SEK ($120/£60) per person.

Ulriksdals Royal Park, S-170 79 Solna. © **08/85-08-15.** www.ulriksdalswardshus.se. Reservations required. Lunch main courses 85SEK–385SEK ($17–$77/£8.50–£39); dinner main courses 225SEK–320SEK ($45–$64/£23–£32); fixed-price menus 385SEK–675SEK ($77–$135/£39–£68). AE, DC, MC, V. Jan–Apr and Sept–Nov Tues 11:30am–3pm, Wed–Fri 11:30am–11pm, Sat 2–11pm, Sun 12:30–7:30pm; May–Aug Mon–Fri 11:30am–11pm, Sat 2–11pm, Sun 12:30–7:30pm; Dec daily 11:30am–11pm. Closed July 18–Aug 2 and Dec 24–27. Take Sveavägen toward Arlanda Airport (exit E18), 5km (3 miles) north of Stockholm.

AT SOLLENTUNA

Edsbacka Krog ★★ (Finds SWEDISH/FRENCH   Chances are you'll fall for the cuisine of Chef Christer Lindstrom and want to wrap him up and haul him back to your own personal kitchen. At least that was our temptation—he's that good. A dedicated chef, he uses top local ingredients in original ways, and his market-fresh cuisine is designed to please. Don't take our word for it: Try such starters as thinly sliced scallops with an orange consommé, or else the sweet Swedish lobster with a terrine of vegetables and a lobster vinaigrette. We like the way he doesn't try to overly adorn dishes, serving you a perfect filet of sole with lemon and a potato purée, or wild duck with a sauce of juniper berries. The warm soufflé of sea buckthorn with a rye ice cream is better than anything dear old mum served us. The historic, thick-walled building from 1626 was the first licensed inn in Stockholm and still oozes upscale country atmosphere. It's 10 minutes by taxi from the town center.

Sollentunavägen 220, Sollentuna. © **08/96-33-00.** www.edsbackakrog.se. Reservations recommended. Main courses 300SEK–470SEK ($60–$94/£30–£47); fixed-price menus 870SEK–1,300SEK ($174–$260/£87–£130). AE, DC, MC, V. Mon–Fri 5:30pm–midnight; Sat 2pm–midnight. T-bana: Sollentuna.

5

SETTLING INTO STOCKHOLM

WHERE TO DINE

Tips   **The Best Panorama in Old Stockholm**

If you don't mind going farther afield, into the industrial landscapes of Söder-malm, the mostly residential once-working-class island directly to the south of Gamla Stan, the finest panorama in Stockholm is visible from the **Fåfängan Café,** Klockstapelsbacken 3 (② **08/642-99-00;** www.fafangan.se). Perched high on a cliff top, directly above the channel from which the warship *Vasa* was excavated, and with a view that sweeps out over the Old Town, this is a simple, modern, and unpretentious self-service cafe with a sprawling outdoor terrace and an interior that might remind you of a school cafeteria. Thanks to its view, you'll get a sense of the ironies and growing pains that Stockholm experienced through the centuries. In the foreground, you'll see flotillas of some of the biggest cruise ships in the world, smaller ships heading out for tours of the archipelago, the copper-sheathed rooftops of Skansen, and the vestiges of imperial Sweden as represented by Gamla Stan's compound of royal buildings.

Main courses cost from 70SEK to 180SEK ($14–$36/£7–£18), and might include Caesar and Greek salads; nacho platters; various pastas; fish soup with fresh salmon, shrimp, and aioli sauce; and open-faced sandwiches. From May to October, it's open daily from 11am to 10pm, and from November to April, it's open only on Saturday and Sunday from 11am to 8pm. To reach it, take bus no. 53.

AT FJÄDERHOLMARNA

Fjäderholmarnas Krog ★ **Finds** SWEDISH This restaurant is worthy not only because of its sublime cuisine but because it gives you an excuse to visit the beautiful Fjäderholm archipelago that lies at the doorstep of Stockholm. Just a 25-minute ferry ride from the center of the city, it's reached by traveling to the closest island in the chain, Fjäderholmarna. You have a choice of dining on the veranda (ideal in summer), at a table in the loft, or in the traditionally decorated main dining room. Backed up by a good wine list, the menu offers well-balanced dishes, and chefs show off impeccably sharp skills in the kitchen. The chef is strongest with fish dishes, including steamed halibut in a butter sauce with trout roe, or roasted filet of salmon with sweet peppers, artichokes, and walnuts. (At last we've found a chef willing to serve salmon in a less-than-traditional method.) Meat courses feature the likes of Swedish meatballs with cream sauce and lingonberries (how Swedish can you get?). Appetizers are also imaginative, including spinach salad with fried oysters and shallot vinaigrette, and the dessert specialty—dark chocolate with brittle and buckthorn sorbet—is suitably decadent.

Stora Fjäderholmarna. ② **08/718-33-55.** www.fjaderholmarnaskrog.se. Reservations required. Main courses 225SEK–645SEK ($45–$129/£23–£65); fixed-price menus 495SEK–725SEK ($99–$145/£50–£73). AE, DC, MC, V. Only Apr 26–Sept 21 and Nov 29–Dec 20 Mon–Fri 11:30am–12:30am; Sat noon–12:30am; Sun noon–11:30pm. Take ferry to Fjäderholmarna.

Discovering Stockholm

No one will argue that Stockholm isn't an expensive city. We hold onto our wallets during every visit. But it's wise to keep in mind that studies cite 10 cities that are more expensive, including Kobe, Japan; Oslo; and Geneva. So cheer up—it isn't as costly as you might have thought, and Stockholm is loaded with sights and activities, many of them bargains. If the *Vasa* Ship Museum doesn't pique your interest (highly unlikely), perhaps the changing of the guard at the Royal Palace or the Gröna Lunds Tivoli amusement park will. Even window shopping for beautifully designed Swedish crafts can be an enjoyable way to spend an afternoon. And after dark, Stockholm becomes the liveliest city in the north of Europe.

1 SEEING THE SIGHTS

THE TOP ATTRACTIONS
On Gamla Stan & the Neighboring Islands
Kungliga Slottet (Royal Palace) & Museums ★★ Sweden has been a monarchy for 1,000 years, and this is your best chance to observe official court life. We don't consider it a match for Buckingham Palace, but a visit offers a real insider's look at the daily place of work for His Majesty and his Queen, plus the other people who make up the royal court. Kungliga Slottet is one of the few official residences of a European monarch that's open to the public. Although the King and Queen prefer to live at Drottningholm, this massive 608-room showcase remains their official address.

Nothing inside the palace is as impressive to us as the **Royal Apartments** ★★★ on the second floor of the north wing. Decorated in the 1690s by French artists, they have the oldest interiors in the palace. The lavish **ballroom** ★★ here is called "The White Sea," and **Karl XI's Gallery** is the venue for official banquets. Privileged guests have called the ballroom and gallery the most spectacular in the north of Europe.

In **Rikssalen** (Hall of State), you can take in Queen Christina's **silver throne** ★, on which she sat during her ill-fated reign. This is a rare piece of silver furniture, and it was created for the queen's coronation in 1650. In the **Bernadotte Apartments,** designed by Carl Hårleman, investitures of foreign ambassadors take place. We'd like to be invited to spend a night in the **Guest Apartment** in the west wing, a sort of marriage of rococo and Gustavian classicism. Because the interiors were designed over a period of centuries, expect a hodgepodge of decorative styles, including Louis XVI and Empire. When Gustav III lived in these apartments, he sent out invitations—highly valued at the time—to Swedish noblemen to watch him wake up in the morning.

Second in importance to the state apartments is the **Skattkammaren** ★★★ or Royal Treasury, entered through Södra Valvet or the south arch. These dark vaults contain the greatest collection of royal regalia in all of Scandinavia, a virtual gold mine when compared to the collections of Oslo or Copenhagen. The competition is rough here, but we think the most impressive exhibits are Gustava Vasa's etched sword of state from 1541 and the ornate silver baptismal font of Karl XI. Especially dazzling to our eyes are the crown, scepter, and orb used at the coronation of King Erik XIV in 1561. They have come to symbolize the principal emblems of the State of Sweden. You can also see the coronation cloak of King Oscar II, the last king of Sweden actually crowned. (These days, a crown is no longer placed on a king's head but is placed symbolically on a chair beside the new monarch.)

The original palace that stood here, destroyed in a fire in 1697, was called Tre Kronor (Three Kronors). On the ground floor of the palace's northern wing, the **Tre Kronor Museum** features objects rescued from that fire. The museum traces the development of the castle from the original defensive fort to the splendid Renaissance palace of today. To enter, you pass through thick—really thick (5m/16 ft.)—walls from the 13th century. You can walk through the old cellar and look down into the creepy excavations from the past, taking in such sights as an old well from the former courtyard and arched brick ceilings.

But don't think you've seen everything; there's more, including **Slottskyrkan,** entered by the south arch. That master of the rococo, Carl Hårleman, came here in 1754, adding his adornments to the existing baroque chapel. The sculptures, statues, and ceiling paintings were the work of the foremost craftsmen in Sweden in the 18th century. Ever since the time of Magnus Ladulas in the 1200s, there has been a royal chapel on this spot.

Before palace fatigue sets in, visit **Gustav III's Antikmuseum ★**, entered on Lejonbacken. This is one of Europe's oldest museums, having opened its doors in 1794. The nucleus of this museum was purchased when the king toured Italy in the 1700s. The sculptures, some 200 in all, were placed in the gallery just exactly as they were originally exhibited. We found the masterpiece here to be *Apollo and His Nine Muses*, but you may be drawn to *The Sleeping Endymion.*

Finally, we've spent years wandering through royal armories, but we must say that **Livrustkammaren ★★** is among the most impressive we've ever viewed. Founded in 1633, it is also Sweden's oldest museum. Set in the palace vaults, this armory isn't just about weapons but displays some of the world's most magnificent **state coaches ★★** and coronation robes, even the costume worn by Gustav III at a fatal masked ball. (The king was assassinated at the 1792 ball, and the incident inspired Verdi to write his opera *The Masked Ball.*)

The greatest oddity we found here was a stuffed horse—called Streiff—which was ridden by Gustav II Adolf when he was killed in the battle of 1632. The most revolting curiosity is a glass jar that preserves the stomach contents of one of the conspirators of Gustav III's assassination. If you like mounted knights, magnificent swords, and muskets too, you have arrived at Valhalla.

Outside the palace, military units from all over Sweden take turns at the **Changing of the Royal Guard ★**. A German women's magazine, having made a "scientific survey," claimed one summer that the Swedish guards are "far handsomer" than Queen Elizabeth II's Buckingham brigade. Come to make a comparison for yourself. Royal Guards have been stationed at the palace since 1523.

In summer, you can watch the military guard parade daily. In winter, parades take place on Wednesdays and Sundays; on other days there are no parades, but you can see the changing of the guard. The parade route Monday to Saturday begins at Sergels Torg and proceeds along Hamngatan, Kungsträdgårdsgatan, Strömgatan, Gustav Adolfs Torg, Norrbro, Skeppsbron, and Slottsbacken. On Sunday, the guard departs from the Army Museum, going along Riddargatan, Artillerigatan, Strandvägen, Hamngatan, Kungsträdgårdsgatan, Strömgatan, Gustav Adolfs Torg, Norrbro, Skeppsbron, and Slottsbacken. For information on the time of the march, ask at the Tourist Center in Sweden

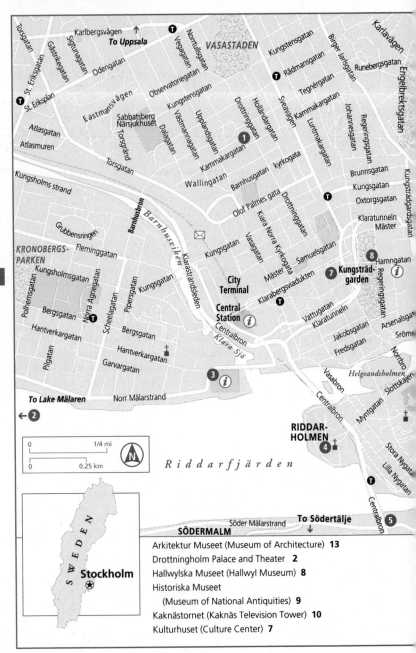

To Uppsala

VASASTADEN

KRONOBERGS-PARKEN

City Terminal

Central Station

To Lake Mälaren

To Södertälje

RIDDAR-HOLMEN

Riddarfjärden

Helgeandsholmen

SÖDERMALM

Söder Mälarstrand

Kungsträd-garden

0   1/4 mi
0   0.25 km

SWEDEN

Stockholm

Arkitektur Museet (Museum of Architecture) **13**
Drottningholm Palace and Theater **2**
Hallwylska Museet (Hallwyl Museum) **8**
Historiska Museet
  (Museum of National Antiquities) **9**
Kaknästornet (Kaknäs Television Tower) **10**
Kulturhuset (Culture Center) **7**

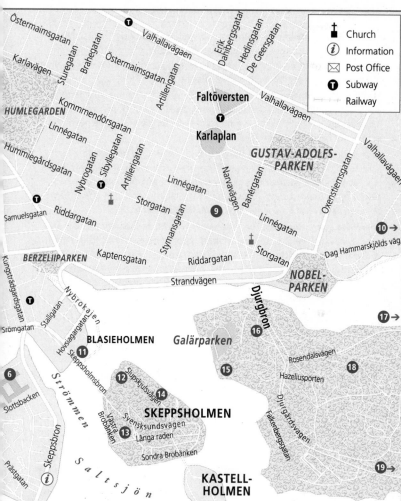

Legend:

- † Church
- ⓘ Information
- ✉ Post Office
- Ⓣ Subway
- +—+ Railway

Kungliga Slottet (Royal Palace) & Museums **6**

Moderna Museet (Museum of Modern Art) **14**

Nationalmuseum (National Museum of Art) **11**

Nordiska Museet (Nordic Museum) **16**

Operahauset (Royal Opera House) **11**

Östasiatiskamuseet
(Museum of Far Eastern Antiquities) **12**

Prince Eugens Waldemarsudde **19**

Riddarholm Skyrkam **4**

Rosendals Trädgård
(Rosendal Botanical Garden) **17**

Skansen **18**

Stadshuset (Stockholm City Hall) **3**

Stadsmuseet (Stockholm City Museum) **5**

Strindbergsmuseet (Strindberg Museum) **1**

Thielska Galleriet (Thiel Gallery) **19**

Vasamuseet (Royal Warship *Vasa*) **15**

Frommer's Favorite Stockholm Experiences

Experiencing Skansen: Be it butter churning or folk dancing, there's always something to intrigue people of all ages here. Wander at leisure through the world's oldest open-air museum (which covers about 30 hectares/74 acres of parkland; p. 120), getting a glimpse of ancient Swedish life.

Strolling through Gamla Stan at night: To walk the narrow cobblestone alleys of the Old Town at night is like going back in time. During your stroll, it'll take little imagination to envision what everyday life must have been like in this "city between the bridges."

A smorgasbord at the Grand Hotel: Unless you're lucky enough to attend a wedding or extended family reunion, you'll have to seek out the lavish but high-maintenance gastronomic display known as a smorgasbord—they happen rarely in Sweden today. One of the few establishments that offers them on a regular, ongoing basis is Stockholm's Grand Hotel (p. 77).

Searching out panoramas: The city's terrain is rocky, and sometimes involves vertigo-inducing heights. Getting a bit of distance from the Old Town helps you visualize it more clearly. The Monteliusvägen on the residential island of Södermalm rarely makes it outside the inner sanctum of the consciousness of local residents, but it should. Tracing the cliff tops of northern Södermalm, and wide enough for hill climbers but not for cars, Monteliusvägen features

House. The changing of the guard takes place at 12:15pm Monday to Saturday and at 1:15pm on Sunday in front of the Royal Palace.

To wrap up your visit, call at the **Royal Gift Shop,** with unique gifts and souvenirs for the King or Queen in your life. Much of the merchandise here is produced in limited editions, including textiles based on designs from the 16th and 17th centuries.

Kungliga Husgerådskammaren. ℂ **08/402-61-30** for Royal Apartments and Treasury, 08/402-61-67 for the Skattkammaren, 08/402-61-30 for Royal Armory, or 08/402-61-06 for Museum of Antiquities. www. royalcourt.se. Entry to Royal Apartments, Royal Armory, Museum of Antiquities, and Treasury is 90SEK ($18/£9) adults, 35SEK ($7/£3.50) seniors and students, free for children under 7. A combination ticket to all parts of palace is 130SEK ($26/£13) adults, 65SEK ($13/£6.50) students and children. Apartments and Treasury Sept–May Tues–Sun noon–5pm (closed in Jan); June–Aug daily 10am–5pm; closed during government receptions. Royal Armory daily 10am–5pm. Museum of Antiquities May 15–May 31 and Sept daily 10am–4pm; June–Aug daily 10am–5pm. T-bana: Gamla Stan. Bus: 43, 46, 59, or 76.

On Norrmalm

Moderna Museet (Museum of Modern Art) ★★ (Kids)   This museum has grown from its 1958 opening in a former drill house on the island of Skeppsholmen to its present reincarnation as one of the greatest repositories of modern art in the north of Europe. In the 1960s and 1970s, it introduced the likes of Andy Warhol and Robert Rauschenberg to Stockholmers; since 1998, the museum has been housed in these avant-garde quarters. Today it has a great showcase of modern art and is especially strong in Cubist paintings, with works by Picasso, Braque, and Léger. Standouts include Matisse's *Apollo decoupage* ★ and the celebrated *Enigma of William Tell* ★★, by Salvador Dalí. You'll also see works by Brancusi, Max Ernst, Giacometti, Arp, and sculpture by the great views that sweep out over the heart of imperial Sweden. Additional panoramas sweep out from the also-recommended Fåfängan Café (p. 113) on Södermalm.

A trip to Riddarholmen: One of our favorite area attractions is the Gamla Stan's satellite island of Riddarholmen, where time seems to have stopped sometime around 1600, and where there's a lot less crowding than on Gamla Stan, just across the channel.

Visiting the Rosendal Botanical Gardens: No other experience in Stockholm will impress upon you the deep-seated sense of responsibility that the Swedes feel for their ecology than a visit to this fervently organic, and utterly enchanting, fortress of the horticultural world. Combine it with a visit to Skansen (p. 120), preferably during the peak of midsummer, when fruits and vegetables, dormant throughout the brutal winters and benefiting from the extended daylight hours of summer, literally explode into maturity at a dizzyingly rapid pace.

Watching the summer dawn: In midsummer, at 3am, you can get out of bed, as many Swedes do, and sit on a balcony to watch the eerie blue sky—pure, crystal, exquisite—emerge from a swath of peach. Swedes don't like to miss a minute of their summers, even if they have to get up early to enjoy them.

Louise Nevelson. In all, the present collection includes 5,000 paintings and sculptures, plus around 25,000 watercolors, graphics, and 100,000 photographs, as well as a large number of videos and films.

As enthralled as we are by the permanent collection, we mainly visit to see the often-stunning temporary exhibitions. One program called "The First at Moderna" offers a new exhibition on the first of every month. Yet another well-attended event is "Moderna by Night" from 6pm to midnight on Fridays. You get food, drink, entertainment . . . and great art. Musical concerts and the best children's workshops in Stockholm are also presented here periodically.

Time your visit to have a good yet affordable lunch at the self-service restaurant offering views toward Östermalm, or for a stop at the modern espresso bar near the main entrance.

Skeppsholmen. ✆ **08/519-552-00.** www.modernamuseet.se. Free admission. Temporary exhibit fees vary. Tues 10am–8pm; Wed–Sun 10am–6pm. T-bana: Kungsträdgården. Bus: 65.

Nationalmuseum (National Museum of Art) ★★★   It's true that this museum cannot compare to the national museum collections in France, Italy, Spain, and England. But as Spencer Tracy said of Katharine Hepburn, "There's not much meat on her bones, but what there is, is choice."

Founded in 1792, the National Museum is one of the oldest museums in the world, and it's Sweden's largest and best museum of world art. The museum grew out of a small collection of art from Gustav Vasa's collection at Gripsholm Castle. Over the years the collection expanded from bequests, purchases, and even spoils of war acquired during the country's emergence as a military powerhouse in the 1600s. Many of the best paintings derived from the Royal Collection of the Swedish monarchs, which became the property of the Swedish nation in the late 19th century and early 20th century.

This treasure house of painting and sculpture lies at the tip of a peninsula, a short walk from the Royal Opera House and the Grand Hotel. In all, the museum owns 600,000 artworks (only a few of which are on display at any given moment) from the late Middle Ages up to the 20th century, with an emphasis on Swedish 18th- and 19th-century art. The collection of Dutch painting from the 17th century is rich, and the **18th-century collection of French paintings** ★★ is regarded as one of the best in the world. Carl Gustaf Tessin, during the years he was the Swedish ambassador to France in the 1740s, brought contemporary French art of the highest quality back to Stockholm. Naturally, the museum is also a good showcase for Sweden's two most famous artists, Anders Zorn and Carl Larsson.

The first floor focuses on applied arts (silverware, handicrafts, porcelain, Empire furnishings, and the like). First-time visitors, if pressed for time, may want to head directly to the second floor. Here, among the paintings from northern Europe, is Lucas Cranach's amusing *Venus and Cupid.* Also displayed is a rare collection of **Russian icons** ★, most of them—such as *St. George and the Dragon*—from the Moscow School of the mid–16th century. Note that only a few of these pieces are usually on display.

The museum also shows an exceptional number of masterpieces by such artists as Perugino *(St. Sebastian),* Ribera (his oft-rendered *Martyrdom of Bartolomé*), El Greco *(Peter and Paul),* Giovanni Bellini *(Portrait of Christ),* Lotto *(Portrait of a Man),* and Poussin *(Bacchus).* The gallery contains some outstanding Flemish works, notably Rubens's *Bacchanal at Andros* and *Worship of Venus,* and Jan Brueghel's *Jesus Preaching from the Boat.*

The most important room in the museum has one whole wall featuring the **works of Rembrandt** ★★—*Portrait of an Old Man, Portrait of an Old Woman,* and *Kitchen Maid* (one of the most famous works in Stockholm). In yet another room is Watteau's *Lesson in Love,* and another salon is noted for its select Venetian works by Guardi and Canaletto, as well as English portraits by Gainsborough and Reynolds.

Modern works on display include Manet's *Parisienne;* Degas's dancers; Rodin's nude male *(Copper Age)* and his bust of Victor Hugo; van Gogh's *Light Movements in Green;* landscapes by Cézanne, Gauguin, and Pissaro; and paintings by Renoir, notably *La Grenouillère.*

Södra Blasieholmshamnen. Ⓒ **08/519-543-00.** www.nationalmuseum.se. Free admission. Tues 11am–8pm; Wed–Sun 11am–5pm. T-bana: Kungsträdgården. Bus: 2, 62, 65, or 76.

At Djurgården

The forested and sparsely populated island of Djurgården (Deer Park) lies about 3km (1¼ miles) to the east of Gamla Stan (Old Town). Crisscrossed with bicycle paths and permeated with parklands, it's distinctly different from the densely populated urban vibes that characterize such neighborhoods as Gamla Stan, Södermalm, and Norrmalm. Its most extensive and most visible attraction is Skansen, reviewed below.

Skansen ★★★   This was the first open-air museum to open in the world, back in 1891—and it's still going strong. It's even better than when we first discovered it on visits to Stockholm as teenagers. Even if you can't escape into the Swedish countryside, head here for a look at how Swedes lived in the days of yore.

Often called "Old Sweden in a Nutshell," this open-air museum features more than 150 reconstructed dwellings scattered over some 30 hectares (74 acres) of parkland. They were originally erected in sites throughout Sweden, from the northern frontier of Lapland to the southern edges of Skåne. Most date from the 18th and 19th centuries, and each has benefited from the lavish attentions of scores of scholars, librarians, and craftspersons. The exhibits include windmills, manor houses, blacksmith shops—even a complete town quarter that was meticulously rebuilt. Visitors can explore old workshops to see where book publishers, silversmiths, and druggists plied their trades in olden days. Many handicrafts for which Swedes later became noted (glass blowing, for example) are demonstrated, along with traditional peasant crafts, such as weaving and churning. For a tour of the buildings' interiors, arrive no later than 4pm.

On-site is a small zoo with 70 different animals, most of which are Swedish fauna, including wild animals from the cold north such as reindeer, seal, lynx, brown bear, and wolverine. Most impressive is the elk, the largest mammal in Sweden; the greatest predator is the fierce brown bear, considered the best "salmon fisherman" in the north.

Although it's hardly comparable to the Tivoli Gardens in Copenhagen, Skansen is also a summer playground for Stockholmers. Folk dancing and open-air concerts, in some cases featuring international stars, are occasionally scheduled during summertime. Check at the Tourist Center for information on special events, and see "Stockholm After Dark," later in this chapter, for info on nightlife options.

Djurgården 49–51. ⓒ **08/442-80-00.** www.skansen.se. Admission 40SEK–100SEK ($8–$20/£4–£10) adults, depending on time of day, day of week, and season; 30SEK–50SEK ($6–$10/£3–£5) children 6–15; free for children under 6. Historic buildings Oct–Apr daily 10am–4pm; May daily 10am–8pm; June–Aug daily 10am–10pm; Sept daily 10am–5pm. Bus: 47 from central Stockholm. Ferry from Slussen.

Vasamuseet (Royal Warship Vasa) ★★★   This 17th-century man-of-war is the most frequently visited attraction in Scandinavia—and for good reason. Housed near the main entrance to Skansen, within a cement-sided museum that was specifically constructed for its display, the *Vasa* is the world's oldest complete and identified ship.

On its maiden voyage in 1628, in front of thousands of onlookers, the Royal Warship *Vasa* capsized and sank almost instantly to the bottom of Stockholm harbor. Its salvage in 1961 was an engineering and archaeological triumph. Onboard were more than 4,000 coins, carpenters' tools, sailors' pants (in a color known as Lübeck gray), fish bones, and other items of archaeological interest. Best of all, 97% of the ship's 700 original decorative sculptures were found. Carefully restored and impregnated with preservatives, they are now back onboard the stunning ship, whose exterior is ornamented with dozens of baroque carvings. They include grotesque replicas of human faces, lion masks, fish-shape bodies, and other carvings, some with traces of their original paint and gilt.

A full-scale model of half of the *Vasa*'s upper gun deck has been built, together with the admiral's cabin and the steering compartment. Several carved wooden figures represent the crew. By walking through the "gun deck" and the exhibit of original objects (including the appallingly primitive medical equipment, preserved clothes, and a backgammon board), you can get an idea of life aboard the ship. Captioned exhibits describe the almost unimaginable hardships of life at sea for the ordinary soldier and sailor. If you're like us, you'll be struck by the drama behind the ship's creation: Designed to terrify Sweden's enemies across the sea, the ship's fatal design flaws were directly commissioned by the king. Its sinking was a great blow to national prestige, but its successful recovery from the muddy bottom became a symbol of restored national pride.

Free tours are conducted at widely varying schedules depending on the season. During the most visited months, June to August, tours in English are conducted every half-hour from 9:30am to 5:30pm.

Galärvarvsvägen 14, Djurgården. ℂ **08/519-548-00.** www.vasamuseet.se. Admission 95SEK ($19/£9.50) adults, 50SEK ($10/£5) students, free ages 18 and under. Sept–May Thurs–Tues 10am–5pm; June–Aug Thurs–Tues 8:30am–6pm, Wed 10am–8pm. Closed Jan 1, May 1, Dec 23–25, and Dec 31. Bus: 47 or 69. Ferry from Slussen year-round, from Nybroplan in summer only.

Rosendals Trädgård (Rosendal Botanical Garden) ★★ For anyone who has ever dug a hole in the fertile earth and tried to cultivate a plant, this is among the most appealing sites in Sweden. Its origins go back to the early 18th century, when Djurgården was dotted with small farms producing fruits, vegetables, and dairy products. In 1817, it was commandeered by the Swedish crown prince (Karl Johan) as the site of what became a small-scale summer palace. **Rosendal Palace,** a pink, ornamental confection, stands in elegant isolation on a hillock above what functions today as the biggest and most varied commercial organic garden in Stockholm.

In 1861, the Swedish Horticultural Society, whose aim involves "promoting more widespread and more orderly gardening in Sweden," moved into their headquarters on this site. In 1988, the Friends of Rosendal Garden was also set up on the site, with the aim to cultivate the land organically. Today, the site contains greenhouses, a sweeping mass of meticulously weeded beds for all kinds of plants, and meeting spaces for public courses on the environment, landscape gardening, composting techniques, and the cultivation of flowers, vegetables, and fruit trees. One of the greenhouses contains a cafe for organically grown "slow food"—the antithesis, the staff will tell you, of fast food. Don't expect culinary glamour (or frankly, any real glamour at all) within the cafe. Set amid potted plants and flowering vines, the restaurant boasts a chalkboard menu and casual vibe. Main courses, priced at 95SEK to 155SEK ($19–$31/£10–£16) each, might include glasses of strictly organic "ecologically correct" wines, red beet salads, breaded and fried filets of rainbow trout served with creamy potato salad, gazpacho made from ingredients grown on-site, and pastries, many made from whole-wheat grains.

Visitors are encouraged to walk along the brick paths, gathering fruits, flowers, and vegetables directly from the beds for preparation within their homes or apartments. A caretaker, from a base within a delicate-looking glass-sided pavilion rising above the fields, charges by the kilo for whatever is gathered. A shop sells unusual canned goods, gift items, baked goods, and vegetables and fruits grown within the garden.

In the surrounding park, you'll find at least one example of every species of tree that's native to the vast landmass of Sweden. Fruits and vegetables in these northern climes have a very short time to mature, but thanks to the prolonged sunlight of Swedish summers, they seem to race through their life cycles, roaring from seedlings to mature plants in a dauntingly short time. Watching Stockholmers cherish the fertility of the site brings a sense of joy—at least to those with the heart of a gardener.

Rosendalsterrassen 12, Stockholm. ℂ **08/545-812-70.** www.rosendalstradgard.se. Free admission. Hours of access to the gardens vary wildly with the season, but the best way to see this place is in conjunction with a visit to its cafe and gift shop, which are open Mon–Fri 11am–5pm, Sat–Sun 11am–4pm. Closed during Jan. Bus: 47.

On Kungsholmen

Stadshuset (Stockholm City Hall) ★★ When you are awarded the Nobel Prize, this is where you'll go to receive your acclaim and pick up the prize. Built in the

"National Romantic Style," the Stockholm City Hall on the island of Kungsholmen is one of the finest examples of modern architecture in Europe. Designed by Ragnar Ostberg, it was completed in 1923. A lofty square tower bearing three gilt crowns, the symbol of Sweden, and the national coat of arms dominates the red-brick structure. In summer you can climb the 100m-high (328-ft.) tower for what we consider the finest **panoramic view** ★★ of Gamla Stan (Old Town) in the area. There are also two courts here: the open civic court and the interior covered court. The Blue Hall is used for banquets and other festive occasions, including the Nobel Prize banquet. About 18 million pieces of gold and colored-glass mosaics cover the walls of the **Golden Hall** ★★. The southern gallery contains murals by Prince Eugen, the painter prince. The 101 City Council members still meet in the council chamber here.

Hantverksgatan 1. ☎ **08/508-29-05.** www.stockholm.se/stadshuset. Admission 60SEK ($12/£6) adults, 30SEK ($6/£3) ages 12–17, free for children 11 and under. Tower additional 20SEK ($4/£2). Apr–Sept daily 10am–4:15pm. City Hall tours (subject to change) June–Aug daily at 10am, 11am, noon, 2pm, 3pm, and 4pm; Sept–May daily at 10am, noon, and 2pm. T-bana: Centralen or Rådhuset. Bus: 3 or 62.

Near Stockholm

Drottningholm Palace and Theater ★★★   No palace in the north of Europe is as grand and spectacular as this regal complex of stately buildings sitting on an island in Lake Mälaren. The royal family still lives here, but don't expect to discover the king walking the corridors in his underwear. The royal apartments are guarded and screened off.

The palace is dubbed the "Versailles of Sweden," and so it is. In fact, work began on this masterpiece in 1662 about the same time as Versailles. Nicodemus Tessin the Elder (1615–81), one of the most celebrated architects of the 17th century, was the master builder.

Listed as a UNESCO World Heritage Site, Drottningholm needs about 3 hours of your time to visit it. Must-stops include the palace itself, the theater, the magnificent gardens, and the Chinese Pavilion. One highlight of any tour is the **State Apartments** ★★★, with a spectacular staircase decorated by Giovanni Carove, the Italian master. The apartments dazzle with opulent furniture and art from the 17th to the 19th century. You'll be as awed as we are by the painted ceilings, the precious Chinese vases, and the ornate gold chandeliers, as well as Hedvig Eleonora's state bedroom designed by Tessin the Elder and completed in 1663.

The Golden Age of Drottningholm came under the reign of Queen Lovisa Ulrika and her son, King Gustav III, who entertained lavishly. Lovisa married Crown Prince Adolf Fredrik in 1744 and demanded more rococo adornments, even going so far as to add another floor. A great patron of the arts, she was also responsible for ordering the building of the theater (see below). Her **library** ★★ is a work of grand beauty, an excellent example of the Gustavian style by Jean Eric Rehn.

After checking out the grand interior, you should retreat to the **Kina Slott (Chinese Pavilion)** ★. Built during the European craze for the exotic architecture of Asia, the pavilion was constructed in Stockholm in 1753. Later it was floated downriver to surprise Lovisa on her 33rd birthday. The pavilion, lying in the southeast corner of the park, is like an exotic silhouette of the Grand Trianon at Versailles. It was a favorite rendezvous place for Gustav III, who loved to pass summer days here with his court.

Allow as much time as you can to stroll through **Drottningholm Gardens** ★★★, the wonderful creation of Tessin the Younger in 1681. The baroque garden is flanked by an avenue of lime trees. The **Hercules Fountain** ★★ here is a famous bronze work, created by Adriaan de Vries and brought by Swedish soldiers from Prague in 1648. Other features of the park include English-style bridges, ornamental pools, canals, and a "water garden" with nearly a dozen water jets.

Drottningholm Court Theater ★★★ is the grandest theater in all of Scandinavia. If we could grant five stars instead of the mandated three, they would go to this gem of baroque architecture designed by Carl Fredrik Adelcrantz for arts-oriented Lovisa. A previous theater on this site was destroyed by fire. The first performance was presented here back in 1766, and the theater reached its apogee under Gustav III. Even more so than Lovisa, Gustav (1742–92) was a patron of the arts, founding the Royal Music Academy and the Royal Opera, which presented performances here. The theater retains its original backdrops and props today. Even the same 18th-century ballets and operas are performed here, the productions authentic down to the original costumes. Between June and July, some two dozen performances are staged; seating only 450, the theater offers one of the most unusual entertainment experiences in Sweden. Many performances sell out far in advance to season ticket holders. The theater can be visited only as part of a guided tour, which focuses on the original sets and stage mechanisms. But theater buffs can visit the **Theatre Museum,** the setting for exhibits tracing the history of European theater since the 1700s, including displays of costumes, stage models, drawings, and paintings.

For tickets to the evening performances, which cost 165SEK to 610SEK ($33–$122/ £17–£61), call ⓒ **08/660-82-25.** For more information about the theater, call ⓒ **08/ 759-04-06** or 08/556-931-07, or visit **www.dtm.se.**

Ekerö, Drottningholm. ⓒ **08/402-62-80.** www.royalcourt.se. Palace 70SEK ($14/£7) adults, 35SEK ($7/£3.50) students and children ages 7–18; theater guided tour 70SEK ($14/£7) adults, 35SEK ($7/£3.50) children 7–18; Chinese Pavilion 60SEK ($12/£6) adults, 30SEK ($6/£3) students. All free for children under 7. Palace Oct–Apr Sat–Sun noon–3:30pm; May–Aug daily 10am–4:30pm; Sept daily noon–3:30pm. Theater guided tours in English May noon–4:30pm; June–Aug daily 11am–4:30pm; Sept daily 1–3:30pm. Chinese Pavilion Apr and Oct daily 1–3:30pm; May daily 11am–4:30pm; June–Aug daily 11am–3pm; Sept Tues–Sun noon–3pm. Lies 11km (6³/₄ miles) west of Stockholm. T-bana: Brommaplan, then bus no. 301 or 323 to Drottningholm. Ferry from the dock near City Hall.

Millesgården ★★★ The island of Lingingö, northeast of Stockholm, houses this former villa and sculpture garden of Sweden's greatest sculptor, Carl Milles (1875–1955). Had we been here for 3 days in 1917, we would have done anything to prevent his plan to destroy all his work and start over again. (Fortunately, he ultimately decided against it.)

After emigrating to Michigan in the U.S. in 1931, Milles became a professor of art, and he created nearly 75 sculptures, many of which are on display around the United States today. It is with shame that we report that some Michiganders insisted that Milles put fig leaves on his nudes. "That's like telling Michelangelo to put a fig leaf on David," Milles responded in anger.

Some of the artist's major works are on view here, including his monumental and much-reproduced sculpture *Hands of God* ★★★. Sculptures sit atop columns on terraces in this garden, set high above the harbor and the city landscape. These are copies of his most famous works; the originals are found all over Sweden and also in the United States. In his early works, you can see how much he was influenced by the French sculptor Auguste Rodin (1840–1917), and also by Art Nouveau. But his later works took on a simpler quality that was both dramatic and expressive. The villa displays a unique collection of art from both the Middle Ages and the Renaissance, plus rare artifacts excavated in the ruins of ancient Rome and Greece. The site also includes his personal collection of works by other leading sculptors.

Carl Milles Väg 32, Lidingö. ℰ **08/446-75-80.** Admission 80SEK ($16/£8) adults, 60SEK ($12/£6) seniors and students, children under 19 free. May–Sept daily 11am–5pm; Oct–Apr Tues–Sun noon–5pm. T-bana: Ropsten, then bus to Torsviks Torg or train to Norsvik. Bus: 207.

MORE TO EXPLORE

On Gamla Stan & the Neighboring Islands

Östasiatiskamuseet (Museum of Far Eastern Antiquities) ★ **Finds** Although it's a short journey to Skeppsholmen, a small island in the middle of central Stockholm, you're really making a trip to the Far East. The collection of archaeological objects, fine arts, and handicrafts from China, Japan, Korea, and India form one of the finest and most extensive museums of its kind outside Asia.

Among the outstanding displays are Chinese Neolithic painted pottery, bronze ritual vessels, archaic jades, wood carvings, ivory, lacquerwork, and enamelware. You might see Chinese glass, Buddhist sculpture, Chinese painting and calligraphy, Tang tomb pottery figurines, Sung classical stoneware (such as *celadon* and *temmoku*), Ming blue-and-white wares, and Ching porcelain made for the Chinese and European markets. The building was erected from 1699 to 1700 as stables for Charles (Karl) XII's bodyguard.

Skeppsholmen. ℰ **08/519-557-50.** www.ostasiatiska.se. Admission 60SEK ($12/£6) adults, free 19 and under. Tues 11am–8pm; Wed–Sun 11am–5pm. T-bana: Kungsträdgården. Bus: 65 to Karl XII Torg; 7-min. walk.

Riddarholm Skyrkam ★ The second-oldest church in Stockholm is located on the tiny island of Riddarholmen, next to Gamla Stan. It was founded in the 13th century as a Franciscan monastery, but today is a virtual pantheon of Swedish kings. The last king buried here was Gustav V in 1950. Before that, some of the greatest monarchs in Swedish history were interred inside, including Gustav III and Gustav II Adolf—but excluding Queen Christina. During one of our visits, two American ladies from Kentucky were demanding to know where Queen Christina was buried. We informed them they'd have to go to Rome to see her tomb.

As you walk across the ancient floor, you'll in essence be walking on the tombstones of royalty and nobility. Although the church is relatively devoid of art, it does contain a trio of royal chapels. On one occasion, we saw the King and his Queen arriving to worship in the Bernadotte Wing. Karl XIV Johan, the first king of the present Bernadotte ruling dynasty, is buried in a large marble sarcophagus here. We always make some little discovery every time we visit. On our last trip, we learned that many Swedish soldiers from the Thirty Years' War were also buried here.

Riddarholmen. ℰ **08/402-61-30.** www.royalcourt.se. Admission 30SEK ($6/£3) adults, 10SEK ($2/£1) children 7–18, under 7 free. May 10am–4pm; June–Aug daily 10am–5pm; Sept daily 10am–4pm. Closed Oct–Apr. T-bana: Gamla Stan.

On Norrmalm

Hallwylska Museet (Hallwyl Museum) ★ **Finds** The filthy-rich Countess Wilhelmina von Hallwyl was a collector of almost anything that was valuable and expensive. She also had a sentimental streak, leaving behind a cutting from the beard of her husband, Count Walther von Hallwyl, for posterity. Although we don't suggest you take a bite, she also preserved a slice of her wedding cake. The countess carefully cataloged her acquisitions and left them to the state upon her death, who placed them here, in a town house occupied by the aristocratic Hallwyl family from 1898 to 1930. Today, the turn-of-the-20th-century residence is both a fine example of the skilled craftsmanship of its day and the most eccentric of Stockholm's museums.

The countess's catalog totaled 78 volumes, so you can imagine the amount of decorative art on display. Open to the public since 1938, the collection includes classic paintings, rare tapestries, silver, armor, weapons, antique musical instruments, glassware, even umbrellas and buttons (but only the finest ones). One of the three daughters became a sculptor and studied with the great Carl Milles. On the tour, you'll learn historical tidbits; for example, this house had a modern bathroom even before the royal palace got one. Ask about summer evening concerts presented in the central courtyard.

Hamngatan 4. ⓒ **08/402-30-99.** www.hallwylskamuseet.se. Guided tours 70SEK ($14/£7) adults, 50SEK ($10/£5) for ground-floor rooms. Free ages 19 and under. Guided tours in Swedish Tues–Sun noon, 1pm, 2pm, and 3pm; extra tour Wed 6pm. In English Sun 1pm. T-bana: Kungsträdgården.

Historiska Museet (Museum of National Antiquities) ★★ A visit to this museum is like a journey to the past. We always feel like we're time-traveling here, from as far back as the Stone Age to the 16th century. The Viking era especially comes to life, through more than 4,000 objects and artifacts that reveal the lives of those rugged seafarers who terrorized the world.

We always head first for the Goldrummet or **Gold Room** ★★★, a virtual treasure chest that, amazingly, goes back to the Bronze Age. Inaugurated in 1994, in the presence of King Carl XVI Gustaf and Queen Silvia, the Gold Room features Viking silver and gold jewelry, large ornate charms, elaborate bracelet designs found nowhere else in the world, and a unique neck collar from Färjestaden. The valuable treasury is underground, along long corridors and behind solid security doors. These precious objects were dug up all over the country, and the state paid the finders of the objects the equivalent of today's market value—in kronor, not in gold.

After all this gold, the other exhibitions are a bit of a letdown. Still, you might want to check out the remaining highlights, including the Gothic Hall, with one of Scandinavia's finest collections of sculpture, church triptychs, and other ecclesiastical objects from the 12th century onward. In the Textile Chamber, fabrics from ecclesiastical and secular textiles from the Middle Ages to the modern era are on display.

Narvavägen 13–17. ⓒ **08/519-556-00.** www.historiska.se. Free admission. May 2–Sept daily 10am–5pm; Oct–May 1 Fri–Wed 11am–5pm, Thurs 11am–8pm. T-bana: Karlaplan or Östermalmstorg. Bus: 47 or 69.

Kaknästornet (Kaknäs Television Tower) (Moments) In the northern district of Djurgården stands the tallest manmade structure in Scandinavia—a 152m-high (499-ft.) radio and television tower. The 1967 tower itself may be ugly, but, once you reach the top, the view of greater Stockholm is the best there is. Two elevators run to an observation platform, where you can see everything from the cobblestone streets of Gamla Stan (Old Town) to the city's modern concrete-and-glass structures and the archipelago beyond. A moderately priced restaurant that serves classic Swedish cuisine is on the 28th floor. (The view from the restaurant is better than the food.)

Mörkakroken. ⓒ **08/667-21-05.** www.kaknastornet.se. Admission 30SEK ($6/£3) adults, 15SEK ($3/£1.50) children 7–15, free for children under 7. Jan–Mar Sun–Wed 10am–5pm, Thurs–Sat 10am–9pm; Apr and Sept daily 10am–9pm; May–Aug daily 9am–10pm; Oct–Dec Mon–Sat 10am–9pm, Sun 10am–5pm. Closed Dec 24–25. Bus: 69.

Nordiska Museet (Nordic Museum) ★★ Aren't you itching to see men's matching garters and ties or women's purple "flowerpot hats" that were worn by Stockholmers in the 1890s? If so, know that a million such objects are preserved in this showcase of Swedish cultural life, inside a massive building from 1907. Prosperous Swedes must have emptied their attics to fill this mammoth repository.

The first object you encounter when entering the Great Hall is a mammoth pink-tinted statue of Gustav Vasa, the work of Carl Milles, Sweden's foremost sculptor. The piece of oak embedded in the statue's forehead was said to have come from a massive tree planted by the king himself.

It's easy to experience museum fatigue here, so pace yourself. The halls are laid out like museums in pre–World War I Europe, before user-friendly museums were ever heard of. You know what to expect: 16th-century dining tables, period costumes, dollhouses, photographs of that mad genius August Strindberg, textiles (some from the 17th c.), and even an extensive exhibit of tools of the Swedish fish trade, including relics of the nomadic Laps or Sami in the north.

Djurgårdsvägen 6–16, Djurgården. © 08/519-546-00. www.nordiskamuseet.se. Free admission. Mon-Fri 10am–4pm; Sat-Sun 11am–5pm. Bus: 44, 47, or 69.

Prince Eugens Waldemarsudde ★★ The youngest of Oscar II's four children, Prince Eugen (1865–1947) was more interested in becoming an artist than in inheriting the throne. Turns out he was no Sunday painter; he became one of the great landscape artists of his day, referred to as the "The Painting Prince" by Swedes. Today, his former home and studio, one of the most visited museums in Sweden, serves as an art gallery and a memorial to his talents.

This lovely three-story mansion on the water was acquired by the prince in 1899, and he lived here until his death. The house and park were willed to the Swedish government upon his death and opened to the public in 1948. The rooms on the ground floor are furnished just as the prince left them. You can see the prince's paintings upstairs and in the gallery adjoining. The prince was not only a painter, but a collector, acquiring works by such great Scandinavian artists as Edvard Munch, Carl Larsson, and Anders Zorn. The prince's studio is on the top floor and is used for temporary exhibitions.

Allow time to wander through the garden to take in its centuries-old trees and panoramic views of Stockholm harbor. That's not all: The park is filled with sculptures by some of the greatest masters in Europe—Carl Milles to Auguste Rodin—and is also studded with classical Roman and Greek sculptures acquired by the art-loving prince. While at Waldemarsudde, also see the **Old Mill,** a windmill built in the 1780s.

Prins Eugens Väg 6. © 08/545-837-00. www.waldemarsudde.se. Admission 85SEK ($17/£8.50) adults, 65SEK ($13/£6.50) seniors and students, free for children under 19. Tues-Sun 11am–5pm. Bus: 47 to the end of the line.

Thielska Galleriet (Thiel Gallery) ★★ It's inevitable to draw comparisons between this world-class gallery and Prince Eugen's Waldemarsudde. Though both of the palatial art-filled mansions at Djurgården were constructed roughly at the same time by architect Ferdinand Roberg, the art collection at Thielska far surpasses that of the Painting Prince's.

Ernest Thiel was once a wealthy banker and art collector who commissioned the mansion, drawing upon architectural influences from both the Italian Renaissance and the Far East. Over the years, Thiel began to fill his palatial rooms with great art. However, in the wake of World War I, he went bankrupt and the state took over his property in 1924, eventually opening it as a museum.

Regrettably, we can't see all of Thiel's masterpieces today. In a robbery that made headlines around the world in 2002, many of the finest works were stolen. They have never been recovered. Perhaps some rich private collector is enjoying all this great art himself. Have no fear: The thieves still left behind a treasure trove—the art-loving thugs couldn't take everything. The remaining highlights include Gustav Fjaestad's furniture; a portrait of Nietzsche, whom Thiel greatly admired; and works by Manet, Rodin, Toulouse-Lautrec, Edvard Munch, and Anders Zorn (see his nude *In Dreams*).

Thiel is buried on the grounds beneath Rodin's statue *Shadow*.

Sjötullsbacken 6–8, Djurgården. ℂ **08/662-58-84.** www.thielska-galleriet.se. Admission 50SEK ($10/£5) adults, 30SEK ($6/£3) students, free for children under 16. Mon–Sat noon–4pm; Sun 1–4pm. Bus: 69.

On Södermalm

Stadsmuseet (Stockholm City Museum) (Kids)

Skip this museum if your time is fading; otherwise, give it a look for an hour or so. For architectural buffs, the building may be more intriguing than its exhibits. Constructed in the Italian baroque style, it was designed by the famous Tessin the Elder as the City Hall for southern Stockholm.

The history of Stockholm is presented in stages on different floors; the first floor depicts Stockholm when it was a great maritime power in the 17th century, although massive poverty also existed in the city at that time. The second floor is devoted to showing Stockholm's emergence as a multicultural city, including information on how its population soared to more than a million people, causing a housing shortage. Finally, on the third floor you are shown what a local factory looked like in 1897. (Get the labor board on the phone.) Relics of Sweden's first Industrial Exhibition, also from 1897, are on view as well.

Intriguing, quirky exhibits are sprinkled throughout, such as a room that re-creates the aura and sounds of a raucous pub in the 1700s. Another room contains a detailed model of Stockholm's layout as it looked in the mid–17th century. If you're curious, you can even check out two reconstructed apartments that poor Stockholmers lived in as neutral Sweden sat out World War II. Talk about cramped conditions.

Torget, a replica of a main square, is found on the ground floor, along with a playground for kids. Daily at 1pm, a 30-minute slide show in English describes Stockholm from the 16th century to the present.

Ryssgården, Slussen. ℂ **08/508-316-00.** www.stadsmuseum.stockholm.se. Admission free. Tues–Sun 11am–5pm; Thurs 11am–8pm. T-bana: Slussen. Bus: 43 or 46.

ESPECIALLY FOR KIDS

The open-air park Skansen (see earlier in this chapter), on Djurgården, offers **Lill-Skansen,** the children's own "Little Skansen." There's a petting zoo with lots of child-friendly animals, including pigs, goats, and horses. Lill-Skansen offers a break from the dizzying (and often tantrum-inducing) excitement frequently generated by a commercial amusement park. A miniature train ride through the park is about as wild as it gets. Lill-Skansen is open daily in summer from 10:30am to 4pm.

Kids can easily spend a day or several at Skansen and not get bored. Before going to Skansen, stop off at the *Vasa* **Museum** (see above), which many youngsters find an epic adventure. The evening can be capped by a visit to **Gröna Lunds Tivoli** (see "Stockholm After Dark," later in this chapter), which also is on Djurgården.

A LITERARY LANDMARK

Strindbergsmuseet (Strindberg Museum)   If you'd like to pay your respects to Sweden's Emile Zola, here is your chance. This late-19th-century apartment, which is located on the fourth floor of a 1907 apartment house popularly known as the "Blue Tower," is Stockholm's most-visited literary shrine. It's where August Strindberg (1849–1912), the dramatist and novelist, spent his last 4 years. Built in 1907, it is set on the uppermost stretches of the Drottninggatan, a shop-lined, all-pedestrian street. The avenue widens and becomes more densely trafficked with pedestrians as it continues its descent toward the sea. The apartment contains a library, a bedroom, and three rooms with a Spartan-looking assemblage of his furnishings, books, articles, and letters that offer insights into the last years of Strindberg's life. The library contains both fiction and nonfiction works, including encyclopedias in Swedish, German, English, and French. Many of the volumes are highlighted with pen and pencil markings—comments on the contents, heavily marked deletions of points he did not approve of, and underlines indicating his diligent research into matters that concerned him. Of special interest to those familiar with Strindberg's plays is that he furnished his rooms like stage sets from his plays, down to the color schemes. The dining room contains sculpture, casts of busts, and masks evoking people and events that played a role in his life.

Drottninggatan 85. ✆ **08/411-53-54.** www.strindbergsmuseet.se. Free admission. Nov–Feb Wed–Sun noon–4pm; Mar–Oct Tues noon–7pm, Wed–Sun noon–4pm. T-bana: Rådmansgatan.

ARCHITECTURAL HIGHLIGHTS

In Stockholm, architecture buffs are often captivated by such grand buildings as **Drottningholm Palace** and **Riddarholm Church.** But many of Stockholm's expanding suburban "cities" also are worth seeing for their urban planning and architecture, which is among the most advanced in the world.

One of these model developments is **Farsta,** completed in 1960 (although much altered since then). It lies 10km (6¼ miles) from the heart of Stockholm and can be reached by the Farsta train departing from the Central Station, or by taking bus no. 18 to the end of the line. With its traffic-free shopping mall, bright and airy modern apartment houses, and contemporary stores and restaurants, it makes for a pleasant afternoon tour.

Arkitektur Museet (Museum of Architecture)   This museum is only for aficionados—it's simply not of interest to the ordinary visitor. Founded in 1962 in a building designed by the Spanish architect Rafael Moneo, the museum illustrates the art of architecture combined with social planning. It displays copies of rooms, buildings, places, and cities from different eras, covering 1,000 years of Swedish architecture. The history of the buildings is presented in chronological sections. The collection consists of some two million sketches, drawings, and documents, plus a half-million photographs and about 1,000 architectural models. The library alone has some 25,000 volumes, most donated by Swedish architects. It's dedicated to the memory of the Swedish diplomat Raoul Wallenberg, known for his humanitarian efforts in Hungary in 1944 and 1945. Less well known is that Wallenberg was a trained architect; his few existing drawings, mainly from his student days in the United States, are in the museum's archives.

Skeppsholmen. ✆ **08/587-270-00.** www.arkitekturmuseet.se. Admission 50SEK ($10/£5) adults, free 18 and under, free for all Fri 4–6pm. Tues 10am–8pm; Wed–Sun 10am–6pm. Bus: 65.

START:	Gustav Adolfs Torg
FINISH:	Slussplan
TIME:	3 hours
BEST TIMES:	Any day it's not raining
WORST TIMES:	Rush hours (Mon–Fri 8–9:30am and 5:30–7pm)

(side margin) DISCOVERING STOCKHOLM

(side margin) 6

(side margin) WALKING TOUR 1: GAMLA STAN (OLD TOWN)

Begin at:

❶ Gustav Adolfs Torg

In the Royal Palace facing the square, Gustavus III, patron of the arts, was assassinated here at a masked ball in 1792.

Walk across Norrbro (North Bridge) heading toward the Royal Palace, passing on your right the:

❷ Swedish Parliament

The Parliament building at Helgeandsholmen dates from 1897, when its foundation stone was laid. It can be visited only on guided tours.

Along the bridge on your left are stairs leading to the:

❸ Medeltidsmuseet (Museum of Medieval Stockholm)

This museum on Strömparterren contains objects and settings from medieval Stockholm, including the Riddarholmship and parts of the old city wall.

TAKE A BREAK
One of Stockholm's hidden cafes, **Café Strömparterren**, Helgeandsholmen (ℰ **08/21-95-45**), is also one of the most centrally located—just next door to the Medeltidsmuseet. Many Stockholmers come here for a morning cup of coffee and a stunning view of the waterfront. In summer, tables are placed outside; the interior of the cafe is built into the walls under Norrbro.

After leaving the museum, continue along the bridge until you come to Slottskajen. Here, directly in front of the Royal Palace, make a right turn and head to:

❹ Mynttorget (Coin Square)

This square is the site of the Kanslihuset, a government office building erected in the 1930s. The neoclassical, columned facade remains from the Royal Mint of 1790.

Continue straight along Myntgatan until you reach Riddarhustorget. On your right is the:

❺ Riddarhuset

The Swedish aristocracy met in this 17th-century House of Nobles during the Parliament of the Four Estates (1665–68).

Continue straight across Riddarholmsbron bridge until you come to the little island of:

❻ Riddarholmen

Called the "Island of the Knights," Riddarholmen is closely linked to the Old Town. You'll immediately see its chief landmark, the **Riddarholmskyrkan** church with its cast-iron spire. Founded as an abbey in the 13th century, it has been the burial place of Swedish kings for 4 centuries.

Walk along the north side of the church until you reach Birger Jarls Torg. From there, take the 1-block-long Wrangelska Backen to the water. Then go left and walk along Södra Riddarholmshamnen.

Veer left by the railroad tracks, climb some steps, and go along Hebbes Trappor until you return to Riddarholmskyrkan. From here, cross over Riddarholmsbron and return to Riddarhustorget.

Cross Stora Nygatan and take the next right onto Storkyrkobrinken, passing the landmark Cattelin Restaurant on your right. Continue along this street, past the Lady Hamilton Hotel, turning right onto Trångsund, which leads to:

❼ Stortorget (Great Square)

Take a seat on one of the park benches—you've earned the rest. This plaza was the

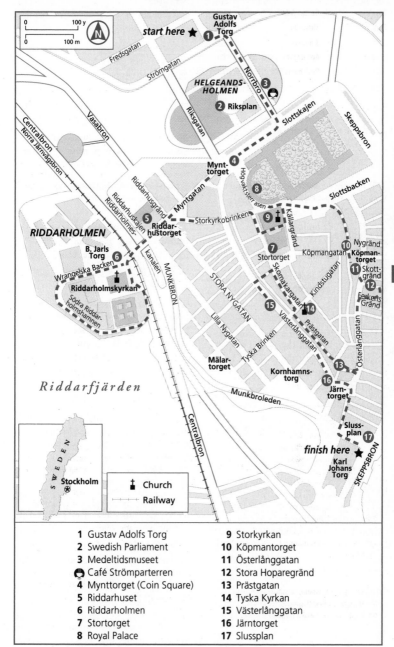

start here ★

1 Gustav Adolfs Torg
2 Swedish Parliament
3 Medeltidsmuseet
🔵 Café Strömparterren
4 Mynttorget (Coin Square)
5 Riddarhuset
6 Riddarholmen
7 Stortorget
8 Royal Palace
9 Storkyrkan
10 Köpmantorget
11 Österlånggatan
12 Stora Hoparegränd
13 Prästgatan
14 Tyska Kyrkan
15 Västerlånggatan
16 Järntorget
17 Slussplan

✝ Church
Railway

finish here ★

DISCOVERING STOCKHOLM

WALKING TOUR 1: GAMLA STAN (OLD TOWN)

6

site of the Stockholm Blood Bath of 1520 when Christian II of Denmark beheaded 80 Swedish noblemen and displayed a "pyramid" of their heads in the square. The Börsen on this square is the Swedish Stock Exchange, a building dating from 1776. This is where the Swedish Academy meets every year to choose the Nobel Prize winners in literature.

At the northeast corner of the square, take Källargränd north to view the entrance, opening onto Slottsbacken, of the:

❽ Royal Palace

The present palace dates mainly from 1760 after a previous one was destroyed by fire. The changing of the guard takes place on this square.

To your right is the site of the:

❾ Storkyrkan

This church was founded in the mid-1200s but has been rebuilt many times since. It's the site of coronations and royal weddings; kings are also christened here. The most celebrated sculpture here is *St. George and the Dragon,* a huge work dating from 1489. The royal pews have been used for 3 centuries, and the altar, mainly in ebony and silver, dates from 1652. This is still a functioning church, so it's best to visit when services are not in progress. It's open Monday through Saturday from 9am to 7pm, and Sunday from 9am to 5:30pm; admission is free.

Continue right along Slottsbacken, either visiting the palace now or saving it for later. Go right as you reach Bollshusgränd, a cobblestone street of old houses leading to:

❿ Köpmantorget

One of the most charming squares of the Old Town, Köpmantorget contains a famous copy of the *St. George and the Dragon* statue.

From the square, take Köpmanbrinken, which runs for 1 block before turning into:

⓫ Österlånggatan

Now the site of many restaurants and antiques shops, Österlånggatan was once Old Town's harbor street.

Continue along Österlånggatan, but take the first left under an arch, leading into:

⓬ Stora Hoparegränd

Some buildings along this dank street, one of the darkest and narrowest in Gamla Stan, date from the mid-1600s.

Walk down the alley toward the water, emerging at Skeppsbron bridge. Turn right and walk for 2 blocks until you reach Ferkens Gränd. Go right again up Ferkens Gränd until you return to Österlånggatan. Go left on Österlånggatan until you come to Tullgränd. Take the street on your right:

⓭ Prästgatan

This street was named after the priests who used to live here. As you climb the street, look to your left to Mårten Trotzigs Gränd, a street of steps that's the narrowest in Gamla Stan.

Continue along Prästgatan, passing a playground on your right. Turn right onto Tyska Brinken until you see on your right:

⓮ Tyska Kyrkan

Since the beginning of the 17th century, this has been the German church of Stockholm. The church has a baroque interior and is exquisitely decorated.

After you leave the church, the street in front of you will be Skomakargatan. Head up this street until you come to Stortorget once again. From Stortorget, take Kåkbrinken, at the southwest corner of the square. Follow this little street until turning left at:

⓯ Västerlånggatan

This pedestrian street is the main shopping artery of Gamla Stan and the best place to purchase Swedish gifts and souvenirs.

Follow Västerlånggatan to:

⓰ Järntorget

This street used to be known as Korntorget when it was the center of the copper and iron trade in the 16th and 17th centuries. At times in its long history, Järntorget has been the place of punishment for "wrongdoers." The most unusual statue in Stockholm stands here—a **statue of Evert Taube,** the troubadour and Swedish national poet of the early 1900s. He's carrying a newspaper under his arm, his coat draped nonchalantly, his sunglasses pushed up high on his forehead.

From the square, take Järntorgsgatan to:

⑰ Slussplan

Here you can catch a bus to return to the central city, or you can board a ferry to Djurgården and its many museums.

| WALKING TOUR 2 | ALONG THE HARBOR |

START:	Stadshuset
FINISH:	Museum of Architecture
TIME:	3 hours
BEST TIMES:	Any day it's not raining
WORST TIMES:	Rush hours (Mon–Fri 8–9:30am and 5:30–7pm)

Start at Hantverkargatan 1, on Kungsholmen, at:

❶ Stadshuset (Stockholm City Hall)

It took 12 years, 8 million bricks, and 19 million gilded mosaic tiles to erect this city hall, which can be visited on a guided tour. Go inside the courtyard on your own and admire the architecture.

When exiting the building, turn right and walk across Stadshusbron (City Hall Bridge) to Norrmalm. On your right is the Stadshuscafeet, where sightseeing boats depart on canal cruises in summer. Walk past the boats and go under an underpass (watch out for fast-riding bicyclists).

Continue along the canal until you reach Tegelbacken, a waterfront square. At the entrance to the Vasabron bridge, cross the street and continue along Fredsgatan. Veer right at the intersection to Strömgatan, hugging the canal. This will take you past Rosenbad, a little triangular park.

The building on your right, across the canal, is the:

❷ Swedish Parliament

You can visit this building on a guided tour, though we won't be stopping there on this walking tour.

Continue on Strömgatan to:

❸ Gustav Adolfs Torg

From here you have a panoramic view of the Royal Palace across the canal and of the Royal Opera straight ahead. This is one of the most famous landmark squares in Stockholm, and the most scenically located.

Strömgatan resumes at the corner of the Opera House, site of the Operakällaren, for many years the finest restaurant in Stockholm. Continue along until you reach the southern tier of the:

❹ Kungsträdgården

These royal gardens, the summer living room of Stockholm, reach from Hamngatan on the north side down to the water. Established in the 1500s as a pleasure garden for the court, they are now open to all, with cafes, open-air restaurants, and refreshment kiosks.

 TAKE A BREAK

Since the late 1800s, the **Café Victoria,** Kungsträdgården (② **08/21-86-00**), in the center of Stockholm, has attracted crowds. It's an ideal spot for a refreshing drink or snack at any time during the day or evening. It's open Monday to Friday 11:30am to 10pm, Saturday noon to 3am, and Sunday from noon to 6pm. (See "Stockholm After Dark," later in this chapter, for more information.)

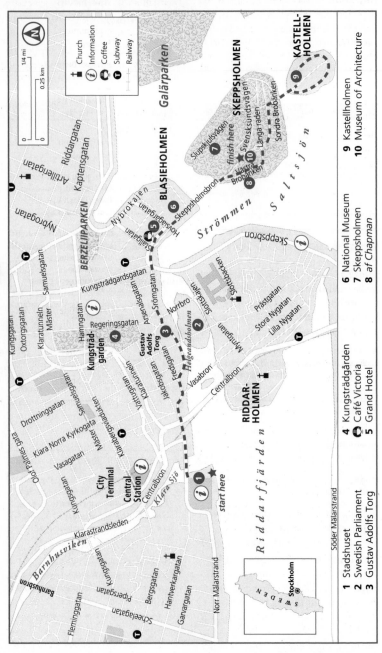

1 Stadshuset
2 Swedish Parliament
3 Gustav Adolfs Torg
4 Kungsträdgården
5 Café Victoria
5 Grand Hotel
6 National Museum
7 Skeppsholmen
8 af Chapman
9 Kastellholmen
10 Museum of Architecture

Continue along the waterfront, past Strömbron, a bridge leading to Gamla Stan, and emerge onto Södra Blasieholmshamnen. At no. 8 is the:

❺ Grand Hotel

For decades this has been the most prestigious address in Stockholm, attracting Nobel Prize winners as well as most visiting dignitaries and movie stars. On your right, any number of sightseeing boats depart in summer for tours of the Stockholm archipelago. From this vantage point, you'll have a good view of the Royal Palace and Gamla Stan.

Continue along Södra Blasieholmshamnen until you reach the:

❻ National Museum

Here you'll find a repository of the state's art treasures—everything from Renoir to Rembrandt.

Cross the Skeppsholmsbron bridge leading to the little island of:

❼ Skeppsholmen

The island holds a number of attractions (see "Gamla Stan & Neighboring Islands," under "The Top Attractions," earlier in this chapter).

After crossing the bridge, turn right along Västra Brobänken. On your right you'll pass the:

❽ Af Chapman

This "tall ship," with fully rigged masts, once sailed the seas under three different flags before being permanently anchored in 1949 as a youth hostel.

Turn left onto Flaggmansvägen. Continue along Holmamiralens väg, passing the Nordiska Institute on your right. Cut right toward the water at Södra Brobänken. Take Södra Brobänken until you reach a bridge on your right. Cross the bridge, which leads to:

❾ Kastellholmen

This is one of the most charming, but least visited, islands in Stockholm.

Head right along the water, going around Kastellholmskajen. Circle around and turn left at the end of Kastelleton. Walk back along Örlogsvägen, which runs through the center of the small island.

Cross the Kastellholmsbron bridge and return to the larger island of Skeppsholmen. This time go straight along Amiralsvägen, turning left onto Långa Raden. Cut right and continue to walk along Långa Raden. The first building on your left is the:

❿ Museum of Architecture

The collection contains slides and thousands of architectural drawings and sketches from the past 100 years.

From this point at the end of the walking tour, you can catch bus no. 65 to take you back to the heart of Stockholm.

2 ORGANIZED TOURS

CITY TOURS   The quickest and most convenient way to see the highlights of Stockholm is to take one of the bus tours that leave from the Square of Gustaf Adolff, near the Kungsträdgården.

Stockholm Sightseeing (also known as City Sightseeing), Svenskundsragen 17 (© **08/ 12-00-4000;** www.stockholmsightseeing.com), offers a variety of tours, mostly in summer. Tours depart from Gustaf Adolfs Torg in front of the Dansmuseet. "Panoramic Stockholm," a 1^1/$_2$-hour tour for 210SEK ($42/£21), purports to show you Stockholm in record time. At least you'll see the landmarks and several waterscape views. This tour is conducted from March 24 to December 31. For "Stockholm in a Nutshell," you can take a 2^1/$_2$-hour tour costing 330SEK ($66/£33), with departures from March 24 to December 17. This tour shows you the highlights of Stockholm, including a sail around the royal park at Djurgården. A more comprehensive tour, the "Grand Tour" lasts 3^1/$_2$ hours and costs 395SEK ($79/£40). This tour is by both boat and bus. A tour known as "Old Town Combination" departs June 26 to August 27, lasts 2^1/$_2$ hours, and costs 290SEK ($58/£29). The combined bus and walking tour includes a guided walking tour through Old Town with its narrow alleys and tiny courtyards. Finally, from June 26 to

August 27, you can go on a 45-minute "Horse and Carriage Tour," costing 140SEK ($28/£14), which departs from Mynttorget by the Royal Palace.

OLD TOWN STROLLS   Authorized guides lead 1-hour walking tours of the medieval lanes of Stockholm's Old Town. These walks are conducted daily from mid-June until late August, departing from the Royal Opera House at Gustav Adolfs Torg. The cost is 110SEK ($22/£11). Tickets and times of departure are available from **Stockholm Sightseeing** (see above).

CANAL CRUISES   Stockholm Sightseeing (see above) offers the "Royal Canal Tour," March 24 to December 17 daily, at 30 minutes past the hour all day. Tours cost 140SEK ($28/£14) for adults, 70SEK ($14/£7) for children 6 to 11, and are free for children 5 and under. Visitors are ferried around the canals of Djurgården.

3 SPECTATOR SPORTS

Soccer and **ice hockey** are the two most popular spectator sports in Sweden, and Stockholm has world-class teams in both. The major venue for any spectator sport in the capital, the **Stockholm Globe Arena (Globen),** lies less than 6.5km (4 miles) south of central Stockholm. Built in 1989, it's the biggest round building in the world, with a seating capacity of 16,000. It offers everything from political rallies, motorcycle competitions, and sales conventions to basketball and ice hockey games, tennis matches, and rock concerts. Its ticket office (✆ **077/131-00-00;** www.globearena.se) also sells tickets Monday to Friday 9am to 6pm and Saturday 11am to 4pm for most of Stockholm's soccer games, which are played in an open-air stadium nearby. The Globen complex lies in the southern suburb of Johnneshov (T-bana: Globen).

Another popular pastime is watching and betting on horse **trotting races.** These races usually take place on Wednesday at 6:30pm and on an occasional Saturday at 12:30pm in both summer and winter. (In winter an attempt is made to clear snow and ice from the racecourse; slippery conditions sometimes lead to unpredictable results.) Admission to **Solvalla Stadium** (✆ **08/635-90-00**), which lies about 6.5km (4 miles) north of the city center, is 40SEK ($8/£4). From Stockholm, take the bus marked SOLVALLA.

For schedules and ticket information, inquire at your hotel or the city's tourist office, or buy a copy of the monthly magazine *What's On,* which is available free at hotels and select shops throughout the city.

4 ACTIVE PURSUITS

GOLF   For those who want to play golf at the "top of Europe," there is the **Bromma Golf Course,** Kvarnbacksvägen 28, 16874 Bromma (✆ **08/704-91-91;** www.bromma golfhall.se), lying 5km (3 miles) west of the center of Stockholm. It's a 9-hole golf course with well-maintained greens. Greens fees are 150SEK ($30/£15) or 200SEK ($40/£20) on Saturday and Sunday, and golf clubs can be rented.

TENNIS, SQUASH & WEIGHTLIFTING   Aside from playing tennis at the **Kungliga Tennishallen (Royal Tennis Hall),** Lidingövägen 75 (✆ **08/459-15-00** for reservations; www.kltk.se), you can lift weights and enjoy a sauna and solarium. The center has 16 indoor courts, 5 outdoor clay courts, and 8 squash courts. Tennis courts cost 200SEK to

325SEK ($40–$65/£20–£33) per hour, squash courts are 30SEK to 250SEK ($6–$50/ £3–£25) for a 30-minute session, and the weight room entrance fee is 65SEK ($13/£6.50). The center is open Monday to Thursday 7am to 11pm, Friday 7am to 9pm, and Saturday and Sunday 8am to 9pm.

5 SHOPPING

THE SHOPPING SCENE

Stockholm is filled with shop after shop of dazzling merchandise—often at dazzlingly steep prices that reflect the high esteem in which Swedish craftspeople are held.

Bargain shoppers should proceed with caution. Some good buys do exist, but it takes a lot of searching. If you're a casual shopper, you may want to confine your purchases to handsome souvenirs and gifts.

Swedish glass, of course, is world famous. Swedish wooden items are works of great craftsmanship, and many people like to acquire Swedish functional furniture in blond pine or birch. Other items to look for include playsuits for children, silver necklaces, reindeer gloves, stainless-steel utensils, hand-woven neckties and skirts, sweaters and mittens in Nordic patterns, Swedish clogs, and colorful handicrafts from the provinces. The most popular souvenir is the Dala horse from Dalarna.

SHOPPING STREETS AND DISTRICTS Everybody's favorite shopping area in Stockholm is **Gamla Stan (Old Town).** Site of the Royal Palace, it even attracts such shoppers as the queen. The main street for browsing is **Västerlånggatan;** many antiques stores are found here, but don't expect low prices.

Skansen is most fun to explore in the summer because many craftspeople display their goods here. There are gift shops (some selling "Skansen glass") as well as individuals who offer their handmade goods at kiosks.

In the **Sergels Torg** area, the main shopping street is **Hamngatan,** site of the famous shopping center **Gallerian,** at the corner of Hamngatan and Sergels Torg, and crossing the northern rim of Kungsträdgården at Sweden House. Big department stores, such as NK and Åhléns, are located nearby.

The **Kungsgatan** area is another major district for shopping, stretching from Hötorget to the intersection of Kungsgatan and Vasagatan. **Drottninggatan** is one long pedestrian mall, flanked with shops. Many side streets branching off from it also are filled with shops. Hötorget, home to the PUB department store, is another major shopping district.

Since around the turn of the millennium, a new shopping district **(SOFO)** has been identified on the rapidly gentrifying island of **Södermalm,** to the south of that island's busy Folkungatan. Streets that have emerged since this neighborhood's gentrification include **Götgatan, Kokgatan, Bondegatan,** and **Skånegatan.** Expect a youth-oriented, funky, hipster consciousness within the SOFO district, where there has been an explosion in housing prices on an island (Södermalm) where 60% of all households are composed of a single person.

SHOPPING HOURS Stockholm shops are open Monday to Friday 10am to between 6pm (for large department stores) and 7pm (for smaller, boutique-style shops). Saturday shopping is possible between 10am and somewhere between 1 and 4pm. Once a week, usually on Monday or Friday, some of the larger stores are open from 9:30am to 7pm (July–Aug to 6pm).

Tips **Avoiding Mr. Taxman**

The **value-added tax** in Sweden, called MOMS, is imposed on all products and services, but you can avoid MOMS if you spend a total of at least 1,200SEK ($240/£120) in each shop. Just give the store your name, address, and passport number and ask for a tax-free check. Don't unwrap your purchase until after you've left Sweden. The customs official will want to see both the tax-free check and your purchase; you'll be given a cash refund, minus a small commission, on the spot. If you're departing by plane, hold on to your luggage until after you've received your refund, and then you can pack your purchase in your bag and check it (or carry the purchase with you, if it's not too big). At the **Tourist Center,** Hamngatan 27 (© **08/508-285-08**), you can pick up a pamphlet about tax-free shopping in Sweden. (For more information, see "Taxes," under "Fast Facts," in the appendix.)

Auctions

Stockholms Auktionsverket (Stockholm Auction Chambers) ★★★ The oldest auction company in the world—it dates from 1674—holds auctions 2 days a week from noon to "whenever." You can view the merchandise Monday to Friday from 9am to 5pm. An estimated 150,000 lots are auctioned each year—everything from ceramics to Picassos. Nybrogatan 32. © **08/453-67-50.** www.auktionsverket.se. T-bana: Östermalmstorg.

Books & Maps

Akademibokhandeln ★★ The biggest bookstore in Sweden carries more than 100,000 titles. A wide range of fiction and nonfiction is available in English. Many travel-related materials, such as maps, are also sold. Stadsgarden 10. © **08/769-81-00.** www. akademibokhandeln.se. T-bana: Hötorget.

Sweden Bookshop Whatever's available in English about Sweden can be found at this bookstore above the Tourist Center. The store also sells many rare items, including recordings of Swedish music. Slottsbacken 10. © **08/453-78-00.** www.swedenbookshop.com. T-bana: Gamla Stan.

Ceramics

Blås & Knåda ★ **Finds** This store features the best products made by members of a cooperative of 50 Swedish ceramic artists and glassmakers. Prices begin at 200SEK ($40/£20) for a single teacup and rise to as much as 25,000SEK ($5,000/£2,500) for museum-quality pieces. Hornsgatan 26. © **08/642-77-67.** www.blasknada.com. T-bana: Slussen.

Keramiskt Centrum Gustavsberg Bone china, stoneware dinner services, and other fine table and decorative ware are made at the Gustavsberg Ceramics Center. A museum at the center displays historic pieces such as *parian* (a type of unglazed porcelain) statues based on the work of the famous Danish sculptor Torvaldsen and other artists. You'll also see hand-painted vases, Toby jugs, majolica, willowware, examples of Pyro (the first ovenware), royal dinner services, and sculpture by modern artists. Visitors can watch potters at work and see artists hand-painting designs. You can even decorate a mug or plate yourself. A shop at the center sells Gustavsberg-ware, including seconds. Värmdö Island (21km/13 miles east of Stockholm). © **08/570-356-58.** Bus: 422 or 440.

Department Stores

Åhléns City   In the center of Stockholm, the largest department store in Sweden has a gift shop, a restaurant, and a famous food department. We often come here to buy the makings for a picnic to be enjoyed later in one of Stockholm's city parks. Also seek out the fine collection of home textiles, and Orrefors and Kosta Boda crystal ware. The pewter with genuine Swedish ornaments makes a fine gift item. Klarabergsgatan 50. 𝄞 08/676-60-00. www.ahlens.se. T-bana: Centralen.

Nordiska Kompaniet (NK) ★★   A high-quality department store since 1902, NK displays most of the big names in Swedish glass, including Orrefors (see the Nordic Light collection) and Kosta. Thousands of handcrafted Swedish items can be found in the basement. Stainless steel, also a good buy in Sweden, is profusely displayed. Hamngatan 18–20. 𝄞 08/762-80-00. www.nk.se. T-bana: Kungsträdgården.

PUB   Greta Garbo worked in the millinery department here from 1920 to 1922. It's one of the most popular department stores in Stockholm; the boutiques and departments generally sell midrange clothing and good-quality housewares, but not the international designer names of the more prestigious (and more expensive) NK. Massive and bustling, with an emphasis on traditional and conservative Swedish clothing, it offers just about anything you'd need to stock a Scandinavian home. There's also a restaurant. Hötorget 13. 𝄞 08/782-19-30. www.pub.se. T-bana: Hötorget.

Fashion

Acne   With a name like this, you wouldn't know that this is a showcase for an award-winning Swedish jeans company and fashion label. The store has some 400 retailers worldwide, including Barney's in New York, Selfridges in London, even Colette in Paris. Launched in 1996, Acne created 100 pairs of unisex designer jeans, which are known for their bright-red stitching. Nytorgsgatan 36. 𝄞 08/640-04-70. www.acnestudios.com. T-bana: Medborgaplatsen.

Artillery 2 ★   This is one of the most fashionable unisex boutiques in Stockholm. If the fashion were created yesterday, it is likely to be on sale here today. Expect all the trendy brand names such as Dolce & Gabbana, Paul & Joe, Nicole Fahri, Blue Cult, and Seven. Artillerigatan 2. 𝄞 08/663-29-20. www.artilleri2.com. T-bana: Östermalmstorg.

Bruno Götgatsbacken   Some of the top names in local Swedish fashion, including Whyred Tiger or Filippa K, are sold in this restored industrial building that dates from the 1600s. This is a chic modernist mall with a cafe and shops, well worth a detour. Götgatan 36. 𝄞 076/871-50-84. www.brunogotgatsbacken.se. T-bana: Slussen.

Filippa K   One of the leading clothiers in Stockholm operates what they define as a large-scale boutique entrenched in the middle-bracket cost category—this is the kind of place where a mother might take her young daughter for her first cotillion dress. Expect a wide array of casual dresses, cocktail dresses, and formal evening wear, along with the business uniforms that are so favored by Scandinavian office workers. There's also a collection of clothing for men—suits, blazers, and casual wear—that's a bit less extensive than for women. There's the added advantage of a small-scale collection of fur coats—perfect for that chilly late-autumn sojourn in the football bleachers of your old alma mater. Grev Turegatan 18. 𝄞 08/545-882-57. www.filippa-k.com. T-bana: Östermalmstorg.

Grandpa   What a misleading name. In Södermalm, the hippest neighborhood in Stockholm, this chic outlet does sell old-fashioned board games. But it's mainly known for its trendy Swedish fashion statement, including such designs as Whyred and Junk de Luxe.

Expect an array of Swedish jeans and slacks, Scandinavian sweaters, shirts, and handbags. Södermannagatan 21. ℭ **08/643-60-80.** www.grandpa.se. T-bana: Medborgarplatsen.

Gunilla Pontén ★ This designer creates clothing for women that are neither faddish nor trendy, but of high quality with good needlework. Clothing comes in such colors as cerise, olive, black, and aubergine. The collection is also distinguished by fun accessories, including specially designed jewelry, handbags, caps, scarves, hats, and fingerless gloves. Mäster Samuelsgatan 10. ℭ **08/611-10-22.** www.ponten.com. T-bana: Östermalmstorg.

H&M ★★ "Of course, everybody in Stockholm buys their clothing at H&M," said the manager of our hotel. "It's the thing to do." This is not always true, as there are many other houses of fashion, but H&M is the first thing that comes to mind when you think of Swedish fashion. H&M stores are found around the world today from Tokyo to New York. The company carries fashion to the far limits, from flamboyant dogtooth check suits with wide lapels to Jodhpur style pants. The design firm also makes an oversize scarf the centerpiece of an outfit, or else can outfit you in faux fur. Their cardigans are the peak of fashion, as are their lumberjack shirts. And for the man who has everything, there is a pair of Jackson Pollock–inspired yellow splattered trousers. 22 Hamngatan in Östermalm. ℭ **08/5246-3530.** www.hm.com. T-bana: Sundbyberg.

J. Lindeberg ★ With its fashion collections for men and women, this chain store definitely lives in the 21st century. Johan Lindberg, along with his partner, the designer Magnus Ehrland, designs menswear for the urban man of taste. There's a smaller collection of clothing for women. Igeldammsgatan 22A. ℭ **08/56-850-00.** www.jlindeberg.com. T-bana: Fridhemsplan.

Marzio In the heart of Stockholm, this chic outlet has a wide array of Italian shoes and bags, among the most sophisticated in the city. Marzio also produces its own brand of shoes and bags, which are made in Italy of the finest leather. Shoes are trendy or classic. The outlet also sells many hot independent brands of shoes for women. Nybrogatan 10. ℭ **08/661-86-37.** www.marzio.se. T-bana: Östermalmstorg.

NK In the realm of menswear, this subdivision of the previously noted Nordiska Kompaniet (see "Department Stores," above) is Stockholm's answer to Harrods in London or Bloomingdale's in New York. From Armani, Prada, and Gucci suits and shoes to the latest fashions in Levi's and casual wear—it's all here. The largest of a chain of menswear stores scattered throughout Sweden, this has been around for more than a hundred years. In addition to stocking outdoor gear and swimsuits, the store also maintains a boutique-within-the-boutique for the Swedish label TIGER (ℭ **08/762-87-72**), which sells fine suits, shoes, and casual wear that's specifically tailored to Swedish tastes and builds. Hamngatan 18–20. ℭ **08/762-80-00.** www.nk.se. T-bana: Kungsträdgården.

Flea Market
Loppmarknaden i Skärholmen (Skärholmen Shopping Center) ★ At this, the biggest flea market in northern Europe, you might find an antique from an attic in Värmland or some other only-in-Sweden trinket. Try to go on Saturday or Sunday (the earlier the better), when the market is at its peak. Admission is 15SEK ($3/£1.50) on Saturday and 10SEK ($2/£1) on Sunday, but free the rest of the week. Skärholmen. ℭ **08/710-00-60.** Bus: 13 or 23 to Skärholmen (20 min.).

Food Markets
Cajsa Warg This food shop is the one most visibly associated with the rapidly gentrifying SOFO neighborhood in Södermalm. Foodies will quickly identify it as the kind of

Funky Items for Counterculture Shoppers

Hornstullstrand Street Market—often known simply as "Street"—is a funky, battered market positioned at the western waterfront on the rapidly gentrifying island of Södermalm. This relative newcomer to Stockholm's punk underground scene is often compared to London's Camden Market.

In cold weather, its booths are confined to the impersonal perimeter of a city-owned, cement-sided former parking garage that evokes a penitentiary. Dozens of stalls here sell costume jewelry, secondhand clothing, and budget-conscious products of struggling, up-and-coming designer wannabes. In clement weather, the venue expands into rows of outdoor booths.

For an organic food break in between shopping, we like to drop into a nearby pub and restaurant, **Hornstulls Strand 4** (✆ **08/658-63-50**), where main courses cost 155SEK to 255SEK ($31–$51/£16–£26). Hours are Monday to Tuesday 11:30am to 11pm, Wednesday to Friday 11:30am to 1am, Saturday noon to 1am, and Sunday noon to 6pm. The market (www.streetinstockholm.se; T-bana: Hornstull) is open year-round Saturday and Sunday 11am to between 5 and 6pm.

market where some of the most esoteric food in Sweden (strawberries from Chile, pâté from France, organic vegetables from everywhere) sit adjacent to the kind of staples (very fresh fish, produce, and meats, including reindeer) that many Swedes associate with their childhoods. If you're preparing a picnic, this is a prime grazing ground within a cozy setting that's paneled and appealingly country-ish. They even maintain a menu that lists four varieties of picnic baskets they'll compile for you, each priced at 75SEK to 125SEK ($15–$25/£7.50–£13) per person. Renstiernas gata 20, in Södermalm. ✆ **08/642-23-50**. www.cajsawarg.se. T-bana: Medborgarplatsen.

NK Saluhall ★   The variety of displays at this hyperfabulous food mall in the Nordiska Kompaniet department store will blow most foodies away. It occupies about a third of a basement level that's otherwise loaded with the kind of cook- and tableware that chefs will salivate over. Then there are the food displays, which are, quite simply, the most visually appealing and lavish of any food market in Stockholm. In addition to rack after rack of produce, meats, and canned goods, there are three separate wine bars on-site, one devoted to wines by the glass accompanied by charcuterie and smoked fish, the other (our favorite) immediately adjacent to the most lavish display of cheeses in Scandinavia. It's open Monday to Friday 10am to 8pm, Saturday 10am to 6pm, Sunday noon to 6pm. Hamngatan 18–20. ✆ **08/762-80-00**. www.nk.se. T-bana: Kungsträdgården.

Östermalms Saluhall   One of the most colorful indoor food markets in Scandinavia features cheese, meat, vegetable, and fish merchants who supply food for much of the area, and a red-brick design from the late 19th century that might remind you of a medieval fortress. If the food on display works up an appetite, you can stop for a snack or a meal at one of the market's restaurants. Nybrogatan 31. No central phone. www.saluhallen.com. T-bana: Östermalmstorg.

Gems & Minerals

Geocity ★ ⓕ**inds**   Geocity offers exotic mineral crystals, jewelry, Scandinavian gems, Baltic amber, and lapidary equipment. The staff includes two certified gemologists who will cut and set any gem you select and do appraisals. The inventory holds stones from

Scandinavia and around the world, including Greenland, Madagascar, Siberia, and South America. Kungsgatan 57. ℂ 08/411-11-40. T-bana: Hötorget.

Gifts & Souvenirs

Stockholm Tourist Center Gift Shop   There are dozens of souvenir shops scattered throughout Stockholm, especially on Gamla Stan, but the merchandise within this official tourism arm, or gift shop emporium, of the Swedish government is superior. Expect Dalarna horses, embroideries, Viking statuettes, and glassware. Stockholm Tourist Center, Sweden House, Hamngatan 27, off Kungsträdgården. ℂ 70/712-02-33. T-bana: Kungsträdgården.

Glass & Crystal

Nordiska Kristall ★★   Since 1918, this company has been the vanguard of Swedish glassmakers. Your pick of Swedish glass is on sale here, anything from classic to more adventurous designs. The company often stages pioneering exhibitions in order to showcase its more daring pieces. Kungsgatan 9. ℂ 08/10-77-18. www.nordiskakristall.se. T-bana: Hörtorget.

Orrefors Kosta Boda ★★★   Two famous companies combined to form this "crystal palace" outlet in the center of Stockholm. Orrefors focuses on clear vases and stemware, while Kosta Boda boasts more colorful and artistic pieces of glass. One of the best-selling items is the "Intermezzo Glass" with a drop of sapphire glass in its stem. 15 Birger Jarlsgatan. ℂ 08/545-040-84. www.kostaboda.com. T-bana: Östermalmstorg.

Handicrafts & Gifts

Brinken Konsthantverk   On the lower floor of a building near the Royal Palace in the Old Town, this elegant purveyor of gift items will ship handcrafted brass, pewter, wrought iron, or crystal anywhere in the world. About 95% of the articles are made in Scandinavia. Storkyrkobrinken 1. ℂ 08/411-59-54. T-bana: Gamla Stan.

DesignTorget ★★ (Finds)   In 1994, the government-owned Kulturhuset (Swedish Culture House) reacted to declining attendance by inviting one of Stockholm's most influential designers and decorators, Jerry Hellström, to organize this avant-garde art gallery. Swedes modestly refer to it as a "shop." In a large room in the cellar, you'll find a display of handicrafts created by 150 to 200 mostly Swedish craftspeople. The work, including some of the best pottery, furniture, textiles, clothing, pewter, and crystal in Sweden, must be approved by a jury of connoisseurs before being offered for sale. The organization maintains several other branches, including a store in southern Stockholm at Götgatan 31 (ℂ 08/462-35-20; www.designtorget.se). It stocks clothing for men, women, and children, and furniture, with less emphasis on ceramics and handicrafts. In the Kulturhuset, Sergelgangen 29. ℂ 08/646-16-78. T-bana: Centralen.

Duka   A large selection of carefully chosen crystal, porcelain, and gifts is available in this shop near the Konserthuset (Concert Hall). It also offers tax-free shopping and shipping. Kungsgatan 5. ℂ 08/440-96-00. T-bana: Hötorget.

Gunnarssons Träfigurer ★ (Finds)   This store boasts one of the city's most appealing collections of Swedish carved wooden figures. All are by Urban Gunnarsson, a second-generation master carver. Highlights include figures from World War II, such as Winston Churchill, U.S. presidents from Franklin D. Roosevelt to Bill Clinton, and a host of mythical and historical European personalities. The carvings are usually made from linden or basswood. Drottninggatan 77. ℂ 08/21-67-17. T-bana: Rådmansgatan.

a wide selection of glass, pottery, gifts, and wooden and metal handicrafts by some of
Sweden's best artisans. Other wares include hand-woven carpets, upholstery fabrics,
hand-painted materials, tapestries, lace, and embroidered items. You'll also find beautiful
yarns for weaving and embroidery. Sveavägen 44. ✆ **08/23-21-15.** www.svenskhemslojd.com.
T-bana: Hötorget.

Home Furnishings

Carl Malmsten This home-furnishings boutique is devoted to the sale and distribu-
tion of the designs of Swedish über-designer Carl Malmsten (1888–1972), and shares
basically the same clientele with the also-recommended (and more plush-looking) Svensk
Tenn (see below), which lies only a few steps away. Expect a relatively simple venue that
focuses on tables, chairs, footstools, and sofas, the designs for which call to mind those
popular during many Swedes' childhoods. What we like best here are the whimsical
upholstery fabrics, each inspired by botanical and garden themes, which manage to cheer
up even the coldest of Scandinavian winters. Strandvägen 5B. ✆ **08/23-33-80.** www.carl
malmsten.se. T-bana: Östermalmstorg.

IKEA ★★ Slightly outside the city, but worth the trip, this local branch of the world-
famous chain has the most comprehensive assortment of Swedish kitchen accessories and
textiles available anywhere. IKEA began when its founder, Ingvar Kamprad, started selling matches to his neighbors back in the 1920s. Today it has stores in 24 countries,
including Britain and the United States. Everything for rooms from the bedroom to the
kitchen is found in the showrooms here. Edgårdsvågen 1, Skäxholmen. ✆ **04/768-1000.** www.
ikea.com.

Nordiska Galleriet This two-story store features the finest in European furniture
design, including the best from Scandinavia. The store can arrange shipment. Boasting
everything from sofas to tables, from vases to avant-garde lamps, and some of the most
daring chairs ever designed, this showroom carries the "masterpieces" of famous designers
of yesterday but also the more daring designers of the 21st century. You might get a lamp
designed by the famous Philippe Starck or a three-legged stool by Arne Jacobsen (the
20th c.'s most famous Danish designer), or even a chair by the innovative Charles Mack-
intosh of Scotland. Also for sale are reproductions of the furniture of Alvar Aalto, Finland's most famous designer. Nybrogatan 11. ✆ **08/442-83-60.** www.nordiskagalleriet.se.
T-bana: Östermalmstorg.

Svenskt Tenn ★★ "Swedish Pewter" (its English name) has been one of Sweden's
most prominent stores for home furnishings since 1924. Pewter is no longer king, but
the shop now sells Scandinavia's best selection of furniture, printed textiles, lamps, glassware, china, and gifts. The inventory is stylish, and although there aren't a lot of bargains,
it's an excellent place to see the newest trends in Scandinavian design. It carries an exclusive collection of Josef Frank's hand-printed designs on linen and cotton. It will pack,
insure, and ship your purchases anywhere in the world. Strandvägen 5. ✆ **08/670-16-00.**
www.svenskttenn.se. T-bana: Östermalmstorg.

Linens

Solgården ★★★ For the dwindling few who really care about luxury linens and
elegant home wares, such as lace and embroidery, this shop is the finest of its kind in

Scandinavia. It was conceived by owner Marianne von Kantzow Ridderstad as a tribute to Gustav III, the king who is said to have launched the neoclassical style in Sweden. Ridderstad designed her shop like a country house, with rough-hewn wood and whimsical furnishings. Each of her linens is virtually a work of art, and the tablecloths are heirloom pieces. You'll cherish the work for its originality and loveliness. **Karlavägen 158.** *(C)* **08/663-93-60.** www.cdecor.com. T-bana: Rådmansgatan.

Shopping Malls

Gallerian ★★★ A short walk from Sweden House at Kunådgården, this modern two-story shopping complex is, to many, the best shopping destination in Sweden. Merchandise in most of the individually managed stores is designed to appeal to local shoppers, not the tourist market—although in summer that changes a bit as more souvenir and gift items appear. **Hamngatan 37.** *(C)* **08/791-24-45.** www.gallerian.se. T-bana: Kungsträdgården.

Sturegallerian ★★ In the center of Stockholm, this renovated and expanded mall has a dazzling array of foreign and domestic merchandise that's sold within at least 60 specialty shops. Summer brings out more displays of Swedish souvenirs and gift items. There are also restaurants and cafes. Sturegallerian opened in 1989 and a year later was named "Shopping Center of the Year in Europe" by the International Council of Shopping Centers. **Stureplan.** *(C)* **08/453-50-67.** www.sturegallerian.se. T-bana: Östermalmstorg.

Textiles

Handarbetets Vänner This is one of the oldest and most prestigious textile houses in Stockholm; founded in 1874, today it is one of the few remaining textile art studios in the country and sells art weaving and embroidery items in a spacious headquarters. The skilled craftspeople here have brought textile design to an art form, as reflected in their "art weaving" and embroidery. Their wall hangings—some of which are virtually heirloom pieces—are the finest in the city. The studio even repairs historic textiles. **Djurgårdsslatten 82–84.** *(C)* **08/545-686-50.** Bus: 47.

Toys

Bulleribock (Kids) Since it opened in the 1960s, this store has carried only traditional, noncomputerized toys made of wood, metal, or paper. You won't find any plastic toys or objectionable war games here. Many of the charming playthings are suitable for children up to age 10, and as many as possible are made in Sweden, with wood from Swedish forests. **Sveavägen 104.** *(C)* **08/673-61-21.** www.bulleribock.se. T-bana: Rådmansgatan.

---

6 STOCKHOLM AFTER DARK

Djurgården (p. 120) is the city's favorite spot for both indoor and outdoor evening events. Although the more sophisticated may find it corny, this is your best early-evening bet. Afterward, you can make the rounds of Stockholm's jazz venues and nightclubs, some of which stay open until 3 or 4 in the morning.

Pick up a copy of ***What's On,*** distributed at virtually every hotel in town as well as at the Tourist Center at Sweden House to see what entertainment and cultural venues are scheduled during your time in Stockholm.

All the major opera, theater, and concert seasons begin in the fall, except for special summer festival performances. Fortunately, most of the major opera and theatrical performances are funded by the state, which keeps ticket prices reasonable.

Concert Halls

Berwaldhallen (Berwald Concert Hall)   This hexagonal concert hall is Swedish Radio's big music studio. The Radio Symphonic Orchestra performs here, and other high-quality musical programs include *lieder* (classical music) and chamber music recitals. The hall has excellent acoustics. The box office is open Monday to Friday noon to 6pm and 2 hours before every concert. Dag Hammarskjölds Väg 3. © **08/784-18-00.** www. sr.se/berwaldhallen. Tickets 60SEK–450SEK ($12–$90/£6–£45). T-bana: Karlaplan.

Filharmonikerna i Konserthuset (Concert Hall)   Home of the Stockholm Philharmonic Orchestra, this is the principal place to hear classical music in Sweden. The Nobel Prizes are also awarded here. Constructed in 1920, the building houses two concert halls. One seats 1,600 and is better suited to major orchestras; the other, seating 450, is suitable for chamber music groups. Besides local orchestras, the hall features visiting ensembles, such as the Chicago Symphony Orchestra. Some series sell out in advance to subscription ticket holders; for others, visitors can readily get tickets. Sales begin 2 weeks before a concert and continue until the performance begins. Concerts usually start at 7:30pm, with occasional lunchtime (noon) or "happy hour" (5:30pm) concerts. Most performances are broadcast on Stockholm's main classical music station, 107.5 FM. The box office is open Monday to Friday 11am to 6pm, Saturday 11am to 3pm. Hötorget 8. © **08/786-02-00.** www.konserthuset.se. Tickets 125SEK–575SEK ($25–$115/£13–£58). T-bana: Hötorget.

Opera & Ballet

Drottningholm Court Theater ★★★   Positioned on an island in Lake Mälaren, 11km (6³/₄ miles) from Stockholm, this is the most famous 18th-century theater in the world. It stages operas and ballets with performers done up in full 18th-century regalia, from period costumes to wigs, and the 18th-century music is performed on antique instruments. Its machinery and 30 or more complete theater sets are intact and in use. The theater, a short walk from the royal residence, seats only 450, which makes it difficult to get tickets. The season is from May to September. Most performances begin at 7:30pm and last 2¹/₂ to 4 hours. You can order tickets in advance by phone with an American Express card. Even if you're not able to get tickets for an actual performance, you can tour the theater as part of a visit to Drottningholm Palace (p. 123). Drottningholm. © **08/660-82-25.** www.dtm.se. Tickets 165SEK–610SEK ($33–$122/£17–£61). T-bana: Brommaplan, then bus no. 301 or 323. Boat from the City Hall in Stockholm.

Operahauset (Royal Opera House) ★★★   Founded in 1773 by Gustav III (who was later assassinated here at a masked ball), the Opera House is the home of the Royal Swedish Opera and the Royal Swedish Ballet. The building dates from 1898. Performances are usually Monday to Saturday at 7:30pm (closed mid-June to mid-Aug). The box office is open Monday to Friday noon to 6pm (until 7:30pm on performance nights), and Saturday noon to 3pm.Gustav Adolfs Torg. © **08/791-44-00.** www.opera.se. Tickets 100SEK–700SEK ($20–$140/£10–£70); 10%–30% senior and student discounts. T-bana: Kungsträdgården.

The Capital of Gay Scandinavia

Copenhagen thrived for many years as a refreshingly raunchy city with few inhibitions and fewer restrictions on alternative sexual preferences. Beginning in the mid-1990s, Stockholm witnessed an eruption of new gay bars, discos, and roaming nightclubs. Copenhagen's more imperial and, in many ways, more staid competition made the Danes' legendary permissiveness look a bit weak. Today, thanks partly to the huge influence of London's gay subcultures, no other city in Scandinavia offers gay-friendly nightlife options as broad and diverse as Stockholm's. Some of the gay bars and clubs maintain fixed hours and addresses. Others, configured as roving parties, constantly change addresses. Listings for gay entertainment venues appear regularly in *QX,* a gay magazine published in Swedish and English. It's available at gay bars and news kiosks throughout Stockholm. You can also check out the magazine's website (www.qx.se). And don't overlook the comprehensive website **www. rfsl.se** maintained by RSFL, a Swedish organization devoted to equal rights for gays.

GAY VENUES IN SÖDERMALM

Looking for a nonconfrontational bar peopled with regular guys who happen to be gay? Consider a round or two on the island of Södermalm at **Sidetrack,** Wollmar Yxkullsgatan 7 (© **08/641-16-88;** www.sidetrack.nu; T-bana: Maria-torget). Small, amicable, committed to shunning trendiness, and located deep within a cellar a few blocks from the also-recommended Hotel Rival, it's named after the founder's favorite gay bar in Chicago. It's open Tuesday to Saturday from 6pm to 1am. Tuesday nights here seem to be something of a gay Stockholm institution. Other nights are fine, too—something like a Swedish version of a bar and lounge at the local bowling alley, where everyone happens to be into same-sex encounters. Prefacing the bar is a well-managed restaurant, serving dinner only, Tuesday to Saturday 6pm to 1am (June–Aug Tues–Sat 8pm–1am). Main courses cost from 89SEK to 155SEK ($18–$31/£9–£16).

To find a Viking, or Viking wannabe, in leather, a 2-minute walk from the above-recommended Sidetrack, head for **SLM** (Scandinavian Leather Men), Wollmar Yxkullsgatan 18 (© **08/643-31-00;** www.slmstockholm.se; T-bana: Mariatorget). Technically, this is a private club. But if you look hot and not creepy, and if you wear just a hint (or even a lot) of cowhide or rawhide, or happen to have spent the past 6 months felling timber in Montana, you stand an excellent chance of getting in—if you don't object to paying a "membership fee" of around 100SEK ($20/£10). On Wednesdays, Fridays, and Saturdays from

Theater

The theater season begins in mid-August and lasts until mid-June.

Kungliga Dramatiska Teatern (Royal Dramatic Theater) ★★★   Greta Garbo got her start in acting here, and Ingmar Bergman staged two productions a year until his death in 2007. The theater presents the latest experimental plays and the classics—in

10pm to 2am, the place, located within what might be the deepest basement in Stockholm, functions as Stockholm's premier leather bar. You'll find lots of masculine-looking men on the street level and a handful of toys and restrictive accoutrements in the cellar-level dungeon. Most of the staff on duty here are volunteers, some of them expatriates from neighboring Finland looking to promulgate the aesthetics of, among others, Tom of Finland (the world's most famous gay male erotica artist). On Saturday from 10pm to 2am, a DJ spins highly danceable music. It's closed on other nights.

Södermalm's most trend-conscious dining venue is the **Roxy,** a boxy, modern-looking site on the Nytorg 6 (✆ **08/640-96-55;** www.roxysofo.se). Funky and whimsical, it has a decor that might have been inspired by a meeting in heaven between the last of Vienna's Hapsburgs and the design team at SAS. The sofas evoke a Danish airport lounge in 1966, and mismatched crystal chandeliers seem to echo the sounds of a Strauss waltz. Art Deco objets d'art might have been salvaged from a 1930s-era ocean liner, and two or three porcelain incarnations of pink flamingos are strictly from 1950s Miami. Drinks of choice include an Assburner (Jack Daniels with ginger, lime juice, and red-hot chilis); a Razz (raspberry liqueur, vodka, and 7-Up), and a Cosmo spiked with ginger. You can always drop in just for a drink (the crowd tends to be youngish and cute-ish), but if you want dinner, main courses cost from 182SEK to 245SEK ($36–$49/£18–£25). The place opens Tuesday to Sunday at 5pm, and closes anytime between 11pm and 1am, depending on business and the night of the week.

GAY VENUES ON GAMLA STAN

If you need a caffeine fix and a slice of chocolate cake before all that leather and latex, you might want to drop into Stockholm's most appealing, best-managed gay cafe, **Chokladkoppen,** Stortorget 18–20 (✆ **08/20-31-70;** T-bana: Gamla Stan). On the street level of a house erected in the 15th century, across from the Nobel Museum, it's open daily from 9am to 11pm. It specializes in sandwiches, gorgeous pastries, and all manner of chocolate confections that appeal even to straight people. The staff is charming, and the clientele more gay than not. The consistently most popular item on the menu is a steaming cupful of white hot chocolate, priced at 35SEK ($7/£3.50), which—if you're really hooked on calories—might be accompanied by a slice of white chocolate cheesecake, for 40SEK ($8/£4).

Swedish only. It's open year-round (with a slight slowdown in July), and performances are scheduled Tuesday to Saturday at 7pm and Sunday at 4pm. The box office is open Monday to Saturday 10am to 6pm. Nybroplan. ✆ **08/667-06-80.** www.dramaten.se. Tickets 120SEK–450SEK ($24–$90/£12–£45); student discount available. T-bana: Östermalmstorg.

Oscars Teatern Oscars is the flagship of Stockholm's musical entertainment world. It's been the home of classic operetta and musical theater since the turn of the 20th century. Known for its extravagant staging of traditional operettas, it was also one of the first theaters in Europe to produce such hits as *Cats* in Swedish. The box office is open Monday to Saturday from 11am to 6pm. Kungsgatan 63. © **08/20-50-00**. www.oscarsteatern. se. Tickets 305SEK–625SEK ($61–$125/£31–£63). T-bana: Hötorget.

Regina Theater This is the only permanent English-language theater in Sweden, although its yearly repertoire is not always in English—you'll have to check to see what's playing at the time of your visit. Originally built in 1911 as a cinema, the building was converted into a theater in 1960. The Regina Theater Company, established in 1980, presents everything from Victorian thrillers to Dickensian Christmas musicals. Its London-style theater pub is unique in Sweden. Shows are presented dinner-theater-style, with entertainment and food costing 600SEK ($120/£60) per person. The box office is open Monday to Saturday noon to 6pm. American Express cardholders can reserve by phone. Drottninggatan 71A. © **08/411-63-20**. T-bana: Hötorget.

Local Culture & Entertainment

Skansen Skansen arranges traditional seasonal festivities, special events, autumn market days, and a Christmas Fair. In summer, concerts, singalongs, and guest performances delight visitors and locals alike. Folk-dancing performances are staged in July and August, Friday and Saturday at 7pm and Sunday at 2:30 and 4pm. In July and August, outdoor dancing is presented with live music Monday to Saturday from 10 to 11:30pm. Djurgården 49–51. © **08/442-80-00**. www.skansen.se. Admission 40SEK–140SEK ($8–$28/£4–£14) adults, 40SEK–50SEK ($8–$10/£4–£5) children 6–15, free under 6. Fee depends on the time of the year. Bus: 44 or 47. Ferry from Slussen.

AN AMUSEMENT PARK

Gröna Lunds Tivoli ★ **Kids** Unlike its Copenhagen namesake, this is an amusement park, not a fantasyland. For those who like Coney Island–type amusements, it can be a nighttime adventure. The park is filled with some hair-raising rides, including a roller coaster as well as a Ferris wheel and bumper cars. The most dramatic is the Power Tower, rising to 107m high (351 ft.)—the tallest free-fall amusement park ride in Scandinavia. At the peak, you have only about 5 seconds to see one of the most dramatic views of Stockholm and its archipelago before you plummet, along with other screaming passengers, to the earth once again. The park is open daily from the end of April to September, usually from noon to 11pm or midnight. Call for exact hours. Djurgården. © **08/587-501-00**. www.gronalund.com. Admission 70SEK ($14/£7) for ages 7 and up, free 6 and under. Bus: 44 or 47. Ferry from Nybroplan.

THE CLUB & MUSIC SCENE
A Historic Nightclub

Café Opera ★★ By day a bistro, brasserie, and tearoom, Café Opera becomes one of the most crowded nightclubs in Stockholm in the evening. Visitors have the best chance of getting in around noon during lunch. A stairway near the entrance leads to one of the Opera House's most beautiful corners, the clublike **Operabaren (Opera Bar)**. It's likely to be as crowded as the cafe. The bar is a monumental but historically charming place to have a drink; a beer costs 60SEK ($12/£6). After 10pm, there is less emphasis on food and more on disco activities. Don't confuse this establishment with the opera's main (and far more expensive) dining room, the **Operakällaren.** To enter, you must be at least 23 years old. The bar is open daily from 5pm to 3am. Operahauset,

Dance Clubs & Discos

Göta Källare   Stockholm's largest supper-club-style dance hall has a reputation for successful matchmaking. Huge, echoing, and paneled with lots of wood in faux-*Español* style inside, it also boasts an outside terrace. The restaurant serves platters of food priced at 124SEK ($25/£12). Menu items include tournedos, fish, chicken, and veal. The live orchestra (which performs "Strangers in the Night" a bit too frequently) plays every night, and pulls in a middle-aged crowd. The hall opens nightly at 10pm. In the Medborgplatsen subway station, Södermalm. ℂ **08/642-08-28.** Cover 140SEK ($28/£14) after 11pm. T-bana: Medborgplatsen.

Laroy ★   Located on the ground floor of Arnoldshuset, this hot bar and club attracts the young and beautiful who are definitely in a party mood. Don't be surprised if the bartender says he won't give you that drink until you give him a kiss. Open Wednesday and Friday to Saturday 10pm to 3am. Biblioteksgatan 23. ℂ **08/545-076-50.** Cover 150SEK ($30/£15). T-bana: Östermalmstorg.

White Room ★   With its snow-white interior and theatrical lighting, this has been called the wildest late-night club in Stockholm. Attracting an under-30 crowd, it is stylish and known for its euphoric atmosphere. After midnight, the scene gets frenetic. Some of the best DJs in Sweden rule the night here. Hours are 11pm to 5am on Wednesday, Friday, and Saturday nights (closed otherwise). Jakobsbergsgatan 29. ℂ **08/545-076-00.** Cover 150SEK ($30/£15). T-bana: Östermalmstorg.

Rock & Jazz Clubs

AG925 (Allmänna Gallieriet 925)   This is about as underground and counterculture an environment as we're willing to recommend. If it were even a bit more extreme or eccentric, it might run the risk of being closed down by the police. The club occupies the sprawling, grimy premises of what functioned for many years as a manufacturer of decorative silver. (AG925, by the way, is a designation of the purity of silver, and as such, it was stamped into the bottom of each tea service or silver vase this factory ever produced.) Today, it's a sprawling, serpentine, much-battered labyrinth of rooms, many of them sheathed in white tiles, that's peppered with bars, artfully conceived graffiti, exhibition spaces for a changing array of artworks, rickety tables and chairs that long ago saw better days, and stages where rock 'n' roll and punk rock bands blare into the night. Dress as you might for a date with rocker Patti Smith or Courtney Love. Friday and Saturday nights often feature a DJ who keeps the place rocking. Patronize the restaurant only to stave off starvation. Open Tuesday to Saturday 7pm to 1am. Kronobergsgatan 37, 2nd floor. ℂ **08/410-681-00.** www.ag925.se. Entrance usually free, but during special concerts, as high as 110SEK ($22/£11). T-Bana: Fridhemsplan.

Fasching ★★   This club attracts some of Sweden's best-known jazz musicians. Well known among jazz aficionados throughout Scandinavia, it is small but fun. The venue varies according to the night of the week and the availability of the artists performing. At the end of the live acts, there's likely to be dancing to salsa, soul, and perhaps R&B. The club is open nightly from 7pm to 1am. Kungsgatan 63. ℂ **08/534-829-60.** www.fasching.se. Cover 100SEK–300SEK ($20–$60/£10–£30). T-bana: Centralen.

Hard Rock Cafe   The Swedish branch of this chain is fun and gregarious. Sometimes an American, British, or Scandinavian rock band presents a live concert; otherwise, rock blasts from the sound system. Burgers begin at 120SEK ($24/£12), steaks at 185SEK ($37/£19), and beer at 60SEK ($12/£6). It's open Monday to Thursday 11:30am to midnight, Friday 11:30am to 1am, Saturday noon to 3am, and Sunday noon to midnight. Sveavägen 75. ℂ **08/545-494-00.** www.hardrock.com. T-bana: Rådmansgatan.

Pub Engelen/Nightclub Kolingen   The Engelen Pub, the Restaurant Engelen, and the Nightclub Kolingen (in the 15th-c. cellar) share a single address. The restaurant, which serves some of the best steaks in town, is open daily 5pm to midnight. Live performances, usually soul, funk, and rock by Swedish groups, take over the pub daily from 8:30pm to midnight. The pub is open Tuesday to Thursday 4pm to 1am, Friday and Saturday 4pm to 3am, Sunday 5pm to 3am. Beer begins at 46SEK ($9.20/£4.60), and items on the bar menu cost 95SEK to 145SEK ($19–$29/£10–£15). The Nightclub Kolingen is a dance club nightly from 10pm to about 3am. It charges the same food and drink prices as the pub, and you must be at least 23 to enter. Kornhamnstorg 59B. ℂ **08/20-10-92.** Cover 60SEK–80SEK ($12–$16/£6–£8) after 8pm. T-bana: Gamla Stan.

Stampen   This pub attracts crowds of music lovers in their 40s and 50s, who crowd in to enjoy live Dixieland, New Orleans, and mainstream jazz, and swing music from the 1920s, 1930s, and 1940s. On Tuesdays, guests come for rock 'n' roll from the 1950s and 1960s. In summer, an outdoor veranda is open when the weather permits. Year-round, a menagerie of stuffed animals and lots of old, whimsical antiques are suspended from the high ceiling. The club has two stages, and there's dancing downstairs almost every night. It's open Monday to Thursday 8pm to 1am, Friday to Saturday 8pm to 2am. Stora Nygatan 5. ℂ **08/20-57-93.** www.stampen.se. No cover. T-bana: Gamla Stan.

Casinos

Casino Cosmopol   Stockholm's world-class casino is installed in the Palladium, a grand old movie house dating from 1918. Housing two restaurants and four bars, the casino is spread across four floors. Guests, who must be at least 20 years old, can play such classic games as American roulette, blackjack, Punto Banco, and seven-card stud. It's open daily 1pm to 4am. Kungsgatan 22. ℂ **08/781-88-00.** www.casinocosmopol.se. Cover 40SEK ($8/£4). T-bana Hötorget.

The Bar Scene

Blue Moon Bar   This street-level bar and basement bar functions as a bar, restaurant, and nightclub. Its chic, modern decor attracts a bevy of supermodels and TV actors, who also come to hear a wide range of recorded music—everything from ABBA to Bob Marley. It's open nightly from 8pm to 4am. Birgerjarlsgatan 29. ℂ **08/20-14-11.** www.bluemoon bar.se. Cover 85SEK–125SEK ($17–$25/£8.50–£13). T-bana: Östermalmstorg.

Cadier Bar ★   This bar, positioned on the lobby level of the also-recommended Grand Hotel, is one of the most famous and plushest in Europe. From its windows, you'll have a view of a venue that was lavishly renovated in 2006, as well as Stockholm's harbor and its Royal Palace. Light meals—open-faced sandwiches and smoked salmon—are served throughout the day and evening. Drinks cost from 120SEK to 195SEK ($24–$39/£12–£20); imported beer runs 65SEK ($13/£6.50). It's open Monday to Saturday 11am to 2am, Sunday 11am to 12:30am; a piano player performs Wednesday to Saturday from 9:30pm to 1:30am. In the Grand Hotel, Södra Blasieholmshamnen 8. ℂ **08/679-35-85.** T-bana: Kungsträdgården.

Gondolen　We think the architecture here is as impressive as the view, and that's saying a lot—the view encompasses Lake Malar, the open sea, and huge areas of downtown Stockholm. Partly suspended beneath a pedestrian footbridge that soars above the narrow channel separating the island of Gamla Stan from the island of Södermalm, this engineering triumph was executed in 1935. An elevator hauls customers (without charge) up the equivalent of 11 stories to the '40s-style restaurant. You'll pay 90SEK ($18/£9) for a whiskey with soda. It's open Monday to Friday 11:30am to 1am, Saturday from 4pm to 1am. Stadtsgården 6. ✆ 08/641-70-90. www.eriks.se. T-bana: Slussen.

Icebar ★★ (Finds　Located in the Nordic Sea Hotel, this is literally Stockholm's "coolest" bar—it's the world's first permanent ice bar, opened in 2001 in the heart of Stockholm. Amazingly, the interior is kept at temperatures of 27°F (–3°C) all year. The decor and all the interior fittings, right down to the cocktail glasses themselves, are made of pure, clear ice shipped down from the Torne River in Sweden's Arctic north. Dress as you would for a dog-sled ride in Alaska; if you own one of those fabulous Swedish fur coats, the Icebar would be the place to wear it. Otherwise, a staff member will give you a parka, with a hood, to keep you warm within this architectural, constantly refrigerated oddity. In the bar, you can order any drink from a Bahama Mama to an Alabama Slammer, although you may have to order liquor-laced coffee to keep warm. Be warned that advance reservations are required; reservations are also tightly controlled, with groups entering and leaving at intervals of about every 40 minutes. Vasaplan 4–7. ✆ 08/50-56-31-24. www.nordicseahotel.se. T-bana: Centralen.

Fenix Bar and Mest Bar　These loosely related bars lie within a few steps of one another on a busy pedestrian street in the heart of Södermalm. Both are decorated with late Victorian accessories. The Mest Bar emphasizes sports more than the Fenix, which is more suitable to pickups, mainly of the straight variety. Both bars are open daily 5pm to 1am, with a beer costing 55SEK ($11/£5.50). Fenix Bar: Götgatan 40. ✆ 08/640-45-06. Mest Bar: Götgatan 44. ✆ 08/641-36-53. T-bana: Björnsträdgård.

Pontus! ★　Near the Stureplan in the very heart of Stockholm, this is a three-level nightlife beacon promising a hot night on the town. It's fashionable and fun, and if you really want to make a night of it, hang out in the chic oysters-and-champagne bar. There's also a cocktail bar on site, plus a sushi bar, even a dim sum station. For more formal dining, there's also a full-fledged restaurant. The bartender's special is called a "Dragon's Kiss" (with fresh ginger juice and Absolut). Open Monday 11am to 2pm and 5pm to midnight; Tuesday to Friday 11:30am to 2pm and 7pm to 1am; Saturday 5pm to 1am. Brunnsgatan 1. ✆ 08/545-273-00. T-bana: Östermalmstorg.

Sturehof　Since 1897, this pub and restaurant has been one of Stockholm's major drinking and dining venues. In the exact center of the city, it is now surrounded by urban sprawl and is attached to an arcade with other restaurants and shops. It remains a pleasant refuge from the city's congestion and is popular as both an after-work bar and a restaurant. It's open Monday to Friday 11am to 2am, Saturday noon to 2am, and Sunday 1pm to 2am. Stureplan 2. ✆ 08/440-57-30. www.sturehofgruppen.se. T-bana: Östermalmstorg.

LATE-NIGHT BITES

Mississippi Inn　For that late-night snack, this is a good choice if you dig American grub with some South of the Border specialties, such as huevos rancheros or quesadillas with fresh salsa. A lot of night-prowling young people show up here before midnight to dig into the barbecue ribs or juicy burgers. The inn also makes the best pancakes in town.

Often the Swedes eat these at night instead of at breakfast, and they come with assorted berries (the blueberries are a particular favorite), chocolate chips, or pecans. Wine is sold by the glass along with a selection of beers and Guinness, even apple cider. Open Monday to Friday 5pm to midnight, Saturday and Sunday noon to midnight. Nytorgsgatan 33. ✆ 08/642-43-80. T-bana: Medborgarplatsen.

---

7 SIDE TRIPS FROM STOCKHOLM

Some of Sweden's best-known attractions are clustered around Lake Mälaren, including the centuries-old villages and castles of Uppsala and Gripsholm that revive the pomp and glory of the 16th-century Vasa dynasty. You can spend a very busy day exploring Sigtuna, Skokloster Castle, Uppsala, and Gamla Uppsala, and stay overnight in Sigtuna or Uppsala, where there are good hotels. Another easy day trip is to Gripsholm Castle in Mariefred or Tullgarn Palace.

The boat trip from Klara Mälarstrand in Stockholm is justifiably popular. It leaves at 9:45am, goes along the beautiful waterway of Mälaren and the Fyris River to Sigtuna—where it stops for 2 hours—and arrives at Uppsala at 5pm. Here you can visit the cathedral and other sights, dine, and then take the 45-minute train trip back to Stockholm. Trains run daily every hour until 11pm.

SIGTUNA ★

48km (30 miles) NW of Stockholm

Sigtuna is Sweden's oldest town and its first capital. This time-warped village—founded in A.D. 980—lies on the shores of Lake Mälaren, northwest of Stockholm. You'll want to allot 2 or 3 hours of your time to soaking up the past here, namely the traces of Sigtuna's Viking and early Christian heritage that can be seen throughout town.

The prime attraction in town is **Stora Gatan ★★**, the main street since the Middle Ages. It's lined with pastel-painted wooden-framed buildings from the 1800s and shops and cafes likely to distract you from your stroll. This street is believed to be the oldest one in Sweden that still follows its original route.

In the Middle Ages, Sigtuna was a great place of worship and became known for its churches, which are mostly in ruins today. Along Prästgatan you can still see the ruins of **St. Lars** and **St. Per.** St. Per was actually Sweden's first cathedral. Nearby stands **Mariakyrkan,** the oldest brick-built building in Sigtuna; originally a Dominican friars' abbey, it was consecrated back in 1247. After Gustav Vasa demolished the monastery, Maria became a parish church in 1529. We like to come here to listen to the summer concerts, though the display of restored medieval paintings is also worth a look. It is open daily from 9am to 8pm in July and August (or 9am–4pm off-season).

If you have time, visit the **Sigtuna Museum,** Storgatan 55 (✆ **08/591-266-70;** www. sigtunamuseum.se), an archaeological museum that features early medieval artifacts found in the surrounding area. You'll see gold rings, runic inscriptions, and coins, as well as exclusive objects from Russia and Byzantium. You can also skip this one with no harm done. Admission is 20SEK ($4/£2) for adults, 10SEK ($2/£1) for seniors and students, or free for those under 20. Hours are June to August daily noon to 4pm; September to May Tuesday to Sunday noon to 4pm.

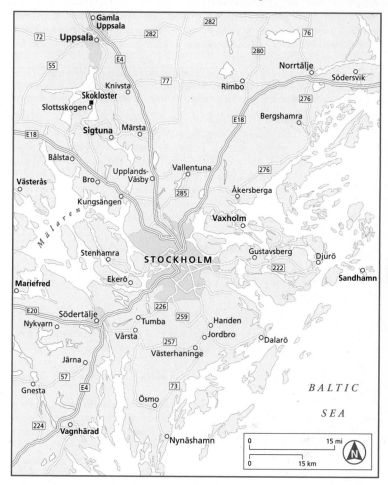

One of the reasons for Sigtuna's resurgence is the **Sigtuna Foundation** (see below), a Lutheran retreat and cultural center founded near the turn of the 20th century and often frequented by writers. It's open to the public daily from 1 to 3pm.

Daily buses and trains connect Stockholm to Sigtuna and Uppsala. From Stockholm, take a train to Märsta, then a bus for the 10-minute ride to Sigtuna.

Where to Stay & Dine

Sigtuna Foundation (Finds)   A stay at this massive building might provide one of your most memorable stopovers in Sweden. Intended as a center where sociological and philosophical viewpoints can be aired, the 1917 structure is more a way of life than a hotel. Over the years, guest lecturers have included the Dalai Lama, various Indian gurus, and many of postwar Europe's leading theologians. The establishment functions as both a conference center and a guesthouse. There's no proselytizing, although there might be opportunities to share experiences. The guest rooms have been refurbished in a bland style, and modern bathrooms with tub/showers were added; the grounds are more appealing, with secluded courtyards, lush rose and herb gardens, and fountains. To guarantee a room, be sure to make arrangements in advance. The foundation is less than 1.5km (1 mile) from the town center.

Manfred Björkquists Allé 2–4, S-193 31 Sigtuna. ✆ **08/592-589-00.** Fax 08/592-589-99. www.sigtuna stiftelsen.se. 62 units. 1,500SEK ($300/£150) double. Rates include breakfast. AE, DC, MC, V. Free parking. Bus: 570 or 575. **Amenities:** Restaurant; lounge; rooms for those w/limited mobility. *In room:* No phone.

Sigtuna Stads Hotell ★ The Sigtuna Foundation may be a bit stifling unless you're stalking the Dalai Lama seeking to learn "the word." We prefer the graciousness of this Victorian-style hotel in the town center. It not only offers the most comfortable, albeit old-fashioned, rooms in town, but it has the best cuisine. Full meals are served daily Monday to Friday 11:30am to 4pm and 5 to 11pm, Saturday noon to 4pm and 5 to 11pm, with dinners costing 275SEK to 330SEK ($55–$66/£28–£33). Sample such dishes as steamed halibut with lobster sauce and the milk-fed veal with a pumpkin and goat-cheese ravioli. For starters, try cauliflower soup graced with truffles or the duck-liver terrine with rose hip.

Stora Nygatan 3, S-193 00 Sigtuna. ✆ **08/592-501-00.** Fax 08/592-515-87. www.sigtunastadshotell.se. 26 units. Mon–Thurs 2,490SEK–2,590SEK ($498–$518/£249–£259) double, 3,975SEK ($795/£398) suite; Fri–Sun 2,090–2,190SEK ($418–$438/£209–£219) double, 2,990SEK ($598/£299) suite. Rates include breakfast. AE, DC, MC, V. Free parking. Bus: 570 or 575. **Amenities:** Restaurant; bar; spa; sauna; room service. *In room:* TV, minibar, hair dryer.

A Side Trip to Skokloster

Skokloster Castle ★★ The best way to plan a day trip from Stockholm is to spend the morning touring the old streets of Sigtuna, followed by an afternoon touring Skokloster, one of the great baroque museums of the north. The village of Skokloster lies at Lake Mälaren, 65km (40 miles) northwest of Stockholm, but only a 26km (16 mile) drive northeast of Sigtuna—it's signposted.

The great Nicodemus Tessin the Elder, whose name appears frequently in books devoted to European architecture, collaborated with others on this grand pile of baroque architecture (1654–76). Flanked by two towers at each end, which are crowned by cupolas and lanterns, the castle represents perfect symmetry. Its recreation of Sweden's golden age comes across most strongly through the richly decorated apartments, boasting an abundance of stucco ornamentation. Antiques, applied art, tapestries, textiles, ceramics, and even arms are on display. The collection of paintings alone has been called priceless.

Who could afford to buy all this loot? The palace was commissioned by Field Marshal Carl Gustav Wrangel, but he didn't pay for all these objets d'art. They came from the spoils of war. If the weather's fair, you can request a picnic basket at the on-site cafe and enjoy it on the landscaped grounds.

S-746 96 Sklokloster. ✆ **018/402-30-70.** www.skoklostersslott.se. Admission 75SEK ($15/£7.50) adults, free 18 and under. Guided tours in English are offered on the hour: May daily noon–3pm; June–Aug daily 11am–4pm; Sept Mon–Fri 1pm and 3pm; Sat–Sun noon–3pm; Oct Mon–Fri 1pm, Sat–Sun noon–3pm; Apr Sat–Sun noon–3pm. Closed Nov–Mar. From Stockholm, take the train to Bålsta, then bus 894.

Skokloster Motor Museum ★ On the palace grounds, this museum houses the largest collection of vintage automobiles and motorcycles in the country. One of the most

notable cars is a 1905 8-horsepower De Dion Bouton, but the oldest car dates from
1898. In all, there are about 40 vintage vehicles in the collection.

S-746 96 Sklokloster. ✆ **018/38-61-06.** Admission 75SEK ($15/£7.50) adults, free 18 and under. Apr–Sept daily noon–4pm. From Stockholm, take the train to Bålsta, then bus 894.

UPPSALA ★★★
68km (42 miles) NW of Stockholm

Uppsala, Sweden's major university city, is so approachable, it may appear smaller than it is. Yet it is the fourth largest city in this country, and the single most popular day trip from Stockholm—for good reason. Not only does it have a great university, but it has a grand 15th-century cathedral and a lot of history. Even Queen Christina once held court here, and the church is still the seat of the archbishop, making it the ecclesiastical capital of Sweden.

As for the university, it's got quite a pedigree, going back to 1477. With a student population hovering around 30,000, Uppsala is the Oxford of Sweden. The city, lying at the northern tip of Lake Mälaren, is also riddled with beautiful green parks, which isn't surprising, considering that this was the hometown of the world's most famous botanist, Carl von Linné (1707–78), also known as Carl Linnaeus.

Film buffs know that Uppsala was the birthplace of the great director Ingmar Bergman (no relation to another great Swede, Ingrid Bergman). Ingmar used Uppsala as a setting for one of his most classic films, *Fanny and Alexander.*

The best time to visit Uppsala is on April 30, Walpurgis Eve, when the academic community celebrates the rebirth of spring with a torchlight parade. The festivities last until dawn throughout the 13 student "nations" (residential halls).

Essentials
GETTING THERE The **train** from Stockholm's Central Station takes about 45 minutes. Trains leave about every hour during peak hours. Some visitors spend the day in Uppsala and return to Stockholm on the commuter train in the late afternoon. Eurailpass holders ride free. **Boats** between Uppsala and Skokloster depart Uppsala daily at 11am and 7:30pm, returning to Uppsala at 5:45 and 11:30pm. Round-trip passage costs 200SEK ($40/£20). For details, check with the tourist office in any of the towns or call ✆ **070/293-81-61.**

VISITOR INFORMATION The **Tourist Information Office** is at Fyris Torg 8 (✆ **018/727-48-00;** www.uppsalatourism.se). It's open Monday to Friday 10am to 6pm, Saturday 10am to 3pm, and Sunday 11am to 3pm (July to mid-Aug).

GETTING AROUND Buses come in from the surrounding suburbs to the center of Uppsala and arrive at the Central Station, where the trains also arrive. Once you arrive in the center of Uppsala, all the major attractions are within easy walking distance. However, if you're going to explore Gamla Uppsala (see the box below), you need to take bus no. 2 or 54, departing from the Central Station.

To get your bearings, it helps to know that the small Frysiån River runs through the town, and the main square, Stora Torget, leads to a pedestrian shopping district.

Seeing the Sights
Carolina Rediviva (University Library) ★ This is one of the greatest of all Scandinavian libraries. At the end of Drottninggatan is the Carolina Rediviva, with more than 5 million volumes and 40,000 manuscripts, including many rare works from the Middle

Ages. The most treasured manuscript is the *Codex Argenteus* or **Silver Bible** ★★★. Displayed in the exhibit room, it was translated into Gothic in the middle of the 3rd century and copied in about A.D. 525. It's the only book extant in old Gothic script, having been written in silver ink on purple vellum. Also worth seeing is the 1539 *Carta Marina,* the earliest map of Sweden and its neighboring countries.

Drottninggatan. ☏ **018/471-39-00.** Admission 20SEK ($4/£2) adults, free for children under 12. Exhibit room Mon–Fri 9am–8pm, Sat 10am–5pm. Bus: 6, 7, or 22.

Linnaeus Garden & Museum ★   You don't have to be a botanist to pay a visit to the house and gardens of Uppsala's most famous son. (Forgive us, Ingmar Bergman.) Swedish botanist Carl von Linné (or Linnaeus) developed a classification system for the world's plants and flowers, and his garden and former home are on the spot of Uppsala University's miniature baroque botanical garden. Linnaeus, who arranged the plants according to his "sexual classification system," left detailed sketches and descriptions of the garden, which have been faithfully followed.

Linnaeus was a professor of theoretical medicine, including botany, pharmacology, and zoology, at Uppsala University. You can visit his house, which has been restored to its original design, and an art gallery that exhibits the works of contemporary local artists.

Svartbäcksgatan 27. ☏ **018/13-65-40** for the museum, or 018/471-25-76 for the garden. www.linnaeus. uu.se. Museum and gardens 50SEK ($10/£5) adults, free for children under 16. Museum May–Sept 30 daily 11am–5pm. Closed Sept 30–Apr 30. Gardens May–Sept daily 11am–8pm. Closed Oct–Apr. Walk straight from the train station to Kungsgatan, turn right, and walk about 10 min.

Uppsala Domkyrka ★★   It is said that medieval church builders in Uppsala set out to create a cathedral that would outdazzle the great Trondheim Cathedral in the ancient city in Norway. Although they didn't achieve that lofty mission, they did create Sweden's most celebrated Gothic building, which has remained the country's coronation church for 3 centuries. It's a notable, elegant building, but a bit soulless, perhaps because of all the fires that have swept through it over the ages. The largest cathedral in Scandinavia, this twin-spired Gothic structure stands nearly 120m (394 ft.) tall. Founded in the 13th century, it received the most damage in 1702 in a disastrous fire.

Among the regal figures buried in the crypt is Gustav Vasa. The remains of St. Erik, patron saint of Sweden, are entombed in a silver shrine, and one of the chapels is filled with 14th-century wall paintings recounting his legend. The botanist Linnaeus and the philosopher-theologian Swedenborg are also interred here. A small museum displays ecclesiastical relics.

Domkyrkoplan 2. ☏ **018/18-71-73.** www.uppsaladomkyrka.se. Free admission to cathedral. Museum 30SEK ($6/£3) adults, free for children under 16. Cathedral daily 8am–6pm. Museum May–Sept daily 10am–5pm; Sept–Mar daily 10:30am–1:30pm. Bus: 1.

Museum Gustavianum ★ ⓕ**Finds**   Across from the cathedral stands the best of this university city's museums and Uppsala University's oldest preserved building. It even houses one of only seven ancient anatomical theaters in the world to get by on natural light. Gruesome public dissections that took place in the 1663 theater were lit by a sun-crested cupola, one of Uppsala's distinctive landmarks. The museum has a number of other attractions, none more attention-grabbing than the **Augsburg Cabinet of Curiosities** ★★, a gift to King Gustav II Adolf from the German city of Augsburg in 1632. It is an ebony cabinet encrusted with gemstones and filled with drawers and "pigeonholes" in which the king placed his precious objects (though someone moved them long

ATTRACTIONS ●
Carolina Rediviva (University Library) **10**
Gamla Uppsala **2**
Linnaeus Garden & Museum **4**
Museum Gustavianum **9**
Uppsala Domkyrka **8**

DINING ◆
Domtrappkällaren **7**
Flustret **11**
Restaurant Odinsborg **1**

ACCOMMODATIONS ■
Clarion Hotel Gillet **5**
Diakonistiftelsen Samariterhemmet **12**
First Hotel Linné **3**
Scandic Hotel Uplandia **6**

6

Gamla Uppsala ★★

About 15 centuries ago, **"Old Uppsala"** ★ was the capital of the Svea kingdom. In its midst was a grove set aside for human and animal sacrifices. Viking burial mounds dating from the 6th century are believed to contain the pyres of three kings.

Nearby, on the site of an old pagan temple, is a 12th-century **parish church,** once badly damaged by fire and never properly restored. Indeed, some people describe it as a stave church that turned to stone. Before Uppsala Cathedral was built, Swedish kings were crowned here.

Across from the church is the **Stiftelsen Upplandsmuseet,** Sankt Erikstoth 10 (© 018/16-91-00), an open-air museum with reassembled buildings that depicts peasant life in Uppland. Admission is free, and it's open year-round from Tuesday to Sunday noon to 5pm.

Gamla Uppsala, about 5km (3 miles) north of the commercial heart of Uppsala, is easily accessible by bus no. 2 or 24, both of which leave frequently from the Central Station.

ago). The museum also includes archaeological exhibitions, from Swedish prehistory to the Middle Ages. Some of the rarer pieces are from the Mediterranean and the Nile Valley, including the sarcophagus of Khonsumes, a priest from the 21st dynasty. In the historical exhibition on the ground floor, you can see everything from student lecture notes from the first term in 1477—the year the university was founded—to photographs and historical artifacts showing the development of the institution over the years as a seat of learning.

Akademigatan 3. © 018/471-75-71. www.gustavianum.uu.se. Admission 40SEK ($8/£4) adults, 30SEK ($6/£3) students and seniors, free for children under 12. Mid-May to mid-Sept Tues–Sun 10am–4pm; off season Tues–Sun 11am–4pm. Bus: 1, 2, 51, or 53.

Where to Stay

Diakonistiftelsen Samariterhemmet Ⓥalue   One of the best bargains in town, this large guesthouse, run by a Christian charity, has spotless rooms with comfortable beds. Some units have neatly kept bathrooms with shower units. You can use the kitchenette with a refrigerator, and there's a TV lounge. Most of the units evoke a ritzy college dormitory.

Samaritergränd 2, S-753 19 Uppsala. © **018/56-40-00.** Fax 018/10-83-75. www.svenskakyrkan.se/ samariterhemmet. 25 units, 12 with bathroom. 760SEK ($152/£76) double without bathroom; 860SEK ($172/£86) double with bathroom. Rates include breakfast. MC, V. **Amenities:** Breakfast room; lounge; nonsmoking rooms. In room: No phone.

First Hotel Linné ★   At the edge of Linnaeus Garden, this is one of the best-managed and most inviting hotels in town. You'll probably be able to see Linnaeus's lovely garden from your window. The great botanist would probably find the interior of the hotel compatible with his garden, because the decorators used floral patterns with warm red tones. It's especially inviting in winter when a large open fire blazes away. The rooms feature modern furniture and plumbing, and each unit has a neatly kept bathroom. One drawback is that the less expensive doubles are a bit cramped.

Skolgatan 45, S-75332 Uppsala. ✆ **018/10-20-00.** Fax 018/13-75-97. www.firsthotels.com. 116 units.
Sun–Thurs 751SEK–1,549SEK ($150–$310/£75–£155) double, from 1,899SEK ($380/£190) suite; Fri–Sat
829SEK–1,129SEK ($166–$226/£83–£113) double, from 1,299SEK ($260/£130) suite. Rates include break-
fast. AE, DC, MC, V. Parking 100SEK ($20/£10). **Amenities:** Restaurant; bar; sauna; limited room service;
laundry service; dry cleaning; nonsmoking rooms; rooms for those w/limited mobility. *In room:* TV, minibar, hair dryer, safe, Wi-Fi.

Clarion Hotel Gillet ★   Although it was built in 1972, this attractively designed
hotel comes in second when stacked up against the Scandic Hotel (see below). Favored
by businessmen, it also attracts parents who are visiting their sons and daughters at the
university. The bedrooms are well furnished and spacious, with comfortable furnishings
standing on hardwood floors set against a backdrop of pastel walls. Doubles are rated
superior or deluxe, and you can rent large or "mini" suites. The location is in the center
of Uppsala, about a 5-minute walk from the Central Station. The building itself dates
from the 19th century but has known many restorations and owners over the years.
Dragarbrunnsgatan 23, S-75320 Uppsala. ✆ **018/68-18-00.** Fax 018/68-18-18. www.clariongillet.se. 161
units. 850SEK–1,795SEK ($170–$359/£85–£180) double; from 2,200SEK ($440/£220) suite. Rates include
breakfast. AE, DC, MC, V. Parking 170SEK ($34/£17). Bus: 801. **Amenities:** Restaurant; bar; indoor heated
pool; fitness center; sauna; room service; massage; laundry service; dry cleaning; nonsmoking rooms;
rooms for those w/limited mobility. *In room:* A/C, TV, minibar (in some), hair dryer, Wi-Fi.

Scandic Hotel Uplandia ★★   Its location may not be glamorous—it's next to the
bus terminal—but this is the best hotel in town. It's more cutting edge than the Clarion
because of its sophisticated aura and high-tech amenities. Construction took place in two
stages in the 1960s and early 1980s, but architects harmoniously blended it all together.
Rooms in the older section are just as well appointed and comfortable as in the newer
wings, and all units are furnished with renovated, tiled bathrooms equipped with tub/
shower combinations. There is much use of blond wood. We've found the staff helpful
and efficient, and the designers have softened some of the impersonal corners, making
for a warm, inviting ambience. However, the cuisine is better at the Gillet.
Dragarbrunnsgatan 32, S-753 20 Uppsala. ✆ **018/495-26-00.** Fax 018/495-26-11. www.scandic-hotels.
com. 133 units. 740SEK–1,860SEK ($148–$372/£74–£186) double; 1,700SEK–2,620SEK ($340–$524/£170–
£262) suite. Rates include breakfast. AE, DC, MC, V. Parking 30SEK ($6/£3). **Amenities:** 2 restaurants; bar;
fitness room; sauna; room service (7am–11pm); laundry service; dry cleaning; nonsmoking rooms; rooms
for those w/limited mobility. *In room:* A/C (in some), TV, hair dryer, Wi-Fi.

Where to Dine

Domtrappkällaren ★★ SWEDISH   No other restaurant in Uppsala can compete
with this one for charm and atmosphere, although it was previously a prison. It was built
in the town center on the ruins of 12th-century cathedral buildings. The vaulted ceilings
and copies of Jacobean paintings in the main dining room complement the low-ceilinged, sun-flooded intimacy of the upper floors. On request, you can dine in a narrow
room where unruly students were imprisoned in the Middle Ages, or in one that served
as a classroom in the 17th century. The chef invariably chooses the very finest ingredients, which he handles with a razor-sharp technique in dishes from poached filet of
reindeer with a horseradish-flavored zabaglione to filet of beef flambé served with a sauce
flavored with Parma ham and thyme. Some dishes come as a surprise: We think we won't
like it; the chef insists, and then we love it—one example being the potato pancakes
served with sautéed bits of salt pork and accompanied by lingonberry jam. We don't
know who's in charge of desserts, but we applaud their inventiveness: Two perfect end-
ings to any meal are the cold cloudberry soup with an almond-and-caramel sweet bread
or the passion fruit soufflé with homemade vanilla ice cream.

Sankt Eriksgränd 15. ℭ **018/13-09-55.** www.domtrappkallaren.se. Reservations recommended. Lunch main courses 165SEK–185SEK ($33–$37/£17–£19), dinner main courses 165SEK–275SEK ($33–$55/£17–£28); 2-course menu 235SEK ($47/£24); 3-course menu 275SEK ($55/£28). Mon–Fri 11am–2:30pm and 5–11pm; Sat 1–11pm; Sun 1–8pm. Closed Dec 24–26. Bus: 2.

Flustret FRENCH   This is a good choice if you're overnighting in Uppsala and want to combine fine cuisine with entertainment. In a riverside setting near the castle, this pavilion is an exact replica of its predecessor, a demolished Victorian building. Its spacious ground-floor dining room serves first-rate meals, offered by one of the best wait-staffs in town (some of whom are university students). We found nothing on the menu more elegant and good tasting than the lobster soup as an appetizer. Although the kitchen relies a bit on the always-dependable salmon, the chefs are daring enough to take on such classic dishes as veal steak Oscar or pheasant Veronique. The most festive dessert is bananas flambé. A dance club on the second floor is open Thursday to Saturday 3pm to 3am, charging no cover.

Svandammen. ℭ **018/10-04-44.** www.flustret.se. Reservations recommended. Main courses 125SEK–220SEK ($25–$44/£13–£22). AE, DC, MC, V. Thurs–Sat 5pm–midnight. Bus: 24.

Restaurant Odinsborg ★ (Value) SWEDISH   Come here if you have an appetite like those Vikings of yore who once roamed the grounds of Gamla Uppsala. In a century-old former private house, this restaurant serves strictly old-fashioned Swedish food. The culinary highlight in the Viking-theme dining room is the smorgasbord—this place laboriously prepares and lays out the sort of traditional roster of foods you might expect at a Swedish family celebration. Menu items include excellent preparations of fried herring, marinated salmon, smoked eel, and whitefish with a dill-flavored butter sauce. You might also try roasted lamb, chicken filets, or steak. The smorgasbord is served only from May to August, attracting far more visitors from abroad than locals. Otherwise, chefs prepare a finely honed a la carte menu during the cold months.

Near the burial grounds, Gamla Uppsala (there's no actual street address). ℭ **018/32-35-25.** www. odinsborg.com. Reservations recommended. Main courses 119SEK–199SEK ($24–$40/£12–£20); set menus 259SEK–359SEK ($52–$72/£26–£36). AE, DC, MC, V. Daily noon–6pm.

GRIPSHOLM CASTLE ★★

60km (37 miles) W of Stockholm

On one of the precious few sunny Stockholm summer days, we would suggest leaving the city altogether—by boat—for **Mariefred** ("Marie's Place") and Gripsholms Slott. Mariefred, an idyllic little town painted in pastels, invites wandering, but it is really the gateway to Gripsholms, constructed as a fortress for King Gustav Vasa in 1537 and one of the best-preserved castles in Sweden.

To the south of town, Gripsholms Slott eats up a small island in Lake Mälaren with its massive structures, including four round brick towers and two courtyards. This castle was often used by royals to stash bothersome fellow royals. Queen Hedvig Eleonora, reportedly a busybody interfering in politics, was banished here after her husband's death. The son of Gustav Vasa, King Erik XIV, exiled his brother Johan here.

There are worse places to have been banished. Today, you can visit three floors filled with antiques and objets d'art collected over a period of 4 centuries. The castle also houses a national portrait gallery of Sweden, with paintings that range from the great Gustav Vasa himself to today's ruling King and Queen.

During the reign of the 18th-century "actor-king," Gustav III, the **Gripsholm theater** ★★ was erected here. A ham actor, the king cast himself as the star in both comedy and drama. It is one of the best-preserved theaters of its era in Sweden, though not as magnificent as the Drottningholm Theater (p. 145).

Gripsholm Castle is 68km (42 miles) southwest of Stockholm. By **car,** follow E20 south; you can drive right to the castle parking lot. To get to Gripsholm Castle, take the train from Stockholm central to Läggesta. From Läggesta, catch a bus to the center of Mariefred. Better yet, **boats** leave from mid-May to September at 10am from Klara Mälarstrand Pier (250SEK/$50/£25 round-trip) in Stockholm. The castle is a 10-minute walk from the center of Mariefred.

Even though Gripsholm (© **0159/101-94;** www.royalcourt.se) was last occupied by royalty (Charles XV) in 1864, it's still a royal castle. It's open May 15 to September 15 daily 10am to 4pm; September 16 to May 14 Saturday and Sunday from noon to 3pm, and closed December 21 to January 1. Admission is 70SEK ($14/£7) for adults, 35SEK ($7/£3.50) ages 7 to 18, free for children 7 and under.

Where to Stay

Gripsholms Värdshus & Hotel ★★   Most visitors leave Mariefred in the late afternoon and return to Stockholm at night. But if you have a night to spend in the surrounding environs of Stockholm, stay at this oldest inn in Sweden, dating from 1609. During the reign of King Karl XI, local townspeople protested over having to house and feed His Majesty's entourage when he was visiting Gripsholms. This led to the creation of this inn, which in 1989 was restored and opened to the public.

A few steps from the village church from 1624, Mariefreds Kyrka, the inn also lies only a 10-minute walk from the castle. Painted a golden yellow and built of wood, it was constructed on the site of an old monastery. Public rooms are filled with art, antiques, timbers, and other artifacts discovered during the renovations. The comfortable bedrooms are spacious and airy with wooden floors—they're the finest in the area. Each room is individually decorated and bathrooms are equipped with tub/shower combinations and, as a bow to modern tastes, heated floors and towel racks.

The hotel has the best restaurant in the region (see "Where to Dine," below).

Kyrkogatan 1, S-647 23 Mariefred. © **0159/347-50.** Fax 0159/347-77. www.gripsholms-vardshus.se. 45 units. 1,690SEK–2,290SEK ($338–$458/£169–£229) double; 500SEK–1,500SEK ($100–$300/£50–£150) supplement for suite. Rates include breakfast. AE, DC, MC, V. **Amenities:** Restaurant; bar; sauna; 24-hr. room service; laundry service; dry cleaning; 1 room for those w/limited mobility. *In room:* A/C, TV, minibar, hair dryer, trouser press, safe, Jacuzzi (in suites), Wi-Fi.

Where to Dine

Gripsholms Värdshus Restaurant ★ SWEDISH/INTERNATIONAL   You'll get panoramic views and the finest food in town if you wisely make this your dining choice. In summer we always opt for a table on the veranda that opens onto a panoramic sweep of Gripsholm Bay. The menu is adjusted to take advantage of the best produce, meats, or game of any given season. We like the way the chefs can turn out tasty Swedish fare based on traditional recipes but can also segue into modern cooking using global cuisine for inspiration.

Breast of guinea fowl has always been served in Sweden, but here it comes with caramelized turnips and a lemon and Szechuan pepper gravy. Grilled halibut is made even more delectable when accompanied by a red paprika cream sauce and a basil-flavored ratatouille. Lamb cutlets are spiced up with a shallot-studded mustard sauce, and herb-flavored baked saddle of venison comes with a feathery-light mushroom pastry. We still remember that raspberry mousse parfait we had for dessert. Tastings in the wine cellar can also be arranged.

Kyrkogatan 1. ℂ **0159/347-50.** Reservations recommended. Main courses 145SEK–295SEK ($29–$59/£15–£30). AE, DC, MC, V. Midsummer daily noon–10pm; rest of year Mon–Fri noon–2pm, Mon–Sat 6–10pm, Sun 12:30–4pm.

TULLGARN PALACE ★

72km (45 miles) S of Stockholm

A visit to this former royal palace near Trosa in Sörmland—just an hour's drive from Stockholm—can be turned into so much more. You can feast on wild hogs cooked over an open fire, eating your meal by the cool lake, or you can picnic beside one of the dams in the area. If you're lucky, your visit can be tied in with one of the outdoor cultural performances presented here. At the very least, you can enjoy a cup of coffee and a Swedish pastry at the Stable Café or the Orangery.

As for the palace itself, it occupies a panoramic setting on a bay of the Baltic Sea, and was a favorite of Gustav V (1858–1950), the great-grandfather of Sweden's present king. The palace dates from the early part of the 1800s. In 1772, Gustav's younger brother, Fredrik Adolf, turned it into his summer retreat.

The grounds invite exploring, with a theater, an orangery, sculptured parks, and ponds. But the **palace interiors** ★★ are also filled with riches. The facade is austere, while the rooms themselves are a hodgepodge of elegant styles—rococo, Gustavian, and Victorian—that hold their own fascination. Much of the decor came about during the reigns of King Gustaf V and Sweden's Queen Victoria, who spent their summers here in those Belle Epoque days around the turn of the 20th century.

The palace (ℂ **08/555-720-11**) is 60km (37 miles) south of Stockholm. By **car,** take E4 south about 60km (37 miles) and turn right at the sign that directs you to Tullgarns Slott, near Vagnhärad. It's another half-kilometer (1/3 mile) to the palace. Getting here by public transportation is extremely inconvenient and not worth the trouble. You first have to take a train to Södertälje Södra (about 20 min.), and then wait for a bus to Trosa, which lies 7km (4 1/3 miles) south of the castle. From Trosa, you have to take a taxi the rest of the way. You could spend all morning just trying to get to the castle, so we recommend skipping it unless you have private transportation or endless amounts of time.

Admission is 60SEK ($12/£6) for adults, 30SEK ($6/£3) for students and children ages 7 to 18. The palace is open to the public on weekends from June to August. Guided tours leave the main entrance every hour from 11am to 4pm.

Where to Stay

Romantik Stadtshotell Trosa ★   The most charming and historically evocative hotel in the region lies in the heart of Trosa, a quiet hamlet 7km (4 1/3 miles) south of Tullgarns Castle. Built in 1867 of yellow-tinged bricks and set in the center of the town, it was enlarged and modernized in the early 1990s. Today it provides cozy, comfortable rooms with a hint of the aesthetics of yesteryear: wooden floors and a scattering of antique accessories, always coupled with color schemes of yellow and green. There are spalike facilities and a first-class restaurant on the premises that's open every day, year-round, for lunch and dinner.

Västra Langgatan 19, S-61921 Trosa. ℂ **0156/170-70.** Fax 0156/166-96. www.trosastadshotell.se. 44 units. July and Fri–Sat year-round 1,400SEK ($280/£140) double; rest of year 1,760SEK ($352/£176) double. Rates include breakfast. AE, DC, MC, V. **Amenities:** Restaurant; bar; fitness center; spa; Jacuzzi; sauna; massage; nonsmoking rooms; rooms for those w/limited mobility; solarium. *In room:* TV, hair dryer, Wi-Fi.

Tullgarns Värdshus SWEDISH/FRENCH   It's not often that you get to dine in a Swedish royal palace without an invitation. But you can do just that in a wing of Tullgarn Palace. Even better, you can order a picnic lunch to be consumed in the royal park. We've had better picnics, but it's the setting that counts here.

The restaurant has its own kind of charm and is a summer-only operation. The cooks here don't try to compete with the master chefs in the environs of Stockholm, but they serve substantial, reliable fare and even a few surprises such as pâté of wild boar. Though all the old favorites are available, including salted salmon with creamed potatoes, we recommend that you also try such dishes as breast of wild duck with a chicken liver mousse or poached filet of salmon with a chive-flavored butter sauce.

In Tullgarn Palace, Vagnhärad. (✆ **08/551-720-26.** Main courses 120SEK–250SEK ($24–$50/£12–£25); Sat–Sun buffet 250SEK ($50/£25). MC, V. May 15–Aug 29 Mon–Fri noon–2:30pm and 5–7pm; Sat–Sun noon–7pm. Closed Aug 30–May 14.

SANDHAMN, VAXHOLM & THE ARCHIPELAGO OF STOCKHOLM ★★★

50km (30 miles) E of City Center

Stockholm is in what the Swedes call a "garden of skerries," an archipelago with more than 24,000 islands and islets (and rocks merely jutting out of the water). The islands nearest the city have become part of the suburbs, thickly populated and connected to the mainland by car ferries or bridges. Many others are wild and largely deserted, attracting boaters for picnics and swimming. Summer homes dot still others. July is the peak vacation month, when yachts crowd the waters.

You can see the islands by taking a boat trip from Stockholm harbor. If you'd like to stop at a resort island, consider **Sandhamn,** where you'll find shops and restaurants. It takes about an hour to explore the entire island on foot. The beaches at the eastern tip are the best in the archipelago. **Vaxholm,** a bathing resort known as "the gateway to the northern archipelago," also makes a good stopover—it's one of our favorites. Artists and writers have traditionally been drawn to Vaxholm, and some hold exhibits during the summer, when the tourist influx quadruples the population. The west harbor and the main sea route to the north are filled with pleasure craft.

Essentials

GETTING THERE   Throughout the year (but more often in the summer), boats operated by several companies depart from in front of the Grand Hotel at Södra Blasieholmshamnen. Most of them are marked VAXHOLM and usually continue to Sandhamn after a stop in Vaxholm. Be sure to ask before boarding.

The trip from Stockholm through the archipelago to Sandhamn takes 3¹⁄₂ hours each way and costs 150SEK ($30/£15) one-way. The ferry trip to Vaxholm from Stockholm takes less than 40 minutes and costs 85SEK ($17/£8.50) one-way. There are no car ferries. If you plan lots of travel around the archipelago, consider buying an **Inter-Skerries Card** for 300SEK ($60/£30). The card allows 30 days of unlimited travel anywhere within the Stockholm archipelago for much less than the cost of individual tickets. Vaxholm-bound boats depart every hour during the summer (about five times a day in winter) from the Strömkagen, the piers outside the Grand Hotel. For information, call the steamship company **Vaxholmes Bolaget** (✆ **08/679-58-30;** www.waxholms bolaget.se).

Buses depart from the Central Station daily (unless inclement weather prevents it) every 30 minutes beginning at 6am. The last bus from Vaxholm leaves at 1am. A round-trip fare is 55SEK ($11/£5.50).

Organized Tours

Strömma Kanalbolaget (© **08/587-140-00;** www.strommakanalbolaget.se) offers a guided cruise in English through the canals and bays to Sandhamn. Tours depart from June to August at 10am and last 8 hours. The "Canal Cruise to Sandhamn" costs 275SEK ($55/£28); children under 12 pay half fare. The company also offers the "Thousand Island Cruise" through the Stockholm archipelago. From July to August 13, the cruise costs 995SEK ($199/£100) and includes lunch and a two-course dinner. Children under 12 enjoy the same deal for half price.

Where to Stay

Waxholms Hotell   A substantial, sturdy, and exceedingly comfortable hotel, the Waxholms opens onto views over the bay. Built in 1902, the bright yellow hotel lies at the pier where the ferries from Stockholm dock. Our favorite pastime here is sitting out on a starry night watching the archipelago's ships drift by. The midsize-to-spacious bedrooms are tastefully furnished and modernized, each with a well-kept bathroom. Even if you are visiting just for the day, as most people do, this hotel is your best bet for dining and drinking. An informal pub, Kabyssen, is at street level. One floor above is the Waxholms Hotell Restaurant (see "Where to Dine," below).

Hamngatan 2, S-185 21 Vaxholm. © **08/541-301-50.** Fax 08/541-313-76. www.waxholmshotell.se. 42 units. 1,125SEK–1,600SEK ($225–$320/£113–£160) double; 2,850SEK ($570/£285) suite. Rates include breakfast. AE, DC, MC, V. Closed Dec 24–Jan 1. Free parking. **Amenities:** 2 restaurants; bar; sauna; babysitting; laundry service; dry cleaning; nonsmoking rooms. *In room:* TV, hair dryer, Wi-Fi.

Where to Dine

In Vaxholm

Waxholms Hotell Restaurant ★ SEAFOOD   The chef says his specialties are "fish, fish—and more fish," and this is one cook who's telling the truth. Overlooking the water from the second floor of the previously recommended hotel, the dining room is the best place for cuisine in Vaxholm. We knew our meal would be good after we launched into the savory, garlic-laced mussel soup appetizer. The kitchen isn't ashamed to serve one of the most basic of all Swedish dishes—fried Baltic herring with mashed potatoes—and the cooks do it well. Taking advantage of the boundless sea here, the chefs also serve fried perch with a chanterelle sauce with bacon or an especially good sautéed filet of char dressed up with a grilled shellfish sausage and a mussel sauce. For dessert, we like the apple-and-nut pastry with homemade cinnamon ice cream and the raspberry and buckthorn mousse.

Hamngatan 2. © **08/541-301-50.** Reservations required in summer. Main courses 139SEK–308SEK ($28–$62/£14–£31). AE, DC, MC, V. Summer daily noon–10:30pm; off season daily noon–9pm. Closed Dec 24–Jan 1.

In Sandhamn

Sandhamns Värdshus ★ SWEDISH   This old favorite has been feeding hungry visitors from Stockholm since 1672; though some things have changed, the panoramic vista of the harbor remains timeless. The food has been much improved since when it served ordinary boiled fish and fried steak years ago. The present chefs are far more imaginative and know how to bring flavor to their concoctions. The chef's fish and shellfish casserole is the best we've sampled in the archipelago—it's flavored with fresh tomatoes, fennel, and lemongrass, and enhanced by a lime aioli and a slab of home-baked bread. Other dishes are loaded with tantalizing accompaniments without destroying their natural flavor, as with the grilled filet of pikeperch with fresh chanterelles, whitefish roe sauce, and a potato cake with fresh dill and chives.

Harbourfront. ℂ **08/571-530-51.** www.sandhamns-vardshus.se. Reservations required Sat–Sun. Main courses 112SEK–250SEK ($22–$50/£11–£25). AE, DC, MC, V. Mon–Thurs noon–2:30pm and 5–10pm; Fri noon–2:30pm and 5–10:30pm; Sat noon–10pm; Sun noon–3pm.

7

Gothenburg & Beyond

Let's face it: Every visitor to Sweden heads to Stockholm—and rightly so. But as any Gothenburger will tell you, they've got something to show you, too. Indeed, the city has one of Europe's largest student populations, and a general *joie de vivre* permeates the atmosphere. Prices are mercifully cheaper than in Stockholm, and the informal, relaxed mood is immediately catching. Locals think Stockholmers are a bit snobbish to strangers, as aloof as the late Greta Garbo. But in Gothenburg (pronounced *Yo*-te-bor-ee in Swedish), visitors are welcomed into local life and embraced with enthusiasm.

Regrettably, the whirlwind group tours that cover Gothenburg don't give visitors enough time to take in the town. The Göta River runs through the city, and boat trips here can be just as delightful as those in Stockholm; you can even go island hopping. Gothenburg also still suffers from its early-20th-century reputation of being a dull industrial center. Those days are long gone; what awaits you now is a sprawling, youthful metropolis filled with some of the brightest and best-looking people in Europe, a city in the process of escaping from its past.

Gothenburg, which received its city charter from Gustavus Adolphus II in 1621, has always been proud of its links to the sea, and of the shipbuilding industry that flourished here during the early 20th century. Now, alas, shipbuilding is in deep decline, so the city has shifted its economic base toward tourism and conventions. But Gothenburg, the "gateway to northern Europe," remains the country's chief port and second largest city. Canals, parks, and flower gardens enhance its appeal, as do a large number of museums (featuring everything from the world's only stuffed blue whale to modern art) and the largest amusement park in northern Europe. Gothenburg also is a convenient center for excursions to a spectacularly pristine archipelago that's the home of fishing villages, wildlife refuges, and several lovely vacation resorts.

The port of Gothenburg contains a shipyard, Cityvarvet, which today limits itself only to the repair of ships, not their construction. The city also is the home of Volvo, the car manufacturer (whose plant is about a 15-min. drive from the city center). Despite this heavy industry, Gothenburg's environmental programs have made it a European leader in developing new products and procedures for dealing with waste. Today, Gothenburg is an attractive interface between high-tech savvy and old-world charm. It's not surprising that locals refer to it as "the biggest small town in Sweden."

1 ORIENTATION

ARRIVING

BY PLANE   SAS (© **800/221-2350** in the U.S.; www.flysas.com) operates 8 to 10 daily flights from Copenhagen to Gothenburg (most of them nonstop) between 7:30am and 11:05pm. (Many Swedes who live on the west coast of Sweden consider Copenhagen a more convenient airport than the one in Stockholm.) SAS also operates 10 to 15 daily flights between Stockholm and Gothenburg, beginning about 7am and continuing until early evening.

Planes arrive at **Landvetter Airport** (℘ 031/94-10-00; www.lfv.se), 26km (16 miles) east of Gothenburg. A *Flygbuss* (www.flygbussarna.se) or airport bus departs every 30 minutes for the 30-minute ride to the central bus terminal, just behind Gothenburg's main railway station. Buses run daily between 5:15am and 12:15am. A one-way trip costs 82SEK ($16/£8.20). A more modern airport, Gothenburg City Airport, opened in 2002. Positioned 18km (11 miles) northwest of the city center, it receives mostly low-cost flights, many of them charters, from other parts of Europe.

BY TRAIN The Oslo–Copenhagen express train runs through Gothenburg and Helsingborg. Trains run frequently on a north–south route between Gothenburg and Helsingborg/Malmö in the south. The most traveled rail route is between Gothenburg and Stockholm, with trains leaving hourly in both directions; the trip takes between 3 and 4^1/$_2$ hours, depending on the train.

Trains arrive at the **Central Station,** on one side of Drottningtorget. Inside the station is a currency-exchange bureau and an office of the Swedish National Railroad Authority (also known as the Statens Järnvägar, "The State's Railways," or, more commonly, SJ), which sells rail and bus tickets for connections to nearby areas. For information, call ℘ 771/75-75-75.

BY BUS There are several buses from Gothenburg to Helsingborg/Malmö (and vice versa) daily. Trip time from Gothenburg to Helsingborg is 3 hours; Gothenburg to Malmö, 3 to 4 hours. Several buses connect Stockholm and Gothenburg daily. The trip takes 6 to 7 hours. Gothenburg's bus station, at Nils Ericson Platsen, is located behind the railway station. For information in Gothenburg, call **Swebus,** Sweden's largest bus company (℘ 036/290-80-00; www.swebusexpress.se).

BY FERRY The **Stena Line** (℘ 031/704-00-00; www.stena.com) has six crossings per day in summer from North Jutland (a 3-hr. trip); call for information on specific departure times, which vary seasonally. They also offer a daily connection from Kiel, Germany, which departs daily at 7pm, arriving at 9am the following morning in Gothenburg. Vessels for both of these routes have excellent dining rooms.

From June to mid-August, there's service from Newcastle-upon-Tyne (England) to Gothenburg twice a week, taking 24 hours. This service is operated by **DFDS Scandinavian Seaways** (℘ 031/65-06-50 for information; www.dfdsseaways.se). There's no rail-pass discount on the England–Sweden crossings.

BY CAR From either Malmö or Helsingborg, the two major "gateways" to Sweden on the west coast, take E6 north. Gothenburg is 280km (174 miles) north of Malmö and 226km (140 miles) north of Helsingborg. From Stockholm, take E4 west to Jönköping and continue west the rest of the way through Borås to Gothenburg, a distance of 470km (292 miles).

VISITOR INFORMATION

The **Gothenburg Tourist Office** is at Kungsportsplatsen 2, SE-411 10 Göteborg (℘ 031/61-25-00; www.goteborg.com), and it's open September to April Monday to Friday 9:30am to 5pm, Saturday 10am to 2pm, May to June 21 daily 9:30am to 6pm, June 22 to August 19 daily 9:30am to 8pm, and August 20 to 31 daily 9:30am to 6pm.

Ⓕun Facts **High Bridge**

Spanning the Göta River, **Älvsborg Bridge** (one of the longest suspension bridges in Sweden) is almost 900m (2,953 ft.) long and built high enough to allow ocean liners to pass underneath.

CITY LAYOUT

The layout of Gothenburg, with its network of streets separated by canals, is reminiscent of Amsterdam—not surprisingly, as it was designed by Dutch architects in the 17th century. Its wealth of parks and open spaces has given it a deserved reputation as Sweden's greenest city.

Some of the old canals have been filled in, but you can explore the major remaining waterway and the busy harbor by taking one of the city's famous **Paddan sightseeing boats** (Ⓒ **031/60-96-60;** www.paddan.se). Their circular tour through the waterways and canals of Gothenburg strike us as one of the most absorbing and intriguing boat tours offered in Scandinavia. *Paddan* is the Swedish word for "toad," and the allusion is to the squat shape of the boats that enables them to navigate under the many low bridges. A Paddan service takes you from the point of embarkation, Kungsportsplatsen (near the Central Station), direct to the Liseberg amusement park. The park is the most popular visitor attraction in the area, attracting some three million visitors annually.

The best place to start sightseeing on foot is **Kungsportsavenyn** (or just "The Avenyn"), a wide, tree-lined boulevard with many sidewalk cafes. (Take a look at the "Gothenburg" map later in this chapter.) Avenyn leads to **Götaplatsen,** a square that's the city's artistic and historic center. Its centerpiece is a huge bronze fountain with a statue of the sea god Poseidon, sculpted by the great Carl Milles.

Gothenburg's old commercial section lies on either side of the central canal. At the central canal is **Gustav Adolfs Torg,** dominated by a statue of Gustav himself. Facing the canal is the **Börshuset (Stock Exchange building).** On the western side is the **Rådhuset (Town Hall),** originally constructed in 1672. Around the corner, moving toward the river, is the **Kronhuset** (off Kronhusgatan), a 17th-century Dutch-designed building—the oldest in Gothenburg.

Gothenburg is dominated by its **harbor,** which is best viewed from one of the Padden boats. The major attraction here is the **Maritiman** center (see "Seeing the Sights," later in this chapter). The shipyards, whose spidery forms appear as if they were made from an Erector Set, are dominated by the IBM building. Part of the harbor is connected by an overhead walkway to the shopping mall of **Nordstan.**

The most rapid growth in Gothenburg has occurred recently on **Hisingen Island,** now home to about 25% of the town's population. Set across the Göta River (the mouth of which functions as Gothenburg's harbor) from the rest of the city, it's the fourth largest island in Sweden, and home of heavy industry, which includes the Volvo factories. In 1966, a bridge was built across the harbor (that is, the Göta River), connecting—for the first time in history—the island to Gothenburg. Despite its growing population and its manufacturing plants, Hisingen Island retains wide swaths of uninhabited scrubland and forest, and we've often gone here for summer hikes.

2 GETTING AROUND

The cheapest way to explore Gothenburg (aside from on foot) is to buy a **Göteborgs-passet (Gothenburg Card).** Available at hotels, newspaper kiosks, and the city's tourist office, it entitles you to unlimited travel on local trams, buses, and ferryboats; a free pass for most sightseeing tours; free admission to the city's major museums and sightseeing attractions; discounts at certain shops; free parking in certain centrally located parking lots; and several other extras that usually make the card worthwhile. A ticket valid for 24 hours costs 225SEK ($45/£23) for adults and 150SEK ($30/£15) for children up to 17 years old; a 48-hour ticket is 310SEK ($62/£31) for adults and 225SEK ($45/£23) for children.

BY PUBLIC TRANSPORTATION (TRAM) A single tram ticket goes for 20SEK to 25SEK ($4–$5/£2–£2.50) or half price for children. If you don't have an advance ticket, board the first car of the tram—the driver will sell you a ticket and stamp it for you. Previously purchased tickets must be stamped in the automatic machine as soon as you board the tram.

BY TAXI Taxis are not as plentiful as we'd like. However, you can always find one by going to the Central Station. To call a taxi, dial ✆ **031/27-27-27** or 031/64-40-00. A taxi traveling within the city limits now costs 100SEK to 250SEK ($20–$50/£10–£25), although a ride from the center to either of the airports will run up a tab of around 400SEK to 450SEK ($80–$90/£40–£45).

BY CAR Parking is a nightmare, so we don't recommend driving through Gothenburg. You'll need a car to tour the surrounding area, but there is good public transportation within the city, as well as to many sights. **Avis** (✆ **031/80-57-80**) has a rental office at the Central Station and another at the airport (✆ **031/94-60-30**). Its rival, **Hertz,** also has an office at the center of town at the Central Station (✆ **031/80-37-30**) and one at the airport (✆ **031/94-60-20**). Compare rates and, of course, make sure you understand the insurance coverage before you sign a contract.

> (**Fun Facts** **Shipping Out from Gothenburg**
>
> If you're a Swedish American, chances are your ancestors spent their last night in their mother country in the city of Gothenburg. The port here was the departure point for the half-million or so Swedes who came to the United States in the late 1800s and the early 1900s.

> (**Fast Facts** **Gothenburg**
>
> **Area Code** The international country code for Sweden is **46;** the city code for Gothenburg is **031.** (If you're calling Gothenburg from abroad, drop the 0; within Gothenburg, drop the 031.)
>
> **Bookstores** The biggest and most central is **Akademi Bokhandeln,** Norra Hamngatan 26 (✆ **031/61-70-31**).

Business Hours Generally, **shops** are open Monday to Friday 10am to 6 or 7pm and Saturday from 10am to 3 or 4pm. Large department stores, such as NK, are also open on Sunday, usually from 11am to 4pm. Most banks are open Monday to Friday from 9:30am to 3pm, and **offices** are open Monday to Friday 9am to 5pm.

Currency Exchange Currency can be exchanged at **Forex,** in the Central Station (✆ **031/15-65-16**), daily 7am to 9pm. There are also currency exchange desks at both Landvetter and Gothenburg City Airport, each open daily 5:15am to 10:45pm.

Dentists Call the referral agency, Stampgatan (✆ **031/80-78-00**), Monday to Friday 8am to 8pm and Saturday to Sunday 8am to 4pm.

Doctors If it's not an emergency, your hotel can call a local doctor and arrange an appointment. If it's an emergency, go to **Axess Akuten,** Södra Allegatan 6 (✆ **031/725-00-00**).

Drugstores A good pharmacy is **Apoteket Vasen,** Götgatan 12, Nordstan (✆ **0771/45-04-50;** www.apoteket.se), open daily 8am to 10pm.

Embassies & Consulates Neither Britain nor the U.S. maintains a consulate in Gothenburg; Americans and citizens of Australia, Britain, Ireland, and New Zealand must contact their embassies in Stockholm.

Emergencies The number to call for nearly all emergencies (fire, police, medical) is ✆ **112.**

Eyeglasses Go to **Wasa Optik,** Vasaplatsen 7 (✆ **031/711-05-35**). It's open Monday to Friday 9am to 6pm.

Hairdressers & Barbers We like the skilled staff at **Salong Noblesse,** Södra Larmgatan 6 (✆ **031/711-71-30**), open Monday to Friday 9am to 7pm and Saturday 9am to 3pm.

Internet The city library, **Stadsbibliotek,** Götaplatsen (✆ **031/61-65-00**), offers free Internet access from a half-dozen stations, although it's best to phone in advance to the English-speaking staff for insights into the library's reservations policies that might be in effect at the time. It's open Monday to Friday 10am to 8pm, and Saturday and Sunday 11am to 5pm (closed Sun May–Aug). There are also seven or eight computers available for access at Centralhuset (no phone), a service center within Gothenburg's Central Railway Station. They're usually available daily from 9am to 7pm.

Laundry & Dry Cleaning Because most Swedes have access to washing machines of their own, and because most hotels make laundry and dry-cleaning part of their service packages, self-service laundromats are hard to find. One that's centrally located, however, close to the Scandic Hotel Europa, is the **Nordstan Service Center,** Lilla Klädpressare 1 (✆ **031/15-03-00**), which also does dry-cleaning.

Liquor Laws You must be 18 to consume alcohol in a restaurant, but 20 to purchase alcohol in liquor stores. No alcohol can be served before noon. Most pubs stop serving liquor at 3am, except special nightclubs with a license to stay open later. Liquor can be purchased at state-owned liquor shops known as *Systembolag,* but only Monday to Friday 10am to 6pm, and Saturday 10am to 2pm.

Lost Property Go to the police station (see "Police," below).

Luggage Storage & Lockers You can store luggage and rent lockers at the Central Station for 20SEK to 85SEK ($4–$17/£2–£8.50), depending on the size of the luggage.

Photography Supplies An excellent store is **Expert,** Arkaden 9 (✆ **031/80-20-70**), open Monday to Friday 10am to 6pm and Saturday 10am to 2pm.

Police The main police station is Polismyndigheten, Ernst Fortells Plats (✆ **031/739-20-00**), opposite Ullevi Stadium.

Post Office Gothenburg doesn't define any particular branch of its many post offices as preeminent or "central," but a branch of the Swedish Postal Service that's convenient to everything in the city's commercial core is at **Nordstan** (✆ **031/80-65-29**), a 5-minute walk from the Central Station. It's open Monday to Saturday 10am to 3pm.

Radio & TV Gothenburg has Swedish-language TV broadcasts on TV1 and TV2, both of which are government-funded stations, and TV3 and TV4, both of which are commercially (that is, privately) funded. It also receives such British channels as Super Sky and BBC. National radio stations include P1, P2, P3, and P4; Radio Gothenburg broadcasts on 101.9 MHz (FM).

Shoe Repair Try **Mister Minit,** Nordstan (✆ **031/15-21-27**). Repairs are made while you wait.

Taxes Gothenburg imposes no special city taxes other than the value-added tax (MOMS, usually calculated at 25%), which applies nationwide.

Transit Information For tram and bus information, call ✆ **0771/41-43-00.**

3 WHERE TO STAY

Reservations are important, but if you need a place to stay on the spur of the moment, try the **Gothenburg Tourist Office,** at Kungsportsplatsen 2 (✆ **031/61-25-00;** www.goteborg.com). There's also a branch of the tourist office in the Nordstan shopping center (no phone), near the railway station. It's open Monday to Friday from 9am to 7pm, Saturday from 9am to 3pm. It lists the city's hotels and boardinghouses and reserves rooms in private homes. Reservations can be made by letter, or by phone. The tourist office charges a booking fee of 60SEK ($12/£6), but if you reserve your own accommodations on the website (www.gothenburg.com), the booking will be free. Double rooms in private homes start at around 250SEK ($50/£25) per person and breakfast always costs extra.

The hotels listed in the following section as "expensive" actually become "moderate" on Friday and Saturday and during midsummer.

EXPENSIVE

Elite Park Avenue Hotel ★ After more than half a century in business, this hotel is once again a prestige address, even though it still lacks a certain character. Built in 1950, and radically renovated in 2005 and 2006 after its takeover by Sweden's Elite Hotel Group, this 10-story contemporary hotel stands as a highly visible fixture on the city's most central boulevard. With a pedigree that attracted, under different ownership, Henry Kissinger, The Beatles, The Rolling Stones, and David Rockefeller, it earned a new lease on life and a shot of additional glamour after its most recent reconfiguration. Its midsize-to-spacious bedrooms are attractive and comfortable, with tile or marble-trimmed bathrooms and lots of contemporary comforts. We go for the rooms on the upper floors because they have the most panoramic views of the water and the cityscape itself. On the premises are a restaurant, the Park Avenue Cafe; a bistro; and a second branch of a cozy English/Irish pub, the Bishop's Arms, whose clone (which lies in the cellar of this hotel's affiliate, the also-recommended Elite Plaza Hotel) is separately recommended in "Where to Dine," later in this chapter. A few steps from the hotel's entrance is the popular nightclub the Madison, which is loosely affiliated with this hotel.

Kungsportsavenyn 36–38, S-40015 Göteborg. © **031/727-10-00.** Fax 031/727-10-10. www.elite.se. 318 units. Mon–Thurs 1,250SEK–2,950SEK ($250–$590/£125–£295) double; Fri–Sun 1,400SEK–1,600SEK ($280–$320/£140–£160) double; 1,800SEK–4,650SEK ($360–$930/£180–£465) suite. Rates include breakfast. AE, DC, MC, V. Parking 195SEK–275SEK ($39–$55/£20–£28) per night. Tram: 1, 4, 5, or 6. Bus: 40. **Amenities:** Restaurant; bistro; bar/pub; room service; babysitting; laundry service; dry cleaning; nonsmoking rooms; rooms for those w/limited mobility. *In room:* TV, minibar, coffeemaker, hair dryer, trouser press, safe, Wi-Fi.

Elite Plaza ★★★ Equaled in Gothenburg only by the Radisson SAS Scandinavia, this 1889 insurance company was stunningly converted into a superior first-class hotel. During the conversion, all of the major architectural features of this palatial structure were preserved, including the stucco ceilings, mosaic floors, and high ceilings, all of which contribute to a rather formal, but not particularly cozy, collection of bedrooms. The public lounges are adorned with an impressive collection of modern art, and all the midsize-to-spacious bedrooms and the plumbing have been updated. Lying in the center of town, the hotel is within a short walk of the Central Station and the Opera House. The less formal (and less expensive) of its two restaurants (the Bishop's Arms) is separately recommended in "Where to Dine," later in this chapter, and its breakfast buffet is particularly lavish. Two of our favorite spots in this hotel include the elegant bar area, which is sheathed in wood paneling, staffed with formally dressed waiters, and lined with dramatic, large-scale modern paintings; and its first-rate sauna facilities.

Vastra Hamngatan 3, S-404 22 Göteborg. © **031/720-40-00.** Fax 031/720-40-10. www.elite.se. 130 units. Sun–Thurs 2,050SEK–3,450SEK ($410–$690/£205–£345) double, 4,850SEK ($970/£485) suite; Fri–Sat 1,500SEK–3,200SEK ($300–$640/£150–£320) double, 4,550SEK ($910/£455) suite. Rates include breakfast. AE, DC, MC, V. Tram: 1, 6, 9, or 11. **Amenities:** Restaurant; bar; exercise rooms; 2 saunas, room service; babysitting; laundry service; dry cleaning; nonsmoking rooms. *In room:* TV, minibar, hair dryer, trouser press (in some), safe, Wi-Fi.

Hotel Flora In 2008, this stylish hotel blossomed anew with a daringly modern and sophisticated design. Its bedrooms today are among the most desirable in town, with state-of-the-art technology and grand comfort. Near the heart of the old city, it is also a convenient address; the entertainment street of Avenyn lies only a stone's throw away. There is taste and a pleasing decor evident throughout, and the staff is one of the most welcoming and efficient in Gothenburg.

Grönsaktorgt 2, 411 17 Göteborg. © **031/13-86-16.** Fax 031/13-24-08. www.hotelflora.se. 68 units. 1,545SEK–1,595SEK ($309–$318/£155–£159) double. AE, DC, MC, V. Tram: 1, 6, or 9. **Amenities:** Bar; room service; laundry service/dry cleaning; nonsmoking rooms. *In room:* TV, minibar, hair dryer, safe, Wi-Fi.

Hotel Gothia Towers ★★ The twin towers of this well-run government-rated four-star hotel, which rise 18 mirror-plated stories above Sweden's largest convention center,

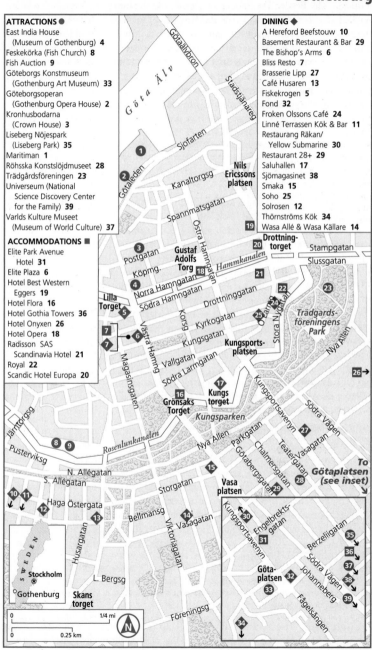

ATTRACTIONS ●

East India House
  (Museum of Gothenburg) **4**
Feskekörka (Fish Church) **8**
Fish Auction **9**
Göteborgs Konstmuseum
  (Gothenburg Art Museum) **33**
Göteborgsoperan
  (Gothenburg Opera House) **2**
Kronhusbodarna
  (Crown House) **3**
Liseberg Nöjespark
  (Liseberg Park) **35**
Maritiman **1**
Röhsska Konstslöjdmuseet **28**
Trädgårdsföreningen **23**
Universeum (National
  Science Discovery Center
  for the Family) **39**
Varlds Kulture Museet
  (Museum of World Culture) **37**

ACCOMMODATIONS ■

Elite Park Avenue
  Hotel **31**
Elite Plaza **6**
Hotel Best Western
  Eggers **19**
Hotel Flora **16**
Hotel Gothia Towers **36**
Hotel Onyxen **26**
Hotel Opera **18**
Radisson SAS
  Scandinavia Hotel **21**
Royal **22**
Scandic Hotel Europa **20**

DINING ◆

A Hereford Beefstouw **10**
Basement Restaurant & Bar **29**
The Bishop's Arms **6**
Bliss Resto **7**
Brasserie Lipp **27**
Café Husaren **13**
Fiskekrogen **5**
Fond **32**
Froken Olssons Café **24**
Linné Terrassen Kök & Bar **11**
Restaurang Räkan/
  Yellow Submarine **30**
Restaurant 28+ **29**
Saluhallen **17**
Sjömagasinet **38**
Smaka **15**
Soho **25**
Solrosen **12**
Thörnströms Kök **34**
Wasa Allé & Wasa Källare **14**

were the tallest buildings on the west coast until they were surpassed in the late 1990s by a newer building in Malmö. The Towers' brisk, friendly format places it among Scandinavia's best business-oriented hotels. Rooms are comfortable, contemporary, and tasteful. Touches of wood, particularly the hardwood floors, take the edge off any sense of cookie-cutter standardization. Bathrooms are spacious, with sleek, tiled tub/shower combinations. We gravitate to the rooms on the top three floors of the towers, which are plusher than those at lower levels, and feature enhanced amenities and services. (A total of 410 rooms lies in the Gothia West Tower, the others in the Gothia East.) A covered passageway runs from each of the towers directly to the convention center.

Mässans Gata 24, S-402 26 Göteborg. (C) **031/750-88-00.** Fax 031/750-88-82. www.gothiatowers.com. 704 units. Mon–Thurs 1,865SEK–2,565SEK ($373–$513/£187–£257) double, Fri–Sun 1,145SEK–1,745SEK ($229–$349/£115–£175) double; 2,900SEK–4,500SEK ($580–$900/£290–£450) suite. AE, DC, MC, V. Tram: 4 or 5. **Amenities:** 2 restaurants; 3 bars; fitness center; sauna; room service; laundry service; dry cleaning; nonsmoking rooms; rooms for those w/limited mobility. *In room:* TV, minibar, coffeemaker, hair dryer, iron, trouser press, safe, Wi-Fi.

Quality Inn 11 ★   Facing central Gothenburg from its waterfront position on Hinsinge Island, this sprawling red-brick hotel opened in 1992 within the premises of what originated around 1890 as a machinists' shop for the shipbuilding industry. In addition to its hotel facilities, its interior contains a movie theater and a convention center. The modern sections of this hotel are angular and very modern and its lobby is outfitted in tones of "toreador red" and black; the antique sections reek of the sweat and hard work of the Industrial Revolution. Views, from both the bedrooms and the endless hallways of this ultramodern convention complex, sweep out over the harbor and the remnants of the heavy industry that used to dominate both the harbor and the town. Select this hotel if you're looking for an out-of-the-way hideaway that's very far from the bustle of Gothenburg's downtown scene. Otherwise, be prepared to make your own entertainment within a quiet corner of the city with absolutely no sense of urban edginess.

Maskingatan 11, Hinsingen, 41764 Göteborg. (C) **031/779-11-11.** Fax 031/779-11-10. www.hotel11.se. 260 units. 1,290SEK–2,578SEK ($258–$516/£129–£258) double. AE, DC, MC, V. Bus: 16. **Amenities:** Restaurant; bar; room service; laundry service; dry cleaning; rooms for those w/limited mobility. *In room:* A/C, TV, minibar, safe (at additional charge), Wi-Fi.

Radisson SAS Scandinavia Hotel ★★★   If you want the most modern and spectacular hotel in Gothenburg, check in here. This unusual deluxe hotel surrounds a large greenhouse-style atrium, which seems like a tree-lined city square indoors. It stands opposite the railroad station, and it's one of the best-run and best-equipped hotels in Sweden. Opened in 1986, but extensively renovated since, the hotel offers among the finest rooms in town; they're large and luxuriously appointed. The fifth floor of the hotel contains the exclusive concierge rooms with extended service and speedier check-ins, and upgraded accommodations are most often booked by the business community.

Södra Hamngatan 59–65, S-401 24 Göteborg. (C) **800/333-3333** in the U.S., or 031/758-50-00. Fax 031/758-50-01. www.radissonsas.com. 349 units. 1,390SEK–2,445SEK ($278–$489/£139–£245) double; 2,500SEK–4,500SEK ($500–$900/£250–£450) suite. AE, DC, MC, V. Parking 255SEK ($51/£26). Tram: 1, 2, 3, 4, 5, or 7. Bus: 40. **Amenities:** Restaurant; bar; indoor pool; fitness center; sauna; room service; babysitting; laundry service; dry cleaning; nonsmoking rooms; rooms for those w/limited mobility. *In room:* TV, minibar, hair dryer, safe, Wi-Fi.

Scandic Hotel Europa ★★   If you're seeking a cozy Swedish inn, this is not it. This is one of the largest hotels in Scandinavia—a big, bustling blockbuster of a building that rises eight bulky stories across from Gothenburg's railway station. Built in 1972 of concrete and glass, the hotel underwent a massive renovation, which added thousands of slabs of russet-colored marble. Today it's a member of Hilton International, and the well-trained staff includes dozens of young graduates from hotel training schools. Midsize-to-spacious bedrooms are outfitted in monochromatic tones of either autumn-inspired browns or pale Nordic tones of blue, and have conservative, modern furniture as well as up-to-date bathrooms. The largest and plushest rooms lie on the hotel's second, eighth, and ninth floors.

Köpmansgatan 38, P.O. Box 11444, S-404 29 Göteborg. ⓒ **031/751-65-00.** Fax 031/751-65-11. www. scandic-hotels.com. 452 units. 900SEK–2,350SEK ($180–$470/£90–£235) double; 2,025SEK–5,000SEK ($405–$1,000/£203–£500) suite double occupancy. Rates include breakfast. AE, DC, MC, V. Parking 100SEK–150SEK ($20–$30/£10–£15). Tram: 1, 2, 3, 4, 5, 6, 7, 8, 9, or 10. **Amenities:** Restaurant; 2 bars; indoor pool; sauna; room service; laundry service; dry cleaning; nonsmoking rooms; rooms for those w/ limited mobility. *In room:* A/C, TV, minibar, hair dryer, safe, Wi-Fi.

MODERATE

Hotel Best Western Eggers ★ (Value) For our kronor, this inn has more old-fashioned charm and authentic character than any other hotel in town. The third oldest hotel in Gothenburg was built in 1859, predating the Swedish use of the word to describe a building with rooms for travelers. Many emigrants to the New World spent their last night in the old country at the Hotel Eggers, and during World War II, the Germans and the Allies met here for secret negotiations. Today it's just as good as or better than ever, with stained-glass windows, ornate staircases, wood paneling, and a distinct sense of history. (If you ask, one of the older staff members here will discuss the role of the hotel as a trysting spot, many decades ago, for Prince Albert, a member of Sweden's Royal Family, and his longtime—then-secret—companion, Lillian, who is today revered within Sweden for her sense of loyalty, discretion, and charm.) Rooms vary in size, but they are all individually furnished and beautifully appointed, with large bathrooms. In the hotel dining room, gilt leather tapestry and polished mahogany evoke the 19th century, a perfect backdrop for the classic Swedish dishes served here.

Drottningtorget, SE 40125 Göteborg. ⓒ **800/528-1234** in the U.S. and Canada, or 031/333-44-40. Fax 031/333-44-49. www.hoteleggers.se. 69 units. June 14–Aug 10 and Fri–Sat year-round 995SEK–1,530SEK ($199–$306/£100–£153) double; rest of year 1,780SEK–2,305SEK ($356–$461/£178–£231) double. Rates include breakfast. AE, DC, MC, V. Parking 100SEK–150SEK ($20–$30/£10–£15). Tram: 1, 2, 3, 4, 5, 6, 7, 8, or 9. Bus: 40. **Amenities:** Restaurant; bar; room service; laundry service; dry cleaning; nonsmoking rooms. *In room:* TV, hair dryer, Wi-Fi.

Hotel Onyxen ★ (Finds) This hotel should be better known, but instead it's one of the relatively unknown gems of Gothenburg. We've anxiously watched its prices rise—it used to be featured in budget guides—but it still offers decent value in spite of inflation. Well run and family managed, it is housed in a building from Gothenburg's Belle Epoque days, meaning around the turn of the 20th century. Originally it was a many-balconied apartment house, until its owners decided to convert it into a good hotel in the 1980s. There's a residents' pub and cocktail lounge near the lobby, but the only meal served is breakfast.

Sten Sturegatan 23, S-412 52 Göteborg. ⓒ **031/81-08-45.** Fax 031/16-56-72. www.hotelonyxen.com. 34 units. Mon–Thurs 1,390SEK–1,890SEK ($278–$378/£139–£189) double; Fri–Sat 990SEK–1,190SEK ($198–$238/£99–£119) double. Rates include breakfast and access to an evening soup-with-fresh-bread buffet served Mon–Sat in the lobby. Parking 120SEK ($24/£12). Extra bed 200SEK ($40/£20) for adults and 100SEK ($20/£10) for children under 16. AE, DC, MC, V. Tram: 2, 4, or 5. **Amenities:** Breakfast room; bar; laundry service; dry cleaning; nonsmoking rooms. *In room:* TV, hair dryer, iron, trouser press, Wi-Fi.

Hotel Opera In high-priced Sweden, this hotel is known for its moderate tariffs. Even though its prices would buy you luxurious accommodations in many parts of the world, what you get here is comfort. From the outside, you'll look at this boxy, white-fronted building and swear that it's a single structure. But it includes two distinctly different divisions, one with three stories, the other with four, which resulted from the interconnection of two once-separate hotels back in 1994. Rooms come in categories of "recently renovated" (that is, slightly larger, brightly accessorized units) and "not so recently renovated" (usually with decors dating back to the mid-1990s, with spaces that are a bit more cramped).

Norra Hamngatan 38, S-401 26 Göteborg. ✆ 031/80-50-80. Fax 031/80-58-17. www.hotelopera.se. 75 units. Sun–Thurs 1,295SEK–1,599SEK ($258–$320/£130–£160) double; Fri–Sat 895SEK–995SEK ($179–$199/£90–£100) double. Rates include breakfast. AE, DC, MC, V. Parking 120SEK ($24/£12). Tram 1, 4, 5, 6, 7, 8, or 9. **Amenities:** Restaurant; bar; Jacuzzi; sauna; laundry service; dry cleaning. *In room:* TV, hair dryer, trouser press, Wi-Fi.

Novotel Göteborg ★★ Most Novotels are dull and boring, with chain-format rooms and cafeteria-like food. This one is an exception—in fact, it's one of our preferred Novotels in the north. The recycling of this red-brick Industrial Age old brewery was done with style and sophistication, and we've spent several comfortable nights here over the years. The converted building is set on the harborfront 4km (2¹/₂ miles) west of the city center. It is a stylish hotel run by the French hotel conglomerate Accor. Each plushly carpeted room offers panoramic views of the industrial landscape. The room style is Swedish modern, with many built-in pieces, good-size closets, and firm sofa beds.

Klippan 1, S-414 51 Göteborg. ✆ 800/221-4542 in the U.S., or 031/720-22-00. Fax 031/720-22-99. www.novotel.se. 149 units. Mon–Thurs 1,590SEK–1,820SEK ($318–$364/£159–£182) double, Fri–Sat 990SEK–1,190SEK ($198–$238/£99–£119) double; 2,290SEK–2,490SEK ($458–$498/£229–£249) suite. Rates include breakfast. AE, DC, MC, V. Free parking. From Gothenburg, follow the signs on E20 to Frederikshavn, then the signs to Kiel; exit at Klippan, where signs direct you to the hotel. Tram: 3 or 9. Bus: 91 or 92. **Amenities:** Restaurant; bar; sauna; room service; laundry service; dry cleaning; nonsmoking rooms; rooms for those w/limited mobility. *In room:* A/C, TV, minibar (in some), hair dryer, safe, Wi-Fi (in some).

Quality Panorama Hotel ★ (Finds) Guidebooks tend to ignore this 13-story hotel, a 10-minute walk west of the center of town, but we consider it a discovery. Even though it is little publicized, it is one of the better choices in the so-called "moderate" category in pricey Sweden. It is spacious with a sense of drama, as evoked by its sky-lit and plant-filled lobby. Each of the midsize-to-large bedrooms is furnished in a comfortable, tasteful style, with soft lighting and double-glazing on the windows. The finest accommodations, and certainly those with a view, are found on the 13th floor. The hotel also boasts a balcony-level restaurant serving good and reasonably priced food made with market-fresh ingredients.

Eklandagatan 51–53, S-400 22 Göteborg. ✆ 031/767-70-00. Fax 031/767-70-70. www.panorama.se. 338 units (some with shower only). 840SEK–1,240SEK ($168–$248/£84–£124) double. Rates include breakfast. AE, DC, MC, V. Parking 100SEK ($20/£10). Closed Dec 22–Jan 7. Tram: 4 or 5. Bus: 49 or 52. **Amenities:** Restaurant; bar; Jacuzzi; sauna; room service; laundry service; dry cleaning; nonsmoking rooms; rooms for those w/limited mobility. *In room:* TV, minibar, hair dryer, Wi-Fi.

Royal ★ This hotel was founded in 1852, making it the oldest in Gothenburg. That in itself is not a recommendation. What makes this a good choice is that it is completely renovated, and is today better than ever. There is a certain inconvenience in staying here, however, as it lies half a kilometer (¹/₃ mile) from the railroad station, but all bus and tram lines pass close by, whisking you to the city center in little time. In spite of its overhaul, it protected some of its 19th-century architectural styling with wrought-iron banisters and heavy cast bronze lamps on the stairs. Of course, the unique hand-painted glass ceiling at the reception area remains. All of the midsize-to-spacious bedrooms are individually decorated and modernized.

Drottninggatan 67, S-411 07 Göteborg. ℂ **031/700-11-70.** Fax 031/700-11-79. www.hotelroyal.nu. 82 units. 1,495SEK–1,695SEK ($299–$339/£150–£170) double (no discount on weekends). Rates include buffet breakfast. AE, DC, MC, V. Parking 125SEK ($25/£13). Tram: 1, 2, 3, 4, 5, or 6. Bus: 60. **Amenities:** Breakfast room; lounge; nonsmoking rooms. *In room:* TV, hair dryer, Wi-Fi.

INEXPENSIVE

A budget hotel in Gothenburg could be considered expensive in many parts of the world. To get low rates, time your visit to Gothenburg on a Friday or Saturday night, when rates are generally slashed.

Hotel Örgryte Though lacking a lot of character, this longtime favorite is a good, safe choice for overnighting. It has its devotees from the Swedish countryside—some of its fans insist they would "stay nowhere else in Gothenburg." Or that was the claim made to us. Named after the leafy residential district of Örgryte, where this hotel is situated, this family-owned hotel lies 1.5 km (about 1 mile) east of the commercial core of Gothenburg. It was originally built around 1960 and renovated many times since. Rooms were upgraded and outfitted with pastel-colored upholstery and streamlined, uncomplicated furniture that makes use of birch-veneer woods. Most units are medium-size, often big enough to contain a sitting area. Both the exterior and the public areas are not particularly inspired in their design, but overall, the place provides decent, safe accommodations at a relatively reasonable price.

Danska Vägen 68–70, SE-41659 Göteborg. ℂ **031/707-89-00.** Fax 031/707-89-99. www.hotelorgryte.se. 70 units. Sun–Thurs 1,350SEK–1,560SEK ($270–$312/£135–£156) double, Fri–Sat 830SEK–990SEK ($166–$198/£83–£99) double; 1,500SEK–2,230SEK ($300–$446/£150–£223) suite. Rates include breakfast. AE, DC, MC, V. Parking 100SEK ($20/£10). Bus: 60 or 62. **Amenities:** Restaurant; bar; sauna; laundry service; dry cleaning; nonsmoking rooms. *In room:* TV, hair dryer, iron, Wi-Fi.

Quality Hotel Winn Chain-run but also chain-efficient, this no-nonsense but comfortable and affordable four-story hotel lies in an isolated wooded area about 3km (1³/₄ miles) north of Gothenburg's ferryboat terminal. Functional and modern, its bedrooms are more comfortable than you might imagine from the uninspired exterior. Each is outfitted in pastel shades, with well-kept bathrooms equipped with tub/shower combinations. If your hopes aren't too high, you may come away pleased with this hotel.

Gamla Tingstadsgatan 1, S-402 76 Göteborg. ℂ **031/750-19-00.** Fax 031/750-19-50. www.winnhotel. com. 121 units. 1,090SEK–1,540SEK ($218–$308/£109–£154) double. Rates include breakfast. AE, DC, MC, V. Free parking. Bus: 40, 45, 48, or 49. **Amenities:** Restaurant; bar; indoor pool; sauna; laundry service; dry cleaning; nonsmoking rooms; rooms for those w/limited mobility. *In room:* TV, minibar, hair dryer, Wi-Fi.

Tidblom's Hotel ★ (Finds) This is a good if offbeat choice, recommended if you're seeking an off-the-record weekend. It's better for motorists because of its location, although it can also be reached by public transportation. Set 3km (1³/₄ miles) east of Gothenburg's center, in a residential neighborhood filled with other Victorian buildings, this hotel was built in 1897 as a dormitory for Scottish craftsmen imported to work at the nearby lumber mill. Despite its functional purpose, its builders graced it with a conical tower, fancy brickwork, and other architectural adornments that remain in place today. After stints as a warehouse, a delicatessen, and a low-rent hotel, the building was upgraded in 1987 into a cozy, charming, and well-accessorized hotel. Guest rooms have good, firm beds; ample bathrooms; and wooden floors—and have more flair and character than you'll find at many larger, more anonymous hotels in Gothenburg's center.

Olskroksgatan 23, S-416 66 Göteborg. ℂ **031/707-50-00.** Fax 031/707-50-99. www.tidbloms.com. 42 units. Sun–Thurs 995SEK–1,235SEK ($199–$247/£100–£124) double; Fri–Sat 795SEK ($159/£80) double. Rates include breakfast. AE, DC, MC, V. Free parking. Tram: 1, 3, or 6. **Amenities:** Restaurant; bar; sauna; room service; laundry service; dry cleaning; nonsmoking rooms; rooms for those w/limited mobility. *In room:* TV, minibar, hair dryer, safe, Wi-Fi.

4 WHERE TO DINE

Gothenburg, as you'll soon discover, is a great restaurant town. It may never compete with the sublime viands of Stockholm, but outside the capital it at least comes in number two in Sweden for fine dining. You can still find your grandmother's dishes here, but Gothenburgers today are on the cutting edge for cuisine in Northern Europe.

EXPENSIVE

Basement Restaurant & Bar ★★★ CONTINENTAL   One of the grandest and best restaurants of Sweden has such an unpretentious name. Don't be put off by that. The cuisine is creative and wonderfully delicate, the ingredients market fresh, the chefs skilled. The set menus are the tastiest in the city, and are changed every day to take advantage of the morning shopping's best ingredients. Magnus Larsson and Ulf Wagner will treat you to a superb menu with one glass of wine selected to suit each dish. Most meals consist of a shellfish plate, a fish course, and a meat dish, followed by a freshly made dessert. If available, the lobster salad is unbeatable. Likely to be featured are such fish dishes as pan-fried turbot on the bone or else filet of beef Rossini, followed perhaps by a yummy crème brûlée.

Gotabergsgatan 28. ℂ **031/28-27-29.** Reservations required. Set 4-course menu 660SEK ($132/£66); 6-course 850SEK ($170/£85); 8-course 1,050SEK ($210/£105). AE, DC, MC, V. Mon–Thurs 5–11pm; Fri–Sat 5pm–1am. Tram: 4, 5, or 6.

Fiskekrogen ★★ SEAFOOD   What is there not to like about a restaurant that offers you a choice of some three dozen fish and shellfish dishes, each fresh? One of the most appealing seafood restaurants in Gothenburg occupies a building across the canal from the Stadtsmuseum, in a handsome, internationally modern setting whose sea-green and dark-blue color scheme reflects the shades of the ocean. Fiskekrogen prides itself on a medley of fresh seafood that's artfully displayed and prepared with a zest that has earned it many loyal customers throughout the city. One of the most appealing aspects of the place is the display of seafood on ice—succulent oysters, fresh lobster, fat crayfish, clams, and mussels. Dishes include poached tournedos of cod with Swedish caviar, asparagus, and an oyster-enriched vinaigrette; and butter-fried halibut with chanterelles, fava beans, truffled new potatoes, and merlot sauce.

Lilla Torget 1. ℂ **031/10-10-05.** www.fiskekrogen.com. Reservations recommended. Main courses 285SEK–315SEK ($57–$63/£29–£32); set menus 645SEK–845SEK ($129–$169/£65–£85). AE, DC, MC, V. Mon–Fri 11:30am–2pm and 5:30–11pm; Sat 1–11pm. Tram: 6, 9, or 11. Bus: 16.

Fond ★★★ SCANDINAVIAN/CONTINENTAL   We are more than just "fond" of this place. It's not quite a love affair, but we honestly consider it to be one of the best restaurants on the west coast of Sweden. It truly lives up to its fine reputation and richly deserves its Michelin star (awarded in Sweden like diamond tiaras are handed out). An

Tips **Picnic Fare**

Go to **Saluhallen,** Kungstorget, for the makings of an elegant picnic. This colorful indoor market was built in 1888 and sells meat, fruit, vegetables, delicatessen products, and everything in between. You can find quail, moose, and reindeer; fruits and vegetables from all over the world; and bread, coffee, olives, pâtés, and more. Much of the food is already cooked and will be packaged for you to take out. If you don't feel like venturing outside, there are four restaurants and a coffee bar in the building. The hall is open Monday to Thursday 8:30am to 6pm, Friday 8am to 6pm, and Saturday 8am to 1pm. Take tram no. 1, 4, 5, or 6 to Kungsportsplatsen.

Once you've packed your picnic basket with goodies, go to any of Gothenburg's major parks (see "Parks & Gardens," later in this chapter). Especially recommended is **Trädgårdsföreningen,** across from the Central Station, although there's a 100SEK ($20/£10) entrance fee. (It's free for ages 14 and under.)

address patronized by the town's discerning gourmets, this is the culinary domain of Stefan Karlsson, a media darling and winner of several culinary citations. He has chosen an attractive modern backdrop for his restaurant, in the Lorensberg sector of town. Light Scandinavian wood furnishings, wall panels, and Italian chairs form a backdrop for the cooking, which shows more finesse than most rival establishments and reflects the personality and style of the chef. In other words, he's puts his personal stamp on everything in the restaurant.

We always select a table with a panoramic view over the Avenyn to watch the world go by as we eat one delectable course after another, each one prepared with market-fresh ingredients. Memorable dishes include a choice loin of Swedish lamb with wine gravy and a side of sugar-glazed cabbage; the deep-fried crayfish with a black-pepper glaze and baby carrots with an orange sauce; the classic boiled crayfish, so beloved in Sweden; or fried filets of brill with chanterelles, artichokes, and white-wine gravy. Desserts are made fresh daily and are meticulously crafted and full of flavor.

Götaplatsen. ✆ **031/81-25-80.** www.fondrestaurang.com. Reservations required. Dinner main courses 225SEK–375SEK ($45–$75/£23–£38); lunch main courses 115SEK–195SEK ($23–$39/£12–£20); 6-course set menu 775SEK ($155/£78). AE, DC, MC, V. Mon–Fri 11:30am–2:30pm; Mon–Sat 5–11pm. Closed 2 weeks at Christmas, 4 weeks in midsummer.

Restaurant 28+ ★★★ INTERNATIONAL/FRENCH   This cozy, intimate, chic, and stylish restaurant sits in the pantheon of Gothenburg's great restaurants, enjoying equal rank with Fond and Sjömagasinet, all of which are in a neck-in-neck race for culinary supremacy. The trio of dining rooms here is lit with flickering candles and capped with soaring vaulted ceilings. It's the city's hippest culinary venue, featuring main courses that include cooked crayfish with a fennel-flavored *nage* (an aromatic broth), smoked filet of char in a red-wine and butter sauce, grilled breast of pigeon, and saddle of reindeer with Jerusalem artichokes and blackberry vinaigrette—the most consistently imaginative cuisine in Gothenburg. The items taste fabulously fresh, and the food is handled faultlessly in the kitchen and delicately seasoned. The service is among the city's best.

Götabergsgatan 28. ✆ **031/20-21-61.** www.28plus.se. Reservations recommended. Main courses 325SEK–445SEK ($65–$89/£33–£45); fixed-price menus 775SEK–1,525SEK ($155–$305/£78–£153). AE, DC, MC, V. Mon–Sat 6–9:30pm (last order). Bus: 40. Tram: 1, 4, 5, or 6. Closed July 1–Aug 21.

Sjömagasinet ★★★ SEAFOOD The most elegant and atmospheric restaurant in town, Sjömagasinet is located near the Novotel in the western suburb of Klippan, about 4km (2½ miles) from the center. The building, erected in 1775, was originally a warehouse, and today it retains its low-ceilinged, heavily timbered sense of rustic craftsmanship of a bygone age. Amid dozens of nautical artifacts from the late 19th and early 20th centuries, you can have predinner drinks in either of two separate bars, one of them outfitted in a cozy, English colonial style.

Only the freshest of seafood is served, from lightly salted cod filled with a truffle-and-cauliflower cream, to a platter containing three different preparations of salmon, to shrimp-stuffed crepes with dill, to shellfish with curry sauce, to poached filet of sole with crayfish, to a succulent house version of bouillabaisse. Our favorite dishes are the *pot-au-feu* of fish and shellfish, served with a chive-flavored crème fraîche, and the poached filet of halibut with a warm cabbage salad and potato salad.

Klippans Kulturreservat. ✆ **031/775-59-20.** Reservations recommended. Dinner main courses 250SEK–495SEK ($50–$99/£25–£50); lunch main courses 325SEK–425SEK ($65–$85/£33–£43). AE, DC, MC, V. Mon–Fri 11:30am–2pm and 6–10pm; Sat 5–10pm; Sun 2–8pm in summer. Tram: 3 or 9. From the town center, head west on E3, following the signs to Frederikshavn, and then to Kiel; exit at Klippan and then follow the signs for the Novotel.

Thörnströms Kök ★★ INTERNATIONAL This is arguably the most discreetly fashionable restaurant in Gothenburg. It's also a bastion of fine cuisine; the chefs shake up tradition while respecting the innate flavors of their ingredients. The restaurant is tucked away in a quiet residential neighborhood, on the street level of a dignified-looking compound of brown-brick apartment buildings, on a hillside that rises above the terminus of the Avenyn. Everything about it is haute, from its social ambitions (you'll get the impression that everyone here is terribly polite about being terribly wealthy) to its prices. Begin perhaps with a bowl of lobster soup delectably flavored with lime butter and succulent chunks of lobster, along with mussels simmered in white wine and served, surprisingly, with fresh papaya. Main courses are even more rewarding, especially those fast-seared filets of turbot married to crab-stuffed agnolotti, glazed carrots, and a lemon-flavored chervil sauce. If only Julia Child were still alive to tell us what she thinks about serving an entrecôte of lamb with a pumpkin purée. The combination works, at least for us. We like how the pastry chef takes real care to create imaginative desserts such as a strawberry *bavaroise* (Bavarian cream) with rhubarb purée and even a rhubarb-flavored sorbet.

Teknologatan 3. ✆ **031/16-20-66.** www.thornstromskok.com. Reservations recommended. Main courses 150SEK–375SEK ($30–$75/£15–£38); set-price menus 745SEK–995SEK ($149–$199/£75–£100). AE, MC, V. Tues–Sat 6pm–1am. Closed 7 weeks in midsummer. Tram: 5.

MODERATE

A Hereford Beefstouw ★ Value STEAK The true carnivore may want to skip some of the fancy restaurants recommended above and head here. This is the best and most appealing steakhouse in Gothenburg, with a reputation for expertly prepared Brazilian beef, and a salad bar that's the most varied and copious in town. One of the three separate dining rooms is smoke free, and all have thick-topped wooden tables, lots of varnished pine, and touches of African oak. The only sauces available to accompany your beef are béarnaise butter sauce, parsley butter sauce, and garlic butter sauce: The management believes in allowing the flavor of the meat to come through, unmasked by more elaborate seasonings. The largest platter is a 500-gram (18-oz.) T-bone steak, a portion

so large that we advise you to finish it at your own risk. Other platters, such as filet steaks, **181**
veal sirloins, and tenderloins, are more reasonably sized. A full list of wines and beers is
available.

Linnégatan 5. ℂ **031/775-04-41.** Reservations recommended. Main courses 145SEK–498SEK ($29–
$100/£15–£50); salad bar as a main course 95SEK–142SEK ($19–$28/£9.50–£14). AE, DC, MC, V. Mon–
Thurs 11:30am–2pm and 5–10pm; Fri–Sat 5–11pm; Sun 3–9pm. Tram: 2, 3, 6, 9, or 11.

Bliss Resto ★ (**Finds**) INTERNATIONAL   In its way, this is one of the hippest and
most appealing dining and drinking spots in Gothenburg, thanks to a setting that was
described to us by a local resident as "the kind of place that you can imagine yourself
having sex in." The staff is charming and there is a sense of whimsical internationalism
to the place. Most patrons range in age from 25 to 40. There are tables set outside during
clement weather, zebra-skin upholsteries that Marlene Dietrich would've loved, great
music, and an ambitious cuisine that's entirely composed of tapas that you'll share with
the other members of your dining party. Management usually recommends that five or
six of them will create an adequate meal for a party of two. There's a provocative drink
menu; the bartender might not even describe the ingredients of, say, the Sunset Boulevard or the Bondi Beach Block at all, but instead, he'll describe the feeling (red and
raucous? pink and dizzy?) that drinking one or two of them will induce. Some clients, in
the wee early hours of a Sunday morning, can remember dancing on the bar here. Luck-
ily, at least according to what we were told, no one has ever actually fallen off. Tasty tapas
and their succulent ingredients change with the season, but might include salmon pas-
trami with cream sauce; deep-fried prawn cakes with chili dip; spicy chorizo rolls stuffed
with lemon-flavored cream sauce; and skewered lamb with wasabi and dill-flavored
bouillon. Come here for a drink before or after a meal in another restaurant, or come
here for a full-fledged dining experience. We classify it among our three or four favorite
spots in Gothenburg.

Magasinsgatan 3. ℂ 031/13-85-55. www.blissresto.com. Reservations recommended for dinner. Tapas
70SEK–119SEK ($14–$24/£7–£12). AE, DC, MC, V. June–Aug Wed–Thurs 7pm–midnight, Fri–Sat 7pm–
2am; Sept–May Tues–Thurs 7pm–midnight, Fri–Sat 7pm–2am. Tram: 6, 9, or 11.

Brasserie Lipp SWEDISH/FRENCH   Since the real Brasserie Lipp in Paris, that
Hemingway favorite, has fallen off in its standards, this bistro now serves even better fare
than the original. Opened in 1987 on Gothenburg's busiest avenue, the brasserie serves
cuisine inspired by the legendary Left Bank bistro in Paris, tweaked for Swedish tastes.
For example, the menu includes escargots in garlic-butter sauce, Lipp's Skagen toast
(piled high with fresh shrimp), a tender Swedish entrecôte of beef with Dijon mustard
sauce, grilled halibut with garlic-tomato sauce, and a savory Thai chicken. There's also
choucroute garnie (sauerkraut with sausage and pork, the most famous dish served at its
Paris namesake), as well as many different kinds of fish, most caught in the waters near
Gothenburg.

Kungsportsavenyn 8. ℂ **031/10-58-30.** www.brasserielipp.com. Reservations required. Main courses
179SEK–319SEK ($36–$64/£18–£32); daily lunch platters 79SEK–109SEK ($16–$22/£8–£11). AE, DC, MC,
V. Mon–Wed 11:30am–1am; Thurs–Fri 11:30am–3am; Sat noon–3am; Sun noon–midnight. Tram: 1, 4, 5,
or 6. Bus: 40.

Linné Terrassen Kök & Bar SWEDISH   One of the best restaurants within its
neighborhood, this eatery occupies an outlandish-looking covered deck that has
disfigured the front of a 19th-century Swedish house. In winter, the venue moves inside
into a cozy antique bar that's flanked on two sides with a well-appointed network of

dining rooms that still retain the panels, coves, and architectural accessories, including depictions of cherubs cavorting on the ceiling, of their original construction; the well-heeled Gothenburg student-types who eat here "shun flashiness." The cookery is predictable and respectable—and we don't mean that as a put-down. Menu items include a goat's-cheese mousse with beetroot salad and walnut dressing; a platter of charcuterie and cheeses with cured meats from Sweden and cheeses from Spain; grilled black Angus sirloin with red-wine sauce; and filet of lamb with cider-flavored mustard and chives and a fondant of potatoes and rosemary sauce. Dessert might be a selection of sorbets with marinated strawberries. This place roars into action as a bar as well as a restaurant. As such, it's separately recommended in the "Gothenburg After Dark" section of this chapter.

Linnégatan 32. ✆ **031/24-08-90.** Reservations recommended. Main courses 95SEK–260SEK ($19–$52/£9.50–£26). AE, DC, MC, V. Mon–Fri 4pm–1am; Sat–Sun 11am–2am. Tram: 6.

Restaurang Räkan/Yellow Submarine ★ SEAFOOD The Beatles are long gone, of course, but this stalwart favorite from the 1970s still survives. This restaurant has evolved into something that's artfully shabby, with a kind of "counterculture cool" that continues to remain popular despite the changing times. Not surprisingly, it has a nautical decor with buoy lamps, wooden-plank tables typical of the Swedish west coast, and a shallow-bottomed re-creation of a Swedish lake. Your seafood platter arrives on a battery-powered boat with you directing the controls. You can order various combinations of crayfish (in season), along with prawns, poached sole, mussels, lobster, filet of gray sole, and fresh crabs. One standby is Räkan's hot and spicy fish and shellfish casserole. If you don't want fish, a choice of chicken and beef dishes is available, but those aren't anything special. Attached to the restaurant is a popular pub, Yellow Submarine, named for The Beatles' song.

Lorensbergsgatan 16. ✆ **031/16-98-39.** www.rakan.se. Reservations recommended. Main courses 235SEK–345SEK ($47–$69/£24–£35). AE, DC, MC, V. Mon–Sat 4–11pm; Sun 3–10pm. Tram: 1, 3, 4, 5, or 6. Bus: 40.

Smaka SWEDISH Smaka (or "Taste") is a solid and much-visited staple for conservative and flavorful Swedish cuisine within the Vasaplatsen neighborhood, a residential area near the main downtown campus of Gothenburg University. The blue-painted dining room evokes an old-fashioned Swedish farmhouse. Food is served on the bare boards of wide-planked, well-scrubbed pinewood tables, without tablecloths, like your Swedish grandmother used to do. Begin your meal with filets of sweet pickled herring, with browned butter, chopped egg, and dill; or whitebait roe with toast, chopped onions, chopped hard-boiled egg, and boiled potatoes. These offerings have staved off hungry Swedes for years. You could follow that with one of the most typical Swedish dishes—Swedish meatballs, the size of ping-pong balls, served with lingonberries. (Beware: The lingonberries are addictive.) If you want to keep sampling Swedish staples, you might try the sautéed filet of pork with fried potatoes or the minced veal steak flavored with herbs and served in a mustard sauce. One of the best dishes, though, is a soup studded with fish and shellfish and given the added flavor of aioli. Don't expect culinary experimentation or innovation here: The clients who frequent this place appreciate its old-fashioned agrarian virtue, and would probably resist any attempts to change it.

Vasaplatsen 3. ✆ **031/13-22-47.** Reservations recommended. Main courses 98SEK–198SEK ($20–$40/£10–£20); set-price menu 340SEK ($68/£34). AE, DC, MC, V. Mon–Thurs and Sun 5pm–1am; Fri–Sat 5pm–2am. Tram: 13 or 16.

Soho ★ INTERNATIONAL   The owner of this cozy and well-managed place enjoyed
New York City's Soho so much that he named his restaurant in its honor. It's the kind of
hip, in-the-know place where publishers entertain prospective best-selling authors. The
decor is Iberia-inspired, something like the living area of a prosperous hacienda in Spain,
even though the thick wood tables and accessories derive from the Czech Republic, India,
and Central America. A wine bar fills up a substantial corner of the place. In winter, up
to 40 reds and 40 whites are sold by the glass. (That number is somewhat reduced in July
and Aug). There's a series of simple platters available at the bar, and more substantial food
is served in the dining area. Menu items include platters with pickled herring and cured
salmon, served with regional cheese; pasta with strips of veal, mushrooms, goat cheese,
citrus sauce, and arugula; or creamy blue mussel soup with herb-and-garlic–flavored
toast. The filet of lamb with a tomato-flavored Parmesan sauce is especially good.

Östra Larmgatan 16. ⓒ **031/13-33-26.** www.sohogothenburg.se. Reservations recommended. Lunch
main courses 129SEK–155SEK ($26–$31/£13–£16); dinner main courses 159SEK–289SEK ($32–$58/£16–
£29). AE, DC, MC, V. Mon–Wed 9am–11pm; Thurs 9am–midnight; Fri 9am–1am; Sat 10am–1am; Sun
11:30am–5pm. Tram: 1, 2, or 3.

Wasa Allé & Wasa Källare ★★ SWEDISH/FRENCH/BRAZILIAN/ASIAN   This
is one of the most appealing restaurants in Gothenburg, an elegant, even posh, enclave
of good times and fine dining that's the culinary focal point of the Wasastan neighborhood, just across the avenue from the downtown campus of the University of Gothenburg. Set within what functioned for many years as a pharmacy, the restaurant contains
a large and angular bar, contemporary-looking crystal chandeliers, touches of stained
glass from its earliest incarnation, and a high-ceilinged sense of grandeur that stands in
quirky contrast to the animation at the bar and at the dining tables. Menu items in the
restaurant include such favorites as shellfish lasagna with squid, crayfish, and scallops,
served with "sugarpea foam" and a confit of tomatoes; or else oyster and parsley soup
with a sashimi of Swedish fish and shellfish. The grilled halibut is set off perfectly with
fresh rosemary and garlic, though we find ourselves gravitating to the *pot-au-feu* of tender
veal served with beans, lentils, roasted garlic, apple mash, horseradish, and a purée of root
vegetables.

Menu items are simpler and cheaper in the street-level Källare, where Swedish home-
style food, displayed in refrigerated glass cases, stands in distinct contrast to the more
exotic cuisine served upstairs. Daily platters might include filet of chicken in parsley-
flavored wine sauce; roasted elk with chanterelles and mashed potatoes; that standard,
Swedish meatballs; a platter of Spanish-style *tapas;* or vegetarian lasagna. Glasses of wine
in the cellar cost around 55SEK ($11/£5.50) each. Although service in the restaurant is
attentive and fast-paced, in the cellar-level cafe, you'll place your food order at the counter, then carry it to a table, either outdoors or inside.

Vasagatan 24. ⓒ **031/13-13-70.** Reservations recommended in the restaurant, not necessary in the cafe.
Restaurant main courses 275SEK–325SEK ($55–$65/£28–£33); set-price menus 395SEK–495SEK ($79–
$99/£40–£50). Cafe platters 55SEK–119SEK ($11–$24/£5.50–£12). AE, DC, MC, V. Restaurant Mon–Thurs
11:30am–2pm and 5:30–11pm; Fri 5:30pm–1am; Sat 5:30pm–1am. Cafe Mon–Sat 10am–6pm. Tram:
1 or 3.

INEXPENSIVE

The Bishop's Arms BRITISH/SWEDISH   Okay, so it's a member of a citywide
chain, but don't expect fast-fried burgers with fries: The venue celebrates Olde England
but with a Swedish accent. Although this is the largest, with a wider selection of beer than
at any of its twins, there are clones of its basic format within other members of the Elite

Hotel group in Gothenburg. The decor is appropriately woodsy and rustic, with black slate floors. The iron beams and brick vaulting of the ceiling recall the original 19th-century insurance company headquarters; there is also lots of stained glass. Note that some of the platters are prepared within the kitchens of the hotel's more expensive main restaurant, thereby providing some high-quality food at "pub grub" prices. The food, though good and filling, hardly taxes the imagination of the busy chefs in back. Menu items include Greek salads, Caesar salads with strips of grilled chicken or shrimp, shrimp sandwiches, salmon toasts, platters piled high with cheese and cold cuts, pork filets in mushroom-flavored cream sauce, and rib-sticking soups. This place operates in the British style: Place your food orders at the bar, and a staff member will carry the final product directly to your table.

In the cellar of the Elite Plaza Hotel. Vastra Hamngatan 3. © 031/720-40-00. Main courses 100SEK–165SEK ($20–$33/£10–£17). AE, DC, MC, V. Mon–Sat 5pm–1am. Tram: 1, 4, 5, or 6. Bus: 40.

Café Husaren INTERNATIONAL   Past lives have included stints as a pharmacy, a milliner, and a bank. Today it is the best known, most animated, and most popular cafe in the Haga district of Gothenburg. The century-old decor includes a reverse-painted glass ceiling conceived in 1890 in tones of cerulean blue with flowers. Place your order for well-stuffed sandwiches, freshly made salads (the shrimp salad is very good), and pastries, which include the biggest, most fattening, and most succulent cinnamon rolls in town. (They're the size of small pizzas, and a lot thicker.) You carry your food to one of the indoor or, in summer, outdoor tables.

Haga Nygata 24. © 031/13-63-78. www.cafehusaren.se. Sandwiches 25SEK–65SEK ($5–$13/£2.50–£6.50); pastries 15SEK–45SEK ($3–$9/£1.50–£4.50). MC, V. Mon–Fri 9am–8pm; Sat–Sun 9am–6pm. Tram: 3, 6, 9, or 11.

Froken Olssons Café SWEDISH   Looking for one of the most central cafes in Gothenburg? If so, head here. Less than 2 blocks from the Avenyn, this is a traditional favorite of Gothenburgers. It tends to be crowded and noisy at lunchtime. Even though there's a large interior, the crowd overflows onto an outdoor terrace in summer. Pastas, chicken dishes, and a hot pie served with a salad are featured. Ongoing staples include baguette sandwiches filled with such ingredients as shrimp or ham and cheese. Beer, wine, and exotic coffees are served, but liquor isn't available. Basically, this is a place that features light coffee shop–style dining, with homemade soups and such main courses as entrecôte.

Östra Larmgatan 14. © 031/13-81-93. Coffee 30SEK ($6/£3); *dagens* (daily) menu 55SEK–72SEK ($11–$14/£5.50–£7.20); hot pie with salad 65SEK ($13/£6.50); sandwiches 35SEK–80SEK ($7–$16/£3.50–£8). AE, DC, MC, V. Mon–Fri 9am–10pm; Sat–Sun 10am–10pm. Tram: 1, 4, 5, or 6. Bus: 40.

Solrosen (Value) VEGETARIAN   "Sunflower" is the best vegetarian restaurant in Gothenburg. Diners take advantage of the all-you-can-eat salad bar, returning again and again for a good "tuck in." (You serve yourself at the counter.) And everything looks fresh and recently prepared. There's even unlimited coffee, with your cup refilled if you want. Unlike at many veg restaurants, beer and wine are available. "Why not?" the cook told us. "Beer and wine are natural ingredients." The Sunflower blooms in the Haga district, a low-rise neighborhood of 18th- and early-19th-century buildings. "It used to be called a working-class neighborhood, but a lot of people in Haga don't work anymore," a local patron informed us.

Kaponjärgatan 4. © 031/711-66-97. Daily platters 50SEK–75SEK ($10–$15/£5–£7.50). AE, DC, MC, V. Mon–Fri 11:30am–10pm; Sat 2pm–1am. Tram: 1, 6, or 9.

5 SEEING THE SIGHTS

Don't panic: Gothenburg has only a fraction of the attractions that Stockholm has, and you can comfortably tour the highlights of the city in a day or two. If it's summer, you might like another day or so to explore some of the resorts, attractions, bodies of water, and islands in the environs.

As with any new destination, often the problem is having too much to do. Following the itineraries below will help you plan your time so you can see as much as possible.

SUGGESTED ITINERARIES

IF YOU HAVE 1 DAY

Enjoy a cup of coffee at one of the cafes along the Avenyn in the center of Gothenburg; then take the classic Padden boat ride, traveling through the moat and canal out to the harbor and the giant docks. Return for a stroll along the Avenyn; then take one of the summertime vintage trams to see part of the city ashore. Go to Liseberg amusement park in the evening.

IF YOU HAVE 2 DAYS

For your first day, follow the suggestions above. On Day 2, take a boat trip to Elfsborg Fortress, leaving from the Stenpiren in the Gothenburg harbor and continuing under the Älvsborg Bridge to Elfsborg. In the afternoon, visit the Göteborgs Konstmuseum and the Botanical Garden.

IF YOU HAVE 3 DAYS

For the first 2 days, follow the itineraries suggested above. On Day 3, get up early to visit the fish auction at the harbor (begins at 7am); then go to the

Feskekörka (Fish Church) nearby. Take tram no. 6 to Guldhedens Våttentorn (water tower) for a panoramic view of Gothenburg. Go to Götaplatsen to see the famed Poseidon fountain by Carl Milles. In the afternoon, visit the Röhsska Museum of Arts and Crafts and stroll through the rose-filled Trädgårdsföreningen across from the Central Station.

IF YOU HAVE 4–5 DAYS

For Days 1 to 3, follow the itineraries suggested above. On Day 4, take an excursion to Marstrand, north of the city. On Day 5, visit Nordstan, the biggest shopping center in Scandinavia. Spend the remaining part of the day exploring the southern archipelago, which you can do free with your Gothenburg Card (see "Getting Around," earlier in this chapter). The MS *S:t Erik* departs from Lilla Bommen, near Gothenburg's Opera House, and the steamboat *Bohuslän* leaves from Skeppsbron/Stenpiren for trips around the archipelago.

THE TOP ATTRACTIONS

The best way to get your bearings when you set out to see the city is to go to the 120m-tall (394-ft.) **Guldhedens Vattentorn** (water tower), Syster Estrids Gata (© 031/82-00-09). To get there, take tram no. 10 or bus no. 51 or 52 from the center of the city, about a 10-minute ride. The elevator ride up the tower is free, and there's a cafeteria/snack bar on top. The tower is open February to November (and sometimes in Dec) daily 11am to 9pm.

Early risers can visit the daily **fish auction** at the harbor, the largest fishing port in Scandinavia. The amusing auction begins at 7am sharp. We suggest that you do as we do and sample some freshly made fish cakes at one of the stands here. You also can visit the **Feskekörka (Fish Church),** on Rosenlundsgatan (no phone), which is in the fish market. Built in 1874, it's open Tuesday to Friday 9am to 5pm and Saturday from 9am to 1pm. Take tram 3, 6, 9, or 11.

The traditional starting point for seeing Gothenburg is the cultural center, **Götaplatsen,** with its *Poseidon Fountain* ★★, sculpted by Carl Milles. This fountain is a powerful symbol of maritime Gothenburg. The trio of buildings here are the **Concert Hall,** the municipally owned **theater,** and the **Göteborgs Konstmuseum.**

East India House (Museum of Gothenburg) ★   This old house is filled with mementos of a more prosperous day, and on each visit we make some new intriguing discovery. The building itself was constructed in 1750 and was the headquarters, warehouse, and auction room of the East India Company. It was filled with the riches of the Orient, including exotic spices, silks, and fine porcelain. Despite great success in the beginning, the company went bankrupt in 1809.

After being taken over by the city, the warehouse was turned into three museums: for archaeology, history, and industry. To some, that will sound dull, but there is much to amuse here, including artifacts from the heyday of the Swedish Vikings.

If you're Sally Field planning to make another labor movement movie, you might be interested in the exhibits detailing harsh working conditions in the textile factories in the early 1900s. Of greater fascination to us is the collection from the "attics" of Gothenburg that include rare antiques, folkloric costumes, a stunning porcelain collection, period interiors, and even medieval artifacts from the west coast of Sweden.

Norra Hamngatan 12. ✆ **031/61-27-70.** www.stadsmuseum.goteborg.se. Admission 40SEK ($8/£4) adults, free for students under 25 and children. June–Aug daily 10am–5pm; Sept–May Tues–Sun 10am–5pm (to 8pm Wed). Tram: 1 or 9. Bus: 40, 58, or 60 to Brunnsparken.

Göteborgs Konstmuseum (Gothenburg Art Museum) ★★★   You could watch Ingmar Bergman films to get the impression that Swedes are mired in moody introspection—but a visit to this museum will do too. Boasting the most significant repository of Swedish art outside Stockholm, the museum's array of 19th- and 20th-century Swedish art is vast; it also possesses a treasure-trove of Dutch and Flemish art from the 1600s, Italian and Spanish art from the 1500s to the 1700s, and French painting from the 19th and 20th centuries. The museum's holdings are beefed up by large bequests of modern art: Bonnard, Cézanne, van Gogh, and Picasso are represented, along with sculpture by Carl Milles and Rodin.

The gallery is also noted for its collection of works by 19th- and 20th-century Scandinavian artists (Anders Zorn and Carl Larsson of Dalarna, and Edvard Munch and Christian Krohg of Norway). Of more local interest is the work of the "Göteborg Colorists" who painted for 20 years beginning in 1930. On every subsequent visit, we always head first for the **Fürstenberg Gallery** ★★★, named to honor its benefactor, Pontus Fürstenberg (1827–1902). He collected an amazing group of paintings by some of Sweden's leading artists, even works by Prince Eugen (the "painting prince"). Look for a display of Swedish artists who lived in Paris's Montmartre section during its artistic heyday in the 1880s and the works from the National Romantic period in the 1890s.

If you need an escape from all the morose, wander into the **Arosenius Room** ★★★, where the wit, charm, and humor of the artist Ivar Arosenius (1878–1909) are on display. The late actress Greta Garbo once came here pronouncing Arosenius's work as "divine, darling," and she rarely called anything divine or anyone darling. Arosenius was an artist of Gertrude Stein's "Lost Generation," and he worked in the shadow of the National Romantic artists but strove to find his own form of expression. The artist, who led a bohemian life, often turned to themes from folklore and myth. He died far too early at the age of 30.

Götaplatsen. (*C*) **031/368-35-00.** Admission 40SEK ($8/£4) adults, 80SEK ($16/£8) adult entry to special exhibitions, free for students and children under 20. Tues 11am–6pm; Wed 11am–9pm; Thurs–Fri 11am–5pm; Sat–Sun 11am–5pm. Tram: 4, 5, 6, or 8. Bus: 40, 41, or 58.

Liseberg Nöjespark (Liseberg Park) ★★ (**Kids**) It's almost unfair to compare this amusement park to Copenhagen's Tivoli, which is the best of its kind. But Liseberg stands on its own as the top tourist attraction in Sweden in terms of number of visitors. It lacks the lavish sense of nostalgic kitsch of Tivoli, but in terms of size, it is the biggest amusement park in northern Europe. From roller coasters to live bandstand music to flower gardens, it is a world of yesterday. In business for some 8 decades, it makes more frequent concessions to popular (usually American) culture than you're likely to find within Tivoli. Singles and romantic couples stroll frequently along paths flanked with immaculately maintained flowerbeds, and entire families sometimes make visits here the focal point of their summer holiday. Some of Sweden's best performing artists entertain every summer at Stora Scenen, the park's main stage. An ongoing attraction within the park is the Gasten Ghost Hotel, filled with things that go bump in the night. Other adventure rides include the Källerado rapid river, a simulated white-water trip through the wilds of northern Sweden, and the HangOver, the most harrowing roller coaster in northern Europe, which travels at a frightening speed along the usual bends and loops. The Tornet is a circling observation platform, visible from most points in Gothenburg, that carries its participants to dizzying heights above the cityscape, where they remain aloft for up to 7 panoramic minutes. The Rocket Launcher fires you 60m (197ft.) into the air; at the top, you'll be weightless before you come screaming back down.

For the younger set, there's a children's playground with a circus, a kiddie roller coaster, and a rabbit house where the Liseberg rabbits live. Like in Disneyland, there also is a Fairy Tale Castle where knights, fair damsels, and other period figures amuse children, plus a Dragon Boat ride straight from Sweden's Viking era. Many Gothenburgers like to come here in summer to dine, as there are at least two dozen dining spots within the park, about two thirds of them devoted to wursts, sausages, and fast food and the rest to more elaborate seafood and steaks.

Korsvägen. (*C*) **031/40-01-00** or 031/40-02-20. www.liseberg.se. Admission to park, but not including rides inside the park, is 70SEK ($14/£7) adults, free for children under 7. An all-inclusive 1-day pass valid for access to all rides within the park costs an additional 290SEK ($58/£29) per person (no discount for children). Hours and opening days during Apr–May and Sept–Oct vary, depending on school holidays and advance reservation for groups; June usually daily 11am–10pm; July–Aug usually daily 10 or 11am to 9 or 11pm. Tram: 4 or 5 from the city.

Maritiman (**Kids**) This is the largest floating ship museum in the world. Located on the harbor, and dedicated to Gothenburg's 19th- and 20th-century shipyard and maritime history, this museum consists of 19 ships, boats, and barges, the largest and most dramatic of which is the destroyer *Småland.* Decommissioned from the Swedish navy in 1979, but still equipped with guns and torpedoes, it's the largest of a collection of vessels that require visitors to navigate lots of ramps, staircases, and—for the truly intrepid, ladders. Designed to be as authentic a maritime experience as possible, the museum includes lightships, steamships, and tugboats, as well as a submarine. The museum includes at least one cafe, or, during midsummer, at least two cafes.

Packhuskajen 8. (☎) **031/10-59-60.** www.maritiman.se. Admission 80SEK ($16/£8) adults, 40SEK ($8/£4) children 7–15, free for children under 7. Mar–Apr and Sept–Oct daily 10am–4pm; May–Aug daily 10am–6pm; Nov Sat–Sun 10am–4pm. Closed Dec–Feb. Tram: 5 to Lilla Bommen.

Röhsska Konstslöjdmuseet (Museum of Arts and Crafts) ★★

Dating from 1916, this is Sweden's only museum of applied art. The museum is well laid out, almost in textbook fashion, with each floor devoted to a different epoch of decorative art. Some of the artifacts shown here date back 1,000 years, from the early Chinese dynasties right up to the modern era that produced the Absolut Vodka bottle. The nostalgic journey includes displays of antiques, old manuscripts, intricate tapestries, glassware, and household objects from the 20th century. Temporary exhibits of modern art and crafts are a regular feature on the ground floor, and the third floor is permanently devoted to East Asian art. There is not one exhibit here that towers over another—it's the sum total of the museum that packs them in. The only exceptions to the rule are the two marble lions from the Ming dynasty (1368–1644) flanking the entrance to this National Romantic–style building.

Vasagatan 37–39. (☎) **031/36-83-150.** Admission 40SEK ($8/£4) adults, free for students and those under 20. Tues noon–8pm; Wed–Fri noon–5pm; Sat–Sun 11am–5pm. Tram: 3, 4, 5, 7, or 10. Bus: 40, 41, or 58.

Universeum (National Science Discovery Center for the Family) (Kids)

Devoted to inculcating a respect for the environment in young children and adults alike, this relative newcomer to the Gothenburg museum scene includes a simulated rainforest, various aquatic environments in oversized saltwater and freshwater holding tanks, and an array of live animals living within re-creations of their native habitats. Frankly, whether you like this museum—or not—will depend largely on the special exhibitions mounted here.

Korsvägen. (☎) **031/335-64-50.** www.universeum.se. Admission 165SEK ($33/£16) adults, depending on special exhibitions, 135SEK ($27/£13) children 4–16, free for children under 4. Daily 10am–7pm. Tram 4, 5, 6, 8, 13, or 14.

Varlds Kultur Museet (Museum of World Culture)

Gothenburg's newest museum (opened in 2004), and the pride of many of its residents, manages to combine aspects of sociology with idealism in ways that seem to have been perfected in Sweden. Expect a respectful celebration of the diversity of human cultures, with an emphasis on "why can't everyone just get along?" Most of the interior is devoted to temporary exhibitions that explore issues of global importance, including religion and racism, global warming, and famine and biodiversity in Africa.

Korsvägen. (☎) **031/63-27-30.** www.varldskulturmuseet.se. Admission 40SEK ($8/£4). Tues and Fri–Sun noon–5pm; Wed–Thurs noon–9pm. Tram: 4, 5, 6, 8, 13, or 14.

PARKS & GARDENS

Botaniska Trädgården (Botanical Garden) ★★

This park is Gothenburg's oasis of beauty and is, in fact, the most dramatic cultivated bit of nature in western Sweden. The botanical gardens were first opened to the public in 1923 and have been improved considerably over the years with better landscaping and more stunning plantings. Winding paths stretching for a few kilometers have been cut through the gardens, and you can stroll along at leisure, absorbing the beauty of nature at every turn. There are plants and landscape scenes from around the world, including a bamboo grove evoking Southeast

Asia and a Japanese dale. In spring, the blooming **Rhododendron Valley** ★★ is one of the most stunning sights of Gothenburg. The splendid **Rock Garden** ★ alone is worth the journey, featuring ponds, rugged rocks, cliffs, rivulets, and a cascade.

Carl Skottsbergsgata 22A. © **031/741-11-06.** Free admission to garden; greenhouses 20SEK ($4/£2), free for children under 17. Garden daily 9am–sunset. Greenhouses May–Aug daily 10am–5pm; Sept–Apr daily 10am–4pm. Tram: 1, 7, or 8.

Slottsskogen (Castle Park) ★★ **Kids** With 110 hectares (272 acres), this is the largest park in Gothenburg, and it's perfect for a picnic on a summer day. First laid out in 1874 in a naturally wooded area, today it has beautiful walks, animal enclosures, a saltwater pool, bird ponds, and an aviary, as well as a children's zoo (open May–Aug). A variety of events and entertainment take place here in summer. There's an outdoor cafe at the zoo, plus restaurants at Villa Bel Park and Björngårdsvillan.

Near Linnéplatsen. © **031/365-37-00.** www.goteborg.se/slottsskogen. Free admission. Daily 24 hr. Tram: 1 to Linnéplatsen.

Trädgårdsföreningen (Horticultural Society Park) ★★ **Kids** If we lived in Gothenburg, we'd make seasonal visits here, coming in February for the camellias, in March and April for the orchids, or in July for the giant waterlilies that burst into bloom. Most definitely we'd show up in early July and again in late August when the roses are at their peak. Located across the canal from the Central Station, this park boasts a large rosarium that flourishes with about 4,000 rose bushes and about 19,000 other species. The park's centerpieces include the **Palmhuset** ★★, a fanciful and ornate greenhouse dating to 1876 (whose design was inspired by London's Crystal Palace, which was built as part of London's World Exhibition) maintained at subtropical temperatures even in the depths of winter; and a butterfly house containing beautiful butterflies that flutter through a simulation of a natural habitat. The city of Gothenburg hosts exhibits, concerts (sometimes during the lunch hour), and children's theater pieces in the park.

Entrances on Slussgatan (across from the Central Station) and Södra Vägen. © **031/365-58-58.** www. tradgardsforeningen.se. Park 15SEK ($3/£1.50) adults, free for children under 18, free for everyone Sept–Apr. Palmhuset 100SEK ($20/£10) adults, free for children 14 and under. Daily 10am–8pm. Butterfly House is open only for private art exhibitions.

ARCHITECTURAL HIGHLIGHTS

Göteborgsoperan (The Gothenburg Opera House) It's the pride of Gothenburg, a sprawling, glass-fronted building erected at the edge of a harbor that a century ago was known throughout the world for its shipbuilding prowess. Today, views from this dramatic postmodern building—inspired by an ocean liner—encompass what remains of Gothenburg's heavy industry. The opera is completely closed during July and August. For more details, see "Opera & Ballet" under "Gothenburg After Dark," later in this chapter.

Packhuskajen. © **031/13-13-00.** www.opera.se. Tickets 95SEK–565SEK ($19–$113/£9.50–£57), depending on the venue. Box office daily noon–6:00pm or until the performance starts (closed on Sun and public holidays, if there is no performance). 90-min. guided tours, scheduled on an as-needed basis by an outside tour operator, cost around 150SEK ($30/£15) per person. Call © 031/10-80-00 for info. Tram: 5 or 10.

Kronhusbodarna (Crown House) One of the architectural showpieces of Gothenburg, Kronhusbodarna originally was built in the 1650s; it's the oldest nonecclesiastical building in town. In the 1660s, it was pressed into service as the meeting place for the Swedish Parliament, which convened here hastily to welcome a visit from Charles X

Gustav during his wars with Denmark. For many years, the building functioned as a warehouse and repair center for the Swedish military, stockpiling sailcloth and armaments. Today its echoing interior accommodates a number of small-scale and rather sleepy artisans' studios, including a chocolate maker, a goldsmith, and the glass-blowing studio of Helena Gibson, whose trademark is glass she crafts in a heavenly shade of cerulean blue.

Kronhusgatan 1D. (℄ **031/40-01-00**. www.kronhusbodarna.nu. Free admission. Mon–Fri 10am–7pm; Sat–Sun 11am–6pm. Tram: 1, 3, 4, 5, 6, 7, 9, 10, or 11 to Brunnsparken.

ESPECIALLY FOR KIDS

At **Liseberg Park** (p. 187), every day is children's day. The Liseberg Cirkus is a fun and charming amusement park with rides and lots of stimulating visuals, and there are always comic characters (some of them developed in close cooperation with the management of Disney) around to play with children. At least some of the rides, including the pony merry-go-round, the kids' boats, and a fun-on-wheels merry-go-round, are free for tots. Liseberg contains more flowers, and more acreage, than Tivoli.

Your children may want to stay at the amusement park's hotel, in the city center, a shorter walk from the park than any other lodgings in Gothenburg. **Hotel Liseberg Heden,** Sten Sturegatan S-411 38 Göteborg (℄ **031/750-69-00;** fax 031/750-69-30; www.liseberg.com), offers year-round rates of 1,120SEK to 2,110SEK ($224–$422/£112–£211) in a double. They include breakfast and coupons for free admission to the amusement park and many of its rides and shows. The hotel accepts major credit cards. It was built in the 1930s as an army barracks and later functioned as a youth hostel. Today, after tons of improvements, it's a very comfortable first-class hotel. To reach the 179-room hotel, take tram no. 4 or 5 to Berzeliegaten.

Naturhistoriska Museet, Slottsskogen (℄ **031/775-24-00;** www.gnm.se), displays stuffed and mounted animals from all over the world, including a stuffed elephant, a giant stuffed blue whale, and lots of big wooden drawers you'll slide open for views of hundreds of carefully preserved insects from around the world. It's open Tuesday to Sunday 11am to 5pm. Admission is 40SEK ($8/£4) for adults, free for students up to 19 years old and children. Take tram 1, 2, or 6, or bus 51 or 54 to Linnéplatsen.

There's also a **children's zoo** at Slottsskogen from May to August (see "Parks & Gardens," above).

A restaurant that kids find especially intriguing is **Restaurang Räkan/Yellow Submarine** (see "Where to Dine," earlier in this chapter), where seafood platters arrive at your table in battery-powered boats.

ORGANIZED TOURS

A sightseeing boat trip along the canals and out into the harbor will show you the old parts of central Gothenburg and take you under 20 bridges and out into the harbor. **Paddan Sightseeing Boats** ★★ (℄ **031/60-96-70**) offers 55-minute tours, with a brisk multilingual commentary. The schedule is as follows: April 4 to 27 Friday and Sunday 11:30am to 3pm; April 28 to May 18 daily 10:30am to 5pm; May 19 to June 15 daily 10am to 7pm; June 16 to August 10 daily 10:30am to 8:15pm; August 11 to 31 daily 10am to 6pm; September 1 to 28 Monday to Thursday 11:30am to 4pm, Friday to Sunday 10:30am to 5pm; September 29 to October 19 noon to 3pm (weather permitting). Boats depart from the Paddan terminal at Kungsportsplatsen, which straddles the Avenyn in the city center. The fare is 125SEK ($25/£13) for adults, 70SEK ($14/£7) for children 6 to 16, and free for kids under 4. A family ticket (two adults and two children) costs 350SEK ($70/£35). We advise you to dress warmly for this trek, as part of the itinerary takes you out into the sometimes-wind-lashed harbor for views of the dockyards and ship-repair docks. If it's less than perfect weather, it's even a good idea to buy a poncho from the ticket window for around 95SEK ($19/£9.50). When it gets truly drenching out in the harbor, you'll be glad you did. Frankly, we really enjoy this tour—it really helps you understand the layout of Gothenburg and its harbor.

Nya Elfsborg (© 031/60-96-70) is docked in the 17th-century *Fästning* fortress at the harbor's mouth. This boat takes you on a 90-minute tour from Lilla Bommen through the harbor—to and around Elfsborg Fortress, built in the 17th century to protect the Göta Älv estuary and the western entrance to Sweden. Elfsborg still bears traces of hard-fought sea battles against the Danes. Carvings on the prison walls tell tales of the threats to and hopes of the 19th-century life prisoners. A guide will be waiting for you at the cafeteria, museum, and souvenir shop for a 30-minute guided tour, in English and Swedish, of the fortress. There are five departures per day from mid-May to the end of August. The fare is 140SEK ($28/£14) for adults, or 70SEK ($14/£7) for children 6 to 16.

The meticulously restored **MS S:t Erik,** originally built in 1881, is available for evening cruises along the waterways of Gothenburg's southern archipelago. For information about tours, check with the tourist office (see "Orientation," earlier in this chapter). Or contact **Borjessons Line** (© 031/60-96-70), which provides excursion packages, brochures, tickets, and timetables. The tour costs 180SEK ($36/£18) for adults and 90SEK ($18/£9) for children 6 to 16. Departure times vary widely with the season and with demand.

For a guided 1-hour **bus tour** of Gothenburg, go to the tourist office or call © **031/60-96-70** (see "Visitor Information," earlier in this chapter) for details. Between June and August, city tours are offered between five and seven times daily depending on demand. From September to May, the tour runs only on Saturday twice a day. The fare is 125SEK ($25/£13) for adults, 70SEK ($14/£7) for children and students. Passengers buy their tickets directly aboard the bus, which departs from a clearly signposted spot adjacent to the Stora Theatern.

GOTHENBURG & BEYOND

7

SHOPPING

6 SHOPPING

Many residents of Copenhagen and Helsingør come to Gothenburg just for the day to buy Swedish merchandise. You can, too, but you should shop at stores bearing the yellow-and-blue tax-free shopping sign. These stores are scattered throughout Gothenburg (see "Fast Facts: Sweden," in the appendix, for more information).

MAJOR SHOPPING DISTRICTS **Nordstan** ★★ (www.nordstan.se), with its 150 shops and stores, restaurants, hotels, patisseries, coffee shops, banks, travel agencies, and the post office, is the largest shopping mall in Scandinavia. We are dazzled at the array of high-quality merchandise on sale here, from exclusive clothing boutiques to outlets for the major confectionery chains to bookshops—though you'll find pink plastic elephants and other junk as well. There's also a tourist information center. Most shops here are open Monday to Friday from 10am to 7pm, Saturday 10am to 6pm, and Sunday 11am to 5pm.

Kungsgatan/Fredsgatan is Sweden's longest pedestrian mall (3km/1³/₄ miles in length). The selection of shops is big and varied. Near these two streets you'll also find a number of smaller shopping centers, including Arkaden, Citypassagen, and Kompassen.

Another pedestrian venue, in this case one that's protected from inclement weather with an overhead roof, is the **Victoria Passagen,** which opens onto the Vallgatan, near the corner of the Södra Larmgatan. Inside, you'll find a cafe or two and a handful of shops devoted to handicrafts and "design" objects for the home, kitchen, and garden.

At **Grönsakstorget/Kungstorget,** little carts are put up daily with flowers, fruits, handicrafts, and jewelry, among other items. It's right in the city center, a throwback to the Middle Ages.

The often-mentioned **Avenyn,** with its many restaurants and cafes, also has a number of stores selling quality merchandise that has earned it an enviable reputation as the Champs Elysées of Sweden.

Kronhusbodarna, Kronhusgatan 1D (© **031/711-08-32;** www.kronhusbodarna.nu; see "Architectural Highlights," above), houses a number of small-scale and rather sleepy studios for glass blowers, watchmakers, potters, and coppersmiths, some of whom sell their goods to passersby. They can be visited, if the artisans happen to show up (call ahead to make arrangements). Take tram no. 1 or 7 to Brunnsparken.

The **Haga District** houses a cluster of small-scale boutiques, fruit and vegetable stands, art galleries, and antiques shops, most of them in the low-slung, wood-sided houses that were built as part of an expansion of Gothenburg during the early 1800s. Defined as Gothenburg's first suburb, it's set within a short distance of the Avenyn.

SHOPPING A TO Z
Antiques
Antik Hallarna ★★ What was originally conceived in the 19th century as a bank is now the site of at least 21 independent antiques dealers who peddle their wares in an urban location across the street from the Elite Plaza Hotel. Expect lots of somewhat dusty, small-scale collectibles and *objets d'art,* coins, stamps, antique watches and clocks, and the remnants, some of them intriguing, of what your grandmother—had she lived in a large house in Sweden—might have been storing for several generations in her attic. Västra Hamngatan 6. Each of the dealers in this place maintains its own phone number, but the phone of one of the largest dealers is © **031/774-15-25.** www.antikhallarna.se. Tram: 1, 6, 9, or 11.

Department Stores
Bohusslöjd ★★ This store has one of the best collections of Swedish handicrafts in Gothenburg. Amid a light-grained birch decor, you'll find wrought-iron chandeliers, unusual wallpaper, fabric by the yard, and other items such as hand-woven rugs, pine and birchwood bowls, and assorted knickknacks, ideal as gifts or souvenirs. In 2006, this outfit celebrated its 100th birthday. Kungsportsavenyn 25. © **031/16-00-72.** http://aos.se. Bus: 5B or 40.

C. J. Josephssons Glas & Porslin ★★★ This store, which celebrated its 140th birthday in 2006, has been selling Swedish glass since 1866 and has established an enviable reputation. The selection of Orrefors crystal and porcelain is stunning. There are signed original pieces by such well-known designers as Bertil Vallien and Goran Warff. There's also a tourist tax-free shopping service plus full shipping service. Korsgatan 12 and Kyrkogatan 34. © **031/17-56-15.** Tram: 6, 9, 11, or 41. Bus: 16 or 60.

Nordiska Kompaniet (NK) ★ Because this is a leading and decidedly upscale department store, shoppers are likely to come here first as a one-stop emporium for some of the most appealing merchandise in Sweden. (The Swedish headquarters of the same

purchases home for you. Typical Swedish and Scandinavian articles are offered here—
more than 200,000 items, ranging from Kosta Boda "sculpture" crystal, Orrefors crystal
in all types and shapes, Rörstrand high-fired earthenware and fine porcelain, stainless
steel, pewter items, dolls in national costumes, leather purses, Dalarna horses, Finnish
carpeting, books about Sweden, Swedish records, and much, much more. Östra Hamngatan 42. ✆ **031/710-10-00.** www.nk.se. Bus: 40.

Design
Design Torget (Kids)   Assembled into one all-encompassing venue, you'll find at least
40 different purveyors of intensely "designed," intensely thought-out items for the
kitchen, home, and garden, as well as some children's toys that would make fine and
thoughtful presents for nephews and nieces back home. Vallgatan 14. ✆ **031/774-00-17.**
www.designtorget.se. Tram: 6, 9, or 11.

Embroideries
Broderi & Garn   Virtually every (female) long-term resident of Gothenburg is familiar with this shop: The grandmothers and mothers of many working women here have
patronized the place seemingly since it was established nearly a century ago. If you're
looking for a pastime to make the long winter evenings go more quickly, or a pastime
that integrates handicrafts with a sense of Swedish nationalism, come here for embroidery yarns, needles, and patterns that incorporate everything from scenes of children
playing to replicas of the Swedish flag. The staff will explain the differences between
cross-stitching and crewelwork, and show you any of dozens of patterns, most of which
reflect nostalgic visions of long ago. Kits, with thread, needles, patterns, and everything
you'd need for the completion of your own embroidered masterpiece, range in price from
100SEK to 2,500SEK ($20–$500/£10–£250) each. Drottninggatan 31. ✆ **031/13-33-29.**
Tram: 1 or 5.

Fashion
Hennes & Mauritz   Established in the 1940s, this is a well-established clothing
store—part of an international Swedish chain—that keeps an eye on what's happening
in cutting-edge fashion around the world. The spirit here is trendy, with an emphasis on
looking chic and youthful for nights out on the town. Despite its undeniable sense of
flair, garments are less expensive than you might assume, with lots of marked-down
bargains for cost-conscious shoppers. Deltavagen 16. ✆ **031/65-33-80.** www.hm.com. Tram: 1,
4, or 5.

Ströms   This is the most visible emporium for clothing for men in Gothenburg, with
a history at this location dating back to 1886. We've purchased a number of smart items
here over the years, some of which still rest proudly in our closets. Scattered over two
floors of retail space, you'll find garments that range from the very formal to the very
casual, and boutique-inspired subdivisions that contain ready-to-wear garments from the
leading fashion houses of Europe. Although most of its fame and reputation derive from
its appeal to men, to a lesser extent it also sells garments for women and children. Kungsgatan 27–29. ✆ **031/17-71-00.** www.stroms.se. Tram: 1, 2, or 3.

Handicrafts
Lerverk   This is a permanent exhibit center for 30 potters and glassmaking craftspeople. We can't recommend any specific purchases because the offerings change from

month to month. Although glassworkers are more readily associated with the east coast, on our latest trip we were astonished at the skill, sleek contemporary designs, and imaginative products of these west-coast potters and glassmakers. Västra Hamngatan 24–26. ℭ 031/13-13-49. www.lerverk.se. Tram: 1, 2, 3, 4, or 7 to Grönsakstorget.

---

7 GOTHENBURG AFTER DARK

To the Gothenburger, there's nothing more enticing than sitting outdoors at a cafe along the Avenyn enjoying the short-lived summer season. Residents also like to take the whole family to the Liseberg amusement park (see "Seeing the Sights," earlier in this chapter). Although clubs are open in the summer, they're not well patronized until the cool weather sets in.

For a listing of entertainment events scheduled at the time of your visit, check the newspapers (*Götenborgs Posten* is best) or inquire at the tourist office.

THE PERFORMING ARTS
Theater
The Gothenburg Card (see "Getting Around," earlier in this chapter) allows you to buy two tickets for the price of one. Call the particular theater or the tourist office for program information. Performances also are announced in the newspapers.

Folkteatern   This theater stages productions of Swedish plays or foreign plays translated into Swedish. The season is from September to May, and performances are Tuesday to Friday at 7pm and Saturday at 6pm. Olof Palmes Plats (by Järntorget). ℭ 031/60-75-75. www.folkteatern.se. Tickets 100SEK–190SEK ($20–$38/£10–£19). Tram: 1, 3, or 4.

Stadsteatern   This is one of the major theaters in Gothenburg, but invariably the plays are performed in Swedish. Ibsen in Swedish may be too much of a challenge without knowledge of the language, but a musical may still be enjoyed. The season runs from September to May. Performances usually are Tuesday to Friday at 7pm, Saturday at 6pm, and Sunday at 3pm. Götaplatsen. ℭ 031/70-871-00. Tickets 190SEK–275SEK ($38–$55/£19–£28). Bus: 40.

Opera & Ballet
Göteborgsoperan (Gothenburg Opera House) ★★   This elegant modern opera house was opened by the Swedish king in 1994, and was immediately hailed as one of the most exciting major pieces of public architecture in Sweden. Overlooking the grimy industrial harbor landscape, with a big-windowed red-and-orange-trimmed facade, it features some of the finest theater, opera, operettas, musicals, and ballet performances in Sweden. There are also five bars and a cafe in the lobby. The main entrance (on Östra Hamngatan) leads to a foyer with a view of the harbor; here you'll find the box office and cloakroom. Big productions can be staged on a full scale. You'll have to check to see what performances are scheduled at the time of your visit. Packhuskajen. ℭ 031/10-80-00 or 031/13-13-00 for ticket information. www.opera.se. Tickets 150SEK–550SEK ($30–$110/£15–£55). Tram 5 or10.

Classical Music
Konserthuset ★★   Ironically, the symphony orchestra of Gothenburg functions as Sweden's national symphony, not its counterpart in Stockholm. And this, the Konserthuset, built in 1935 and noteworthy for its acoustics, is the Gothenburg orchestra's

official home. Between September and June, it's the venue for world-class performances of classical music. During July and August, with the exception of two or so outdoor concerts, one of which is conducted on the Götaplatsen, the concert hall is closed. Götaplatsen. ⌀ **031/726-53-00.** www.konserthuset.se. Tickets 280SEK ($56/£28). Bus: 40. Tram: 3 or 5.

THE CLUB & MUSIC SCENE
Bars & Nightclubs

Berså Bar   There's a lot about this place that might remind you of a sudsy, talkative, neighborhood bar, except that it lies astride one of the busiest intersections in Gothenburg, a prime spot for drop-ins, and for checking out who and what's on the prowl on a typical night in Sweden's "second city." There's a dance floor on the premises, a brisk big-city feeling to the bar area, and a dining menu. If you happen to engage someone here in a dialogue, ask him or her how to translate this bar's name; even the locals will give differing answers, as it was conceived as a deliberate play on Swedish words. The answer you'll usually get is "a cozy and comfortable campsite." Kungspanplatsen 1. ⌀ **031/ 711-24-80.** Sun–Thurs 11am–1am; Fri–Sat 11am–3am. Tram: 1, 4, 5, or 6.

Glow   In stark contrast to the sprawling size of the Trädgår'n (see below), this nightclub and cocktail lounge is small-scale and intimate. Outfitted in pale colors and attracting a clientele over 30, it's the most popular late-night venue in Gothenburg, sometimes attracting workers from restaurants around town who relax and chitchat here after a hard night's work. There's a small dance floor, but most visitors ignore it in favor of mingling at the bar. Open daily from 8pm to 5am. Avenyn 8. ⌀ **031/10-58-20.** Tram: 1, 4, 5, or 6.

Linné Terrassen Kök & Bar   If you linger after your evening meal here, you might be surprised at the way the bar area of this also-restaurant grows increasingly crowded, often surpassing the volume of clients in the dining room. As such, it's fun and charming and favored by attractive and usually available singles.

At the bar, you'll find 40 kinds of wine served by the glass, at least 10 beers on draft, 50 single-malt whiskies, and a daunting collection of wines by the bottle. In winter, live jazz is performed every Wednesday and Friday from 7 to 9pm, often to standing-room-only crowds. Linnégatan 32. ⌀ **031/24-08-90.** Tram: 6.

Oakley's   This is one of the most popular and visible supper clubs in Gothenburg, a frequently reconfigured longtime survivor of the entertainment industry that has chugged out food and cabaret for as long as anyone can remember. Set within a short walk of the Avenyn, behind a red-and-white facade of what was originally a fire station, it offers a changing array of dancers and impersonators (ever hear a Madonna clone singing in Swedish?) who work hard to keep the audience amused or at least visually distracted. Expect a changing array of musical acts, plenty of musical and showbiz razzmatazz, and imitations of Swedish pop stars that you might not have heard of. Food items are derived from "international" sources from around the world; well-prepared renderings of fish and meat (salmon terrine with champagne sauce, roast beef with purée of Idaho potatoes, turbot with a wasabi-flavored cream sauce) are served, supper-club-style, at tables within sightlines of a stage. There's an automatic cover charge of 130SEK ($26/£13) per person, which is added to the cost of your meal. Main courses cost from around 200SEK to 265SEK ($40–$53/£20–£27) each. The club is open Tuesday to Saturday 7pm to 1am. Tredje Långgatan 16. ⌀ **031/42-60-80.** www.oakleys.nu. Reservations recommended. Tram 1, 3, 4, or 9.

Park Lane   In this leading nightclub along Sweden's west coast, the dinner-dance room sometimes features international stars. Past celebrities have included Marlene Dietrich and Eartha Kitt. The dance floor is usually packed. Many of the musical numbers performed here are devoted to songs and lighthearted cabaret acts, so even if you don't speak Swedish, you can still appreciate the entertainment. The international menu consists of light supper platters such as crab salad or toasted sandwiches. Beer begins at 55SEK ($11/£5.50). Open Tuesday to Saturday 11:30pm to 3am. Elite Park Avenue Hotel, Kungsportsavenyn 36–38. ⓒ 031/20-60-58. www.parklane.se. Cover 80SEK–125SEK ($16–$25/£8–£13); hotel guests enter free. Tram: 1, 4, 5, or 6. Bus: 40.

Trädgår'n   This is the largest and most comprehensive nightspot in Gothenburg, with a cavernous two-story interior that echoes on weekends with the simultaneous sounds of a restaurant and a dance club. No one under 25 is admitted to the cosmopolitan and urbane venue. Cover charge for the disco is 100SEK ($20/£10). Main courses in the restaurant are 185SEK to 275SEK ($37–$55/£19–£28). The restaurant is open Monday to Friday 11:30am to 2pm and Wednesday to Saturday 6 to 10:30pm. The disco is open Friday to Saturday 11pm to 5am. Allegaten 8. ⓒ 031/10-20-80. www.tradgarn.se. Tram: 1, 3, or 5.

Tranquilo   Tranquilo is fun, colorful, and Gothenburg's newest nightspot. It features a pan-Latino aesthetic of ultrabright colors (plum, pink, and fiesta orange), all of them laid out in rectangles of color that manage, despite the ongoing background of salsa and meringue, to look like they were designed by Scandinavians—something like what Alvar Aalto might have designed on psychedelics, or on a color binge. Although food is served throughout the evening, with main courses priced from 165SEK to 235SEK ($33–$47/£17–£24), the place feels more like a bar (a singles bar), where the women are predominantly svelte, long-legged, and gorgeous. Three kinds of tacos, grilled tuna or chicken, burgers, surf-and-turf skewers, ceviche, mangos stuffed with grilled roast beef, sweet desserts, and mojitos and caipirinhas are all the rage—especially the caipirinhas, which cost around 165SEK ($33/£17) each. Food is served daily from 11:30am to 10:30pm, with the bar remaining open until between 1 and 3am, depending on business. Kungstorget 14. ⓒ 031/13-45-55. www.tranquilo.se. Tram: 1, 2, or 3.

Casinos

Casino Cosmopol   In a whimsically ornate Victorian-era building constructed on the harborfront in 1865, this palace of amusement offers food, drink, entertainment, and, of course, casino games such as blackjack, poker, Punto Banco, and American roulette. Naturally, there are slot machines—204 in all. The better of the casino's two restaurants is Casanova, offering panoramic views of the harbor from the second floor. The stage next to the Jackpot Bar Bistro, located just beside the games, features occasional entertainment. Guests must be 21 years of age and have some form of official photo ID. The entrance fee is 30SEK ($6/£3) for a day pass. It's open daily from 1pm to 4am. Packhusplatsen 7. ⓒ 031/333-55-00. www.casinocosmopol.se. Tram: 1 or 2.

Dance Clubs

Valand/Lilla London   Gastronomically and socially, this combination restaurant and dance club, both under the same management and both within the same glass-fronted building on the Avenyn, has it all. Many clients move restlessly between the two venues, ordering stiff drinks, pastas, seafood, and steaks at Lilla London, then dancing, drinking, and flirting at the congenially battered and irreverent Valand located immediately upstairs. On the premises is a small-stakes casino with blackjack and roulette, and a lot of good-looking, sometimes raucous and sometimes available, singles. The minimum age for entry is 25. Valand is open only on Friday and Saturday from 8pm to 3am. Lilla London is open Monday to Thursday from 5pm to 1am and Friday to Sunday from 4pm to 3am. Vasagatan 41. ℰ 031/18-30-93. www.valand.nu. Cover 80SEK–100SEK ($16–$20/£8–£10) for disco after 10pm. Main courses at Lilla London 119SEK–189SEK ($24–$38/£12–£19); 3-course menu 330SEK ($66/£33). Tram: 1, 4, 5, or 6. Bus: 40.

GAY GOTHENBURG

Greta's Named in honor of Greta Garbo, whose memorabilia adorns the walls of its upper floor, this is the leading gay bar and restaurant in Gothenburg, with a clientele that includes all ages and all types of gay men and lesbians. There are two animated bars, the larger of which is a wood-topped sinuous affair that fills part of the ground floor with an undulating series of curves. Decor is a mixture of the kitschy old-fashioned and new wave, juxtapositioned in ways that are almost as eye-catching as the clientele. Menu items change at least every season but might include fish and lime soup, lamb filet with mushrooms in a red-wine sauce, breast of duck with potato croquettes, or a creamy chicken stew baked in phyllo pastry. Every Friday and Saturday night from 10pm to 3am, the place is transformed into a disco, and every Saturday night beginning at 1am, there's some kind of show, often drag, sometimes not. Open Tuesday to Thursday 5 to 11pm, Friday 4pm to 3am, and Saturday 5pm to 3am. There's a cover charge of 80SEK ($16/£8), but only on Friday and Saturday nights after 10pm. Drottningsgaten 35. ℰ 031/13-69-49. www.gretas.nu. Reservations recommended Fri–Sat. Main courses 98SEK–149SEK ($20–$30/£10–£15). Tram: 1, 2, or 3.

8 THE BOHUSLÄN COAST & HALLAND

As fascinating as Gothenburg is, excursions along the west coast of Sweden can be even better. The Bohuslän Coast north of Gothenburg is called "The Golden Coast," and it's riddled with islands and skerries. This is the most idyllic sailing country in Sweden. The coast of Halland south of Gothenburg is also renowned, and it contains the most chic summer resort in Sweden, the town of Båstad. Here you'll find miles of sandy beaches lined by dunes, especially in **Skummeslovsstrand** and **Melbystrand.** Arm yourself with a good map from the Gothenburg Tourist Office before setting out.

THE BOHUSLÄN COAST ★★

The coast north of Gothenburg consists of waterways winding their way past myriad islands, sunken rocks, sounds, inlets, and waterside communities. Away from the coast, the countryside is varied, with forests, mountains, and lakes offering wonderful opportunities for outdoor activities. You can cycle along carefully laid-out tracks, hike the Bohusleden Trail (tourist offices have maps), go fishing, play golf, or take out a canoe.

Many Swedes have summer cottages along the northern coast's chain of islands, which are linked by bridges or short ferry crossings. Train service is possible from Gothenburg through to Uddevalla (which is industrial) and on to Strömstad. Buses also cover the coast, but service is infrequent. It's best to take a **driving tour** of the coast, following the E6 motorway north from Gothenburg to one of the following destinations.

Kungälv ★

If you're pressed for time, at least see Kungälv, 17km (11 miles) north of Gothenburg by bus no. 301, 302, 303, or 330 from the Central Station. We recommend it as a day trip, not necessarily as an overnight venture.

The 1,000-year-old town of Kungälv, known by the Vikings as Kongahälla, has a panoramic position by the river of Nordre Älv. The well-preserved old town consists of **Gamla torget** (the old square), a parish church, and the cobbled streets of **Östra gatan** and **Vastra gatan,** where you'll find wooden houses built centuries ago. An island in the river, **Fästningsholmen,** is an idyllic spot for a picnic.

On the E6 highway lie the ruins of the 14th-century **Bohus Fästning** (Bohus castle and fortress), Fästningsholmen (✆ **0303/156-62**). This bastion played a leading role in the battles among Sweden, Norway, and Denmark to establish supremacy. Bohus Fästning was built by order of Norway's King Haakon V on Norwegian territory; after being ceded to Sweden in 1658, it was used as a prison. Climb the tower known as *Fars Hatt* ("Father's Hat") for the most panoramic view of the coast. Hours of operation are from May 1 to August 31 daily 10am to 7pm; from September 1 to September 30 daily 11am to 5pm; closed off season. Admission is 45SEK ($9/£4.50) for adults; 25SEK ($5/£2.50) for children 7 to 16, students, and seniors; and free for ages under 7.

Where to Stay & Dine

Hotel Fars Hatt ★   The best place in town for food and lodging was established in the 17th century in the town center, close to the river. This site was used to refresh travelers with fish, game, and ale. Today the tradition continues, albeit in a four-story building from the 1960s, which has been continuously renovated ever since. The restaurant menu offers a wide selection of good-tasting Swedish and international dishes, and nonguests are welcome. The small to midsize bedrooms are well furnished, each modern and well maintained, with ample bathrooms.

Torget S-442 31 Kungälv. ✆ **0303/109-70.** Fax 0303/196-37. www.farshatt.se. 120 units. Mon–Thurs 1,325SEK ($265/£133) double; Fri–Sun 975SEK ($195/£98) double; from 1,475SEK ($295/£148) suite. Rates include breakfast. AE, DC, MC, V. Free parking. **Amenities:** Restaurant; bar; lounge; outdoor pool; sauna; laundry service; dry cleaning; nonsmoking rooms; rooms for those w/limited mobility. *In room:* TV, hair dryer (in some), Wi-Fi.

Marstrand ★★

The coast is riddled with evocative villages oozing charm and character, which makes choosing a single place to stay difficult. Although Kungälv is a good option in the area if you have time for only one stopover, Marstrand is the most evocative island in the archipelago. The resort town, formerly frequented by the Swedish king Oscar II, boasts little shops, art galleries, and idyllic scenery that's reminiscent of Nantucket, Massachusetts. Part of the fun of Marstrand is the ferry journey here; it lies 25km (16 miles) west of Kungälv.

To reach the island, drive north along E6 from Gothenburg, exiting at the signs pointing to Marstrand. These lead you to the village of Koön, where you'll park your car. (Only service vehicles with special permits are allowed on the island, thereby creating an islandwide zone that is basically reserved exclusively for pedestrians and bicyclists.) From the wharf at Koön, ferryboats depart every 15 minutes for Marstrand. Round-trip ferryboat passage costs 20SEK ($4/£2) per person. For ferryboat information (no advance reservations are necessary) call ✆ **0303/603-22.**

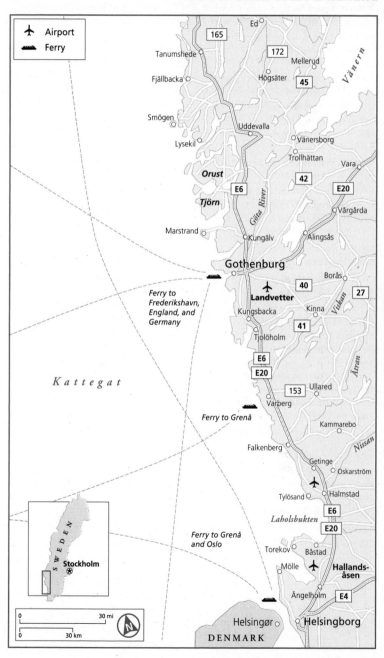

Another alternative is the no. 312 bus, which departs from Gothenburg's Central Station. Between May and September, buses leave every hour; the rest of the year, depending on business and the weather, they're less frequent and no advance reservations are necessary. For 110SEK ($22/£11), you can purchase a combined bus and ferry ticket to the island. The bus stops first in the hamlet of Tjuvkil and then continues on to the wharf at Koön.

Young people from Gothenburg and its environs flock to Marstrand on weekends, filling up the clapboard-sided hotels. The town, quiet all week, comes alive with the sounds of folk singers and the twang of guitars. The major historical site is the 17th-century **Carlsten Fortress** (© 0303/602-65) that towers over the island. After you climb up Carlsten's hill, visit the chapel and then walk through the secret tunnel to the fortress, which dates from 1658, when Charles X Gustav decided that it should be built to protect the Swedish west-coast fleet. The bastions around the lower castle courtyard were constructed from 1689 to 1705, and then completed during the first half of the 19th century. Admission is 70SEK ($14/£7) for adults, 25SEK ($5/£2.50) for children 7 to 15, and free for children under 7. It's open March to October daily from noon to 4pm, and on a limited basis the rest of the year for clients who prearrange their visits a few days, or even hours, in advance.

Where to Stay

Grand Hotel Marstrand ★   Standing head and shoulders above virtually every other hotel on the island, this yellow-fronted grande dame derives most of its midsummer business from individual clients, often families, and most of its off-season business from the many conventions which are scheduled here during the cold-weather months. Built at the close of the 19th century, it was called "the grand old lady of Marstrand," back in the days when people tended to speak in such politically incorrect terms. Although today's clients are not as elegant as those who arrived with steamer trunks long ago, the Grand still holds its own. Renovations, including the latest round completed in 2006, have preserved the original architectural charm while adding modern conveniences. Bedrooms are well furnished and spacious, opening onto views of a nearby swath of greenery (Paradise Park) and the boat-filled harbor. Bathrooms are the winners here: Decorated in classic white with brass fittings, all include showers and those old-fashioned bathtubs. Even if you're not a guest, consider patronizing the hotel's restaurant on the ground floor.

Radhusgatan 3, S-440 30 Marstrand. © **0303/603-22.** Fax 0303/600-53. www.grandmarstrand.se. 23 units. 1,795SEK–2,195SEK ($359–$439/£180–£220) double; 2,195SEK ($439/£220) suite. Rates include breakfast. AE, DC, MC, V. **Amenities:** Restaurant; bar; sauna; limited room service; babysitting; laundry service; dry cleaning; nonsmoking rooms. *In room:* TV, minibar, hair dryer.

Where to Dine

Restaurant Tenan INTERNATIONAL   The most sophisticated and the best restaurant in town lies on the street level of the Grand Hotel, within a trio of rooms that combine memorabilia and photos of the America's Cup Race with dark colors and respectful references to Sweden's royal family. During July and August you can dine on a spacious outdoor terrace. The cooks are experts at smoking fish (or do they import it?). At any rate it's served with the perfect accompaniment: dill sauce. Terrines of foie gras are served with warm brioches and fresh butter. The chefs also excel at seafood soups and piquant shellfish stews, although the menu offers other temptations, including anglerfish in a garlic-flavored saffron sauce and trout with almonds. Meat eaters should favor the grilled filet of beef with a pepper and mushroom sauce.

Lysekil ★ & Fjällbacka ★

This 200-year-old town, with its wooden houses and narrow alleyways, is another good base for exploring the coast. Today it also contains a number of workshops for artisans, artists, and craftspeople who find the area a perfect retreat from the world.

Lysekil lies directly on the seashore, set against a backdrop of pink granite rocks. Fishing areas, as well as some of the best waters for diving in northern Europe, are found here. In summer, there are occasional seal-watching trips, as well as sailing trips.

If you're driving, take Route E6 north from Gothenburg to Uddevalla, then head west along Route 161. An express bus from Gothenburg (no. 840 or 848) runs every 2 hours during the day.

The best sight in town is **Havets Hus,** Rosvikstorg (© **0523/66-81-61;** www.havets hus.lysekil.se), a sea aquarium with a collection of animal and plant life from the Gullmaren and North Sea. The main attraction here is a tunnel aquarium showing a variety of different species such as cod, ray, halibut, lobster, shark, and much more. At this tunnel, massive fish swim over and around you. At a special pool, children can feel spiky starfish and slimy algae. Wave machines make some biotopes especially realistic. From February 9 to June 13 and August 23 to October 31, it is open daily 10am to 4pm. From June 14 to August 22, hours are daily 10am to 6pm. Admission is 90SEK ($18/£9) for adults and 45SEK ($9/£4.50) for children 5 to 15 years old. The aquarium is a 10-minute walk from the tourist office, heading down toward the water.

The entire shoreline around Lysekil is a nature reserve, with some 275 varieties of plant life. Guided "marine walks" and botanical tours are at times offered in the summer (ask at the tourist office; Sodra Hamngatan 6; © **0523/130-50;** Mon–Sat 9am–7pm, Sun 11am–3pm).

On the way north to Tanumshede (see below), we always continue north along the E6, but cut west near Rabbalshede to follow Route 163 to **Fjällbacka ★**, which, in our view, is one of the most perfect, picture-postcard little fishing villages in Sweden. Houses are painted in bright shades with a wealth of gingerbread. Swedes call this *snickargladje,* although Americans are more familiar with the term "Carpenter's Gothic."

We once traveled here to interview screen legend Ingrid Bergman, star of the classic *Casablanca* and other films. She'd invited us for lunch, which consisted of a loaf of freshly baked bread and a great big red beet. (Such a lunch isn't uncommon in Sweden in the summertime.) Ms. Bergman's summer house was on one of the islands off the coast. In town, Swedes remember her fondly, and the main square is called Ingrid Bergman Square, with a statue of the screen goddess looking out over the water to her former home. Following her death from cancer in 1982, her ashes were scattered over the sea nearby.

Where to Stay & Dine

Hotel Lysekil Built in 1954 in brown brick and copper, with a traditional, gable-roofed design, this is one of the most prominent hotels in town—a focal point for most of the town's business meetings, conventions, and corporate rendezvous. Rooms were renovated in 1992, with ongoing improvements every year since, and are conservatively decorated with angular furniture and comfortable beds, but are smaller than one may hope.

Rosviktstorg 1, S-453 30 Lysekil. ℓ **0523/66-55-30.** Fax 0523/155-20. www.hotellysekil.se. 50 units. 1,190SEK–1,390SEK ($238–$278/£119–£139) double. Rates include breakfast. AE, DC, MC, V. **Amenities:** Restaurant; bar; nightclub; small-scale spa; sauna; laundry service; dry cleaning; nonsmoking rooms. *In room:* TV, Wi-Fi.

Lysekil Havshotell ★ (**Finds**) This place has more of a down-home style than the previously recommended Hotel Lysekil. Less than a kilometer (¹/₂ mile) west of the town center, the Lysekil began business in 1900 as an upscale private home. Set within its own gardens behind a turn-of-the-20th-century scarlet-and-white facade, it has polite, well-rehearsed service, public rooms that evoke a bygone age, and comfortable bedrooms that are renovated. The staff here will prepare you a simple platter of food on request—virtually whenever you want it—but other than breakfast, meals are not served on a regular basis. Access from the center of Lysekil is particularly pleasant, as you can follow the seafront quays most of the way.

Turistgatan 13, S-453 30 Lysekil. ℓ **0523/797-50.** Fax 0523/142-04. www.strandflickorna.se. 15 units. 1,239SEK–1,418SEK ($248–$284/£124–£142) double; 1,328SEK–1,596SEK ($266–$319/£133–£160) suite. Rates include breakfast. AE, MC, V. Free parking. **Amenities:** Breakfast room; bar; outdoor hot tub; laundry service; dry cleaning; nonsmoking rooms. *In room:* TV, minibar (not in summer).

Tanumshede ★★

Back on the E6 heading north, the next destination is Tanumshede, known for the greatest concentration of Bronze Age rock carvings in Scandinavia. They were designated in 1994 as a UNESCO World Heritage Site. If you're not driving, you can take one of the express buses to Tanumshede; they travel from Gothenburg five times each day, and the trip takes 2 hours.

As you enter town, you can pay a visit first to the **Tourist Office,** Bygdegardsplan (ℓ **0525/183-80**). Information regarding the best ways to visit the Bronze Age carvings is available here. The office is open from June to mid-August Monday to Friday 8am to noon and 1 to 4:30pm. Off-season hours are Monday to Friday 8am to noon and 1 to 4:30pm.

Just to the east of Tanumshede is the **Vitlycke Museum** (ℓ **0525/209-50;** www.vitlyckemuseum.se), open May to September daily 10am to 6pm, off season Tuesday to Sunday 11am to 5pm. The museum is free. The museum documents the history of the rock carvings and offers excursions—sometimes by moonlight—to the actual attraction. You also can obtain a map, "The Rock Carving Tour," which guides you easily among the carvings of northern Bohuslän, showing the way to Bohuslän's 10 best rock-carving faces. Four are in Tanum and constitute the World Heritage area. Close to the museum lies a Bronze Age farm, a full-scale reconstruction of a dwelling and farm from the era of the rock carvings. At a restaurant in the museum, the cuisine is inspired by Bronze Age raw materials such as meat and venison, fish and shellfish, parsley root, sorrel, and chickweed. Gooseberry ice cream rounds off the repast.

Where to Stay & Dine

Tanums Gestgifveri ★★ This hotel, one of the oldest continuously operating inns in the district, was established in 1663 in a forest about 10km (6¹/₄ miles) inland from the sea. From the outside, it resembles a prosperous Swedish farmhouse, with rambling porches painted in tones of pale ocher. Bedrooms are old-fashioned, cozy, and, in most cases, accented to some degree with varnished paneling. Within a separate building, also constructed in the early 1600s (but with many additions and improvements during the early 20th c.), there's a well-managed and surprisingly upscale restaurant. Most residents of the hotel opt to dine here as well, but if you're just passing through, you should know

> **(Fun Facts** Sunspot
>
> **Strömstad,** 35km (22 miles) north of Tanumshede, claims to have more annual
> hours of sunshine than anywhere else in Sweden.

that gastronomes go out of their way to visit this spot. Specialties include a succulent version of fish stew served with rice and braised fresh vegetables and freshwater catfish with wine sauce.

Apoteksvägen 7, SS-45731 Tanumshede. ✆ **0525/290-10.** Fax 0525/295-71. www.tanumsgestgifveri. com. 27 units. 980SEK–1,890SEK ($196–$378/£98–£189) double; 1,990SEK–2,290SEK ($398–$438/£199–£229) suite. Rates include breakfast and dinner. AE, DC, MC, V. Closed Dec 24–Jan 15. **Amenities:** Restaurant; pool; sauna; room service; laundry service; dry cleaning; nonsmoking rooms; rooms for those w/ limited mobility. *In room:* TV, minibar.

Strömstad ★ & the Koster Islands ★

Strömstad is a slice of Norway in Sweden—more Norwegians than Swedes summer here. Until 1658, Strömstad actually *was* part of Norway. Today it is a fishing harbor and, in summer, a lively tourist center. (A fish market is held here at 7am Tues–Fri.) Lying on the salty Skaggerrak on the borderline between Sweden and Norway, it's a place of rolling waves, cliffs warmed by the sun, and sandy beaches.

Thirty-two kilometers (20 miles) north of Tanumshede, Strömstad knew greater glory in the 18th century when it was one of the most fashionable spas in Sweden. The town makes an excellent stopover for those heading farther north into the wilds of Sweden. Many Norwegians also pass through here because of ferry links to Sandefjord, Fredrikstad, and Halden in Norway.

For information, head first for the tourist office, **Strömstad Tourist,** Torget (✆ **0526/ 623-30**). It's open July to August daily 9am to 8pm; off season Monday to Friday 9am to 6pm, Saturday 10am to 2pm.

Strömstad is linked by rail to Gothenburg, a 3-hour journey. The E6 Express Bus between Gothenburg and Oslo also stops off here. Motorists should follow Route 176 off the E6 for a distance of 12km (7¹/₂ miles).

Many visitors also use Strömstad merely as a refueling stop for trips over to the **Koster Islands ★**. If you have time for only one island, make it **Nordkoster (North Koster),** which is a large nature reserve. You can explore the whole island on foot in about 2 hours; cars are prohibited. **Sydkoster (South Koster)** is three times the size of North Koster and can be toured by bike. Before heading here, ask at the Strömstad tourist office how to arrange rentals. The waters around both islands are the warmest in Sweden for summer swimming. You can also go bird- or seal-watching on this island, and the islands abound in wildflowers. In Strömstad, ferries leave year-round from Laholmen and cost 120SEK ($24/£12) per person round-trip. The tourist office keeps a list of ferry schedules, which are subject to change because of weather conditions.

Where to Stay & Dine

Hotel Laholmen ★ This is the larger and better-accessorized of Strömstad's two hotels, with a policy of remaining open year-round. Built in 1994, it parallels the shoreline of a small peninsula that juts seaward from the center of town, and is flanked by a busy marina. Low and sprawling, the hotel has a streamlined, modern decor and comfortable bedrooms that, although monochromatic, are well maintained and cozy, with

Halland locals like pointing out that its inhabitants live longer and take less sick leave than other Swedes.

well-kept little bathrooms equipped with tubs/shower combinations. Public areas have big windows, touches of varnished paneling, and a sense of spaciousness. There's no pool or health club on the premises, although the staff will direct you to nearby facilities. There is, however, a big dining room serving good regional food (lots of fish), a disco, and an indoor-outdoor restaurant that operates only between June and early September.

S-452 30 Strömstad. ✆ **0526/197-00.** Fax 0526/100-36. www.laholmen.se. 152 units. 1,600SEK ($320/£160) double; 2,700SEK ($540/£270) suite (breakfast included year-round). AE, DC, MC, V. Parking 75SEK ($15/£7.50). **Amenities:** Restaurant; 2 bars; sauna; room service; laundry service; dry cleaning. *In room:* TV, minibar (in some), hair dryer, safe, Wi-Fi.

HALLAND: THE SWEDISH RIVIERA ★

After experiencing the north-coast islands, skerries, and old fishing villages, it may be hard to pack up and head south. Yet the southern area, what the Swedes call their Riviera, is not without its charms—its beaches and sporting facilities (especially golf) are even better, and the hotels better equipped. Halland lies south of Gothenburg and, because of its white sandy beaches, is the fastest growing tourist district in the country. During the summer months, the population of the region doubles.

Windsurfing is the major regional sport here, and Halland has produced many champions. Consistent, steady winds and shallow shoreline waters provide ideal conditions. **Mellbystrand, Tylösand, Ringenäs,** and **Skrea** are the beaches most favored by windsurfers.

In addition to the beaches, Halland's network of rivers and lakes gives the region its life and character. There are more than 900 bodies of water in the province, and many of these inland lakes and rivers are ideal for canoeing and camping. Many places have public access areas with docks, swimming areas, and barbecues. Some lakes boast blossoming waterlilies and flowering meadows that extend down to the water's edge. Many salmon waters have been restored in recent years, and both salmon and trout make their way over the Atlantic to Halland's rivers. A number of lakes offer good perch and pike fishing.

Halland's mild winters and early springs help make it Sweden's most golf-intensive region. In all, there are 30 golf courses in the province. Try either the **Båstad Golf Club** at Boarp (✆ **0431/783-70**) or the **Bjäre Golf Club** at Solomonhög (✆ **0431/36-10-53**). Newest of the lot is the **New Äppalgårdans Golf Club,** Hallansvagen (✆ **0431/223-30**). Positioned 3km (1¾ miles) east of Båstad, it opened in 2006. At any of these courses, greens fees cost around 250SEK ($50/£25) for a full day's play, and golf clubs can be rented for around 125SEK ($25/£13) per day.

Our favorite places (as either bases or stopovers) include the following resorts.

Halmstad ★

Once a grand walled town and a major stronghold of Danish power, Halmstad lies 145km (90 miles) south of Gothenburg and 40km (25 miles) south of Falkenberg, and

is the golf capital of Sweden. Aside from the fabled **Tylösand golf course** ★★★ at
Halmstad Golfklubb (*€* **035/17-68-01;** www.hgk.se; greens fees 600SEK/$120/£60
adult, 300SEK/$60/£30 junior 21 years old and under), there are six courses in town. In
summer, Swedes and Danes (in the main) flock to Halmstad's famous wide strip of white
sand called **Tylösand beach** ★★. Along with the adjacent Ringenäs and Frösakull
beaches, this is one of the longest beaches in Scandinavia.

Long a Swedish resort, Halmstad today is one of the fastest-growing towns in the
country. Halmstad is forever linked to the memory of Christian IV, king of Denmark
(1588–1648), who left his mark on the town. He spent a lot of time here and built
Halmstad Castle, where in 1619 he entertained the Swedish king Gustav Adolf II with 7
solid days of festivities.

Shortly after that meeting, a fire destroyed most of the town but spared the castle.
After the fire, Christian created a Renaissance town with a high street, Storgatan, and a
grid of straight streets unlike the narrow, crooked ones of old. If you walk along Storgatan, you'll see many Renaissance-style merchants' houses from that rebuilding period.
The Danes were driven out in 1645 and Halmstad returned to Sweden. Because the town
had lost its military significance, the walls were torn down. All that remains is *Norre Port,*
one of the great gateways.

Motorists can follow E6 southeast from Falkenberg. Halmstad lies on the major rail
lines between Malmö and Gothenburg, so there is frequent service throughout the day.

Halmstads Turistbyrå, in Halmstads Slott (Halmstads Castle), Aschebergsgatan 1
(*€* **035/13-23-20**), is open in midsummer (Jun 25–Aug 13), Monday to Saturday 9am
to 7pm, Sunday 11am to 6pm. From May 15 to June 24 and from August 14 to October
15, it's open Monday to Friday 9am to 6pm, Saturday 10am to 3pm. The rest of the year,
it's open Monday to Friday 9am to 5pm.

Seeing the Sights

In the town center, **Stora Torg** (the market square) contains *Europa and the Bull* ★, a
fountain group designed by Carl Milles with mermen twisted around it. Flanking one
side of the plaza is the **St. Nikolai kykra,** Kyrkogatan (*€* **035/15-19-00**), a 14th-cen-
tury church. It and the castle were the only major structures to survive from the era of
Christian IV. The church contains some of the finest **stained-glass windows** ★★★ in
Sweden. The tall windows were created by Einar Forseth (1892–1988), who designed the
golden mosaics in Stockholm's Stadshuset and the mosaic paving for England's Coventry
Cathedral. Erik Olson (1901–86), part of the fabled Halmstad Group—Sweden's first
surrealists—conceived the two smaller circular windows. The church is open daily
8:30am to 6pm and charges no admission.

The town's major landmark is **Halmstad Slott** ★, which King Christian IV commissioned Hans van Steenwinckel, a Dutchman, to build in 1620 as part of Halmstad's
defense system. Currently, it is the residence of the county governor and with the noteworthy exception of the small area that's devoted to the city's tourist office (see above),
its interior is not open to the public. An exception to this occurs during a weeklong
period in early June every year, when a limited number of guided tours of its interior are
offered to the public. (Ask at the tourist office for information about this.) Most of the
year, you'll have to satisfy yourself with views of its outside, and with walks through its
gardens, which are open 24 hours a day free of charge.

Along the river stands **Museet i Halmstad** ★, Tollsgatan (*€* **035/16-23-00;** www.
hallmus.se), 2km (1¼ miles) north of the town center (to reach it, follow the river-
front promenade), which contains exhibits from local archaeological digs of only minor

interest. The chief treasure of the museum is its **painted wall hangings** ★★, known in Swedish as *bonader,* on the second floor. This collection of folk paintings mostly depicting scenes from the Bible is stunning and very typical of this part of western Sweden. Curiously, the costumes and the settings are not from ancient days at all but evoke the 18th and 19th centuries in which they were painted. In the upper-floor rooms are cozy home interiors from the 1600s through the 1800s; here you'll find an array of artifacts, from Gustavian harps to 1780s square pianos. On the top floor are paintings by the Halmstad Group, the Swedish surrealists, as well as a changing roster of temporary exhibitions. The museum is open Wednesday from noon to 8pm, and Tuesday to Sunday noon to 4pm. (It's closed Mon.) Admission is 45SEK ($9/£4.50) for adults and 25SEK ($5/£2.50) for children ages 7 to 9. It's free for children under 7.

Three kilometers (1³⁄₄ miles) northwest of the center of Halmstad (follow the signs to the airport), **Mjellby Konstgård,** Mjellby (✆ **035/13-71-95**), also displays art of the Halmstad Group. This group was composed of six artists, including the brothers Axel and Erik Olson and their cousin Waldemar Lorentzon, along with Esaias Thorén, Stellan Mörner, and Sven Jonson. They were post-Cubists who first worked here in 1929. In time, they developed a Nordic form of surrealism that was deeply rooted in the landscapes of Halland. Many members of the group continued to produce until the 1980s. Set in the beautiful Halland countryside, the art center here was established by the daughter of Erik Olson. Along with permanent exhibitions from the Halmstad Group, the site is host to temporary exhibitions, often by great masters such as Le Corbusier. To reach the center if you're not driving, take bus no. 20, then change to bus no. 330, and ask to be let off at the nearest stop. (*Warning:* The museum is still a brisk 5-min. walk from the bus stop.) The hours are Tuesday to Sunday 1 to 5pm. Admission is 55SEK ($11/£5.50) per adult. Persons under 20 enter free.

Where to Stay & Dine

Best Western Grand Hotel ★   Originally built in 1905, this hotel sports a mock-medieval block tower jutting skyward from its exposed corner. Set a short walk from the railway station, traditionally it has attracted artists and business travelers to its well-upholstered, well-heeled interior. Look for solid comfort and a no-nonsense (and sometimes rather brusque) approach to the business of innkeeping, as reflected by the spick-and-span bathrooms with shower units.

Stationsgatan 44, S-302 45 Halmstad. ✆ **800/780-7234** or 035/280-81-00. Fax 035/280-81-10. www.grandhotel.nu. 108 units. July to mid-Aug and Fri–Mon year-round 890SEK–1,295SEK ($178–$259/£89–£130) double; rest of year 1,295SEK–1,995SEK ($259–$399/£130–£200) double. Rates include breakfast. AE, DC, MC, V. Free parking. **Amenities:** Restaurant; bar; fitness center; sauna; room service; laundry service; dry cleaning; nonsmoking rooms; rooms for those w/limited mobility. *In room:* TV, hair dryer, Wi-Fi.

Hotel Tylösand ★★ **Kids**   We return again and again to this place, one of the most dramatically modern resorts in the region. The hotel occupies a parcel of rock-and-scrub-covered seafront land on a south-facing peninsula about 9km (5¹⁄₂ miles) west of Halmstad. In summer, it's filled with families on holiday enjoying the nearby beaches and wide-open landscapes. The rest of the year, management works hard to fill the place with corporate conventions and theme weekends during which guests participate in wine tastings and its limited array of spa treatments. Rooms are airy, well furnished, and stylish, each decorated with light touches and pale colors, and all have adequate-size bathrooms. Throughout the premises, in both bedrooms and public areas, views extend over an eerie, sometimes surreal landscape that can be equally soothing, invigorating, isolated, and wild.

This hotel is well-known within Sweden for its ownership by a locally famous rock and pop singer, Per Gessle, the leading force behind the music group Roxette. It's also known for containing a trio of restaurants ranging from an informal bistro to a formal modern area with light that floods in from a Nordic interpretation of a greenhouse. One of them sporadically features live dance music.

Tylöshusvägen P.O. Box 643, S-301 16 Halmstad. © **035/305-00.** Fax 035/324-39. www.tylosand.se. 230 units. Sun–Thurs 1,600SEK ($320/£160) double, 4,190SEK ($838/£419) suite; Fri–Sat 1,800SEK ($360/£180) double, 4,390SEK ($878/£439) suite. Rates include breakfast. AE, DC, MC, V. Free parking. **Amenities:** 3 restaurants; 4 bars; 2 pools (1 indoor); health spa; sauna; 24-hr. room service; babysitting (June–Aug only); laundry service; dry cleaning; nonsmoking rooms; rooms for those w/limited mobility. *In room:* A/C (in some), TV, minibar, hair dryer, safe, Wi-Fi.

Båstad ★★★

Tennis rules the day here. Jutting out on a peninsula surrounded by hills and a beautiful landscape, Båstad is the most fashionable international seaside resort in Sweden, 179km (111 miles) south of Gothenburg and 105km (65 miles) north of Malmö.

All the famous international tennis stars have played on the courts at Båstad. Contemporary Swedish players—inspired by the feats of Björn Borg—receive much of their training here. There are more than 50 courts in the district, in addition to the renowned Drivan Sports Centre. Tennis was played here as early as the 1880s and became firmly established in the 1920s. King Gustaf V took part in these championships for 15 years from 1930 onward under the pseudonym of "Mr. G," and Ludvig Nobel guaranteed financial backing for international tournaments.

Golf has established itself almost as much as tennis, and the Bjäre Peninsula offers a choice of five courses. Båstad's first golf course was built in 1929 in Boarp on land purchased by Nobel. The bay also provides opportunities for regattas and different kinds of boating. Windsurfing is popular, as is skin diving. In summer, sea bathing is popular along the coast.

The Bjäre Peninsula, a traditional farming area, is known for its early potatoes, which are served with pickled herring all over Sweden.

By car, head west on Route 115 from Båstad. If you're not driving, you'll find trains running frequently throughout the day between Gothenburg and Malmö. Six buses a day also arrive from Helsingborg; the trip takes 1 hour. For tourist information, **Båstad Turism,** Kyrkgatan 1 at Stortorget (© **0431/750-45;** www.bastad.com), is open from June 20 to August 7 Monday to Friday 10am to 6pm, Saturday 10am to 4pm, and Sunday 11am to 5pm; off season Monday to Saturday 10am to 4pm. You can book hostel rooms here from 135SEK to 200SEK ($27–$40/£14–£20) per person or rent bikes for 70SEK to 95SEK ($14–$19/£7–£9.50) per day. They also will provide information about booking tennis courts, renting sports equipment, or reserving a tee time for a round of golf.

Exploring the Area

The best sights are not in Båstad itself but on the Bjäre Peninsula (p. 208). However, before leaving the resort, you may want to visit **Mariakyrkan (Saint Mary's),** Köpmansgatan (© **0431/787-00**). Open daily from 9am to 4pm, it's one of Skåne's landmark churches. Saint Mary's was built between 1450 and 1500. Inside are many treasures, including a sculpture of Saint Mary and Christ from about 1460 (found in the sanctuary). The altarpiece is from 1775, but the crucifix is medieval. The angel with trumpet above the altar is from about the same time. The pulpit is from 1836, its hourglass from 1791. In the northern nave are various fresco paintings and a church clock from 1802.

Båstad is the site of the **Norrvikens Trädgårdar (Norrviken Gardens)** ★★★, in Kattvik (*C* **0431/36-90-40**), 2.5km (1½ miles) west of the resort's center, the most splendid gardens on the west coast of Sweden. Founded in 1906 by Rudolf Abelin, these gardens have been expanded and maintained according to his plans, embracing a number of styles. One is Italian baroque, with a pond framed with pyramid-shape boxwood hedges and tall cypresses. A Renaissance garden's boxwood patterns evoke the tapestry art of 15th-century Italy; in the flower garden, bulbs compete with annuals. There is also a Japanese garden, an Oriental terrace, a rhododendron dell, a romantic garden, and a water garden.

At Villa Abelin, designed by the garden's founder, wisteria climbs the walls and blooms twice a year. The villa houses shops, exhibits, and information facilities, and there is also a restaurant and a cafeteria on the grounds.

The gardens can be viewed from May 1 to September 1 daily from 10am to between 5 and 8pm, depending on business and the hour of sunset. Admission is 90SEK ($18/£9) for adults, and it's free for children under 15.

With the time you have remaining after exploring the gardens, turn your attention to the **Bjäre Peninsula** ★★, the highlight of the entire region, where the widely varied scenery ranges from farm fields to cliff formations. Before exploring in depth, it's best to pick up a detailed map from the Båstad tourist office (see above).

The peninsula is devoted to sports, including windsurfing, tennis, golf, hiking, and mountain biking. It has white, sandy beaches reaching down to the sea, as well as riding paths and cycle roads set aside for these activities. You can play golf on at least five different 18-hole courses from early spring. The Båstad tourist office can provide more information; see below for some golf and tennis recommendations.

If you don't have a car, public transport is provided by bus no. 525, leaving Båstad every hour Monday through Saturday. It traverses the center of the peninsula. The **Skåneleden walking trail** ★★ runs the entire perimeter of the island and is also great for cycling. However, the terrain is quite hilly in places, so you need to be in fabulous shape.

On the peninsula's western coast is the sleepy village of **Torekov,** a short drive from Kattvik. Here you'll find a beach and pier where early morning bathers can be seen walking down to the sea in bathing gowns and sandals. From Torekov, you can take a boat to explore **Hallands Väderö,** an island off the west coast of Sweden. Ferryboats, some of them old-fashioned wooden vessels used during part of the year for fishing, make the 15-minute crossing every hour between June and August. From September to May, departures are every 2 hours. The cost is 80SEK ($16/£8) round-trip, with the last departure at 4pm daily. For more information, call Hallands/Väderö Billettkassan (*C* **0431/36-30-20**).

One of Sweden's few remaining seal colonies exists on **Hallands Väderö.** "Seal safaris" come here to view, but not disturb, these animals. In addition to seals, the island is noted for its rich bird life, including guillemots, cormorants, eiders, and gulls.

Outdoor Activities

GOLF　The region around Båstad is home to five separate golf courses. Two of them accept nonmembers who want to use the course during short-term visits to the region. They include the **Båstad Golf Club,** Boarp, S-269 21 Båstad (*C* **0431/783-70;** to reach it, follow the signs to Boarp and drive 4km/2½ miles south of town), and the **Bjäre Golf**

Club ★, Solomonhög 3086, S-269 93 Båstad (© **0431/36-10-53;** follow the signs to Förslöv, driving 10km/6¹/₄ miles east of Båstad). Newest of the lot is the **New Äppalgår-dans Golf Club,** Hallansvagen (© **0431/223-30**). Positioned 3km (1³/₄ miles) east of Båstad, it opened in 2006. All the above courses charge greens fees of around 250SEK ($50/£25) for a full day's play, and golf clubs can be rented for around 125SEK ($25/£13) per day. Advance reservations for tee times are essential, but because most of the golf clubs are open to the public, membership in any of them is not.

TENNIS Båstad is irrevocably linked to the game of tennis, which it celebrates with fervor, thanks to its role as the longtime home of the **Swedish Open.** If you want to improve your game, consider renting one of the 14 outdoor courts (available Apr–Sept) or one of the six indoor courts (available year-round) at the **Båstads Malen Tennis Säll-skat** (also known as the Drivan Tennis Center), Korrödgatan, S-26922 Båstad (© **0431/ 685-00**). Set about a half-kilometer (¹/₃ mile) north of Båstad's town center, it's the site of a corps of tennis professionals and teachers, who give lessons for 400SEK ($80/£40) per hour. Indoor courts rent for 160SEK ($32/£16) per hour.

Where to Stay
Hotel-Pension Enehall On a slope of Hallandsåsen Mountain, only a few minutes' walk from the sea, this cozy, intimate place caters mainly to Swedish families and the occasional Dane or German. Built in 1924 as an elegant private home, it was trans-formed into a personalized and (charmingly) eccentric hotel in 1960. The rooms, although small, are adequately equipped with good beds and tiny bathrooms. The food at the on-site restaurant is tasty, and the service polite and efficient.

Stationsterrassen 10, S-26936 Båstad. © **0431/750-15.** Fax 0431/750-14. www.enehall.se. 70 units. 895SEK–1,350SEK ($179–$270/£90–£135) double. Rates include breakfast. AE, DC, MC, V. Free park-ing. **Amenities:** Restaurant; bar; sauna; nonsmoking rooms; 1 room for those w/limited mobility. *In room:* TV.

Hotel Riviera Often a favorite venue for conferences, this yellow-fronted hotel, originally built in 1932 and frequently upgraded at almost yearly intervals, is one of the better hotels in the area. It takes on a somewhat festive air in summer. Located by the sea, about a kilometer (²/₃ mile) from the railroad station and about 3km (1³/₄ miles) east of the town center, it offers views from many of its modern bedrooms, as well as from its 300-seat restaurant. Bedrooms are comfortably and attractively furnished. Excellent housekeeping results in impeccably clean accommodations. Guests can relax by sitting out in the gardens or on the terrace. The kitchen serves a superb combination of Scan-dinavian and international food; when it's nice out, there's often a live band.

Rivierävägen 33, S-269-39 Båstad. © **0431/36-90-50.** Fax 0431/761-00. www.hotelriviera.nu. 50 units. 1,445SEK–2,410SEK ($289–$482/£145–£241) double. Rates include breakfast. AE, DC, MC, V. Closed Oct–Mar. Free parking. **Amenities:** Restaurant; bar; nonsmoking rooms. *In room:* TV.

Hotel Skansen ★★ Comfortable, sprawling, and contained within a compound of mostly brick-fronted buildings, this is *the* tennis venue in Sweden—it's surrounded by six tennis courts, most of them ringed with bleachers, that are home every year to the Swed-ish Open. As such, it has housed the most famous tennis stars in Sweden, including Björn Borg, Anders Järryd, and Henrik Holm. A few minutes' walk from the marina and 5m (16 ft.) from the beach, it was originally built in 1877 as a warehouse for grain and food supplies. The hotel's original building (listed as a national monument) has been supplemented by three more recent structures. The interior of the main building has a beamed roof, pillars, and views of the sea. Renovated bedrooms are airy, elegant, and traditionally outfitted with conservative furniture, including good beds with ample private bathrooms.

The in-house restaurant is open daily year-round but is closed on Sundays in the winter. Set within the oldest of the four buildings, it serves excellent Swedish and international cuisine. A cafe operates year-round and offers seating in the courtyard during warm weather.

Kyrkogatan 2, S-269 33 Båstad. (℃) **0431/55-81-00.** Fax 0431/55-81-10. www.hotelskansen.se. 173 units. 1,475SEK–1,670SEK ($295–$334/£148–£167) double; 2,800SEK ($560/£280) suite. Rates include breakfast. AE, DC, MC, V. Free parking. **Amenities:** 2 restaurants; 2 bars; indoor pool; 6 tennis courts; fitness center; sauna; babysitting; nonsmoking rooms; rooms for those w/limited mobility. In room: A/C (in some), TV, minibar, hair dryer, safe.

Where to Dine

The preceding hotels all have good restaurants, although you should call in advance for reservations. But if you're just passing through, consider dropping in at the **Solbackens Café & Wåffelbruk,** Italienska Vägen ((℃) **0431/702-00**). This bustling, gossipy cafe is locally famous, known since 1907 for serving Swedish waffles and other snack-style foods. If the weather is fair, opt for a table on the terrace overlooking the water.

Centrecourten SWEDISH/INTERNATIONAL   In a town as obsessed with tennis as Båstad, you'd expect at least one restaurant to be outfitted with a tennis theme—and Centrecourten's cozy and small-scale dining room is adorned with photos of such stars as Björn Borg, a scattering of trophies, old-fashioned tennis memorabilia, and tennis rackets. The best menu items include fresh fish, such as mussels, lemon sole, and cod. You can dine fancier if you like, by ordering house specialties of duck with a bacon-flavored purée of potatoes and a brisket of beef with fresh chanterelles and shallots. All the cuisine is merely good, but the ingredients are fresh and the flavors often enticing, especially in the seafood selections.

Köpmansgatan 70b. (℃) **0431/752-75.** Reservations recommended. Pizza 50SEK–85SEK ($10–$17/£5–£8.50); main courses 95SEK–150SEK ($19–$30/£9.50–£15). AE, MC, V. Daily noon–11pm.

Båstad After Dark

One good option for nightlife is **Pepe's Bodega,** Warmbadhuset Hamnen ((℃) **0431/36-91-69**), where spicy food and festive cocktails evoke southern Spain, northern Mexico, or some undefined hideaway in a forgotten corner of South America. It's open Wednesday to Sunday both for food and for its active bar life (from 5–11pm for food, and until 1am for drinks). There's also an on-site disco.

8

Skåne (Including Helsingborg & Malmö)

Skåne strikes us like another little country that's attached to—but not part of—Sweden. Pronounced *Sk*-neh, Skåne is the southernmost province of the country. Because of its greater sunshine and fertile plains, it is also the "granary" of the country.

Like Stockholm, Skåne, and especially the emerging city of Malmö, strikes a more Continental pose than other spots in Sweden—and for good reason. A long-anticipated bridge between Sweden and Denmark became a reality in 2000, opening up the southernmost corner of Sweden as never before. With three million people living within a 49km (30-mile) radius of the link, the region has the largest concentrated population in all of Scandinavia—and it's still growing. An artificial island was also constructed halfway across the Öresund in 2000 to connect 3km (1³/₄ miles) of immersed railway and motorway tunnels and a 7.7km (4³/₄-mile) bridge.

Denmark used to govern Skåne before the Swedes reclaimed their beloved southern frontier in 1658. To judge from a recent visit, when we encountered more Danes than locals wandering the streets of Malmö, it appears that Denmark is set on taking control of the country once again. (Then again, it's possible that all the Swedes were off enjoying one of Skåne's golden sandy beaches.) It is now so easy to reach Malmö from Copenhagen that many Danes simply drive to Malmö for a long, lingering Sunday lunch or elegant dinner.

Skåne may not have Scandinavia's snowcapped mountains or famous fjords, but it seems to possess about everything else, including some of Sweden's most varied scenery, from dark forests to pristine waterways to the best beaches in Sweden (though the water is often too cold for visitors from warmer climes). Its rolling landscape and sand-studded coastline are simply made for wandering and exploring. Skåne also has medieval cities with some of the country's stateliest cathedrals, and more castles than any other region in Sweden. For those who are fans of Viking history, several ancient sites, and Bronze Age remains, are in the area.

Skåne is even easy to reach. You have a wide choice of flights, either to Malmö's Sturup Airport or to the Copenhagen airport, from which there are frequent hovercraft connections directly to the center of Malmö. Hovercraft also run between downtown Copenhagen and Malmö, and every 15 or 20 minutes, day and night; connections are possible by car ferry from Helsingør, Denmark, to Helsingborg, Sweden. If you're traveling by car, there are ferry routes from Denmark, Germany, and Poland. Or you can simply rent a car in Copenhagen and drive across the bridge we've been raving about.

1 HELSINGBORG

230km (143 miles) S of Gothenburg, 560km (348 miles) SW of Stockholm, 63km (39 miles) N of Malmö

Helsingborg, the "pearl of the Öresund," likes to call itself Sweden's gateway to the Continent. But it took us a long time and several visits before we warmed to its charms. We once viewed it as a not very impressive provincial town with a large ferry terminal, a passageway between Sweden and Denmark.

After having spent a lot more time in Helsingborg, we've changed our minds. More and more, the city is taking great care to make itself a more inviting and user-friendly destination. Now, at least there are enough attractions to make for a very busy day of sightseeing before you rush over to Denmark to see Hamlet's Castle or head south to sample the more continental charms of Malmö.

This industrial city and major port sits at the narrowest point of the Øresund (Öresund in Swedish) strait that separates Sweden and Denmark. Many people from Copenhagen take the 5km (3-mile) 25-minute ferry ride (leaving every 20 min.) across the sound for a look at Sweden.

What they get is a modern city with an ancient history. In the Middle Ages, Helsingborg and Helsingør together controlled shipping along the sound. Helsingborg is mentioned in the 10th-century Njal's-Saga (an ancient Viking document), and other documents indicate that there was a town here beginning in 1085. The city now has more than 100,000 inhabitants and the second busiest harbor in the country. This is the city that introduced pedestrian streets to Sweden, and it has long promenades along the shore of the sound.

In the 1990s, Helsingborg (Hålsingborg) rebuilt large, vacant-looking sections of its inner city into one of the most innovative urban centers in Sweden. The centerpiece of these restorations lies beside the harbor and includes an all-glass building, the **Knutpunkten,** on Järnvägsgatan. Contained within are the railroad, bus, and ferryboat terminals; an array of shops similar to an American mall; and a heliport. The sunlight-flooded railroad station is the cleanest, brightest, and most memorable we've seen in Sweden. In addition, many dozens of trees and shrubs have transformed the center city into something like a verdant park, with trees between the lanes of traffic.

ESSENTIALS

GETTING THERE **By Ferry** Ferries from Helsingør, Denmark, leave the Danish harbor every 20 minutes day or night (trip time: 25 min.). For information about ferryboats in Helsingborg, call © **042/18-61-00;** for information on the Danish side, call

---

Fun Facts **The Goose of Honor**

The tip of the Scandinavian peninsula was where Selma Lagerlöf's **The Wonderful Adventures of Nils** began. This story, translated into every major language, tells of a hero who travels on the back of a wild goose. In reality, however, the web-footed, flat-billed, large-bodied geese of Skåne are tame and never travel far from home. No doubt they regret this on November 10, when Scanians celebrate the almost-sacred bird with a gargantuan dinner—one enjoyed by everyone but the geese.

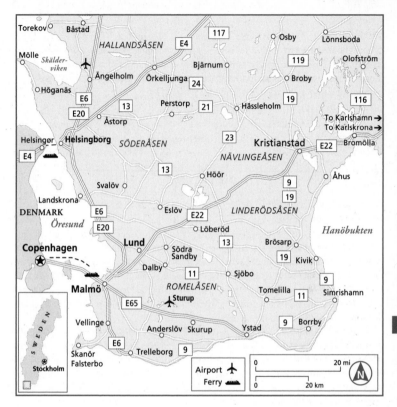

Map labels:
Torekov, Båstad, HALLANDSÅSEN, 117, E4, Osby, Lönnsboda, Mölle, Skälder-viken, Ängelholm, Örkelljunga, 24, Bjärnum, 119, Olofström, Höganäs, E6, 13, Perstorp, 21, Hässleholm, 19, Broby, E20, Åstorp, 23, To Karlshamn →, To Karlskrona →, 116, Helsingør, Helsingborg, SÖDERÅSEN, Kristianstad, E22, Bromölla, NÄVLINGEÅSEN, E4, 13, Höör, Åhus, Svalöv, 9, Landskrona, 19, DENMARK, E6, Eslöv, E22, LINDERÖDSÅSEN, Öresund, E20, Löberöd, Hanöbukten, Lund, 13, Brösarp, Copenhagen, Södra Sandby, 19, Kivik, Dalby, 11, Sjöbo, Malmö, ROMELÅSEN, Tomelilla, 11, Simrishamn, 9, E65, Sturup, Vellinge, SWEDEN, Anderslöv, Skurup, Ystad, 9, Borrby, E6, Skanör, Falsterbo, Trelleborg, 9, Stockholm, Airport ✈, Ferry ⛴, 0 20 mi, 0 20 km, N

℃ 33/15-15-15. The cost of the ferryboat for pedestrians is 28SEK ($5.60/£2.80) each way or 54SEK ($11/£5.40) round-trip. The regular round-trip cost of the ferryboat for a car with up to five passengers is 670SEK ($134/£67).

By Plane   The **Ängelholm/Helsingborg Airport** (℃ 011/19-20-00; www.lfv.se) lies 30 minutes from the center of the city, with regular connections to Stockholm's Arlanda Airport. There are between two and four flights per day (flying time: 1 hr.). For SAS reservations, call ℃ **0770/72-77-27.**

By Train   Trains run hourly during the day between Helsingborg and Malmö, taking 50 minutes. Trains arrive four times per day on the 5-hour trip from Stockholm, and they also leave Helsingborg twice per day for Stockholm. Trains between Gothenburg and Helsingborg depart and arrive twice a day (trip time: 2¹/₂ hr.). Call ℃ **042/10-43-50** for information or visit **www.railrocket.com.**

By Bus   Three buses per day link Malmö and Helsingborg. Two leave in the morning and one in the afternoon, the trip taking 1 hour and 10 minutes. Buses leave twice per day from Gothenburg and arrive in Helsingborg in 3¹/₄ hours. Buses to and from Stockholm leave once per day (trip time: 9 hr.). Call ℃ **0200/218-18** for more information.

By Car   From Malmö, head north on E6 for 1 hour; from Gothenburg, drive south on E6 for 2¹/₂ hours; from Stockholm, take E4 south for 7¹/₂ hours until you reach Helsingborg.

VISITOR INFORMATION   The tourist office, **Helsingborg Turistbyrå**, Rådhuset, 251 89 Helsingborg (✆ 042/10-43-50; www.helsingborg.se), is open from mid-June to mid-August Monday to Friday 9am to 9pm, Saturday and Sunday 10am to 2pm; mid-August to mid-June Monday to Friday 10am to 6pm and Saturday 10am to 2pm.

GETTING AROUND   Most of Helsingborg's sights are within walking distance; however, if your legs get tired and the weather is less than perfect, you can always take a city bus, numbered 1 to 7. Most buses on their way north pass the Town Hall; those heading south go by Knutpunkten. You can buy tickets onboard the buses for 15SEK ($3/£1.50) for one zone or 6SEK ($1.20/60p) for an extra zone. Tickets are valid for transfer to another city bus line as long as you transfer within 1 hour from the time the ticket was stamped. For information, call ✆ 042/10-43-50.

SEEING THE SIGHTS

Built in 1897, the turreted, neo-Gothic **Town Hall** (Rådhuset), Drottninggatan 1 (✆ 042/10-50-00), has beautiful stained-glass windows depicting scenes from the town's history. The artist, Gustav Cederström, took great pride in the epic history of his hometown and painted these scenes. But, frankly, the reason to stop here at any of five times a day (9am, noon, 3pm, 6pm, and 9pm) is to listen to the songs ringing from the 66m (217-ft.) bell tower. Two memorial stones outside were presented by the Danes and the Norwegians to the Swedes for their assistance during World War II. There is also a sculpture relief representing the arrival of Danish refugees.

In the main town square, the **Stortorget** is a monument commemorating Swedish general Magnus Stenbock's victory over Denmark at the Battle of Helsingborg in 1710. Today the statue is virtually ignored, as ferry-bound travelers pass it by, but it marked a turning point in Danish/Swedish history. (In 1709, the Danes invaded Skåne once again and wanted to take it back, but they were finally defeated the following year in a battle just outside Helsingborg.)

Fredriksdal Friluftsmuseum ★★ (Kids)   If you have time for only one open-air museum in Skåne, make it this one 2km (1¹/₄ miles) northeast of the Helsingborg center in the Fredriksdal district. It's that special. Built around a manor house constructed in 1787, the park covers 28 hectares (69 acres) of landscaping. Allow yourself at least 2 hours to wander and explore the streets and take in the old, evocative houses. There's something here to attract the whole family: Kids will like the children's farm with animals, and everyone should like the rose garden—the single most beautiful one we've ever visited in Skåne. We lost count of the different types of roses on display here, but it has to be 450 or more. On-site is a French baroque style open-air theater, built in 1927, where major cultural performances are staged in the summer months. Check locally to see what's happening at the time of your visit.

Gisela Trapps Vag 1. ✆ 042/10-45-00. www.fredriksdal.se. Admission May–Oct 80SEK ($16/£8) adult, 70SEK ($14/£7) students and senior citizens, free for children 18 and under; Nov–Apr free. May and Sept daily 10am–5pm; June–Aug daily 10am–7pm; Oct–Apr daily 11am–4pm; closed Christmas Eve, Christmas Day, and New Year's Eve. Bus: 1 or 7.

Kärnan (The Keep) ★   You might see the ghost of Hamlet delivering a soliloquy in his castle if you climb the 146 steps here to a panoramic terrace that, on a clear day, gives you a grand view of Danish Helsingør across the sound. One of the most important

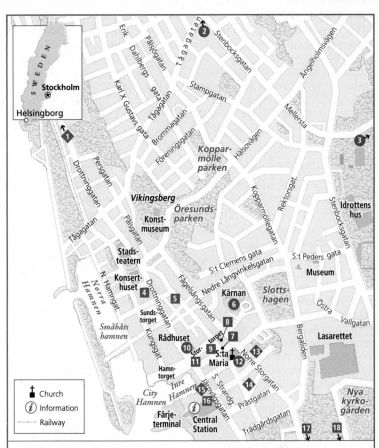

ATTRACTIONS ●

Fredriksdal
  Friluftsmuseum **3**
Kärnan (The Keep) **6**
Mariakyrkan (Church of St. Mary) **12**
Sofiero Slott **2**
Stortorget **8**
Town Hall (Rådhuset) **10**

Dining ◆

Gastro **13**
Pälsjö Krog **1**
Restaurang La Petite **14**
SS Swea **15**

ACCOMMODATIONS ■

Best Western Hotel Helsingborg **7**
Clarion Hotel Grand **9**
Comfort Hotel Nouveau **17**
Elite Hotel Marina Plaza **4**
Elite Hotel Mollberg **11**
Hotell Linnéa **16**
Hotell Viking **5**
Scandic Horisont **18**

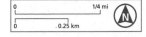

0   1/4 mi
0   0.25 km

medieval monuments in Sweden, and the symbol of Helsingborg, Kärnan rises from the crest of a rocky ridge in the city center. The origins of this 30m-tall (98-ft.) square tower—built in the 11th century—are mysterious; it adopted its present form in the 1300s. Its name translates as "the keep," a moniker related to its original position as the most central tower (and prison) of the once-mighty Helsingborg Castle. (The castle and its fortifications were demolished in 1679 after generations of bloody fighting between the Swedes and the Danes; only Kärnan, which was restored and rebuilt in 1894, remains.) The thickness of its walls (about 4m/13 ft.) make it the most solidly constructed building in the region.

The easiest way to reach Kärnan is to board the elevator, which departs from the *terrasen* (terrace) of the town's main street, the Stortorget. For 5SEK ($1/50p) per person, you'll be carried up the rocky hillside to the base of the tower. However, many visitors avoid the elevator, preferring instead to climb a winding set of flower-flanked steps as part of their exploration of the city.

Kärngränden (off the Stortorget). ✆ **042/10-59-91.** Admission 20SEK ($4/£2) adults, 10SEK ($2/£1) children 8–16. Apr–May Tues–Fri 9am–4pm, Sat–Sun 11am–4pm; June–Aug daily 11am–7pm; Sept–Mar Tues–Sun 11am–5pm. Bus: 1 or 6.

Mariakyrkan (Church of St. Mary)   In lieu of a grand cathedral, Helsingborg has this modest church filled with treasures. It's one of the best examples we know of Danish Gothic architecture. It actually dates from the 14th century, but it took a century to finish it. You can take a look at it by strolling east from the harbor, but don't be disappointed as you approach the plain facade; the gems are concealed inside, including a trove of silver in the Vestry and Silver Chamber. Note the intricately carved Renaissance pulpit (1615) and the triptych from 1450, which always catches our eye. If the sun is shining, the modern **stained-glass windows** ★★ take on a particularly jewel-like tone. Artists such as Ralph Bergholtz, Erik Olson, and Martin Esmond created these windows, whose themes range from the Tree of Life to epic moments in the history of Helsingborg.

Södra Storgatan. ✆ **042/37-28-30.** Free admission. June–Aug Mon–Sat 8am–6pm, Sun 9am–6pm; Sept–May Mon–Sat 8am–4pm, Sun 9am–4pm. Bus: 1 or 6.

Sofiero Slott ★★   Before the Swedish royal family moved their summer slot (palace) to Öland (see chapter 10), they used to spend their precious weeks of sunshine right outside Helsingborg. When you first take in the glories of Sofiero, you'll have two immediate reactions: You'll want to move in, and you'll be puzzled why the royals decamped from such a beautiful castle in the first place.

One of the most famous buildings in southern Sweden, lying 5km (3 miles) north of Helsingborg, this castle was constructed in 1864 and 1865 to be the summer residence of King Oscar II and his wife, Sofia. It was bequeathed in 1905 to their grandson, Gustav Adolph, and his wife, Margareta, who enlarged the site and created some of the most memorable gardens in the country. Their interests supposedly sparked a nationwide interest in landscape architecture, which continues stronger than ever throughout Sweden today. After his coronation, Gustav Adolph spent his last days here, eventually bequeathing Sofiero as a gift to the city of Helsingborg in 1973. In 1993, many of the original gardens were re-created in memory of their designer, Queen Margareta. Today the most visited sites include the 1865 castle, which contains a cafe and restaurant; the rose garden; and the Rhododendron Ravine, with an estimated 10,000 rhododendrons, which are in their full glory in early June.

Sofierovägen. ✆ **042/13-74-00.** www.sofiero.helsingborg.se. Admission 80SEK ($16/£8) adults, 20SEK ($4/£2) children 7–18, free 6 and under. Daily 11am–5pm. Closed Oct to mid-Apr. Bus: 219 or 221.

SHOPPING

In the center of Helsingborg, you'll find a number of shopping possibilities, including **Väla Centrum,** which is one of the largest shopping centers in all of Scandinavia. To reach it, follow Hälsovägen and Ängelholmsvägen north about 6km (3³/₄ miles; it's sign-posted), or take bus no. 202 from Knutpunkten. Seemingly everything is here under one roof, including two large department stores and 42 specialty shops, selling everything from shoes to tropical fish.

The best bookstore in town is **Bengt Bökman,** Bredgattan 22 (© **042/10-71-00**), with many English-language editions. The best place to buy glass is **Duka Carl Anders,** Kullag 17 (© **042/24-30-20**), which carries the works of such prestigious manufacturers as Kosta Boda and Orrefors.

Pottery ★★

Northwest Scania is known as Sweden's pottery district. The first Scanian pottery factory was founded in 1748 in Bosarp, 15km (9¹/₃ miles) east of Helsingborg. The city of Helsingborg got its first factory in 1768 and another began manufacturing in 1832. Since then, the tradition has been redeveloped and revitalized, making the area famous far beyond the borders of Sweden.

At a point 7km (4¹/₃ miles) south of Helsingborg, you can visit **Raus Stenkarlsfabrik,** less than a kilometer (¹/₂ mile) east of Råå (look for signs along Landskronavagen). It is open May to August Monday to Friday 10am to 6pm, Saturday 10am to 4pm; in the off season, you must make an appointment. Call © **042/26-01-30** for more information, or visit **www.martensson.net**.

In Gantofta, 10km (6¹/₄ miles) southeast of Helsingborg, lies **Jie-Keramik** (© **042/22-17-00**), one of Scandinavia's leading manufacturers of hand-painted decorative ceramics, wall reliefs, wall clocks, figures, and other such items. You can visit a factory shop or patronize a cafe on-site. From Helsingborg, drive south to Råå, then follow the signs to Gantofta. You also can take bus no. 209 from Knutpunkten in the center of Helsingborg. The outlet is open June to August daily noon to 6pm. Off-season hours are daily 10am to 4pm.

If you drive 20km (12 miles) north of Helsingborg to Höganäs, you'll find two famous stoneware factories. **Höganäs Saltglaserat** (© **042/21-65-40;** www.hoganassaltglaserat. se) has been manufacturing salt-glazed stoneware since 1835. Today the classic, salt-glazed Höganäs jars with their anchor symbol are still in production. Everything is made by hand and fired in coal-burning circular kilns from the turn of the 20th century. The shop here is within the factory, so you can see the throwers in action and go inside the old kilns. It's open year-round Monday to Friday 9am to 4pm, and Saturdays in June, July, August, and September 10am to 1pm. The other outlet, **Höganäs Keramik** (© **042/35-11-31;** www.hoganaskeramik.se), is Scandinavia's largest stoneware manu-facturer. Its factory shop, inaugurated in 1994, sells flawed goods from both Höganäs Keramik and Boda Nova at bargain prices. This outlet is open May to August Monday to Friday 9am to 6pm, Saturday and Sunday 10am to 5pm. Off-season hours are Monday to Friday 10am to 6pm, Saturday 10am to 4pm, and Sunday 11am to 4pm.

WHERE TO STAY

Expensive

Clarion Hotel Grand ★★★ This is Helsingborg's grandest hotel, an imposing brick-built pile from 1926 that has been completely modernized—though its classic details remain. After its takeover by the Clarion chain, it is even better than it was as a

Radisson SAS: The hotel combines high-ceilinged, richly paneled public areas and spacious, well-accessorized guest rooms with elaborate ceiling moldings, old-world decorative touches, and lots of modern comforts and conveniences. After all the hustle and bustle of crossing over from Denmark, it's great to work off tension on the nearby jogging track along the Strandpromenaden.

Stortorget 8–12, Box 1104, S-251 11 Helsingborg. **©** **800/333-3333** in the U.S., or 042/38-04-00. Fax 042/38-04-04. www.choicehotels.se. 164 units. 960SEK–1,295SEK ($192–$259/£96–£130) double; from 2,376SEK ($475/£238) suite. Rates include breakfast. MC, V. Parking 150SEK ($30/£15). Bus: 1A or 7B. **Amenities:** Restaurant; bar; sauna; room service; laundry service; dry cleaning; nonsmoking rooms; rooms for those w/limited mobility. *In room:* TV, minibar, hair dryer, iron, Wi-Fi.

Moderate

Best Western Hotel Helsingborg ★
This lovely old hotel occupying four floors of a 1901 bank headquarters has historic luxuries, such as marble stairs, a heroic neoclassical frieze, and three copper-sheathed towers. But it has also kept abreast of the times: The high-ceilinged rooms are pleasantly modernized and flooded with sunlight on many a summer day. They retain a certain *Jugendstil* (Art Nouveau) look, with strong colors and many decorative touches. Of the three hotels that lie along the grand main avenue, this one is closest to the city's medieval tourist attraction, the Kärnan.

Stortorget 20, Box 1171, S-252 23 Helsingborg. **©** **800/780-7234** or 042/37-18-00. Fax 042/37-18-50. www.hotelhelsingborg.se. 56 units. 695SEK–995SEK ($139–$199/£70–£100) double; 1,295SEK–2,000SEK ($259–$400/£130–£200) suite. Rates include breakfast. AE, DC, MC, V. Parking 100SEK ($20/£10). Bus: 7A, 7B, 1A, or 1B. **Amenities:** Restaurant; bar; sauna; laundry service; dry cleaning; nonsmoking rooms; rooms for those w/limited mobility. *In room:* TV, hair dryer, Wi-Fi.

Comfort Hotel Nouveau ★ (Finds)
This tastefully decorated building built of ocher brick and touches of marble lives up to its namesake and delivers solid comfort. The decor throughout draws on upscale models from England and France, and includes chintz curtains, varnished mahogany, often with wood inlays, and warm colors inspired by autumn. Rooms are nice and cozy—not particularly large, but well maintained, with tasteful fabrics and frequently renewed linen. As a thoughtful touch, a fresh flower is often placed on your pillow at night.

Gasverksgatan 11, S-252 25 Helsingborg. **©** **042/37-19-50.** Fax 042/37-19-59. www.choice.se. 95 units. 950SEK–1,449SEK ($190–$290/£95–£145) double; 1,575SEK ($315/£158) suite. Rates include breakfast. AE, DC, MC, V. Free parking. Bus: 1A or 7A. **Amenities:** Restaurant; bar; indoor pool; sauna; laundry service; dry cleaning; nonsmoking rooms; rooms for those w/limited mobility. *In room:* TV, minibar, hair dryer, Wi-Fi.

Elite Hotel Marina Plaza ★★
This place is like a glittering palace at night, its reflection cast in the waters of Öresund. Marina Plaza is Helsingborg's most innovative and most talked-about hotel, and is adjacent to the city's transportation hub, the Knutpunkten, opening onto panoramic views. The atrium-style lobby overflows with trees, rock gardens, and fountains. Midsize-to-spacious guest rooms line the inner walls of the hotel's atrium and have a color scheme of marine blue with nautical accessories, as befits its waterfront location. Bedrooms are attractively furnished, and the bathrooms are state of the art. The on-site dining and drinking facilities are the best in town, becoming even more so in summer when the Oceano BBQ opens. Guests in the major restaurant, Aqua, can dine on first-rate cuisine while taking in views of the harbor life.

1,250SEK–1,750SEK ($250–$350/£125–£175) double; 1,550SEK–2,850SEK ($310–$570/£155–£285) suite. Midsummer discounts available. AE, DC, MC, V. Parking 150SEK ($30/£15). Bus: 41, 42, 43, or 44. **Amenities:** Restaurant; bar; pub; sauna; limited room service; laundry service; dry cleaning; nonsmoking rooms; rooms for those w/limited mobility. *In room:* TV, dataport, minibar, hair dryer, safe.

Elite Hotel Mollberg ★ This landmark hotel is arguably Sweden's oldest continuously operated hotel and restaurant. It still attracts traditionalists, though trendsters infinitely prefer the more glamorous Elite Hotel Marina Plaza (see above). Although a tavern has stood on this site since the 14th century, most of the building was constructed in 1802. Its elaborate wedding-cake exterior and high-ceilinged interior have long been its hallmarks. Kings, counts, and barons used to check in here, although there aren't too many of those fellows around anymore. The Swedish king Gustav IV Adolf, on the way home from Pomerania, checked in for 2 months, not wanting to go back to Stockholm right away.

As is typical of a building of this age, bedrooms come in different shapes and sizes, but each has been modernized and furnished in a comfortable, tasteful way. On-site is a modern French-style brasserie with special musical evenings, and a rather successful clone of a London pub, the Bishop's Arms, with the town's largest selection of different beers and whisky.

Stortorget 18, S-251 14 Helsingborg. ⓒ **042/37-37-00.** Fax 042/37-37-37. www.elite.se. 104 units. 1,000SEK–1,650SEK ($200–$330/£100–£165) double; 1,700SEK–2,500SEK ($340–$500/£170–£250) suite. Rates include breakfast. AE, DC, MC, V. Parking 125SEK ($25/£13). Bus: 7A, 7B, 1A, or 1B. **Amenities:** Restaurant; bar; sauna; room service; laundry service; dry cleaning; nonsmoking rooms; solarium. *In room:* TV, minibar, hair dryer, Wi-Fi.

Scandic Horisont If you'd like to escape the traffic and the hysteria at the center of the city, you can check into this more tranquil choice about a kilometer (^{2}/$_3$ mile) south of the ferryboat terminal. Hiding behind one of the most striking modern facades in town, this 1985 hotel offers free transportation Monday to Thursday (mainly for the benefit of its business clients) between its precincts and central Helsingborg. Guest rooms are comfortably furnished and well accessorized, and come in various shapes. You can live here at a moderate price or more expensively, depending on your demands. A carefully crafted international menu is served at the on-site restaurant, along with Swedish classics.

Gustav Adolfs Gate 47, S-250 02 Helsingborg. ⓒ **042/49-52-100.** Fax 042/49-52-111. www.scandichotels.com. 164 units. 770SEK–1,660SEK ($154–$332/£77–£166) double; 1,470SEK–2,350SEK ($294–$470/£147–£235) suite. Rates include breakfast. AE, DC, MC, V. Free parking. Bus: 7B, 1B, or 2. **Amenities:** Restaurant; bar; Jacuzzi; sauna; laundry service; dry cleaning; nonsmoking rooms; rooms for those w/limited mobility. *In room:* TV, hair dryer, Wi-Fi.

Inexpensive

Hotell Lìnnéa ★ (Finds) "To travel is to live," the receptionist said when checking us in. Considering that Hotell Lìnnéa is conveniently located a few yards from where ferries from Denmark pull in, the statement—a Hans Christian Andersen quote—seems fitting. Occupying a pink Italianate house built in 1897, this small hotel boasts detailing that might remind you of something in a historic neighborhood of pre-Katrina New Orleans. Guest rooms are appealingly outfitted, with comfortable beds and high-quality furnishings that include tasteful reproductions of 19th-century antiques. Only breakfast is served, but many reliable dining choices are close by.

Prästgatan 4, S-252 24 Helsingborg. ℭ **042/37-24-00.** Fax 042/37-24-29. www.hotell-linnea.se. 28 units. July–Aug and Fri–Sat year-round 895SEK–1,095SEK ($179–$219/£90–£110) double; rest of year 1,445SEK–1,480SEK ($289–$296/£145–£148) double; 1,880SEK ($376/£188) suite. Rates include breakfast. AE, DC, MC, V. Parking 125SEK ($25/£13). Bus: 7A or 7B. **Amenities:** Breakfast room; bar; laundry service; dry cleaning. *In room:* TV.

Hotell Viking   In the center of town, less than 2 blocks north of the Drottninggatan, this hotel looks more historic, cozier, and a bit more artfully cluttered than many of its more formal and streamlined competitors. It was built during the late 19th century as a row of shops where the owners usually lived upstairs from their businesses. Today, after a radical remodeling, you'll find a carefully preserved sense of history; a pale color scheme of grays, beiges, and ochers; and a hands-on management style by the resident owners. The individually designed bedrooms are cozy, neat, and functional. Some of the rooms are superior to the regular doubles, complete with adjustable beds, computers, stereos, and plasma-screen TVs, and these go first.

Fågelsångsgatan 1, S-252 20 Helsingborg. ℭ **042/14-44-20.** Fax 042/18-43-20. www.hotellviking.se. 40 units. Mid-June to July and Fri–Sun year-round 1,025SEK–1,225SEK ($205–$245/£103–£123) double; rest of year 1,475SEK–1,576SEK ($295–$315/£148–£158) double. Rates include breakfast. AE, DC, MC, V. Free parking. Bus: 7A, 7B, 1A, or 1B. **Amenities:** Breakfast and dining room; bar; laundry service; dry cleaning; nonsmoking rooms; rooms for those w/limited mobility. *In room:* TV, minibar, hair dryer, Wi-Fi.

WHERE TO DINE

Gastro ★★ CONTINENTAL/FRENCH   In the wake of the closure of the two finest restaurants in Helsingborg, this first-class choice has emerged as the best. It's set within a modern, big-windowed building of yellow brick overlooking the city's historic core. Within a room decorated with birchwood veneer, pale tones of monochromatic gray, and a medley of riveting modern paintings, you can enjoy specialties based on Swedish ingredients prepared using Mediterranean culinary techniques. Menu items vary with the season, but our favorites are the pan-fried scallops with sun-dried and marinated tomatoes, served with a terrine of green peas, or a superb fried breast of duckling with onions, carrots, and prosciutto. Expect lots of fresh fish from the straits of Helsingborg and the Baltic, and lots of savoir-faire from the well-versed, attentive staff.

Södra Storg 11–13. ℭ **042/24-34-70.** www.gastro.nu. Reservations recommended. Main courses 140SEK–360SEK ($28–$72/£14–£36); fixed-price menu 465SEK ($93/£47). AE, DC, MC, V. Mon–Sat 7–10pm. Closed July. Bus: 11.

Pälsjö Krog SWEDISH   For traditional and home-style Swedish cooking, we head here, despite its inconvenient location. A 10-minute drive north of the center of Helsingborg, this brightly painted yellow wood-sided building was originally constructed around 1900 as a bathhouse beside the beach. As such, it was filled at the time with cubicles for sea bathers to change clothes. In the late 1990s, it was transformed into a cozy Swedish restaurant, the kind of place where local families—with grandmothers in tow—come to enjoy recipes that haven't changed much since the end of World War II. Within a large dining room painted in tones of pale yellow and decorated with hints of Art Deco, you'll find grilled pepper steak, poached Swedish salmon with dill sauce, and aromatic local mussels steamed with herbs in white wine. Drinkers and smokers appreciate the cozy aperitif bar near the entrance, where cigars are welcomed and where the staff can propose a wide assortment of after-dinner cognacs.

Drottninggatan 151. ℭ **042/14-97-30.** Reservations recommended. Main courses 165SEK–200SEK ($33–$40/£17–£20). AE, DC, MC, V. Mon–Fri 11:30am–3pm and 6–10pm; Sat–Sun 1–10pm. Bus: 1A or 1B.

Restaurang La Petite (Value FRENCH/MEDITERRANEAN No one's ever accused the chefs here of being too inventive. But that's the way the habitués like it, preferring tried-and-true recipes to "experiments." In a charming old house that evokes provincial France, this bistro has been going strong ever since it opened its doors in 1975. Still relatively undiscovered by foreign visitors, it serves classics based on time-tested French recipes. We're talking about those longtime favorites that for decades have characterized French bistro fare: onion soup, savory frogs' legs, and steaming kettles of mussels in a wine-laced sauce studded with garlic. Basically, what you'll get is good French comfort food.

Bruksgatan 19. ✆ **042/21-97-27.** www.lapetite.se. Reservations required on weekends only. Main courses 175SEK–285SEK ($35–$57/£18–£29). AE, DC, MC, V. Tues–Sat 11:30am–2pm; Mon–Thurs 6–10pm; Fri–Sat 6–11pm.

SS Swea ★ SEAFOOD/SWEDISH Go here for some of the most freshly caught fish and shellfish at the port, both of which are presented in a wide-ranging menu that appeals to most tastes. Housed on a Kungstorget ship furnished like the luxury cruisers that used to cross the Atlantic, the restaurant offers market-fresh food deftly handled by skilled chefs and served in a cozy ambience by a thoughtful waitstaff. Appetizers might range from iced gazpacho to a Greek salad studded with feta cheese. However, most diners prefer one of the fish starters, especially the delectable smoked salmon. Fish platters, which depend on the catch of the day, also dominate the main courses. Our juicy flounder, served with bacon-flavored mushrooms, was superb in every way. Carnivores will find comfort in a classic pepper steak with *pommes frites,* or the filet mignon, laced with Black and White scotch.

Kungstorget. ✆ **042/13-15-16.** www.swea.nu. Reservations required. Main courses 170SEK–255SEK ($34–$51/£17–£26); fixed-price 3-course menu 335SEK–389SEK ($67–$78/£34–£39). AE, DC, MC, V. Mon–Thurs 6–10pm; Fri 6–11pm; Sat 1–11pm; Sun 1–8pm. Bus: 7A or 7B.

HELSINGBORG AFTER DARK

Helsingborg has had its own city symphony orchestra since 1912. In 1932, its concert hall, or **Konserthuset,** opened at Drottninggatan 19 (✆ **042/10-42-70**). One of the finest examples of 1930s Swedish functionalism, today the hall is still the venue for performances by the 50-piece orchestra. The season opens in the middle of August with a 10-day Festspel, a festival with a different theme every year. Tickets are available at the **Helsingborg Stadsteater City Theater,** Karl Johans Gata (✆ **042/10-68-00** or 042/10-68-10; www.helsingborgsstadsteater.se), which dates from 1817 but is one of the most modern in Europe; of course, performances are in Swedish.

With a decor that includes crystal chandeliers and lots of original paintings (which often are rotated with works by various artists), **Marina Nightclub,** Kungstorget 6 (✆ **042/19-21-00**), is set within the Hotel Marina Plaza. It admits only clients 24 or older. It's open Friday and Saturday from 11pm to around 5am.

An English-inspired pub that draws a busy and convivial crowd is **Telegrafen,** Norra Storgatan 14 (✆ **042/18-14-50;** www.restaurangtelegrafen.se), where live music, especially jazz, is presented on either of two levels devoted to maintaining a cozy environment for drinking, chatting, and flirting. Live-music enthusiasts should also consider an evening at one of the largest jazz venues in Sweden, **Jazzklubben** ★, Nedre Långvinkelsgatan 22 (✆ **042/18-49-00;** www.jazztime.nu). Live Dixieland, blues, Celtic ballads, and progressive jazz are featured on Wednesday, Friday, and Saturday nights beginning around 8:30pm. Most other nights, based on a schedule that varies with the season and the whims of the staff, the place functions as a conventional bar.

2 MALMÖ ★★

285km (177 miles) S of Gothenburg, 618km (384 miles) SW of Stockholm

Now that it's linked to the Continent via Denmark by the bridge over Öresund, Malmö is taking on an increased sophistication. We find each visit more appealing than the one before. Once the staid old capital of Skåne, Malmö is today a vibrant, modern city with a definite young vibe. Or, as one former city official told us, "Gothenburg lives on via its great maritime past; Malmö represents the Sweden of tomorrow." A fine sentiment indeed, but not one to belt out in a Gothenburg pub full of soccer fans.

Nothing seems to evoke Malmö's entry into the 21st century more than the avant-garde and controversial **"Turning Torso"** ★★★, rising over the Western Harbor. You'll gaze in awe at Sweden's tallest building, which rises 190m (623 ft.) and consists of nine cubes—a total of 54 floors—with a 90-degree twist from base to top. The creation of architect Santiago Calatrava, it was inspired by a sculpture called *Turning Torso* by (you guessed it) Calatrava himself. Today it is the most spectacular apartment building in all of Sweden.

If you can, allow at least 2 days to tour Malmö, Sweden's third largest city. The old city, dating from the 13th century, makes a good base for exploring the attractions of western Skåne. Or you might prefer to use ancient Lund (see later in this chapter) for a base for touring basically the same sights. It's your choice: big, bustling, modern city or beautiful old university town.

From its early days, Malmö (pronounced *Mahl*-mer) prospered because of its location on a sheltered bay. In the 16th century, when it was the second largest city in Denmark, it vied with Copenhagen for economic and cultural leadership. (Reminders of that age are **Malmöhus Castle** [see below], the **Town Hall,** and the **Stortorget,** plus several homes of rich burghers.) Malmö has been a Swedish city since the end of a bloody war in 1658, when the Treaty of Roskilde incorporated the province of Skåne into Sweden.

ESSENTIALS

GETTING THERE **By Plane** Malmö's airport (© **040/613-11-00;** www.lfv.se) is at Sturup, 30km (19 miles) southeast of the city. It receives international flights from London, plus flights from cities within Sweden and Stockholm (trip time: 1 hr.). Airlines winging their way into Malmö include **Malmö Aviation** (© **771/44-00-10;** www.malmoaviation. se), **SAS** (© **770/72-77-27;** www.sas.se), and **Sterling** (© **4608/5876-9148;** www.ster-ling.nu). The city's major international link to the world is Copenhagen Airport at Copenhagen, to which Malmö is connected via the Öresund Bridge.

By Car From Helsingborg, motorists can head southeast along Route E6 directly into the center of Malmö. Another option is the car ferry from Denmark. See p. 40 for info.

By Train Railway service is frequent between Gothenburg and Malmö (trip time: 3¹/₂ hr.), and since the construction of the bridge, rail service is now direct, quick, and easy to both central Copenhagen and its airport. From Helsingborg to Malmö (trip time: 45 min.), trains leave hourly. From Stockholm, travel is 4¹/₂ hours aboard the high-speed X-2000 train, 6 to 7 hours aboard slower trains. There also is train service between Copenhagen and Malmö. Trains depart from the central railway stations of both cities at 20-minute intervals, stopping en route at the Copenhagen airport. The cost each way between the centers of each city is 100SEK ($20/£10).

By Bus   Two buses daily make the 4¹/₂-hour run from Gothenburg to Malmö. For bus information, call **Travelshop,** Skeppsbron 10, Malmö (© 040/33-05-70). They specialize in the sale of bus tickets within Sweden and to other points within Europe as well.

VISITOR INFORMATION   The **Malmö Tourist Office,** Central Station Skeppsbron 2, 205 80 Malmö (© 040/34-12-00; www.malmo.se), is open as follows: May to September Monday to Friday 9am to 7pm, and Saturday and Sunday 10am to 4pm; October to April Monday to Friday 9am to 5pm, Saturday and Sunday 10am to 3pm.

GETTING AROUND   It's easy to walk around the city center, although you may need to rely on public transport if you're branching out to sights on the periphery. An individual bus ticket costs 16SEK ($3.20/£1.60) and is valid for 1 hour. For rail information within Sweden call © 771/757-575. Individual tickets are sold aboard the bus by the driver. Discount cards can be bought or refilled at the automated vending machines in the Central Station and at other strategic transport junctions throughout the city.

SEEING THE SIGHTS

The **Malmö Card,** which is available from the Malmö Tourist Office, entitles visitors to free admission to most of the city's museums. It also grants free parking and free bus travel within the city limits. A card that's valid for 1 day costs 130SEK ($26/£13); one that's valid for 2 days goes for 160SEK ($32/£16); one that's valid for 3 days is 190SEK ($38/£19). An adult who has a Malmö Card can be accompanied, with no additional charge, by two children up to 16 years of age.

You have to begin your exploration somewhere, and we find that the best place to do that is around **Stortorget** ★, the main square of Malmö, dating from the 1530s. The vast square was more of a market square than it is today. In its center stands an equestrian statue of King Karl X Gustav, who took Skåne back from the Danes. That event in 1658 is also commemorated with a fountain that is one of the most imaginative in Scandinavia and includes a nightingale, the symbol of Malmö.

Bordering the eastern side of the square is the **Rådhuset** (Town Hall), once imbued with a look of Renaissance splendor back in 1546. It has undergone major changes over the years, most notably in the 1860s when Helgo Zettervall redesigned the facade in the Dutch Renaissance style, which is more or less what you'll see today. Unless you have official business, the interior cannot be visited except for its cellar restaurant (Rådhuskällern, p. 233).

Nearby lies **Lilla Torg** ★★, Malmö's most charming square and the centerpiece of much of its nightlife and cafe culture. An attractive cobble-covered plaza ringed with fine half-timbered buildings dating from the 16th to the 18th century, it looks like a film set. In addition to its status as a place to see and perhaps meet other people, many handicraft shops are found here. For many centuries this was the bustling open-air marketplace of Malmö; however, in the early 20th century, a covered market (the sturdy brick-built Saluhallen) replaced the open-air booths and stalls. Today, the Saluhallen houses a small-scale shopping mall with handicrafts, foodstuffs, and a number of restaurants, the best of which are recommended in "Where to Dine," later in this chapter

While on this square, check out the **Form Design Centre** at Lilla Torg 9 (p. 228, under "Shopping").

THE MAJOR ATTRACTIONS

Malmöhus Slott ★★   There is so much to see and do at this impressive fortress that we always allow a minimum of 3 hours to preview some of the highlights. (If you're very

SKÅNE (INCLUDING HELSINGBORG & MALMÖ)

8

MALMÖ

ACCOMMODATIONS■
Best Western Mäster
  Johan Hotel **17**
Best Western Noble House **8**
Elite Hotel Residens **20**
Elite Hotel Savoy **23**
Hilton Malmö City **28**
Hotel Plaza I Malmö **27**
Hotell Baltzar **13**
Quality Hotel Konserthuset **26**
Radisson SAS Hotel **24**
Rica Hotel Malmö **9**
Scandic Hotel Kramer **19**
Teaterhotellet **30**

ATTRACTIONS●
Kommendanthuset **1**
Konstmuseet **2**
Lilla Torg **10**
Malmöhus Slott **5**

Malmö Konsthall **29**
Naturmuseum **3**
Rådhuset **15**
Sankt Petri kyrka **22**
Stadsmuseum **4**
Stortorget **16**

DINING◆
Årstiderna I Kockska
  Huset **18**
Johan P **11**
Kramer Gastronomie **19**
Wallman's Salonger **6**
Anno 1900 **25**
Lemongrass **7**
Rådhuskällern **21**
Victor's **12**
Casa Mia **14**
Restaurant B&B
  (Butik och Bar) **11**

Ångbåtsbron
Stormgatan
Inre hamnen
Nordenskiöldsgatan
Hjälmarekajen
Skeppsbron
Carlsgatan
Beijerskajen
Köpenhamns-
båtarna
**Central-
stationen**
ⓘ
Neptuni-
parken
Adelgatan
Norra Vallgatan
Västergatan
**Stor-
torget**
**Råd-
huset**
Engelbrektsgatan
**GAMLA
STADEN**
Söderg

Malmöhusvägen
Slottsbron
**Malmöhus
Castle**
MALMÖHUS
Kungsparken
Grynbodgatan
Stora Nygatan
**Gustav
Adolfs
torg**
Mariedals-
parken
Mariedalsvägen
Slottsgatan
Torggatan
Gamla
begravnings-
platsen
Isak
Södra
Linnéplatsen
Slottsparken
Kung Oscars väg
Regementsgatan
Storgatan

**KRON-
PRINSEN**
Regementsgatan
Tärningsholms-
gatan
Mariedalsvägen
Fågelbacksgatan
† **Helgeands-
kyrkan**
HÄSTHAGEN
Erik Dahlbergsgatan
Fosens väg
Vår Frälsares
kyrka
Holmgatan
DAVIDSHALL
Östra Rönneholms vägen
Davids Hallgatan
Södra Förstadsgatan

Rönneholmsvägen
**FÅGEL-
BACKEN**
Kramersv.
Törnskärsgatan
Edward Lindahlsgatan
Krutmeijersgatan
Kronborgsvägen
Carl Gustafs väg
Pildammsvägen
Stadsteatern
30
TEATERN
INNERSTADEN
29 Konsthall
S:t Johannes-
gatan
S:t Johannes
kyrka
28
Köpenhamnsvägen

rushed, skip all but the Konstmuseet, Skåne's great treasure trove of art.) Malmö's greatest monument was founded in the 15th century by Eric of Pomerania but rebuilt by Christian III in the 16th century. The Earl of Bothwell, third husband of Mary Queen of Scots, was incarcerated here from 1568 to 1573. But those sad memories are long gone today, as it's been turned into a series of museums offering a repository of culture. The castle lies a 10- to 15-minute walk west of the Stortorget. It is split into the following divisions:

Kommendanthuset   Part of the 18th-century arsenal, this member of the museum cluster lies across the street from the castle. Check out what's going on here at the time of your visit, as this house is host to a frequently changing roster of traveling exhibits, many related to photography. Near Kommendanthuset is the **Teknikens och Sjöfartens Hus (Science and Maritime Museum)**. This is only for technology buffs who'll appreciate the flight simulator, submarine, cars (old and new), and relics of trams and ferries.

Konstmuseet ★★   These second-floor art galleries boast a collection of old Scandinavian masters, especially those from southern Sweden. Notable among the artists is Carl Fredrik Hill (1849–1911), one of Sweden's most revered landscape painters and a forerunner of European modernism. But we're most drawn to the display of **Russian oil paintings** ★★, created in the 1890–1914 revolutionary period. This is the largest collection of such works outside Russia itself. Almost equally intriguing is the museum's collection of **Nordic art** ★★ painted in the volatile 1920s and 1930s; Christian Berg, Max Walter Svanberg, and Carl Fredrik Reutherswärd seem to tower over their competition here.

Naturmuseum   This museum hardly stacks up against similar museums in New York or London. But you might give it a look if time remains. It covers the geology of Skåne, including its flora and fauna. Its most compelling exhibits are an **aquarium** and a **tropicarium** in the basement.

Stadsmuseum   Regrettably for a historic city such as Malmö, the city museum is a disappointment. City officials have moved some artifacts from their "attic" to display here. Unless you're writing a book on the history of Malmö, you might want to skip this one. Another drawback is that the exhibits are all in Swedish, so it is hardly user-friendly.

Malmöhusvägen. ✆ **040/34-10-00**. Admission free with Malmö Card. All-inclusive ticket 40SEK ($8/£4), 10SEK ($2/£1) children 7–15, free for children under 7. Sept–May noon–4pm; June–Aug 10am–4pm. Bus 14 or 17.

Malmö Konsthall   One of Europe's largest contemporary art centers, this museum hosts exhibitions of avant garde and experimental artwork—chicken blood or dung on canvas and such—but it also appreciates the classics of modern art as well. With a rich core of art by both modern masters and cutting-edge painters, it's a visual feast for anyone who appreciates recent developments in painting and sculpture. In our view, no other venue in southern Sweden so effectively mingles contemporary architecture with modern paintings. It's unpredictable what will be on parade at the time of your visit, though.

St. Johannesgasse 7. ✆ **040/34-12-93**. www.konsthall.malmo.se. Free admission. Daily 11am–5pm (until 9pm Wed).

Sankt Petri kyrka ★★★   Malmö doesn't possess a great cathedral. For that, you have to travel to Lund (see later in this chapter). But it does have a grand church, lying a block east of the Rådhuset (see above). Dark and a bit foreboding on the exterior, it is light and airy within. This Gothic church originated in the 14th century, when Malmö was under the control of the Hanseatic League, and was modeled on Marienkirche, a famous church in Lübeck, Germany. Other than the slender pillars and supporting ogive vaulting, the church's most stunning feature is its **Krämarkapellet ★★**, or tradesmen's chapel, from the 1400s. Amazingly, the original artwork remains. At the Reformation, the artwork here was viewed as "redundant," and the chapel was sealed off, which, in effect, protected its paintings from the overzealous "restoration" of the reformers. Look for the impressive New Testament figures surrounded by decorative foliage on the vaulted ceiling. Also notice the tall retable from 1611 and an exquisitely carved black limestone and sandstone pulpit from 1599. The octagonal baptismal font from 1601, as well as the pulpit, were the work of master craftsman Daniel Tommisen.

Göran Olsgatan. ✆ **040/35-90-43.** Free admission. Mon–Fri 10am–4pm; Sat–Sun 10am–6pm.

Svaneholm ★★   The province of Skåne is known for its castles, but this is the best one to visit while based in Malmö. Lying 40km (25 miles) to the east of Malmö by E65, this impressive Renaissance fortress dates from 1530. Many aristocratic families have lived here, but the castle's most colorful character was Baron Rutger Macklean (1742–1816), who introduced crop rotation to Sweden, an unheard-of concept. The castle was partially converted into an Italian-style palace. Today it houses a museum of paintings, furnishings, and tools dating primarily from the 18th and 19th centuries. The establishment is owned by the Svaneholm Castle Cooperative Society Ltd. For information, write **Svaneholm Museum,** S-274 00 Skurup (✆ **0411/400-12**). An on-site restaurant (✆ **0411/450-40**) serves regional specialties, costing 155SEK to 265SEK ($31–$53/£16–£27) for main courses.

Hamlet of Skurup. ✆ **0411/400-12.** www.svaneholms-slott.se. Admission 25SEK ($5/£2.50) for adults, 5SEK ($1/50p) children 6–14. May–June and Aug Tues–Sun 11am–5pm; July daily 10am–5pm; Sept Wed–Sun 11am–4pm. The castle is open other times upon request. Reaching Svaneholm is difficult by public transportation; a train from Malmö stops at Skurup, but it's a walk of about 3km (1³⁄₄ miles) from there. Therefore, many visitors opt to go by taxi the rest of the way. During the summer, the castle offers free transportation from Skurup, but you must call 1 hr. in advance.

SHOPPING

Malmö's two main pedestrian shopping streets include **Södergatan,** which leads south of Stortorget toward the canal, and **Södra Förstadsgatan.** And for shoppers who haven't found what they wanted in any of the specialty shops listed below, try **Hansa,** Stora Nygatan 50 (✆ **040/770-00;** www.mitthansa.se), a shopping complex with more than 40 shops, cafes, and restaurants. The latest fashions and items for the home are among the many specialties featured here, including the finest in Swedish glassware. Most stores are open Monday to Saturday from 10am to 5pm.

Crystal & Glassware

Juvelerare Hugo Nilsson   This shop, established in 1927, features some of the most famous names in Danish jewelry making, including Georg Jensen, Rauff, and Ole Lynggaard. Jewelry by Finnish designers such as Lapponia is also sold. Södra Tullgatan 2. ✆ **040/12-65-92.** www.hugonilsson.se. Bus: 17.

Fashion

Mattssons Päls   This is one of Sweden's leading furriers. Saga mink coats and jackets are the most luxurious buys, but Mattssons has a full range of fine furs at prices lower than in the United States. In the boutique are fur-lined poplins and accessories, all tax-free for tourists. The store lies a 5-minute walk from the Central Station and the Copenhagen boats. Norra Vallgatan 98. ☎ **040/12-55-33**. Bus: 17.

Form Design Centre Nearby, at 16th-century Lilla Torg, you can visit this museum-like exhibition space with boutiques selling upscale handicrafts, including Swedish textiles by the yard, woodcarvings, and all manner of other crafts. Lilla Torg 9. ☎ **040/664-51-50**. www.formdesigncenter.com. Bus: 17.

WHERE TO STAY
Expensive

Best Western Mäster Johan Hotel ★★ Our favorite hotel in Malmö, this well-run and comfortable hotel lies in the heart of town. It's a lot newer than you might think, thanks to good design and a respect for the history of its neighborhood. Built in 1990 and renovated frequently since then, it skillfully blends the avant-garde with a sense of the antique, always with lavish use of expensive stone, wood, and marble. The result is a very charming and very personalized hotel. Bedrooms are midsize to large, each beautifully maintained with cherrywood reproductions of Provençal antiques and equipped with stone or marble-trimmed bathrooms. Grace notes include oaken floors, Asian carpets, deep cove moldings, and a sense of privacy thanks to soundproofing. Staff is helpful, cheerful, and discreet, and the morning breakfast buffet—served adjacent to a glass-topped replica of a baroque courtyard—is appropriately lavish.

Mäster Johansgatan 13, S-211 21 Malmö. ☎ **800/780-7234** or 040/664-64-00. Fax 040/664-64-01. www.masterjohan.se. 69 units. Fri–Sat 1,400SEK–1,600SEK ($280–$320/£140–£160) double; Sun–Thurs 2,220SEK–2,625SEK ($444–$525/£222–£263) double; 3,325SEK ($665/£333) junior suite. AE, DC, MC, V. Bus: 2, 3, 4, 5, 7, 8, or 32. **Amenities:** Bar; gym; sauna; room service; laundry service; dry cleaning; non-smoking rooms; rooms for those w/limited mobility. *In room:* TV, kitchenette in suites, coffeemaker (in some), hair dryer, iron, safe, Wi-Fi.

Hilton Malmö City ★★★ Encased in a steel-and-glass ultramodern structure, the city's most visible international luxury hotel rises 20 stories from a position in the commercial heart of town. (It's the third tallest building in Malmö, but still hardly competition for the "Turning Torso," above.) Originally conceived in 1989 as a Sheraton, then transformed into a Scandic Hotel, and now a member of Hilton International, it boasts sweeping views of the Öresund region from almost all its bedrooms. The top three floors contain only upgraded "executive level" rooms and suites and a well-engineered health club. Many of its guests are business travelers, often attending one of the dozens of conventions that attract participants from throughout Europe. The spacious rooms are tastefully and comfortably appointed, with light colors and many electronic amenities. Suites are the best in town, with kitchenettes and large sitting areas; some even have their own Jacuzzi.

Triangeln 2, S-200 10 Malmö. ☎ **040/693-47-00**. Fax 040/693-47-11. www.hilton.com. 214 units. Sun–Thurs 1,140SEK–3,720SEK ($228–$744/£114–£372) double; Fri–Sat 1,090SEK–2,920SEK ($218–$584/£109–£292) double; 3,290SEK–4,360SEK ($658–$872/£329–£436) suite. Rates include breakfast. AE, DC, MC, V. Parking 95SEK ($19/£9.50). Bus: 14 or 17. **Amenities:** Restaurant; bar; fitness center; sauna; business services; room service; babysitting; laundry service; dry cleaning; nonsmoking rooms; rooms for those w/limited mobility. *In room:* A/C, TV, minibar, hair dryer, iron, Wi-Fi.

Radisson SAS Hotel ★★ This chain-run hotel competes for the same clients as the Hilton, but the Hilton skyscraper has little to fear from its competition—more successful businessmen seem to check in there. If that deal hasn't come through yet, this is a viable alternative, and is also a suitable choice for vacationers. The Radisson SAS contains tastefully decorated rooms with elegant bathrooms. Built in 1988, the seven-story hotel lies only a 5-minute walk from the train station, which provides transportation to Copenhagen in only 40 minutes. As an added convenience, the hotel bus stops nearby. If you don't want to go out at night, try the hotel's excellent Thott Restaurant, serving both Swedish traditional dishes and international specialties.

Östergatan 10, S-211 Malmö. © **800/333-3333** or 040/698-40-00. Fax 040/698-40-01. www.radissonsas. com. 229 units. Mon–Thurs 1,695SEK–2,695SEK ($339–$539/£170–£270) double; Fri–Sun 1,190SEK–1,490SEK ($238–$298/£119–£149) double; Mon–Sun 2,200SEK–2,800SEK ($440–$560/£220–£280) suite. Rates include breakfast. AE, DC, MC, V. Parking 130SEK ($26/£13). Bus: 14 or 17. **Amenities:** Restaurant; bar; sauna; room service; babysitting; laundry service; dry cleaning; nonsmoking rooms; rooms for those w/limited mobility. In room: A/C, TV, minibar, hair dryer, iron, Wi-Fi.

Scandic Hotel Kramer ★

A top-to-bottom redesign has extended the shelf life of this long-time favorite. At the side of the town's main square, this château-style twin-towered building is one of Malmö's landmarks. Built in 1875, it's been renovated regularly since, including the construction of a modern wing in the mid-1980s. Most recently, the rooms were redecorated with an old-fashioned sense of nostalgia, which is vaguely reminiscent of staterooms on a pre–World War II ocean liner. Each has a marble bathroom with a tub/shower combination, dark paneling, curved walls, and kitschy 1930s-style accessories.

Stortorget 7, S-201 21 Malmö. © **040/693-54-00.** Fax 040/693-54-11. www.scandic-hotels.com. 113 units. 850SEK–2,390SEK ($170–$478/£85–£239) double; from 3,420SEK ($684/£342) suite. Rates include breakfast. AE, DC, MC, V. Parking 95SEK ($19/£9.50). Bus: 14, 17, or 20. **Amenities:** Restaurant; bar; sauna; room service; laundry service; dry cleaning; nonsmoking rooms. In room: A/C, TV, minibar, hair dryer, Wi-Fi.

Moderate

Best Western Noble House ★★

Elegance at a moderate price is the keynote here. One of the most modern and up-to-date hotels in town—and certainly one of the most glamorous—is named after the best-selling novel by James Clavell. (The former owner was a great devotee of his writings.) The comfortable pastel-colored rooms are decorated with copies of early 20th-century Swedish paintings. Because of the four-story hotel's convenient location in the town center, its quietest rooms face the interior courtyard.

Gustav Adolfs Torg 47, S-211 39 Malmö. © **800/780-7234** or 040/664-30-00. Fax 040/664-30-50. www. hkchotels.se. 130 units. 825SEK–1,625SEK ($165–$325/£83–£163) double; 1,625SEK–2,995SEK ($325–$599/£163–£300) suite. Rates include breakfast. AE, DC, MC, V. Parking 160SEK ($32/£16). Bus: 1, 2, 5, 6, 7, or 8. **Amenities:** Restaurant; breakfast room; bar; sauna; laundry service; dry cleaning; nonsmoking rooms; rooms for those w/limited mobility. In room: TV, minibar, hair dryer (in some), safe, Wi-Fi.

Elite Hotel Residens ★ (Value)

Not the market leader that its sister hotel, Elite Hotel Savoy, is, this is still a most recommendable choice. In 1987, a team of local investors enlarged the beige and brown-sided premises of a historic 1517 inn by linking it with a brick-and-stone structure erected during the '70s. The interconnected structures provide solid, comfortable, and upscale lodgings near the railroad station. Except for certain corners where an effort was made to duplicate a woodsy-looking men's club in London, many of the public areas are outfitted in a glossy, modern setup with lots of mirrors, touches of chrome, and polished marble floors. Guest rooms, each renovated between 2006 and 2007, are traditionally outfitted and fairly spacious. They have hardwood floors or wall-to-wall carpeting, well-upholstered furnishings, and, in some cases, Oriental carpets. Windows are large and double-insulated against noise from the urban landscape outside.

Adelgatan 7, S-211 22 Malmö. (C) **040/664-48-90.** Fax 040/664-48-95. www.elite.se. 69 units. 893SEK–1,850SEK ($179–$370/£89–£185) double; 1,148SEK–3,150SEK ($230–$630/£115–£315) suite. Rates include breakfast. AE, DC, MC, V. Parking 195SEK ($39/£20). Bus: 2 or 4. **Amenities:** Breakfast room; on-site sauna and free access to a nearby fitness club; room service; laundry service; dry cleaning; nonsmoking rooms. *In room:* TV, minibar, hair dryer, iron, safe (in some), Wi-Fi.

Elite Hotel Savoy ★★   Set immediately across the square from the railway station, this landmark hotel has figured prominently in Malmö history, as its origins date back to the 14th century. Famous guests have included actress Liv Ullmann, actor Alan Alda, and Johnny ("Tarzan") Weissmuller. We're impressed with the careful restoration of the regular bedrooms and suites; everything has been modernized with respect for the classic decor. In fact, the hotel boasts some of the most plushly decorated accommodations in Sweden. Rooms contain champagne-colored upholstery, cabriole-legged or Chippendale-style furniture, excellent beds, and all the extras of a deluxe hotel. In the hotel restaurant, you can order from an international menu, perhaps stopping for a before-dinner beer in the British-style pub, the Bishop's Arms.

Norra Vallgatan 62, S-201 80 Malmö. (C) **040/664-48-00.** Fax 040/664-48-50. www.savoy.elite.se. 109 units. 978SEK–2,150SEK ($196–$430/£98–£215) double; 1,148SEK–4,650SEK ($230–$930/£115–£465) suite. Rates include breakfast. AE, DC, MC, V. Parking 195SEK ($39/£20). Bus: 14 or 17. **Amenities:** Restaurant; bar; fitness center; sauna; room service; laundry service; dry cleaning; nonsmoking rooms. *In room:* TV, minibar, hair dryer, iron, safe, Wi-Fi.

Hotell Baltzar ★ Finds   Around 1900, an entrepreneur who had made a fortune selling chocolate moved into a private home whose turrets, towers, and fanciful ornamentation evoked a stone-carved confection. Several decades later, when it became a hotel, it expanded into one of the neighboring buildings. Today you'll find a somewhat eccentric hotel with many charming corners and cubbyholes, and a reception area set one floor upstairs from street level. Grace notes include frescoed ceilings (in some of the public areas and also in about 25% of the bedrooms), substantial-looking antiques, and elaborate draperies in some of the public areas. The comfortable, high-ceilinged guest rooms were upgraded with the kind of furnishings and parquet floors that would suit a prosperous private home. The location on an all-pedestrian downtown street, about a block south of the heartbeat Stortorget, keeps things relatively quiet inside. Breakfast is the only meal served.

Södergatan 20, S-211 24 Malmö. (C) **040/665-57-00.** Fax 040/665-57-10. www.baltzarhotel.se. 40 units. Mon–Thurs 1,500SEK–1,900SEK ($300–$380/£150–£190) double; Fri–Sun 950SEK–1,300SEK ($190–$260/£95–£130) double. Rates include breakfast. AE, DC, MC, V. Free parking. Bus: 10. **Amenities:** Breakfast room; room service; laundry service; dry cleaning; nonsmoking rooms. *In room:* TV, minibar, hair dryer, safe.

Rica Hotel Malmö ★   Built in 1914, with many subsequent changes and improvements since, this hotel lies on Malmö's main square facing the Town Hall, a short walk from the railway station. Since 2007, most of the guest rooms have been rebuilt in a tasteful modern format. Originally, this hotel was owned by the Salvation Army, which strictly forbade the consumption of alcohol on the premises; but since its sale to the Rica chain, all of that is a distant memory, and there's now a bar adjacent to the lobby. The rooms are generally spacious, but bathrooms tend to be cramped.

Stortorget 15 S-211 22 Malmö. (C) **040/660-95-50.** Fax 040/660-95-59. www.rica.se. 82 units. Mon–Thurs 1,095SEK–2,195SEK ($219–$439/£110–£220) double; Fri–Sun 875SEK–1,095SEK ($175–$219/£88–£110) double. Rates include breakfast. AE, DC, MC, V. Parking 145SEK ($29/£15). Bus: 6 or 10. **Amenities:** Breakfast room; lounge; sauna; laundry service; dry cleaning; nonsmoking rooms. *In room:* TV, minibar, hair dryer, Wi-Fi.

Teaterhotellet   The only negative aspect of this hotel is its banal-looking 1960s-era facade; it's no uglier than hundreds of other contemporaneous Scandinavian buildings, but that doesn't make it particularly inviting or pleasing. Inside, however, you'll find a cozy, tasteful, and colorful establishment that attracts many repeat clients. Appealing touches include beige and tawny-colored marble floors, lots of elegant hardwood paneling, lacquered walls in neutral tones of pale amber and beige, and spots of vibrant colors in the guest rooms (especially jewel tones of red and green) that perk up even the grayest of Swedish winter days. Rooms are renovated with modern furniture, plus restored bathrooms. Less than a kilometer (about ¹/₂ mile) south of the railway station, the hotel is near a verdant park and the Stadsteater. Only breakfast is served, but you can usually get someone to bring you a sandwich and coffee.

Rönngatan 3, S-211 47 Malmö. ✆ **040/665-58-00.** Fax 040/665-58-10. www.teaterhotellet.se. 44 units. Sun–Thurs 1,500SEK–1,700SEK ($300–$340/£150–£170) double; Fri–Sat 950SEK ($190/£95) double; 1,800SEK ($360/£180) junior suite. Rates include breakfast. AE, DC, MC, V. Parking 125SEK ($25/£13). Bus: 5. **Amenities:** Breakfast room; bar; room service; laundry service; dry cleaning; nonsmoking rooms. *In room:* TV, minibar (in some), hair dryer, Wi-Fi.

Inexpensive

Hotel Plaza I Malmö   This is one of the least pretentious and most nondescript hotels in town, yet it's conveniently located a half-block from an important all-pedestrian shopping thoroughfare, and 3 blocks from the better-accessorized (and more expensive) Hilton. With its three-story red-brick contemporary-looking facade and its stripped-down and dull but respectable lobby, it might remind you of an upgraded youth hostel. Though everything here is simple and basic, it's well scrubbed. Staff members are also friendly and spontaneous and, at their best, humorous; and there are some amenities you might not have expected, including a sauna and an exercise area. Beer and wine are served from a small dispensary in the lobby, and there are many different dining options within a short walk from this place.

Kasinogatan 6, P.O. Box 17550, S-200 10 Malmö. ✆ **040/33-05-50.** Fax 040/33-05-51. www.hotel-plaza. se. 48 units. Sun–Thurs 1,395SEK ($279/£140) double; Fri–Sat 940SEK ($188/£94) double. AE, MC, V. **Amenities:** Health club/exercise area; sauna. *In room:* TV, minifridge (without liquor), iron.

Quality Hotel Konserthuset ⟨Value⟩   The most unusual thing about this cost-efficient hotel involves the way it shares its premises, a bulky, boxy-looking mirrored cube on the southeast outskirts of town, with the headquarters of the Malmö Symphony Orchestra. Don't expect luxury: Everything about the place is designed for no-nonsense efficiency, with no superfluous frills. As such, it's favored by corporations as lodging for conventions, and by families with children looking for simple, unfrilly lodgings. Rooms are well maintained and comfortable, despite their angular and relatively spartan venues.

Amiralsgatan 19, S-211 55 Malmö. ✆ **040/664-60-00.** Fax 040/664-60-65. www.choicehotels.se. 154 units. 995SEK–1,995SEK ($199–$399/£100–£200) double. **Amenities:** Restaurant; bar; nightclub (Tues and Fri–Sat only); health club; spa; sauna. *In room:* TV, iron, safe, Wi-Fi.

WHERE TO DINE

Expensive

Årstiderna I Kockska Huset ★★★ SWEDISH/INTERNATIONAL   The best restaurant in Malmö lies behind a red-brick facade on a "perpetually shadowed" medieval street in the city's historic core. It was built in the North German style in 1523 as the home and political headquarters of the Danish-appointed governor of Malmö, Jürgen Kock. In its own richly Gothic way, it's the most unusual restaurant setting in town, with vaulted brick ceilings, severe-looking medieval detailing, and an undeniable sense of the posh and plush good life. Owners Marie and Wilhelm Pieplow have created an environment where the prime ministers of Sweden and Finland, as well as dozens of politicians, artists, and actors, have dined on exceedingly good food. Menu items change with the seasons; the establishment's name, Årstiderna, translates from Swedish as "The Four Seasons." Likely to be featured are scallops and Norwegian lobster "du jour"; gin-cured salmon with asparagus and melted, mustard-flavored butter; grilled salted cod with clams and a lemon-flavored beurre blanc; filets of sole poached in white wine with grilled lobster, asparagus, and Parmesan sauce; filet of beef flambéed with grappa; and raspberry and licorice–glazed venison with gravy and a ragout of mushrooms. All dishes are prepared with infinite care using the best and freshest ingredients.

Frans Suellsgatan 3. ✆ **040/23-09-10** or 040/703-20. www.arstiderna.se. Reservations recommended. Main courses dinner 235SEK–375SEK ($47–$75/£24–£38), lunch 155SEK–235SEK ($31–$47/£16–£24); fixed-price lunch 295SEK–345SEK ($59–$69/£30–£35), fixed-price dinner 350SEK–585SEK ($70–$117/£35–£59). AE, DC, MC, V. Mon–Fri 11:30am–11pm; Sat 5–11pm. Bus: 7, 14, or 31.

Johan P ★★ (Finds) FISH/SEAFOOD   The most appealing seafood in Malmö is prepared and served in this artfully simple, mostly white dining room whose terraces spill out, during clement weather, onto the cobble-covered street on one side, and into the corridors of the Saluhall (food market) on the other. The result is a bustling but almost pristine setting where the freshness of the seafood is the main draw. Menu items are prepared from scratch every day, based on whatever is available within the Saluhallen, and the kitchens are visible to whomever happens to pass by. Diners are served brimming bowlfuls, one after another, of this restaurant's cream-based, and then its tomato-based, fish soups, accompanied by fresh bread and a salad. Other examples include a half-lobster with lemon-flavored mayonnaise; lobster-larded monkfish with vinegar sauce; light-grilled tuna with truffled mayonnaise, roasted peppers, and artichokes; and grilled veal with morels in white sauce with a compote of onions. Dessert might include a mousse made with bitter white chocolate, served with dark-chocolate madeleines and coffee sauce.

Saluhallen, Landbygatan 3. ✆ **040/97-18-18.** Reservations recommended. Daily specials (lunch only) 89SEK ($18/£9); main courses 220SEK–398SEK ($44–$80/£22–£40); 3-course fixed-price menu 345SEK–798SEK ($69–$160/£35–£80). AE, DC, MC, V. Mon–Fri 11:30am–10pm (last order); Sat noon–11pm. Bus: 14 or 17.

Kramer Gastronomie ★ CONTINENTAL/FRENCH   This restaurant serves the best food of any hotel dining room in Malmö. There's an upscale, vaguely baroque-looking bar that's separated from the brown and off-white dining room with a leaded-glass divider, and an attention to cuisine that brings a conservative, not particularly flashy clientele back again and again. The composition of the fixed-price menus changes every week. The chef is dedicated to his job, personally shopping for market-fresh ingredients. Menu items include shots of shellfish bouillon served with Parmesan chips and coriander salsa; scallops with grilled tuna and bacon; blackened filet of beef with pecorino cheese, lemon wedges, arugula, and a sauce made with a reduction of court bouillon and red wine; and chargrilled halibut with glazed turnips, truffle butter, and dill oil. Pastas here are upscale and esoteric, including a version with spinach, crayfish, fried filet of sole, and dill sauce.

In the Scandic Hotel Kramer, Stortorget 7. ✆ **040/693-54-00.** Reservations recommended. Main courses 235SEK–385SEK ($47–$77/£24–£39); 3-course fixed-price menu 360SEK ($72/£36). AE, DC, MC, V. Mon–Fri 5–11pm; Sat 6–11pm. Bar open till 1am. Bus: 10.

Wallman's Salonger ★ CONTINENTAL   Malmö's leading supper club and cabaret, painted a heady shade of bordeaux red, is the most entertaining restaurant in the
city—with an entertaining staff as well. Tables have views over a stage and dance floor
upon which members of the staff—each an aspiring actor or at least a candidate for a job
in the theater—will sing, dance, and amuse you. The razzle-dazzle array of songs and
cabaret acts might range from a number evoking ABBA during their musical heyday to
something with a top-hat-with-tails allure suitable for a Nordic revival of *A Chorus Line.*
Set menus are identified by names that include "Elvis Presley," "Judy Garland," and
"Golden Hits," and exude lots of culinary ambition. The finest examples include a catch
of the week from the Baltic served with risotto verde and a tomato cassoulet; a cashew,
chestnut, and prosciutto tart served with creamy roasted garlic; and an array of steaks,
salads, seafood, veal, or pork dishes, plus vegetarian dishes. They're usually flavorful and
well prepared, but because most clients are watching the good-looking, mostly blond
performers on stage or gyrating on the dance floor themselves, no one seems especially
concerned. An evening here can get a bit pricey, but because it incorporates dining and
the hard-working efforts of an entire crew of theatrical hopefuls, the relatively high tab
seems understandable.

Generalsgatan 1. ✆ **040/749-45** for reservations (before 5pm) or ✆ 040/97-03-76 after 5pm. Reservations recommended. 3-course fixed-price menus 345SEK–1,690SEK ($69–$338/£35–£169). AE, DC, MC, V.
Wed–Sat 7:30pm–3am. Kitchen closes at 11pm. Closed May to mid-Aug. Bus: 5.

Moderate

Anno 1900 ★ (Finds) SWEDISH   If you have a Swedish grandmother, bring her
here—she'll feel right at home. The name of this place gives a hint about its turn-of-the-
20th-century decor, which includes lots of antique woodwork and accessories from the
heyday of the Industrial Revolution. There's a garden in back that's open during warm
weather, and a worldly management team that seems to cherish memories of their youthful heydays in New York City. Menu items derive from tried-and-true *husmanskost*
(home-cooked) classics: old-fashioned versions of cauliflower soup, roasted pork with
onion sauce, braised calf's liver, poached halibut with horseradish sauce, grilled sausages
with dill-flavored cream sauce, chicken dumplings with noodles, *frikadeller* (meatballs),
or fried herring.

Norra Bultoftavagen 7. ✆ **040/18-47-47.** Reservations recommended. Main courses 125SEK–245SEK
($25–$49/£13–£25); fixed-price lunch 115SEK–235SEK ($23–$47/£12–£24). AE, DC, MC, V. Mon–Fri
11:15am–2pm; Thurs–Sat 6–11pm. Bus: 14 or 17.

Lemongrass ASIAN   When we begin to tire of a Swedish diet, we book a table here.
Lemongrass is set in a large, spartan room that's devoid of the artsy clutter of many Asian
restaurants. Instead, against sand-colored walls, you'll find occasional clusters of exotic-
looking plants and, within an otherwise artfully minimalist setting, tufted bunches of the
lemongrass for which the restaurant was named. There's a bar where you can wait for
your table, if you have to, and a menu that contains food items from Japan (including
sushi), China, and Thailand. A staff member will help you coordinate a meal from disparate culinary styles in ways that you might have expected only in Los Angeles, London,
or New York.

Grunbodgatan 9. ✆ **040/30-69-79.** www.lemongrass.se. Reservations recommended. Main courses
134SEK–208SEK ($27–$42/£13–£21). AE, MC, V. Mon–Thurs 6pm–midnight; Fri–Sat 6pm–1am. Bus: 4.

Rådhuskällern (Value) SWEDISH   This is the most atmospheric place in Malmö,
located in the cellar of the Town Hall. Even if you don't eat here, at least drop in for a

drink in the pub or lounge. The severe exterior and labyrinth of underground vaults were built in 1546; the dark-vaulted dining room was used for centuries to store gold, wine, furniture, and food. Menu staples include halibut with lobster sauce, fried redfish with mango sauce, tournedos of beef with red-wine sauce and creamed morels, and roast duck, and there's always an array of daily specials. Although the fare is first-rate here, it never overexcites the palate.

Kyrkogatan 5. (C) **040/790-20.** www.profilrestauranger.se. Reservations recommended. Main courses 110SEK–215SEK ($22–$43/£11–£22); set menus 105SEK–230SEK ($21–$46/£11–£23); set menu for lunch 225SEK ($45/£23). AE, DC, MC, V. Mon–Fri 11:30am–2pm and 5–10:30pm; Sat 5–11pm. Closed July 1–Aug 21. Bus: 14 or 17.

Salt & Brygga ★ (Finds) SWEDISH/MEDITERRANEAN

Opening onto a large patio with a panoramic view of the Öresund, this postmillennium restaurant was hailed as restaurant of the year the moment it opened. On our last visit, we found that it lived up to its initial praise. It prides itself on the use of mostly organic (that is, grown without synthetic fertilizers or pesticides) food, most of which derives from nearby suppliers and is prepared with a respect for the culinary traditions of the Mediterranean. It's an atmospheric and artfully contemporary place that's brisk, internationally hip, and pleasing. Guests dine in relative simplicity, enjoying freshly prepared dishes that include lots of seafood and fresh produce, an enticing assortment of risottos, and a large selection of organic wine, cider, and beer. The smoked coalfish ("saithe" on the menu) makes a fine and tasty appetizer, and vegetarians should appreciate the savory vegetable lasagna. Desserts are prepared fresh daily and don't over-rely on sugar for their appeal.

Sundspromenade 7. (C) **040/611-59-40.** www.saltobrygga.se. Reservations recommended. Main courses 195SEK–249SEK ($39–$50/£20–£25); fixed-price lunch 99SEK ($20/£10). AE, DC, MC, V. Mon–Fri 11:30am–3pm and 6–10pm; Sat noon–10pm. Bus: 3 or 5.

Victor's SCANDINAVIAN

Set cheek by jowl among about a dozen competitors that line the perimeter of the historic Lilla Torg, this restaurant is a bit hipper and more popular than many of the others. Of course, on the crush of a midsummer evening, when every cafe and restaurant on the square is packed with seers who enjoy being seen, it looks a lot like its neighbors. But in winter, when the action moves into its interior, its coziness becomes more obvious. Its principal draw is an Old Sweden theme: Menu items are old-fashioned and conservative, but undeniably flavorful. The best examples include toast Skagen (layered with shrimp, mayonnaise, and dill); gravlax (marinated salmon) cured with fennel; a spicy version of fish soup; pan-fried loin of cod; and vegetarian tomato stew with chickpeas. Dessert might feature a dark chocolate parfait with almond-studded crisps.

Lilla Torget 1. (C) **040/12-76-70.** Lunch platters 69SEK–75SEK ($14–$15/£7–£7.50); dinner main courses 155SEK–225SEK ($31–$45/£16–£23). AE, DC, MC, V. Daily 11:30am–3pm and 6–10:30pm. Bus: 17.

Inexpensive

Casa Mia ITALIAN

The staff here works hard to maintain Italian bravura amid the snows of Scandinavia. Venetian gondola moorings ornament the front terrace of this Nordic version of a neighborhood trattoria; schmaltzy Neapolitan ballads play in the background; and your waiter is likely to address you in Italian. You might begin with a steaming bowl of *stracciatella alla romana* (egg-and-chicken soup) or the fish soup of the house, then move on to penne with shrimp, basil, cream, and tomatoes, or spaghetti with seafood. Later you can dig into *saltimbocca alla romana* (veal with ham), grilled scampi with asparagus, roasted lamb with new potatoes, or an array of grilled meats with

aromatic herbs. There are about a dozen types of savory pizza on the menu, and pastries
are offered for dessert. Okay, it's not as good as the food served in a typical trattoria in
northern Italy, but the cuisine is a refreshing change of pace.

Södergatan 12. (*C*) **040/23-05-00.** www.casamia.se. Reservations recommended. Pastas and pizzas
70SEK–135SEK ($14–$27/£7–£14); main-course platters 162SEK–245SEK ($32–$49/£16–£25). AE, DC, MC,
V. Mon 11:30am–11pm; Tues–Sat 11:30am–midnight; Sun 1–10pm. Bus: 14 or 17.

Restaurant B & B (Butik och Bar) SWEDISH/ITALIAN   This well-managed, relatively inexpensive bistro occupies a corner of the Saluhallen (the food market directly
adjacent to Lilla Torget, the landmark square), which provides the fresh ingredients that
go into each menu item. Within a simple, old-fashioned setting, with glowing hardwood
floors, pristine white walls, and a scattering of antiques that evoke the Sweden of long
ago, you'll find flavorful, unpretentious food firmly rooted in the old-fashioned traditions of both Italy and Sweden. The menu includes the Swedish staples: Skagen toasts
(with shrimp, hard-boiled eggs, and dill-flavored mayonnaise), elk steak with cloudberry
sauce, and fried flank steak with roasted potatoes. Italian offerings include saltimbocca,
various kinds of pastas, and grilled steaks with Mediterranean herbs.

Saluhallen, Landbygatan 1. (*C*) **040/12-71-20.** Reservations recommended. Main courses 139SEK–
189SEK ($28–$38/£14–£19); fixed-price lunch 65SEK–85SEK ($13–$17/£6.50–£8.50). AE, DC, MC, V. Mon–
Sat noon–10pm. Bus: 2, 3, 4, 5, or 7.

MALMÖ AFTER DARK
Those seeking cultural activities after dark should get tickets to the **Malmö Symphony
Orchestra** ★★★, which is renowned across Europe. It performs at the Konserthus,
Föreningsgatan 35 ((*C*) **040/630-45-06**). The tourist office distributes programs of its
upcoming schedule as well as schedules and descriptions of other cultural events.

Cafes & Bars
For other serious after-dark pursuits, many locals, especially young people, head for
nearby Copenhagen. But for people-watching, no place in Malmö is more popular than
the Lilla Torg, with its plethora of outdoor cafes and restaurants that shelter an attractive
mix of locals and visitors. The most popular of the dozen or so watering holes surrounding the square include Victor's (recommended in "Where to Dine," above) and the
Moosehead Bar.

At the **Moosehead Bar,** Lilla Torget 1 ((*C*) **040/12-04-23;** www.moosehead.se.; bus
17), the clientele might seem a bit less concerned with etiquette and social niceties than
the patrons of more sedate hangouts in other parts of the square. Its woodsy-looking,
brick-lined decor and its emphasis on the biggest animal of the northern forests and
tundra might remind you of a college hangout in Maine, but the conversation and the
proliferation of blondes is pure Sweden. Don't expect gourmet cuisine here: Everybody's
favorite meal is a juicy burger made from either beef or moose meat (it's up to you to
specify which), accompanied by a foaming mugful of Åbro, the local lager. Barring that,
consider ordering a green melon or pineapple daiquiri, priced at between 85SEK and
120SEK ($17–$24/£8.50–£12), depending on the size.

One of the most packed and long-lived hipster bars in Malmö is **Centiliter &
Gram** ★, Stortorget 17 ((*C*) **40/12-18-12;** bus 17). When it was inaugurated in the mid-
1990s, "Cl. & Gr." was one of Malmö's hottest restaurants, but since then it's emerged
as a popular bar with a hot clientele age 25 and up—although the food is still entirely
respectable. It occupies an artfully minimalist herb-and-grass-colored space whose focal
point is a centrally placed bar that rocks with an ongoing stream of electronic, usually

house, music. Guests often stay to flirt long after their dishes have been cleared away. Main courses cost from 135SEK to 240SEK ($27–$48/£14–£24), with an emphasis on salads, pastas, grilled fish and grilled steaks, and light vegetarian fare. The establishment's name, incidentally, derives from wine (which is measured in centiliters) and food (which is measured in grams). It's open Wednesday to Saturday 5pm to 3am.

Nostalgic for Britain? Then check out the **Bishop's Arms,** Norra Vallgatan 62 (℃ 040/664-48-88; bus 14 or 17), a cozy and highly appealing replica of an Anglo-Irish pub. Located within the Elite Savoy Hotel, it serves generous platters, priced at 120SEK to 185SEK ($24–$37/£12–£19) each, of such Anglo and Celtic staples as fish and chips, burgers, buffalo wings, and pepper steaks, as well as some of the coldest beer in town. There's always a congenial crowd. As is common in the U.K., you'll place your drink and/or food order directly at the bar, and then a staff member will carry it to your table. It's open Monday to Saturday 4pm to 1am, Sunday 4 to 11pm. Take bus 4, 5, or 7.

Dance Clubs

The hippest and most appealing dance club in the area is **Slagthuset,** Jörgen Köcksgatan 7A (℃ 040/10-99-31). It's set within the red-brick premises of what was conceived in the 19th century as a slaughterhouse for cattle and hogs, in a location directly behind the railway station. This high-energy and much-talked-about place now functions as the largest dance club in Scandinavia. You can wander freely over three floors, each with its own bars, dance floor, labyrinth of interconnected rooms, music, and crowds of good-looking, sometimes raucous clients. It's open only on Friday and Saturday nights, from 10pm to 5am. The entrance fee is 100SEK ($20/£10).

Slaghuset's most visible competitor is **Club Skeppsbron,** Skeppsbron 2 (℃ 040/30-62-02). Outfitted for a relatively mature clientele that, in the words of a good-looking local woman, includes "cute guys, rich men, and strong drinks," this nightclub incorporates a restaurant, an outdoor terrace, big windows overlooking a canal, and a mixture of antique nautical paneling with postmodern angularity. It's open only on Saturday nights, from 10pm to 5am, year-round. The entrance fee is 100SEK ($20/£10).

Dancing is also the rage at the creatively designed **Nightclub Étage,** Stortorget 6 (℃ 040/23-20-60; bus 17). Initially conceived as an upscale bar and restaurant in the late 1980s, this nightspot lowered its prices and began marketing to a mass audience in the early 1990s. Despite its lowered expectations, the bar has not suffered as a result. It's reached by climbing a circular staircase from an enclosed courtyard in the town's main square. The complex is open Monday and Thursday to Saturday 10pm to at least 4am, depending on the crowd. The cover for the dance club ranges from 75SEK to 90SEK ($15–$18£7.50–£9).

Many love affairs, both long and short, a few of which have segued into marriages, have gotten their start at the **Malmborgen Compound,** a sprawling antique warehouse on Hamburgsgatan. There's a restaurant within the building's courtyard (Gränden; ℃ 040/12-38-95; bus 14 or 17) serving pizzas, shish kebabs, and Swedish meatballs with salad for 98SEK to 175SEK ($20–$35/£9.80–£18) daily from 11:30am to 11:30pm. The compound also contains a somewhat nondescript scattering of minor bars and cafes, but its most visible venue is the **Swing Inn,** Stadt Hamburgsgatan 3 (℃ 040/12-22-21), where romantic dancing is the norm. Attendees tend to be over 35, and the recorded music is reminiscent of a '60s variety show. There's a restaurant on the premises serving platters of traditional Swedish food Thursday to Saturday between 10 and 11:30pm. Main courses cost from 135SEK to 205SEK ($27–$41/£14–£21). Music and bar activities are scheduled on Thursdays from 10pm to 1am, Fridays 10pm to 3am, and Saturdays 10pm to 4am. The cover charge is 90SEK ($18/£9) after 11pm.

Gay & Lesbian Nightlife

Many gays and lesbians now take the train across the bridge to the fleshpots of Copenhagen. But gay nightlife in Malmö recently took a distinct turn for the better thanks to the involvement of Claes Schmidt, creator of such mainstream clubs as the also-recommended Slagthuset (see above). Claes "came out" publicly to the Swedish press in 2003 as a (mostly heterosexual) cross-dresser. Immediately in the wake of this "confession," the local paper sold an additional 20,000 copies (huge by local standards). (For more on the story of the double life he'd been leading as his now-famous stage name Sara Lund, check out his website, www.saralund.se.) In the wake of these confessions, Claes became the most famous cross-dresser in Europe, working occasionally as a paid consultant at corporate consciousness-raising conventions and at universities throughout Scandinavia. Claes's nightclub sensation, which has surpassed his smashing success Slagthuset and is now the most popular cutting-edge dance club in Malmö, is **Indigo** ★★, 15 Monbijou-gatan (© **040/611-99-62;** www.rfsl.se/malmo). Don't expect to find it easily: It lies in a former warehouse within a drab industrial neighborhood in the Triangeln neighborhood, a 12-minute walk from the Hilton Hotel. You'll climb solid, industrial-strength stairs to the third floor of this brick-built fortress, encountering some amicably punkish people en route.

   Inside, you'll find a vast and echoing space with enormous dance floors and bars that host the city's various drag or leather events. The best known of these is Switch, which defines itself as "a bar for men and women of all genders." Switch hosts a drag ball and elegance contest that occurs on the second Friday of every month—but the scheduling can and often does change according to the whim of whoever's monitoring the event. Don't expect regularity in anything associated with Indigo. It plays host to all manner of counterculture splinter groups of all persuasions: Some weekends, it's an old-fashioned gay bar for old-fashioned Swedes and Danes; other nights, thanks to the welcome flash and flair of Claes/Sara, it can get a lot more exotic. In most cases, Indigo is open only on Friday and Saturday nights from 11pm to 3am, and usually charges an entrance fee of 60SEK to 85SEK ($12–$17/£6–£8.50). If you really want to be sure it's open, telephone in advance, or check the website noted above.

An Amusement Park

Between May and September, locals, often accompanied by their children, and roaming hordes of young and sometimes boisterous teenagers head for **Folkets Park** (People's Park), Amiralsgatan 35 (© **040/709-90**), where a battered compound reminiscent of a B-rated Tivoli draws crowds. Children might enjoy the playhouse, small zoo, reptile center, and puppet theater. Restaurants, some devoted to fast food, also dot the grounds, and at random intervals there might be a live concert from a pop or rock-'n'-roll group. Hours are daily from 3pm to midnight in summer, noon to 6pm in winter. Admission is free; however, some performances require an admission price of 50SEK to 110SEK ($10–$22/£5–£11). Take bus no. 5.

3 LUND ★★

18km (11 miles) NE of Malmö, 302km (188 miles) S of Gothenburg, 602km (374 miles) SW of Stockholm

The second oldest town in Sweden, this mellow old place with a thousand-year history holds more appeal for us than its rival university city, Uppsala, north of Stockholm. In some respects, Lund is more comparable to Cambridge in England.

Lund was probably founded in 1020 by Canute the Great, ruler of the United Kingdom of England and Denmark, when this part of Sweden was a Danish possession. However, the city's 1,000-year anniversary was celebrated in 1990 because archaeological excavations showed that a stave church was built here in 990. The city really made its mark when its cathedral was consecrated in 1145, after which Lund quickly became a center of religion, politics, culture, and commerce for all of Scandinavia.

The town's medieval streets and its grand cathedral are compelling reasons to come and take a look, but the vibrant student life is even more persuasive. Lund University, founded in 1666, continues to play an active role in town life. The most exciting time to be in Lund, as in Uppsala, is on Walpurgis Eve, April 30, when student revelries signal the advent of spring, but a visit to Lund anytime is a pleasure.

ESSENTIALS

GETTING THERE **By Plane** **Kastrup (Copenhagen)** airport is very convenient, especially because trains from Copenhagen pass through Kastrup, then go directly to Lund, a travel time of 50 minutes and a one-way fare of 120SEK ($24/£12). The nearest Swedish airport is the Malmö/Lund airport, which lies in the village of Sturup, 30km (19 miles) and a 30-minute bus ride from Lund. "Airport Coach Services" (aka the "Flygbuss") charge 95SEK ($19/£9.50) and time their departures from Sturup to correspond to the arrivals of flights at Sturup.

By Train Trains run hourly from Malmö (see earlier in this chapter), only a 15-minute ride. Both the bus and the train stations here are in the center of town. Call ☎ 0771/77-77-77.

By Bus Buses also arrive hourly from Malmö, but they take 30 minutes. Call ☎ 0771/77-77-77.

By Car From Gothenburg, head south along E6; Malmö and Lund are linked by an express highway, only a 20-minute drive.

VISITOR INFORMATION The tourist information office is at **Lunds Turistbyrå,** at Kyrkogatan 11 (P.O. Box 41), SE-221 00 Lund (☎ 046/35-50-40; www.lund.se). Hours for this bureau are complicated and can vary. In peak season, hours are generally Monday to Friday 10am to 7pm, Saturday 10am to 3pm, and Sunday 11am to 3pm.

SEEING THE SIGHTS

Botaniska Trädgården (Botanical Gardens) Just follow the students on their bikes if you want to check out Lund's favorite gardens—they are no doubt headed here. A block east of the cathedral, these gardens contain some 7,500 specimens of plants gathered from all over the world. On a sunny day, you'll spot clusters of students stretching out beneath the trees and families enjoying picnic lunches. Serious horticulturists should visit when the greenhouses are open.

Östra Vallgatan 20. ☎ 046/222-73-20. Free admission. Gardens daily 6am–8pm; greenhouses daily noon–3pm. Bus: 1, 2, 3, 4, 5, 6, or 7.

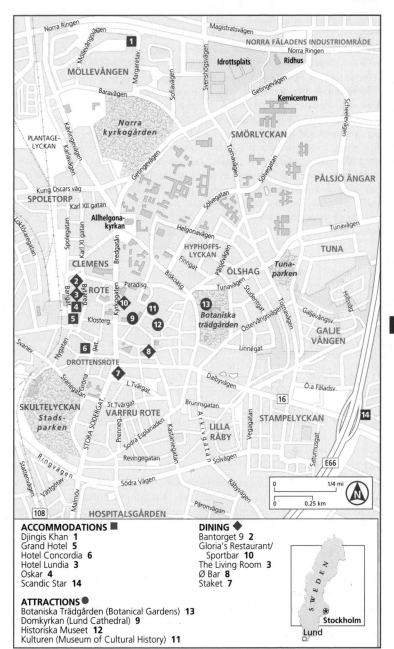

SKÅNE (INCLUDING HELSINGBORG & MALMÖ)

8

LUND

ACCOMMODATIONS ■
Djingis Khan **1**
Grand Hotel **5**
Hotel Concordia **6**
Hotel Lundia **3**
Oskar **4**
Scandic Star **14**

ATTRACTIONS ●
Botaniska Trädgården (Botanical Gardens) **13**
Domkyrkan (Lund Cathedral) **9**
Historiska Museet **12**
Kulturen (Museum of Cultural History) **11**

DINING ◆
Bantorget 9 **2**
Gloria's Restaurant/
  Sportbar **10**
The Living Room **3**
Ø Bar **8**
Staket **7**

Stockholm
Lund

240 **Domkyrkan (Lund Cathedral)** ★★★ This imposing twin-towered, gray-sand-stone cathedral that dominates the town is magnificence itself. Work began on it in 1080, coming to an end at its consecration in 1145. Today it represents the zenith of Romanesque design in Sweden—in fact, the **eastern facade** ★★ of the church is one of the finest expressions of Romanesque architecture in northern Europe.

The interior is filled with splendor and wonder, especially the **apse** ★★★ from 1130, a masterpiece of Romanesque styling with its Lombard arcading and third-tier gallery. The **mosaic** ★★★ of the apse vault, representing the Resurrection in true Byzantine tradition, was the creation of Joakim Skovgaard between 1925 and 1927. Look for the elaborately carved 1370 **choir stalls** ★★★ depicting Old Testament scenes. Then look again: Beneath the seats are grotesque engravings.

Nothing is more dramatic here than the remarkable **astronomical clock** ★★★ from the 14th century. It depicts days, weeks, and even the courses of the moon and the sun in the zodiac. The clock was silent for 3 centuries until it was restored in 1923. If you're here at noon or 3pm daily, you'll be treated to a splashy medieval tournament complete with clashing knights and blaring trumpets. That's not all—the Three Wise Men come out to pay homage to the Virgin and Child. On Sunday, the noon show doesn't begin until 1pm.

Finally, head for the **crypt** ★★★, little changed since the 12th century. The pillars of the crypt are carved with zigzagging and twisting patterns, an eerie sight in these dimly lit, dramatic precincts. One tomb contains the remains of Birger Gunnarson, the last archbishop of Lund.

Kyrkogatan. ℂ **046/35-88-80.** Free admission. Mon–Fri 8am–6pm; Sat 1–5pm; Sun 1–6pm. Bus: 1, 2, 3, 4, 5, 6, or 7.

Historiska Museet Founded in 1805, this is the second largest museum of archaeology in Sweden. Collections trace the development of the people of Skåne from the Stone, Bronze, and Iron to the Middle Ages. One of the exhibits displayed here is that of the **skeleton of a young man** ★★ dating from around 7000 B.C.—one of the oldest human skeletons found in northern Europe. Another displays jewelry and weapons unearthed from a large grave field during excavations in eastern Skåne. The medieval exhibition is predictably dominated by church art removed from Skånian churches.

Kraftstorg 1. ℂ **046/222-79-30.** www.historiska.se. Admission 60SEK ($12/£6) adults, 40SEK ($8/£4) seniors and students 12–18, free for ages 18 and under. May–Sept Tues–Sun 10am–5pm; off season Tues–Sun 11am–5pm. Bus: 1, 2, 3, 4, 5, 6, or 7.

Kulturen (Museum of Cultural History) ★★ After you visit the Lund cathedral, walk across the university grounds to Adelgatan, which the local citizens consider their most charming street. (We agree.) Here you'll find Kulturen, another of Sweden's open-air museums. This one contains reassembled sod-roofed farms and manor houses—some of which were saved before they disappeared forever—a carriage museum, ceramics, peasant costumes, Viking artifacts, old handicrafts, and even a wooden church moved to this site from the glassworks district.

Established in 1892, it's one of the best organized and maintained open-air museums in Sweden. You can walk back in time in effectively 2 hours—well spent, especially if you take in the 17th-century houses, still perfectly preserved today. The on-site outdoor restaurant near several runic stones dug up and brought here serves home-cooked Swedish specialties.

Tegnérsplatsen. ℂ **046/35-04-00.** www.kulturen.com. Admission 70SEK ($14/£7) adults, free for children. Apr 15–Sept daily 11am–5pm; Oct–Apr 14 Tues–Sun noon–4pm. Bus: 1, 2, 3, 4, 5, 6, or 7.

SKÅNE (INCLUDING HELSINGBORG & MALMÖ)

8

LUND

The tourist office (see above) can help you obtain housing in private homes for as little as 225SEK ($45/£23) per person per night.

Djingis Khan ★ (Finds)   At first this struck us as the worst-named hotel in Sweden. Why Djingis Khan? Actually, it makes sense when you learn that Djingis Khan is the name of a revue written by Hasse Alfredsson and presented by Lund students in 1954. Since that time, this same show has been performed every 5 years. The building itself looks like an upmarket student dormitory, but it's one of the best hotels in town, though not a rival of the Grand (see below). We found the staff the most helpful in town. "We can help you book flights, order a taxi, or arrange for a shirt to be washed," the hotel proclaims—and it's all true. The midsize bedrooms are sleek and modern and comfortably arranged with all the gadgets you'll need. Public areas contain lots of English-inspired dark paneling, Chesterfield sofas, and an ambience that evokes a private men's club in London.

Margarethevägen 7, S 222 40 Lund. © **046/33-36-00.** Fax 046/46-33-36-10. www.djingiskhan.se. 73 units. Sun–Thurs 1,595SEK ($319/£160) double; Fri–Sat 950SEK ($190/£95) double. Rates include breakfast. AE, DC, MC, V. Closed July. Free parking. Bus: 3 or 93. **Amenities:** Restaurant; bar; indoor pool; fitness center; sauna; room service; laundry service; dry cleaning; nonsmoking rooms; rooms for those w/limited mobility. *In room:* TV, minibar, hair dryer, Wi-Fi.

Grand Hotel ★★★   In 1899, every man, woman, and child who could walk, or so it is said, turned out for the opening of the châteaulike Grand. At last Lund had a fashionable hotel. The decades and world wars (fought without Sweden) have come and gone, and the Grand has changed and evolved over the years, but it has also kept its elegant architecture and remains the number-one choice of discerning visitors to Lund, including the most well-heeled parents of students enrolled at the university. In spite of its fashion and formality, the Grand is not "stiff and starched"; office workers will assemble here for a beer after a hard day's work, and it provides a welcoming setting for family feasts. The tone is set by the supremely elegant marble lobby, which basically justifies the hotel's name.

As befits the late 1890s, no room is like any other—each has its own character, some spacious, others smaller. But each is comfortably furnished with a mix of modern and traditional. Overlooking the fountains and flowers of a city park, many patrons also come here to dine, even if they aren't staying at the hotel. The magnificent surroundings are somewhat enhanced by the Grand's traditional Scanian and Swedish menu and carefully crafted selection of international specialties. We are astonished by the wine list, which boasts 500 different vintages from some three dozen countries around the world. At the hotel's wine bar, you can sample these exclusive wines by either the glass or the bottle.

Bantorget 1, S-221 04 Lund. © **046/280-61-00.** Fax 046/280-61-50. www.grandilund.se. 84 units. June 7–Aug 8 and Fri–Sat year-round 1,200SEK–1,750SEK ($240–$350/£120–£175) double, 3,200SEK ($640/£320) suite; Aug 9–June 6 1,950SEK–2,550SEK ($390–$510/£195–£255) double, 4,500SEK ($900/£450) suite. Rates include breakfast. AE, DC, MC, V. Parking 120SEK ($24/£12). Bus: 1, 2, 3, 4, 5, 6, or 7. **Amenities:** Restaurant; wine bar; fitness center; sauna; room service; laundry service; dry cleaning; nonsmoking rooms. *In room:* TV, minibar, hair dryer, Wi-Fi.

Hotel Concordia ★   A classic, elegant landmark from 1882, Concordia was originally built as a private home, but for many years it served as a student hotel. You'd never know to look at the building today—it has been successfully converted to a government-rated four-star hotel, a bastion of comfort, charm, and elegance. Although the public rooms have what is known as a "Lundian character," that style does not extend to the modernized, comfortably furnished midsized bedrooms. However, their parquet floors, warm colors, and tiled bathrooms help a lot. We like the addition of two armchairs to every double room—in so many hotels, you only get one. It's next door to the brick house where August Strindberg lived in 1897 and is only a 5-minute walk south of the railway station.

Stålbrogatan 1, S-222-24 Lund. ✆ **046/13-50-50.** Fax 046/13-74-22. www.concordia.se. 63 units. 995SEK–1,695SEK ($199–$339/£100–£170) double; 1,995SEK ($399/£200) suite. Rates include breakfast. AE, DC, MC, V. Parking 100SEK ($20/£10). Bus: 1, 2, 3, 4, 5, 6, or 7. **Amenities:** Breakfast room; lounge; fitness center; sauna; business center; laundry service; dry cleaning; nonsmoking rooms. *In room:* TV, minibar, hair dryer, iron, Wi-Fi.

Hotel Lundia ★★ (Finds)

The design concept of this hotel is "sushi and lingonberries." The reference is baffling until architect Jonas Lloyd explains that, while renovating this long-established property near the railway station, he wanted to combine Swedish modern (symbolized by lingonberries) with Japanese simplicity (as evoked by the sushi reference). Much of the success of this hotel's overhaul is in Lloyd's use of natural materials; he also must be in love with blondes, because that Nordic shade prevails throughout. Lundia is under the same management as the Grand Hotel (see above) but is hardly a rival, although its interior is graced with winding staircases, white marble sheathing, and large windows. Guest rooms are quite special, with softly curved furniture in birchwood with accents of cherrywood. We were impressed that the raw walls were treated with beeswax glazing. The tasteful, comfortable furnishings rest on floors made of massive oak, each board nailed by hand.

Knut den Stores Gata 2, S-221 04 Lund. ✆ **046/280-65-00.** Fax 046/280-65-10. www.lundia.se. 97 units. Late June to early Aug and Fri–Sat year-round 1,025SEK ($205/£103) double; rest of year 2,050SEK ($410/£205) double; 2,225SEK–4,125SEK ($445–$825/£223–£413) suite. Rates include breakfast. AE, DC, MC, V. Parking 110SEK ($22/£11). Bus: 1, 2, 3, 4, 5, 6, or 7. **Amenities:** Restaurant; bar; room service; laundry service; dry cleaning; nonsmoking rooms; rooms for those w/limited mobility. *In room:* TV, minibar, hair dryer, trouser press, safe, Wi-Fi.

Oskar ★★ (Finds)

Those who prefer to overnight in more intimacy than that offered by the Grand might well check in here if they can afford it. It's a charmer, a boutique hotel that was created by restoring two townhouses constructed sometime in the 1800s. The hotel is imbued with a sophisticated Scandinavian design—chairs and tables by Gunilla Allard for Lammhults, lamps by the legendary Arne Jacobsen. Frankly, we've inspected hotel after hotel in Lund and found the beds from Dux used here to be the most relaxing in town. Bedrooms are bright and relatively large, furnished with contemporary pieces against a backdrop of original art adorning the white walls. Each room is an individual design statement. On summer days breakfast is served in the garden, and even on rainy days, you can join fellow guests or students at the downstairs cafe.

Bytaregatan 3, SE 222 21 Lund. ✆ **046/188-085.** Fax 046/373-030. www.hotelloskar.se. 6 units. Sun–Thurs 1,495SEK–1,595SEK ($299–$319/£150–£160); Fri–Sat 995SEK–1,095SEK ($199–$219/£100–£110) double. AE, DC, MC, V. **Amenities:** Cafe; room service; laundry service; nonsmoking rooms. *In room:* TV, hair dryer, safe, Wi-Fi.

Scandic Star ★★

Lying a 20-minute walk from the city center, this hotel doesn't have the grace and tradition of the Grand, but it's one of the most comfortable hotels in southern Sweden. In fact, rock stars and film actors seem to prefer it. Though it also caters to individual travelers, and does so exceedingly well, it's often used for business conventions. What makes it so special is that nearly all the double rooms are configured as minisuites, with separate sitting areas and traditional, conservative furnishings that 243 would fit into a well-appointed upper-middle-class Swedish home. No other hotel in Lund has public facilities equal to the ones here, including a pool. The on-site **Garda's Restaurant** zealously guards the recipes for the Skåne specialties served. "However, we're not just regional," says the chef. "My inspiration comes from the four corners of the globe—that is, if the world has four corners." The bar in the spacious courtyard has become a town meeting point.

Glimmervägen 5, P.O. Box 11026, SE-220 11 Lund. © **046/285-25-00.** Fax 046/285-25-11. www.scandichotels.com. 196 units. Mid-June to mid-Aug and Fri–Sat year-round 770SEK ($154/£77) double; rest of year 1,090SEK–2,250SEK ($218–$450/£109–£225) double; 1,780SEK–3,060SEK ($356–$612/£178–£306) suite. AE, DC, MC, V. Free parking. Bus: 3 or 7. **Amenities:** Restaurant; bar; indoor pool; fitness center; sauna; room service; laundry service; dry cleaning; nonsmoking rooms; rooms for those w/limited mobility. *In room:* TV, minibar, hair dryer, iron, safe, Wi-Fi.

WHERE TO DINE

Bantorget 9 ★ SWEDISH/CONTINENTAL   Charming and traditional, this restaurant occupies a white-painted, wood-sided structure that, at the time of its construction in the 1860s, contained three separate residences; the building later functioned as a bakery, a motorcycle repair shop, and a clothing store. Today, in much-gentrified form—amid frescoed ceilings, flowerpots, and holders for the candles (up to 120 per night) that illuminate this place—you'll enjoy a sophisticated medley of ingredients cooked in Swedish, and sometimes vaguely French, ways. The best examples include marinated mussels and snails in garlic sauce, traditional Swedish meatballs and duck breast with orange sauce, and an old-fashioned Swedish favorite, minced veal with cream-based gravy and mashed potatoes. Other excellent choices include roast lamb, tournedos of veal, braised pikeperch, and pan-fried lemon sole. It lies within a very short walk of Lund's railway station.

Bantorget 7–9. © **046/32-02-00.** www.bantorget9.com. Reservations recommended. Main courses 245SEK–315SEK ($49–$63/£25–£32). AE, DC, MC, V. Mon–Thurs 6pm–midnight; Fri–Sat 6–11pm. Bus: 2 or 4.

Gloria's Restaurant/Sportbar AMERICAN   The success of this American-inspired sports and western bar would warm the heart of any U.S.-born ideologue. It has a crowded and likable bar in the cellar and an even larger bar upstairs. Scattered throughout the premises are photographs and posters of American sports heroes, baseball and football memorabilia, and Wild West artifacts. Foam-topped draft beer comes in mugs. (One local student from Stockholm, studying at the university, told us that he downs 12 a night here. When does he ever get any studying done?) The restaurant serves copious portions of such rib-stickers as hamburgers and steaks, and an array of Cajun-inspired dishes. The staff wears jeans, cowboy boots, and shirts emblazoned with Gloria's logo. Various styles of live music are performed between 9:30 and 11:30pm each Thursday. Friday and Saturday nights feature a disc jockey spinning rock.

St. Petri Kyrkogata 9. © **046/15-19-85.** www.glorias.se. Reservations recommended. Main courses 139SEK–239SEK ($28–$48/£14–£24). AE, DC, MC, V. Mon–Wed 11:30am–midnight; Thurs 11:30am–1am; Fri 11:30am–3am; Sat 12:30pm–3am; Sun 1–11pm. Bus: 1, 2, 3, 4, 5, 6, or 7.

The Living Room ★ SWEDISH/INTERNATIONAL   The chefs here believe that when you go out to dine, you have "the right to expect something more than the usual, something different." That's what you get here. If the dishes you're served come as a surprise, it'll be the good kind. The chefs constantly vary their menu to take advantage of market conditions and seasonal produce; they also achieve a perfectly balanced mix between inspired international cuisine and traditional Swedish fare. Follow the chef's suggestions and sample the most frequently ordered dish, a skillet-grilled entrecôte (perfectly tender and full of flavor) served with Béarnaise sauce. The rack of lamb arrives aromatically baked and accompanied by grilled sweet potatoes. Other dishes include a juicy grilled trout with root vegetables and a grilled tuna with risotto cooked with a zesty lemon oil. If you arrive for lunch, you can have a lighter meal, such as a freshly made salad, well-stuffed sandwich, or delectable burger. Two desserts are memorable: a chocolate crème brûlée (our favorite) and the blueberry pie. As its name suggests, the environment is like a laid-back living room filled with sofas.

In the Hotel Lundia, Knut den Stores Gata 2. ✆ **046/280-65-00.** Reservations required Fri–Sat. Main courses 190SEK–295SEK ($38–$59/£19–£30). AE, DC, MC, V. Daily 11:30am–11pm. Bus: 1, 2, 3, 4, 5, 6, or 7.

Ø Bar ★ (Finds INTERNATIONAL This intriguing restaurant defines itself as a "laboratory for chefs" because its experimental menu changes every week. The venue looks like it might have been designed by a Milanese postmodernist, with blue and ash-white walls and a severe kind of angularity. It's usually mobbed every night, both with diners and with clients of the convivial bar area, where you're likely to meet animated students from the university and their professors. If you've been hankering for filet of elk, you'll find the town's best version here. It's enhanced by a sauce made with fresh thyme and a side of apple- and potato-laced muffins. Each night the chef also makes a homemade pasta dish with various sauces. The standard of the Swedish kitchen, grilled halibut, comes alive again with its zesty flavorings of horseradish and lemon oil. To get you going, the cooks even come up with such offerings as a lime-flavored clam chowder (a most unusual dish for Sweden) or Vietnamese spring rolls.

Mårtenstorget 9. ✆ **046/211-22-88.** Reservations recommended. Main courses 125SEK–220SEK ($25–$44/£13–£22). AE, DC, MC, V. Daily 11:30am–midnight; bar until 1 or 2am. Bus: 1 or 2.

Staket (Value SWEDISH/INTERNATIONAL This old tavern, a favorite with students, serves good food in a step-gabled brick facade that is a historic landmark. Food and drink are offered in the cellar—our favorite place for a rendezvous—but also at street level. Both dining rooms have their appeals, but fondues (a ritual in which skewers of meat are cooked at your table in pots of heated oil) are served only in the cellar. For appetizers, try a succulent crab cocktail and a tasty goulash soup evocative of Budapest. For a main course, the mixed grill is a winner, as is the tender, flavorful tournedos of beef.

Stora Södergatan 6. ✆ **046/211-93-67.** Reservations recommended. Main courses 155SEK–215SEK ($31–$43/£16–£22). AE, DC, MC, V. Mon–Thurs 11am–11pm; Fri 11am–midnight; Sat noon–midnight; Sun 1–11pm. Bus: 1, 2, 3, 4, 5, 6, or 7.

LUND AFTER DARK

Most dance clubs in Lund operate only on weekends, when the clientele includes many students from the university. The hottest spot is **T-Bar,** in the basement of Tegnérs Matsalar restaurant, Sandgatan 2 (✆ **046/13-13-33**). There's also a dance floor in the basement of the already-recommended **Gloria's Restaurant/Sportbar,** every Friday and Saturday beginning at 10:30pm. Entrance is free. Another dance choice, also open only Friday and Saturday, is the **Palladium,** Stora Södergatan 13 (✆ **046/211-66-60**), a beer pub with a college-age clientele. Admission is free.

With its small dance floor, **Basilika,** Stora Södergatan 13 (© **046/211-66-60**), occasionally hosts live bands from England or Europe. The big nights here are Friday and Saturday, when a 75SEK ($15/£7.50) cover charge is imposed. A final hot spot is **Stortorget,** Stortorget 1 (© **046/13-92-90**), which has a DJ at night and a surprising age requirement (for a university town): You must be over 22 to enter.

SIDE TRIPS FROM LUND

From Lund, you may want to make a side trip to **Dalby Church** ★, 5-240 12 Dalby (no phone), in Dalby, 13km (8 miles) east of Lund. This starkly beautiful, well-preserved 11th-century former bishop's church built of stone is the oldest church in Scandinavia; be sure to visit its creepy crypt. It's open daily from 9am to 4pm. Several buses a day (nos. 158 and 161) run between Lund center and Dalby.

About a 30-minute drive northeast of Lund (off Rte. 23) is the **Castle of Bosjö-kloster** ★★, Höör (© **0413/250-48;** www.bosjokloster.se). Once a Benedictine convent founded around 1080, it was closed during the Reformation in the 16th century. The **great courtyard** is spectacular, with thousands of flowers and exotic shrubs, terraces, a park with animals and birds, and a 1,000-year-old oak tree. Indoors is the vaulted refectory and the stone hall where native arts and crafts, jewelry, and other Swedish goods are displayed. You can picnic on the grounds or enjoy lunch at a simple restaurant in the garden for 110SEK ($22/£11). The entire complex is open daily from May 1 to September 30 from 8am to 8pm; the museum and exhibition hall inside the castle are open daily from 10am to 6pm. Admission is 75SEK ($15/£7.50) for adults, seniors, and students; it's free for children up to age 16. The castle lies 45km (28 miles) from Malmö and 29km (18 miles) from Lund. From Lund, there's a train link to Höör. Once at Höör, take the "ring bus" marked BÖSJOKLOSTER, which travels 5km (3 miles) south on Route 23 to the castle.

4 YSTAD ★★

55km (34 miles) E of Malmö, 46km (29 miles) W of Simrishamn

Time has passed Ystad by, and that's why we like it. Its **Gamla Stan** ★★★ contains an astonishing 300 well-preserved half-timbered antique houses along cobbled streets. They're scattered about town, but we found the greatest concentration of them on **Stora Östergatan.**

Most of the houses date from the latter 1700s, although one we discovered, **Ånglahu-set,** on Stora Norregatan, was from around 1630. You can also launch yourself into the past by exploring **Stortorget** ★★, the impressive main square of Ystad, which was a big smuggling center during the Napoleonic wars. You'll want to check out another charming square, **Tvättorget,** Ystad's smallest, as well. Surrounded by half-timbered houses, it's hard to find, reached only by walking up a narrow lane called Bäckahästgränd.

At one time, Ystad was much more important than the provincial town you see today. Back in the 17th century, it was "Sweden's window to the world." Amazingly, the first automobile in Sweden was driven on the old streets of Ystad. The town also opened Sweden's first bank, and its first building that could be called a hotel. There is still some activity here, with ferries leaving for the Danish island of Bornholm—even to Poland.

If you're a fan, like us, of the best-selling Inspector Karl Wallander crime thrillers—all written by Henning Mankell—you probably already know that Ystad is also a setting for his suspense tales. If you don't have time to wade through all of Mankell's books, opt for the fourth, *The Man Who Smiled.* It's the best and most evocative. Devotees of the series can tour the sights associated with the inspector with a volunteer fire brigade every Tuesday and Thursday from July to mid-August. Fans are taken around town on an antique fire engine. The tourist office (see below) will have details.

Devotees of the silent screen might know of Ystad as the birthplace of Valentino's "beautiful blond Viking" Anna Q. Nilsson, who was born here in 1890 and whose fame at one time was greater than that of Greta Garbo, a fellow Swede. Some of Nilsson's greatest films were *In the Heart of a Fool* (1921); *Ponjola* (1923), in which she played a boy; and *Midnight Lovers,* finished in 1925, the year of a horseback-riding accident that ended her career. Today she is remembered mainly for appearing in a cameo role as one of the "waxworks" in the 1950 Gloria Swanson classic *Sunset Boulevard.*

ESSENTIALS

GETTING THERE By Plane The nearest regional airport is at **Sturup,** 37km (23 miles) in the direction of Malmö, and a taxi there costs 450SEK ($90/£45) each way. The closest international big-time airport is at **Kastrup,** outside of Copenhagen, via the Øresund Bridge.

By Train There are good rail connections between Malmö and Ystad. From Monday to Saturday, trains run roughly on the hour between Malmö and Ystad, taking 1 hour. On Sunday, there are only six daily trains from Malmö. In Ystad, both the bus station and the railway station lie immediately adjacent to one another, half a kilometer (about ¹/₃ mile) south of the town center. City bus nos. 1, 2, 3, and 4 all make runs from the railway/bus station to the town center, and a taxi will charge 80SEK ($16/£8). For more information, call © **0771/777-77-77.**

By Bus There are three daily buses Monday to Saturday from Malmö to Ystad, taking 1 hour. On Sunday, there is only one bus.

By Car From Malmö, head east on Route 65. For more information, call © **0200/21-82-18.**

VISITOR INFORMATION The tourist bureau, **Ystads Turistbyrå,** St. Knuts Torg, 271 80 Ystad (© **0411/57-76-81;** www.ystad.se), is at the bus station in the same building as the art museum (Konstmuseum). It's open from June to August Monday to Friday 9am to 7pm, Saturday 10am to 6pm, Sunday 10am to 6pm; September to May Monday to Friday 9am to 5pm.

SEEING THE SIGHTS

As we've already told you, Ystad's main sight is **Gamla Stan (Old Town)** itself. But there are a few other specific targets to check out as you wander about.

St. Maria Kyrka ★ This church, dating from the early 1200s, is the focal point of town. It certainly respects tradition: A night watchman still sounds the hours of the night from here, just as his distant ancestor did back before clocks were invented. (Fortunately, night watchmen have it better today than in olden times; in the medieval era, if the watchman fell asleep, he was beheaded.) Though many of its richest decorative features were removed in the 1880s because of changing tastes, some of the most precious ones were brought back in a restoration program occurring 4 decades later. The chancel with the ambulatory is late Gothic, and the church spire dates from 1688. Inside, look for the baptismal chapel with a richly carved German altar from the 15th century. The font came from Lübeck, Germany, in 1617, and the iron candelabra is a very early one from the 1300s. Of all the treasures here, we think the **Renaissance Pulpit** ★★ by an unknown craftsman from North Germany is the most remarkable.

Stortorget. ✆ **0411/69-20-0.** Free admission. June to mid-Sept daily 10am–6pm.

Stadsmuseet i Gråbrödraklostret (City Museum in the Grey Friars Monastery) Part of the fun of visiting this museum is getting here. From the main square, Stortorget, take a stroll up Garvaregränd (where you'll be distracted by the high-quality arts and crafts for sale in the workshops). When you reach Klostergatan, you'll be near the entrance to the museum, which is the only one in Sweden inside a monastic house from the Middle Ages.

Gråbröder, or "Greyfriars," dates from 1267, when it was occupied by monks. At the Reformation, these guys were booted out, marking a long decline for the building. It went from hospital to distillery to seedy poorhouse. And just when the townspeople thought the building had reached its lowest point, it hadn't: It soon became a dumping ground for garbage. It wasn't until 2001, when city fathers intervened, that the building was rescued.

Once in charge of the building, the city had to do something with it. They rounded up most of their valuables and housed them here. Despite that effort, the building is more intriguing than the exhibits, which consist mainly of antiquities from the area—the usual, boring history exhibits. Local textiles and silverware aren't likely to grab you. Perhaps the display of bridal costumes from the 1700s will attract your notice. Or you might agree with us that the 80 gravestones from the 1300s to the 1700s have a certain ghoulish fascination. Just save the best for last—the **gardens** ★, which are open 24 hours. The monks originally created these gardens, and many of the same spices, vegetables, and medicinal herbs they grew bloom again today in honor of their long-ago commitment. They're most glorious in July.

St. Petri Kykoplan. ✆ **0411/57-72-86.** Admission 30SEK ($6/£3), free 16 and under. Mon–Fri 10am–5pm; Sat–Sun noon–4pm.

Ystads Konstmuseum (Museum of Modern Art) This is a very minor museum and could easily be missed if you're on a tight schedule. But if you want to check it out, it does contain one of the most evocative collections of Danish and southern Swedish painters over the past century. "We may not have the greatest collection," the curator told us, "but at least we're representative." There is also a small military museum that would not have impressed General Eisenhower. The Ystad Tourist Office is in the same building as the museum.

St. Knuts Torg. ✆ **0411/57-72-85.** Admission 30SEK ($6/£3). Tues–Fri noon–5pm; Sat–Sun noon–4pm.

WHERE TO STAY

Hotell Continental ★★ This 1829 landmark was constructed over the site of an old customs house when Ystad was the major port link between Sweden and the Continent. In 1996, a family-owned company took it over and began a program of refurbishing and redecorating that continues to this day. These owners seem to take a personal interest in their guests, many of whom arrive by train or by ferry from Europe; the hotel is convenient to both terminals. Marble sheeting in the lobby and gleaming crystal chandeliers add grace notes. The midsize-to-spacious bedrooms are furnished with sleek modern stylings that are both comfortable and tasteful. Consider visiting the dining room here even if you're not a guest. Chefs prepare Swedish classics and often use regional produce in summer. Breakfast highlights such classic Swedish dishes as *Äggakaka*, a thick pancake with crispy bacon and lingonberries.

Hamngatan 13, S-271 00 Ystad. ℂ **0411/137-00.** Fax 0411/125-70. www.hotelcontinental-ystad.se. 52 units. 940SEK–1,595SEK ($188–$319/£94–£160) double. Rates include breakfast. AE, DC, MC, V. Parking 40SEK ($8/£4). **Amenities:** Restaurant; bar; room service; babysitting; laundry service; nonsmoking rooms; rooms for those w/limited mobility. *In room:* TV, hair dryer, Wi-Fi.

Hotel Tornväktaren (Value)

This is the best choice in Ystad for those who don't want to check into the more expensive hotels we've recommended. A simple bed-and-breakfast, it derives much of its charm from its hard-working owner, Mr. Roy Saifert. His home is a turn-of-the-20th-century stone-built, red-trimmed structure with a garden, 10 minutes on foot from the railway station. Rooms are outfitted in pale pastels with lots of homey touches that include frilly curtains, wall-to-wall carpeting, and lace doilies covering painted wooden furniture. Not all rooms have a private bathroom, and we have found that the corridor facilities are adequate. The breakfast served is generous and home cooked, mostly to order; no other meals are served.

St. Östergatan 33, S-271-34 Ystad. ℂ **0411/784-80.** Fax 0411/729-27. 9 units, 5 with bathroom. 895SEK ($179/£90) double with bathroom; 795SEK ($159/£80) double without bathroom. Rates include breakfast. AE, MC, V. Free parking. **Amenities:** Breakfast room; lounge; nonsmoking rooms. *In room:* TV, Wi-Fi.

Ystads Saltsjöbad ★ (Finds)

This hotel is a classic, made all the more so by its helpful owners, Ann and Kent Nyström. Beautifully situated on 4 hectares (10 acres) of forested land beside the sea, the hotel is close to Sweden's southernmost tip. It was built in 1897 by one of the most famous opera stars of his day, Swedish-born Solomon Smith. Designed as a haven for the Gilded Age aristocracy of northern Europe, it consists of three connected four-story buildings with big-windowed corridors, set close to the sands of an expansive beach. The guest rooms are comfortably furnished in turn-of-the-20th-century style. The clientele changes throughout the year: In the summer, the hotel caters to beachgoers; in the winter, it's often filled with corporate conventions. The neighborhood also provides good opportunities for healthy pastimes such as tennis and golf. Both the main dining room and a smaller, more intimate a la carte restaurant, **Apotheket,** open onto views of the sea; both menus feature an international cuisine that's married to traditional Swedish fare. Fresh produce is delivered several times a day, and the local suppliers are "environmentally aware."

Saltsjöbadsgatan 6, S-271 39 Ystad. ℂ **0411/136-30.** Fax 0411/55-58-35. www.ystadssaltsjobad.se. 109 units. June 19–Aug 31 1,565SEK–1,665SEK ($313–$333/£157–£167) double; Sept–June 18 1,345SEK–2,990SEK ($269–$598/£135–£299) double; year-round Mon–Thurs 3,500SEK ($700/£350) suite, Fri–Sun 2,200SEK ($440/£220) suite. AE, DC, MC, V. Closed Dec 23–Jan 6. Free parking. **Amenities:** 2 restaurants; 2 bars; cafe; 2 pools (1 indoor); spa; sauna; room service; laundry service; dry cleaning; nonsmoking rooms. *In room:* A/C, TV, hair dryer, Wi-Fi.

WHERE TO DINE

Lottas Restaurang INTERNATIONAL   Fans praise it as one of the most popular and bustling restaurants in town; detractors avoid it because of slow service by a small staff that sometimes seems impossibly overworked. Everyone awards high marks, however, for the well-prepared cuisine. Meals are served in a brick dining room within a century-old building that once functioned as a private home. The menu runs to conservative, old-fashioned Swedish cuisine, which might include fried and creamed filet of cod with dill-flavored boiled potatoes, pork schnitzels with asparagus and Béarnaise sauce,

and marinated breast of chicken with roasted potatoes. For dessert, try warm chocolate
cake with ice cream. Although overly familiar to anyone who has dined in Sweden for
more than a week, each of these dishes is made with fresh ingredients—and is satisfying
and filling.

Stortorget 11. ☏ **0411/788-00.** www.lottas.se. Reservations recommended. Main courses 152SEK–225SEK ($30–$45/£15–£23). AE, DC, MC, V. Mon–Sat 5–10pm.

Sandskogens Vardshus ★ (Finds) SWEDISH

Set about 1.5km (1 mile) east of
Ystad's center, this structure was originally built in 1899 as a summer home for the town's
mayor. It was converted into a restaurant in the 1930s and has provided local diners with
well-prepared Swedish specialties ever since. One of the most popular appetizers in Sweden is a toast served with white bait roe, sour cream, and onions. When in Sweden, do
as the locals do and give it a try. We'd go for it, if we didn't find the pot of marinated
mussels even more tempting. Other appealing choices here are the freshly caught brill,
greatly enhanced with a caramelized butter sauce; the turbot, dressed up with shrimp and
Swedish caviar; or the even grander gratin of lobster accompanied by a lemon sole. In
summer, we'd walk a mile for one of the pastry chef's cloudberry parfaits made with
golden berries picked in the Arctic.

Saltsjøvagen, Sandskogen. ☏ **0411/147-60.** Reservations recommended. Main courses 180SEK–225SEK ($36–$45/£18–£23); fixed-price dinner 273SEK ($55/£27). MC, V. Daily noon–9pm. Closed Jan–Feb.

Steakhouse Bruggeriet ★ SWEDISH/INTERNATIONAL

With such a name,
you would expect the best steaks in Lund. And this place delivers. The novel restaurant
was originally built in 1749 as a warehouse for malt; in 1996, a team of local entrepreneurs installed a series of large copper vats and transformed the site into a pleasant, cozy
restaurant and brewery. Today they specialize in two "tastes" of beer—a lager and a
dark—that are marketed under the brand name Ysta Färsköl. Food items served here
seem carefully calibrated to taste best when consumed with either of the two beers. The
kitchen doesn't like to go in for culinary experiments, adopting the concept that if it was
good enough for grandfather, it is good enough for today's patrons. That seems to sit well
with the patrons, who order such dishes as fried herring marinated in mustard and sour
cream, or the grilled salmon in a red-wine sauce. Swedish lamb is well flavored with
garlic and fresh herbs, and the tenderloin steak meets the perfect match in a brandy
sauce. On some occasions, we've seen succulent versions of barbecued ribs, just like they
serve them in Dixie, on the menu.

Långgatan 20. ☏ **0411/69-99-99.** Reservations recommended. Main courses 84SEK–184SEK ($17–$37/£8.40–£18). AE, DC, MC, V. Mon 11:30am–2pm; Tues–Fri 11:30am–10pm; Sat noon–midnight; Sun 3–8pm.

Store Thor SWEDISH/FRENCH

One of the most reliable lunchtime restaurants in
Ystad occupies a series of vaulted cellars that were part of a monastery in the 1500s. A
disastrous fire destroyed the monastery, but the Rådhus (Town Hall) was reconstructed
over the cellars several hundred years later. Today, amid small tables and romantic candlelight, you can enjoy such tasty dishes as grilled anglerfish enlivened with a basil cream
sauce; saddle of lamb roasted with fresh herbs; and shellfish soup, rescued with saffron.
As a waitress here put it, the "dishes are cute and brave."

Stortorget 1. ☏ **0411/185-10.** www.storethor.se. Main courses 98SEK–235SEK ($20–$47/£9.80–£24). AE, DC, MC, V. Mon–Sat 11:30am–midnight; Sun 4pm–midnight.

630km (391 miles) S of Stockholm, 95km (59 miles) E of Malmö, 40km (25 miles) E of Ystad

If you're trying to decide between visiting Ystad or Simrishamn, make it Ystad. That doesn't mean that this old fishing village is without its charms. Actually, with its cobblestone streets and tiny brick houses, it's one of the most idyllic villages in Skåne. It's also the best center for exploring some of the major attractions of the province, including Dag Hammarskjöld's farm, a medieval castle, and a Bronze Age tomb.

Because of its proximity to Ystad, Simrishamn can also be treated as a day trip. At some point, wander down by the harbor where the fishing boats pull in with cod, eel, and herring. If you're here during summer, you'll also notice hundreds of holiday makers eating ice cream while waiting for a ferry to take them to the vacation island of Bornholm in Denmark.

Once you arrive at the southeastern tip of Skåne, you'll find good sandy beaches, especially at **Sandhammaren.**

ESSENTIALS

GETTING THERE By Car Because buses or trains from Sturup to Simrishamns require a time-consuming 2-hour transit from the nearest airport (the Lund/Malmö Airport at Sturup), most people opt to rent a car instead of flying. From Ystad, our last stopover, continue east along Route 10.

By Train Ten trains a day (eight on Sat and Sun) make the 45-minute run between Malmö and Simrishamn. Simrishamn's train and bus stations are both in the town center. For information, call ☎ **0771/77-77-77.**

By Bus Nine buses per day arrive from Kristianstad (four a day Sat–Sun), and 10 buses per day arrive from Ystad (three Sat–Sun). From Lund, there are eight daily buses. Tickets can be purchased onboard these buses. Call ☎ **0771/77-77-77.**

VISITOR INFORMATION For information about hotels, boardinghouses, summer cottages, and apartments, check with the tourist bureau. **Simrishamns Kommun Turistbyrå,** Tullhusgatan 2, 272 80 Simrishamn (☎ **0414/81-98-00;** www.turistbyra. simrishamn.se), is open June to August Monday to Friday 9am to 8pm, Saturday 10am to 8pm, and Sunday 11am to 8pm; September to May Monday to Friday 9am to 5pm.

SEEING THE SIGHTS

The chief attraction here is a stroll through the town's **Gamla Stan** ★ or Old Town, which is the historic core, a maze of fondant-colored tiny cottages that in some ways evokes a movie set. If you're driving, there is parking down by the harbor. As you stroll along, follow Strandvägen to **Sjöfartsplatsen,** which is a garden studded with works of art (you may disagree) made from the debris of shipwrecks. On our last visit, we made a surprising discovery when we wandered into **Frasses Musikmuseum,** Peder Morks Väg 5 (☎ **0414/145-20**). Here we found the world's most complete collection of Edison phonographs. The museum also has a collection of antique musical curiosities, including self-playing barrel organs. It's open June and August only on Sunday 2 to 6pm. In July, hours are Monday to Wednesday and Sunday 2 to 6pm. Admission is 35SEK ($7/ £3.50).

The chief monument in Gamla Stan is **St. Nicolai Kirke,** Storgatan (☎ **0414/41-24-80**). It's open June to September from 10am to 6:30pm, Sunday noon to 6:30pm;

October to May Monday to Friday 10am to 3pm, and Saturday 10am to 1pm. Originally constructed as a fisherman's chapel in the 12th century, the church literally dominates the town. It's built of chunky sandstone blocks, with a brick porch and step gables. Over the years there have been many additions, with a nave added in the 1300s, although the vault dates from the 1400s. Inside, look for the flamboyantly painted pulpit from the 1620s. The pews and votive ships on display were installed much later, in the 1800s. Outside you'll see two sculptures, both by Sweden's greatest sculptor, Carl Milles, called *The Sisters* and *Angel with Trumpet.*

The main square and the center of local life is **Storgatan. Östergatan** and **Stora Norregatan** are the best streets for charming little 19th-century houses; nearly all of them have carved wooden doors and potted plants on their doorsteps.

Nearby Attractions

Backakra ★ Located off the coastal road between Ystad and Simrishamn is the farm that Dag Hammarskjöld, the late United Nations secretary-general, purchased in 1957 and intended to make his home. Although he died in a plane crash before he could live there, the old farm has been restored according to his instructions. The rooms are filled with gifts to Mr. Hammarskjöld—everything from a Nepalese dagger to a lithograph by Picasso.

The site is 31km (19 miles) southwest of Simrishamn and can be reached by the bus from Simrishamn marked YSTAD. Likewise, a bus from Ystad, marked SIMRISHAMN, goes by the site. Scheduling your return might be difficult because of infrequent service—check in advance.

Other than the caretakers, the site is unoccupied most of the year, with the exception of 18 members of the Swedish Academy, who are allowed to use the house for meditation and writing whenever they want.

S-270 20 Loderup. (✆ **0411/52-60-10.** Admission 30SEK ($6/£3) adults, free for children under 15. June 8–Aug 16 daily noon–5pm; May 16–June 7 and Aug 17–Sept 20 Sat–Sun noon–5pm. Closed Sept 21–May 15.

Glimmingehus ★★ Even more than Kivik (see below) and Backakra (see above), this is the top attraction in the area. The somewhat Gothic castle, built between 1499 and 1505, appears much as it did at the time of its construction. Nearly all other such castles in Sweden are in ruins or else have been extensively tampered with—so this one is for purists. This majestic edifice was constructed by Adam van Büren for a member of the Danish aristocracy, who demanded strong fortresslike walls and tiny windows. Naturally the fortress had a moat. In time, the aristocrats, finding the castle far too austere, moved out—and the rats moved in. There were so many rats here at one time that Selma Lagerlöf, in her book *The Wonderful Adventures of Nils,* describes an epic battle between the gray and the black rats. Like a Pied Piper, the fictional Nils lures away the gray rats by playing from his enchanted pipe, plucked from a wise old owl who inhabited the tower of Lund Cathedral. Swedish schoolchildren still read this adventure story today.

Hammenhög 276 56. (✆ **0414/186-20.** Admission 60SEK ($12/£6) adults, free for children 7–18. Daily 10am–6pm. Closed Nov–Mar. From Simrishamn follow Rte. 10 southwest for 10km (6¼ miles) to the village of Hammenhög and then follow the signs.

Kivik Tomb ★ The drive here is worth the journey, as it takes you through fields planted with fruit, mainly pears and apples, and to the little village of **Kivik,** where the cider is said to taste better than anywhere else in Scandinavia.

Discovered in 1748, this remarkable find, Sweden's most amazing Bronze Age relic, is north of Simrishamn along the coast of Kivik. In a 1931 excavation, tomb furniture, bronze fragments, and some grave carvings were uncovered. Eight floodlighted runic slabs depict pictures of horses, a sleigh, and what appears to be a fun-loving troupe of dancing seals.

Bredaror. No phone. Admission 20SEK ($4/£2). Daily 10am–6pm. Closed Sept–Apr. From Simrishamn follow Rte. 10 northwest to the village of Kivik, at which point the tomb is signposted.

WHERE TO STAY

Hotel Kockska Gården (Value) This unspoiled black-and-white half-timbered former coaching inn looks like one of those old places in the English countryside—except this inn is in Sweden and right in the town center. The hotel is built around a large medieval courtyard where horses were once sheltered during the bitter Swedish winter. Much modernized, updated, and greatly altered over the years—and now more comfortable than ever—it is an inviting choice. The bedrooms have tasteful furnishings and soothing pastel colors. Breakfast is the only meal served, but there are places to eat within an easy walk of the front door.

Storgatan 25, S-272 31 Simrishamn. © 0414/41-17-55. Fax 0414/41-19-78. www.kockskagarden.se/dk/hotellet.html. 18 units. 1,690SEK–1,990SEK ($338–$398/£169–£199) double. Rates include breakfast. AE, MC, V. Free parking. **Amenities:** Breakfast room; lounge; nonsmoking rooms. *In room:* TV.

Hotel Svea ★ We wouldn't want to check in forever, but for an overnight stay, this is the best choice in town. It also has the finest restaurant (see below). Right on the waterfront, in the town center, Svea was built around the turn of the 20th century; it's painted yellow, with a red-tile roof typical of other buildings nearby. Much of what you see today was rebuilt and radically renovated, so everything is modernized. Many of its well-appointed, conservatively comfortable rooms overlook the harbor. The hotel's only suite, the Prince Eugen, is named after a member of the royal family of Sweden who stayed here shortly after the hotel was built.

Strandvägen 3, S-272 21 Simrishamn. © 0414/41-17-20. Fax 0414/143-41. www.hotellsvea.se. 59 units. 1,290SEK–1,590SEK ($258–$318/£129–£159) double; 1,890SEK ($378/£189) suite. AE, DC, MC, V. Free parking. **Amenities:** Restaurant; bar; sauna; laundry service; dry cleaning; nonsmoking rooms; rooms for those w/limited mobility. *In room:* TV, hair dryer, safe, Wi-Fi.

WHERE TO DINE

Restaurant Svea ★ SWEDISH/INTERNATIONAL The best restaurant in town lies within the pale yellow walls of the above-recommended Hotel Svea. Within a modern, mostly beige room whose windows overlook the harbor, the kitchen focuses on very fresh fish caught in local waters. However, the kitchen also turns out beef, pork, chicken, and some exotic meats, such as grilled filet of ostrich. (The chef added it to the menu mainly as a conversational oddity.) Other menu items include strips of smoked duck breast in lemon sauce, a platter of artfully arranged herring that can be prepared at least three different ways, filet of fried sole with white-wine or tartar sauce, medallions of pork with béarnaise sauce, and a succulent filet of beef with salsa-style tomato sauce. On a number of visits, we have found all these dishes deftly prepared with fresh ingredients. As a waiter said to us, "Guests come here for an hour or two of enjoyment, and we feed them well—what more can they ask?"

In the Hotel Svea. Strandvägen 3. © 0414/41-17-20. Reservations recommended. Main courses 195SEK–235SEK ($39–$47/£20–£24); 3-course menu 275SEK ($55/£28). AE, DC, MC, V. Daily 6:30–10am, 11:30am–1pm, and 6:30–10pm. Closed Dec 21–Jan 8.

6 KRISTIANSTAD ★

73km (45 miles) N of Simrishamn, 95km (59 miles) NE of Malmö, 126km (78 miles) SE of Växjö

Try to see all the towns we've recommended in the preceding pages. And then, if you have an extra day, head over to Kristianstad. With its former ramparts; moats; and broad, tree-lined boulevards, we always find a visit here rewarding. It's also the best base for exploring the country palace of Charles XV, one of the outstanding attractions of southeast Skåne.

Called the "most Danish of Sweden's towns," Kristianstad actually was a part of Denmark—for 44 years. Its founder, Christian IV of Denmark, still makes his presence felt in many ways. In fact, the town, originally known as Christianstat, was issuing bank notes with a Danish king imprinted on them as late as 1898.

The city was founded in 1614 to defend the Danish kingdom against Swedish attacks. The fort laid out by Christian IV was northern Europe's most modern. The fortification period ended in 1847, and once the ramparts were leveled, Kristianstad expanded, building Parisian-style boulevards that earned it the name "Little Paris." The only parts of the fortification still left are portions of the northernmost system surrounding what now is the residential district of Utanverken. After a century and a half without the restricting fortifications, Kristianstad has expanded to become the largest town in the county, just as Christian IV had hoped.

ESSENTIALS

GETTING THERE **By Plane** The nearest airport (the Kristianstad Airport) is 20km (12 miles) southwest of town. Accessing the town from the airport requires transit by taxi (310SEK/$62/£31 each way), or by **Flygbuss** for a charge of 100SEK ($20/£10) per person each way. Transit time takes 15 minutes, and bus departures are timed to coincide with the arrivals of airplanes.

By Train There is frequent rail service throughout the day from Malmö; the trip takes 1 hour and 15 minutes. The train and the bus stations here are both within a 10-minute walk of the town's major hotels. Call © 0771/75-75-75.

By Bus Local buses arrive several times a day from Ystad (trip time: 1 hr., 30 min.) and also from Simrishamn (same trip time). Call © 0711/77-77-77.

By Car From Simrishamn, our last stopover, head northwest along Route 10 until you come to the junction with Route 118, at which point you go north into Kristianstad.

VISITOR INFORMATION The **Kristianstads Turistbyrå** is at Stora Torg, 291 80 Kristianstad (© 044/13-53-35; www.kristianstad.se). It is open in summer Monday to Friday 9am to 7pm, Saturday 9am to 3pm, and Sunday 2 to 6pm. Off-season hours are Monday to Friday 10am to 5pm, and the last Saturday of each month 10am to 2pm.

SEEING THE SIGHTS

A Renaissance town created in 1614 by Christian IV, the "builder king" of Denmark, Kristianstad is eastern Skåne's most historic center. Thanks to a grid plan laid out by this long-ago king, it is also still easy to find your way around.

Those arriving at the train station are greeted by one of the city's major landmarks, **Trefaldighertskyrkan ★★**, or the Holy Trinity Church, Västra Storgatan (© 044/20-64-00); it's the most beautiful Renaissance church in Scandinavia. Construction on it took place between 1617 and 1628, and it remains the apogee of all that was spectacular about the Renaissance-minded King Christian IV of Denmark. The grandiose exterior contains seven splendid spiraled gables; the high windows allow the light to flood inside. Inside, the vaulted design and slender granite pillars create an unusually beautiful architectural setting. Most of the church appointments date from the time of Christian IV, including the carved oak benches, the altarpiece, and the marble-and-alabaster pulpit, as well as the magnificent organ facade built in 1630. It's open daily 9am to 6pm year-round.

Directly across from the church lies **Storatorg,** the major town square, and the setting for the 19th-century **Rådhus,** or Town Hall, located on Västra Storgatan. The current town hall replaced an older building in 1891 and is built in Christian IV's Renaissance style like structures in Copenhagen. In a niche under the hands of the Town Hall clock stands a statue of Christian IV, a zinc copy of Bertel Thorvaldsen's bronze original that is in Christian IV's sepulcher in Denmark's Roskilde Cathedral. Step through the arms-emblazoned portal and you'll also be greeted by a bronze bust of Christian IV sculpted with exceptional skill by François Dieussart in 1643. The original stands in Rosenborg Palace in Copenhagen.

North of Storatorg is the **Regionmuseet,** Östra Boulevarden (© **044/13-52-45**), sheltered in a structure that was originally intended as a royal palace for Christian IV in 1616. In time, however, it became an arsenal for Danish partisans during the bloody conflicts with Sweden. The building acquired its present look in the 1780s, becoming a regional museum in 1959. The art and handicraft collections here are worth seeing, especially the treasure-trove of silver. The works of local artists also are displayed, and there is an array of antique textiles of very minor interest. The museum is open June to August daily 11am to 5pm. Off-season hours are Tuesday to Sunday noon to 5pm (first Wed of every month until 9pm). Admission is free.

A short walk east of Storatorg will take you to the **Filmmuseet (Film Museum),** at Östra Storgatan 53 (© **044/13-57-29**). It comes as a surprise to many visitors that Kristianstad—not Stockholm—was the cradle of the Swedish film industry. This unique museum is housed in the oldest film studio (from 1909) still standing in Sweden. Outside the door, you're greeted by an early movie camera; on videotape inside you can view the flickering works of Sweden's first film directors. It charges no admission and is open Tuesday to Friday and Sunday from 1 to 4pm.

When you tire of museums, head for **Tivoli Park,** which can be reached from the Film Museum by wandering down any of the roads to its right. The avenues of horse chestnut trees are perfect for strolling. In the park is a theater built in the Art Nouveau style in 1906 by Axel Anderberg, who designed the Stockholm Opera. At the north end of the park is **Barbacka Cultural Center,** a lively home for the town's art gallery.

The best way to admire the topography around Kristianstad involves taking a boat ride on the nearby lakes and rivers. From early May to mid-September, **a sightseeing steamer ★** departs from Kristianstad for 2-hour tours of **Lakes Araslövs and Hammar,** with time spent on the River Helgeå as well. Departures usually are daily at 11am, 2pm, and 6pm, and the cost is 120SEK ($24/£12) adults, 60SEK ($12/£6) children 4 to 14 years old. You can stake out some of the generous deck space to view the midsummer sunlight even at night. For information and reservations, contact the tourist office (see above).

A Nearby Palace

Bäckaskog Slott ★ You've heard of living like a king. That cliché can be taken literally at this favorite 19th-century summer address for royalty, because it's open for hotel bookings. This country palace of King Charles XV stands in a 16-hectare (40-acre) park managed by the Swedish Forest Service. The castle, a National Trust building, was a monastery founded in the early 13th century. The chapel dates from 1230, but its tower is from 1640. At Bäckaskog, you'll find a **Biblical Garden** ★★ featuring trees, bushes, and herbs mentioned in the Bible or having some other religious connection.

The on-site restaurant, plus 15 hotel rooms and 4 suites (all in a contemporary style), are open to guests all year. A double goes for 1,050SEK to 1,550SEK ($210–$310/£105–£155); suites range from 1,450SEK to 1,650SEK ($290–$330/£145–£165).

Exhibitions and sales of art and country furniture can be attended even when the castle is not open to visitors. The palace can be reached by taxi from Kristianstad; call Taxi Allians at ⏾ **044/24-62-46.** If you're driving from Kristianstad, go 15km (9¹/₃ miles) north along E66 until you reach the turnoff for Fjälkinge, at which point Bäckaskog is signposted.

S-290 34 Fjälkinge. ⏾ **044/530-20.** www.backaskogslott.se. Free admission. Apr–Sept daily 8am–6pm; Oct–Mar daily 10am–5pm.

WHERE TO STAY

Hotel Anno 1937 ★ (Finds) This is the most atmospheric hotel in Kristianstad. Near the heart of town, it was originally built in the 1700s as the private home of the local bailiff. Today it boasts some of the most elaborate brickwork in town, especially on its second floor, where windows are gracefully arched and mullioned. Bedrooms are outfitted with more style and taste than you might have guessed from the hotel's relatively moderate rates. None is particularly large, but in view of their coziness, soft beds, and carefully chosen decorations, guests find that the rooms are very comfortable.

Vestre Storgatan 17, S-291-32 Kristianstad. ⏾ **044/12-61-50** or 044/10-30-99. www.hotelanno.se. 31 units. June to mid-Aug and weekends 1,295SEK–1,395SEK ($259–$279/£130–£140) double; 1,595SEK–1,995SEK ($319–$399/£160–£200) suite. Rates include breakfast. AE, DC, MC. V. Parking 70SEK ($14/£7). **Amenities:** Breakfast room; bar; sauna; laundry service; dry cleaning; nonsmoking rooms. *In room:* TV, Wi-Fi.

Quality Hotel Grand This is a good, reliable choice, and sometimes that is just what you're looking for when you overnight in a provincial Swedish town. The largest and most centrally located hotel in Kristianstad occupies a position near the railway station; it was built in the early 1960s and features a conservative brick facade. In 1985, its size was doubled with a new four-story wing, and the interior was radically modernized; it is now one of the best in town, though lacking the character of the previous choice. Today you'll find a series of busy conference rooms and bedrooms that are conservatively outfitted in a style that's just a bit banal but very comfortable, with ample bathrooms.

An in-house restaurant serves lunch and dinner daily. The bar is a two-story space named **Grands.** A separate restaurant, open only on Saturday nights, features a live orchestra that offers contemporary and supper-club dance music for cheek-to-cheek dancing. Computers are available for use by guests.

Storgatan 15, Box 45, SE-291 21 Kristianstad. ⏾ **044/28-48-00.** Fax 044/28-48-10. www.choicehotels.no. 137 units. Mid-June to mid-Aug and Fri–Sun year-round 693SEK–880SEK ($139–$176/£69–£88) double; rest of year 1,050SEK–1,735SEK ($210–$347/£105–£174) double. Rates include breakfast. AE, DC, MC, V. Free parking. Bus: 11. **Amenities:** Restaurant; bar; sauna; limited room service; laundry service; dry cleaning; nonsmoking rooms; rooms for those w/limited mobility. *In room:* TV, minibar, hair dryer, Wi-Fi.

WHERE TO DINE

For a quick but enjoyable drink and snack in Tivoli Park, try the **Fornstugan Café,** 29180 Kristianstad (no phone), open from May to September only.

Den Lilla Tavernan GREEK Go to Stockholm for great dining—Kristianstad doesn't make it on the culinary map. But that doesn't mean you can't find satisfying food here. This is Kristianstad's only Greek restaurant—opened in part because it reminds so many locals of their holidays in the Mediterranean. The decor evokes a simple taverna on one of the Greek islands, with solid wooden furniture, a low-key and decidedly unpretentious decor, and a blue-and-white color scheme that reflects the colors of the Greek flag. Menu items include all the Greek standards: stuffed grape leaves, moussaka, many different preparations of lamb (including well-seasoned kabobs), and fish. A honey-drenched portion of baklava makes a worthy dessert. A few of these dishes lose a little something in their transmigration to frigid Sweden, but it's at least a change of pace from standard Swedish fare.

Nya Boulevarden 6B. (🕿 **044/21-63-04.** Reservations recommended on weekends. Main courses 70SEK–189SEK ($14–$38/£7–£19). AE, DC, MC, V. Daily 4–11pm.

---

7 KARLSHAMN

508km (316 miles) S of Stockholm

For many Swedes who sailed to America, Karlshamn was the last they saw of the old country before heading to a new life in the wilds of the Dakotas or such. Long a rival of Karlskrona (see later in this chapter), this old port city has often been a battleground between the Danes and the Swedes. In 1658, the Swedish king, Karl X Gustav, a cousin of his predecessor, Queen Christina, decided to found a naval port here, and the great city architect Erik Dahlberg drew up plans to defend the city from attack. After defeating the forces of Fredrik III of Denmark, Karl entered into the Peace of Roskilde, which on February 26, 1658, granted Sweden control of the province of Skåne as well as Blekinge.

In time, the port proved difficult to defend, and the big naval plans envisioned for it were abandoned. The last garrison at Frisholmen came to an end in 1864. In the 19th century, the town became a den of thieves and smugglers, its economy based on the production of liquor, snuff, tobacco, and playing cards.

From its lowly beginnings as a small fishing village, Karlshamn developed because of its location in a deep, well-sheltered bay at the mouth of the Mieån River, where it flows into the Baltic. On the border of Skåne, Karlshamn is actually in Sweden's smallest province of Blekinge. A rival tourist officer in a neighboring town once told us, "Go to Karlskrona, not Karlshamn—there's nothing to see in Karlshamn." Well, that isn't exactly true: It's true that it's a fairly sleepy town, but it's also one that invites you to wander its old cobblestone streets, and it's a good stopover for those traveling from Kristianstad in the west to Kalmar in the north on the road to Stockholm.

ESSENTIALS

GETTING THERE The nearest **airport** is an inconveniently far-away Sturup (aka Malmö/Lund), 150km (93 miles) away, and there is no direct and easy public transport from Sturup to Karlshamn. Consequently, most air arrivals for Karlshamn are funneled through Kastrup in Copenhagen. From here, train transit is easy and efficient, funneling passengers through (1) Malmö, and then (2) Kristianstad, and then (3) Karlshamn, all for a combined rail ticket price of 300SEK ($60/£30).

hours to the train station in the city center. Transit requires a transfer in the town of
Hessleholm, a 90-minute ride from Karlshamn. There are four **buses** per week from
Stockholm, traveling with many stops en route, but without a change of bus required,
from Stockholm. They depart Monday, Thursday, Friday, and Sunday at 9am, and arrive
in downtown Karlshamn at 6pm. For more information, call the local bus company at
© **771/75-75-75.**

VISITOR INFORMATION For information about Karlshamn and the area, go to the
Karlshamn Tourist Office at Ronnebygatan 1, S-374 81 Karlshamn (© **454/812-03;**
www.karlshamn.se). From mid-June to mid-August, it's open Monday to Friday 9am to
6pm, Saturday 10am to 6pm, and Sunday noon to 6pm. The rest of the year, it's open
Monday to Friday 9am to 5pm.

SPECIAL EVENTS One of the town's best events occurs for a few days in July (exact
dates vary) every summer: the **Karlshamn Baltic Festival.** Visitors from all over Sweden,
and even Copenhagen, flock here for the festivities, which take place at many venues
throughout town. Music and live entertainment fill the town, mixed with the smell of
fish frying to feed the hordes. (Herring sandwiches are a big favorite.) Samba orchestras
provide exotic rhythms, dance, and naked flesh; brass bands march up and down the
streets. On one street corner you might find someone playing a barrel organ; on the next
corner classical music will fill the air; and farther on, you can listen to African tunes or
else American rock from the 1970s. The revelry and good times continue into the wee
hours in the pubs. The tourist office (see above) will have dates and more details on
events.

SEEING THE SIGHTS

As you'll soon learn from visiting its museums and galleries, or even looking at its architecture, the golden age of Karlshamn was the 19th century.

The chief attraction in town is the **Karlshamns Kulturkvarter** ★★, at the corner of
Vinkelgatan and Drottninggatan. Here one finds the town's most historic buildings,
some of which have been turned into small galleries and museums.

The **Karlshamns Museum** (Vinkelgatan; © **454/148-68**) is the center point of Kulturkvarter. This is a treasure trove of relics from the "attic" of the little province of Blekinge. There's a little bit of everything, ranging from intriguing folk art and costumes, to
remnants of the tobacco industry, to nautical and maritime trinkets, to the lost Swedish
art of painted ceilings. One room even commemorates Alice Tegnér (1864–1943), a name
still known to all Swedish schoolchildren because of the songs she wrote for them.

After visiting the Karlshamns Museum, head into the courtyard to some of the other
galleries of the Kulturkvarter, including the **Stenhuset,** with its exhibitions of elaborate
wrought-iron work, 18th- and 19th-century wall decorations, and antique organ fronts.
The quaint **Holländarhuset,** the seat of Dutch merchants who once had a lucrative trade
with Karlshamn, has been converted into a workshop, which you can visit. One gallery,
Tobaksladen ★★, is now a tobacco museum, with artifacts from the days when processing tobacco and snuff was the major industry in Karlshamn, in the 17th and 18th
centuries.

On the far side of the Vinkelgatan, you can drop in to visit an art gallery, **Konsthall,**
installed in an old tobacco warehouse. The museum features displays of modern Swedish
art and has some beautiful samples of Swedish mural paintings and painted ceilings,
which were originally in the old town hall.

(Finds) **A Cafe with a View**

We like to spend an hour or two in summer sitting at the **Café Utsikten,** Vägga (© **454/103-25**), set about 1.2km (³/₄ mile) south of the town center. It was originally built as a private villa in the 17th century. It's open only from early June to September. Right on the sea, the cafe offers the best view of the Firth of Karlshamn and the 17th-century citadel, the **Katellet,** on the island of Frishol- men (see below). On a summer day, we also like to walk along the seafront prom- enade; there's a tiny harbor where fishmongers hawk smoked eel, mackerel, and fresh salmon.

The last attraction in the museum compound is the **Punschmuseet.** This museum relives the grand heyday when "Karlshamns Flagg" was the punch of choice in many a home in western Europe. Flavored with arrack, this was a sweet, spirits-based drink; one type was distilled from the juice of the coconut palm, the other from molasses and rice. You can still see some of the equipment used in the original 19th-century distillery. The punch was launched by J. N. von Bergen, who became celebrated in Sweden as a great entrepreneur in the 19th century. He was also the largest producer of playing cards in Sweden, but was mainly known for his "Punsch" liqueur, and aquavit. The factory show- cases authentic equipment, machinery, bottles, wooden barrels, and other relics.

The admission fee for the Kulturkvarter's main core is 25SEK ($5/£2.50) for adults, free for children under 17. Between mid-June and mid-August, the museum's "satellites" (Holländarhuset, Tobaksladen, the art gallery, and the Punschmuseet) are included in the fare; they're all open Tuesday to Sunday noon to 5pm. The rest of the year (mid-Aug to mid-June), only the museum's main core is open, Monday to Friday 1 to 4pm. Admission is the same, regardless of the time of year you visit.

Thanks to the town's prosperity and industries, many wealthy merchants built lavish homes here. Several are gone today, but some still stand. We think that the best of these is **Skottsbergska Gården,** at Vinkelsgata 6 (© **454/148-68**), near the Karlshamns Museum. This is an impressive example of an 18th-century merchant town house, and it's still filled with valuable antiques and wall paintings specially commissioned by local artists. It's open only between mid-June and mid-August every Tuesday to Sunday noon to 5pm. Admission for adults, children, and students costs 20SEK ($4/£2).

At the harbor and **Hamnparken (Harbor Park),** you can see one of the most famous statues ★★ in Sweden, erected here in 1959. Axel Olsson created this much-reproduced monument to honor the Swedes who emigrated to America from southern Sweden. The characters represented, Kristina and Karl-Oskar, are those depicted in Vilhelm Moberg's monumental work *The Emigrants,* which was made into a film starring Liv Ullman and Max von Sydow. The book detailed the hardships that drove Swedes to leave their home- land for America. The farmer looks out to the sea, whereas his wife turns her head back to the land she is leaving. An exact duplicate of this statue graces the center of Lindstrom, Minnesota. The relief in Olsson's work is of the emigrant ship, **Charlotta.**

In a beautiful little rose garden to the west stands another statue, that of a barefooted girl named Maja, a character created by Alice Tegnér, the famous writer of children's songs.

In summer, boats leave from the quay, taking you over to the **Kastellet (castle),** the old fortress built on the island of Frisholmen to protect Karlshamn from the Danes and Baltic invaders. In 1676, the Danes overpowered the fortifications here, but the Swedish forces retook the castle the following year. The Danes returned victoriously in 1710 and took the fortress once more. But after the Swedes paid a huge ransom, the Danes sailed back to Copenhagen within the year. But that wasn't the end of Karlshamn's troubles: About half the members of the garrison, as well as half the inhabitants of Karlshamn, were afflicted with the plague in 1711. The fortifications date from 1675, and at its peak the garrison had a force of 400 soldiers. However, all of them pulled out at the end of 1864, and Kastellet is no longer used for military purposes. Once on the island, you can visit the fortifications, including the wall and gun emplacements, each well preserved. You're also allowed to visit the dungeon and look at a "poisoned well."

Today Kastellet is merely a ruin, without barriers, and open to view by anyone who wants to wander among the battlements. The ferryboat ride takes 10 minutes each way, departs every hour between early June and late August, and costs 40SEK ($8/£4) per person round-trip. (There are no discounts for children, but children under 5 ride free if they're with guardians.) For more information, contact the **Hauglund Shipping Company,** Gästhamn (the harbor front), Karlshamn (© 414/149-58).

Some visitors carry a picnic from the mainland. Others visit the **Kastellet Cafeteria** (© 454/125-27), which is positioned at the point where the ferryboats land. Congenial owner Rolf Bildström serves pastries, coffee, and sandwiches, and displays the works of local artists for sale. The cafe maintains completely erratic summer-only hours, opening only during the operation of the ferryboat that connects this island to the Swedish mainland.

Motorists can also drive 10km (6¼ miles) along E22 to reach **Eriksberg Natturreser-vat,** a beautiful park and nature reserve where some 800 animals roam freely. The collection of animals is particularly rich in red and fallow deer, along with European bison. The drive involves a trip through deciduous woodland, leading to a little lake that is known as a setting for the increasingly rare red waterlily, best seen in late spring and early summer. On-site are a children's zoo and a cafeteria.

From E22, take exit Åryd east of Karlshamn and follow the signposts. Eriksbergs Nature Park (© 454/600-58) is open only as follows: June and August daily noon to 8pm, July daily noon to 9pm. Once inside, you'll drive your car in a 14km (8⅔-mile) circle, getting out only at clearly designated "safety points" en route. (The danger from wild animals is a cause for concern.) Admission costs 110SEK ($22/£11) per adult, 60SEK ($12/£6) for children 8 to 15, free for children 7 and under; a family ticket costs 250SEK ($50/£25).

ⓂMoments Sailing the Turbulent Baltic

One midsummer diversion you should try in Karlshamn is an ocean cruise, operated by **Hauglund Shipping Company,** on the harborfront, Gästhaum (© 414/149-58). Boats depart twice a day between mid-June and mid-August. It costs 180SEK ($36/£18) per person, lasts for 2½ hours, and sails through the scenic harborfront and along the jagged coastline.

First Hotel Carlshamn ★ This is one of the most reliable stopovers along the Swedish coast. In the 1980s, the builders of this hotel discovered blueprints for a Market Hall that stood here in the 19th century. They ended up constructing the hotel using the same plan, which explains why this relatively modern building (completed in 1987) has such old-fashioned charm. Most of its rooms, either public or private, open onto panoramic views of the historic harborfront. The bedrooms offer first-class comfort, although the decor is a bit bland; they're decently sized, with twins or a queen-size bed, and all accommodations have small, tiled bathrooms with showers (five with bathtubs as well). There are Jacuzzis and small living rooms in the suites. The on-site restaurant, **Arrak,** isn't run by the hotel, but the staff will gladly make reservations for you.

Varvsgatan 1, S-374 35 Karlshamn. ✆ **454/890-00.** Fax 454/891-50. www.firsthotels.com. 99 units. 999SEK–1,199SEK ($200–$240/£100–£120) double; 2,020SEK ($404/£202) suite. Rates include continental breakfast. Children under 15 stay free in parent's room. AE, DC, MC, V. Closed Dec 20–Jan 2. **Amenities:** Restaurant; bar; sauna; laundry service; dry cleaning; nonsmoking rooms; rooms for those w/limited mobility. *In room:* TV, hair dryer, trouser press, Wi-Fi.

Scandi Karlshamn Typical of the rather modern and impersonal hotels erected along the Baltic in the late 1960s, this well-run establishment lacks excitement, but it will house you in comfort and give you a good "tuck-in" in its restaurant—and charge you a moderate price for the privilege. The interior of the three-story, white-brick building is much more inviting than its exterior suggests. The staff is helpful, and the furnishings are kept up-to-date. The rooms are decorated in bright pastels, such as lemon yellow, to chase away the gloom of a gray day.

Jannebergsvagen 2, S-374 32 Karlshamn. ✆ **454/58-87-00.** Fax 454/58-87-11. www.scandic-hotels.se/SiteHomePage. 101 units. 750SEK–1,390SEK ($150–$278/£75–£139) double. Children under 13 stay free in parent's room. Rates include continental breakfast. AE, DC, MC, V. **Amenities:** Restaurant; bar; indoor pool; fitness center; sauna; nonsmoking rooms. *In room:* TV, hair dryer, iron, Wi-Fi.

WHERE TO DINE

Kopmanngarden ITALIAN The cuisine is modern, but there's a certain nostalgia about the setting—considering the building itself dates from the 1600s. Boasting casual, relaxing surroundings, this family-run place is one of the most inviting in town, and it serves the best pizza pies in the area. Recipes are time-tested and familiar, including spaghetti Bolognese and a tender and well-flavored chateaubriand. They even dish up an old-fashioned banana split, evocative of America in the 1950s, for dessert. In summer, you can dine at tables in the garden.

Drottninggatan 88. ✆ **454/157-40.** Reservations recommended. Main courses 79SEK–169SEK ($16–$34/£8–£17). AE, DC, MC, V. Mon and Wed–Thurs 4–10pm; Fri 4–11pm; Sat 12:30–11pm; Sun 12:30–10pm.

Restaurant Terrassen ★ SWEDISH/ITALIAN This is the best restaurant in town, an intimate and candlelit place that can comfortably handle 80 discerning patrons every night. Ingredients of the first-rate quality are skillfully handled by the well-trained kitchen staff. Lots of fresh fish, depending on the catch of the day, are featured on the menu, and the salmon, trout, and sole are particularly delectable. The chef's real specialty, however, is 30 different types of steak, especially a succulent cut of chateaubriand. Although this is primarily a Swedish restaurant, the chefs prepare a number of Italian dishes as well. For dessert, dare you try the fried Camembert with a special orange marmalade? There is also a moderately priced and well-chosen wine list.

KARLSHAMN AFTER DARK

Many nightclubbing locals gravitate to the **Loch Ness Pub and Restaurang,** Ronneby-gatan 22 (ℭ **454/126-00**). Living up to its namesake, the club is decorated with "memories of Scotland," including tartan patterns everywhere. On some nights they have live rock-'n'-roll bands but don't charge a cover. Many Scotch whiskeys, from Talisker to Glen Livet, are sold, as well as beer on tap. It's open daily from 5pm to 1am.

---

8 KARLSKRONA ★★

111km (69 miles) E of Kristianstad, 201km (125 miles) NE of Malmö, 107km (66 miles) SE of Växjö, 500km (311 miles) SW of Stockholm

Even if you have to skip Karlshamn or Kristianstad (see earlier in this chapter), try to plan for at least an overnight to this ancient port city. Karlskrona is a major bastion for the Swedish Navy on the country's southern flank. By royal command of King Karl XI in 1680, the port for the navy base was founded here. Today it's one of the few remaining naval ports in the world that is almost fully intact. In 1998, UNESCO declared Karls-krona a World Heritage Site.

As such, hundreds of women on the prowl from both Sweden and other parts of Europe flock here to hook up with those handsome blond sailors. The sexually charged atmosphere of Karlskrona is featured in dozens of gay guides to destinations in Europe.

The city makes a good stopover for visitors en route between Kristianstad and Kalmar to the north. It opens onto an archipelago of more than 30 islands (depending on how many islets you want to count), but many of these are off-limits and under the control of the Swedish military. In the heyday of the cold war, in 1981, a Soviet submarine spy-ing on Swedish military installations ran aground here, and Karlskrona made world headlines. Today, Karlskrona is likely to make the papers only as host port for the Inter-national Cutty Sark Tall Ships' race.

Immediately east of Skåne, Karlskrona is the capital of the old province of Blekinge, which coincides with the modern county of the same name. Blekinge is the smallest province in Sweden and, like Skåne itself, once belonged to Denmark until Sweden reclaimed it in 1658.

ESSENTIALS

GETTING THERE   The nearest airport is the **Ronneby airport,** which lies 30km (19 miles) north of Karlskrona. The **Flygbuss** from the airport costs 120SEK ($24/£12) per person each way, and a taxi costs 300SEK ($60/£30) each way. Transit time is 25 min-utes, and bus departures are timed to coincide with the arrivals of airplanes.

Karlskrona lies on the main rail link between Stockholm and southern Sweden and points west. There are frequent **trains** throughout the day. **Svenda Bus** services the area from Stockholm (take no. 31). Both the train and the bus stations lie within a 5- to 7-minute walk of the town center. Motorists can follow E66 north from Kristianstad or the same motorway southwest from the port of Kalmar (also the same route from Stock-holm farther north).

VISITOR INFORMATION For information about the town and the area, go to the **Karlskrona Tourist Office,** Stortorget 2, 371 83 Karlskrona (© **0455/30-34-90;** www. karlskrona.se). In summer, hours are Monday to Friday 10am to 8pm, Saturday and Sunday 9am to 8pm. Off-season hours are Monday to Friday 10am to 6pm, Saturday 10am to 1pm. Boat trips of the archipelago are often available in summer; ask at the tourist office for details.

SPECIAL EVENTS Lövmarknad, on the day before Midsummer's Eve, is one of the liveliest and most attended events on the southern coast of Sweden. It takes place on the Stortorget, the main square of Karlskrona. During the celebration, Swedes decorate their houses, churches, and other structures with flowers, and raise a maypole. All members of the community dance around the maypole until late in the evening. Dancing to traditional music, drinking, and dining, including the eating of the first potatoes of the year, highlight the festivities. Contact the tourist office, above, for more information.

SEEING THE SIGHTS

Stortorget ★★, or the main square of town, is one of the biggest and most beautiful in northern Europe. In the middle of it is a statue of Karl XI, who founded the town, and two baroque churches designed by Nicodemus Tessin the Younger dominate the square. Both of these escaped the great fire of 1790. The fire, started by a laundry maid, forced massive rebuilding—which resulted in the town's baroque style giving way to a more neoclassical motif.

The first church in Stortorget, **Fredrikskyrkan,** is from 1744 and named after King Fredrik (1720–51). If something about it looks unfinished, it is—Tessin actually planned for the church to have spires on its squat towers. A series of Ionic pilasters graces the interior, and the three dozen bells in the south tower are rung daily. Standing opposite the church is the neoclassical **Rådhus,** or town hall, from 1795.

The other church, **Trefaldighetskyrka,** is circular in shape and is referred to as "the German church," even though that community stopped worshiping here in 1846. The church was completed in 1750, and Tessin based his design on the Pantheon in Rome. The roof burned in the great fire, and the present wooden roof is painted with *trompe l'oeil* coffering. The oldest artifact in the church is a red Öland limestone font from 1685. The church shelters the tomb of one of Sweden's greatest naval heroes, Admiral Hans Wachmeister, who in July 1700 sailed from the harbor with 38 ships and 8 frigates. With his ship loaded with 1,000 men and 108 guns, he defeated the Danish fleet at Öresund.

Marinmuseum (Naval Museum) ★, at Admiralitetsslatten (© **0455/35-93-02**), dates from 1752 and is one of the oldest naval museums in Sweden. Lying on the island of Stumholmen, the museum traces the country's naval heritage through various exhibits, including a marvelous collection of **figureheads ★** and ship models from the 18th to the 19th century. Old maps, maritime charts, plans for ship designs, navigating equipment, artifacts pulled up from the sea (including parts of actual ships), weapons, uniforms, and shipyard handicrafts are on parade. You can also see a full-scale replica of the *Hiorten,* a post ship from 1692. The museum is located along a long pier. Moored along the quays are the minesweeper *Bremon,* the *Spica* torpedo boat, and a fully rigged training ship, *Jarramas.* It's open June to August daily 10am to 6pm, September to May Tuesday to Sunday 11am to 5pm. Admission is free.

Church; © **0455/103-56**), lies on Bastiongatan on the naval island, a few minutes from
Stortorget. Built in 1685, the church was supposed to be temporary, but its stone replace-
ment was never built. Originally called Ulrica Pia, after Queen Ulrica Eleonora, wife of
Karl XI, the church may have been designed by Erik Dahlberg, the original town planner.
(Dahlberg gave Karlskrona its broad streets, monumental buildings, and large squares.)
The church contains a number of treasures, including a pulpit hourglass from 1693 and
an altarpiece that's a copy of *Thrust of the Lance,* by Rubens. Crowning the altar is a cross
given to a Swedish sea captain by the Patriarch of Constantinople in 1744. The church
is open from June to August daily from 9am to 5pm. In the off season, you have to make
an appointment with the tourist office to see it. Admission is free.

In front of the Admiraliteskyrkan is Karlskrona's most beloved **statue.** It depicts ex-
constable Matts Rosenbom, who froze to death on New Year's Eve in 1717. He was
found in the morning with his hand outstretched, his hat pulled over his ears, and a
beggar's bundle on his back. Since then, the wooden statue of Rosenbom has tipped its
hat to all who give alms to the poor.

To reach the oldest part of Karlskrona, take Hantverkargaten to **Björkholmen,** a hilly
island settled by shipbuilders, where many 18th-century houses still stand. The occupants of these little wooden houses with their small gardens lived in exceedingly cramped
conditions. The streets in the area are named after types of boats and Swedish admirals.

After a visit, you can head back to the north quay and the **Fisktorget,** the site of an
antique covered market. This spot, with its fishing boats tied up along the pier, is the
landing stage for any boats touring the archipelago.

You can also visit the **Blekinge Lans Museum** ★ here, at Fisktorget 2 (© **0455/30-
49-60**), which opened in 1899. The museum consists of a row of old houses, one of
which holds the **Blekinge County Museum** ★, exhibiting artifacts from this small
maritime province. The main building, **Greevagården,** dating from 1705, was the mansion of Admiral Hans Wachtmeister. Inside you'll find rooms filled with antiques and
paintings, all evocative of the rich life enjoyed by some in the 18th century. The mansion
adjoins a lovely garden. It is open mid-June to mid-August daily 10am to 6pm. During
other months, hours are Tuesday to Sunday 11am to 5pm and Wednesday 11am to 7pm.
Admission is 30SEK ($6/£3), free for ages under 18.

Museum Leonardo da Vinci Ideale ★, Drottninggatan 28 (© **0455/255-73;** www.
museumldv.com), is a museum created from the private collection of the Kulenovic family. Its chief treasure is *The Youngest Madonna* ★, by da Vinci himself. Although this is
the painting that gets all the press, we have a lot of other favorites here, including *A
Stolen Kiss,* by Jea Honoré Fragonard; *Stilleben,* or still life, by Georges Braque; another
Stilleben by Henri Matisse; plus a startling *Medical Care,* by Peter Bruegel. Two paintings
are by Vincent van Gogh: *Portrait* and *Sheep.* Other exhibits include a drawing by Da
Vinci, rare porcelain from the Topkapi Palace in Istanbul, a stunning gem-studded gold
piece from South Asia (ca. 1900), and a cabinet by the French architect André Charles
Boulle (1642–1732). The museum can be visited May to August Wednesday to Sunday
11am to 6pm. Admission is 20SEK ($4/£2).

Still partly a military base, **Kungsholm Fort,** on the island of Kungshomen (© **0455/
30-34-90**), can be visited in the summer. You must go with a guide, because some of the
area is restricted. This impressive fortress was constructed in 1680 to protect Karlskrona
from frequent Danish intrusions. But Denmark wasn't Karlskrona's only enemy: The

port was also blockaded by the Russians in the 1780s and faced British attempts at domination in the 19th century. The fortress is an architectural curiosity, containing an artificial circular harbor constructed into the island itself, with only a narrow passage leading out into the Baltic. Excursions can be arranged through the tourist office (see above) from May to August at 10am and 3pm on Tuesday, Thursday, and Saturday. Tours cost 150SEK ($30/£15) for adults and 75SEK ($15/£7.50) for children ages 12 to 16 (free for children under 12).

In summer, you can also take **boat tours of the archipelago,** to see dozens of small islands—really "islets"—in the impressive harbor. Some boats visit the islands, and many visitors often take along a picnic lunch. Many of the islands also have small trails for hiking. **Affärs Verken Bättrafik,** at Fisktorget (*©* 0455/783-30), offers the best cruises, lasting half a day and costing 115SEK to 150SEK ($23–$30/£12–£15) for adults or 55SEK to 85SEK ($11–$17/£5.50–£8.50) for children 7 to 16. Departures are daily June through August at 8am and 11am, with a final tour at 3:45pm.

Outdoor Pursuits

Many Swedes visit Karlskrona during summer for its 30 beaches, 7 of which lie in the center. The most central, **Stumholmen Beach** is the best. This sandy beach, ideal for kids, has a bridge and diving tower, along with a restaurant. Next to the beach is the famous Marinmuseum (see above).

Drägsö Beach is another favorite in the archipelago, lying only 5 minutes from the historic core and linked to the main island with a bridge. You'll find beaches and towering cliffs along with such activities as canoeing, water-skiing, and fishing.

Karlskrona also opens onto great waters for both saltwater and freshwater fishing. To become part of a fishing trip, call **Senoren's Sportfishing Tours** (*©* 0455/440-10), which takes fishermen to the far reaches of the archipelago. **Hasslö Island Touring & Fishing Service** (*©* 0455/33-21-24) also offers great fishing in freshwater streams or in the Baltic.

WHERE TO STAY & DINE

If you're just passing through for the day, or if you're sticking around for dinner, your best bet for food is the dining room at the **First Hotel Statt** (see below).

First Hotel Statt ★ . This turn-of-the-20th-century property in the center of the port is the hotel of choice in Karlskrona. After getting a little tattered, it was completely refurbished and now looks much better than when we first stayed here. Guests enjoy such architectural grace notes as candelabras and grand stairwells throughout. Every room is decorated individually; some are carpeted and others contain hardwood floors. For locals, the hotel is a dining and entertainment hub, offering first-rate food prepared with market-fresh ingredients.

Ronnebygatan 37-39, S-371 33 Karlskrona. *©* **045/55-55-50.** Fax 045/51-69-09. www.firsthotels.com. 107 units. 998SEK–2,198SEK ($200–$440/£100–£220) double; 2,300SEK ($460/£230) minisuite. Children under 12 stay free in parent's room. Rates include continental breakfast. AE, DC, MC, V. **Amenities:** Restaurant; bar; pub; nightclub; sauna; laundry service; dry cleaning; nonsmoking rooms. *In room:* TV, hair dryer, iron, trouser press, Wi-Fi.

Hotel Conrad The Wenström family, owners of this hotel, enjoy a deserved reputation as the most welcoming hosts in Karlskrona. Their Hotel Conrad actually is a trio of buildings, the oldest of which, the Culture House, is from the late 18th century. Two other buildings date from the 1970s and 1980s. Being traditionalists, we naturally opt for one of the six minisuites in the Culture House. Not only are they more luxurious, but they cost the same as the regular doubles. Naturally, they are the most requested and go first. All the rooms are comfortable, each with modernized bathrooms.

Västra Köpmansgatan 12, S-371 34, Karlskrona. ((C)) **0455/36-32-00.** Fax 0455/36-32-05. www.hotel conrad.se. 58 units. Mon–Thurs 1,195SEK ($239/£120) double, 1,295SEK ($259/£130) suite; Fri–Sun and summer 895SEK ($179/£90) double, 1,095SEK ($219/£110) suite. Children under 6 stay free in parent's room. Rates include continental breakfast. AE, DC, MC, V. **Amenities:** Breakfast lounge; sauna; laundry service; dry cleaning; nonsmoking rooms. *In room:* TV, minibar, hair dryer, iron, Wi-Fi.

KARLSKRONA AFTER DARK

The leading after-dark diversion is at **Kino's Nightclub,** Borgmästaregatan 17 ((C) **0455/ 31-11-00**), a bar, nightclub, and restaurant that rocks to a DJ all night long. The cover charge ranges from 45SEK to 120SEK ($9–$24/£4.50–£12).

Kalmar & the Southeast

During the 17th century, Denmark and Sweden fought bitterly over this area—and with good reason. Now that the wars are over, Sweden's southeast is a sleepy but idyllic place for a holiday. If you're on the most rushed of schedules, we suggest staying at least 1 night in Kalmar and another night in Växjö, especially if you want to buy some Swedish glass. Swedes call the latter town the "King of Crystal," because some of the world's most stunning pieces of glass artworks are produced here.

But the region has a lot more going for it than glass. It has a rich history, evident in its medieval towns with cobblestone streets and so-called "fairy-tale" castles. The province also boasts natural beauty, with abundant elk, large forests, flowering meadows, long stretches of *gädesgårdar* (the timber fences typical of this region), and some 5,000 lakes teeming with fish. And then there's the nightlife: In July and August, some of the coastal resorts with beaches become hard-partying towns.

Olaus Magnus wrote back in the 16th century, "The forces of nature work in a more secretive and wonderful way on Lake Vättern than they do anywhere else." Indeed the stuff of myth and legend, Lake Vättern (not to be confused with the even larger lake of Vänern) is one of the oldest cultural areas in the north of Europe, and it extends out to four provinces, including Småland. The water here is so pure that some 400,000 people use it as their drinking water supply. Despite the clarity of its water, the lake is notorious for its unpredictability; many a ship now lies at the bottom.

We've found that the towns along Vättern are just as appealing to visitors as Kalmar and the glassworks. The city of Jönköping lies on the southern shores; other more charming centers are Gränna, Vadstena, and Motala, and you should budget time for visits there. If time remains afterward, you can visit Örebro, beyond Motala and 60km (37 miles) north of Lake Vättern. Örebro is Sweden's sixth most populous city, lying on the shores of Lake Hjälmaren, the country's fourth largest lake.

---

1 KALMAR ★★

292km (181 miles) NE of Malmö, 110km (68 miles) E of Växjö, 409km (254 miles) S of Stockholm, 340km (211 miles) E of Gothenburg

Perhaps we've read too many novels about Kalmar's seafaring past. On our first visit long ago, we were a bit disappointed, expecting more of a medieval aura. But after settling in and wandering for hours through its old streets, we found that Kalmar became strangely appealing. Today we eagerly await another visit. There is much to discover here if you ignore the expanding industrial suburbs and concentrate on the historic core that Danish soldiers came to capture centuries ago.

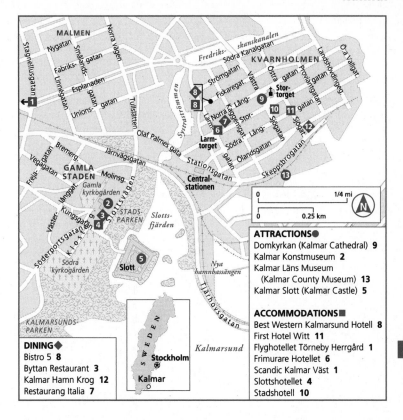

Map labels:
MALMEN · Nygatan · Norra vägen · Stagnellusgatan · Smålands- gatan · Fabriks- gatan · Esplanaden · Linnégatan · Unions- gatan · gatan · Tullslätten · Fredriks- · skanskanalen · Södra Kanalgatan · KVARNHOLMEN · Strömgatan · Fiskaregat. · Västra · Östra · gatan · Provian- tgatan · Landshövdingeg. · Ö:a Vallgat. · Stor- torget · Olaf Palmes gata · Systrströmmen · Norra K. · Lång- · Larmg. · Kaggens · Stor- · Södra · Lång- · gatan · Sjögatan · Spögat. · Bremerg. · Järnvägsgatan · Stationsgatan · Olandsgatan · Skeppsbrogatan · GAMLA STADEN · Molinsg. · Vegagatan · Frejagatan · Slottsvägen · väster- Långgat. · Kungsgatan · Söderportsgatan · Kl:o:st · Gamla kyrkogården · STADS- PARKEN · Slotts- fjärden · Larm- torget · Central- stationen · Södra kyrkogården · Slott · Nya hamnbassängen · Tjärhovsgatan · KALMARSUNDS- PARKEN

DINING◆
Bistro 5 **8**
Byttan Restaurant **3**
Kalmar Hamn Krog **12**
Restaurang Italia **7**

SWEDEN · Stockholm · Kalmar · Kalmarsund

0   1/4 mi
0   0.25 km

ATTRACTIONS●
Domkyrkan (Kalmar Cathedral) **9**
Kalmar Konstmuseum **2**
Kalmar Läns Museum
  (Kalmar County Museum) **13**
Kalmar Slott (Kalmar Castle) **5**

ACCOMMODATIONS■
Best Western Kalmarsund Hotell **8**
First Hotel Witt **11**
Flyghotellet Törneby Herrgård **1**
Frimurare Hotellet **6**
Scandic Kalmar Väst **1**
Slottshotellet **4**
Stadshotell **10**

A coastal town opposite the Baltic island of Öland, historic Kalmar contains Sweden's best-preserved Renaissance castle. And though today it is a thriving commercial center, it also still retains many 17th-century buildings and sea captains' houses, many clustered around the *Stortorget* (main square) in the center of town. The first large-scale Swedish emigration to America, more than 3 centuries ago, originated in Kalmar (and ended up in Wilmington, Delaware).

Historically, the town is forever linked to the Kalmar Union, the treaty that three northern crowns signed here in 1397 linking Denmark, Norway, and Sweden into an ill-fated but united kingdom. Queen Margrethe of Denmark headed the union, which was dissolved in 1523.

ESSENTIALS

GETTING THERE By Plane Kalmar Airport (© **0480/45-90-00;** www.kalmar airport.se) receives two to four daily 50-minute flights from Stockholm. The airport is 5km (3 miles) west of the town center. The **Flygbuss** (www.kalmarflyg.se) makes the 10-minute drive to the center of Kalmar for a per-person price of 50SEK ($10/£5). Buses are timed to depart with the arrivals of flights at the airport.

By Train   Seven trains a day make the 6¹/₂-hour run between Stockholm and Kalmar. Eight daily trains arrive from Malmö, taking 3 hours and 20 minutes. Both the train and bus stations lie in the center of town. Call ✆ **771/75-75-75.**

By Bus   Three to seven buses a day make the 7-hour trip from Stockholm. From Gothenburg, there is one bus on both Friday and Saturday, taking 6 hours. For information, call ✆ **0200/21-82-18** (within Sweden only).

By Car   From Stockholm, take E66 south.

VISITOR INFORMATION   The Kalmar Tourist Office, **Turism I Kalmarbygåden,** is located at Ölandskajen 9 (P.O. Box 23), 391 20 Kalmar (✆ **0480/41-77-00;** www.kalmar. se/turism), near the railway station right in the town center. The office is open June 1 to July 27 and August 16 to August 31 Monday to Friday 9am to 7pm, and Saturday and Sunday 10am to 4pm; July 28 to August 15 Monday to Friday 9am to 9pm, and Saturday and Sunday 10am to 5pm; September to May Monday to Friday 9am to 5pm.

CASTLES, CATHEDRALS & MORE

Still surrounded by parts of its old fortified walls, the 17th-century New Town is a warren of cobblestone streets and market squares. Despite the name, this town was created in 1647, after a devastating fire that caused the townspeople to move away from the old town to this one on Kvarnholmen. If you're pressed for time, you can feel secure in knowing that only Kalmar Slott, the Renaissance castle, ranks as a "must see."

Domkyrkan (Kalmar Cathedral)   From the town's marketplace, you can wander over to Stortorget to visit this 17th-century cathedral. Kalmar Cathedral is the only one in Sweden without a bishop, but it's still an impressive building. The bright, massive space of the interior is a reminder that the cathedral was built when Sweden was one of the great European powers. It was designed in 1660 by Nicodemus Tessin the Elder in the Italian Renaissance style. (Tessin visited Rome and found his inspiration there.) The altar was designed by Tessin the Younger, and it shimmers with gold. It's surrounded by a series of sculptures, such as a depiction of "Faith" and one of "Mercy."

Stortorget. ✆ **0480/123-00.** Free admission. June 12–Aug 30 daily 8am–8pm. Off season daily 10am–6pm. Bus: 1, 2, 7, or 9.

Kalmar Konstmuseum   This is Kalmar's leading museum of art, though naturally it can't compete with the treasures found in Gothenburg and Stockholm. But it has its own particular charm, especially if you're drawn to two of the best-known Swedish artists, Anders Zorn and Carl Larsson. (We weren't particularly thrilled with some of the other 19th-c. Swedish painters.) The best reason to come here is to see the temporary modern exhibitions, part of "traveling shows" that bring great art to the provinces of Europe. Sketches and finished works by important Swedish designers are displayed in the design gallery.

Slottsvägen 1D. ✆ **0480/42-62-82.** www.kalmarkonstmuseum.se. Admission 40SEK ($8/£4) adults, free for ages under 20. Fri–Wed 11am–5pm; Thurs 11am–8pm. Bus: 1, 2, 7, or 9.

Kalmar Läns Museum (Kalmar County Museum)   County museums in Sweden can be particularly dull, but this one intrigues with its setting in an old mill along the harbor. Inside, the obvious highlights are relics from the royal flagship *Kronan* ★★, which sank in the Baltic Sea off the island of Öland during a battle against the Danes and the Dutch in 1676. Only 42 of the 840 men aboard survived. The museum was responsible for excavation at the wreck site. Objects found by the marine archaeologists—glass bottles,

tin plates, nautical instruments, a seaman's chest, and many old coins—are on display. In **269**
another exhibit, the museum re-creates the world of Jenny Nyström (1854–1946), a native of Kalmar who went to Paris and became a prominent painter. Her artistic mind was filled with elves and pixies, and her enchantment touched the Swedish heart. Even today, many of her traditional motifs appear on Christmas cards. Models, reproductions, and original paintings evoke her world and art. Outside the exhibits is a cafe.

Skeppsbrogatan 51. 📞 **0480/45-13-00.** www.kalmarlansmuseum.se. Admission 50SEK ($10/£5) adults, 25SEK ($5/£2.50) seniors and students, free for children under 19. June 15–Aug 15 daily 10am–4pm; off season Tues–Fri 10am–4pm. Bus: 1, 2, 7, or 9.

Kalmar Slott (Kalmar Castle) ★★★   It's got the kind of realism that Disney just can't create, right down to the dank dungeon where you can still imagine the cries of the damned. There are enough secret passages here to enthrall Dracula, along with the more fairy-tale architectural adornments such as pepper pots and turrets. For romantics, there are even a moat and a drawbridge. This is Sweden's best-preserved Renaissance castle, and you might want to allow 2 hours to see it. Founded in the 12th century, the strategically situated fortress was once called the key to Sweden. It was here that the Danish Queen Margrethe of Denmark launched the Kalmar Union, uniting the crowns of Denmark, Norway, and Sweden. Then, in the 16th century, under order of King Gustavus Vasa and two of his sons, Erik XIV and Johan III, the medieval stronghold was transformed into a Renaissance palace. Be sure to see the restored castle chapel as well as the prison for women, which was in use in the 18th and 19th centuries. English-language tours are conducted from mid-June to mid-August daily at 11am and 3pm. To get here from the train station, turn left on Tullbron.

Kungsgatan 1. 📞 **0480/45-14-90.** Admission 80SEK ($16/£8) adults, 50SEK ($10/£5) students, 20SEK ($4/£2) children 5–16, free for children under 5. Apr–Oct daily 10am–6pm; Nov–Mar only on the 2nd weekend of each month 10am–4pm. Bus: 1, 2, 7, or 9.

WHERE TO STAY

Kalmar offers an adequate range of accommodations, although many choose to stay on the island of Öland (see chapter 10).

The Kalmar Tourist Office (see above) can help you rent rooms in **private homes** for 350SEK ($70/£35) for a single and from 450SEK ($90/£45) for a double. Some of the private homes charge an additional 50SEK ($10/£5) for sheets.

Expensive

Slottshotellet ★★   In the center of Kalmar, close to the castle, this traditional hotel is our nostalgic favorite. A gracious old house on a tranquil street, facing a waterfront park, it lies an easy walk from the train station. Each of the bedrooms has a different style of decoration and furnishing, with touches such as wallpaper, wooden floors, old-fashioned chandeliers, and brass or wood headboards reminiscent of a country house in England. Rooms vary widely in shape and style, but all are equipped with average-size bathrooms. Everything is kept spotlessly clean. The hotel consists of both a main building from 1864 and three annexes. Even the annexes have charming rooms. Breakfast is served in the pavilion, and on winter evenings tea and coffee are offered in the lounge. The hotel also offers facilities for those who want to cook their own meals. In summer, full restaurant service is offered on the terrace; otherwise, only breakfast is served.

Slottsvägen 7, S-392 33 Kalmar. 📞 **0480/882-60.** Fax 0480/882-66. www.slottshotellet.se. 44 units. 1,390SEK–1,790SEK ($278–$358/£139–£179) double; 1,990SEK ($398/£199) suite. Often weekend reductions. Rates include breakfast. AE, DC, MC, V. Free parking. **Amenities:** Restaurant; bar; sauna; breakfast-only room service; laundry service; dry cleaning; nonsmoking rooms; solarium. *In room:* TV, minibar.

Moderate

Best Western Kalmarsund Hotell   This is a serviceable, durable, reasonably priced hotel that was designed to give you a good night's sleep—not to thrill you. Set in the heart of Kalmar, near the railway station, the well-maintained, well-managed hotel you see today was converted in 1982 from a 40-year-old complex of shops and offices. The staff here is responsible and motivated, and bedrooms are snug, modern, cozy, and nicely decorated with conservative modern furniture. There's an attractive restaurant, **Bistro 5,** on site (see below) serving good food.

Fiskaregatan 5, S-392 32 Kalmar. ⓒ **800/780-7234** or 0480/48-03-80. Fax 480/41-13-37. www.kalmarsund hotel.se. 85 units. Sun–Thurs 1,175SEK–1,255SEK ($235–$251/£118–£126) double, 2,500SEK ($500/£250) suite; Fri–Sat 680SEK–800SEK ($136–$160/£68–£80) double, 1,750SEK ($350/£175) suite. Rates include buffet breakfast. AE, DC, MC, V. Parking 95SEK ($19/£9.50). **Amenities:** Restaurant; bar; sauna; room service; laundry service; dry cleaning; nonsmoking rooms; rooms for those w/limited mobility. *In room:* TV, minibar, hair dryer, iron, trouser press, Wi-Fi.

First Hotel Witt ★ (Kids)   This is not the best hotel in town, but the helpful staff seems to care more about the comfort and welfare of their guests than most of their competitors. Although the foundations and some of the inner walls of this building date from the 1600s, most of what you'll see, both inside and out, is from the 1970s, when what remained of the decrepit original was rebuilt and reconfigured. Bedrooms are renovated and furnished with conservatively dignified and very appealing furniture, hardwood floors, and, in some cases, good copies of Oriental carpets. In addition to appealing to the ordinary traveler—often couples or businesspeople—the hotel designer planned some units especially for female travelers, families, persons with disabilities, and those with allergies. Rooms are generous in size, with attractive styling and excellent bathrooms. Views usually extend out over Kalmar Sound, and the hotel's position in the heart of the old town is convenient to virtually everything in the center.

Södra Långgatan 42, S-392 31 Kalmar. ⓒ **0480/152-50.** Fax 0480/152-65. www.firsthotels.com. 112 units. Mid-June to Aug and Fri–Sun year-round 899SEK–1,199SEK ($180–$240/£90–£120) double, 1,525SEK ($305/£153) suite; rest of year 1,290SEK–1,790SEK ($258–$358/£129–£179) double, 1,850SEK ($370/£185) suite. Rates include breakfast. AE, DC, MC, V. Free on-street parking, 100SEK ($20/£10) in hotel garage. **Amenities:** Restaurant; bar; indoor heated pool; gym; sauna; room service; laundry service; dry cleaning; nonsmoking rooms; rooms for those w/limited mobility. *In room:* TV, hair dryer, iron, Wi-Fi.

Scandic Kalmar Väst (Value)   Comfortable, conservative, and well managed, this hotel is a low-rise two-story building erected in the 1970s and located about 2.5km (1¹⁄₂ miles) west of Kalmar's central core. This hotel appeals to motorists who don't want to encounter parking problems in the historic district. It has long been a family favorite with visiting Swedes, but more and more foreign visitors are discovering its advantages. The bedrooms are modern, well-maintained, and outfitted with comfortable beds.

Dragonvagen 7, S-392 39 Kalmar. ⓒ **0480/46-93-00.** Fax 0480/46-93-11. www.scandichotels.com. 148 units. 890SEK–1,390SEK ($178–$278/£89–£139) double. Rates include breakfast. AE, DC, MC, V. Free parking. **Amenities:** Restaurant; bar; indoor heated pool; sauna; children's playroom; room service; nonsmoking rooms; rooms for those w/limited mobility; solarium. *In room:* TV, hair dryer, iron, safe, Wi-Fi.

Stadshotell ★   Every provincial Swedish city has an unimaginatively named Stadshotell ("City Hotel," its English equivalent). Many are merely decent places to hang your hat for the night, but the Kalmar establishment is better than most. Located on the main square in the heart of the city close to the train station, the 1906 Stadshotell still retains

its romanticized architecture, with gables and a bell tower overlooking the cathedral. And
many of its original Art Nouveau touches are still in place—cut-glass chandeliers and
even a library give the aura of a rich private home. Modular bathrooms with showers are
adjoined by large bedrooms (among the most spacious in town) with bedside TV controls, feather pillows and duvets, hardwood floors, and distinctive built-in furniture.
There's also a nightclub that is open on weekends.

Stortorget 14, S-392 32 Kalmar. ✆ **0480/49-69-00.** Fax 0480/49-69-10. www.profilhotels.se. 126 units. June
6–Aug 2 and Fri–Sat year-round 915SEK–1,015SEK ($183–$203/£92–£102) double, 1,150SEK–1,350SEK
($230–$270/£115–£135) suite; rest of year 1,395SEK–1,595SEK ($279–$319/£140–£160) double, 1,795SEK–
1,995SEK ($359–$399/£180–£200) suite. AE, DC, MC, V. Parking 95SEK ($19/£9.50). **Amenities:** Restaurant;
bar; sauna; nonsmoking rooms; 1 room for those w/limited mobility. *In room:* TV, hair dryer, Wi-Fi.

Inexpensive

Flyghotellet Törneby Herrgård ★ (Finds)　If you're seeking a place more homelike
and personal than a city chain, this oasis hits the spot. This stately hotel lies on 1.2 hectares
(3 acres) of verdant parkland, near clear springs and streams, 5km (3 miles) west of Kalmar, and a 1-minute drive from the airport. Although there has been an inn on this site
since 1616, the elegantly symmetrical building you see today dates from the 1870s, when
it was constructed as a manor house in a style similar to the classical ruins of Pompeii.
Inside, Dagmar and Agneta Herlin have decorated their hotel and home with a roster of
worthy antiques and color schemes that are almost universally pink- or salmon-toned.
Bedrooms are cozy, well maintained, and charming, each with a small bathroom.

Flottiljvägen 9, S-392 41 Kalmar. ✆ **0480/200-24.** Fax 0480/267-40. www.torneby.se. 18 units. Sun–
Thurs 1,195SEK ($239/£120) double, 1,695SEK ($339/£170) suite; Fri–Sat 895SEK ($179/£90) double,
1,395SEK ($279/£140) suite. Rates include breakfast. AE, DC, MC, V. **Amenities:** Restaurant; bar; outdoor
pool; sauna; room service; laundry service; dry cleaning; nonsmoking rooms. *In room:* TV, hair dryer.

Frimurare Hotellet　If for no other reason, we'd recommend this hotel for its tranquil
setting; it's tucked away in a large park. Fortunately, it's also an old-fashioned place full of
charm and character. The richly detailed Italianate building was constructed in 1875 as a
headquarters for the local branch of the Freemasons. Today, after extensive renovations,
the two lowest floors of the three-story building are devoted to a comfortable, cozy hotel;
the stately top floor is still the domain of the Freemasons, one of Kalmar's most active
social and charitable organizations. Bedrooms are well maintained and, in most cases, have
high ceilings and appealingly formal furnishings, including well-maintained private bathrooms. There's a copious breakfast buffet included in the room price.

Larmtorget 2. S-39232 Kalmar. ✆ **0480/152-30.** Fax 0480/858-87. www.frimurarehotellet.gs2.com. 34
units. Fri–Sat 995SEK–1,045SEK ($199–$209/£100–£105) double; Sun–Thurs 925SEK–1,460SEK ($185–$292/
£93–£146) double. Rates include breakfast. AE, DC, MC, V. **Amenities:** Breakfast lounge; sauna; solarium.
In room: TV, dataport, hair dryer, Wi-Fi.

WHERE TO DINE

Bistro 5 INTERNATIONAL　No one need call *Gourmet* magazine after dining here,
but the food is reliable, attractively priced, and fresh. Set on the lobby level of the also-
recommended Best Western Kalmarsund Hotell, this is a warm, denlike spot that celebrates an American-Italian alliance in food. Expect painted depictions on the walls of
both the Italian and the U.S. flags, red-and-white-checkered tablecloths, flickering candles, a long and hospitable bar area, and food that includes pasta, quesadillas, Caesar
salads, baby back ribs, burgers, grilled fish—most caught within Swedish seas and
lakes—and all kinds of juicy steaks.

In the Best Western Kalmarsund Hotell, Fiskaregatan 5. ✆ **0480/181-00.** Reservations recommended. Main courses 199SEK–329SEK ($40–$66/£20–£33). AE, DC, MC, V. Mon–Sat 6–10pm.

Byttan Restaurant ★ SWEDISH   In the city park near the base of the castle, a 10-minute walk south of the town center, is one of the best spots for dining in Kalmar. From a terraced pavilion overlooking the water or in the vine-covered courtyard, you can sample one of the many soups Byttan Restaurant specializes in; they too are some of the best in town. The finest examples include cream of lobster and cream of mushroom. Main courses range from omelets to filet of beef with red-wine sauce and forest mushrooms. Other dishes that might tantalize your palate include veal steak in a pepper-flavored cream sauce, sliced tenderloin of pork with red-wine and herb sauce, and our all-time favorite here: salmon with a Riesling sauce. (You also can order it with butter sauce.) Even if you don't come for a meal, the restaurant is a good place to have afternoon tea.

In 1994, the restaurant was enlarged with the addition of a bistro-inspired annex known as **Däcket.** Outfitted with wood paneling and shades of pale green, in summer it serves the same menu, during the same hours, as the main dining area. In winter, however, it features a simpler menu costing about 15% less than in the main dining area.

Slottsvägen 1. ✆ **0480/163-60.** www.byttan.nu. Reservations recommended in summer. Fixed-price lunch 85SEK ($17/£8.50); main courses 120SEK–180SEK ($24–$36/£12–£18). Buffet Mon–Fri 189SEK ($36/£19). AE, DC, MC, V. Mon–Fri 11am–11pm; Sat–Sun 3–11pm. Closed Sept–Nov.

Kalmar Hamn Krog ★★ INTERNATIONAL   After much searching (and many bad meals), we've found the cuisine here the best and most gastronomically sophisticated in town. It's also just a stylish place to dine. Established in 1988, Kalmar Hamn Krog is usually the local spot for celebratory meals and anniversary parties—it's that special. The restaurant was built from scratch on an old pier where steamships used to deposit passengers from the neighboring island of Öland. Today the interior is all blue and white. The kitchen staff slaves away to maintain the restaurant's high-ranking position in Kalmar, and the products that go into the cuisine are the best in the city. The best dishes include the pork filet with a port-wine sauce; the grilled halibut with a dill and lemongrass stew; or the filet of pikeperch in a sweet-and-sour curry sauce. One unusual specialty is the grilled steak with piña colada sauce. The latter gives the meat a scent of coconut-flavored rum and a hint of the tropics—most unusual in these northern climes. The wines are from Austria, the United States, and France, among other countries.

Skeppsbrogatan 30. ✆ **0480/41-10-20.** www.calmarhamnkrog.se. Reservations required. Main courses 185SEK–345SEK ($37–$69/£19–£35). AE, MC, V. Mon–Sat 5–10pm.

Restaurang Italia Ⓥalue ITALIAN   For pizza and pasta, and one of the best and most affordable luncheon buffets in town, head here. Because so many locals vacation in Italy, the entrepreneurs decided to cater to a newfound market. Something may be lost in translation from the Mediterranean to the Baltic, but the food is good, the pizzas and pastas savory. The beef and chicken dishes come in many varieties and taste fresh and succulently seasoned.

Storgatan 10. ✆ **0480/870-87.** Reservations recommended. Fixed-price lunch 75SEK ($15/£7.50); main courses 95SEK–185SEK ($19–$37/£9.50–£19). DC, MC, V. Mon–Sat 11am–11pm.

SHOPPING

If you're searching for antiques, head for **Anderssons Antik,** Esplanaden 6 (✆ **0480/47-41-62,** but call first to make an appointment). For one of the best selections of ceramics

and glassware, try **Noshörningen,** Olof Palmes Gata 1 (© **0480/151-25**). Another good
selection is found at **Mats Nordell,** Milingsgatan 7 (© **0480/41-11-01**).

KALMAR AFTER DARK

If a major cultural event is being staged, it'll likely be at the local concert hall, **Kalmar-Salen,** Skeppsbrogatan 49 (© **0480/42-10-00**). Otherwise, most of the nighttime activity centers on **Krogers,** Larmtorget 7 (© **0480/265-50**), which is merely a bar and does not offer live entertainment.

---

2 VÄXJÖ

110km (68 miles) W of Kalmar, 443km (275 miles) S of Stockholm

Sweden's reputation for high quality and often imaginative glasswork has spread to every corner of the globe—and Växjö, the country's "Glass Kingdom," has a lot to do with that. Some 16 factories here produce world-renowned Swedish crystal. Yet we recommend visiting even if you're not a glass aficionado. The name Växjö comes from *Vägsjön,* or "lake where the roads meet" and, true to that name, this 14th-century city offers scenic lakes and forests, dotted with traditional red-timbered cottages. Many ancestors of Swedes who emigrated to America also came from here, so odds are good that you'll encounter other travelers, often from Minnesota, researching their roots.

ESSENTIALS

GETTING THERE **By Plane** There are two daily flights between Stockholm and Växjö, arriving at the Växjö Airport, 9km (5¹⁄₂ miles) north of the center. For flight information, call © **0470/75-85-00;** www.smalandairport.se.

By Train There are train connections from Gothenburg, leaving at 7am daily and arriving in Växjö at noon; from Malmö, leaving at 6:14am and arriving in Växjö at 12:18pm. Trains arrive hourly throughout the day from Kalmar. Call © **771/75-75-75.**

By Bus From Stockholm, buses leave Monday to Saturday (take Express Bus) at 9am and 4pm; Sunday at noon, 1:30, 3, and 5pm. Call © **771/67-67-67.**

By Car From Stockholm, take E4 south to Norrköping, then continue south along E66 to Kalmar. At Kalmar, head west on Route 25.

VISITOR INFORMATION The **Växjö Tourist Information Centre,** Stadsbiblioteket, Västra Esplanaden 7 (P.O. Box 1222), 351 12 Växjö (© **0470/414-10;** www.vaxjo.se), is open mid-June to mid-August Monday to Friday 9:30am to 6pm, Saturday 10am to 3pm; off season, it's open Monday to Friday 9:30am to 4:30pm. Closed June 20 through 22.

SEEING THE SIGHTS

In summer, between mid-June and late August, tours on **Lake Helgåsjön** are conducted aboard the century-old steamer **S/S** *Angaren Thor* (© **0470/510-43-70**), which reigns as one of the oldest wood-fired steamships in Scandinavia today. Don't expect state-of-the-art hardware aboard this ship: Part of the allure derives from old-fashioned brass fittings and a maritime dowdiness that is rapidly on the way to achieving high camp. A 2¹⁄₂-hour tour costs 125SEK ($25/£13); a 7-hour tour, which includes some kind of dinner, goes for 500SEK ($100/£50). Other tours to more distant parts of the lake are arbitrarily scheduled, and are canceled and reactivated according to the weather, prior

---

(Finds) **The World's Oldest Working Paper Mill**

The small town of Lessebo, on Route 25, 35km (22 miles) west of Orrefors in the heart of the glassworks district, is home to the **Lessebo Papermill** ((℃ **0478/476-91**), the world's oldest working producer of handmade paper. In existence since 1693, the mill is open to the public, so you can watch as paper passes through the various stages of production, from cotton pulp to individual sheets that are pressed and hung to dry. There's a gift shop where you can purchase handmade products, and tours are available in English, costing 350SEK ($70/£35) for anywhere from 10 to 22 persons. You should call in advance and make arrangements if you want a formal tour; however, most visitors just show up, collect the English-language pamphlets, stroll around the property, drop into the gift shop, and ask questions of the friendly, polite staff, most of whom speak English. It's open Monday to Friday 7am to 4pm; admission is free.

---

bookings, and the whim of the owners. For information and reservations, inquire at the local tourist office (above).

Småland Museum   Established in 1792, this is the oldest provincial museum in Sweden. It's not the best—just one of the oldest. Even so, it's been much improved and enlarged, with an added wing focusing on the history of Swedish glassmaking. You'll see tools and archives from the early days of the craft, with a special collection of more than 25,000 pieces. A separate exhibit displays the finest artistic examples of **Swedish glass** ★★★ produced over the centuries. In other areas of the museum you can view one of Sweden's largest art exhibits, collections of coins, religious objects, weapons, and a special room housing an ethnological collection. Forestry and agricultural exhibits are also included. (Unless you're a farmer or a forest ranger, you might want to skip these.) The museum is near the train station—so at least it's easy to find.

Södra Järnvägsgatan 2. (℃ **0470/70-42-00**. www.smalandsmuseum.se. Admission 40SEK ($8/£4) adults, 20SEK ($4/£2) students, free for those under 20. June–Aug Mon–Fri 10am–5pm, Sat–Sun 11am–5pm; Sept–May Tues–Fri 10am–5pm, Sat–Sun 11am–5pm.

Svenska Emigrantinstitutet (House of Emigrants) ★★   This is one of the real "roots" museums of Scandinavia. Swedish-Americans come here to trace their ancestry to see if they descended from royalty or highway robbers. This institution, founded in 1968, documents the 1.3 million Swedish people who left their homeland during the "America fever" years—the 1850s to the 1920s—and moved to the United States, often facing harsh conditions en route. The house contains exhibits on emigrant history as well as archives and a research library. A permanent exhibition, the "Dream of America," presents insights into the causes and consequences of the emigration. Minnesota Day, a folk festival held here the second Sunday in August each year, draws thousands of Swedes and Swedish-Americans.

Museiparken. (℃ **0470/201-20**. www.swemi.se. Admission 40SEK ($8/£4) adults, 5SEK ($1/50p) age 18 and under. May–Aug Tues–Fri 10am–5pm, Sat–Sun 11am–5pm; Sept–Apr Tues–Fri 9am–4pm, Sat 11am–5pm.

Växjö Cathedral   As Swedish cathedrals go, this is low on the totem pole—you might drop in for a 30-minute visit. Legend has it that this cathedral stands on the spot where St. Sigfrid (an 11th-c. missionary to Småland from York, England) erected a little

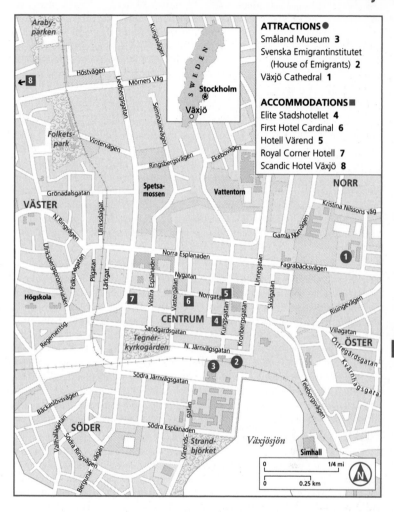

ATTRACTIONS ●
Småland Museum **3**
Svenska Emigrantinstitutet
   (House of Emigrants) **2**
Växjö Cathedral **1**

ACCOMMODATIONS ■
Elite Stadshotellet **4**
First Hotel Cardinal **6**
Hotell Värend **5**
Royal Corner Hotell **7**
Scandic Hotel Växjö **8**

wooden church. The cathedral has copper-clad towers and a bright interior, and its chimes are heard three times a day. Summer concerts are held in the cathedral Thursdays at 8pm.

Adjacent to the cathedral is **Linnéparken (Linné Park),** named for Carl von Linné (Carolus Linnaeus), the Swedish botanist who developed the scientific categories of plants. In the park, an arboretum displays 24 categories of perennials. There also are other flower gardens throughout and a playground for children. The cathedral is in the town center.

Linnégatan. ℂ **0470/70-48-24.** Free admission. Daily 9am–5pm.

Between Kalmar and Växjö—within an hour's drive—are several glassworks, including **Orrefors** and **Kosta Boda.** Kosta Glassworks and Boda Glassworks have been the leading names in Swedish crystal since the 19th century. However, they have pooled their resources to become "Kosta Boda" and now operate as one empire, although many of their original factories still maintain separate identities. Not only can you go on Sweden's grandest shopping trip here, but you also can see master glass blowers—among the world's finest—at work.

Åfors Glasbruk ★★ At a point 29km (18 miles) west of Nybro and 50km (31 miles) south of Växjö is Åfors, the domain of glass designers Bertil Vallien and his wife, Ulrica Hydman-Vallien, two of the most famous names in Swedish glass. Bertil is known for his stout Château Bohème glasses, rustic and masculine with a satisfying heft. His wife Ulrica's work is simple and clean, using strong colors. This also is the showcase of Gunnel Sahlin, who often brings experiences of nature into the blowing room with her. She likes to combine contrasting elements—soft round forms and simple lines, and silky smooth surfaces and bright, brilliant color. This place is especially popular with Christmas shoppers, as it is known for its ornaments. The factory shop is open Monday to Saturday 10am to 6pm, and Sunday 11am to 5pm. Glasbruksvägen 50, Eriksmala. ✆ **0471/ 411-22.**

Boda Glasbruk ★ Although the Boda Glassworks (founded in 1864) long ago merged its administration with that of the Kosta Glassworks, this is the showroom for production of the Boda division of the conglomerate. Playful, even cheeky design is given free rein. Designers make wine glasses that dance, salad bowls that evoke the sweet smells of summer, and vases in which you can hear whispers of the jungle. The glass innovators here love to goad your senses and are never afraid to test the limits of their material. Sometimes glass might be combined with iron, while at other times, it's decorated with feathers. Located in the village of Boda, about 19km (12 miles) west of Nybro, it offers a discounted collection of seconds. We think that the flaws are almost imperceptible, but their prices are substantially lower than normal retail for more perfect pieces. It's open from Monday to Friday 11am to 5pm, Saturday noon to 3pm. Storgatan (Hwy. 25). ✆ **0481/242-62.** Free admission. Bus: 218 from Lessebo, which has rail links to Växjö.

Kosta Glasbruk This main headquarters of the Kosta complex was founded in 1742 by two former generals, Anders Koskull and Georg Bogislaus Stael von Holstein, who at first brought in glass blowing talent from Bohemia, which was then the reigning kingdom of crystal. Kosta pioneered the production of crystal, which must, by law, contain one quarter oxide. Here you can see the old Kosta Museum, with articles from the 18th and 19th centuries, as well as exhibitions of contemporary glass. Despite Kosta's merger with the nearby Boda Glassworks, this entity retains much of its separate identity. Over the years we have concluded that the best buys here are on items that have been discontinued (not necessarily because they were unsuccessful or bad, but because the company wanted to move on with new creations). Artists here tell us they get their inspiration from just about anything—the dew on a meadow, the morning mist on a lake, or a Swedish summer sky. It's open late June to early August Monday to Friday 10am to 5pm, Saturday 10am to 5pm, Sunday 11am to 5pm; off season Monday to Friday 10am to 5pm, Saturday to Sunday 10am to 3pm. Storavägen 96, Hwy. 28. ✆ **0478/345-00.** Located between Eriksmala and the junction with Rte. 31, 19km (12 miles) east of Orrefors.

Buying Swedish Glass

The temperature inside the furnace is 2,066°F (1,130°C). The gatherer reaches into its flaming interior, gathers the glowing melt on the blowing iron, and hands it over to the blower. The caramel-soft material sizzles as it is shaped against wet newsprint in the hands of the gaffer. Only an expert's touch will do now—a touch schooled by years of experience. When it's time for the gaffer to put the handle on a pitcher, he has to "see" how hot the glass is. If it's too hot, the attachment will run off or go through the pitcher. If it's too cold, it will be impossible to attach. Handblown glass is a living craft, born in the hands of glass workers.

Shopping in the Kingdom of Crystal is one of Sweden's best activities, especially if you keep the following points in mind: An ordinary purchase can save you as much as 75% off stateside prices—and if you're willing to settle for seconds or glass with certain flaws, you can save still more. On other items, assuming you're getting a bargain, the cost of glass purchased in the "kingdom" can still be about 50% cheaper in Sweden than in the United States, even when shipping costs are added. Even if it is flawed, the glassware sold in the area is superior to what you are likely to find in your local shopping mall back home. Still, it's always best to do some advance scouting of the glass outlets in Stockholm so you'll be familiar with the prices when you arrive. Seek out the red tags in the Växjö outlets; they signal that the glass has been greatly reduced in price for quick clearance. You can always look for special promotional deals that might be offered at any time of the year, depending on an outlet's inventory.

Bumps, discoloration, nicks, and bubbles are the most common faults in "seconds," but sometimes they are virtually unnoticeable except to a trained eye. Ask a factory if it's selling any discontinued styles. These products are invariably marked down for quick clearance. If you're a collector, you no doubt already know that a signed piece of art glass has value, whereas an unsigned piece does not.

Before leaving the store, make absolutely certain that the piece of glass you purchased (obviously not art glass) can go into the dishwasher. If it can't, you'll have to wash the glass by hand. Detergents can cause glass to lose some of its luster.

If you're a light shopper, you can hand-carry your purchases back on the plane, providing they are carefully wrapped. You can also have the store ship your glass home for you. As a rule, shipping costs equal about 30% of the marked price on the item. If your glass arrives broken, take a picture of the damaged merchandise and send it with a letter along with a copy of your receipt to the factory at which you made the purchase. All breakage is replaced.

Finally, count on visiting no more than five outlets per day. Pick up a map at the tourist office in Växjö and devise your attack plan from that.

Målerås Glasbruk A 10-minute drive from Orrefors (see below), this factory belongs to one of the few independent glassmakers still left in the glass district, the Målerås company. Much of their production revolves around the engravings of master artisan Mats Jonasson, whose trademark involves vivid images that are a bit less formal than those produced by competing (larger) manufacturers—images such as a Dalmatian pup, his eyes glowing with mischief, or of flora and fauna—captured in the clearest of crystal. The Black Magic collection, consisting of bowls in dramatic black glass with a sandblasted rim, is especially intriguing. The effect has been likened to one of Småland's deep forest ponds. After careful inspection of the seconds here, we could find no flaws, but the designer could—hence the reduced prices. Prices here are about half what you'd pay for similar purchases in Stockholm. It's open June to August weekdays 9am to 6pm, Saturday 10am to 5pm, and Sunday 11am to 5pm; September through May it's open weekdays 10am to 6pm, Saturday 10am to 4pm, and Sunday 11am to 4pm. Rte. 31, 15km (9¹/₃ miles) northwest of Orrefors. ✆ **0481/314-00.** Free admission.

Orrefors Glasbruk ★★ Orrefors, between Nybro and Lenhovda, 40km (25 miles) west of Kalmar, has been one of the most famous names in Swedish glass since it was established in 1898. Guided tours are conducted Monday to Friday from 9:30am to 2:30pm, anytime someone shows up. During most of the year, a visit incorporates tours of divisions that include glass blowers, cutters, and engravers of fine glass. In July, the cutters and engravers are on vacation, although demonstrations of glass blowing are still available. It's possible to purchase seconds (in most cases, hardly distinguishable from perfect pieces), and gift shipments can be arranged. Tax-free shopping can also be arranged in the factory's shop.

Although a handful of Orrefors subsidiaries (including Sandvik and Strömbergshyttan) also offer tours of their factories, the tours at this main factory are the most complete and comprehensive. The best plan may be to tour Orrefors first and then inquire about specialized tours of the company's subsidiaries. It's open June to July weekdays 8am to 4pm, Saturday 11am to 4pm, and Sunday noon to 4pm; August to May it's open weekdays 10am to 4pm, Saturday 10am to 4pm, and Sunday noon to 4pm. Rte. 31, Orrefors. ✆ **0481/34-19-95.** Free admission.

Studioglas Strömbergshyttan Lying 31km (19 miles) east of Växjö, along Route 25, is this domain of three master blowers: Håkan Gunnarsson, Leif Persson, and Mikael Axenbrandt. The trio started this studio in 1987 determined to experiment to the utmost limit. Staying true to that ambition, the three glass blowers let loose their creativity in front of the furnace, creating dishes, vases, and decorative pieces with an utterly free approach to the glowing melt. Colors are brilliant and freely combined. Look for Anna Örnberg's work, which has a youthful audacity and a warm sense of humor; her vases and small bowls seem to burst with joy. For example, Anna puts pouting lips on fruit-colored fish vases that balance on their tail fins. The best days to visit are Monday and Wednesday, when you can see more artisans at work. It's open weekdays 9am to 6pm, Saturday 10am to 4pm, and Sunday noon to 4pm. Hovmantorp. ✆ **0478/310-75.** Free admission.

WHERE TO STAY

Elite Stadshotellet (Value) This venerable old hostelry from 1853 has, after several restorations, become a choice place to stay, successfully combining old and new elements. Bedrooms have a bit of style and flair—they often have hardwood floors and provide a homelike feeling with Oriental carpeting. Bathrooms are larger than average and often luxuriously appointed—some with Jacuzzis, and all with a tub/shower combinations. The hotel's cozy restaurant is outfitted like a rustic Swedish tavern, with strong, dark colors and a traditional menu of *husmanskost* (country cooking). The only reason we didn't give this place a star is that it tends to book a lot of tour groups.

Kungsgatan 6, S-351 04 Växjö. ℂ **0470/134-00.** Fax 0470/448-37. www.elite.se. 134 units. June 19–Aug 9 and Fri–Sun year-round 893SEK ($178/£89) double, 1,250SEK ($250/£125) suite; rest of year 1,495SEK ($299/£150) double, 1,795SEK ($359/£180) suite. Rates include breakfast. AE, DC, MC, V. Free parking. **Amenities:** Restaurant; bar; nightclub; 24-hr. room service; laundry service; dry cleaning; nonsmoking rooms; 1 room for those w/limited mobility. *In room:* TV, minibar (in some), Wi-Fi.

First Hotel Cardinal ★ We recommend this four-story hotel for its central location on Storgatan (the main street of town) and for its traditional charm and comfort. In the late 1980s, the owners radically renovated a turn-of-the-20th-century apartment building and turned it into the current hotel. It now provides first-class service and comfort to a clientele that includes lots of business travelers. Bedrooms are well upholstered and decorated with more formality than you might expect—in some cases, with Oriental carpets and a scattering of exposed timbers and beams under the eaves. Beds are especially comfortable, often with hypoallergenic coverings.

Bäckgatan 10, S-352 30 Växjö. ℂ **0470/72-28-00.** Fax 0470/72-28-08. www.firsthotels.com. 71 units. 896SEK–1,096SEK ($180–$190/£90–£110) double; 1,250SEK ($250/£125) suite. Rates include breakfast. AE, DC, MC, V. Parking 110SEK ($22/£11). **Amenities:** Restaurant; bar; gym; sauna; room service; laundry service; dry cleaning; nonsmoking rooms; rooms for those w/limited mobility. *In room:* TV, minibar, hair dryer, Wi-Fi.

Hotell Värend ★ (Finds) Under the management of the hardworking Wadsworth family, this hotel emerged from the premises of what was originally a four-unit apartment house in the 1890s. Richly renovated and upgraded, but with very few of its original architectural adornments, it lies just a 5-minute walk north of Växjö's main square, within a quiet residential neighborhood filled with private homes. Good-size bedrooms are well maintained, tasteful, and well insulated against the harsh winters of central Sweden—safe havens for a cost-effective night or two. The beds are very comfortable and the bathrooms, though small, are well maintained.

Kungsgatan 27, S-352 33 Växjö. ℂ **0470/77-67-00.** Fax 0470/362-61. www.hotellvarend.se. 24 units. July and Fri–Sat year-round 695SEK ($139/£70) double; rest of year 850SEK ($170/£85) double. Rates include breakfast. AE, DC, MC, V. Free parking. **Amenities:** Restaurant (breakfast only); nonsmoking rooms; 1 room for those w/limited mobility. *In room:* TV, Wi-Fi.

Royal Corner Hotell ★ You get predictably good comfort here and no surprises, but no excitement either. In other words, it's a standard, always-reliable choice. In the town center, this first-class hotel rises six floors, taller than any other structure in town. The view from the upper floors offers panoramic vistas of Småland. Built in 1985, the hotel—with its bedrooms outfitted with Nordic pieces and functional style—might remind you of a good American chain hotel. Rooms are only slightly larger than average, and bathrooms are small and clean.

Liedbergsgatan 11, S-352 32 Växjö. ℂ **800/780-7234** in the U.S., or 0470/70-10-00. Fax 0470/70-10-10. www.royalcorner.se. 158 units. Sun–Thurs 848SEK–1,565SEK ($170–$313/£85–£157) double; Fri–Sat 648SEK ($130/£65) double; daily 1,198SEK–1,895SEK ($240–$379/£120–£190) suite. AE, DC, MC V. Free parking outside, 120SEK ($24/£12) in garage. **Amenities:** Restaurant; bar; fitness center; Jacuzzi; sauna; room service; massage; laundry service; dry cleaning; nonsmoking rooms; rooms for those w/limited mobility. *In room:* A/C, TV, hair dryer, Wi-Fi.

Scandic Hotel Växjö (**Value**) It's little more than a roadside motel, but this is one of the best value hotels in the area. Built in 1979, the Scandic offers well-furnished bedrooms, including some large enough for families. Each room is fitted in bright pastel shades, with small but well-maintained bathrooms with tub/shower combinations. The hotel lies 3km (1³/₄ miles) west of the center of town on the road going to the airport.

Hejaregatan 19, S-352 46 Växjö. ⓒ **0470/73-60-00.** Fax 0470/73-60-11. www.scandichotels.com. 123 units. Sun–Thurs 1,150SEK–1,390SEK ($230–$278/£115–£139) double; Fri–Sat 750SEK–890SEK ($150–$178/£75–£89) double. Rates include breakfast. AE, DC, MC, V. Free parking. **Amenities:** Restaurant; bar; indoor heated pool; sauna; nonsmoking rooms; 1 room for those w/limited mobility. *In room:* TV, Wi-Fi.

WHERE TO DINE

Throughout the environs of Växjö and Orrefors, you'll find lots of separate and independent restaurant options. One of the most unique options involves an enduring dining tradition: This area is known for the age-old method of cooking fish, potatoes, and sausages in the cooling chambers of the glassworks. Inaugurated during an era when fuel was conserved with something approaching religious zeal, the tradition, known as *Hyttsill,* developed into a slow-cooking style that turned out simple, hearty, but succulent food, well suited to the hungry factory workers toiling in the cold.

This antique presentation is duplicated today as part of randomly scheduled evening entertainment provided by three of the region's biggest glassmakers. After the day's factory closings, usually around 3pm, trestle tables and simple chairs are carried onto the factory floor as a means of duplicating the simple communal meals of long ago. During the summer months, the large glassworks usually rotate the days and hours of their presentations.

Advance reservations are necessary, and per-person fees average 325SEK ($65/£33) for a full meal. The meals invariably include such traditional glassmakers' dishes as herring with cream and onions, roasted or baked potatoes (traditionally these were baked in the hot ashes produced as a byproduct of the firing process), pork sausages, mustard, bread and butter, local cheeses, and cheesecake.

As part of the package, the organizers of these events usually include live musical entertainment and demonstrations of glass blowing. Be warned in advance that this is very much a movable feast. Even during the peak of midsummer, there's likely to be only about three of them scheduled during any week; during the winter, they might occur only once a month as a specially arranged group event that individuals can attend if they reserve a spot in advance. To be certain of getting a place, phone each of the glassworks individually, or phone any of the tourist offices within the area, for information and confirmations. For reservations or information about meals served on the factory floor, call the **Kosta Glassworks** (ⓒ **0478/345-29**), or the **Orrefors Glassworks** (ⓒ **0481/340-00**).

Orrefors Inn ★ SWEDISH We like to dine here for an authentic "taste of Sweden." Set in the center of the cluster of glass factories that have always dominated the economy of Orrefors, this historic inn was established in 1898; today the wood-sided building and its four dining rooms remain very similar to the originals—the space calls to mind a rustic farmhouse. You'll dine on a menu that's unrelentingly Swedish and in many ways authentic to the cuisine that many locals remember from childhood. Menu items include grilled salmon or steak served on a wooden platter, Swedish meatballs with brown sauce and roasted potatoes, and local moose steak with forest mushrooms and boiled potatoes. Don't expect the grand or experimental cuisine you might find in Stockholm; instead, you'll get rib-sticking fare that can perk you up for a round of glass shopping at any of the nearby gift shops.

3 ALONG THE SHORES OF LAKE VÄTTERN ★★

This is Sweden's second largest lake and the fifth largest in Europe, measuring some 129km (80 miles) from north to south. The average depth of the lake is 38m (125 ft.) and the deepest measured depth, south of Visingsö, is 127m (417 ft.).

The lake is known for its sudden storms. At times, we've sailed on it and the waters were placid. But on one occasion a sudden storm arose, whipping the water into dangerously choppy waves and almost overturning our boat. That said, the inland lake, which once was a sea bay, is always great for angling. There are 28 different fish species remaining in its freshwater. Some of these species have lived here since the Ice Age, including the famous Vättern alpine char. There is also an array of pike, perch, and pikeperch, along with grayling, salmon, and brown trout.

When it comes to swimming, Lake Vättern has both a good and a bad reputation. On the one hand, not many inland lakes can offer such long, Riviera-like beaches with water that is virtually drinkable; on the other hand, its temperature varies greatly because of its depth—one day it's suitable for swimming, and the next day it's icy cold.

Jönköping (350km/217 miles southwest of Stockholm or 150km/93 miles northeast of Gothenburg) can serve as your gateway to Lake Vättern, especially if you're driving north from Småland. However, even more charming places can be found along the lake, especially the towns of Gränna and Vadstena, as well as Motala.

Following the eastern shore, E4 offers the most scenic route, providing panoramic vistas across the lake.

GRÄNNA ★

Gränna boasts great scenery, but it also suffers from some tacky tourist overlay. Because so many Swedish honeymooners have chosen Gränna for their wedding nights, it is even sometimes referred to as a "baby factory." The sugary nature is in keeping with the town, though. This is the place that invented peppermint candy, after all; the red-and-white candy sticks, or *Polkagris,* were first made here in 1859 by widow Amalia Eriksson.

Gränna was founded in 1652 by Count Per Brahe, one of the first Swedish counts to be governor of Finland. Nowadays it is mainly a summer town with boutiques, arts and crafts stalls, hot-air ballooning sites, and a harbor area with camping, bathing, and restaurants. In addition, it has great pears: Per Brahe encouraged the planting of pear orchards in the environs, and pears from Gränna are ranked as the finest in Scandinavia today.

To reach the lakeside town, head north from Jönköping along E4. After a distance of 40km (25 miles), you reach Gränna, which lies at a point 280km (174 miles) southwest of Stockholm and 230km (143 miles) east of Gothenburg. The town of Tranås lies 40km (25 miles) from Gränna and is on the main rail route between Stockholm and Malmö. From Tranås, several buses make the final run to Gränna.

You should head first for the **Gränna-Visingsö Turistbyrå,** Brahegatan 48 (© **0390/410-10;** www.grm.se/grm/turistinfo), open June to September daily 10am to 6pm. The rest of the year, hours are Monday to Friday 11am to 4pm. Once you tire of wandering the town's cobbled streets, lined with painted wooden houses, you can take a ferry across Gränna harbor to the island of Visingsö (see below).

Seeing the Sights

Grännaberger, or Gränna Mountain, can be reached either by car from the road between Gränna and Tranås or by climbing the steps that begin in a couple of places in town. At the top, you'll be rewarded with a fine view. If you're energetic, you can walk along a trail to **Skogstornet (Forest Tower),** from which you'll get a panoramic view of the area around Lake Vättern.

The Gränna area is a rich repository of Iron Age weapons, tools, *menhirs* (monoliths), and burial grounds, some 4,000 years old. Gränna was also the birthplace of the North Pole balloonist-explorer Salomon August Andrée, who made an ill-fated attempt in 1897 to cross the pole in the balloon *Ornen* ("Eagle"). The remains of the expedition were found in 1930 and can be seen in the **Andrée Museum,** Brahegatan 48 (✆ **0390/410-15;** www.grennamuseum.se). With funding by Alfred Nobel and King Oscar, the flight north toward the pole lasted only 3 days. The balloon was forced to make a landing on ice. After 6 weeks of trekking, Andrée and his men died, from either the cold or trichinosis, contracted when they ate raw meat from a polar bear they'd speared. Their frozen but well-preserved bodies and their equipment were discovered by a Norwegian sailing ship, and the artifacts of that trip are on display at this museum. **Museigården,** a part of the museum, houses exhibits illustrating the history of the area. The museum is open from mid-May to mid-September daily 10am to 6pm, from mid-September to mid-May daily 11am to 4pm. Admission is 50SEK ($10/£5) for adults, 30SEK ($6/£3) for students, and 20SEK ($4/£2) for children 7 to 15.

Nearby Visingsö Island ★★

The heyday of the offshore island of Visingsö, reached by ferry from Gränna Harbor, was in the 12th and 13th centuries. A journey to the island is for us an evocative trip back to the past. It's a chance to glimpse Sweden as it was before it joined the modern world.

This has been an important site since humans first set foot here some 6,000 years ago; large Viking-era graves indicate how busy the area once was. On the southern part of the island are the remains of Sweden's oldest secular building, **Näs Castle,** built around 1150. According to the Icelandic sagas, it had a large treasury and was an important target in the fighting between the eastern and western parts of southern Sweden in the Middle Ages. The castle burned down in 1319.

The remains of another castle, **Visingsborg,** are by the harbor. This was the seat of the Brahe family. The most illustrious member of the clan was Per Brahe (1520–90), Count of Visingsö. Brahe was one of Gustavus Vasa's privy councillors. The Brahe family also built the island's **parish church** in the 1680s, using the walls of the Stroja medieval church as the foundations. The tower and the door of the sacristy are from the old church; the door has old runic writing signifying that it was made in the 11th century. The church is baroque, which is unusual by Swedish standards. You can visit Count Brahe's reconstructed 17th-century garden here, too; there's no admission fee.

At the harbor near Visingsborg is **Kumlaby Church,** whose oldest parts date from the 12th century, though it also has some well-preserved 15th-century murals. Visitors can climb the tower to a small roof balcony, where they'll get a panoramic view of the island. The church is open only May to August daily from 10:30am to 5pm, charging an admission of 10SEK ($2/£1) adults, 5SEK ($1/50p) children 5 to 16 years old.

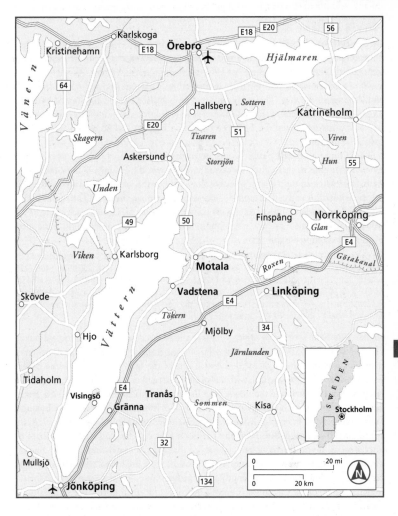

KALMAR & THE SOUTHEAST

9

ALONG THE SHORES OF LAKE VÄTTERN

A 20-minute ferry trip will take you from Gränna to the island of Visingsö, 6.5km (4 miles) across the water, for 50SEK ($10/£5) adults, 25SEK ($5/£2.50) children round-trip. Ferryboats leave every 20 minutes during the day in summer and eight times per day in winter. Boats depart from the central harbor at Gränna; for information, call ℂ **0390/410-25** or visit **www.visingso.net**. There's a tourist office (open during odd summer hours) near the point where the ferryboat docks.

The island is long but very narrow; it can be traversed by car in about 5 minutes. There are no road names or street numbers. In summer, some of the island residents meet arriving ferries with horse-drawn carriages for an excursion past the architectural highlights of the island. The cost is 90SEK ($18/£9) per adult, 45SEK ($9/£4.50) for children 6 to 16, for a 90-minute tour. There is no phone to call for information—it's all very casual.

Where to Stay & Dine

Hotel Gyllene Uttern ★   The Hotel Gyllene Uttern, or "Golden Otter," is this area's honeymoon Shangri-La, complete with a baroque wedding chapel in the basement. A step-gabled imitation castle built in 1937 overlooking Lake Vättern, 4km (2¹/₂ miles) south of Gränna on the highway (E4) to Stockholm, Gyllene Uttern offers the best food and lodgings in the area. The main dining room is highlighted by gilt-framed paintings (copies of great masters), medieval suits of armor, deeply set windows with views of the lake, and a bas-relief fireplace. Food is served to both guests and nonguests, and regional specialties are featured.

The dining room and public rooms are in the main building, which contains only nine guest rooms; the rest of the rooms are spread across the grounds in the annexes that were constructed in the 1960s. Note that the rooms in the (ca. 1930) main building are the most nostalgic and old-fashioned—and they will remain that way. The rooms within the two more modern annexes have more contemporary decor. Cabins, each crafted from wood in a rustic style, are available only in summer and contain the most basic (hot-plate-style) cooking equipment.

On E4, S-563 92 Gränna. © **0390/108-00.** Fax 0390/418-80. www.gylleneuttern.hotelgroup.com. 52 units, 6 cabins. Sun–Thurs 1,465SEK–1,780SEK ($293–$356/£147–£178) double, 2,250SEK ($450/£225) suite; Fri–Sat 1,255SEK–1,788SEK ($251–$358/£126–£179) double, 2,250SEK ($450/£225) suite; 800SEK–4,000SEK ($160–$800/£80–£400) cabin (available in summer). AE, DC, MC, V. Free parking. **Amenities:** Restaurant; bar; sauna; room service; laundry service; dry cleaning; nonsmoking rooms; rooms for those w/limited mobility. *In room:* TV, hair dryer, Wi-Fi.

Hotell Västanå Slott ★★ (Finds)   This is one of Sweden's most romantic old inns, a very special place that's long been a favorite of ours. Although there are dozens of stately manors scattered throughout Sweden, this is one of the few that is open to the public. Formal and rigidly symmetrical, with a neoclassical design and a red-tile roof, it was built in 1590 and by 1641 was the power base for what eventually became the Vasa family dynasty. Ironically, the building was rendered smaller (not larger) during two subsequent renovations. In 1770, parts of its original roof were demolished and rebuilt; in 1928, the entire third floor was pulled down and the castle achieved the design aesthetic that's on display today. If you overnight here, be warned that to some extent you'll be invading the much-treasured precincts of what some still consider a private home. Bedrooms are high-ceilinged, spacious reminders of another era, with antiques, good carpets, and dramatic, sometimes allegorical paintings; however, they lack the usual amenities. Public rooms include suits of armor, frescoed ceilings, and historic mementos. No meals are served other than breakfast, but a nearby 18-hole golf course, where greens fees cost 150SEK to 350SEK ($30–$70/£15–£35), maintains a clubhouse where robust platters of food are served at both lunch and dinner every day. There's a tennis court within a short walk of the historic castle.

S-563-92 Gränna. © **0390/107-00.** Fax 0390/418-75. www.vastanaslott.se. 20 units. 1,490SEK–2,090SEK ($298–$418/£149–£209) double. MC, V. Closed Jan–Apr. Free parking. **Amenities:** Restaurant; laundry service; dry cleaning; nonsmoking rooms; rooms for those w/limited mobility, Wi-Fi in lobby. *In room:* No phone.

VADSTENA ★

In this hometown of St. Birgitta (1303–73), patron saint of Sweden, the Middle Ages never died. The world has long passed by this sleepy former pilgrimage center—and that's precisely why we love it. An evocative town, filled with narrow streets and medieval buildings, Vadstena enjoys a lakeside setting on the eastern shore of Lake Vättern. It's the most nostalgic stop along the Göta Canal—far less touristy than Gränna.

St. Birgitta's convent and church were once known far and wide, and pilgrims thronged to see the saint's relics. King Gustav Vasa was a regular visitor in the 16th century and built the famous Vadstena castle. In fact, there was a royal palace in Vadstena as early as the 13th century, when Birgitta was a lady-in-waiting, before she went on to found the convent. Today there are still Sisters of St. Birgitta at Vadstena Convent. Vadstena is also known all over Sweden for its handmade lace—to see samples of this delicate product, walk along Stora Gatan, the main street.

Vadstena lies 256km (159 miles) southwest of Stockholm, 260km (162 miles) northeast of Gothenburg, and 60km (37 miles) north of Gränna. From the last stopover at Gränna, continue north along E4 until you reach the junction with Route 50, at which point you veer off the main highway and continue along 50 until you reach Vadstena. Bus no. 840 runs daily from Jönköping, and bus no. 855 departs from the Central Station in Stockholm, but only on Friday and Sunday. If you're driving here from Stockholm, take E4 southwest; at the junction of Route 206, head northwest.

The tourist bureau, **Vadstena Turistbyrå,** is located in Vadstena Castle, S-592 80 Vadstena (✆ **0143/315-70;** www.vadstena.se). The bureau is open daily 10am to 6pm from June to September; off season hours usually are daily 11am to 4pm.

Seeing the Sights

Vadstena Abbey ★★★
You'll learn a lot about St. Birgitta (Bridget) of Sweden during a visit here, notably that she married at the age of 13 and gave birth to eight children, so she's hardly a nun. Inside you can see a red velvet box that holds her bones, and the abbey still has the coffin in which she was returned from Rome. We think the 15th-century statue of her, located near the altar, looks a lot like the Madonna (no, not that one).

Built between the mid-14th and mid-15th centuries to specifications outlined by Bridget, this Gothic church is rich in medieval art. Parts of the abbey date from 1250. The abbey housed the nuns of St. Birgitta's order until their expulsion in 1595.

The New Monastery and Church, built in 1973, show the same traditional simplicity St. Birgitta prescribed for her order. The view to the huge windows is the only decoration in this otherwise stark church. The nuns, who returned to Sweden in 1963, will show the church and their guesthouse to interested visitors at times convenient to their own schedule. It's a 3-minute walk from Stora Torget.

Grasgatan 31. ✆ **0143/298-50.** Free admission. May and Sept daily 9am–5pm; June and Aug daily 9am–7pm; July daily 9am–8pm; Oct–Apr Mon–Sat 9am–3pm, Sun 11am–1pm.

Vadstena Castle
Founded in 1545 by Gustavus Vasa, king of Sweden, but not completed until 1620, this is one of the most splendid Vasa castles, erected in Renaissance style during a period of national expansion. It dominates the town from its position on the lake, just behind the old courthouse on the south end. Vadstena was last inhabited by royalty in 1715 and was restored in the 19th century. Since 1899, the greater part of the castle has been used for provincial archives.

Slottsvägen. ✆ **0143/315-70.** Admission 55SEK ($11/£5.50) adults, 10SEK ($2/£1) children 7–15, free for children under 7. June–Aug daily 11am–4pm; Sept–May Mon–Fri 11am–4pm.

Starby Kungsgård ★★ As an estate, this place dates from the 1200s, when it was known for the fertility of its soil and its feudal prestige. In 1520, Swedish king Gustav Vasa added it to his roster of houses and castles, thereby beginning a fashion: Members of the royal family and members of their entourage (including the legendary courtesan Hedwig Eleanora) would drop in to the king's residences for rest and relaxation. The building as you see it today, which lies less than a kilometer (about ¹/₂ mile) south of the town center, dates mostly from the late 1800s, except for wings built in 1984 that contain most of the establishment's bedrooms. Each of these is furnished with sleek, functional furniture and done up in pastel colors, with small bathrooms. Some of the big attractions are the indoor swimming pool, the health club, and the **Valven** restaurant, which is recommended separately below.

Ödeshögsvägen, S-592 30 Vadstena. ℭ **0143/751-00.** Fax 0143/751-70. www.starbgkungsgard.se. 61 units. 1,395SEK ($279/£140) double. Rates include breakfast. AE, DC, MC, V. Free parking. **Amenities:** Restaurant; bar; spa; Jacuzzi; sauna; nonsmoking rooms; rooms for those w/limited mobility. *In room:* TV, Wi-Fi.

Vadstena Klosterhotellet ★ (Finds) What once was the premier religious stronghold in Sweden has been transformed into a hotel and conference center that welcomes individuals (and occasional church and civil groups) into its sprawling and echoing medieval premises. Set adjacent to the abbey church, about 640m (2,100 ft.) from Vadstena Castle, it's contained within one wing of an *L*-shape building that was constructed in the 12th century as a convent. The remainder of the building—which includes 59 nuns' cells and the longest triple-barrel vault (57m/187 ft. long) in northern Sweden—can be explored without hindrance.

Accommodations are severely dignified and deliberately spartan-looking, with dark-stained copies of furniture inspired by medieval models, stark white walls—which gives a vague sense of their original anything-but-plush function as lodgings for penitents. They are nonetheless comfortable, with high ceilings and simple, small, but adequate bathrooms. Rooms that overlook the lake are at the high end of the price spectrum; units fronting the town and forest are at the low end.

Klosterområdet, S-592 00 Vadstena. ℭ **0143/315-30.** Fax 0143/136-48. www.klosterhotel.se. 70 units. 1,595SEK–1,695SEK ($319–$339/£160–£170) double; 2,700SEK ($540/£270) suite. Rates include breakfast. AE, DC, MC, V. Free parking. **Amenities:** 2 restaurants; bar; sauna; laundry service; dry cleaning; nonsmoking rooms; rooms for those w/limited mobility. *In room:* TV, Wi-Fi.

Where to Dine

Rådhuskällaren (Value) SWEDISH If St. Birgitta were to return to earth today, she probably wouldn't be surprised by this longtime favorite. First of all, a meal here affords the opportunity to visit the interior of the oldest courthouse and town hall in Sweden—the restaurant lies within an early-14th-century cellar, beneath vaulted ceilings and above medieval flagstone floors. Second, menu items are rib-sticking, substantial fare designed to ward off the cold of a Swedish winter. Examples include such staples as roasted beef with horseradish sauce, fried filets of codfish with dill sauce and boiled potatoes, tenderloin of pork with mushrooms in cream and béarnaise sauce, poached filet of lemon sole with an asparagus and leek ragout, and halibut steak with horseradish sauce. Dessert might be a slice of warm chocolate cake with elderflower ice cream.

Rådhustorget. ℭ **0143/121-70.** www.radhuskallaren.com. Reservations recommended. Main courses 119SEK–195SEK ($23–$39/£12–£20). AE, DC, MC, V. Sun–Tues noon–10pm; Wed–Fri noon–1am; Sat noon–2am.

Valven ★ SWEDISH/INTERNATIONAL This is the best place to eat in town. Set beside Vadstena's busiest commercial thoroughfare, the restaurant occupies a series of vaulted stone rooms that originally were built in the 15th century by the local church. Today the place is warmly illuminated, partially by candlelight, and maintained as the showcase restaurant of the also-recommended **Starby Kungsgård Hotel,** which lies within a 5-minute walk to the south. Regardless of where you sit, a staff member will hand you two different menus, the simpler of which contains dishes such as cheese platters, steaks, salads, sandwiches, and grilled chicken with herb sauce. The more elaborate menu offers a more upscale and finely honed cuisine, including grilled turbot with saffron sauce, tournedos with pepper sauce, smoked filet of reindeer, and bouillabaisse. Dessert might include a gratin of chocolate with forest berries and homemade ice cream.

Storgatan 18. © **0143/123-40.** www.valven.se. Reservations recommended. Main courses on bistro menu 105SEK–135SEK ($21–$27/£11–£14); main courses on "restaurant menu" 205SEK–285SEK ($41–$57/£21–£29). AE, DC, MC, V. Mon–Thurs 11:30am–2pm and 6–9pm; Fri 11:30am–10pm; Sat noon–10pm; Sun noon–8pm.

MOTALA

Before reaching Stockholm, Göta Canal cruises go to Motala. And before reaching the canal, waters of the lake go to a flight of five locks, a dramatic sight that makes Motala one of the highlights of the Göta Canal cruises. Motala was designed by Baltzar von Platen, one of the waterway's creators, and he remains a popular local hero. His grave and statue lie side by side on the canal sidewalk.

On the eastern shore of Lake Vättern, a stone's throw from the Göta Canal, Motala is called the "bicycle town," as it contains 50km (31 miles) of designated bicycle paths, which many local residents use year-round. Every June sees the running of the world's largest bicycle exercise race around Lake Vättern. The town lies 210km (130 miles) southwest of Stockholm, 472km (293 miles) northeast of Helsingborg, and 263km (163 miles) northeast of Gothenburg.

From Vadstena, continue north along Route 8, with Lake Vättern on your right, and you'll come to Motala after a drive of 13km (8 miles). If you're not driving, you can take bus no. 16, which runs along the eastern side of Lake Vättern.

For information about Motala and the surrounding area, call the **Motala Turistbyrå,** Hamnen (© **0141/22-52-54;** www.motala.se), open June to August Monday to Friday and Sunday 10am to 6pm, Saturday 10am to 3pm. Off-season hours are Monday to Friday 9am to 5pm.

Seeing the Sights

Motala is rather bland but makes an excellent center for exploring nearby attractions. It also boasts outdoorsy options, the best of which is cycling. Bikes can be rented at the tourist office kiosk down by the harbor from June to mid-August daily from 9am to noon and 4 to 8pm, for 100SEK ($20/£10) per day.

Another good bet is the boat trip along the canal to Borensberg, 20km (12 miles) east of Motala. In summer, this 5-hour trip leaves Motala at 10:30am and costs 300SEK ($60/£30) round-trip, 240SEK ($48/£24) one-way.

Varamon Beach lies just 3km (1¾ miles) east of town. The beach offers a kilometer (⅔ mile) of golden sand, making it one of Scandinavia's largest inland bathing beaches. It has the warmest waters in Lake Vättern (which isn't saying much), and the sand is often thick with milk-white bodies soaking up the summer sun. It's also a venue for windsurfing. Locals like to call Varamon their "Riviera of Lake Vättern."

Motala has some museums, but all are of only minor interest. The best is the **Motala Motor Museum** (ℂ **0141/588-88;** www.motala-motormuseum.se), lying at the edge of the harbor. Cars of various eras are intriguingly exhibited here—for example, parked outside an Esso Station. All the vintage cars displayed in the showrooms are kept in mint condition. Admission is 50SEK ($10/£5) adults, 40SEK ($8/£4) students, 30SEK ($6/£3) children 7 to 15. Hours are May to September daily 10am to 6pm; October to April Monday to Friday 8am to 4pm, Saturday and Sunday 11am to 5pm.

Where to Stay

Best Western Motala Stadshotell ★   The most highly recommended and most prestigious hotel in town was originally built in 1880 in a location adjacent to Stora Torget (the town's main square) and enlarged in 1923. Rising four floors, with access to a beautiful garden that's centered on a circular reflecting pool, it offers a traditional, consciously upscale decor. For example, dozens of yards of fabric are sewn into the most elaborate draperies in town, and the furnishings are mostly Chippendale or Queen Anne in the public areas. The sense of plush, well-heeled bourgeoisie taste also comes through in the architectural adornments, such as in the ceiling friezes showing cherubs cavorting across vineyards, which are surrounded by formal, usually neoclassical moldings. Bedrooms have high ceilings, austere furnishings, thick carpets, and small but very efficient bathrooms with showers.

Stora Torget, Box 19, S-591 21 Motala. ℂ **800/780-7234** or 0141/21-64-00. Fax 0141/21-46-05. www. motalastadshotell.com. 78 units. Mid-June to mid-Aug and Fri–Sat year-round 900SEK–1,150SEK ($180–$230/£90–£115) double; rest of year 1,150SEK–1,350SEK ($230–$270/£115–£135) double; year-round 3,750SEK ($750/£375) suite. Rates include breakfast. AE, DC, MC, V. Parking 75SEK ($15/£7.50). **Amenities:** Restaurant; bar; sauna; room service; laundry service; dry cleaning; nonsmoking rooms; 1 room for those w/limited mobility; solarium. *In room:* TV, minibar, fridge, coffeemaker, hair dryer, safe, Wi-Fi.

Hotel M   Set within the heart of Motala and favored by business travelers from Germany, France, the United Kingdom, and the United States, this three-story hotel is a well-managed place that was originally built in 1964. Throughout, you'll find a bland but comfortable kind of international modernity, especially in the bedrooms. But even the older members of your management team will feel comfortable in their rooms, amid the wall-to-wall carpeting, frilly curtains, well-padded beds, and writing tables. The more expensive rooms are labeled "Business Class" and are larger and more inviting.

Kungsgatan 1, S-591 30 Motala. ℂ **0141/21-66-60.** Fax 0141/572-21. www.hotelm.se. 55 units. Mid-June to Aug and Fri–Sat year-round 1,040SEK ($208/£104) double; rest of year 1,450SEK ($290/£145) double; year-round 2,200SEK ($440/£220) suite with Jacuzzi. Rates include breakfast. AE, DC, MC, V. Parking: 75SEK ($15/£7.50). Closed Oct–May. **Amenities:** Bar; sauna; laundry service; dry cleaning; nonsmoking rooms; rooms for those w/limited mobility. *In room:* TV, hair dryer, iron, Wi-Fi.

Where to Dine

Harry's Pub ★ SWEDISH/CONTINENTAL   The local favorite for food and drink is this pub installed in the **Best Western Motala Standshotell** (see above). The location is adjacent to the Stora Torget (the town's main square). There has been a restaurant of some sort on this site since 1880. The well-prepared food is based, whenever possible, on local ingredients. In fall you might encounter venison, pheasant, and grouse. A year-round delicacy is freshwater char from the nearby lakes. The menu changes frequently but count on fresh salmon or tasty and tender beef dishes. (Most locals request them with a Béarnaise sauce.) If you're homesick for America, you might even try the spare ribs with coleslaw.

ÖREBRO

Örebro is a bit of a wallflower town compared to the more popular destinations in the area, such as Vadstena. But there are rewards here for those willing to seek them out. The town lies 60km (37 miles) north of Lake Vättern and is strategically located on the main route from southwest Sweden to the capital city of Stockholm. Sweden's sixth most populous city, it borders the shores of Lake Hjälmaren, the fourth largest lake in the country.

Its castle, Örebro Slott (see below), is one of the most famous in Sweden; it also lies at the River Svartån, which is studded with waterlilies in summer. To the immediate west of the town center is **Lake Tysslingen,** which is best reached by bike. Many birders come here to view the lake in the spring when thousands upon thousands of whooper swans temporarily settle on the way to Finland from their winter retreats.

Motorists departing from our last stopover at Motala can continue north along Route 50 until they reach the junction with E3, an express highway that will carry them north into the center of Örebro.

You can also visit Örebro directly on a main east–west train from Stockholm (trip time: 2 hr.). For information about the town, contact the visitor center, **Destination Örebro,** Slottet (in the castle; ℰ **019/21-21-21**). It is open June to August Monday to Friday 10am to 6pm, Saturday and Sunday 10am to 4pm. Off-season hours are Monday to Friday 10am to 6pm, Saturday and Sunday from 10am to 2pm.

Exploring the Area

We suggest you take a bike ride out to **Lake Tysslingen;** you can rent a bike at **Service-centralen,** Hamnplan (ℰ **019/21-19-09**), for 70SEK ($14/£7) per day, 300SEK ($60/£30) weekly. Or, instead of riding around the water, you can sail over it; the tourist office (see above) can provide information about boat tours of **Lake Hjälmaren** on either the M/S *Linna* or the M/S *Gustav Lagerfbjelke.* A 3-hour boat cruise costs 350SEK ($70/£35) round-trip.

The town's major attraction is **Örebro Slott** (ℰ **019/21-21-21**; www.orebro.seslottet), a castle that for more than 700 years has kept a watchful eye on everyone crossing the bridge over the River Svartån. (The castle lies on an island in the Svartån and dominates the town.) The oldest part of the castle, a defensive tower, was erected in the latter half of the 13th century. The tower was expanded in the 14th century to make an even larger stronghold. Over the years, the whole thing has been restored, and then restored again. Today it has a grand, romantic exterior, although not much remains inside. There is no original furniture, and much of the interior is used for county offices. Nevertheless, tour guides valiantly struggle to re-create the romance and lore of the *slott* (castle). The beamed **Rikssalen,** or Parliament Hall, remodeled in 1927, has several portraits, notably those of Karl XI and his family; if you're wondering why their eyes are bulging, that's because of the arsenic used to whiten their faces. The newly organized **Slottsmuseet** functions as a county museum, displaying the saga of the county since the days of the Stone Age. From May to September only, guided tours in English are conducted daily at 2pm, costing 50SEK ($10/£5) per person.

Beautifully situated on the banks of the Svartån in the center of Örebro is the little, wooden, open-air village of **Wadköping** (ℰ **019/21-62-20**). The village consists of a collection of ancient buildings—18th-century timbered structures in traditional barn red, and lovely, bright 19th-century wooden houses—from Örebro and the surrounding countryside, all moved to this site in the **Stadsparfken** (city park) in 1965. Nowadays, Wadköping is a thriving community with a cafe, craftspeople at work, shops, some minor museums, exhibitions, a theater, and puppet shows. The entire area can be visited May to August Tuesday to Sunday from 11am to 5pm, September to April Tuesday to Sunday from 11am to 4pm. Admission is free.

The major church in town is **St. Nicolai Kyrka,** Stortorget (© 019/12-40-25), dating from 1260 and standing on the main square of Örebro. It was extensively restored in the 1860s, so little of its former medieval character remains. The church is a frequent venue for temporary art exhibitions. It was here in 1810 that Jean Baptiste Bernadotte, Napoleon's marshal, was elected successor to the Swedish throne.

Shopping

If you're interested in Swedish handicrafts, the finest outlet along Lake Vättern is **Konsthantverkarna ★**, Järntorgsgatan 2 (© 019/10-79-05), a shop in central Örebro run by professional craft workers. No junk is allowed here, and the crafts are not only well made but charming; they are ideal for gifts and souvenirs.

Where to Stay

Best Western City Hotel   Now part of the Best Western worldwide family of hotels, this fine address has received a complete overhaul. Though the town-center hotel doesn't escape the angular, brick-and-stucco facade its six floors were given when it was built in 1985, added glamour now comes from the parquet floors and the sleek, contemporary furniture. The hotel does a thriving trade with business travelers, but is a suitable choice for the casual visitor intent on sightseeing. All the midsize bedrooms are comfortably furnished and maintained, each with modern bathrooms. We've found the staff to be cheerful and cooperative, but, even so, it's not the equal of the Scandic Grand (see below).

Kungsgatan 24, S-702 24 Örebro. © **019/601-42-00.** Fax 019/601-42-09. www.bestwestern.com. 85 units. July to mid-Aug and Fri–Sat year-round 890SEK ($178/£89) double; rest of year 1,495SEK ($299/£150) double. Rates include breakfast. AE, DC, MC, V. Parking 130SEK ($26/£13) per day in nearby public garage. **Amenities:** Exercise room; sauna; laundry service; dry cleaning; nonsmoking rooms; rooms for those w/limited mobility. *In room:* TV, minibar, beverage maker, hair dryer, safe, Wi-Fi.

Scandic Grand Hotel ★   A seven-story structure erected in the mid-1980s in the center of town, this hotel provides well-maintained accommodations and a thoroughly international and modern style. Despite an upscale decor that includes lots of hardwood panels, marble floors, and a dramatic modern staircase within the lobby, the well-trained staff exudes warmth. Bedrooms contain aspects that evoke a living room in a comfortably contemporary home, partly because of the occasional sofa and, in some cases, reproductions of Turkish or Persian carpets.

Fabriksgatan 21–23, Box 8112, S-700 23 Örebro. © **019/767-43-00.** Fax 0191/767-43-11. www.scandic hotels.com. 221 units. Mid-June to mid-Aug and Fri–Sat year-round 990SEK ($198/£99) double; rest of year 1,040SEK–1,590SEK ($208–$318/£104–£159) double; year-round 1,790SEK–2,390SEK ($358–$478/£179–£239) suite. Rates include breakfast. AE, DC, MC, V. Parking 150SEK ($30/£15). **Amenities:** 3 restaurants; bar; exercise room; Jacuzzi; sauna; room service; laundry service; dry cleaning; nonsmoking rooms; rooms for those w/limited mobility. *In room:* TV, hair dryer, iron, Wi-Fi.

10

The Baltic Islands: Öland & Gotland

We suspect that Sweden would like to keep its Baltic islands, Öland and Gotland, to itself. Each summer, the number of Swedish visitors there reaches almost a million, and for good reason. The islands boast the sort of charming beaches and natural beauty that attract tourists.

Although Öland attracts so many vacationers, life there wasn't always so friendly. Islanders who could not make a living emigrated to America in greater numbers than in any other province in Sweden. Many of the American tourists visiting Öland today are the descendents of those Swedes, returning to see where their great-grandparents came from. But you don't necessarily have to come from Öland to enjoy its beauty and its beaches. Just ask the royal family, who use the island as their vacation retreat.

Called the "island of sun and winds," Öland is Sweden's sunniest province. It is know for its family-friendly, shallow, crystal-clear waters, and for its luxuriant vegetation. Many plants aren't found in any other Scandinavian country, including a profusion of orchids, some 34 species in all. Öland is also a land steeped in prehistoric times. There are plants here from Iberia, the Alps, and eastern Europe that survived the Ice Age and the warmer postglacial period. Remains from 4,000-year-old burial chambers can even be seen, as well as many runic stones from the Viking era.

Two hundred years ago, a British visitor called Ölanders "the Italians of the north," suggesting a more extroverted streak than mainland Swedes. After a visit, you can decide that for yourself. Today the inhabitants of Öland make their living mainly from agriculture, fishing, food production, industry, and tourism. The hub of the flat, rural Baltic island, connected to southern Sweden by one of the longest bridges in Europe, is **Borgholm,** the capital, a small resort with a recreational harbor on the west coast.

As fascinating as Öland is, we recommend touring Gotland, particularly its ancient capital of Visby, if you have time to visit only one island. Because the climate is milder in Gotland than in the rest of Sweden, the scenery here offers a wide variety of flora and fauna, as well as a unique landscape of statuesque limestone formations, cliffs, forests, heaths, and meadows.

In Gotland, some 1,000 farms dating from the Viking era—and medieval times in general—are still in use today. (In Viking times, Gotland was the gateway to Sweden and the scene of many a battle.) Off the coast of Gotland lie several other islands. Farthest to the north is **Gotska Sandön,** a place of myths and legends and the stronghold of Sweden's last pirates. Just a stone's throw off the north coast lies **Fårö,** familiar to many as a once-favorite retreat of Olof Palme, Ingmar Bergman, and other political and cultural personalities. To the west, the twin **Lilla and Stora Karlsö** islands are known for their huge colonies of guillemots and other seabirds.

If you don't have time to absorb all of that, at least check out **Visby,** the capital city. It's surrounded by well-preserved medieval walls, the finest in Scandinavia. Some 2,000 citizens live within these walls today. Once a Viking trading station, Visby developed into a leading commercial center for trade across the Baltic Sea in the 12th century. In time it became one of the most important cities of the Hanseatic League. The city grew and prospered, as the remaining 13 ruined churches, 2 monasteries, cathedral, and 200 buildings resting on medieval foundations attest to today.

1 ÖLAND ★

40km (25 miles) E of Kalmar, 470km (292 miles) S of Stockholm

When we first arrived in Öland long ago, we wondered why so many Swedes left it for America. Obviously, life in the 1800s was rough here, and locals simply could not make a living, so they set out for such places as the Dakotas and Minnesota, states in America they found closer to their own style of living, at least in climate. During that mass exodus in the 19th century, the Baltic island lost a quarter of its population. Many émigrés, however, returned here to retire. That's not surprising, considering how beautiful it is, with its sandy beaches, its treeless *alvaret* (steppe) covered with wildflowers, its bird life, and its profusion of windmills silhouetted against the summer sky.

One of Europe's longest bridges, nearly 6.5km (4 miles) long, connects Kalmar with Öland. At 140km (87 miles) long and 16km (10 miles) wide, this is Sweden's second largest island but its smallest province. Beaches run along both coasts, and there is only one town, Borgholm, a summer retreat. The royal summer residence is at Solliden. To rent a summer house on the beach, get in touch with the tourist office (see below).

ESSENTIALS

GETTING THERE **By Plane** The nearest airport is at Kalmar. From the Kalmar airport, take the Flygbuss to the center of Kalmar, then transfer to bus 101 or 106 for the 40-minute ride across the bridge to the center of Borgholm on Öland. The cost of that ride is 65SEK ($13/£6.50) each way, per person. For a timetable of the buses across the bridge, click on www.klt.se.

By Bus Buses run from the Kalmar terminal to Borgholm on Öland in less than an hour; take no. 101 or 106. Bus transits within Öland cost from 18SEK to 91SEK ($3.60–$18/£1.80–£9.10), depending on the distance traveled. Call ✆ **0200/218-18** (only within Sweden).

By Car From Kalmar, take the bridge over the sound, then turn left onto Route 136 to reach Borgholm.

VISITOR INFORMATION Go to the **Ölands Tourist,** ABSE-386-21, Färjestaden (✆ **0485/56-06-00;** www.olandsturist.se), at the Öland end of the famous 6.5km (4-mile) bridge to Kalmar. It's open January 8 to April Monday to Friday 9am to 5pm; May to June Monday to Friday 9am to 6pm, Saturday 9am to 4pm, and Sunday 10am to 4pm; July to August 6 Monday to Friday 9am to 7pm, Saturday 9am to 6pm, and Sunday 10am to 5pm; August 7 to August 20 Monday to Friday 9am to 6pm, Saturday 9am to 4pm, and Sunday 10am to 4pm; August 21 to August 31 Monday to Friday 9am to 5pm, Saturday 9am to 4pm, and Sunday 10am to 4pm; September Monday to Friday 9am to 5pm and Saturday 10am to 4pm; October to December Monday to Friday 9am to 5pm.

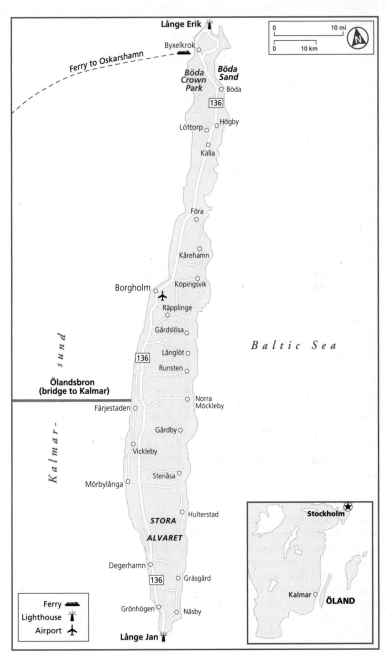

BIKING Öland is a great cycling country. Although there are Olympic-style athletes who bike the entire 129km (80-mile) stretch of the island, others are less ambitious. Whatever your cycling plans, you'll find seemingly endless cycle tracks along flat roads.

Bike rentals—usually summer-only concession stands—are available near the point where the ferryboat will deposit you from the Swedish mainland.

GOLFING **Ekerum Golf Course,** Ekerum, S-387-92 Borgholm (✆ **0485/800-00;** www.ecs.net), is 16km (10 miles) south of Borgholm, surrounded by the rolling lushness of an isolated region near the island's center. This course was created in 1991 as part of the Sunwing Ekerem Hotel. It's open April to November. Driving ranges lie between verdant forests and rolling fields. It charges greens fees of between 295SEK and 440SEK ($59–$88/£30–£44) per day, depending on the season. You can choose from an 18-hole course and a 9-hole course that lies immediately adjacent.

SEEING THE SIGHTS
A Prehistoric Village

Eketorp Ring-Fort ★★★ We've crossed deserts to see ruins, only to find a few stones—but this site is actually impressive. They've reconstructed a large selection of the massive wall that encircled this ring-fort, along with Iron Age houses within the walls, to give you a sense of how a fortified village looked in its heyday. Built inside of a ring-shaped enclosure for defensive purposes, the site is the only rebuilt prehistoric fort in Scandinavia. It's on the island's extreme southern tip, 35km (22 miles) south of Mörbylånga, rising starkly from a treeless landscape of steppelike tundra.

Eketorp is one of 15 known prehistoric forts on the island. Excavations have shown three phases of settlement here from A.D. 300 to 1300. You can see dwellings, cattle byres, and storehouses reconstructed using ancient crafts and materials, as well as species of livestock. Objects found in the excavations include simple tools, skillfully crafted jewelry, and weapons. The best of these finds are exhibited in a museum inside the fort wall, but don't expect to be overwhelmed. After all, these were primitive times. When you arrive on the island, ask about the "reenactment days," when men and women dress up in medieval garb and go through the motions of daily life as it was back then.

Degerhamn. ✆ 0485/66-20-00. Admission 50SEK–70SEK ($10–$14/£5–£7) adults, 20SEK–30SEK ($4–$6/£2–£3) children 7–14. May 1–July 2 daily 10am–4pm; July 3–Aug 20 daily 10am–6pm; Aug 21–Sept 3 daily 10am–4pm. Unless you have a car, getting here is tricky, although 5 buses a day (no. 103) come here from the Mörbylånga bus station. 2 buses make the run on Sat and only 1 on Sun. Check with the tourist office (see above) for bus timetables.

In Borgholm

About the most impressive sight we ever viewed in this capital of Öland was the royal family walking the streets on a shopping expedition. (They have a summer home nearby at **Solliden,** described below, to which they did not invite us.)

Borgholm used to be an important Baltic trading post, and we're certain it was far more intriguing in those days than today. Now it's extremely overcrowded during the month of July, when tourists, mainly the Swedes themselves, overrun its bars, cafes, and pizzerias. At that time it takes on a carnival atmosphere (later settling down for a long winter's nap). Unless you're in the market for a pink plastic alligator or perhaps an ice-cream cone, we suggest you spend little time in this touristy place and seek out the beauty of the island itself.

If you see anything inside the city, make it Borgholms Slott, Borgham's greatest attraction (see below). Just to the north of the town center of Borgholm you can also visit the ruins of **Blårör** (no phone), the island's largest Bronze Age cairn, although there isn't much to look at today. When it was discovered in 1849, the tomb in its center had already been plundered by grave robbers. In 1920, four more tombs were discovered, but they too had been plundered. What remains are a few sunken granite stones. This site is mainly for serious archaeologists.

Borgholms Slott ★★ These evocative ruins are some of the most beautiful in Scandinavia. We've often stood here for an hour just taking in the eerie beauty of this setting at the top of the sheer, steep face of the Landborg Cliffs, just southwest of the center of Borgholm. As the keeper of the castle told us, "Strolling through the ruins is like thumbing through the pages of a history book covering 8 centuries."

In the Middle Ages, this was one of Sweden's major royal castles and was a center of intrigue and endless battles. Subject to frequent attacks, it guarded the sound and was Sweden's southernmost outpost against Denmark. The castle was partially destroyed during the Kalmar War (1611–13). King Karl X Gustav ordered that the castle be restored and turned into a baroque palace, but building was interrupted in 1709 because of a cash shortage. In 1806, fire reduced the palace to its present ruins. Remains of the original fortified circular tower can still be seen in the northwest corner of the inner courtyard.

We like to attend summer concerts here—called "Music in the Ruins"—and there's also a nature reserve nearby good for wandering. From late June through mid-August, children's activities are scheduled.

Lying only a short walk south is the royal family's Italian-style villa, **Solliden,** which they use as their residence in summer. This white palace was built between 1903 and 1906 by Queen Victoria of Sweden. Their home is off-limits, but you can stroll through Solliden Park (see below), the gardens of the villa.

Borgholm. ✆ **0485/123-33.** www.borgholmsslott.se. Admission 50SEK ($10/£5) adults, 20SEK ($4/£2) ages 12–18, free for children under 12. May–Aug daily 10am–6pm; Apr and Sept daily 10am–4pm. To get there, you can walk to a nature reserve signposted from the center of Borgholm. By car, take the first exit south of Rte. 136.

Solliden Park ★★ These formal gardens surround the most famous "summer house" in Sweden. The present king, Carl Gustaf, inherited the mansion from his great-grandfather, Gustaf V, who died in 1950. (We've been told that the man in dirty coveralls who you might mistake for a gardener could be the king himself.) Although you can't go into Solliden Palace itself, you can stroll through the royal family's gardens, which were originally conceived by Sweden's Queen Victoria (not that other monarch in London). The grounds are exceptionally beautiful, especially in late June and July when they're in full bloom. Exhibitions about Swedish royalty are housed in a new pavilion, which also contains a gift shop. On-site is a creperie selling ice cream, crepes, and drinks.

2.5km (1½ miles) south of the center of Borgholm. ✆ **0485/153-56.** www.sollidensslott.se. Admission 65SEK ($13/£6.50) adults, 45SEK ($9/£4.50) students, 35SEK ($7/£3.50) children 7–17, free for children under 7. May 15–Sept 15 daily 11am–6pm.

In Central Öland

Frankly, we prefer to stick to Öland's coastline, as it's more scenic. But if you have an afternoon to spare, you might go inland to visit the well-preserved village of Himmelsberga, now an open-air museum (see below). It's worth the effort to reach it.

(Finds) The Blue Maiden ★★

Off the west coast of Öland lies one of the most remote and "forgotten" islands of the Baltic, **Blå Jungfrun,** whose name translates to the "Blue Maiden." It rises high above the Kalmar Straits, 127m (417 ft.) above the sea bed and 450m (1,476 ft.) above sea level. Inhabited only by colonies of birds and wildlife, it's noteworthy for its bare, windswept cliffs; slabs of red granite; and thousands of rocky outcroppings. To us, it's more of a rock spur than an island, measuring less than 1.5km (1 mile) long and less than a kilometer (¹/₂ mile) wide, covering an area of about 65 hectares (161 acres). Designated as a national park, the island has two separate harbors, both of which lie near the northern tip: Lervik to the east and Sikhamn to the west. The direction and intensity of the wind at the time of your arrival will determine which of the two the crew of your ferry-boat will use for a landing. Seas surrounding the island are tricky: Even a light wind can make it difficult to approach the island's rocky coastline.

Olaus Magnus, a famous Swedish bishop, mentioned Blå Jungfrun as long ago as 1555. Carl von Linné (Linnaeus) was the first to describe the island in detail, having visited it in 1745 during his "Journey to Öland and Gothland."

Later the forest and plant life suffered drought and the foolish mistake of introducing rabbits, which caused much damage to vegetation. Quarrying in 1904 brought more ecological disasters, especially when the largest of the great caves on the island was blown up. After World War I, forces mobilized to save the island; industrialist Torsten Kreuger donated enough money for the island to be purchased and turned over to Sweden as a national park.

Once on the island, you can observe how the granite dome was covered by sediment some 500 million years ago and how the island took shape about

To explore central Öland, you can travel east from Borgholm (bus no. 102 runs here), following signs to Räpplinge. This brings you to Storlinge Kvarna, a row of seven wind-mills. We were startled to learn that this little island once had more windmills than Holland. Less than .5km (¹/₃ mile) south, you'll arrive at **Gärdslösa,** the island's best-preserved medieval church. Inside is a pulpit made in 1666 along with paintings from the 1200s.

Your major stopover will be about 2km (1¹/₄ miles) south in the village of **Himmels-berga ★★**, which is preserved as an open-air museum built along both sides of the narrow village road. The heart of the museum consists of three large farms with buildings dating from the 18th and 19th centuries. You can see furnishings, farm equipment, car-riages, and sleighs common to that period in Öland's history. After soaking in Öland's past, we like to relax in the Cottage Café, where you can order delicious and freshly baked cakes to be consumed under the shade of walnut and maple trees in the garden. The gallery offers a constantly changing array of art and handicraft shows. The site is open from May 15 to September 15 (closed in off season) daily 10am to 6pm (last entrance at 5:30pm). During the summer, activities ranging from open-air theater productions to

1 million years ago during the Quaternary Ice Age. The larger boulder fields in the south of the island always draw much interest, as do the lichens and bird life. Other exotic animals include the island's black guillemot, as well as rare birds such as the water pipit, the velvet scoter, and the white-tailed sea eagle.

The "labyrinth," the only ancient monument on the island, was first mentioned by von Linné, who called it "Trojeborg." An intricate maze of paths, it lies on a level area of rock on the southern slope of the island.

The best way to view the Blue Maiden's attractions involves signing up for one of the summer (June–Aug only) tours of the island conducted by local fishermen. Check with the tourist office (see below) to hook up with such an excursion.

Alternatively, you can reach the Blue Maiden by departing from Oskarshamn, on the Swedish mainland. From the harbor at Oskarshamn, the M.S. *Soltust* departs every day of the week except Monday at 9:30am, with a return scheduled for 4:30pm. Transit takes about 90 minutes each way, allowing about 3 hours to explore, on foot, the hiking trails that crisscross the island. A kiosk on the island dispenses maps and local information about how best to appreciate this sparsely inhabited island's charms. Round-trip transit costs 220SEK ($44/£22) for adults, and 110SEK ($22/£11) for children 6 to 15 years old. For information and reservations, call the tourist office of Oskarshamn at ⓒ 0491/881-88. To contact the local branch (in Kalmar) of the Swedish National Park Service, the organization that oversees the hiking trails on the Blue Maiden, call ⓒ 0480/821-95.

concerts with jazz and folk music captivate visitors. For more information, call ⓒ 0485/56-10-22 or visit www.olandsmuseum.com.

South Öland

If you have time for only one section of Öland, make it the north (see below). South Öland has only a few worthwhile attractions. **Stora Alvaret,** for example, a giant limestone plain, dominates the southern part of the island. This great plateau is almost entirely devoid of trees, covering an area 37km (23 miles) long and 15km (9¹/₃ miles) wide. The thin soil in places gives way to bare limestone outcrops, creating the impression of a barren landscape. Yet the area is teeming with life and is, in fact, the last refuge for a number of unique plant and animal species.

In this eerie landscape, we've always found something to enchant in almost every season, from colorful orchids to soaring skylarks in the spring, from rockroses to golden plovers in summer, and from rose hips to cranes in the autumn. Winter, however, will prove inspirational only to fans of gloom.

The prettiest village here, and a possible refueling stop, is **Vickleby.**

Capellagården   Vickleby is the site of a private craft college founded in the late 1950s by Carl Malmsten, who had a great vision: He bought a number of decaying farmhouses on the island and replanted them here. He transformed the buildings into a living community with student houses, workshops, and studios. He wanted to design furniture and utensils that paid tribute to old Swedish traditions and the "forms of nature." Today the college is a training school for cabinet making, woodworking, ceramics, textiles, design, and horticulture. It also has one of Sweden's largest herb gardens, containing a wide variety of unusual plants. During the summer, the college stages exhibitions and sales in the old Vickleby school.

Vickleby. ✆ **0485/361-32.** www.capellagarden.se. Admission 10SEK ($2/£1) adults, free for children under 16. June 1–Aug 22 daily 10am–5pm, but call first. Reached on Rte. 136 between Färjestaden to the north and Mörbylånga to the south.

Ottenby Naturum ★   At the southern tip of Öland sits this exhibition of nature and culture, one of the best bird-watching sites anywhere in Sweden. The few "birdies" we know in this far-northern landscape appreciate Ottenby for its ornithological station, which conducts research. The surrounding area was an ancient park and the hunting ground of kings. In the 16th century, King Johan III stocked the park with fallow deer, and the strain still thrives here; today, you can still see the coast-to-coast wall built by King Karl X Gustaf in 1650 to fence off the deer and to improve hunting. The park is also the breeding ground for the rare golden oriole.

Ottenby Nature Reserve. ✆ **0485/66-12-00.** Free admission. Mar–Apr daily noon–3pm; May–June daily noon–5pm; July–Aug 10am–5pm; Sept 1–Nov 5 daily noon–3pm. From Borgholm follow Rte. 136 all the way south to the southern tip of the island, where you'll see Ottenby Naturum signposted with hiking trails leading you into the reserve.

North Öland

We like to return to this part of Öland again and again. The coastal villages are idyllic, the forests appropriately dark and spooky—no doubt filled with witches—and in summer, the fields are so pretty they call to mind *The Sound of Music.*

From Borgholm, head north on Route 136 to find a more varied landscape than in the south. At Föra, a village 20km (12 miles) to the north, stands **Die Kirche von Föra,** with its well-preserved defensive tower. (In the Middle Ages, churches often doubled as fortresses.) If it's open, look inside the interior, which still boasts a medieval aura, with a cross dating from the 15th century. North of the village of Sodvik, you come to **Lilla Horns Iovangar (Little Horn Forest Meadows) ★★**, which are abundantly flowering meadows best viewed in the late spring. If seen at the right time, this can be the most beautiful and evocative spot on Öland.

Before you reach the village of Källa, you'll spot **Källa Kyrka,** which stands lonely and deserted today after its last parishioners departed in 1888. In a setting of flowery meadows, this church from the Middle Ages has dry-stone walls; however, its furnishings are long gone. On-site are ancient burial tombs. The church was last "modernized" in the 14th century, and it was frequently attacked during Baltic wars.

Continuing north, you arrive at the village of Högby, site of **Högby Kyrka och Kyrkstallare,** a religious shrine from the Middle Ages, now in evocative ruins.

After leaving Högby, your last major village will be Böda before you reach the island's largest greenbelt, the stunningly beautiful **Böda Kronopark ★★** preserve. This "crown" over Öland is shaped like a bird's head, the beak facing east. The island's best beaches are here, lying for the most part on the eastern coastline. The beaches start at Böda Sand. We sand. One section is signposted and reserved for nudists, where you can see firsthand that some Swedes are blond all over.

The island's most scenic part, **Trollskogen** ★, or "Trolls Forest," is also here. This storm-swept forest with ivy-covered trunks is at the very northeastern tip of Öland. Part of Böda Crown Park, it'll bring to mind the setting from a child's fairy tale. We almost expect to see a wicked witch emerge at any time from the gnarled trunks of the ancient oaks. This forest offers some of the island's most dramatic walks in any direction.

Before going all the way to the northern tip of the Kronopark, though, you can make a slight 9.5km (6-mile) detour west from Böda on Route 136 to see Skäftekarr. The **Skäftekarr Museum,** Lottorp (© 0485/221-11; www.skaftekarr.se), opened in 1998 on the site of the archaeological excavations of an Iron Age village. On the premises is an exhibition showing what farm life was like in the 6th century A.D., and a reconstruction of several of the village's gravesites. The site also contains nearly a dozen well-preserved foundations of stone buildings, each attributed to five separate farms established between A.D. 300 and 700. This location is still in the process of being excavated and enlarged. On-site is an unusual botanical garden planted by a local gardener during the mid–19th century. It boasts 100 or so different trees and bushes and is ideal for country rambles. Midsummer festivities, including musical events and lectures, are staged at this park about once a week. Adjacent to the museum is a 2.5km (1.6-mile) path that's splendid for walks. The path follows a "cultural route," passing the ancient settlements from the Iron Age. You can order a complete meal or light refreshments at the cafe, which dates to 1860. When it's bright and sunny, you'll be able to linger here for 3 to 4 hours, especially if you like long walks. The museum is open August 28 to May 3 Wednesday to Sunday from 10am to 4pm; from May 4 to July 7, hours are daily 11am to 4pm; July 8 to August 20 daily 10am to 6pm; August 21 to 27 daily noon to 4pm. Admission costs 40SEK to 60SEK ($8–$12/£4–£6) for adults and 20SEK to 30SEK ($4–$6/£2–£3) for children 6 to 15. Children under 6 enter free.

SHOPPING ON ÖLAND

The items you haul back from Öland will probably involve either durable clothing suitable for nature walks in the rugged outdoors, or local handicrafts and pottery made by arts-oriented refugees from urban life. One of the most appealing outlets in the area for ceramics and pottery is **Lotta & Mary,** Hamnen, very close to the piers of Färjestaden (© 0485/318-81; www.checkpoint-oland.com), where the idiosyncratic and painstakingly crafted ceramics of a team of local artisans are displayed and sold. Nearby, at **Atelje Ölandssnipan,** Hamnplan, Färjestaden (© 0485/319-95), some of the most artfully crafted miniature ship models in Sweden are displayed, each authentic to one or another of the many vessels that have sought shelter in Öland's harbor.

A collection of antiques is stockpiled and sold at **Antikgården,** Salomonstorp, in the hamlet of Köpingsvik (© 0485/727-83; www.antikgarden.com).

WHERE TO STAY

Ekerum Golf & Resort ★ It's a golfer's Valhalla. Set 15km (9¹⁄₃ miles) south of Borgholm, this hotel was built in 1991 at the same time as the adjacent Ekerum golf courses, the best on the island. The hotel is a complex of buildings, the older of which have red roofs and ocher-colored walls, and retain shades of their former use as farmhouses. The more modern buildings are white-sided structures, the largest of which is a three-story gabled building with prominent bay windows and a design that seems inspired by early-20th-century stylings. Accommodations are well maintained, conservatively furnished, and tasteful, each with a shower-only bathroom, wood-burning stove, and comfortable, not-frilly furniture—the sort of place where a golf enthusiast might feel at home after a long day on the links. The restaurant, boasting a large open-air terrace, is delightful; it's one of the best places in Öland to watch the sunset. **Bistro Ekerum** wins you over with such appetizers as creamy lobster soup flavored with cognac and cheese as an appetizer, followed by such main dishes as pork with watermelon salsa or beefsteak spiced with coriander and chili. The grilled meats are the most aromatic and enticing on the island, especially the lamb chops in garlic.

Ekerum, S-387-92 Borgholm. ✆ **0485/800-00.** Fax 0485/800-10. www.ekerum.com. 700SEK–1,100SEK ($140–$220/£70–£110) per person double occupancy; 610SEK–850SEK ($122–$170/£61–£85) per person in a quad. Rates include breakfast and linen. AE, DC, MC, V. Free parking. Closed Nov–Mar. Bus: 101 or 106. **Amenities:** Restaurant; bar; small indoor pool; gym; sauna. *In room:* A/C, TV, hair dryer, iron.

Guntorps Herrgård ★ (Value)

If you like down-home atmosphere, this is your best choice on the island. You get more of an only-in-Öland vibe here than in other spots, and it's a well-run and -maintained place, often entertaining Americans whose ancestors emigrated to the United States. The original 1918 manor house lies less than a kilometer (¹/₂ mile) southwest of Borgholm's center; it was formerly the home of a family of merchants who controlled much of the island's commerce until around the turn of the 20th century. Bedrooms are midsize to spacious and attractively and comfortably furnished, with shower-only bathrooms. We think the hot and cold smorgasbord in the dining room is among the finest on the island, featuring such delights as pickled herring in ginger and dill-cured salmon filets with gin and juniper berries. Want to go really local? Dig into the liver pudding and pig's trotters in jelly. The gargantuan feast is only 185SEK ($37/£19) per person.

Guntorpsgatan, 387-36 Borgholm. ✆ **0485/130-00.** Fax 0485/133-19. www.guntorp.oland.com. 32 units. 1,195SEK ($239/£120) double (sleeps 4). Rates include breakfast. AE, DC, MC. Free parking. Bus: 101. **Amenities:** Restaurant; bar; indoor pool; Jacuzzi; sauna; limited room service; laundry service; dry cleaning; rooms for those w/limited mobility. *In room:* TV, minibar, hair dryer, iron, Wi-Fi.

Halltorps Gästgiveri ★★

For coziness and charm, this is where we like to hang our hats during repeated visits to Öland. Set near the geographic center of the island, 9.5km (6 miles) south of Borgholm, this tasteful and reliable hotel occupies one of Öland's oldest manor houses, a yellow-sided complex of steep-roofed buildings dating from the 17th century. Launched as a hotel in 1975, it has a tranquil farmland setting, with a view across the Kalmarsund and the Halltorp Forest. It used to be a royal farming estate, and between the end of World War I and the early 1970s, it functioned as a home for the elderly before its limestone walls were reinforced and it was transformed into an inn. Bedrooms are cozy and intimate, often with beamed ceilings, and each is outfitted with artfully old-fashioned decor. About two thirds of the rooms are within a modern annex; the remaining dozen or so are within the original manor house. Each is named after a region of Sweden, with stylistic touches that are inspired by traditional models from that region. Unlike many other hotels on the island, this one remains open all year.

Högstrum, S-387 92 Borgholm. ✆ **0485/850-00.** Fax 0485/850-01. www.halltorpsgastgiveri.se. 36 units. 680SEK–1,695SEK ($136–$339/£68–£170) double; 830SEK–1,840SEK ($166–$368/£83–£184) suite. Rates include breakfast. AE, DC, MC, V. Free parking. From Borgholm, take bus 101 or 106. **Amenities:** Restaurant; bar; 2 saunas; room service; laundry service; dry cleaning; nonsmoking rooms; solarium. *In room:* TV, hair dryer.

Hotell Borgholm

It's good, it's serviceable, and it's most recommendable, though it doesn't inspire us. That said, like a well-run motel, it comes in real handy should you land in Öland without a reservation on a summer night. This establishment, restored after a 2004 fire, has been in the restaurant business far longer (since 1850) than it has been a hotel. But in the 1950s, the site was enlarged with a pleasant and airy set of bedrooms that have been renovated several times since then. The hotel is convenient to everything in Borgholm—it's only about 5m (16 ft.) from the Storgatan, the town's main street—and remains open throughout the winter for the many Swedish and European business travelers who make it their home during their time in Borgholm. Bedrooms have high ceilings and are tastefully decorated in a monochromatic style, with an emphasis on conservative furnishings.

Trädgårdsgatan 15-19, S-387 31 Borgholm. ✆ **0485/770-60.** Fax 0485/124-66. www.hotellborgholm. com. 33 units. 1,390SEK ($278/£139) double; 2,190SEK ($438/£219) suite. Rates include breakfast. AE, DC, MC, V. Free parking. Closed Jan–Feb. **Amenities:** Restaurant; bar. *In room:* TV.

Hotel Skansen　The setting here is even more idyllic than the hotel itself. "It's for sleeping and eating," a local told us. "You don't come to Öland to sit around in a hotel room all day." Positioned among trees, forests, and fields, 34km (21 miles) south of Borgholm, this hotel is targeted at ecologists, nature lovers, and anyone who's interested in getting away from the pressures of urban life. It's composed of three separate buildings, each with an old-fashioned ocher-colored exterior that might remind you of an antique inn, and a tile roof. The oldest of the buildings dates from 1811. Public areas combine modern furnishings, some of them upholstered in black leather, Persian carpets, and hardwood floors. Bedrooms are functional, comfortable, and outfitted with angular modern furniture with an emphasis on white walls and varnished hardwoods.

S-386 21 Färjestaden. ✆ **0485/305-30.** Fax 0485/348-04. www.hotelskansen.com. 60 units. 1,190SEK–1,590SEK ($238–$318/£119–£159) double. Rates include breakfast. AE, MC, V. Free parking. Bus: 101. **Amenities:** Restaurant; bar; outdoor pool; Jacuzzi; sauna; room service; laundry service; dry cleaning; nonsmoking rooms; rooms for those w/limited mobility. *In room:* TV, hair dryer, iron, Wi-Fi.

Strand Hotell ★★　At some accommodations on Öland, you have to rough it a bit. Here you get a little pampering. This is the largest, splashiest, and most glittery hotel on Öland, the closest thing there is to a seafront resort. Built in 1952 and massively enlarged in 1973, it is much better accessorized than any competition on the island. Most accommodations are within a four-story building whose sides taper into a lopsided pyramid as they rise, a design that creates large, sun-flooded terraces for many of the rooms inside. Each is outfitted with pale Nordic colors and modern furniture usually made from blond laminated woods such as birch. Many of them overlook an upscale marina, part of which is owned by the hotel, and which once won an award as the best privately owned yacht harbor in Sweden. About 16 of the units with kitchens are privately owned and used as vacation homes by urbanites. These are rented out by the week (selected weeks only) during some periods when the owners are out of town.

Villagatan 4, S-387 88 Borgholm. ✆ **0485/888-88.** Fax 0485/888-99. www.strandborgholm.se. 1,190SEK–1,690SEK ($238–$338/£119–£169) double; 1,890SEK–2,290SEK ($378–$458/£189–£229) suite; apts with kitchen available only on selected weeks in summer from 10,090SEK ($2,018/£1,009) per week double occupancy. Rates include breakfast. AE, DC, MC, V. Free parking. Bus: 101. **Amenities:** 2 restaurants; 6 bars; indoor pool; sauna; room service; laundry service; dry cleaning; nonsmoking rooms; rooms for those w/limited mobility. *In room:* TV, minibar, hair dryer, safe, Wi-Fi (in most).

WHERE TO DINE

Halltorps Gästgiveri ★ SWEDISH　Over the years, we've become "addicted" to the cuisine—based on time-tested Swedish recipes—served here. Set within the previously recommended inn (see "Where to Stay," above), this is the most nostalgic and appealing restaurant in Öland. The dining rooms evoke old-fashioned Sweden, but in a way that's charming and with none of the drawbacks of that less mechanized, less convenient age. Menu items are seasoned with herbs and vegetables from nearby suppliers, which arrive ultrafresh and at frequent intervals. Two particularly appealing specialties include filets of cod brought in by local fishermen, fried and served with parsley-flavored butter, and filets of island lamb with thyme sauce and au gratin potatoes. Unlike many competing restaurants on the island, this one is open year-round.

In the Halltorps Gästgiveri Hotel, Borgholm. ☎ **0485/850-00.** Reservations recommended. Main courses 235SEK–315SEK ($47–$63/£24–£32); fixed-price menu 355SEK–555SEK ($71–$111/£36–£56); vegetarian menu 355SEK ($71/£36). AE, DC, MC, V. Mon–Thurs 11:30am–9pm; Fri–Sat 11:30am–10pm; Sun noon–7pm. From Borgholm, take bus 101 or 106.

Restaurant Bakfickan ★★ (Finds) INTERNATIONAL Even though this restaurant in the Hotel Borgholm isn't as atmospheric as the Halltorps Gästgiveri (see above), the cuisine here is the best on the island. The food is at the top of the list for international flair, subtle flavors, and panache. The culinary force behind its excellence is German-born Karin Fransson, an entrepreneur who is widely recognized as the most sophisticated chef and culinary mentor in the area. He does marvelous things with local lamb and fish (especially codfish). A memorable meal might include garlic-fried mussels from local waters; smoked and baked salmon served cold with a compote of tomatoes, a timbale of avocados, and a lime-basil sauce; or roasted and aromatic Öland lamb wrapped in bacon and served with a potato and parsnip strudel (a first for us) and marinated peppers.

In the Hotell Borgholm, Trädgårdsgatan 15-19. ☎ **0485/770-60.** Reservations recommended. Main courses 515SEK–565SEK ($103–$113/£52–£57); 3-course menu 565SEK ($113/£57); 4-course menu 625SEK–735SEK ($125–$147/£63–£74). AE, DC, MC, V. June–Aug daily 6–10pm; Sept–May Tues–Sat 6–10pm.

ÖLAND AFTER DARK

The island's most popular pub lies in Borgholm and attracts young clients from throughout the island. The local favorite is **Pubben,** Storgatan 18 (☎ **0485/124-15**). Open September to April nightly from 4pm to 1am, and May to August noon to 1am daily, it stocks nearly 50 brands of whisky—enough to make you feel like you've wandered into a single-malt pub in Scotland.

2 GOTLAND ★★ & VISBY ★★★

219km (136 miles) S of Stockholm, 150km (93 miles) S of Nynäshamn, 89km (55 miles) E of the Swedish mainland

In the middle of the Baltic Sea sits the island of "Gothland"—the ancient home of the Goths—about 121km (75 miles) long and 56km (35 miles) wide. Swedes go to the coast of Gotland—Sweden's most popular tourist island—for sunny holidays by the sea, whereas North Americans tend to be more drawn to the old walled city of Visby. An investment of a little extra time will reveal that both Visby and greater Gotland, with its cliffs, unusual rock formations, bathing beaches, and rolling countryside, are rich territory. If you can visit only one Swedish island, make it Gotland—even if you have to skip Öland. Buses traverse the island (see below for more info), as do organized tours out of Visby.

From the end of the 12th century and throughout the 13th, the walled city of Visby rose to the zenith of its power as the seat of the powerful Hanseatic merchants and the

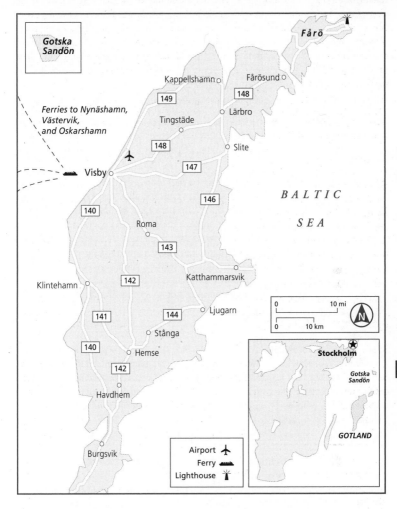

trade center of northern Europe. During its heyday, 17 churches were built, step-gabled stone houses were erected, and the townspeople lived in relative luxury. Visby eventually was ransacked by the Danes, however, and fell into decline. Sometime late in the 19th century, when Visby was recognized as a treasure house of medieval art, it became a major attraction.

ESSENTIALS

GETTING THERE   By Plane   Visitors can fly **SAS** to Gotland from Stockholm; there are three daily flights, which take about 30 minutes. The airport lies 3km (1³/₄ miles) north of Visby. For information and schedules, call © **0770/72-77-27.** The only viable transit from the airport is via taxi; a one-way fare into the center of the city costs 140SEK to 180SEK ($28–$36/£14–£18). Taxis may or may not be waiting at the airport: If one isn't in line, pick up the telephone marked TAXI or TAXI-PHONE and summon one.

By Boat   Those who want to take the boat to Gotland must first go to Nynäshamn; by bus from Stockholm, it's about a 1-hour ride. The last car-ferry to Visby leaves at 11:30pm and takes about 3 hours and 15 minutes. In summer, there also are five daily connections. You can make reservations through your travel agent or directly with the ferry service, **Destination Gotland,** for cabin or car space. It's wise to book deck space if you plan to travel on a weekend. Call ℂ **0771/22-33-00** in Gotland.

VISITOR INFORMATION   In Visby, contact the tourist bureau, **Gotlands Turist Service,** Skeppsbron 4–6 (ℂ **0498/20-33-00;** www.gtsab.se), open May to August Monday to Friday 8am to 7pm, Saturday and Sunday 7am to 6pm; September to April Monday to Friday 8am to 4pm.

SPECIAL EVENTS   We've attended many a festival in Sweden, but not one of them appealed to us as much as this journey back to the Middle Ages. During the annual **Medieval Week ★★** in August, for 8 days Visby once again becomes a Hanseatic town. At the harbor, Strandgatan swarms with people in medieval dress, many of them tending market stalls. Musicians play the hurdy-gurdy, the fiddle, and the flute; jesters play the fool. Toward nightfall a kingly procession comes into the square. The program has more than 100 such events during the festival, along with medieval mystery plays, masses, choral and instrumental music, tournaments, and displays of horses, as well as archery competitions, fire-eaters, belly dancers, and walking tours of the medieval town.

EXPLORING GOTLAND
By Car

If you are pressed for time, we recommend heading straight to Visby. But if you have 4 or 5 hours and have rented a car, we have devised this road tour of Gotland that encapsulates the island in a nutshell. Arm yourself with a good road map before setting out. If you get lost, that's all right, as you won't be lost for long—the island is too small for that.

From Visby, drive north on Route 149, heading toward the fishing port of **Lickershamn.** Look for a narrow trail along the cliffs. This path leads you to a rock that juts into the water. Known as the Maiden, this promontory offers some of the best views on Gotland.

From Lickershamn, continue along Route 149, passing the towns of **Ire** and **Kappelshamn.** From Kappelshamn, follow Route 149 south to the junction with Route 148 in **Lärbro.** Here, go north on Route 148 to **Fårösund.** The village of Fårösund sits on the shores of the 1.5km-wide (1-mile) Fårösund channel, which separates the small island of **Fårö (Sheep Island)** from the main island of Gotland. You can take a ferry to Fårö to visit some of the island's superb beaches.

From Fårösund, take Route 148 back to Lärbro. A few kilometers past Lärbro, take Route 146 southwest toward **Slite.** Follow it down the coast to **Aurungs.** Here, go west on a secondary road heading toward **Siggur.** In Siggur, follow signs south to the village of **Dalhem.** The most remarkable sight in Dalhem is the village church, situated just outside town. Its wall paintings and stained glass are the finest on Gotland.

From Dalhem, continue south on the road that brought you to town. Head toward **Roma.** Look for the ruins of Roma Abbey, a Cistercian monastery destroyed during the Protestant Reformation.

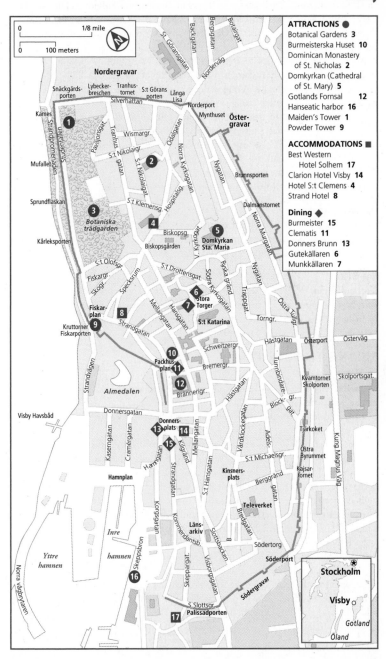

ATTRACTIONS ●
Botanical Gardens **3**
Burmeisterska Huset **10**
Dominican Monastery
of St. Nicholas **2**
Domkyrkan (Cathedral
of St. Mary) **5**
Gotlands Fornsal **12**
Hanseatic harbor **16**
Maiden's Tower **1**
Powder Tower **9**

ACCOMMODATIONS ■
Best Western
Hotel Solhem **17**
Clarion Hotel Visby **14**
Hotel S:t Clemens **4**
Strand Hotel **8**

Dining ◆
Burmeister **15**
Clematis **11**
Donners Brunn **13**
Gutekällaren **6**
Munkkällaren **7**

Head west from Roma on a secondary road toward Route 140 that runs along Gotland's western coast. You'll pass the villages of **Bander** and **Sojvide** before you reach Route 140. Follow it south to **Burgsvik,** a popular port and resort town. Just east of Burgsvik, visit the small hamlet of **Öja.** Its church boasts a triumphal cross dating from the 13th century.

After visiting Öja, return to Burgsvik. Here you head south, passing the villages of **Bottarvegården** and **Vamlingbo.** At the southern tip of Gotland you'll find **Hoburgen,** with its towering lighthouse. Along with the lighthouse, you'll encounter cliffs, many with strange rock formations, and a series of caves.

Return to Burgsvik to connect with Route 140. Turn off after **Fidenäs,** following Route 142 toward **Hemse.** Outside Hemse, take Route 144 to **Ljugarn,** a small port and resort town on Gotland's east coast. Just south of Ljugarn, on a secondary road, is a series of Bronze Age stone sculptures. The seven rock formations, depicting ancient ships, form the largest group of stone settings on the island.

Follow Route 143 northwest from Ljugarn and return to Visby.

By Bus

There are as many as 20 different bus routes on the island. Depending on how many zones you travel, bus fares range from 55SEK to 95SEK ($11–$19/£5.50–£9.50). However, because the bus schedules are inconvenient, renting a car is your best option.

By Bike

Gotlands Resor (© 0498/20-12-60; www.gotlandsresor.se), whose offices lie within the Ferryboat Terminal for all boats arriving from both departure points on the Swedish mainland, is the area's leading purveyor of bike rentals. It charges 70SEK to 130SEK ($14–$26/£7–£13) per day for rentals.

SEEING THE SIGHTS

In Visby

The walled city of Visby—a UNESCO World Heritage site—is made for wandering and getting lost. The city is simply a marvel. From the middle of May to the middle of August, vehicles are banned in the Alstadt, or Old Town, so you'll have the cobbled streets to yourself.

If you're energized, you can walk the entire perimeter of the walls, the **Ringmurer** ★★★, a distance of 3.5km (2¼ miles). We've walked these walls, which are riddled with medieval gates and towers, at least a dozen times and we always find something new and enchanting. There is both a land wall and a sea wall, the latter 5.3m (17 ft.) tall. It was built as a fortification sometime in the late 1200s, incorporating an ancient gunpowder tower, the **Kruttornet** ★. The crenellated land wall is only 6m (20 ft.) high. Amazingly, a total of 27 of the original 29 towers of the Ringmurer are still standing.

Even though Visby is a good town for walkers, you may want to take one of the organized tours that are offered in season. Because so many of the sights, particularly the ruins of the 13th- and 14th-century churches, are better appreciated with some background, we recommend the tours that take 2 hours each and cost 95SEK ($19/£9.50) per participant. They're offered only in summer, between mid-June and mid-August. Between mid-June and mid-July, English-language tours are conducted every Wednesday and Saturday at 10am.

In town, you can walk about, observing houses from the Middle Ages, ruined fortifications, and churches. Notable among these is the **Burmeisterska Huset,** the home of the *burmeister,* or the leading German merchant, at Strandgatan 9. Or you can stroll down to the old **Hanseatic harbor** (not the same harbor in use today) and continue to the **Botanical Gardens,** which have earned for Visby the title "City of Roses." You'll pass two of the most famous towers in the old wall—the **Maiden's Tower** (a peasant girl was buried alive here for helping a Danish king) and the **Powder Tower** (the oldest fortification in Visby).

In its heyday, little Visby boasted 17 churches. Only one, **Domkyrkan (Cathedral of St. Mary)** ★★, is in use today. Found at Kyrkberget, it was built with funds collected by German merchant ships, and was dedicated in 1225—though it didn't obtain its status as a "cathedral" until 1572. The so-called Swertingska chapel was added in 1349, with the blessing and permission of Pope Clement VI in Avignon. But the church was later damaged in four serious fires: in 1400, 1586, 1610, and 1744. The only original fixture left is a sandstone font from the 1200s. The towers of the church are considered Visby's landmarks; the tower at the western front is square, whereas two slimmer ones appear on the east. The interior is worth checking out, especially the fringe of grotesque angels' faces beneath the pulpit. Hours are daily 8am to 8pm and admission is free. For more information, call ☎ **0498/20-68-00.**

The ruins of the former **Dominican Monastery of St. Nicholas** are just down the road from Domkyrkan. Work began on the monastery in 1230, but it was destroyed by Lübeck forces in 1525. Still visible are remnants of the monastery church's rose window, cut from a single big stone, which is more than 3m (10 ft.) in diameter. For more information, call ☎ **0498/20-68-00.**

Another sightseeing recommendation is the impressive **Gotlands Fornsal** ★★, the Historical Museum of Gotland, Strandgatan 14 (☎ **0498/29-27-00**), on a medieval street noted for its step-gabled houses. We consider this one of the best regional museums in the country—it's certainly among the largest, and you'll need to devote about 2 hours to it to take in the highlights. The museum contains artifacts discovered on Gotland, including carved stones dating from A.D. 400, art from medieval and later periods, plus furniture and household items. After five floors of exhibitions, and 8,000 years of history, we like to wind down at the on-site cafe and browse through the bookstore. It's open from May 15 to August daily 10am to 6pm, September to May 14 Tuesday to Sunday noon to 4pm. Admission is 75SEK ($15/£7.50) for adults, and free for children under 17.

On the Island

At the **Turistbyrå,** Skeppsbron 4-6 (☎ **0498/20-17-00**), ask what island tours are scheduled during your visit; these daily tours (different every day) are the best way to get a quick overview of Gotland. The price can be as low as 70SEK ($14/£7) for a brief walking tour or as high as 550SEK ($110/£55) for a complete tour of the island by van.

One thing you can be sure of is that each tour will visit the **Lummelunda Grottan,** Lummelunds Bruk (☎ **0498/27-30-50**), a karst cave formed of limestone bedrock by a subterranean stream. The explored part of the stream cave stretches for 4km (2¹⁄₂ miles) and contains stalactite and stalagmite formations, fossil remains, and subterranean waters. The part of the cave with some of the biggest and most beautiful chambers is open to visitors. It's located 13km (8 miles) north of Visby along Route 149. A bus departs from Österport Visby from June 19 to August 14 daily at 2pm. The cave is open from May to June 25 daily 9am to 4pm, June 26 to August 14 daily 9am to 6pm, August 15 to September 14 daily 10am to 2pm (closed at other times). Visits on your own cost 90SEK ($18/£9) for adults, 70SEK ($14/£7) for children 5 to 15, free for children under 5.

One of the best area tours goes to **northern Gotland and Fårö**. A bus takes you to the ferry port of Fårösund, with a 7-minute ferry ride over the strait followed by an excursion around Fårö (Sheep Island) so that you can see dwarf forests and moors.

The tours take place in summer on Tuesday and Thursday from 8:30am to 5:30pm.

SHOPPING

No one goes to Gotland to shop. But, once here, you'll find some pleasant surprises if you're in the mood to buy. The most memorable goods are produced on the island, usually by individual craftspeople working in highly detailed, small-scale productions. One fave store at which you can find such products is **Yllet,** St. Hansgatan 19, Visby (© **0498/21-40-44**), where clothing made from wool sheared from local sheep is sold in the form of sweaters, scarves, hats, gloves, coats, and other winter wear for men, women, and children. We've found that goods here tend to be natural and soft, deriving from the untinted, unbleached fibers originally produced by the sheep themselves. Also, don't overlook the gift shop that's showcased within the island's historical museum, **Gotlands Fornsal,** Strandgatan 14, Visby (© **0498/29-27-00**), where reproductions of some of the museum's art objects are for sale, as well as handicrafts and textiles made on the island. It's open Monday to Saturday from 10am to 5pm.

As Gotland is home to highly skilled, independent artists, many of whom mostly work out of their own houses or studios, ceramics, textiles, woodcarvings, or examples of metalwork are also on offer. Their merchandise tends to be marketed by cooperatives—loosely organized networks that publicize and display the works of artists. The artists' work is judged by a panel that decides whether their products are qualified to represent the local art and handicraft scene. Objects are displayed and can be purchased at **Galerie Kvinnfolki,** Donnersplats 4 (© **0498/21-00-51**). Kvinnfolki limits its merchandise to items crafted by women, which includes jam made from local berries, textiles, children's clothing, and a line of cosmetics made on the island from all-natural oils, emollients, and pigments.

WHERE TO STAY

If you should arrive without reservations—not a good idea—contact the **Gotland Resort** (© **0498/20-12-60;** www.gotlandsresor.se). The English-speaking staff will try to arrange for rooms in a hotel or private home in or near Visby. The average rate for accommodations in a private home is 440SEK ($88/£44) per person, per night.

In Visby

Best Western Hotell Solhem   It was the setting that first attracted us to this Best Western hotel. Solhem lies in the midst of a beautiful park, **Palissadparken,** and is the most tranquil choice we've found in Visby. The well-run hotel was built in 1987 on a slope overlooking the harbor, a few blocks north of the town center. In 1998, its size was doubled, thanks to an addition designed to match the hotel's existing core with ocher-colored walls, prominent gables, a terra-cotta roof, and a vague sense of the seafaring life of the early 19th century. Bedrooms are comfortable, cozy, and warm, with simple but tasteful furniture and small bathrooms. What we like about this place is that the owners have made an attempt to see that no two rooms look alike. Even so, some of them, though comfortable, look a bit like an upmarket college dormitory in an East Coast (U.S.) university—but that isn't necessarily bad. Speaking of dormitories, some of the rooms house six persons in reasonable comfort, with extra beds costing 375SEK ($75/£38) for adults or 200SEK ($40/£20) for children. If you can, get a room with a

Tips **The Hotel Squeeze in Summer**

Considering all its attractions, Visby doesn't have enough hotels. Because accommodations are packed in summer, you need to reserve in advance. If at all possible, make reservations from Stockholm or from home before you leave.

view of the water and the floodlighted city walls at night. If not, settle for a garden view; at least try to get one of the 17 rooms with a private balcony.

Solhemsgatan 3, S-621 58 Visby. © **0498/25-90-00.** Fax 0498/25-90-11. www.hotellsolhem.se. 94 units. 920SEK–1,710SEK ($184–$342/£92–£171) double. Rates include breakfast. AE, DC, MC, V. Free parking. Closed Sat–Sun Jan–Feb. **Amenities:** Breakfast room; lounge; sauna; babysitting; laundry service; dry cleaning; nonsmoking rooms; rooms for those w/limited mobility. *In room:* TV, hair dryer.

Clarion Hotel Visby ★★ If you want more of a homey hotel, check into the S:t Clemens (see below). But if you want the most glamorous hotel on the island, make it the Clarion, which took the title after it was radically restored and upgraded in the early 1990s. Set close to the harborfront in the town center, its historic core includes medieval foundations and the type of solid stonework you'll see elsewhere in Visby. Radiating outward from the core are additions that span several centuries. The best feature of the hotel, which makes it the finest place to stay off season, is a winter garden, a bold combination of steel, glass, and Gotland sandstone. You can relax in a leather armchair here with a drink and admire the greenery and the changing Nordic light. The bedrooms are conservatively elegant, and some have reproductions of 18th-century furniture. Even if we don't stay here, we try to have a meal at the **Captain's House,** with its genuine turn-of-the-20th-century atmosphere. The food is based on market-fresh, first-rate ingredients that are deftly prepared. You can sample an elegant selection of fine vintages at periodic wine tastings in the restaurant's cubbyhole bar.

Strandgatan 6, S-621 24 Visby. © **0498/25-75-00.** Fax 0498/25-75-50. www.wisbyhotell.se. 134 units. 1,504SEK–2,560SEK ($300–$512/£150–£256) double; 2,500SEK–5,400SEK ($500–$1,080/£250–£540) suite. Rates include breakfast. AE, DC, MC, V. Free parking. **Amenities:** 2 restaurants; 2 bars; lounge; indoor pool; sauna; room service; laundry service; dry cleaning; nonsmoking rooms; rooms for those w/ limited mobility. *In room:* TV, minibar, hair dryer, Wi-Fi.

Hotel S:t Clemens ★ **Value** We've spent so many nights here, it's like coming home again every time we return. We liked it on our first visit way back when we were researching a tome called *Scandinavia on $10 a Day.* It's as comfortable now as it was then, though there have been a number of improvements over the years. Once an 18th-century building, the centrally located hotel is now composed of a series of five antique buildings connected by two idyllic gardens. All renovations were carried out with care, so as not to ruin the architecture, and it boasts a tasteful, modern decor, with light pastels used effectively throughout. It's open year-round, and the staff is helpful and efficient. No two rooms are identical; your choices range from the smallest single in the shoemaker's old house with a view over church ruins, to a four-bed unit with a sloping ceiling and botanical garden greenery framing the window. The old stable even offers rooms for guests with allergies.

Smedjegatan 3, S-621 55 Visby. © **0498/21-90-00.** Fax 0498/27-94-43. www.clemenshotell.se. 30 units. 850SEK–1,480SEK ($170–$396/£85–£148) double; 1,150SEK–2,400SEK ($230–$480/£115–£240) suite.

Additional bed 250SEK ($50/£25) extra. Rates include breakfast. AE, DC, MC, V. Free parking. **Amenities:** Breakfast room; lounge; sauna; nonsmoking rooms; rooms for those w/limited mobility. *In room:* TV, hair dryer, Wi-Fi.

Strand Hotel   This site was once the Visby Brewery, but the owners, the Wiman family, agreed in 1982 to stop making suds and turn the place into a hotel. Even though some of the buildings are from modern times, they had to conform to city zoning that dictates a maximum height of three floors inside the city walls. When we first checked in, there were only 13 rooms, but the Strand has grown to 110 accommodations today, spread across three buildings that look older than they are. Fellow guests can meet in the library or in the adjoining bar—civilized spots for reading Keats or downing a Swedish beer. The comfortable bedrooms are midsize and tastefully modern, and the bathrooms are well maintained with up-to-date plumbing. Breakfast is the only meal served.

Strandgatan 34, S-621 56 Visby. (©) **800/528-1234** in the U.S., or 0498/25-88-00. Fax 0498/25-88-11. www. strandhotel.net. 110 units. 1,060SEK–1,950SEK ($212–$390/£106–£195) double; 2,800SEK ($560/£280) suite. Rates include breakfast. AE, DC, MC, V. Free parking. **Amenities:** Breakfast room; bar; indoor pool; sauna; babysitting; laundry service; dry cleaning; nonsmoking rooms. *In room:* TV, minibar, hair dryer, iron, Wi-Fi.

Nearby Hotels

Toftagården Hotell & Restaurang   Two generations of the Göransson family are always on hand to welcome us back to this time-mellowed old place in the heart of the Gotland countryside, just a stone's throw away from Tofta's long sandy beach. Set adjacent to the island's coast, 19km (12 miles) south of Visby, and separated from the beach only by a windbreak of trees, this cozy hotel developed from a core that was established shortly after World War II. Much improved and enlarged since then, its most visible section was built in the 1980s as a gable-fronted replica of a large private house. The conventional bedrooms and the quintet of cottages are cozy and comfortably outfitted with functional furnishings. The prices vary because a handful of them were renovated less recently than the more expensive units and have older, slightly more worn upholstery and furniture. No place in Gotland is as environmentally friendly as this one—it's big on recycling and the use of "friendly" (not hazardous) products.

Part of the allure of the Toftagården derives from its well-managed **restaurant,** which serves dishes from Gotland and the rest of Sweden every day from noon to 8pm (until 10pm July–Aug). Specialties include roasted Gotland lamb and different preparations of salmon.

Tofta, S-621 98 Visby. (©) **0498/29-70-00.** Fax 0498/26-56-66. www.toftagarden.se. 70 units, plus 10 cottages. 890SEK–1,495SEK ($178–$299/£89–£150) double. Rates include breakfast. AE, DC, MC, V. Free parking. **Amenities:** Restaurant; bar; outdoor pool; sauna; laundry service; dry cleaning; nonsmoking rooms; rooms for those w/limited mobility; solarium. *In room:* TV, hair dryer, iron, safe.

In Burgsvik

As charming as Visby is, many savvy Swedes prefer to stay in southern Gotland in the hamlet of Burgsvik, 90km (56 miles) south of Visby. If you have a car, you may want to check out this popular port and resort town.

Pensionat Holmhällar (Value)   The clientele here seems mainly enthralled by nature, ecology, and life on the beach. "We come to escape the distractions of the outside world," said a very beautiful female client from Stockholm who returns every summer. The origins of this hotel date from 1940, when it was built as a barracks and administrative center by the Swedish army as they pondered the political role they should take vis-à-vis the growing menace of Nazi Germany. In 1949, it was enlarged and adapted into a resort hotel, and further enlarged throughout the course of the 1960s and 1970s. Today it incorporates three separate buildings and 16 simple cottages within an area of natural beauty, 20m (66 ft.) from one of the best beaches in the southern region of Gotland. Bedrooms are a step up from army barracks in comfort, but they are small. Bathrooms also are rather cramped, but each has a shower. There's a restaurant on the premises that maintains impossibly early hours (dinner is served only 5–7pm) and specializes in family-style set menus priced at 95SEK ($19/£9.50) each.

Know in advance that this place is much more appealing in summer than in winter: Between October and March, services and access to most of this hotel are radically cur-tailed. All dining and drinking facilities are closed, and only a handful of the outlying cottages are available for rent. These cost 525SEK ($105/£53) for a double without bathroom, and 675SEK ($135/£68) for a double with bathroom. In addition, no linens or towels are provided in the off season, so you'll have to bring your own.

Vamlingbo, S-620-10 Burgsvik. ✆ **0498/49-80-30.** Fax 0498/49-80-56. www.holmhallar.se. 50 units. 450SEK ($90/£45) double; 1,000SEK ($200/£100) per person for apt. MC, V. Free parking. **Amenities:** Restaurant; sauna.

Värdshuset Björklunda ★ (Value)   If you come looking for problems here, you are likely to find a few, but overall this is a real discovery—and the price is right. On first sight, the inn evokes a villa on a Greek island. It's not, however. An unpretentious farm-house from the 1890s, it developed during the 1970s into a well-respected hotel that's now directed by charming and hardworking members of the Jacobson family. It's set near a small beach, within a forest, and beside the main highway leading south into Burgsvik. Bedrooms are functional, well-maintained, and modern, but not a big selling point. Although fairly comfortable, rooms are small. Bathrooms—each with a shower—also are a bit cramped.

Värdshuset Björklunda draws a loyal clientele to its **restaurant** between June and August. Within a cozy, traditionally decorated dining room, you can order culinary specialties from Gotland and, to a lesser extent, from the rest of Sweden as well. The best examples include smoked filets of lamb, barbecued lamb (a treat available only on Sat nights), and fresh salmon served with saffron sauce. Main courses run 65SEK to 200SEK ($13–$40/£6.50–£20). Menu service is curtailed and presented on an "as needed" basis the rest of the year, so if you arrive between October and April, it's likely that your meal will be served *en famille* with the Jacobsons, without the fanfare of a commercial restau-rant, but with some of the warmth and conviviality of a private home.

S-620 10 Burgsvik. ✆ **0498/49-71-90.** Fax 0498/29-04-90. www.gunnelsbjorklunda.se. 22 units. 840SEK ($168/£84) double. Rates include breakfast. AE, DC, MC, V. Free parking. **Amenities:** Nonsmoking rooms; rooms for those w/limited mobility. *In room:* TV, no phone.

WHERE TO DINE

Burmeister ITALIAN/INTERNATIONAL   Don't expect too much, and you won't be disappointed here. This large restaurant in the town center offers dining indoors or under shady fruit trees in the garden of a 16th-century house originally built for the wealthiest citizen of Visby. Diners can look out on the surrounding medieval buildings from many of the tables. The cuisine is rather standard international—pizza is the most popular menu choice. Though the dishes aren't exceptional, they're far from disappoint-ing. It's incredibly popular during summer—so they must be doing something right.

After 10pm in the summer, the restaurant becomes a dance club; the cover charge ranges from 100SEK to 250SEK ($20–$50/£10–£25).

Strandgatan 6, Visby. ℂ **0498/21-03-73.** Reservations required. Main courses 165SEK–258SEK ($33–$52/£17–£26); pizzas 105SEK–132SEK ($21–$26/£11–£13). AE, DC, MC, V. June 20–Aug 5 Mon–Sat noon–4pm and 6–11pm. Disco mid-June to Aug 5 Mon–Sat 10pm–2am.

Clematis ★ ⒻFinds SWEDISH

Is it a museum or a restaurant? Imbued with a medieval atmosphere, this summer-only spot has been a tourist favorite since it opened in the late 1980s. Medieval feasts, accompanied by jesters, musicians, and fire-eaters, are the standard here, and can be arranged for special parties during December. At times, the costumed staff breaks into medieval tunes while serving the food. Yes, it's all so very campy, but fun, good only if you're in the mood.

The building itself is from the 13th century, and all the props are either real or copies from excavations on Gotland. You are given a flat slab of bread instead of a plate, accompanied by a jug of red wine or a cellar-cooled beer. The only eating utensil is a knife—no forks allowed. Begin with such old-fashioned dishes as salt-pork dumplings or else smoked flounder, and follow with such favorites as a whole chicken stuffed with prunes and apples, or marinated and grilled pork on the bone with honey-fried carrots and turnips. Instead of ordering a la carte, you can also select a full medieval banquet that includes the likes of apples, nuts, candied rose petals, smoked leg of lamb, sausages, honey-fried cabbage, lamb chops, spareribs, and dessert.

Strandgatan 20. ℂ **0498/21-02-88.** www.clematis.se. Reservations not accepted. Main courses 115SEK–310SEK ($23–$62/£12–£31); medieval banquet 310SEK ($62/£31). AE, DC, MC, V. June 26 to mid-Aug daily 6–11pm.

Donners Brunn ★★★ ⒻFinds FRENCH/SWEDISH

If you're feeling adventurous and want to tempt your palate, head here—the finest restaurant on the island. Its chef and owner is Bo Nilsson, the former chef of Operakällaren, arguably the finest restaurant in Stockholm. Branching out on his own, he has taken over this 17th-century building, constructed of orange-colored brick, on a small square in the heart of town and has established a showcase for his own refined cuisine. He makes great use of market-fresh produce and produces seasonally based dishes that are truly sublime. Just a 2-minute walk from the harbor, here diners relax comfortably, perusing an enticing menu of the chef's specialties, the signature dish being Gotland lamb with fresh asparagus served with a freshly made hollandaise. Before that, though, you might begin with a tempting platter of Baltic herring, or else a pot of mussels flavored with chorizo sausage. Always count on a fresh fish platter along with a selection of other main dishes, which can range from the humble to the noble, depending on the night. Desserts are freshly made and frequently changing, but are always a delight.

Donners plats 3. ℂ **0498/27-10-90.** Reservations required in summer. Main courses 185SEK–295SEK ($37–$59/£19–£30). AE, DC, MC, V. June–Sept daily 6pm–2am; off season Mon–Sat 6pm–midnight.

Gutekällaren SWEDISH

The ambience here is considerably more sober than in most of the other restaurants on this fun-loving island, but once the dining is out of the way, the place really livens up (see "Visby After Dark," below). This restaurant and bar in the town center originally was built as a tavern in the early 1600s on foundations that are much older. It was enlarged in 1789 and today is one of the oldest buildings (if not *the* oldest) in Visby. The menu is solid and reliable, featuring fresh ingredients; it offers fish and meat dishes, as well as some vegetarian specialties. You might begin with

a delectable fish soup made with lobster and shrimp, then follow with filet of sole
Waleska or roast lamb chops. The dessert specialty in summer is a parfait made of local
berries.

Stortorget 3, Visby. ℂ **0498/21-00-43**. www.gutekallaren.com. Reservations recommended. 5-course
menu 400SEK ($80/£40); 8-course menu 600SEK ($120/£60). AE, DC, MC, V. Daily 6–11pm.

Munkkällaren ★ SWEDISH/INTERNATIONAL This restaurant is one of the best
in town, although it hardly has the chef at Donners Brunn rattling his pots and pans in
fear of the competition. You'll recognize it in the center of Visby by its brown wooden
facade. The dining room, which is only a few steps from the street, is sheathed in white
stone, parts of which date from 1100. In summer, the management opens the doors to
two more pubs in the compound. The main pub, **Munken,** offers platters of good-tasting
and flavorful *husmanskost* (Swedish home cooking), including *frikadeller* (meatballs). The
restaurant is a bit more refined: You might begin with escargots in creamy garlic sauce,
or toast with Swedish caviar. Specialties include a savory shellfish stew; an ably crafted
salmon-stuffed sole with spinach and a saffron sauce; and, a hunter's delight, venison in
port-wine sauce. Live music is often performed in the courtyard, beginning around 8pm.
After the music stops, a dance club opens Friday to Sunday from 11pm to 2am. Admission to the club is 80SEK to 200SEK ($16–$40/£8–£20).

Lilla Torggränd 2, Visby. ℂ **0498/27-14-00**. www.munkkällaren.se. Reservations required in summer.
Main courses 120SEK–305SEK ($24–$61/£12–£31). AE, DC, MC, V. Restaurant Mon–Sat 6–11pm; pub
Mon–Sat 9pm–2am (June 1–Aug 7 noon–11pm).

VISBY AFTER DARK

There's a lot more energy expended on stargazing, wave watching, and ecology in Gotland than on barhopping and nocturnal flirting. The island's premier venue for folks over
40 who enjoy dancing "very tight" (ballroom style) occurs every Saturday night at the
Borgen Bar, Hästgatan 24 (ℂ **0498/24-79-55**), which contains a restaurant, a dance
floor, and recordings that get patrons hopping. (The music ranges from the big-band era
to more modern, supper-club selections.) A hipper alternative, where dancers are less
inclined to wrap themselves romantically in each other's arms, is the **Munkkällaren,**
which was recommended previously as a restaurant and derives at least some of its business from its role as a bar and late-night, weekend-only dance club. It's a good pickup
spot. A similar atmosphere is found at **Gutekällaren,** another previously recommended
restaurant, whose interior becomes a dance club either 2 or 4 nights a week, beginning
around 10pm, for high-energy dancers mostly ages 35 and under. If you happen to be a
bit older than 35, you'll still feel comfortable hanging out at the establishment's bar,
soaking up aquavit, absorbing the local color, and picking up a blond or blonde.

11

The Göta Canal &
Lake Vänern

When visitors lament that they have only a few days for the Swedish countryside after seeing Stockholm, we tell them to sail along the Göta Canal to see it all in a nutshell. This is deservedly one of Sweden's major attractions, linking the North Sea with the Baltic and connecting Stockholm with a direct inland water route. The canal is called "Sweden's blue ribbon," and it runs to the province of Västergötland between Lake Vänern and Lake Vättern (often confused because of the similarity of their names).

Stretching for 190km (118 miles) and rising more than 90m (295 ft.) above sea level at its highest point, with a total of 65 locks, the Göta Canal makes for an unforgettable journey. It's preferable to see it by water, but you can also drive along the canal, and we once even cycled it. The shifting scenery along the entire length of the canal provides one of the most beautiful panoramas in Europe.

The Göta Canal was begun for the purpose of transporting goods across Sweden, thereby avoiding expensive tolls levied by Denmark on ships entering and leaving the Baltic Sea. Construction started in 1810 under the supervision of former naval officer Baltzar von Platen, assisted by some 60,000 soldiers, and the first of the locks was built in Forsvik in 1813 and is still in use today. However, soon after it was completed, Denmark waived its shipping tolls, and the railway between Stockholm and Gothenburg was created, allowing for the cheaper and faster shipment of goods across Sweden. The canal's importance as a transport artery began to diminish, and it became more of a tourist attraction than a means of transportation. The idea of using it for leisure activities has fully caught on, and today 4,000 boats a year travel the canal, in addition to a significant number of passenger vessels and even canoes.

The towpaths are almost as busy as the canal itself. Where oxen once could be seen giving barges and sailing craft a much-needed tow, you now find walkers and cyclists making their way to the leafy countryside.

One of the highlights of any trip along the Göta Canal is to take in views of Lake Vänern, an inland sea that has existed since 6500 B.C. (although back then it covered a much larger area than today—the present-day Lake Vänern took shape during the Iron Age around 300 B.C.). It is the largest lake in Sweden and the third largest lake in Europe, encompassing 2,130 sq. km (822 sq. miles) and measuring 145km (90 miles) long and 80km (50 miles) wide at one point.

Some 20 tributaries of varying size feed water into the lake, although that water is discharged to just one outflow, the River Göta. The amount of water being discharged is just over 500,000 liters per second, which, in effect, means the water in the lake is changed every ninth year. The lake boasts about 20,000 small islands and rocks, forming the world's largest freshwater archipelago.

1 THE GÖTA CANAL ★★★

During Sweden's summers, everyone seems to take to the water to enjoy the precious few days of sunshine before the long, cold winter. If you have only a few days to spare, do the same and take in a **Göta Canal cruise ★★★**. Each cruise covers a distance of 560km (348 miles) from Gothenburg in the west to Stockholm in the east or vice versa, traveling by way of the canal and other related lakes and rivers. To break up the 4-day journey, captains wisely stop four or five times along the way, but only at the most scenic or intriguing destinations. Day trips and cruises also are offered.

Boats depart Gothenburg heading east along the Göta älv River. About 30 minutes outside Gothenburg, you'll see the 14th-century **Bohus Fortress (Bohus Fästning;** p. 198). This bastion played a leading role in the battles among Sweden, Norway, and Denmark to establish supremacy. The castle was built by order of Norway's Haakon V on Norwegian territory. After the territory was ceded to Sweden in 1658, Bohus Fortress was used as a prison. Climb the tower, **"Father's Hat,"** for what we consider the finest panoramic view on the entire trip. Farther down the river, the boat will pass the town of **Kungälv** (p. 198), known by the Vikings as Kongahälla, whose traditions are 1,000 years old.

As the boat proceeds eastward on the Göta's clear water, the landscape becomes wilder. About 5 hours into the journey, you'll reach the town of **Trollhättan** (see below), home of one of Europe's largest power stations. The once-renowned Trollhättan Falls, now almost dry, can be seen at their full capacity only in July. Today most of the water is diverted to a series of underground channels to the power station.

After passing through a succession of locks, boats enter **Lake Vänern** (see chapter 12), Sweden's largest lake. The trip across Lake Vänern takes about 8 hours. Along the way you'll pass **Lidköping,** home of the famous Rörstrand porcelain. Lidköping received its charter in 1446. North of Lidköping, on the island of Kållandsö, stands **Läckö Slott,** a castle dating from 1298. Originally home of the bishops of Skara, the castle was given to King Gustavus Vasa in 1528 and later presented to Sweden's great hero, Gen. Magnus Gabriel de la Gardie.

Having crossed Lake Vänern, the boats once again enter the canal. A progression of locks, including the canal's oldest at Forsvik, then carry the steamers to Sweden's second largest lake, **Lake Vättern** (see chapter 9). This lake is famous for its beauty and translucent water, and we think it's even more alluring and scenic than noble Vänern. At some points, visibility reaches a depth of 15m (49 ft.).

The medieval town of **Vadstena** (p. 284) on the eastern shore of Lake Vättern is our favorite stopover on the Göta Canal trip because it is the most atmospheric and evocative—it's a regular journey back to the Middle Ages. Within the town are old narrow streets and frame buildings. It's known throughout Sweden for its delicate handmade lace, which you can find in storefronts while walking along Stora Gatan, the main street. Also worth a visit is the **Klosterkyrkan (Abbey Church;** p. 285). Built between the mid–14th and the 15th centuries to specifications outlined by its founder, St. Birgitta (Bridget) of Sweden, this Gothic church is rich in medieval art. Parts of the abbey date from 1250; the abbey sheltered the nuns of St. Birgitta's Order until they were expelled in 1595.

Another major sight is **Vadstena Castle** (p. 285). Construction began under Gustavus Vasa, king of Sweden, in 1545, but was not completed until 1620. This splendid Renaissance castle, erected during a period of national expansion, dominates the town from its

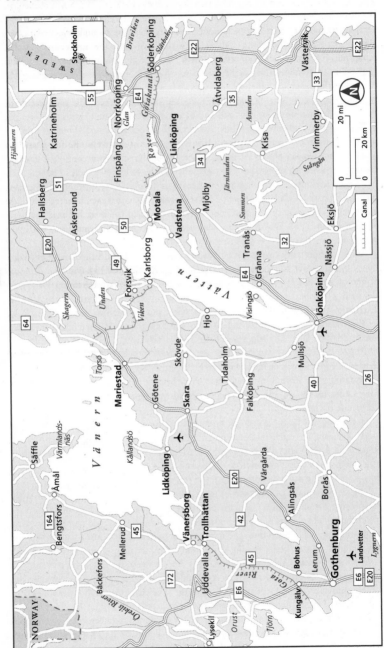

moated position on the lake, just behind the old courthouse on the south end. The caretaker told us that the last royalty seen living here was back in 1715. Since those days, the castle has been restored, but with respect for its original architecture.

Boats bound for Stockholm depart Lake Vättern and pass through two small lakes, Boren and Roxen. Just south of Lake Roxen, you'll find the university town of **Linköping,** site of a battle between Roman Catholic King Sigismund of Poland and Duke Charles of Södermanland (later Charles IX). Charles won the battle and established Linköping as part of Sweden rather than a province of Rome. In the town's main square stands the Folkung Fountain, one of sculptor Carl Milles's most popular works. Northwest of the main square you'll find the cathedral, a not-quite-harmonious blend of Romanesque and Gothic architecture.

From Linköping, boats enter Lake Roxen and continue their journey northeast by canal to **Slätbaken,** a fjord that stretches to the sea. Steamers then continue along the coast to Stockholm.

The **Göta Canal Steamship Company** offers turn-of-the-20th-century steamers, including its 1874 *Juno,* possibly the world's oldest passenger vessel offering overnight accommodations. The line also operates the 1912 *Wilhelm Tham* and the newer—that is, from 1931—*Diana.* Passengers can walk, jog, or bike along the canal path, and there are organized shore excursions at many stops along the way.

A lot of hawkers will try to sell you these Göta Canal cruises, but we think the most reliable and affordable company is **Cruise Scandinavia** (© **800/334-6544** or 212/480-4521; www.cruisescandinavia.com). North Americans can book these tours before leaving home. Cruises cost all sorts of prices, but count on spending 8,195SEK to 11,995SEK ($1,639–$2,399/£820–£1,200) per person, based on double occupancy, for a 6-day package. Discounts are given for early reservations.

2 TROLLHÄTTAN

70km (43 miles) N of Gothenburg, 437km (272 miles) SW of Stockholm

If some director ever remakes the film classic *The Third Man,* which starred Joseph Cotten and Orson Welles, it should be set in Trollhättan instead of Vienna. The town celebrates an industrial legacy of the 1800s—its foggy canals and crashing waterfalls are offset by old warehouses, making for a perfect dramatic backdrop for a film noir.

Once early inhabitants learned how to harness the power of the Göta River, they began to build sawmills along its banks. By the early 16th century, a small community had been established. The building of the Göta Canal in the 18th and 19th centuries gave Trollhättan its first major thrust toward the future. Hundreds of laborers moved in to build the canal and its locks, and houses sprang up on the islands and banks of the river as the community grew.

In time, cheap electricity obtained directly from the power stations at the falls attracted business companies that led to major industries (including Saab). These companies helped put Trollhättan on the Nordic map, and they employ a good percentage of the town's 55,000 inhabitants.

ESSENTIALS

GETTING THERE **By Plane** The Trollhättan/Vänersborg airport (© **0520/42-93-61;** www.lfu.se) lies 5km (3 miles) north of town. Taxis are the only mode of transport.

Passengers either drive their own cars or pick up the "Taxi Phone" adjacent to the luggage pickup stand and summon one. Cost of a taxi into the center of Trollhättan is 150SEK ($30/£15).

By Train   About 22 trains roll into Trollhättan every day from Gothenburg, each of them direct, and each taking about 1 hour. Both the train and the bus stations lie .5km (¹/₃ mile) outside the city center. For information about train service into Trollhättan, call ℂ **771/75-75-75.**

By Bus   Likewise, about 15 buses arrive every day in Trollhättan from Gothenburg, taking 1¹/₂ hours. For schedules and information, call ℂ **0200/21-82-18.**

By Car   From Gothenburg, head north on Route 45.

VISITOR INFORMATION   For facts on the area, go to the **Trollhättan Tourist Office,** Åkerssjövägen 10 (P.O. Box 901), 461 29 Trollhättan (ℂ **0520/49-50-00;** www.trollhattan. se). It is open June to August Monday to Saturday 10am to 6pm, and September to May Monday to Friday 10am to 4pm.

SPECIAL EVENTS   The Göta River and the waterfalls of Trollhättan are celebrated in a 40-year-old festival called **Fallens Dagar,** or "Waterfalls Days." It starts every year on the third Friday in July and lasts for the whole weekend. Food, music, and dancing fill the agenda. There are even fireworks displays, a duck race, a handicraft market, and various activities for kids. We always like to time our visit to Trollhättan during the festival.

SEEING THE SIGHTS

In Trollhättan, the Göta, which has the highest flow of any Swedish river, takes a mighty leap, a spectacular sight that has attracted visitors to the town for centuries. The best spots for viewing the falls include Kopparklinten, Nyckelbergeet, and Spikön Island. The waterfalls, with a drop of 31m (102 ft.), once were an obstacle difficult to overcome; however, they have since been harnessed. Today you can see the water flow into the gorge at a rate of 90,000m (295,276 ft.) per second—but only at certain times, such as during Fallens Dagar in July (see above).

A nearby attraction, about 2km (1¹/₄ miles) south of town, is **Kanalmuseet,** Slussområdet (ℂ **0520/47-22-51**), which lies at the top of a 31m (102-ft.) "staircase" created by the locks. It tells the story of the Trollhättan Canal in pictures, models, and tools. An on-site cinema shows historic footage of the locks throughout their history. It is open between June and August 20 daily from 11am to 7pm, and off season from noon to 5pm Saturday and Sunday. Admission is 20SEK ($4/£2) per person. To reach it from the center of town, follow the signposts pointing to SLUSSARNA ("The Locks").

There's nothing we like doing better here than taking a walk along the falls. The promenade is called **Schleusenpromenade,** and a walk along this pathway will reveal ruins of the failed canals of the 18th century. In the Gamle Dal'n Park area, locks from the early and mid–19th century remain. Information boards tell of the huge obstacle the falls once presented before they were tamed, and how the unique industrial landscape you see today came about.

If you stroll south on the promenade, you'll reach the **Innovatum Kunskapen Hus** (ℂ **0520/48-84-80**), which answers questions about energy and power in the area with slide shows, computers, energy cycles, water pumps, and many more hands-on exhibits. It sounds boring, but you'll find it intriguing even if there's only the tiniest bit of an engineer in you. The 1910 building housing the institute contains 13 massive generators.

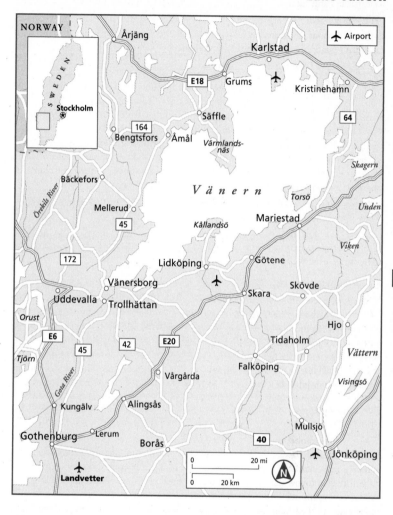

The admission fee is 60SEK ($12/£6) adults, 40SEK ($8/£4) children 7 to 19; hours are daily 9am to 5pm.

If you cross the canal and head into Trollhättan's industrial hinterland, you'll come to the **Saab Bilmuseum,** Åkerssjövägen, Nohans Industriområde (© **0520/843-44**), where you can experience more than 50 years of innovative car engineering. From two-stroke to turbo, the history of Saab is presented dramatically. This museum certainly worked its magic on us: After a visit, we went out and bought a Saab for touring around Europe. The museum displays an example of every model of Saab ever built, as well as future designs. It's open from June 23 to August 24 daily 9am to 5pm; otherwise, Tuesday to Friday 11am to 4pm. Admission is 60SEK ($12/£6) adults, 30SEK ($6/£3) children 6 to 16.

The best place for arts and crafts in town is **Handkraft Trollhättan,** Magasinsgatan 1 (© **0520/42-92-42**), a year-round shop with high-quality arts and crafts made by local artisans. We've often been able to purchase some intriguing Christmas presents here, especially for our friends of Scandinavian origin.

WHERE TO STAY

First Hotel Kung Oscar   We're not sure why this hotel is named after royalty, other than that it lies on a street named Drottninggatan (Queen St.), right in the center of town. Rising five floors, it was once an apartment house back in the 1950s. But by the '80s it had been turned into one of the best-run hotels in the area. We like the little extras here, such as the sports bar and the evening buffet spread out in the lobby bar—which is free. The hotel looks rather plush, at least from the inside. If Laura Bush or Michelle Obama ever showed up, they'd be assigned the First Lady Room with elegant toiletries, sweets, and enough skin-care products to enchant Michael Jackson.

Drottninggatan 17, S-461 32 Trollhättan. © **0520/47-04-70.** Fax 0520/47-04-71. www.firsthotels.com. 76 units. Sun–Thurs 1,198SEK–1,398SEK ($240–$280/£120–£140) double, 1,598SEK ($320/£160) suite; Fri–Sat 798SEK ($160/£80) double, 1,598SEK ($320/£160) suite. Rates include breakfast. AE, DC, MC, V. Free parking. Bus: 11. **Amenities:** Cafe (Mon–Thurs); bar; sauna; laundry service; dry cleaning; nonsmoking rooms; rooms for those w/limited mobility; solarium. *In room:* TV, minibar, hair dryer, trouser press, iron, Wi-Fi.

Hotel Trollhättan (Kids)   This is a good, serviceable hotel that has never escaped its 1950s architecture (when it started out as a small guesthouse above the local post office). But over the years, frequent renovations and expansion—the addition of two extra floors—have turned it into an inviting oasis in spite of its facade. Its appeal picks up considerably in the bedrooms, each with an individual character, often classical in decor. Families gravitate to the hotel as their first choice because it has three- or four-bedded rooms, enough for an average-size brood.

Polhemsgatan 6, S-461 30 Trollhättan. © **0520/125-65.** Fax 0520/154-71. www.hoteltrollhattan.se. 54 units. Mid-June to Aug and Fri–Sun year-round 780SEK ($156/£78) double; rest of year 1,040SEK ($208/£104) double. Rates include breakfast. AE, DC, MC, V. Free parking. **Amenities:** Restaurant; bar; sauna; room service; laundry service; dry cleaning; nonsmoking rooms; rooms for those w/limited mobility. *In room:* TV, dataport, minibar, trouser press, Wi-Fi.

Scandic Swania ★★   Right in the town center and by the waterfront, this is the grandest, most attractive hotel in town. It's completely modernized but has enough old-fashioned charm for traditionalists like us. The hotel resides in a red-brick building from 1916, but frequent renovations have brought it up to modern-day standards—though it has retained the monumental staircases, high ceilings, and, in some cases, elaborate cove moldings of its original incarnation, the city hall. Bedrooms are traditional, conservative, and comfortable, not at all experimental or prone to decorative risk-taking. However, they are the most reliable and biggest in town, and certainly have the best beds.

Storgatan 47–49, S-461-26 Trollhättan. © **0520/890-00.** Fax 0520/890-01. www.scandichotels.com. 198 units. Sun–Thurs 1,390SEK–1,810SEK ($278–$362/£139–£181) double, 1,780SEK–2,010SEK ($356–$402/£178–£201) minisuite for 2; Fri–Sat 740SEK–1,090SEK ($148–$218/£74–£109) double, 1,140SEK–1,290SEK ($228–$258/£114–£129) minisuite for 2. Rates include breakfast. AE, DC, MC, V. Free parking. **Amenities:** Restaurant; bar; disco; indoor heated pool; exercise room; sauna; children's playroom; room service; laundry service; dry cleaning; nonsmoking rooms; rooms for those w/limited mobility. *In room:* A/C, TV, minibar, hair dryer, iron, Wi-Fi.

15km (9¹/₃ miles) north of Trollhättan, 85km (53 miles) N of Gothenburg

The famed poet Birger Sjöberg exaggerated when he called Vänersborg "Little Paris." Frankly, nature lovers like us prefer to spend little time in town itself and more hours exploring the surrounding reserves and walking trails (see below). The town lies at the southern outlet of Lake Vänern, though, which makes it a good refueling stop for those driving along the banks of the Göta Canal.

Vänersborg grew from its roots in Brätte, a medieval trade center in the early 1600s next to Vassbotten. (Brätte was not excavated by archaeologists until 1944.) It took a great many workers in Brätte to unload the Vänern ships and reload the goods onto horse-drawn carriages. In time, it became difficult for ships to enter the bay, as the bottom was silting up. More land was needed for expansion, and Vänersborg grew up as a result of this. It was granted its town charter in 1644 and became the county seat in 1679.

When the Trollhättan Canal was built, shipping became a major source of income. Light industry, administration, and schools later would become part of Vänersborg's profile. In 1834, a fire leveled the town, turning it into a heap of smoking ash in just 14 hours. Only a handful of buildings survived. Afterward, the new city design included a wide firebreak street to avoid another catastrophe.

ESSENTIALS

GETTING THERE **By Plane** The Trollhättan/Vänersborg airport lies 8km (5 miles) west of the town center. Taxis are the only mode of transport from here. Passengers either drive their own cars or pick up the "Taxi Phone" adjacent to the luggage pickup stand and summon one. The cost of a taxi into the center of Vänersborg is around 195SEK ($39/£20).

By Train Ten trains arrive from Stockholm every day; depending on the train, the trip takes between 3 and 5 hours. Most require you to change trains in Herrlgungå en route. About 10 nonstop trains arrive from Gothenburg daily and take about an hour. For information, call ✆ 771/75-75-75.

By Bus At least two buses arrive from Stockholm every day, a travel time of 6 hours, as well as a handful of buses from Gothenburg (travel time: about 90 min.). Bus and railway stations lie a very short walk from the center of town. For bus information affecting Vänersborg and the towns around it, call ✆ 0200/21-82-18.

By Car From Trollhättan, our last stopover, continue north along Route 45 into Vänersborg.

VISITOR INFORMATION The **tourist office** in Vänersborg is one of the few in Sweden that changes its address according to the season. Between June and August, it's at the railway station (✆ 0521/27-14-10; www.vanersborg.se), where it operates Monday to Friday 8am to 7pm, Saturday and Sunday 10am to 4pm. The rest of the year, it operates Monday to Friday 8am to 5pm at Sundsgatan 6B. For written inquiries, address your correspondence to P.O. Box 147, S-46222 Vänersborg, Sweden.

SEEING THE SIGHTS

You can walk around and see Vänersborg's highlights in 2 hours or so. **Torget,** laid out in 1860 and once the town's market area, is still the center of town and a good place from which to start exploring. The chief attraction in town is the **Vänersborg Museet,** Östra Plantaget (© 0521/141-09), which displays objects from around the world. The West African bird collection is its most famous exhibit. A reconstruction of Birger Sjöberg's home is also on display, including many of his personal belongings and authentic pieces from the turn of the 20th century. (He, of course, was the city's great poet and troubadour, who referred to Vänersborg as "Little Paris.") Other collections are devoted to natural history, agriculture, and a history of music. In general, the museum's exhibits have hardly changed since the late 19th century, and it remains appropriately gloomy. It's open June to August Tuesday, Wednesday, Thursday, Saturday, and Sunday noon to 4pm. Off-season hours are Tuesday, Thursday, Saturday, and Sunday noon to 4pm. Admission is 20SEK ($4/£2) for adults, free for children 17 and under.

Anyone interested in handicrafts, particularly doll making, may appreciate the exhibits within the **Vänersborg Doll Studio & Museum,** Residensgatan 2 (© **0521/615-71**). It's open June 15 to August 15 Tuesday to Friday 2:30 to 6pm, and Saturday 10am to 1pm; the rest of the year Tuesday to Friday 2:30 to 6pm, and Saturday 10am to 1pm. It's housed in the oldest wooden structure still standing in Vänersborg—the building was built in the 1790s—but the dolls go back only to the 1890s. You can view Birgitta Person's own prize-winning dolls, and her work is available for purchase in the on-site shop, along with a full range of doll-making materials. The entrance fee is 40SEK ($8/£4) adults, 20SEK ($4/£2) children 5 to 18.

The Swedish scientist Carl Linnaeus called the dramatic, craggy twin bluffs of **Halleberg** and **Hunneberg** ★★ and the surrounding area "earthly paradise." We don't know why great men always wanted to exaggerate when writing about Vänersborg, but Linnaeus was more on target than Birger Sjöberg (see above). The twin bluffs east of town are 500 million years old, and have been used as hunting grounds since the 1500s. Traditionally, this was Swedish elk country, but disease has reduced the stock to around 120 animals. However, there is still a great deal of other wildlife, including deer, hare, and foxes. King Oscar II began the tradition of holding the royal elk hunt here, and hunting rights are still held by the Swedish king. Today the "elk safaris" hunt with cameras rather than guns. Ask at the tourist office in Vänersborg if you'd like to frame some Swedish elk.

You also can visit the **Naturskola Nature Center** at Hunneberg (© 0521/22-37-70), a center that explores the history, flora, and fauna of the twin bluffs. It is open Monday to Friday 9am to 3pm, weekends by appointment. There's a cafe on-site and plenty of information available about the wildlife still living in the surrounding hills. You can also pick up information here about the 50km (31 miles) of hiking trails, the best along the Göta Canal. The cafe is open daily 10am to 4pm.

SHOPPING

At **Konsthantverkarna i Vänersborg** ★, Edsgatan 5 (© **0521/107-47**), more than 20 craftspeople and artisans present their work for sale under one roof. This is one of the best places to shop for handicrafts along Lake Vänern. The work obviously shows a great deal of skill and craftsmanship; in other words, you won't discover any hidden MADE IN TAIWAN stickers on the wares.

WHERE TO STAY

Quality Hotel Vänersborg Though it lacks the charm of the following selection, this is a well-run chain hotel with comfortable bedrooms. Its major advantage is that it lies adjacent to the Göta Canal, only 1.5km (1 mile) south of the city center. A four-story hotel built in 1977, it has been renovated several times since and has kept up-to-date with modern comforts. Inside you'll find colorful public areas. Bedrooms are angular and modern looking, with somewhat spartan lines that are softened by ample use of wood-veneered panels; the spaces seem a bit larger than they are, thanks to large mirrors. Bathrooms, though small, are spotless and contain tub/showers. As a member of a chain, it benefits from a cooperative and well-trained staff.

Nabbensberg, S-462 40 Vänersborg. ✆ **0521/575-720.** Fax 0521/609-23. www.choicehotels.se. 119 units. June 19–Aug 15 and Fri–Sat year-round 790SEK–890SEK ($158–$178/£79–£89) double; rest of year 1,220SEK–1,450SEK ($244–$290/£122–£145) double. Rates include breakfast. AE, DC, MC, V. Free parking. **Amenities:** Restaurant; bar; indoor heated pool; gym; sauna; laundry service; dry cleaning; nonsmoking rooms; 1 room for those w/limited mobility. *In room:* TV, hair dryer (in some), iron, Wi-Fi.

Ronnums Herrgård ★ ⓕⓘⓝⓓⓢ   If you like Swedish country-house living, a beautifully landscaped setting, and gracious comfort, this is the best choice in the area. We're not alone in thinking this—Nicole Kidman chose it for a 2-month stay while shooting *Dogville*. The much-renovated 18th-century manor house is sheathed with yellow clap-boards and a red roof, and lies within its own park, with window views that sweep out over the surrounding forest and the low hills of those majestic plateaus of Halleberg and Hunneberg. Bedrooms are outfitted with pastel colors and furniture that's more contem-porary than what you'll find within the main house. There are also a bar and a cozy **restaurant** where, amid 19th-century Swedish antiques, you can sample excellently pre-pared dinner specialties such as platters of Swedish herring, Swedish caviar, venison with Swedish chanterelles, and a roster of dessert parfaits.

S-468 30 Vargön. ✆ **0521/26-00-00.** Fax 0521/26-00-09. www.ronnums.com. 60 units. Mid-June to mid-Aug and Fri–Sat year-round 995SEK ($199/£100) double, 1,950SEK ($390/£195) suite; rest of year 1,450SEK ($290/£145) double, 1,995SEK ($399/£200) suite. AE, DC, MC, V. Free parking. From Vänersborg, drive south for 5km (3 miles), following the signs to Vargön. **Amenities:** Restaurant; bar; Jacuzzi; sauna; room service; laundry service; dry cleaning; nonsmoking rooms; rooms for those w/limited mobility. *In room:* TV, minibar, hair dryer, iron (in some), Wi-Fi.

WHERE TO DINE

There are a few busy little eateries on the main street in Vänersborg, but nothing special; a few serve pizza and pasta that loses something in its translation to the far north. Motor-ists may consider driving outside of town to **Ronnums Herrgård** for some of the most elegant dining in the area (see "Where to Stay," above).

Koppargrillen INTERNATIONAL   If you like good home cooking—not too fancy—head for the center of town, to Koppargrillen. The well-run dining room cozily outfitted in a Swedish rustic style is in a 1960s-era building (no great compliment). Its dishes are based on tried-and-true recipes, and what you get is not bad, including sautéed salmon with a whitebait roe sauce, or plain poached halibut with melted butter and horseradish. Pork chops are made savory with Madeira sauce, and the standard entrecôte is served with deep-fried onion rings.

Sundsgatan 11. ✆ **0521/181-51.** www.koppargrillen.se. Reservations recommended. Main courses 61SEK–199SEK ($12–$40/£6–£20). AE, DC, MC, V. Mon–Fri 11am–11pm; Sat noon–11pm; Sun noon–10pm.

40km (25 miles) NE of Lidköping, 318km (198 miles) SW of Stockholm, 180km (112 miles) NE of Gothenburg

Its slogan, "Pearl of Lake Vänern," is designed to lure tourists. But in this case Mariestad lives up to the billing. It's the most evocative stopover among the lake towns, both for its architecture and as a center for exploring the district.

Mariestad is known for its many well-preserved old structures in its **Gamla Stan** (or Old Town), including one building from the 17th century, all of which have survived despite several widespread town fires. The town lies on the eastern shore of Lake Vänern, taking its name from Maria von Pfaltz, the first wife of Duke Karl (later Karl IX).

This lakeside city is lovelier and less industrialized than Lidköping. Take along a camera, as its medieval quarter and harbor area have many scenic views. The town contains a wide array of architectural styles, including Gustavian, Carolean, classical, and Art Nouveau. Several magazines have accurately called it a "living museum" of architecture.

ESSENTIALS

GETTING THERE **By Plane** The Gothenburg Airport (p. 167) lies 200km (124 miles) south of Mariestad. Passengers bound for Mariestad take the airport bus from the Gothenburg airport to the center of Gothenburg, then board a train for the ongoing route into Mariestad.

By Train There's about one train per hour arriving in Mariestad from Stockholm, usually with a change in Töreboda Skövde en route. Depending on the train, transit takes from $2^{1}/_{2}$ to 3 hours. There also are two or three trains per day between Mariestad and Lidköping, a trip of about an hour, on a not particularly busy rail line that runs perpendicular to the busier main east-to-west rail routes. For information, call © 771/75-75-75.

By Bus Bus travel to Mariestad from Stockholm is less convenient than equivalent transit by train. There are two buses per day from Stockholm, each requiring between $3^{1}/_{2}$ and 4 hours for the trip, and one or two from Lidköping, taking less than an hour. Both the bus and the train stations lie in the center of town. For information, call © 0200/21-82-18.

By Car From Lidköping (discussed earlier in this chapter), continue northeast along Route 44 until you come to the junction with the express highway, E3, which will carry you into Mariestad.

VISITOR INFORMATION The **Mariestad Turistbyrå,** Hamnplan, 542 86 Mariestad (© 0501/75-50-00; www.mariestad.se), is open June to August Monday to Friday 8:30am to 7pm, Saturday 8:30am to 1pm and 2 to 5pm, and Sunday 9:30am to 1pm and 2 to 5pm. From September to May, hours are Monday to Friday 8:30am to 4pm.

SEEING THE SIGHTS

If time is limited, head first for the **Gamla Stan (Old Town)** ★★, where you can walk medieval streets and see some of the old buildings. The best of these lies along Kyrkogatan. At Kyrkogatan 21 is the **first general hospital** in Mariestad, built in 1760, the third such hospital in Sweden. At Kyrkogatan 31, you'll see a timbered cottage called **Aron's House,** a burgher's house from the 17th century that survived the fire of 1693.

The town's most impressive monument is the cathedral **Mariestad Domkyrka,** Kyrkogatan (no phone), open daily from June 15 to August from 7am to 9pm. The rest of the year, it is open daily 7am to 4pm. Built between 1593 and 1625, it was a source of religious controversy between Duke Karl and his brother, King Johan III: In 1580 Värmland and the northern part of Västergötland were detached from the diocese of Skara and given a superintendent of their own, residing at Mariestad. The duke had the new cathedral built according to plans made by Dutchman Willem Boy for the church of Santa Clara in Stockholm, thereby freely copying his brother's most important building in the Swedish capital. The nave gives a remarkable impression of unbroken unity, as its vaults span a considerable width without supporting pillars, a tradition of the late Middle Ages. The present-day appearance of the cathedral was brought about by a restoration beginning in 1903 by the architect Folke Zetterval, who gave the spire its present height.

Other than the cathedral, the major attraction here is the **cruise** up to Lake Vänern to the start of the Göta Canal's main stretch at Sjotorp, 19km (12 miles) from Mariestad. Between Karlsborg and Sjotorp, boats pass through 21 locks. The most scenic section stretches up to Lyrestad, lying east of Sjotorp and 19km (12 miles) north of Mariestad on the motorway, E20. For information on lake and canal cruises for day trips, contact the tourist bureau (see above). Cruises cost 150SEK to 375SEK ($30–$75/£15–£38), last 5 to 6 hours, and are conducted between June and early September only. Most of them begin at Sjotorp. For more information, call © 0141/20-20-50 or go to **www.gotakanal.se**.

Other attractions in and around the town include the **Vadsbo Museum,** Marieholm (© 0501/75-58-31), located in the wings of the county governor's residence in the town center. The building served as the governor's house in the 18th century. You can skip this one unless you've got an hour or so to spare. Exhibits include artifacts from the city history, a carriage collection, and temporary thematic and art exhibitions. In 1998, a small industry museum opened on the site as well. Admission to Vadsbo, including the industry museum subsidiary, is 20SEK ($4/£2) for adults, or free for children. It is open June to August Tuesday and Thursday to Sunday 1 to 4pm, and Wednesday 1 to 6pm. Off-season hours are only Saturday and Sunday 1 to 3pm.

The **Canal Museum (Kanalmuseet)** at Sjotorp, 19km (12 miles) from Mariestad, lies along the harbor at Hamn (© 0501/514-34), and houses exhibitions showing the building of the Göta Canal and the operations of the Sjotorp shipyard. Because you've been touring the canal, you are likely to find this stopover more intriguing than the Vadsbo Museum. Other displays include a large collection of engine history, and a ship and shipwreck exhibition, as well as various thematic shows. It is open daily June to August 10am to 6pm, and charges 30SEK ($6/£3) for adults, 10SEK ($2/£1) for children. To reach Sjotorp, head north of Mariestad along Route 64. It's closed in the off season.

Lugnås Rocks, on Lugnåsberget Hill, south of Mariestad (take E3 going south from Mariestad and look for signs at the hamlet of Lugnås), once was the site of a major milestone-manufacturing industry begun way back in the 12th century. One of the old caves is open for guided tours daily 11am to 5pm mid-June to August. The rest of the year, tours are conducted Monday to Friday noon to 5pm, Saturday and Sunday 11am to 5pm. Admission is 40SEK ($8/£4). For information about this attraction, inquire at the Mariestad tourist bureau (© 0501/75-58-50).

WHERE TO STAY

Bergs Hotell ★ Finds   An eccentric landlady, "Old Madam Berg," gave her name to this long-favorite hotel back in the 1950s. From an old window mirror outside her sitting room, she watched for the arrival of guests to come knocking on her door. Now and then, today's landlady, the kindlier Elisabeth Åkerloind, follows the same tradition of keeping an eye on the mirror. Part of the allure of this 300-year-old hotel derives from its position in the oldest part of town, in a neighborhood composed only of equivalently antique houses. Set behind a one-story pink facade that from the back side reveals itself as a two-story structure, the hotel boasts bedrooms that are outfitted in a style similar to a Swedish beach house, with painted furniture; cozy, somewhat cramped dimensions; and very few grace notes other than a sense of antique Swedish charm and hints of the many generations who stayed here before you. No meals are served other than breakfast, but the cobble-covered courtyard in back, punctuated as it is with pear trees and flowers, is a charming place to read or write.

Kyrkogatan 18, S-542 30 Mariestad. © 0501/103-24. www.bergshotel.com. 5 units, none with bathroom. 700SEK ($140/£70) double; 900SEK ($180/£90) triple. Rates include breakfast. MC, V. Free parking. **Amenities:** Breakfast lounge; nonsmoking rooms. *In room:* No phone.

Stadshotellet ★ The largest hotel in town appeals to overnight visitors with its nostalgic charms, some of which derive from its construction more than a century ago. Its salmon-colored stones rising three stories above the town's main square were cobbled together in the 1880s. Public rooms have high ceilings and retain some of their original detailing, and the dowdy bedrooms will appeal to anyone with an old-fashioned sense of virtue. Each comes with a small private bathroom with shower.

Nya Torget, S-54230 Mariestad. © 0501/138-00. Fax 0501/776-40. www.stadtshotelletmariestad.com. 29 units. Sun–Thurs 1,160SEK ($232/£116) double; Fri–Sat 850SEK ($170/£85) double. AE, DC, MC, V. Free parking. **Amenities:** Breakfast room; bar; health club; sauna; nonsmoking rooms; rooms for those w/ limited mobility. *In room:* TV, minibar, hair dryer, Wi-Fi.

WHERE TO DINE

St. Michel SWEDISH/INTERNATIONAL This restaurant is associated with the Stadshotellet, which steers its residents here, although it's set within separate premises. Cozy and well maintained, it serves good food that arrives in generous portions, accompanied by a bit of culinary flair. The best include filets "black and white" that mix pork cutlets with Béarnaise sauce and beef filets with wine sauce. Tournedos are served with your choice of three different sauces, and you also can order a tantalizing flambéed pepper steak or succulent grilled filets of sole stuffed with lobster.

Kungsgatan 1. © 0501/199-00. Reservations recommended. Set lunch 75SEK ($15/£7.50); set dinner 160SEK–250SEK ($32–$50/£16–£25). AE, DC, MC, V. Mon–Sat 11am–2pm and 6:30–10pm.

Värmland & Dalarna

It comes as no surprise that many Swedes holiday in the folkloric provinces of Värmland and Dalarna. Dalarna and Värmland are said to be the soul of Sweden; native Swedes particularly cherish the sun-dappled Lake Siljan in Dalarna and Lake Vänern (third largest inland sea in Europe) in Värmland.

In one of her most famous works, *The Saga of Gösta Berling*, Nobel Prize winner Selma Lagerlöf lyrically described **Värmland** life in the early 19th century. Today parts of the province remain much as she saw it. Forests still cover a large part, and the 274km-long (170-mile) Klarälven River carries logs to the industrial areas around Lake Vänern. Sometimes described as "Sweden in miniature," Värmland not only is a land of mountains, rolling hill country, islands, and rivers, but also has its own festivals, music, art, literature, and handicrafts. Karlstad, on the shores of Lake Vänern, makes an ideal stopover for exploring the province. Among its chief waterways are the Göta River and the Göta Canal. A smaller body of water, Lake Vättern, lies to the east of Vänern.

Dalarna, the more traditional province, is known for its maypole dancing, fiddlers' music, folk costumes, and handicrafts (including the Dala horse, Sweden's most popular souvenir). *Dalarna* means "valleys," and sometimes you'll see it referred to as **Dalecarlia,** the Anglicized form of the name. Any time is good for a visit to Dalarna, but to catch the Dalecarlians celebrating the custom of maypole dancing, go from June 23 to June 26. The locals race through the forest gathering birch boughs and nosegays of wildflowers with which they cover the maypole. Then

the pole is raised and, under the midsummer sky, they dance around it until dawn.

There's more to Dalarna, though: Lake Siljan is arguably the most beautiful lake in Europe. It's ringed with resort villages and towns. Leksand, Tällberg, and Rättvik attract visitors during summer with sports, folklore, and music events. In winter, people come for skiing.

It was from Dalarna that Gustava Vasa recruited an army that freed the country from the Danish yoke back in the 1500s. Alfred Nobel, who immortalized himself by creating the Nobel Prize, came from Värmland, and the land has produced some of the country's greatest artists and leaders, including prime minister Tage Erlander, poet Gustaf Fröding, and the aforementioned Nobel Prize-winning novelist Selma Lagerlöf.

The quickest and easiest way to reach these provinces is by train from the Central Station in Stockholm, a 4¹/₂-hour trip. (All the towns in this chapter have good rail connections with each other.) Motorists from Oslo can stop over in Dalarna before venturing on to the Swedish capital. Similarly, visitors to Gothenburg can head north to both Värmland and Dalarna before seeing Stockholm.

If you drive, you can enjoy more scenery, including a spectacular section between Vadstena and Jönköping, where the road winds along the eastern shore of Lake Vättern. On the other hand, if you want to see the area in a hurry and are dependent on public transportation, you can fly to Mora and use it as a center for exploring Dalarna, or fly from Stockholm to Karlstad and use that city as a base for exploring the Värmland district. Both Karlstad and

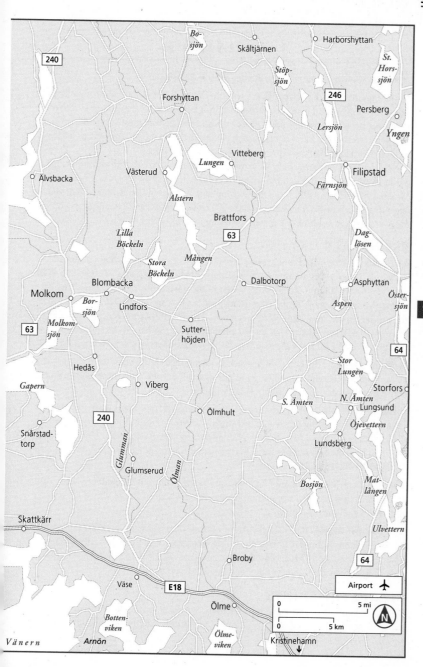

240

Bo-sjön
Skåltjärnen
Harborshyttan
St. Hors-sjön
Stöp-sjön
246
Forshyttan
Persberg
Lersjön
Yngen
Vitteberg
Lungen
Västerud
Älvsbacka
Färnsjön
Filipstad
Alstern
Brattfors
63
Lilla Böckeln
Dag-lösen
Mången
Stora Böckeln
Blombacka
Dalbotorp
Asphyttan
Molkom
Bor-sjön
Lindfors
Aspen
Öster-sjön
12
63
Molkom-sjön
Sutter-höjden
64
Hedås
Stor Lungen
Gapern
Viberg
Storfors
S. Ämten
N. Ämten
Lungsund
240
Ölmhult
Öjevettern
Snårstad-torp
Lundsberg
Glumman
Glumserud
Ölman
Bosjön
Mat-lången
Skattkärr
Ulvettern
Broby
64
Väse
E18
Airport ✈
Botten-viken
Ölme
0   5 mi
0   5 km
N
Vänern
Arnön
Ölme-viken
Kristinehamn

VÄRMLAND & DALARNA

Mora also have good rail connections from Stockholm. Many visitors also take in the "nutshell" version of central Sweden by sailing on a Göta Canal cruise (see chapter 11).

1 KARLSTAD ★

248km (154 miles) NE of Gothenburg, 300km (186 miles) W of Stockholm

At the mouth of the Klarälven River, the port city of Karlstad, capital of Värmland, is sleepy and provincial. There's nothing too exciting here, but the atmosphere is enlivened somewhat by a large student population, which keeps the bars busy at night. The town lies more or less at the halfway mark between Stockholm and Oslo, convenient for those making this scenic drive between the two Scandinavian capitals.

Karlstad has a few attractions of its own, but mainly it's a base for touring the great outdoors of Värmland. It's an old town, founded back in 1584 by Duke Charles (later Sweden's King Charles IX). But a fire, starting in a barley barn, leveled it in 1865, which left only a dozen original buildings standing. The wide streets and open squares you see today are a direct result of city planners who wanted to prevent another tragic fire.

ESSENTIALS

GETTING THERE   By Plane   Nine flights on SAS connect Stockholm and Karlstad daily; the "jump" takes 45 minutes. The airport, **Karlstad Flyggplas** (© **054/556-000;** www.lfv.se), lies 10km (6¼ miles) northwest of the town center. Airport buses haul passengers from the airport to the town center, but it's best to call © **020/32-32-01** after the touchdown of your plane to summon one. The **Flygbuss** costs 65SEK ($13/£6.50) per person each way. Taxis (there's a taxi phone on-site) also have to be summoned, and they charge 250SEK ($50/£25) each way. For flight information, call © **054/455-50-10.**

By Train   Six trains per day run between Gothenburg and Karlstad, ten trains per day arrive from Stockholm, and three trains per day come from Oslo. Each takes about 3 hours. For rail information, call © **711/75-75-75.**

By Bus   Three buses per day arrive from Gothenburg, taking 4 hours; four arrive weekly from Stockholm, taking 4½ hours; and two arrive weekly from Oslo, taking 4½ hours. Check locally for bus schedules, which change from month to month. Note that both the train and the bus stations lie in the center of town. For general information, call © **0200/21-82-18** (within Sweden).

By Car   From Stockholm, take E18 west all the way, and from Gothenburg head north along the E6 expressway, turning northeast at the junction of Route 45, which runs all the way to Karlstad.

VISITOR INFORMATION   Karlstad and most of the region around it are represented by the **Värmlands Tourist Office,** in the city's conference center, Västra Torggatan 26, 651 84 Karlstad (© **054/29-84-00;** www.varmland.org). It's open Monday to Friday 9am to 6pm, Saturday 11am to 6pm, and Sunday 10am to 3pm.

SEEING THE SIGHTS

Although Karlstad has its share of attractions, we think that **Lake Vänern** ★★★ is the most compelling site in the area. So we recommend that, before treading the wide

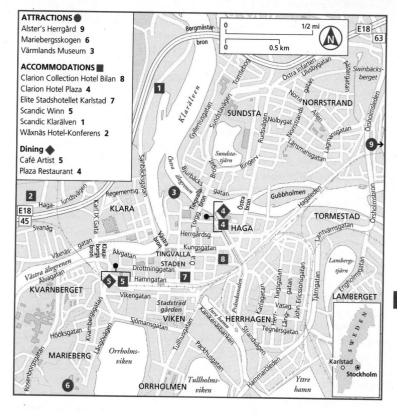

boulevards of Karlstad, you go cruising on this magnificent body of water. As Sweden's largest lake, it has a surface area of 2,152 sq. km (831 sq. miles).

The **Vestrag** is a small-scale lake cruiser with oversize windows and an onboard cafe. Its home port is Karlstad's **Imre Hamn (Inner Harbor),** where it embarks on between two and five cruises a day, depending on the schedule, between mid-June and late August. Tours average 1 hour in length and take in views of the city and the several islands situated near the entrance to its harbor. They cost 19SEK ($3.80/£1.90) for adults and 11SEK ($2.20/£1.10) for children ages 6 to 12 (free for children under 6). Longer cruises that carry you farther away from the waters around Karlstad are scheduled at least twice a week aboard the **Polstjärnan,** the only steam-driven cruiser left in the waters of Lake Vänern. The cruises explore the miniarchipelago near Karlstad in approximately 3 hours; they cost 280SEK to 320SEK ($56–$64/£28–£32) for adults and 180SEK to 200SEK ($36–$40/£18–£20) for kids 7 to 12; they're free for children under 7. Schedules vary from week to week and sometimes are canceled altogether because of inclement weather. For schedules and more information, contact Karlstad's tourist information office, or dial © **054/29-84-00.**

A Nobel Attraction

Alfred Bernhard Nobel (1833–96), the chemist and armaments manufacturer who invented dynamite, hoped to somehow atone for the destruction caused by his creations. In the end, he got his wish: In his will, he created the Nobel Prize, and it's now one of the most prestigious awards in the world. His name is now synonymous with "peace," and the world has mostly forgotten his association with the exploding sticks.

To learn more about this complex man, it's best to go back to his roots. His home, a white-sided manor house otherwise known as **Alfred Nobel's Björkborn,** lies near the hamlet of Karlskoga at the edge of Lake Möckeln (© **0586/ 834-94**). Here you can visit the laboratory where some of the arms that later made Nobel's fortune, and which instilled in him an overwhelming sense of guilt, were developed. The library inside is also considered extremely valuable by scholars. There's a cafe on-site and a staff that is proud of the site's role as the only Nobel-related museum in the world.

Admission is 80SEK ($16/£8), free for children under 10. It's open June to August Tuesday to Sunday 11am to 4pm, and in winter for groups by request. Take E18 56km (35 miles) east of Karlstad to the town of Karlskoga.

Alster's Herrgård ★ **Finds**   Who is Gustaf Fröding and why should you care? We asked ourselves the same question until we began to learn more about him: Both his life and his work proved fascinating. A daydreamer in his youth, he settled down, between bouts of alcohol and woman-chasing, to write poetry. His work was highly celebrated— "against my will"—in his time, and Fröding was named the national poet of Sweden upon his death in 1911. He often wrote his poems in a sanatorium, and, in fact, he's considered one of 300 famous people who were officially diagnosed with mental illness. The Swedish poet is in good company: The list includes Sir Winston Churchill (did you know that?), Lord Byron (we're sure you knew that), and even Napoleon Bonaparte (no surprise there).

Lying 8km (5 miles) east of Karlstad on the Stockholm road, Alster's Herrgård (Manor) is maintained in memory of Fröding, who was born here in 1860. (Gustaf's grandfather, squire Jan Fröding, purchased the estate in 1837.) Today it is an affiliate of the Värmlands Museum and serves as a memorial to Gustaf. There is a Fröding exhibition here depicting the family and its possessions—one entire room is devoted to Gustaf's sisters. There also is a changing array of exhibitions devoted to the art, music, and culture of Värmland. A cafe is on the premises, and you can stroll through Fröding Grove.

Alsters Herrgårdsväg. © **054/83-40-81.** Admission 40SEK ($8/£4) adults self-guided tour, 20SEK ($4/£2) adults conducted tour, free for children under 15. Daily 11am–6pm. Closed Sept–Apr. Bus: 14, 15, or 17.

Mariebergsskogen ★ **Kids**   As provincial city parks go, this is one of the best we've seen in Sweden. It opened in 1925 as an open-air museum; antique buildings were moved to the site, including a chapel, a manor house, a water mill, and a fishing and hunting lodge. Over the years it just grew and grew as more and more facilities were added. It's an active place, with playgrounds for kids and even swimming and ice-skating in (and on) Lake Vänern. There are country walks through an old forest with 300-year-old pines and waterside meadows for picnics. The children's petting zoo contains a collection of tame animals such as rabbits, goats, and lambs. A number of Tivoli-style amusements are also found here, such as a summer sightseeing train. Mariebergsskogen lies in the heart of the Klarälven delta where the river meets Lake Vänern, a 15-minute walk south of the center.

Mariebergs Park. ✆ **054/29-69-90.** www.mariebergsskogen.se. Free admission. Park daily 7am–10pm.

Värmlands Museum ★ (**Kids**) It would be easy to write this off as another sleepy museum in provincial Sweden. But in 2005, the government named it Sweden's best museum, and, the curator assured us, they'll continue to make improvements in the coming years. Usually from the first week of May until the weather turns cold in mid-September, current exhibitions are staged here to enliven the regular displays.

This museum is the best repository of the history of Värmland, tracing the history of the early settlers to the development and subsequent decline of its mill towns and industries. Audiovisual programs add more meaning to the exhibits. There are also sections devoted to Värmland music from folk to modern, and other displays focus on archaeology, textiles, and even Finnish immigration from the 16th and 17th centuries.

Sandgrundsudden. ✆ **054/701-19-00.** www.varmlandsmuseum.se. Admission 40SEK ($8/£4) adults, free for ages under 20. July–Aug daily 10am–5pm; Sept–June Tues–Fri 10am–5pm, Sat–Sun 11am–5pm (closes at 9pm on Wed).

SHOPPING

Connoisseurs seek out Värmland antiques at **Blandorama,** Näckens Väg 2 (✆ **054/56-66-56**). The best center for arts, crafts, and gifts is **Karin Lööf Keramik,** Fagerstagatan 8A (✆ **054/57-25-14**). A very good selection of local jewelry is sold at **Isaksson Porfyr,** Zakridelslingen 6 (✆ **054/56-74-80**).

WHERE TO STAY
Expensive
Clarion Collection Hotel Bilan Those who have fantasies about spending a night in a prison can get their wish granted here—but they'll get comfort too. Back in the mid–19th century, this establishment was a penitentiary, and there remains a prison museum in its basement. Today it's been successfully converted into a hotel where you won't feel imprisoned at all. The exterior is still a bit foreboding, but inside it warms considerably. The public rooms have been tastefully decorated, as have the rather small bedrooms. Even though it's a bizarre setting for a hotel, the place has its devotees and does a lot of repeat business with visiting Swedes.

Karlsbergsgatan 3, S-652 24 Karlstad. ✆ **054/10-03-00.** Fax 054/21-92-14. www.choicehotels.no. 68 units. 1,292SEK–1,840SEK ($258–$368/£129–£184) double. AE, DC, MC, V. Rates include breakfast and evening buffet. **Amenities:** Dining room; pool for dips only; sauna; babysitting; laundry service; nonsmoking rooms; rooms for those w/limited mobility. *In room:* TV, minibar, hair dryer, Wi-Fi.

Clarion Hotel Plaza ★★ If you want to be steeped in tradition, check into the Elite Stadshotellet (see below). But if you like modern comforts and chain hotel efficiency, this establishment is for you. Since it opened in 1984, it has been considerably upgraded and improved. There's not a lot of soul here, but you get comfort instead. The rooms are elegantly decorated and generally spacious, with midsize bathrooms. The most expensive rooms are the business units, which have more work space, including a large desk. These accommodations are equipped with minibars and provide robes.

If there's any place in Karlstad where we like to hang out, it's the **Plaza Restaurant,** which is decorated in a casual yet elegant New York Art Deco style. The menu of Swedish and international dishes is first rate, and the lounge has become a trendy rendezvous point for the town's young professionals. The prestige restaurant, though, is the **Plaza Gourmet,** with its superb menu and well-stocked wine cellar in a gracious 19th-century setting (see "Where to Dine," below).

Västra Torggatan 2, SE-652 25 Karlstad. © **054/10-02-00.** Fax 054/10-02-24. www.clarionplaza.se. 131 units. June–Aug 15 and Sat–Sun year-round 940SEK–1,460SEK ($188–$292/£94–£146) double; rest of year 1,460SEK–1,780SEK ($292–$356/£146–£178) double; year-round 1,800SEK–2,600SEK ($360–$520/£180–£260) suite. AE, DC, MC, V. Parking 90SEK ($18/£9). **Amenities:** Restaurant; bar; night club; Jacuzzi; sauna; business center; room service; laundry service; dry cleaning; nonsmoking rooms; rooms for those w/limited mobility. *In room:* A/C, TV, minibar, hair dryer, iron, Wi-Fi.

Elite Stadshotellet Karlstad ★★ (**Value**) This hotel was founded back in 1870, and the marble, high-grade wood, and cut-glass chandeliers are still here to welcome you today, along with a host of improvements from over the years, thanks to Elite Hotels' purchase of the Stadshotellet in 1984. All of the bedrooms are individually decorated and beautifully furnished; the best ones have open fireplaces, oriel windows, and high ceilings. The **Bishop's Arms** is one of the best pubs in town, and the **Restaurant Munken** offers first-class dining just as it did at the turn of the 20th century. Rail travelers will find the hotel only a 5-minute walk to the south.

Kungsgatan 22, S-651 08 Karlstad. © **054/29-30-00.** Fax 054/29-30-31. www.elite.se. 139 units. Sun–Thurs 1,318SEK–1,750SEK ($264–$350/£132–£175) double; Fri–Sat 978SEK–1,150SEK ($196–$230/£98–£115) double; 1,800SEK–2,700SEK ($360–$540/£180–£270) suite. Rates include breakfast. AE, DC, MC, V. Parking 90SEK ($18/£9). **Amenities:** Restaurant; pub; exercise room; sauna; room service; laundry service; dry cleaning; nonsmoking rooms; rooms for those w/limited mobility. *In room:* TV, hair dryer, trouser press, Wi-Fi.

Scandic Winn ★★ Even though it's part of a chain, this hotel remains charming and graceful, with a distinct, inviting personality of its own. For years, it's been favored by both discerning business travelers and vacationers alike. Even when it expanded, it retained its personalized service; the many nights we've spent here have been so satisfying that we've always returned. Built on the shores of the Klarälven River in the heart of Karlstad, most of the bedrooms are spacious, with ample-size bathrooms. Each has carpeting and traditional furnishings that are replaced when they start to show wear and tear. In 1998, the owners doubled the size of this hotel by buying the building next door and joining it to the hotel's existing core.

Café Artist is the hotel's restaurant, popular for its good food (see "Where to Dine," below). There's also a piano bar.

Norra Strandgatan 9–11, S-652 24 Karlstad. © **054/776-47-00.** Fax 054/776-47-11. www.scandichotels. com. 199 units. Sun–Thurs 1,550SEK–1,610SEK ($310–$322/£155–£161) double; Fri–Sat 950SEK ($190/£95) double; all week 1,650SEK–2,600SEK ($330–$520/£165–£260) suite. Rates include breakfast. AE, DC, MC, V. Parking 130SEK ($26/£13). **Amenities:** Restaurant; bar; Jacuzzi; sauna; room service; laundry service; dry cleaning; nonsmoking rooms; rooms for those w/limited mobility. *In room:* TV, minibar, hair dryer, Wi-Fi.

Moderate

Scandic Klarälven Taking its name from the river that runs through Karlstad, this is a chain hotel that is comfortable, well designed, and well recommended. It's the top choice in the middle bracket and is best for motorists, because it lies just outside town. Set less than a kilometer (about ¹/₂ mile) north of Karlstad's commercial core, on a grassy strip of land midway between the Klarälven River and the E18 highway, this low-slung hotel was built around 1970. Bedrooms contain unremarkable furniture with contemporary, international styling and monochromatic color schemes, plus spotless bathrooms. The **335** rooms at the cheaper end of the spectrum have only one double bed and are actually a bit too small to be considered comfortable. It's better to opt for one of the slightly more expensive rooms because they are a lot bigger and more satisfying.

Sandbäcksgatan 6, S-653 40 Karlstad. ✆ **054/776-45-00.** Fax 054/776-45-11. www.scandichotels.com. 143 units. June 30–Aug 22 and Fri–Sat year-round 950SEK ($190/£95) double; rest of year 1,490SEK– 1,590SEK ($206–$219/£103–£110) double. Rates include breakfast. AE, DC, MC, V. Free parking. **Amenities:** 2 restaurants; bar; indoor heated pool; fitness room; sauna; laundry service; dry cleaning; nonsmoking rooms; rooms for those w/limited mobility. *In room:* TV, hair dryer, iron, Wi-Fi.

Inexpensive

Wåxnäs Hotel-Konferens (Value)   In case you have to face a trivia question, the site of this hotel was famous in the 18th and 19th centuries as Sweden's biggest marketplace for horse trading. Today it's the best value hotel in town. Once again, to save money you have to leave the grand old dames of the historic core and head slightly out of town—in this case to a triangle of land 1.5km (1 mile) away that abuts the E18 highway. The two-story hotel offers internationally modern bedrooms outfitted with angular, motel-style furniture that's comfortable but not particularly plush. The owners are a Swedish-Greek team headed by members of the Apostolidi family. There's a bowling alley on-site, under separate management.

Ventilgatan 1, S-654 45 Karlstad. ✆ **054/56-00-80.** Fax 054/56-88-19. www.waxnashotel.se. 39 units. Mid-June to mid-Aug and Fri–Sun year-round 695SEK ($139/£70) double; rest of year 895SEK ($179/£90) double; year-round 1,095SEK ($219/£110) suite. Rates include breakfast. Free parking. Bus: 33 or 35. **Amenities:** Bar; sauna; room service; babysitting; laundry service; dry cleaning; nonsmoking rooms; Wi-Fi in lobby; rooms for those w/limited mobility. *In room:* TV, minibar, hair dryer, safe.

WHERE TO DINE

Café Artist ★ SWEDISH/FRENCH   We have this thing for restaurants named Café Artist or Cafes des Artistes. But it's not just the name in this case—the cuisine draws us here time and time again. Simply put, the chefs consistently serve the best food in town at this restaurant in the previously recommended Scandic Winn hotel. Its culinary finesse is more obvious at nighttime than at lunch. The setting contains lots of 19th-century pine-wood antiques and carefully finished paneling, which creates a cozy glow of old-fashioned well-being. The only option at lunchtime is a copious buffet attended by many of the town's office workers, who select from a generous medley of fish, meats, soups, salads, and vegetarian dishes. Evening meals are more elaborate, with well-choreographed service and menu items that include well-prepared olive-and-feta–stuffed chicken with herbs, garlic, and potato pie; filet of lamb with sage; or an alpine char with a white-wine sauce. A dessert favorite is homemade vanilla ice cream with a compote of warm cloudberries.

In the Scandic Winn, Norra Strandgatan 9–11. ✆ **054/776-47-00.** Reservations recommended for dinner on weekends. Lunch buffet 155SEK ($31/£16) Mon–Fri; dinner main courses 100SEK–250SEK ($20– $50/£10–£25). AE, DC, MC, V. Mon–Fri 11:30am–2:30pm and 5–11pm; Sat–Sun 6–10pm.

Plaza Restaurant ★ SWEDISH   The restaurant on the ground floor of the previously recommended Clarion Plaza combines contemporary furnishings with antique and traditional. But no one comes here for decor—they patronize the place for a consistently reliable cuisine made with market-fresh ingredients. The chefs here are highly skilled, giving their competitors at Café Artist close chase with imaginative but never far-fetched dishes. One of the best is the marinated salmon flavored with lime, ginger, and coriander. Other specialties include a filet of veal in a creamy morel sauce, or an elegant breast of pheasant with a white-wine sauce and grapes. In autumn, reindeer with fresh chanterelles is a local favorite.

In the Clarion Hotel Plaza, Vastra Torggatan 2. (✆) **054/10-02-00.** Reservations recommended. Main courses 195SEK–230SEK ($39–$46/£20–£23). AE, DC, MC, V. Mon–Fri 11:30am–2pm and 5–10pm; Sat 5–10pm.

KARLSTAD AFTER DARK

Restaurant Sandgrund, Sandgrundsudden (✆ **054/21-16-70**), is Värmland's best-known dance restaurant; it always draws a large friendly crowd, and it's easy to make new acquaintances. **Arena,** Kungsgatan 18 (✆ **054/21-95-95**), a pub and dance club on two floors, also draws a lively, young crowd. One of the town's best pubs is the **Bishop's Arms,** in the Elite Stadshotellet Karlstad, Kungsgatan 22 (✆ **054/29-30-20**). This is a classic pub opening on the Klarälven, and it offers a wide range of beer. Drawing even more business and enjoying greater popularity is **Wollpack Inn,** Järnvägsgatan 1 (✆ **054/ 15-80-16**), a British-style pub.

2 SUNNE

380km (236 miles) W of Stockholm, 61km (38 miles) NW of Karlstad, 288km (179 miles) NE of Gothenburg

Locals romantically refer to this resort town in the Fryksdalen (Frylen Valley) as the "land of legend," and it's forever associated with the writing of the Nobel Prize winner Selma Lagerlöf. Sunne, in fact, was the prototype for the village of Bro in *The Sage of Gösta Berling,* her most famous work, which was turned into a movie starring Greta Garbo.

Stressed out Swedes—but well-heeled ones—come to Sunne for much-needed R&R, because it lies on idyllic Lake Fryken. During summer, you can take boat trips on the glistening waters or play golf on a 9-hole course. In winter, Sunne often attracts skiers, as it has Värmland's highest lift capacity and the most modern cross-country stadium in Europe. Its slalom facility offers a ski school, ski rentals, a ski shop, sports services, a restaurant, and a lodge. There are 10 descents that vary in difficulty; 4 of them are lit when twilight falls. Akka Stadium is the name of Sunne's ski stadium, and there are several cross-country trails starting from here. For information about skiing in the area, call **Ski Sunne** at (✆ **0565/602-80** or visit **www.skisunne.se.**

ESSENTIALS

GETTING THERE   By Plane   Most conventional air traffic flies into Karlstad airport, 70km (43 miles) south of Sunne. From there, you can take regional bus no. 302 into the center of Karlstad or continue the remaining 70km (43 miles) into the center of Sunne.

By Train   Four or five trains arrive daily on the 4¹/₂-hour trip from Stockholm, and from Gothenburg there are another four or five trains a day, which take 3²/₃ hours. You always have to change trains in Kil, and sometimes in Hallsberg, depending on the train. From Oslo there are two trains per day, requiring a change in Kil; trip time is 3 to 4 hours. For more information, call (✆ **771/75-75-75.**

By Bus   If you're traveling from Stockholm, take the train. The bus trip is too complicated and has too many transfers. From Gothenburg, one bus a day arrives Monday through Friday on the 7¹/₄-hour trip; transfer in Karlstad. Both the train and the bus stations are in the town center. Call (✆ **0200/21-82-18** for schedules.

By Car   Drive north along routes 61 or 45 from Karlstad.

byrån 41, 686 80 Sunne (② 0565/167-70; www.varmland.org/sunne). Open June 15 to
August 15 daily 8am to 9:30pm; the rest of the year Monday to Friday 9am to 5pm,
Saturday and Sunday 9am to 2pm.

SEEING THE SIGHTS

Mårbacka Minnesgård ★★
Selma Lagerlöf is one of the most enigmatic figures in
Swedish literature, so it's worth a visit to her former home. Lagerlöf, a limping, ugly
duckling, rose from provincial schoolteacher and great storyteller to Nobel laureate and
literary queen of Sweden. She managed to succeed as both an author of traditional children's books and an innovative, linguistic modernist. Although she was a staunch
defender of public morality—a Swedish puritan, actually—this cultural icon was later
revealed to be a closeted lesbian. Since 1991, her portrait has been featured on the Swedish 20-krona bill.

Lagerlöf (1858–1940) was born at Mårbacka, 10km (6¹⁄₄ miles) southeast of Sunne
and 58km (36 miles) north of Karlstad. The pillared building is kept much as she left it
at the time of her death; the estate is filled with her furnishings and mementos. A thinly
disguised version of the house, called Lövdala, was featured prominently in her masterpiece *The Saga of Gösta Berling.*

Mårbackastiftelsen (Box 306). ② **0565/310-27.** Admission 70SEK ($14/£7) adults, 35SEK ($7/£3.50) children 5–15. May to mid-Aug daily 10am–4pm. Off-season guided tour Sat 2pm.

Sundsbergs Gård
Even if we weren't interested in the exhibits (which we are, incidentally), we'd go here to see this lovely old building. It was used as one of the settings
in Selma Lagerlöf's masterpiece *The Saga of Gösta Berling,* which remains our all-time
favorite novel written by a Swede. Once—in 1780—it was the Sundsberg Manor House,
but the residents died out and the town took it over; it's now a showcase illustrating
domestic life over a period of 300 years. From the kitchen to the elegant drawing room,
various exhibits are painstakingly labeled to indicate what particular century or time
frame they represent. The summer-only museum lies close to the landmark Hotel Selma
Lagerlöf.

Ekebyvagen. ② **0565/103-63.** www.sundsbergsgard.se. Admission 30SEK ($6/£3). June 25–Aug 10 Wed–
Sun noon–4pm. Closed Aug 11–June 24. Off season by appointment only.

WHERE TO STAY & DINE

Hotel FrykenStrand ★ ⟨Value⟩
If you can't afford the grander luxuries of the Quality
Hotel and Spa Selma Lagerlöf (see below), this is a welcoming, charming, and viable
option. Set on well-kept lawns 3km (1³⁄₄ miles) north of the center of Sunne, a meter
(only about 3 ft.) or so uphill from the waters of Lake Fryken, this is a three-story hotel
whose two sections were built in the early 1960s and the early 1980s. During good
weather, many of the hotel's social activities take place on masonry terraces that flank its
edges. The sunny and very well-maintained interior offers big-windowed views—especially from the hotel's dining room—of the surrounding lake and landscapes. Accommodations are comfortable; upholstered with plush, pastel-colored accessories; and
outfitted like cozy nests—not overly large, but appealing and sleep-inducing. The hotel
restaurant is appealingly polite and friendly, with an emphasis on traditional Swedish
specialties.

By 80, S-686 93 Sunne. ② **0565/133-00.** Fax 0565/71-16-91. www.frykenstrand.se. 62 units. 1,250SEK–
1,590SEK ($250–$318/£125–£159) double. Rates include breakfast. AE, DC, MC, V. Free parking. From

Quality Hotel and Spa Selma Lagerlöf ★★   The Selma Lagerlöf is the best and most luxurious hotel in Värmland, and we're not in the minority with this opinion—book ahead. Completed in 1992, this is the only full-service spa in a Swedish hotel. Owned by a conglomerate of Danish and Swedish banks, it was launched in 1982 with the construction of a consciously old-fashioned core ("the hotel") designed like a stately Swedish manor house. Ten years later, a nine-story tower ("the spa") was built 274m (899 ft.) away, with modern bedrooms with balconies and a full array of spa treatments. In the spa section, each of the 184 bedrooms is available only on a full-board basis. In the hotel, breakfast-only guests are accepted. Guests at the hotel must pay for extra activities, whereas spa guests get some activities, such as daily aerobics classes, free. However, all spa treatments require supplemental fees. Note that meals in the spa are diet-conscious and fat-free, whereas the hotel restaurant serves a sophisticated fare of Swedish regional specialties, some from Värmland, and top-rate international dishes—mainly continental—as well. The hotel and spa lie at the edge of Lake Fryken, about a 5-minute drive south of the center of Sunne. Each of the separate buildings has its own reception staff, restaurant, and bars.

Ekebyvägen, S-686 28 Sunne. © **0565/166-00.** Fax 0565/166-31. www.selmahotel.se. 156 units. Spa 1,290SEK ($258/£129) per person double; mid-June to July 1,790SEK ($358/£179) per person double. Rates include full board. Hotel 850SEK ($170/£85) per person double; summer 1,100SEK ($220/£110) per person. Rates include breakfast. All suites 1,000SEK ($200/£100) per person supplement year-round. AE, DC, MC, V. Free parking. **Amenities:** 3 restaurants; 3 bars; 6 pools (1 indoor); health spa; sauna; laundry service; dry cleaning; nonsmoking rooms; rooms for those w/limited mobility. *In room:* A/C, TV, minibar, hair dryer, safe, Wi-Fi.

3 FILIPSTAD

269km (167 miles) W of Stockholm, 309km (192 miles) NE of Gothenburg

Let's admit it: Filipstad is an acquired taste, unless you get off on visiting ancient mining towns. Because thousands of foreign visitors come here, there's obvious interest, so we're including it. Many buffs of America's Civil War also visit Filipstad because of its associations as the hometown of inventor John Ericsson. (See box below.) Ericsson's brother was Baron Nils Ericsson, a noted construction engineer in Sweden who is known for having planned and built Sweden's first main railway. Another well-known Filipstad figure is poet Nils Ferlin, whose realistic statue sits on a park bench in the center of town.

The center for the Bergslag (mining) area of Värmland, Filipstad was founded in 1611. It's almost certain that iron ore was mined in this region even before the black death of the 14th century, and documentary evidence establishes it as being a thriving business in 1413. The main mine products were iron and manganese ore, but silver, copper, lead, and zinc ore were also found. Even gold occasionally has been unearthed. Today the Filipstad Bergslag smelting houses have vanished and only two mines remain in operation, but visitors can see the old open mine shafts, ruins of ironworks, and grand houses where the ironmasters once lived. Other industries here include the making of *knäckebröd* (sold as Wasa Crispbread) and tourism. Canoeing is a favorite summer activity, whereas downhill and cross-country skiing lure winter visitors.

The Swede Who Helped Defeat the South

He may not have figured in *Gone With the Wind*, but John Ericsson, the famous Swedish inventor, helped the Union win the war against the Confederacy. Born near Filipstad on July 31, 1803, Ericsson joined the Swedish army in 1820. Eventually, he migrated to England, where he lost in a competition to create a new locomotive for the Liverpool and Manchester Railway when his "novelty" heat engine developed trouble.

Disappointed, he moved to America, where he gained fame for his other inventions, which included, above all, the marine propeller. His acclaim was cemented when his warship, the Yankee *Monitor*, defeated the Confederate *Merrimac* on May 9, 1862. This victory saved the northern fleet and led to the Union naval forces quickly taking command of the sea, closing off Confederate ports by blockade.

Ericsson also invented the steam fire engine and the hot-air (or caloric) engine, and made several improvements in steam boilers. Even though this son of Filipstad lived abroad for much of his life, he placed his inventions at the disposal of the Swedish navy.

After a successful life as an inventor, John Ericsson died on March 8, 1889, in the United States. Because he had requested to be buried at Filipstad on his native ground, his remains were transported to Sweden on the American armed cruiser *Baltimore*. He arrived back home with full honors and a magnificent hearse bearing his body. All the residents of Filipstad turned out to welcome home their now-famous native son.

On July 31, 1895, the John Ericsson Mausoleum was consecrated on the anniversary of Ericsson's birth. Once more, the town honored its great son, and the streets were decorated with flags, flowers, and several triumphal arches. The mausoleum lies at **Östra Kyrkogården** (✆ **0590/611-00**) today and is often visited by Americans (at least, Yankees), among others. Every year since 1929, the John Ericsson Society places a wreath of flowers, in the shape of a propeller, at this mausoleum. Every July 31, Filipstad also stages a mock naval battle between the *Merrimac*, the armored vessel of the Confederates, and Ericsson's smaller gunboat, the *Monitor*. The *Monitor* always wins, of course.

ESSENTIALS

GETTING THERE   By Train   You can't take the train to Filipstad. The nearest station is at Kristinehamn or Karlstad, from which you can make bus connections to Filipstad. For rail information, call ✆ **771/75-75-75**.

By Bus   Daily connections are possible from Karlstad. Call ✆ **0200/21-82-18** or 0563/532-34 for schedules. The bus ride from Karlstad to Filipstad, a distance of 60km (37 miles), takes about 40 minutes and costs about 50SEK ($10/£5). Most hotels can send a shuttle van to pick up passengers at the bus station, or you can call a cab at ✆ **0590/104-00**.

By Car Follow Route 61 through Arvika to Kil. Drive through Forshaga to Route 63 to Molkom and Filipstad.

VISITOR INFORMATION The **Filipstads Turistbyrå,** Stora Torget 3D, S-682 27 Filipstad (© **0590/613-54;** www.filipstad.se), is open June to July Monday to Friday 9am to 12:30pm and 1 to 6pm and Saturday and Sunday 11am to 4pm; August to May it's open Monday to Friday 10am to 12:30pm and 1 to 4pm.

SEEING THE SIGHTS

Filipstad is known for its mines. For a taste of the industry, visit the mining village of **Langbans Gruvby,** Hyttbacken (© **0590/221-81**), where you'll not only get to see the birthplace of the Swedish-American inventor John Ericsson but will come away with enough knowledge that you can go to work in the West Virginia coal mines. To reach this attraction, you drive 19km (12 miles) northeast of Sunne. Mining on this site was carried out from the middle of the 16th century until 1972. The Långban mines were especially known in the 19th century for producing manganese, and during the last decades of their activity, they were primary sources of dolomite. More than 300 different kinds of minerals have been found here. Långban today is a well-preserved mining village with mine holes, shaft towers, a smelting house, workmen's houses, and a manor house. (In 1803, Ericsson was born in a wing of the old managing director's residence.) The site is open from mid-June to mid-August Monday to Friday 10am to 4pm, and Saturday and Sunday noon to 4pm, and charges 20SEK ($4/£2) admission for adults (free for those up to 16 years old).

Only miners themselves may want to explore **Storbrohhyttan Hembygådsgården** at Munkeberg (© **0590/140-28**), a restored blast furnace and ironworks that have been made into a mining museum with a wealth of artifacts. On-site is a crafts center, Tullhuset, that's open Monday to Friday year-round 10am to 5pm. A well-informed guide at Tullhuset shows newcomers the blast furnace lying a few steps away. The cost of the visit is 30SEK ($6/£3).

Lesjöfors Museum ★ (Finds) This evocative museum illustrates 3 centuries of Värmland history. You'll find yourself transported to different epochs, feeling the spirit of Lesjöfors from the beginning of the 20th century. The museum not only presents the history of the steelworks that once were in the town, but also re-creates the society, organizations, sports, and housing of the workers who lived here. You'll see authentic environments, including the waiting room of the former factory. In the foundry hall you can view exhibits of some of the steel products once created here. (Artist Larseric Vänerlöf shaped an impressive sculpture from some of the different molds left behind when the factory shut down.) One section also re-creates in minute detail a kitchen from the 1950s. All that's missing is Lucille Ball doing her *I Love Lucy* gig.

Lesjöfors. © **0590/311-22.** www.lesjoforsmuseum.com. Admission 50SEK ($10/£5) or free 14 and under. June–Aug Mon–Fri 10am–4pm, Sat–Sun noon–4pm; Sept–May Mon–Fri 2–5pm. Take Rte. 64 north of town 35km (22 miles).

WHERE TO STAY & DINE

Hennickehammars Herrgård ★★ (Finds) There's no contest: This is the best place to stay in the area. Check in after you shake off the mining dust. Built in 1722 as the home of a wealthy landowner, this hotel close to the edge of Lake Hemtjärn, 4km (2¹/₂ miles) south of Filipstad, is a comfortable country spot loaded with personality and charm. Rooms are either in one of several outbuildings or in the main manor house itself, with its elegant detailing and symmetrical facade. The rooms in the outbuildings are comfortable, but we always request the more antique accommodations in the original building. All the units, new or old, are stylishly comfortable thanks to renovation. Guests can swim in the lake, rent horses at a nearby riding school, play tennis, or enjoy golf at a course about 15km (9¹/₃ miles) away.

The best dining in and around Filipstad is found at the hotel **restaurant.**

Lake Hemtjärn, Box 52, S-682 22 Filipstad. ℂ **0590/60-85-00.** Fax 0590/60-85-05. www.hennickehammar. se. 54 units. Fri–Sat 1,292SEK ($258/£129) per person double; Sun–Thurs 795SEK ($159/£80) per person double. Rates include dinner. AE, DC, MC, V. Free parking. **Amenities:** Restaurant; bar; tennis court; fitness center; Jacuzzi; sauna; nonsmoking rooms; rooms for those w/limited mobility. *In room:* TV, hair dryer, Wi-Fi.

Hotel John   Even "Johnny Rebs" are allowed to check in here, although this hotel was named in honor of John Ericsson, who helped defeat the Confederates. Set near the center of town, close to the junction of highways 64 and 65, this low-slung, two-story, white-walled hotel dates from 1974, when it was designed to cater to both roadside traffic and corporate conventions. Inside you'll find a tavern-style restaurant, wood-floored bedrooms with double-glazed windows, and decor typical of middle-bracket hotels. Bedrooms, although rather "motel grade," are comfortable and fine for an overnight stopover.

John Ericssonsgatan 8, S-68230 Filipstad. ℂ **0590/125-30.** Fax 0590/106-68. www.hotelljohn.se. 47 units. Mid-June to mid-Aug and Fri–Sat year-round 730SEK ($146/£73) double; rest of year 980SEK ($196/£98) double. Rates include breakfast. AE, DC, MC, V. Free parking. **Amenities:** 2 restaurants; 2 bars; indoor heated pool; Jacuzzi; sauna; laundry service; dry cleaning; nonsmoking rooms; rooms for those w/ limited mobility. *In room:* A/C, TV, Wi-Fi.

4 FALUN ★

488km (303 miles) NE of Gothenburg, 229km (142 miles) NW of Stockholm

An exploration of the Dalarna region begins in Falun, the old capital of Dalarna. This town, which lies on both sides of the Falu River, is noted for its copper mines; the income generated from copper has supported many Swedish kings.

At this point you may be saying, "Enough with the mines already." But don't dismiss the attractions of Falun. After all, UNESCO inspectors thought it worthy enough to be preserved and added to their World Heritage List for future generations to explore. Even if you don't like mines, you might want to come here to pay homage to one of Sweden's most celebrated painters, Carl Larsson, whose home you can visit.

ESSENTIALS

GETTING THERE   By Plane   The nearest airport is the Dala Airport, at Borlänge, 26km (16 miles) to the west. There's no convenient direct bus, but you can grab a taxi there, priced at around 480SEK ($96/£48) each way.

By Train   There is frequent service during the day from Stockholm (trip time: 3 hr.) and from Gothenburg (trip time: 6 hr.). For schedules, call ℂ **771/75-75-75.**

By Bus   Buses operated by **Swebus** (ℂ **0200/21-82-18;** www.swebusexpress.se) run between Stockholm and Falun either once or twice every Friday, Saturday, and Sunday, depending on the season. Although the distance is greater, buses coming from Gothenburg arrive twice a day every day of the week, making frequent stops along the way.

> ### (Fun Facts) Portrait of the Artist
>
> Admired though painter **Carl Larsson** (see below) was during his lifetime, he could still hold a grudge. When his erstwhile friend, the playwright August Strindberg, published a vicious attack on Larsson, the artist took a knife and stalked Strindberg through the streets of Stockholm.

In Falun, the bus and railway stations lie adjacent to each other, 455m (1,493 ft.) south of the town center. White-sided city bus no. 60 or 70 makes runs from the stations to the Stortorget, the town's central square.

By Car   If you're driving to Falun from Stockholm, take the E18 expressway northwest to the junction with Route 70. From here, continue to the junction with Route 60, where you head northwest. Falun is signposted.

VISITOR INFORMATION   The **Falun Tourist Office,** Trotzgatan 10–12, 791 83 Falun (© **023/830-00**), is open from mid-August to mid-June every Monday to Friday 8am to 5pm. During summer, from mid-June to mid-August, it's open Monday to Friday 8am to 4pm, Saturday 9am to 6pm, and Sunday 10am to 5pm. For more information on Falun, refer to the town's website at **www.falun.se.**

SEEING THE SIGHTS

Before you get down and dirty at some dark pits and mines, head first to the Stora Torget, the market square, to see the **Kristine Church** (© **023/279-10**), a copper-roofed structure dating from the mid–17th century (the tower itself dates from 1865). It's open daily 10am to 4pm, and admission is free. It closes at 6pm in summer.

Bjursås Ski Center   This ski center has six mechanized ski lifts, 10 downhill slopes, and a restaurant or two. It does not, however, resemble a full-fledged ski resort like Gstaad or Chamonix. Don't expect much more than a big parking lot and lots of snow, ice, and midwinter darkness, with illuminated ski trails and a sense of family fun and Scandinavian thrift. Equipment can be rented.

S-790 21, Bjorsås. © **023/77-41-77.** www.bjursäs.com. Day pass 280SEK ($56/£28). Dec 13–Easter only. Bjursberget is about 21km (13 miles) north of the center of Falun; follow the signs pointing to Råttuik.

Carl Larsson-gården ★★★   Carl Larsson (1853–1919) is justifiably acclaimed as Sweden's greatest painter. A 20-minute trip from Falun will take you to a small village, Sundborn, site of Lilla Hyttnas, Carl Larsson's home (now known as Carl Larsson-gården). Through Larsson's watercolor paintings of his own house, the grounds here have become known throughout Sweden. In the United States, reproductions of Larsson's watercolors, mainly of his wife, Karin, and their eight children, appear frequently on prints, calendars, and greeting cards. Larsson claimed in his memoirs that pictures of his family and home here "became the most immediate and lasting part of my life's work." There are guided tours throughout the day, and English-language tours sometimes are available.

While at the home of the artist, you can also ask about viewing **Carl Larsson's porträttsambling ★** (a portrait collection donated by Larsson), displayed in the Congregation House next to the local church. The pictures, painted between 1905 and 1918, depict well-known local residents representing many different occupations. One of the

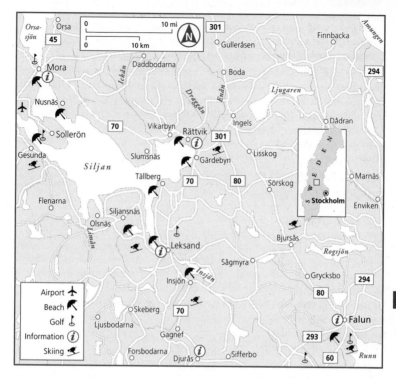

best-known portraits is that of a carpenter, Hans Arnbon, of whom Larsson said: "Before the Devil can get his slippers on, Arnbon is standing there at his lathe or his bench."

Carl Larssons Väg 12, Sundborn. ℭ **023/600-53.** www.clg.se. Admission 100SEK ($20/£10) adults, 50SEK ($10/£5) children 6–18, free for children under 6. May–Sept daily 10am–5pm; Oct–Apr by appointment only (call ℭ 023/600-69 or 023/600-53 for reservations). Bus: 64 from Falun. Lies 13km (8 miles) northeast of Falun.

Dalarnas Museum ★★★ This is Dalarna's most intriguing folk-art museum and the best way to come face to face with the province's folkloric life, be it in painting, music, or native dress. It's especially rich in genuine, old, colorful folk costumes and their accessories, and also exhibits the best collections of peasant wall paintings. The music section is especially appealing to us, and you can hear recordings of fiddlers and young girls blowing the traditional small alphorns. The Falun group of graphic artists is well known in the Swedish art world, and the six artists who made up that elite group in the early decades of the 20th century are displayed here. Of these, Axel Fridell is the finest. A faithful reconstruction of Swedish writer **Selma Lagerlöf's study** ★★, complete with its original furnishings, has been installed in the museum.

Stirgaregatan 2–4. ℭ **023/76-55-00.** www.dalarnasmuseum.se. Free admission. Tues and Thurs–Fri 10am–5pm; Sat–Sun noon–5pm. Sept–Apr also Wed 5–9pm.

Falu Koppargruva ★★★ When Carl von Linné visited here in 1734, he called it "Sweden's greatest wonder, but as terrible as Hell itself." This copper mine, around which the town developed, was the world's largest producer of copper during the 17th century; it supplied the raw material used for the roof of the palace of Versailles. Since 1970, when the mine was opened to the public, more than one million visitors have taken the elevator 54m (177 ft.) below the surface of the Earth and into the mine. Guides take you through old chambers and winding passages dating from the Middle Ages. In one section of the mine, you'll see a shaft divided by a timber wall that's more than 195m (640 ft.) high; this may be the world's tallest wooden structure. Today the only industrial product of the mine is pigment used for producing Sweden's signature red paint (sold under the Falu Rödfärg name), which is used not only on Swedish barns, but on thousands upon thousands of private homes and even commercial and public buildings. Buildings painted this shade of barn red have become virtual symbols of Sweden.

Gruvplatsen. © 023/78-20-30. www.falugruva.se. Admission 150SEK ($30/£15) adults, 50SEK ($10/£5) children 4 and up. May–Sept daily 9am–6pm; Oct–Apr Mon–Fri 11am–5pm, Sat–Sun 11am–4pm. Tours must be booked in advance in winter.

Lugnet ★ This is the best—and also the largest—sports complex we've found in western Sweden. Its main fame derives from its selection in 1974 as the site for the cross-country skiing world championship. Today it contains a large-scale hotel (the below-recommended Scandic), a ski jump, an ice hockey rink, and a sports hall with an indoor heated pool, a sauna, and a steam bath that's the centerpiece for all the other facilities (including miles of cross-country ski tracks and a campground).

S-79131 Falun. © 023/835-00. Admission 50SEK ($10/£5) for a day's use of all the facilities (except massage). Sports hall daily 8am–9pm.

Stora Museum ★ Thinking about mining as a career? After seeing the harsh conditions under which workers labored, you'll think twice. This museum is devoted to the technical and industrial past of the area, and depicts the history of its copper mountain. We're most drawn to the model room with Christopher Polhem's clever inventions. Polhem (1661–1751) was the father of Swedish mechanics and loved using devices such as mechanical alphabets. Entering this museum is like a step into the 18th century; the tiled stoves, antiques, decorative molded plaster, and chandeliers all are of the era—either the genuine article or an exact replica. In the coin cabinet, the entire history of minting copper coins is documented. Various methods of producing iron are described in pictures and models.

Vid Falu Gruva. © 023/78-20-30. www.falugruva.se. Admission 20SEK ($4/£2). May–Sept daily 10am–5pm; off season Mon–Fri 11am–5pm, Sat–Sun 11am–4pm.

WHERE TO STAY & DINE

First Hotel Grand ★ Because of its impressive spa facilities and overall comfort, this hotel has an edge over the Scandic Lugnet (see below), although each establishment has its devotees. This buff-colored hotel 90m (295 ft.) south of the landmark Falun Church was built in 1862, with a modern addition constructed in 1974. The tastefully modern guest rooms are among the best decorated in town. All have ample-size bathrooms equipped with shower units. If you don't mind paying 210SEK ($42/£21) extra, you can book a Grand Room with a free minibar and TV with free premium movie channels, plus a luxurious bathrobe with slippers. For the most elegant living of all, reserve a suite with its own sauna and large private bathrooms. On-site is Harry's Pub and Restaurant, which not only serves good food but might entertain you with jazz, blues, or even a sports

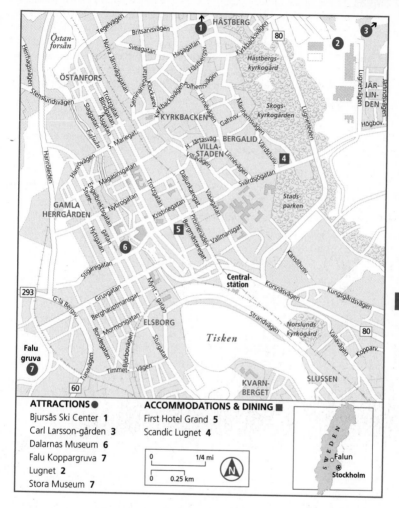

ATTRACTIONS ●

Bjursås Ski Center **1**
Carl Larsson-gården **3**
Dalarnas Museum **6**
Falu Koppargruva **7**
Lugnet **2**
Stora Museum **7**

ACCOMMODATIONS & DINING ■

First Hotel Grand **5**
Scandic Lugnet **4**

0	1/4 mi
0	0.25 km

evening. The spa is the best in town, with many types of treatments followed by a sauna and a relaxing swim.

Trotzgatan 9–11, S-791 71 Falun. ℭ **023/79-48-80.** Fax 023/141-43. www.firsthotels.com. 151 units. Sun–Thurs 1,498SEK–1,698SEK ($300–$340/£150£170) double; Fri–Sat 798SEK–1,040SEK ($160–$208/£80–£104) double; all week 2,750SEK ($550/£28) suite. Rates include breakfast. AE, DC, MC, V. Parking 80SEK ($16/£8). Bus: 701 or 704. **Amenities:** Restaurant; bar; indoor heated pool; fitness center; sauna; room service; laundry service; dry cleaning; nonsmoking rooms; rooms for those w/limited mobility. *In room:* TV, minibar (in some), trouser press, Wi-Fi.

Scandic Lugnet ★ (**Kids**) Rising a dozen floors above a forested landscape, less than a 10-minute walk from the center of Falun, this hotel is one of the tallest buildings in town. As if that weren't enough, its pale green facade and futuristic detailing also make it one of the most unusual. Built in the early 1990s, with vertical rows of bay windows, it has well-crafted public areas outfitted in natural materials that include lots of stone and wood, and contemporary bedrooms. Although it has a chain-hotel feel, the tastefully decorated rooms are nonetheless well designed and furnished. There is an "environmental floor," where 97% of the waste of the room is recycled. Expect tour-bus groups and a hardworking, sometimes slightly harassed staff. There's a bistro-style restaurant and a bar on the premises, offering a wide range of dishes. A children's menu is also offered.

Svärdsjögatan 51, S-791 31 Falun. ⓒ **023/669-22-00.** Fax 023/669-22-11. www.scandichotels.com. 153 units. July–Aug and Fri–Sat year-round 1,020SEK ($204/£102) double; rest of year 1,440SEK ($288/£144) double; year-round 1,270SEK–1,690SEK ($254–$338/£127–£169) minisuite. Rates include breakfast. AE, DC, MC, V. Free parking. **Amenities:** Restaurant; bar; indoor heated pool; sauna; children's playroom; laundry service; dry cleaning; nonsmoking rooms; rooms for those w/limited mobility; bowling alley. *In room:* TV, hair dryer, Wi-Fi.

5 LEKSAND ★★

48km (30 miles) W of Falun, 18km (11 miles) S of Rättvik, 267km (166 miles) NW of Stockholm

No less an authority than Hans Christian Andersen found Leksands Noret—the doorway to Lake Siljan—idyllic. Leksand in its present form dates from the early 1900s, when it was reconstructed following a fire that razed the community. However, some type of settlement has existed on this site since pagan times.

Many of the province's old traditions still flourish here. Women occasionally don traditional dress for church on Sunday, and in June and July the long "church boats" from Viking times may cross the lake carrying parishioners to church. These same boats compete in a church-boat race on the first Sunday in July. Since World War II, a miracle play, *The Road to Heaven,* has been presented here in open-air performances, providing an insight into the customs and folklore of Dalarna. The play runs for 10 days at the end of July.

ESSENTIALS
GETTING THERE **By Plane** You can fly from Stockholm on **Skyways** (ⓒ 0771/95-95-00;** www.skyways.se); the nearest airport is **Dala-Airport** (ⓒ 0243/645-00), in Borlänge, 50km (31 miles) south, from which there is frequent bus and train service to Leksand. Car rentals are available at the airport.

By Train There's a direct train from Stockholm to Mora that stops in Leksand (travel time: 3¹/₂ hr.). For reservations and information, call ⓒ 771/75-75-75.

By Boat Another way to reach Leksand is on the *Gustaf Wasa* ★; call ⓒ 010/252-32-92 for information and reservations. Every Monday at 3pm it makes one long trip from Mora to Leksand (through Rättvik). The round-trip fare is 150SEK ($30/£15) for adults, 75SEK ($15/£7.50) for children. Tickets are sold onboard. The return is by train.

By Car From Falun, our last stopover, head north on Route 80 to Bjursås, then go west on a secondary road signposted as sÅGMYRA. Follow the signs into Leksand.

VISITOR INFORMATION Contact the **Leksands Turistbyrå,** Norsgatan 40, 793 30 Leksand (ⓒ 0247/79-61-30; www.siljan.se), open June 15 to August 10 Monday to Friday 10am to 7pm, Saturday and Sunday 10am to 5pm; rest of the year Monday to Friday 10am to 5pm, and Saturday 10am to 11pm.

(Moments) Sweden's Best White-Water Rafting

The best way to profit from the meltdown of Sweden's winter snows involves floating downstream atop the surging waters of the Klarälven River, a scenic stream that originates in the high altitudes of Norway and eventually flows through Värmland. White-water enthusiasts gravitate to its northern stretches; aficionados of calmer waters move to points near its southern terminus. One of the most respected outfitters for excursions along any length of this historic river is **Vildmark in Värmland,** P.O. Box 209, Torsby SE 68525 (© **0560/140-40;** www.vildmark.se). Established in 1980 and known throughout the region for the quality of its guides, it offers canoe excursions along the northern lengths of the river between April and October, providing instruction and all the equipment and excitement you'll need.

More unusual than its white-water excursions is what the company promotes along the calmer southern stretches: You'll be taught how to lash together a log raft, equivalent to what Huckleberry Finn might have built for treks on the Mississippi. (The logging industry floated as many as six million logs downstream every year until the practice was halted for the most part in 1991.) On a raft lashed together with hemp rope, without metal fasteners or wire of any kind, you'll float downstream, past panoramic vistas, as part of a trek that can last between 1 and 7 days. Participants sleep either aboard their rafts, which consist of three layers of logs stacked atop one another, or in tents along the shore. Rafts are suitable for between two and six passengers, and are eventually disassembled and sent to paper mills to be turned into pulp. A 4-day experience covering about 48 downstream kilometers (30 miles) costs 2,020SEK ($404/£202) per adult; a 7-day jaunt covering twice that distance costs 2,410SEK ($482/£241) per person.

Less structured trips are offered by a competitor in Värmland, **Branäs Fritidscenter,** Branäs Fritidsanläggin, S-680 20 Sysslebäck, 150km (93 miles) north of Karlstad (© **564/475-70;** www.j2ski.com). This operation devotes much of its time to the rental of cross-country skis but also conducts white-water rafting on several nearby streams and rivers.

SPECIAL EVENTS Sweden's biggest music festival, **Music at Lake Siljan** ★★★, takes place during the first week of July. There are some 100 concerts covering a wide range of music at venues in both Leksand and Rättvik. Fiddle music predominates. For information, contact **Music at Lake Siljan,** Karlsviks väg 2, S-795 35 Rättvik (© **0248/ 102-90;** www.musikvidsiljan.se).

ENJOYING THE OUTDOORS

A sports-oriented and health-conscious town, Leksand provides ample opportunity for outdoor sports. The town's tourist office can provide information on local swimming, cross-country skiing, curling, ice-skating, tennis, and boat rides on Lake Siljan, all of which are available in or near the town center, depending on the season and weather conditions. There are downhill skiing facilities at **Granberget,** about 21km (13 miles) to the southwest. Granberget is neither the biggest nor the best ski facility in Sweden, but on the premises are five mechanized lifts and one restaurant (no hotels at all). A 1-day ski pass costs 280SEK ($56/£28). For information, call or write **Ski Leksand Granberget,** S-79327 Leksand (🕾 **0247/223-30;** fax 0247/223-06; www.siljan.se).

SEEING THE SIGHTS

Leksands Kyrka   Founded in the 13th century, Leksand's parish church might be of passing interest. But the frame competes with the picture: The church's pretty lakeside setting and tree-lined churchyard are so picture perfect, they're more idyllic than the church itself. It has retained its present form since 1715 and is still one of the largest rural churches in Sweden. During renovations in 1971, a burial site was found that dates from the period when the Vikings were being converted to Christianity. There are other treasures as well, including Dalarna's oldest organ, a German font from the 16th century, and a crucifix from the 15th century.

Norsgatan, near the lake. 🕾 **0247/807-00.** Free admission to the church. Mid-June to early Aug guided tours (in Swedish and English) Mon–Sat 10am–1pm and 2–5pm; Sun 1–5pm.

Fräsgården   Whoever assembled this open-air summer museum back in the 1920s had some foresight. The oldest farm buildings in Dalarna were being torn down to make way for more modern barns. Before all was lost, many of these structures were moved to this site (near the just-visited parish church), with great difficulty, and saved for future generations. Nearly all of them, as well as many 18th- and 19th-century buildings also on-site, are painted red, typical of Sweden. You'll also find old paintings from the 1700s depicting Christ and his Apostles in Dalarna dress.

Norsgatan. 🕾 **0247/802-45.** Admission 20SEK ($4/£2) adults, free for children. Mid-June to mid-Aug Mon–Fri noon–4pm; Sat–Sun noon–5pm.

Munthes Hildasholm ★   Axel Munthe (1857–1949) was a famous Swedish doctor who is remembered mainly today for his autobiography, *The Story of San Michele,* published in 1929. In the book, Munthe depicted many colorful people he'd met, among them Guy de Maupassant and Louis Pasteur. Munthe is mainly associated with Capri, where he lived on and off for half a century. With monies earned as the special physician to the royal family, including the Swedish Queen Victoria, Munthe also built this country estate on Lake Siljan. At a beautiful site near Leksand Church, it became a summer home for him and his English wife, Hilda, whom he'd married in 1907. The house is built in stone and flanked by two identical wings. Inside you'll find Munthes's art and furniture, mainly from the 18th and 19th centuries. As you walk through its 14 rooms, you'll be left with the feeling that the Munthes have only temporarily departed and are due back at any time. Mrs. Munthe laid out the **gardens** ★★, and they remain today much as she designed, especially the beautiful Peacock Garden (or Yellow Garden) with its peacock sculptures. On-site is a cafe serving coffee and Swedish pastries.

Klockaregatan 5, Kyrkudden. 🕾 **0247/100-62.** www.hildasholm.org. Admission 90SEK ($18/£9). June–Sept Mon–Sat 11am–6pm; Sun 1–6pm.

WHERE TO STAY

During the summer, you may find it fun to rent a *stuga* (log cabin) with four beds for 400SEK to 1,000SEK ($80–$200/£40–£100) per night. You can use it as a base for exploring all of Dalarna. The **Leksands Turistbyrå** (see above) will book you one. You also can inquire about renting a room in a private home.

Masesgården ★★ (**Finds**)   This is one of the most sports-and-fitness–conscious
hotels in Sweden. It has a reputation for educating guests about new eating and exercise
habits, and a philosophy of preventing disease and depression through proper diet and
exercise. Most people spend a week, participating in supervised aerobic and sports
regimes—not indulging in conventional spa-style pampering. Beside a sea inlet, with a
view of Leksand across the fjord, it's a sprawling compound of low-slung buildings.
Guest rooms are more soothing and plush than you might imagine. Each comes with a
well-maintained bathroom equipped with a shower unit.

The daily program includes lectures that stress the link between a healthy body and a
healthy soul ("Astrological Reincarnation and Modern Lifestyles" is a favorite), and
physical exercise in disciplines such as tai chi. Theme weeks concentrate on individual
subjects, such as meditation and modern yoga, and Reiki healing through applied massage. Other activities include aerobics, sometimes in a swimming pool, and weight training. Classes are conducted in Swedish, but most staff members speak English. This is not
a holiday for the faint-hearted. Be prepared to sweat and reevaluate your lifestyle, in ways
that might not always be completely comfortable.

Grytnäs 61, S-793 92 Leksand. (✆) 0247/645-60. Fax 0247/122-51. www.masesgarden.se. 34 units, 23
with bathroom. 6,260SEK–8,240SEK ($1,252–$1,648/£626–£824) per person per week in double without
bathroom; 6,975SEK–9,175SEK ($1,395–$1,835/£698–£918) per person per week in double with bathroom. Rates include all meals and 30 hr. of supervised sports activities. AE, DC, MC, V. Free parking.
Amenities: Restaurant; lounge; indoor heated pool; sauna; wellness programs. *In room:* No phone.

Moskogen Motel   You may not want to go through all the regimes attached to the
previous recommendation. In that case, Moskogen offers very basic and very different
types of accommodations, mostly red-painted summer cottages. And you don't really
have to rough it: The cottages aren't that basic and have a number of facilities. The rooms
are well furnished and comfortable, with good beds. Each unit has a tiny kitchen and a
neatly kept bathroom with shower unit. A restaurant on the premises serves light lunches
and dinners. The Moskogen is 1.5km (1 mile) west of the railway station. The motel and
red wooden huts make a good base for excursions around the Lake Siljan area.

Insjövägen 50, S-793 33 Leksand. (✆) 0247/146-00. Fax 0247/144-30. www.moskogen.com. 49 units.
960SEK ($192/£96) double; 1,430SEK–1,800SEK ($286–$360/£143–£180) suite. Rates include breakfast.
AE, DC, MC, V. Free parking. Bus: 58. **Amenities:** Breakfast room; bar; 2 heated pools (1 indoor); tennis
court; exercise room; Jacuzzi; sauna; laundry service; dry cleaning; nonsmoking rooms; rooms for those
w/limited mobility. *In room:* TV, safe.

WHERE TO DINE

Bosporen SWEDISH/TURKISH   Most guests dine at their hotels, but this little
eatery continues to attract the more independent-minded foodies. The restaurant, 360m
(1,181 ft.) west of the railroad station, maintains longer, more reliable hours than any
other place in town. Its Istanbul-derived name comes from the Turkish-born owners, and
the chefs are equally at home with both Swedish and Turkish cuisine. Shish kebab and
Turkish salads are featured, but you can also order fried Baltic herring, sautéed trout,
fresh salmon, or plank steak. The cooking is fair and even a bit exotic in a town not
renowned for its restaurants.

Torget 1. (✆) 0247/132-80. Main courses 70SEK–220SEK ($14–$44/£7–£22). AE, DC, MC, V. Summer daily
noon–11pm; mid-Sept to May daily 3–10pm.

6 TÄLLBERG ★★★

13km (8 miles) N of Leksand, 280km (174 miles) NW of Stockholm, 518km (322 miles) NE of Gothenburg

This lakeside village, charmingly in tune with the spirit and tradition of Dalarna, is our favorite spot in the whole province, and the area of choice for nature lovers in both summer and winter. Skiing, curling, skating, and sleigh riding are popular sports, and swimming and boating lure summer visitors. Tällberg's beauty was discovered after artists and other cultural celebrities built summer houses in the village, and it has more of a village-like aura than the more built-up Leksand (p. 346).

ESSENTIALS

GETTING THERE **By Plane** The nearest airport is the Dala Airport, at Borlänge, 60km (37 miles) to the east. There are no buses into Tällberg, but the trains that run between Stockholm's Arlanda Airport and Mora stop in Tällberg. Arlanda Airport (in Stockholm) is a 3-hour train ride away.

By Train Trains from Gothenburg take about 7 hours, with a change in Börlange. There are direct trains daily from Stockholm, but with many stops; the trip time is about 3¹/₂ hours. Trains also make the 10-minute run between Leksand and Tällberg. Call ✆ 771/75-75-75 for information.

By Bus There is no direct bus service from Stockholm or Gothenburg. Bus passengers get off at either Leksand or Rättvik, where local bus connections can be made. Call ✆ 0200/21-82-18 for information.

The bus and train stations here lie 2km (1¹/₄ mile) from the densest cluster of hotels, but most hotels can arrange a shuttle van to pick you up. If you prefer taking your own car, you can call for a driver through ✆ 0247/147-00.

By Car Take the E18 expressway northwest from Stockholm; then turn onto Route 70 toward Börlange and drive all the way to Tällberg, a 3-hour drive.

VISITOR INFORMATION If you need information, the **Leksand Tourist Office** handles queries (see above).

SEEING THE SIGHTS

The chief attraction of Tällberg is the village itself. (You could miss all its minor attractions and not suffer any cultural deprivation.) As you wander the main streets, the chic (and expensive) boutiques will tell you that Tällberg is not for backpackers.

For information on outdoor activities, ask the advice of the staff at any of the town's hotels. Of particular merit is the staff within the **Hotel Långbers,** S-79370 Tällberg (✆ 0247/502-90; www.langbers.se). Most indoor sports in Tällberg are guided by the staff at the **Feel House** (✆ 0247/893-86), which lies within a sports compound adjacent to the Hotel Dalecarlia (see below). They know virtually everything about sports in the Lake Siljan region. The complex at the Feel House also contains an indoor heated pool, weight lifting and exercise facilities, and sauna and massage facilities.

For those with a more historical bent, the **Holen Gustaf Ancarcronas,** Holen (✆ 0247/513-31), is old-time charm personified. This re-created village consists of a collection of nine wood-sided buildings that were restored and, in some cases, hauled into position from other parts of Dalarna under the guidance of collector and local resident Gustaf Ancarcronas between 1910 and 1911. Ancarcronas (1869–1933) amassed a considerable collection of folk artifacts during his lifetime, many of which are on display within the compound. It's open only for a limited part of each summer, from mid-June to early August daily from noon to 4pm. Admission and a guided tour costs 20SEK to 40SEK ($4–$8/£2–£4).

Another attraction from yesterday is **Fräsgården**, Ytterboda (© **0247/802-45**), a family farm estate dating from the 18th century, which today is configured as an open-air museum with a collection of Dalarna folk costumes. It maintains the same hours as Holen Gustaf Ancarcronas but charges no admission. To reach Fräsgården from Tällberg, a distance of 5km (3 miles) to the south, follow the signs to Leksand, then the signs to Ytterboda.

WHERE TO STAY

Akerblads i Tällberg ★★ (Finds) No inn in the area puts you in touch with the spirit of Dalarna more than this place. An old-fashioned family hotel since 1910 (the oldest in Tällberg), this establishment is 2km (1¼ miles) south of Tällberg station at the crossroads leading down to Lake Siljan. The core of the house is still the wooden storehouse in the courtyard, but there has been much rebuilding over the years, including an addition of minisuites. All rooms at the hotel are done up in a traditional Dala style (typical of the 18th-c. farms in the area), with comfortable beds and small bathrooms. During the winter, you can take advantage of a sleigh ride and then warm up with a log fire and hot mulled wine. In less snowy weather, bicycles are available for 70SEK ($14/£7) per day. The hotel **restaurant** is locally renowned for its home-style cooking, buffets, and homemade bread.

Sjögattu 2, S-793 70 Tällberg. © **0247/508-00.** Fax 0247/506-52. www.akerblads.se. 69 units. 1,295SEK–1,495SEK ($259–$299/£130–£150) double; 1,595SEK–1,995SEK ($319–$399/£160–£200) minisuite. Rates include breakfast. AE, DC, MC, V. Free parking. **Amenities:** Restaurant; bar; indoor heated pool; Jacuzzi; sauna; nonsmoking rooms; rooms for those w/limited mobility. *In room:* TV, minibar (in some), hair dryer.

Green Hotel ★ Although we infinitely prefer Akerblads (see above), this hotel was a real oasis one night when we arrived and our favorite was closed. It's located on a lawn sloping down toward the lake less than a kilometer (½ mile) west of the railroad station. The staff wears regional costumes, the lounge has a notable art collection, and the wide array of rooms ranges from small to VIP size. On the premises is a swimming pool whose surface is covered every Saturday night with a glass top and converted to a dance floor. Open year-round, the hotel offers an array of summer and winter sports. A few of the more luxurious bedrooms have their own fireplaces and private saunas.

S-793 70 Tällberg. © **0247/50-000.** Fax 0247/501-30. www.greenhotel.se. 101 units. 1,150SEK–1,900SEK ($230–$380/£115–£190) per person double. Rates include breakfast. DC, MC, V. Free parking. **Amenities:** Restaurant; bar; 2 heated pools (1 indoor); Jacuzzi; sauna; room service; nonsmoking rooms; rooms for those w/limited mobility. *In room:* TV, hair dryer.

Hotel Dalecarlia ★★ We especially like this well-established hotel when it's not overrun with conventioneers. This is the largest, most substantial, and most prestigious hotel in Tällberg, with a historic, woodsy-looking original structure that was built in 1910 and a state-of-the-art enlargement that was added in 1991. Set on sloping land near Lake Siljan, it evokes an alpine hotel in Switzerland, thanks to lots of varnished panels and a cozy, elegantly rustic public area that has plenty of comfy chairs for reading, gossiping, or hanging out. Bedrooms are outfitted in pastel tones, with medium-size tiled bathrooms. Although much of its business derives from its appeal to the Scandinavian companies that hold conventions within its meeting rooms, it also offers many of the diversions and outdoor activities of a lakeside resort.

The hotel's **dining room** is a large, woodsy-looking affair with big windows overlooking the lake and attentive service from a uniformed staff. Actually, we enjoy breakfast here more than any other meal. Although lunch and dinner here are good, at breakfast you can bake your own waffles and eat them with cloudberries, and even squeeze your own orange juice.

S-793 70 Tällberg. © **0247/891-00.** Fax 0247/502-40. www.dalecarlia.se. 80 units. 795SEK–1,295SEK ($159–$259/£80–£130) double; 350SEK ($70/£35) per person extra for suite. Rates include breakfast. AE, DC, MC, V. Free parking. **Amenities:** Restaurant; bar; indoor heated pool; health spa; sauna; nonsmoking rooms; rooms for those w/limited mobility. *In room:* TV, minibar, hair dryer, Wi-Fi.

Hotel Klockargården   Thanks to blackened wooden siding, steep roofs designed to shed snowfalls, and an artfully maintained rusticity, this place is evocative of a chalet in Switzerland. The whole thing is built from about a half-dozen 18th- and 19th-century wood-sided buildings, some of which were already here as part of a farmstead; others were hauled in from other parts of Dalarna. Frankly we value this place mostly for its **restaurant** (see below), but the Klockargården rents 43 well-maintained bedrooms, each of which is decorated with hand-woven textiles and woodcarvings created by local artisans.

Siljansvägen 6, S-793 70 Tällberg. © **0247/502-60.** Fax 0247/502-16. www.klockargarden.com. 43 units. 575SEK–1,245SEK ($115–$249/£58–£125) double; 1,545SEK–1,725SEK ($309–$345/£155–£173) suite (per person). Rates include breakfast. **Amenities:** Restaurant; sauna; massage pool; massage treatments. *In room:* TV, minibar (in suites), fireplace (in suites), Jacuzzi (in suites).

Siljansgården (Kids)   If you had a Swedish aunt and uncle, this is the kind of place where you might find them living on your return to the old country. In many ways, Ms. Signe Alm and her staff are part of a Sweden of long ago. Even the Swedish National Trust has recognized that these old premises should be preserved as part of local history. Originally built in 1915, this rustic, timber-sided hotel stands on 5 hectares (12 acres) of lakefront 1.5km (1 mile) west of the railroad station. There's a private bathing beach on the grounds. The hotel bedrooms are simply furnished but comfortable. Each has a neatly kept bathroom. In addition, 12 rustic summer cottages are suitable for up to four occupants, making them family favorites. Because they're not heated, they are available only in the summer. A **restaurant** in the main building is licensed for beer and wine only, and serves a one-course lunch and a three-course dinner. In spite of the winter snows, the hotel is open year-round. Cottage renters need to bring their own sleeping bags, but sheets can be rented.

Sjögattu 36, S-793 70 Tällberg. © **0247/500-40.** Fax 0247/500-13. www.siljansgarden.com. 31 units, plus 11 cottages. Year-round 420SEK–950SEK ($84–$190/£42–£95) double; May–Sept 20 only 900SEK–1,395SEK ($180–$279/£90–£140) cottage. Rates include breakfast. DC, MC, V. Free parking. Minimum stay 3 nights. **Amenities:** Restaurant; lounge; sauna; laundry service; dry cleaning. *In room:* TV.

WHERE TO DINE

Klockargården ★ (Finds) SWEDISH   Though it's known for being a hotel, we enjoy the restaurant at the Hotel Klockargården more. Local specialties here include fried elk steak with juniper berry sauce and such conventional dishes as fried steaks with garlic and wine sauce. The most appealing moment here is during the weekend smorgasbords, when the agrarian bounty of central Sweden makes itself visible on groaning buffet tables in a style that originated about a century ago.

Siljansvägen 6. © **0247/502-60.** Fax 0247/502-16. www.klockargarden.com. Reservations recommended. Main courses 110SEK–185SEK ($22–$37/£11–£19); fixed-price menu 345SEK ($69/£35). June 21–Sept 5 daily 4–10pm; closed off season.

21km (13 miles) NE of Leksand, 275km (171 miles) NW of Stockholm

Tällberg takes top billing in Dalarna, but if you can't stay there because of heavy bookings (a likely possibility in summer), then Rättvik is a most delightful runner-up. With some of the best hotels in the district, Rättvik is one of the most popular resorts bordering Lake Siljan. In summer, conducted tours begin here and go around Lake Siljan. Culture and tradition have long been associated with Rättvik; you'll find peasant costumes, folk dancing, Dalarna paintings, arts and crafts, fiddle music, and "church boats"—flamboyantly painted boats in which entire congregations are floated for Sunday services. The old style of architecture is still prevalent, and you'll see many timber houses. Carpenters and painters from Rättvik are known for their craftsmanship.

ESSENTIALS

GETTING THERE **By Plane** The nearest airport is at Mora, 30km (19 miles) to the north, and city bus nos. 70 and 270 charge 75SEK ($15/£7.50) to haul passengers from the airport to the center of Sunne.

By Train You can reach Rättvik by rail. The Stockholm train to Mora stops in Leksand, where you can catch another train for the short trip to Rättvik. Train information in Stockholm is available at the **Central Station** (✆ 771/75-75-75). Note that both the train and the bus stations lie in the center of town.

By Bus Buses to Rättvik operate Friday to Sunday from Stockholm. There also is a bus connection between Leksand and Rättvik. For schedules, call ✆ **0200/21-82-18.**

By Car From Leksand, head north on Route 70 into Rättvik.

VISITOR INFORMATION The **Rättvik Tourist Office** is in the train station, Riksvägen 40, 795 32 Rättvik (✆ **0248/79-72-10;** www.rattvik.se). It's open from June 15 to August 10 daily 10am to 7pm; from August 11 to June 14 Monday to Friday 10am to 5pm.

SEEING THE SIGHTS

Don't overtax yourself running around taking in Rättvik's minor attractions—this town is more about enjoying nature. For a sweeping view of the natural surroundings that stretches for many kilometers, drive 5km (3 miles) east of town along the road leading to Falun. Here, soaring more than 24m (79 ft.) skyward, is a red-sided wooden tower, originally built in 1897, called the **Vidablick,** Hantverksbyn (✆ **0248/102-30**). (*Warning:* There's no elevator to the top and the stairs are steep.) Admission is 40SEK ($8/£4) for adults, 5SEK ($1/50p) for children 7 to 15. On the premises are a coffee shop and a souvenir stand. The complex is open only from May 1 to September 6 daily from 10am to 5pm.

Gammelgården ★★ (✆ **0248/137-89**) is an antique Dalarna farmstead whose pastures and architecture evoke the 19th century. The Swedes are a bit crazy for open-air museums and you'll run across quite a few during your travels, but try to take in this one. The hours are erratic—basically, it's open whenever a farm resident is able to conduct a tour—so it's important to phone in advance. Upon prior notification, visits can be arranged throughout the year, but regular scheduling is most likely between mid-June and mid-August daily from noon to 5pm. Admission is 20SEK ($4/£2). To reach Gammelgården from the center of Rättvik, 1.5km (1 mile) north of town along Route 70, follow the signs pointing to Mora.

You can also visit the artists' village (established by the Swedish artist Sören Erikson) at **Rättviks Hantverksby,** Gårdebyn ((C) **0248/302-50**).

WHERE TO STAY

The traditional **Green Hotel** ((C) **0248/502-50**), signposted from the center of town and lying less than a kilometer (about ¹/₂ mile) away from the Lerdalshöjden (see below), dates from the 1600s, when it first opened as an inn. Additional rooms were added in the 1960s. With breakfast and dinner included, rooms are around 1,000SEK ($200/£100); the hotel and its restaurant are open year-round.

Hotel Gärdebygården (Value) This hotel, off Storgatan in the town center, is a very good value. Opened in 1906, it lies within a short walk of the lake, and has expanded to include a trio of outlying buildings. The comfortable rooms are sedately outfitted, with conservative furniture, and the bathrooms with shower units are very small. But some units have a view of the lake, and the big breakfast is almost like a Swedish smorgasbord. Some nights are devoted to communal singalongs; cross-country ski trails and jogging paths are a short distance away.

Hantverksbyn 4, S-795 36 Rättvik. (C) 0248/302-50. Fax 0248/306-60. 44 units. 950SEK ($190/£95) double. Rates include breakfast. MC, V. Free parking. Closed Oct–May. Bus: 58 or 70. **Amenities:** Restaurant; bar; laundry service; dry cleaning. In room: TV, minibar, hair dryer.

Hotel Lerdalshöjden ★ (Finds) This hotel has grown and prospered since 1943, when the Hagberg family took over its 11 rooms and one kitchen with a wood stove. In the 60 or so years since, they've built up a lively trade. New owners are now installed, but they carry on the same high standards of the long-ago Hagbergs. We like the panoramic views of Lake Siljan and the distant mountains. Near the top of a hill overlooking Rättvik, right next to a ski slope, the hotel lies a 10-minute walk north of the lake. The only remaining part of the original building is the **Lerdalshöjden restaurant** (see "Where to Dine," below). The guest rooms are well furnished and maintained.

Mickelsgatan, S-795 35 Rättvik. (C) **0248/511-50.** Fax 0248/511-77. www.lerdalshojden.se. 96 units. 1,200SEK ($240/£120) double; 1,900SEK ($380/£190) suite. Children under 12 stay free in parent's room. Rates include breakfast. DC, MC, V. Free parking. Bus: 58 or 70. **Amenities:** Restaurant; bar; fitness center; spa; sauna; room service; laundry service; dry cleaning. In room: TV, trouser press.

WHERE TO DINE

If a hungry visitor arrives off season and the option below is closed, a suitable alternative is the restaurant at the **Green Hotel** (see above), which serves year-round.

Lerdalshöjden SWEDISH This summer-only restaurant sits in the only original section remaining in the turn-of-the-20th-century hotel of the same name. It has long been a favorite with lake-district locals, who like its traditional, tasty Swedish home-style cooking, including fresh fish and beef dishes. Try the steak tartare with bleak (a freshwater fish) roe, or fried ptarmigan with red-currant sauce.

In the Lerdalshöjden Hotel. (C) **0248/511-50.** Reservations recommended. Fixed-price 6-course menu 645SEK ($129/£65); main courses 250SEK–275SEK ($50–$55/£25–£28). DC, MC, V. Daily noon–2pm and 6–9pm. Closed Aug 16–June 14.

8 MORA ★★

45km (28 miles) W of Rättvik, 328km (204 miles) NW of Stockholm

This old resort town in Upper Dalarna is a busy place in both summer and winter, and we find it to be a good base for touring the surrounding area. It's fabled as the town where King Gustav rallied the peasants to form an army to rise up against Denmark. This history-making event is commemorated every year in the 80km (50-mile) Vasa Race. Mora is also the hometown of the once-celebrated Anders Zorn, who is known mainly today for his paintings of nude women bathing. Between Lake Orsa and Lake Siljan, the provincial town of Mora is our final major stopover in the province.

ESSENTIALS

GETTING THERE **By Plane** You can fly from Stockholm on **Next Jet** (© **08/639-85-38;** www.nextjet.se); there are two flights per day Monday to Friday, and the flight time is 50 minutes. On Saturday and Sunday there is only one flight per day. The airport (© **0250/301-75**) is about 6.5km (4 miles) from the center; taxis meet arriving flights.

By Train There's direct rail service daily from Stockholm (trip time: 4 hr.). For information and schedules, call © **771/75-75-75.**

By Bus Weekend buses leave from Stockholm's Central Station for the 4¹/₄-hour trip. Contact **Swebus Vasatrafik** at © **0200/21-82-18.**

By Boat The *Gustaf Wasa* (see "Essentials," in the "Leksand" section, earlier in this chapter) travels between Mora and Leksand. The boat departs Leksand in the afternoon and leaves Mora at 3pm on Monday. Call © **010/252-32-92** for information and reservations.

By Car From Rättvik, continue around Lake Siljan on Route 70 to Mora.

VISITOR INFORMATION Contact the **Mora Turistbyrå,** Strandgatan 14, 792 30 Mora (© **0250/59-20-20;** www.siljan.se). It's open from June 15 to August 31 Monday through Friday 10am to 7pm, and Saturday and Sunday 10am to 5pm; September 1 to June 14 Monday to Friday 10am to 5pm.

SEEING THE SIGHTS

Mora is home to a **Santa complex** (© **0250/287-70**), which features a "replica" Santa's house and factory. Visitors can meet Santa and see his helpers making and wrapping presents for children all over the world, and kids can enroll in Santa School and participate in troll and treasure hunts.

Lisselby is an area near the Zorn Museum made up of old houses that now are used as arts-and-crafts studios and boutiques. The area was formerly home to Anders Zorn (1860–1920), Sweden's most famous painter.

Zornmuseet (Zorn Museum) ★★ The son of a brewer, Anders Zorn was born in Mora in 1860, and showed incredible artistic talent at a very young age. He became Sweden's most internationally recognizable artist, up there in a class with fellow artist Carl Larsson and sculptor Carl Milles. Zorn spent time in the United States, where he painted portraits of President Grover Cleveland and later President William Taft. As an etcher, Zorn was compared to Rembrandt—in fact, many art critics felt that Zorn surpassed the Dutch master in this genre. Zorn was also an accomplished sculptor, and it is his *Gustav Vasa* that greets Vasalopp's skiers when they arrive in Mora.

Of all the paintings here, we think *Midnight* is Zorn's masterpiece, although there are those who'll pay millions for his female nudes. Zorn painted *Midnight* in 1891 and the piece evocatively and eerily portrays a woman rowing in shadowless summer light. The same year, the artist painted his second most memorable work, *Margit,* which depicts a girl braiding her hair in the rays of light from a small window.

The museum also displays works that Zorn collected with the money he amassed from sales of his work. He was able to purchase world-class art, including paintings from his chief rival, Carl Larsson, and also from the painting prince, Eugene, as well as sculptures by Kai Nielsen of Denmark and etchings by Rembrandt. He also gathered together a large collection of the rural art and handicrafts of Dalarna.

Vasagatan 36. (*C*) **0250/59-23-10.** www.zorn.se. Admission 50SEK ($10/£5) adults, free for children under 15. Mid-May to Aug Mon–Sat 9am–5pm, Sun 11am–5pm; Sept to mid-May daily noon–4pm.

Zornsgården ★★   Zorn died here in 1920, at the age of 60—seemingly when he had exhausted all new ideas and artistic projects. He and his wife, Emma, had no children, so when Emma herself died in 1942 during the war, she donated almost all of their holdings, both property and art, to the state. The government decided to allow their home to remain as Emma had left it, hoping that it would give future generations an insight into the artistic world and visions of Sweden's greatest painter. It does so most admirably.

Their former house is large and sumptuous, and furnished with exquisite taste, from the furniture to, of course, the choice of art. Zorn's love of his native countryside is evident in his paintings, and fortunately, in spite of modern encroachments, you'll be able to see many of the unspoiled scenes he painted so long ago. After visiting his former home, we always pay our respects to this great artist by going over to his gravesite in **Mora Cemetery.**

Vasagatan 36. (*C*) **0250/59-23-10.** Admission 60SEK ($12/£6) adults, 20SEK ($4/£2) children 7–15. Mid-May to Sept Mon–Sat 10am–4pm, Sun 11am–5pm; Oct to mid-May Mon–Sat noon–1pm and 2–3pm. Full tours of the house are conducted by guides at noon, 1, 2, and 3pm (in summer every 30 min.).

NEARBY SHOPPING IN NUSNÄS

In Nusnäs, about 9.5km (6 miles) southeast of Mora, you can watch the famous *dalahäst* (wooden Dalarna horse) being made. You're free to walk around the workshops watching the craftspeople at work, and the finished products can be purchased at a shop on the premises. They also sell wooden shoes and other crafts items. **Nils Olsson Hemslöjd** (*C* **0250/372-00**) is open from June to mid-August Monday to Friday 8am to 6pm, and Saturday and Sunday 9am to 5pm; and from mid-August to May Monday to Friday 8am to 5pm, and Saturday 10am to 2pm. To find Nusnäs, take the signposted main road east from Mora, turning off to the right at Farnas. From Mora, bus no. 108 also runs to Nusnäs.

WHERE TO STAY

Best Western Mora Hotell & Spa ★   In terms of overall facilities and comfort, we'd rate this Best Western the best in town—there are no surprises, but no disappointments either. It's in the center of town across from the lakefront, a minute's walk from the tourist bureau. Renovations over the years have added sun terraces and glassed-in verandas. The interior is tastefully decorated with bright colors and folkloric accents. All accommodations—mostly midsize bedrooms—have comfortable furniture, including ample bathrooms. The hotel is known for its **Emma Spa** with superb massage and body treatments, and they certainly relieved us from the stress of checking out Stockholm. The steam rooms and Jacuzzis hit the spot, too.

Strandgatan 12, S-792 30 Mora. (C) **800/780-7234** or 0250/59-26-50. Fax 0250/189-81. www.bestwestern. com. 141 units. Sun–Thurs 1,168SEK ($234/£117) double, 1,688SEK ($338/£169) suite; Fri–Sat 748SEK ($150/£75) double, 1,288SEK ($258/£129) suite. Rates include breakfast. AE, DC, MC, V. Parking 85SEK ($17/£8.50) in the garage, free outdoors. **Amenities:** Restaurant; bar; indoor heated pool; spa; Jacuzzi; sauna; room service; babysitting; laundry service; dry cleaning; nonsmoking rooms; rooms for those w/ limited mobility. *In room:* TV, trouser press, safe, Wi-Fi.

Hotel Mora Parken ★ (Finds)   Although it is a 2-minute drive from the center of Mora, we get the impression that we're deep in the Swedish wilderness here, thanks to the location in a forested park, midway between a pond and the banks of the river Västerdal. Laid out in a low-slung, rustic design with a steeply peaked roof and lots of exposed wood, it was built in 1976 as a restaurant and expanded in 1982 into the sports-conscious establishment you see today. Accommodations are woodsy, simple, and uncomplicated, and although comfortable, are far from particularly plush. This seems to suit the participants in the many conventions held here, who enjoy rowing boats and canoes and swimming in the nearby pond, hiking in the surrounding forest, and attending meals in the **restaurant,** which serves breakfast and lunch.

Pavkuagenl, S-792 25 Mora. (C) **0250/276-00.** Fax 0250/276-01. www.moraparken.se. 75 units. Mid-June to mid-Aug and Fri–Sun year-round 830SEK ($166/£83) double; rest of year 1,295SEK ($259/£130) double. Rates include breakfast. AE, DC, MC, V. Free parking. **Amenities:** Restaurant; bar; sauna; laundry service; dry cleaning; nonsmoking rooms; rooms for those w/limited mobility. *In room:* TV.

WHERE TO DINE

Terrassen (Value) SWEDISH/INTERNATIONAL   This restaurant is a good bet for a meal even if you aren't staying at its attached hotel, the Best Western Mora Hotell & Spa. We've always come away filled and satisfied, although hardly raving about the cuisine, which is of a high standard and reliable—nothing more. Fresh produce is used whenever possible, and fresh fish and Swedish beef dishes are featured. You might begin with herring or a freshly made salad. Service is polite and efficient, and the fixed-price lunch is an exceptional value.

In the Best Western Mora Hotell & Spa, Strandgatan 12. (C) **0250/59-26-50.** Reservations recommended. Main courses 150SEK–395SEK ($30–$79/£15–£40); fixed-price lunch 90SEK ($18/£9). AE, DC, MC, V. Mon–Fri 11am–2pm and 6–9pm; Sat 6–9pm.

13

Swedish Lapland

For some, summer visits to Norrland (the entire north of Sweden) and Swedish Lapland specifically mean nothing but bleakness, unrelenting daylight, and a wilderness foreboding enough to bring a tear to the eye. But for others, it's the adventure of a lifetime: They'll fly in from Stockholm in summer just to see the sunshine after midnight above the Arctic Circle. In other words, Lapland is an acquired taste—a haven of beauty and tranquillity for many, but not all.

Swedish Lapland is Europe's last wilderness—9,400 sq. km (3,629 sq. miles) of more or less untouched nature. (The area of Norrland, which encompasses Lapland and other northern provinces, covers roughly half the area of Sweden, and one quarter of the country lies north of the Arctic Circle.) This wild, undisturbed domain of the midnight sun is a land of high mountains and plateaus; endless forests and vast swamplands; crystal-blue lakes and majestic mountains; and glaciers, waterfalls, rushing rivers, and forests.

Like the Grand Canyon and the Galapagos Islands, Lapland, whose natural wonders include a population of brown bears and alpine flora, is listed as a World Heritage Site. It has been occupied by the Sami people since prehistoric times. Most still make their living from tending reindeer herds.

Surprisingly, the territory can be reached easily. Fast electric trains take you from Stockholm to Narvik in Norway, with stops at Kiruna and Abisko. The express train, *Nordpilen*, takes a day and a night to travel from Stockholm to far north of the Arctic Circle. Once here, you'll find mailcoach buses connecting the other villages and settlements in the north.

It's much quicker to fly, of course, and there are airports at Umea, Lulea, and Kiruna. The last, for example, is reached by air in 4 hours from Stockholm. Those with more time may want to drive here. From Stockholm, just stay on E4, the longest road in Europe. From Stockholm to the Finnish border town of Haparanda, you'll ride along about 1,130km (702 miles) of good surface.

Various towns in Lapland can serve as a center from which to explore the Laponian area. We'll also preview national parks to visit in Laponia under those individual town listings.

1 ENJOYING THE GREAT OUTDOORS

In the north of Sweden you'll find wilderness outside every town, from forests to wild rivers to unspoiled coastlines to thousands of tranquil lakes to high mountains to low farmlands. Of course, getting to those villages is part of the fun, as your trip will take you along roads ranging from express highways to the smallest, winding logging paths.

We come to Norrland mainly to explore Sweden's national parks. The most spectacular of the lot is **Muddus National Park** (see "Gällivare," later in this chapter), some 49,000 hectares (121,082 acres) in all. From Gällivare, you can reach other national parks, including **Stora Sjöfället** and **Padjelanta.** These parks combine to form Europe's largest national park, a landmass of 5,225 sq. km (2,017 sq. miles). Others come to

explore the highest mountain in Sweden, **Kebnekaise,** at 2,090m (6,857 ft.); see "Kiruna," later in this chapter.

Abisko is the best center for exploring **Abisko National Park,** where the mountains tower as high as 1,170m (3,839 ft.). It is also one of the best centers for watching the midnight sun. But that's not all: It's the start of the longest marked hiking trail in Sweden, the **Kungsleden,** or "Royal Trail," which stretches from Abisko to Hemavan, a distance of 338km (210 miles).

As one of the last great wildernesses of Europe, Lapland offers even more outdoor activities. You can play golf at the most northerly courses in the world, go on horseback riding trips, experience white-water rafting along rapids, or even go canoeing. In winter, dog and reindeer teams can take you on adventures through the backcountry. In addition, Lapland has the best grayling fishing in Europe, and you can hunt for small game and elk here.

Fishing trips, golfing jaunts, horseback riding, and especially dog and reindeer sledding should be arranged in advance through a tour group before you go to Sweden. It is usually not possible to just show up and book these activities. To reserve in advance, contact **Lynx Ski Travel** (© **800/422-5969** in the U.S.; www.lynxvacations.com). For general information and bookings once you are in Sweden, most questions can be answered by calling **Destination Kiruna**, at the **Ice Hotel**, Marknadsvägen 63, S-981 91 Jukkasjärvi, Sweden (© **0980/668-00;** fax 0980/668-90). Kiruna may be able to book you on last-minute sporting activities if you've arrived without plans, but again, it's best to reserve beforehand.

GOLFING   If you want to set up a golfing adventure in north Sweden, this too should be arranged in advance. Of course, your chances of playing golf in Lapland will depend heavily on weather conditions, which may be dicey even in the summer. Summer is also the time when mosquitoes plague the golf courses, so be sure to slather on repellent before you hit the links. For information about golf vacations, contact **Idrefjällen Golfklubb,** P.O. Box 32, S-790 91 Idre (© **0253/202-75;** www.idregolf.se). Greens fees range from 190SEK to 370SEK ($38–$74/£19–£37).

HIKING & CAMPING   Swedish Lapland is a Valhalla for hikers and campers (if you don't mind the already-mentioned mosquitoes). Before you go, get in touch with the **Svenska Turistföreningen (Swedish Touring Club),** Stureplan 4c (Box 25), S-101 20 Stockholm (© **08/463-21-00;** www.stf.nu), which maintains mountain hotels and has built bridges, marked hiking routes, and even introduced regular boat service on some lakes.

Locals and visitors can enjoy hundreds of kilometers of marked hiking and skiing tracks (Mar–Apr and even May are recommended for skiing; hiking is best in the warm summer months). Some 90 mountain hotels or Lapp-type huts (called *fjällstugor* and *kåtor,* respectively) are available, with beds and bedding, cooking utensils, and firewood. Huts can be used for only 1 or 2 nights. The club also sponsors mountain stations (*fjällstationer).*

You must be in good physical condition and have suitable equipment before you set out, because most of the area is uninhabited. Neophytes are advised to join one of the tours offered by the Swedish Touring Club (contact the club for more details).

SKIING   In spite of the bitter cold, many visitors come here to ski in winter. At least snow is guaranteed here, unlike at some alpine resorts of Switzerland and Austria. Kiruna, Gällivare, and Arvidsjaur offer some of the best possible conditions for cross-country skiing. Local tourist offices will offer constantly changing advice about how to hook up with many of these activities, which naturally depend a great deal on weather conditions.

2 LULEÅ: THE GATEWAY TO LAPLAND

930km (578 miles) N of Stockholm

This is the northernmost town in all of Sweden, at least the northernmost one of any notable size. You'll suffer no great deprivation if you skip it or simply view the town as a refueling stop. Luleå is not totally devoid of charm, however. This port city on Sweden's east coast at the northern end of the Gulf of Bothnia is 113km (70 miles) south of the Arctic Circle, yet it has a surprisingly mild climate—its average annual temperature is only a few degrees lower than that of Malmö, on the southern tip of Sweden.

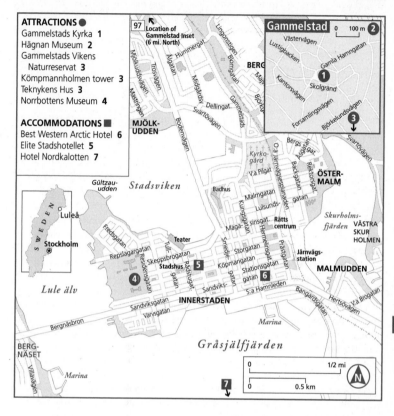

ATTRACTIONS ●
Gammelstads Kyrka **1**
Hägnan Museum **2**
Gammelstads Vikens
　Naturreservat **3**
Kömpmannholmen tower **3**
Teknykens Hus **3**
Norrbottens Museum **4**

ACCOMMODATIONS ■
Best Western Arctic Hotel **6**
Elite Stadshotellet **5**
Hotel Nordkalotten **7**

　　Establishing a city this far north was laden with difficulties. Gustavus Adolphus may have founded the city in 1621, but it wasn't until 1940 that development really took hold. Today, as the seat of the University of Luleå, the town has a population of 70,000 and is liveliest when the students are here in winter, although most foreigners (except businesspeople) see it only in summer. During this season, the town is a port for shipping iron ore; its harbor remains frozen over until May. The state-owned ironworks here have led to a dramatic growth in population since the 1940s.

　　If you have 2 or 3 hours to wander about, you can visit the town's original settlement, which enjoys protection as a UNESCO World Heritage Site.

ESSENTIALS

GETTING THERE　By Plane　SAS runs nine flights each weekday between Stockholm and Luleå (two on Sat and Sun), which take 1¼ hours. There are six flights each weekday between Gothenburg and Luleå (two on Sat, four on Sun), taking 2¼ hours. The airport is 14km (8²/₃ miles) south of Luleå; the Flygbuss costs 45SEK ($9/£4.50) per person each way, and a taxi goes for 235SEK ($47/£24) each way. For information and schedules, call ℂ **0770/72-77-27.**

(Moments) **Northern Lights & the Midnight Sun**

If you visit Lapland and Norrbotten (the remote northeastern province of Sweden) in the winter, you will see the **Aurora Borealis** ★★★, a sparkling display of colors in the sky that becomes visible at dusk.

The northern lights, as it is called, are shimmering lights with surging colors in the sky, a natural phenomenon that can amaze the observer just as much as the most lavish fireworks display. They often can be seen during the dark season, from early in the evening until midnight. The northern lights occur in the Arctic region and are seen more clearly and more frequently the farther north you travel.

The source of energy for the northern lights is the sun and solar winds. Solar wind plasma is constantly emitted by the sun at a velocity of 400km (249 miles) per second. Some of the energy absorbed by the Earth's magnetic field accelerates the ions and electrons. The electrons are steered toward the polar regions, and, at a few hundred kilometers from the Earth, the electrons collide with atmospheric atoms and molecules. On collision, a small amount of the electrons' kinetic energy is transformed into visible light.

You will also experience the **midnight sun** ★★★ above the Arctic Circle. By midnight sun, we mean that it is possible to see more than half of the sun even in the middle of the night when it is directly north. At midsummer, it can be seen south of the Arctic Circle, thanks to the refraction of light in the atmosphere. From a high hill with a good view to the north, the midnight sun can still be seen quite far to the south. The farther north you go, the longer this phenomenon lasts: In the far north, it's from the end of May to the end of July.

The light at night is milder and softer than the harsh, blinding sunshine of the day and creates an impression that time is somehow standing still. Many activities and events are connected with the midnight sun, including trips to the mountains, bike races, and nighttime fishing contests. Local tourist offices will have more information about these events.

By Train Six trains arrive daily from Stockholm (travel time: 15 hr.); an additional six come from Gothenburg (travel time: 19 hr.). Trains from Stockholm to Kiruna usually deposit passengers bound for Luleå at the railway junction at Boden, 9.5km (6 miles) northwest of Luleå. Here they board one of three connecting trains a day going between Boden and Luleå. Train traffic from Gothenburg to Luleå also necessitates a transfer in Boden. For more information, phone ⓒ **0771/75-75-75.**

By Bus A bus runs between Stockholm and Luleå on Friday and Sunday, taking 14 hours. Both the bus and the train stations are in the town center. For further information, call **Swebus** at ⓒ **0200/21-82-18** or visit **www.swebusexpress.se.**

By Car From Stockholm, take the E4 expressway north to Uppsala and continue northward along the coast until you reach Luleå.

VISITOR INFORMATION Contact the **Luleå Tourist Office** at Kulturens Hus at Skeppsbrogatan 17, S-971 85 Luleå (ⓒ **0920/45-30-00;** www.lulea.se), open in summer

Monday to Friday 10am to 6pm, Saturday 10am to 4pm; off season Monday to Friday 10am to 5pm.

SEEING THE SIGHTS

It is a rare privilege to visit any town in the north of Sweden that enjoyed its heyday in the 17th century, and historic Luleå doesn't disappoint. Some of the most evocative and historic architecture here lies 9.5km (6 miles) north of the modern city in **Gammelstad (Old Town)** ★★, the town's original medieval core and a once-thriving trading center. Its demise as a viable commercial center began when the nearby harbor became clogged with silt and was rendered unnavigable. In 1649, a new city, modern-day Luleå, was established, and the Old Town fell into decline and disrepair. Today it serves as a reminder of another era and is the site of the region's most famous church, **Gammelstads Kyrka** ★★, also known as **Neder Lulea Kyrka** (no phone). This is the largest medieval church in the north. Built in 1492, the church is surrounded by clusters of nearly identical red-sided huts, many of which date from the 18th and 19th centuries. The church rented these to families and citizens traveling to Luleå from the surrounding region as temporary homes during holy days. There's no admission fee, and it's open mid-June to mid-August daily 9am to 8pm; mid-August to mid-June Monday to Friday 10am to 2pm.

Gammelstad's other major site is the **Hägnan Museum** (also known as the **Gammelstads Friluftsmuseum**), 95400 Gammelstad (✆ **0920/45-48-66;** www.lulea.se/hagnan), consisting of about a dozen historic buildings hauled in from throughout Norrbotten. It's nothing special—we've seen better compounds in the south—but if you're in the area you might give it a look-see. It's open between June 6 and August 15 daily from 11am to 5pm, depending on the season. Entrance is free. To reach Gammelstad from modern-day Luleå, take bus no. 8 or 9 from Luleå's center.

Adjacent to Gammelstad Bay you'll find some of the richest bird life in Sweden. Ornithologists have counted 285 different species of birds during the spring migrations. The best way to experience this cornucopia of avian life involves following a well-marked hiking trail for 7km (4.3 miles) south of Gammelstad; just look for signs pointing from Gammelstad to the **Gammelstads Vikens Naturreservat** ★★. (For more information, call the Luleå Tourist Office, listed above.) The trail, consisting of well-trod earth, gravel, and boardwalks, traverses marshy, usually forested terrain teeming with bird life. En route, you'll find barbecue pits for picnics and the unstaffed, unsupervised 9m (30-ft.) **Kömpmannholmen tower** (no phone), which is useful for spying on bird nests in the upper branches of nearby trees. The trail ends in Luleå's suburb of Pörson, site of the local university, and site of a small-scale museum, **Teknykens Hus,** Pörson, 97187 Luleå (✆ **0920/49-22-01;** www.teknikenshus.se). Conceived as a tribute to the industries that bring employment and prosperity to Norrbotten, it charges an admission fee of 60SEK ($12/£6) for adults or 30SEK ($6/£3) for ages 5 to 17. In summer the attraction is open Tuesday to Friday 10am to 4pm, Saturday and Sunday 11am to 4pm; off season Tuesday to Friday 10am to 4pm. From Pörson, after your visit to the museum, take bus no. 4 or 5 back to Luleå. Hiking along the above-mentioned trail is not recommended in winter, as heavy snowfalls obliterate the signs and the path, and it's unsafe for all but the most experienced and physically fit residents.

Norrbottens Museum Close to the city center at Hermelin Park, Norrbottens Museum is worth a look because it shelters the world's most complete collection of Lapp artifacts. This is a good place to orient yourself before you move even deeper beyond the

Arctic Circle and actually meet the Lapp people. The museum also showcases how these weather-beaten people forged a living in the northern regions in bygone days.

Storgatan 2. ✆ **0920/24-35-00.** Free admission. Tues–Fri 10am–4pm; Sat–Sun noon–4pm. Bus: 1, 2, 4, 5, 8, or 9.

WHERE TO STAY

Best Western Arctic Hotel ★   This first-rate hotel (and the attached restaurant) in the heart of town is like a fortress of warmth and comfort from the bitter weather outside. With the best and most helpful staff in town, it is both functional and stylish, lying just a stone's throw from both the train station and the bus terminal. Airport buses also stop right at the entrance to the hotel. Unless it's a gray day, guest rooms are bright and fresh, each comfortably and attractively furnished in a modern style. Thoughtful touches abound throughout, including coffee and crackers available during the day in the lobby and a light sandwich buffet with fresh fruit and vegetables served on weekday evenings. Guests can relax in the hotel's whirlpool bathrooms. Even if you're not a guest, consider patronizing the on-site Resaurang Eden. Its first-class cuisine includes such signature dishes as Arctic char with mushroom sauce, or even entrecôte of elk.

Sandviksgatan 80, S-972 34 Luleå. ✆ **800/780-7234** or 0920/109-80. Fax 0920/607-87. www.arctichotel. se. 94 units. 699SEK–1,698SEK ($140–$340/£70–£170) double; 1,200SEK–1,999SEK ($240–$400/£120–£200) suite. AE, DC, MC, V. Parking 70SEK ($14/£7). **Amenities:** Restaurant; bar; sauna; room service; laundry service; dry cleaning; nonsmoking rooms; rooms for those w/limited mobility. *In room:* TV, mini-bar (soft drinks only), coffeemaker (in some), hair dryer, iron (in some), Wi-Fi.

Elite Stadshotellet ★★   This is the finest choice in town, although we are also partial to the just-recommended Arctic Hotel. The Stadshotellet has more tradition, situated as it is in a stately, architecturally ornate, brick-and-stone building that has stood in the center of town next to the waterfront since the turn of the 20th century. The airport bus stops right outside the door at a site near the north harbor, and both the bus and the train stations are within walking distance.

The hotel was conceived by "six local gentlemen" back in 1897, and they demanded a magnificent facade with excellent stone craftsmanship, spires, and towers. In 1959 a devastating fire swept across the third and fourth floors, and the cut-glass chandeliers came crashing down. To rebuild it in an authentic style, the hotel owners of the time had to import stucco workers from the south of Italy, who also restored the original roof and built a dance hall/restaurant opening onto a panoramic view of the harbor.

Each room is individually decorated and accommodations are also the most spacious in town, especially the large and luxurious suites, with bathrooms in Italian marble. Traditional Swedish fare and zestier Italian specialties are served in the signature restaurant, **Tallkotten.** In 2001, the **Bishop's Arms,** a cozy pub in the English style, was added to keep the hotel abreast of the times.

Storgatan 15, S-971 81 Luleå. ✆ **0920/27-40-00.** Fax 0920/670-92. www.elite.se. 135 units. Mon–Thurs 1,232SEK–1,650SEK ($246–$330/£123–£165) double; Fri–Sun 765SEK–1,100SEK ($153–$220/£77–£110) double; all week 1,912SEK–2,700SEK ($382–$540/£191–£270) suite. Rates include buffet breakfast. AE, DC, MC, V. Parking 120SEK ($24/£12). Bus: 1, 2, 4, 5, 8, or 9. **Amenities:** Restaurant; bar; sauna; room service; laundry service; dry cleaning; nonsmoking rooms; 1 room for those w/limited mobility. *In room:* TV, minibar, hair dryer, Wi-Fi.

Hotel Nordkalotten ★★ (Finds   More than any other, this hotel captures the spirit of the north of Sweden. Set 5km (3 miles) south of the town center, the Nordkalotten is the most architecturally intriguing lodge in the region, with some of the most charming

grace notes: In 1984, it was acquired by an independent entrepreneur who was lucky
enough to secure thousands of first-growth pine logs (many between 600 and 1,000 years
old) that had been culled from forests in Finland and Russia. Well-known Finnish architect Esko Lehmola then arranged the logs into the structural beams and walls of the
hotel's reception area, sauna, and convention center. The result, which could never be
duplicated today simply because the raw materials are no longer available, is a comfortable space that showcases the growth rings of the wood, revealing hundreds of years of
forest life—direction of sunlight, climate changes, and rainfall—a source of endless fascination for foresters and botanists.

Most unusual of all is a dining and convention room set within what is shaped like an
enormous tepee—also crafted from ancient trees—that's flooded with sunlight from
wraparound windows. Guest rooms are outfitted in soothing tones of beige and gray,
with conservatively contemporary furnishings, tiled bathrooms, and wall-to-wall carpeting. Some double rooms have their own private saunas.

Lulviksvägen 1, S-972 54 Luleå. (C) **0920/20-00-00.** Fax 0920/20-00-90. www.nordkalotten.com. 172
units. Mon–Thurs 1,940SEK ($388/£194) double room with sauna, 1,440SEK ($288/£144) standard double; Fri–Sun 1,440SEK ($288/£144) double room with sauna, 840SEK ($168/£84) standard double. AE, DC,
MC, V. Free parking. From Luleå's center, follow the signs to the airport. **Amenities:** Restaurant; bar;
indoor heated pool; sauna; laundry service; dry cleaning; nonsmoking rooms; rooms for those w/limited
mobility. *In room:* TV, minibar, Wi-Fi.

WHERE TO DINE

Nordkalotten ★ SWEDISH/LAPPISH   The cuisine here, consisting of flavors that
are unique to Sweden's far north, is one of the best examples we've found in the north of
Sweden of "living off the land." Your palate will welcome such treats as smoked filet of
trout, marinated salmon, and (maybe) the inevitable bleak roe, which for some is an
acquired taste. Other menu items include variations on elk, reindeer, and freshwater char.
Presentations are elegant, in some cases emulating the upscale restaurants of Stockholm,
and is accompanied by polite and friendly service. Of course, some patrons come for a
meal just to see what hundreds of thousands of kronors' worth of exotic and very old
timber can produce. (See the hotel review, above.) Lunch is usually served in the tepee-
shaped building that's the hotel's trademark; dinner, traditionally, is in the **Renhagen
(Reindeer) Restaurant,** where log walls, a flagstone-built fireplace, and flickering candles create a soothing but dramatic ambience.

Lulviksvägen 1. (C) **0920/20-00-00.** Reservations recommended. Main courses 89SEK–195SEK ($18–$39/
£9–£20). AE, DC, MC, V. Daily 6–10pm. From Luleå's center, follow the signs to the airport and drive 5km
(3 miles) south of town.

3 ARVIDSJAUR

699km (434 miles) N of Stockholm, 112km (70 miles) S of the Arctic Circle, 171km (106 miles) SW of Luleå

All this place needs is a modern Mae West to arrive and open a beer joint called "Klon-
dike Annie." Even though Arvidsjaur today is a modern community, it still revolves
around its old Lappish center with well-preserved, cone-shaped huts where reindeer are
rounded up and marked in June and July. Those months are the best time for most visitors to pop in.

Not all the Lapps have gone into the reindeer business. Many of the more traditional
villages still pursue a life based on hunting and fishing. A very small percentage are

nomads, following in the footsteps of their ancestors; sometimes you can see these color-ful characters come into town to pick up supplies. Many of them still wear their genuine folk dress, a sight to behold. We recently spoke to one young man in native garb and were taken aback to hear him answer us in perfect English, proving that educational standards, even in the north of Sweden, are among the highest in the world.

Arvidsjaur lies in a belt of coniferous forests bordering on the highland region; these forests alone would merit a visit. Excellent skiing, an untouched wilderness with an abundance of wildlife, dog sledding, and good fishing at the Pite and Skellefte rivers are a few of the region's temptations.

ESSENTIALS

GETTING THERE   By Plane   Arvidsjaur can be reached by air from Stockholm, with daily departures in both directions. The airport is 12km (7¹/₂ miles) from the town cen-ter. Flight time is 2 hours; there is no specially designated airport bus, but a taxi to the center of town costs 140SEK ($28/£14) per person if it's shared. For information and bookings, call **SAS** (© **0770/72-77-27**).

By Train   Arvidsjaur has rail links with Stockholm. Train schedules change depending on the time of year, so you should call for information at © **0771/75-75-75.** Arvidsjaur is on the inland railway, a line that stretches for nearly 1,290km (802 miles), running between Kristinehamn in Värmland and Gällivare in Lapland. There are rail connections to the Northern Mainline from Stockholm up to the Finnish border.

By Bus   Weekend buses from Stockholm, with a change in Skellefteå, can be booked through **Nyman & Schultz Travel Agency** by calling © **0960/65-45-00.** The distance between the bus station and the railway station is about 455m (1,493 ft.); both are close to Stortoget. For other bus connections in the area, including to Arjeplog, call © **0960/103-07.**

By Car   Most motorists take the eastern coastal road of Sweden, E4, which runs through Umeå to Skellefteå. At Skellefteå, head inland and northwest along Route 94 into Arvidsjaur.

VISITOR INFORMATION   The **Arvidsjaur Tourist Bureau,** at Östra Skolgatan 18C, 933 31 Arvidsjaur (© **0960/175-00;** fax 0960/136-87; www.arvidsjaurlappland.se), is open from June 15 to August 16 daily from 9:30am to 6pm. Otherwise, hours are Monday to Friday 9:30am to noon and 1 to 4:30pm, Saturday and Sunday noon to 4:30pm.

SEEING THE SIGHTS

Various Lapp villages are strewn throughout the north of Finland, Norway, and Sweden. One of the best of the lot is the admission-free **Lappstaden** ★★★ near the center of Arvidsjaur. More than 100 traditional houses have been moved to this site to create a Sami village as it might have appeared in the olden days. The 17th-century Sami Church Village here is the oldest and best preserved in the north of Sweden. And the huts you will see are still used during the great Sami festival on the last weekend in August, when Lapps from the surrounding area flock to Arvidsjaur for the celebration. For 30SEK ($6/£3), guided tours are offered daily at 5pm from June 19 to August 20 (summers are very short here).

The **Glommerstrask Historical Museum,** also near the town center (© **0960/202-91**), used to be an old farming estate back in the 1700s, believe it or not. (How any brave soul attempted farming here with only a few weeks of warm weather is a mystery.) The museum's collection of about a dozen buildings preserves the old way of life and has

The Lapps

The Lapp, or Sami, people have inhabited Swedish Lapland since ancient times. Their area of settlement, known as "Sapmi," extends over the entire Scandinavian Arctic region and stretches along the mountain districts on both sides of the Swedish-Norwegian border down to the northernmost part of Dalarna. Approximately 15,000 to 17,000 Lapps live in Sweden alone.

Many Lapps maintain links to their ancient culture, whereas others have completely assimilated. Some 2,500 still lead the nomadic life of their ancestors, herding reindeer and wearing traditional multicolored dress.

The language of the Lapps belongs to the Finno-Ugric group. Approximately 75% of Lapps speak northern Sami, and a large part of their literature has been published in that language. (One of the classic works of Lapp literature is Johan Turi's *Tale of the Lapps,* first published in 1910.) As with all Arctic societies, oral storytelling has also played a prominent role in Lapp culture. Among Lapps, this oral tradition takes the form of *yoiking,* a type of singing. Scandinavian governments tried to suppress yoiking in the past, but it is now enjoying a renaissance.

Handicrafts are important in the Lapp economy. Several craft designers have developed new forms of decorative art, producing a revival in Lapp handicraft tradition.

Many members of the Sami community feel that the term *Lapp* has negative connotations; as a result, it's gradually being replaced by the indigenous minority's own name for itself, *Sábme,* or with other dialect variations. *Sami* seems to be the most favored English translation of *Lapp,* and the word is used increasingly.

served to protect the fast-fading heritage of the town's locals. As you wander through it, you can see many artifacts from the early colonization of the Lapp region, including a little schoolroom that dates from the 1840s. There is also a smithy and an on-site retail shop for handicrafts made by the Lapps themselves. If you have time for only one look at Sami culture, make it Lappstaden (see above). But this other village has a certain appeal if you can spare the time. It charges 20SEK ($4/£2) for admission and is open from June 14 to August 13 Monday to Friday 10am to 4:30pm.

EXPLORING THE AREA

Directly south of Arvidsjaur lies the exquisite, mountainous preservation region of **Vittjåkk-Akkanålke** ★, a forest reserve with hiking paths cut through its wild and beautiful reaches. The paths are 1.5 to 5km (1–3 miles) in length. Also contained within the nature preserve is **Lake Stenträsket,** which is known for its char fishing. In summer, you can rent boats to tour the lake. The summit of Akkanålke can be reached by car and offers a panoramic lookout perch.

Lappish souvenirs and handicrafts are available at **Anna-Lisas Souvenirbutik,** Stationsgatan 3 (© **0960/106-33**). Other souvenir stores in town are **Handicraft Arvida,**

Storgatan 17 (© **0960/133-20**); and **Lindmarks Slöjd & Snickeri,** Hedgatan 9 (© **0960/ 217-70**).

WHERE TO STAY & DINE

Laponia Hotel ★ This hotel is fine for what it is, but don't expect too much. Nevertheless, it's the best recommended and most substantial place to stay in town, a stopping-off place since 1957. Guest rooms are comfortable, uncontroversial, outfitted the way you'd expect in an upscale motel, and filled with Nordic light from big windows. As a special feature, suites contain their own kitchenettes and sauna. The food at the hotel is the best in town, featuring both regional specialties and international dishes.

Storgatan 45, S-933 33 Arvidsjaur. © **0960/555-00.** Fax 0960/555-99. www.hotell-laponia.se. 200 units. June–Aug 890SEK ($178/£89) double, from 1,190SEK ($238/£119) suite. Rest of year Mon–Thurs 1,170SEK ($234/£117) double, from 1,870SEK ($374/£187) suite; Fri–Sun 890SEK ($178/£89) double, from 1,190SEK ($238/£119) suite. Rates include breakfast. AE, DC, MC, V. Free parking. **Amenities:** Restaurant; bar; indoor heated pool; gym; spa; sauna; laundry service; dry cleaning; nonsmoking rooms; rooms for those w/limited mobility. In room: TV, minibar, Wi-Fi.

EASY EXCURSIONS FROM ARVIDSJAUR

The town of **Arjeplog** sits on the edge of high mountain country on a peninsula between the great lakes of Uddjaur and Hornavan. The highlands in this region are studded with excellent fishing waters (you can practically catch whitefish from the roadside). It was colonized in the 16th century when silver mining started in Nasafjäll on the Norwegian border. Reindeer at that time carried the silver to **Piteä** for shipment. The church at Arjeplog was built in 1767 and contains a bridal crown (made from flowers and tree branches from the forest); legend says that it once was stolen by the Lapps but was found again up in the mountains. In **Aldorfstrom,** the neighboring silver village, you can still see some of the buildings from the old purifying plant. Today, lead ore is mined in the "underwater mine" at **Laisvall.**

Guided visits to the area stop at **Galtispouda,** a mountain range outside Arjeplog, which offers a panoramic outlook over the surrounding lakes and mountains. The Arvidsjaur tourist board (see above) organizes excursions to the area from June 30 to August 5. Tours leave by local bus (© **46/771-100-10**) from Arvidsjaur at 11:15am daily, going to Arjeplog; a one-way ticket costs 90SEK ($18/£9). At Arjeplog, you visit the silver museum and the beautiful old church. At 3pm you're picked up by a guide at the tourist information kiosk and taken by bus to **Båtsuoj,** a Sami camp in the forest where you can later enjoy a Lapp dinner in a hut.

On Friday and Saturday the return to Arvidsjaur is by an old **steam train ★★**, one of the most thrilling such rides in the north. Arrival back in Arvidsjaur is at 10pm, but the midnight light will light your way. The price of the train ride is 190SEK ($38/£19); free for children up to 12. For children under 6, the trip is free. If you visit the silver mine at Arjeplog, you pay another 50SEK ($10/£5), although children under 16 enter free.

4 TÄRNABY & HEMAVAN

360km (224 miles) NE of Umeå, 328km (204 miles) W of Luleå, 440km (273 miles) N of Östersund, 1,008km (626 miles) N of Stockholm

We'd be inclined to skip these villages if they weren't vitally necessary refueling stops in this remote wilderness area. The villages mark the end of the Kungsleden (Royal Trail;

see below), one of the greatest hiking trails in all of Europe. The trail runs from Hernavan
to Abisko, a distance of 338km (210 miles).

Tärnaby was the birthplace of Ingmar Stenmark, double Olympic gold medalist and Sweden's greatest skier. Not surprisingly, Tärnaby also is the center of Sweden's most accessible alpine region, which offers beautiful mountains and a chain of lakes. Hikers can strike out for Artfjället, Norra Storfjället, Mortsfjället, and Atoklinton (only with hired guides). And Laxfjället, with its fine ski hills and gentle slopes, is nearby on the Blå Vägen (European Rd. 79).

Hemaven is the largest tourist resort in the area. Many paths lead toward Norra Storfjället, a small mountain visible from Hemavan. A delta formed by the River Ume is particularly rich in bird life.

ESSENTIALS

GETTING THERE   By Plane   Most visitors use the airport at Umeå rather than the one at Arvisjaur because of the greater frequency of flights. The airport lies only 455m (1,493 ft.) from the center of Hemavan. You can call **SAS** for flight information at Umeå (© **0770-72-77-27**) to see which flight is more convenient for you.

By Train   Two trains depart daily from Stockholm for the far-northern rail junction of Storuman. Trains from Gothenburg headed for Storuman also are routed through Stockholm. From Storuman, it's necessary to go the rest of the way by bus (1¹/₂ hr. or more, depending on the weather). Call © **0771/75-75-75** for rail schedules.

By Bus   From the rail junction at Storuman, five buses per day make the 126km (78-mile) run to the center of Tärnaby. From the airport at Umeå, there are three or four buses a day, but it takes 5 hours. For schedules, call © **0200/21-82-18.**

By Car   Take E4 north to Stockholm, transferring onto Route E75 at the junction to Östersund. From here, take Route 88 north to Storuman, then head northwest on E37 to Tärnaby. From Arvidsjaur, head southwest along Route 45 until you reach the junction with E12 heading west.

VISITOR INFORMATION   Turistinformation, in the town center, Västra Strandvägen 1, S-920 64 Tärnaby (© **0954/104-50;** www.tarnaby.se), is open from mid-June to mid-August Monday to Friday 8:30am to 7pm, Saturday and Sunday 10am to 6pm; off season Monday to Friday 9am to 5pm.

EXPLORING THE AREA

Tärnaby and Hemavan may be tiny mountain villages almost devoid of attractions, but they are popular destinations because they mark the welcome end of the highly acclaimed and touted **Kungsleden Royal Trail ★★★**. Most hikers begin their odyssey at Abisko (see "Abisko," later in this chapter) and finish their journeys at Hemavan. However, you may prefer to go against the flow by starting at Hemavan and ending at Abisko.

Instead of overnighting at Hemavan, you can stay at Tärnaby, the little village nearby. It is much more attractive, with meadows whose midsummer wildflowers run up to the edge of the dark forests that surround the town.

The tourist office (see above) is staffed by helpful people who have the latest information on hiking and fishing in the area. Because conditions are constantly changing, depending on the weather and the day, it is wise to inquire here for advice before heading out into the wilderness on your own.

Our favorite walk, which is signposted from the town center, is across a series of meadows to **Laxfjället Mountain.** From the base of that mountain, you can look back for a panoramic view of Tärnaby. If the day is warm and sunny, you can follow the signs to the "beach" at **Lake Laisan.** Locals go swimming here in July, but if you're from somewhere tropical, the waters will surely be too cold for you.

WHERE TO STAY & DINE

Laisalidens Fjällhotell   This is an oasis, a mountain hotel built in 1953 for hikers and other adventurers. Gloriously isolated amid trees and tundra, the lodge lies 20km (12 miles) west of Tärnaby; both winter and summer trails into the surrounding mountains begin at the inn's doorstep. We'd recommend at least 1 night here; it's one of the most tranquil retreats in the north, although the lack of sound at night is "deafening." (Maybe we've spent far too much time in cities, but we swear it's hard to ignore the stillness of an arctic night.) The steep, sloping roof is designed to shed the winter's heavy snowfalls, and the dark, woodsy facade makes it look like a modern chalet. With windows opening onto views of the lake, the traditionally decorated but functional-looking guest rooms are very pleasant. Bathrooms are tiny, with shower stalls, toilets, and basic sinks. Simple Swedish food is served three times daily in the **restaurant.** The staff will arrange fishing trips and motorboat excursions to nearby lakes in the summer.

S-920 64 Tärnaby. ✆ **0954/211-00.** Fax 0954/211-63. www.laisaliden.se. 16 units. 645SEK ($129/£65) per person double. Rate includes breakfast. MC, V. Free parking. Bus: Vlå Vägen from Umeå. From the center of Tärnaby, follow Rte. 73 west for 20km (12 miles) until you come to the hotel. **Amenities:** Restaurant; bar; sauna; room service (7am–10pm); laundry service; dry cleaning. *In room:* TV, Wi-Fi.

Tärnaby Fjällhotell   You know you're in the far north when the chef at the hotel restaurant sometimes features bear on the menu. Though it may not be on the list of options while you're here, you will find reindeer, elk, game birds, and something we like even better: arctic char. But if you're not looking to devour local wildlife, there is always poultry or even vegetarian choices. Whatever you eat, if you're here in summer, opt for freshly picked cloudberries. They're simply addictive.

The restaurant isn't the only draw here: If you want to stay in the town center, this is your best bet, and it's the largest hotel in the area, which means you can sometimes find a room here when the Laisalidens (see above) is fully booked. No great architectural statements were being made in the north of Sweden in the 1950s, and the hotel reflects its time frame, but it has been improved and renovated over the years. Bedrooms are small, often decorated with pastel colors, and with purely functional furnishings.

Östra Strandvägen 16, S-920 64 Tärnaby. ✆ **0954/104-20.** Fax 0954/106-27. www.tarnabyfjallhotell. com. 36 units. 790SEK–980SEK ($158–$196/£79–£98) per person double. Rates include breakfast. AE, DC, MC, V. Free parking. **Amenities:** Restaurant; bar; gym; sauna; laundry service; dry cleaning. *In room:* TV.

5 JOKKMOKK

198km (123 miles) NW of Luleå, 1,191km (740 miles) N of Stockholm, 204km (127 miles) S of Kiruna

Surrounded by a vast wilderness, this little community on the Luleå River, just north of the Arctic Circle, is the best center for immersing yourself in the culture of the Samis. It has been a cultural center and trading post since the 1600s.

Jokkmokk, meaning "bend in the river," is also the finest base in Norrland we've found for exploring the great outdoors. Bus routes link Jokkmokk to surrounding villages, but the system offers service that is too infrequent to be of practical use by the ordinary visitor, so for most visitors, a car will be vital.

> **(Tips) A Frontier Outpost**
>
> If you're traveling from Luleå on Route 97 toward Jokkmokk, consider stopping at
> **Boden.** Founded in 1809, this is Sweden's oldest garrison town. After losing Fin-
> land to Russia, and fearful of a Russian invasion, Sweden built this fortress to pro-
> tect its interior region. Visit the Garrionmuseet (Garrison Museum), which has
> exhibits on military history, as well as uniforms and weapons used throughout
> Sweden's history.

Who comes to Jokkmokk? Other than summer tourists, visitors are mostly business travelers involved in some aspect of the timber industry or hydroelectric power. Jokkmokk and the 12 hydroelectric plants that lie nearby produce as much as 25% of all the electricity used in Sweden. Most residents of the town were born here, except for a very limited number of urban refugees from Stockholm.

ESSENTIALS

GETTING THERE By Plane The nearest airport is in Luleå, 198km (123 miles) away (see "Getting There," in the "Luleå" section, earlier in this chapter, or call **SAS** at ℭ **0770/72-77-27**). From Luleå, you can take a bus for the final leg of the journey.

By Train No trains run between Stockholm and Jokkmokk. However, three trains make the run from Stockholm to Murjek, a town lying 60km (37 miles) to the south of Jokkmokk. From Murjek, you can take one of three buses a day for the final lap into Jokkmokk.

By Bus There is one scheduled bus per day from Luleå to Jokkmokk, which is timed to meet the plane's arrival. For information, call ℭ **0200/21-82-18.**

By Car From Luleå, take Route 97 northwest.

VISITOR INFORMATION Contact the **Jokkmokk Turistbyrå,** at Stortorget 4 (P.O. Box 124), SE-962 23 Jokkmokk (ℭ **0971/222-50;** www.turism.jokkmokk.se), open from June to mid-August daily from 10am to 6pm, from mid-August to May Monday to Friday 8:30am to noon and 1 to 4pm.

LIFE AMONG THE SAMIS

At a point 7km (4¹/₃ miles) south of Jokkmokk, you'll cross the Arctic Circle, if you're traveling along Route 45. At a kiosk here, you'll even be given a souvenir certificate in case you need to prove to anybody that you're a genuine Arctic explorer.

Jokkmokk is the site of the **Great Winter Market** ★★★, a 400-year-old tradition held annually in February. It's the best place in all of Scandinavia to stock up on smoked reindeer meat if your supply is running low. Samis from all over the north, including Finland and Norway, come to this grand market held the first weekend of February from Thursday to Sunday. At this time, Samis display and sell the precious handicrafts they've been working on during the bitter winter months. Some 30,000 people flock to this market every year. If you're planning a visit, you'll need to make reservations a year in advance.

Salmon fishing is possible in the town's central lake. Locals jump in the river in summer to take a dip, but we suggest you watch from the sidelines unless you like to swim in freezing waters.

(Fun Facts) Chillin' in Jokkmokk

Jokkmokk is one of the coldest places in Sweden in winter, with temperatures plunging below –29°F (–34°C) for days at a time. In the winter, the cold weather forces the Lapp Church to inter corpses in wall vaults until the spring thaw will permit burial in the ground.

Karl IX decreed that the winter meeting place of the Jokkmokk Sami would be the site of a market and church. The first church, built in 1607, was known as the **Lapp Church.** A nearby hill, known as **Storknabben,** has a cafe from which, if the weather is clear, the midnight sun can be seen for about 20 days in midsummer.

It is only fitting that Jokkmokk is home to the national Swedish Mountain and Sami Museum **Ájtte** ★★★, Kyrkogatan (ⓒ 0971/170-70; www.ajtte.com), in the center of town. This museum (whose Sami name translates to "storage hut") is the largest of its kind; its exhibits integrate nature and the cultures of the Swedish mountain region. One part of the museum is the **Alpine Garden** (ⓒ 0971/101-00), which lies close to the museum on Lappstavägen. If you want to learn about the natural environment and the flora of the north of Sweden, this is the place to go. The mountain flora is easily accessible and beautifully arranged. There are also a restaurant and a gift shop. Museum admission is 50SEK ($10/£5) for adults, free for children under 18. The museum is open year-round: in summer Monday to Friday 11am to 5pm, and Saturday and Sunday noon to 5pm; off season it closes at 4pm.

A JOURNEY BACK IN TIME

Vuollerim   This 6,000-year-old winter settlement at the mouth of the Luleå River was created and used by a group of Stone Age people. They lived by hunting, fishing, and gathering berries and plants. They eventually abandoned the site, probably in search of better hunting grounds, and it remained untouched until 1983, when researchers from Umeå found this unique settlement, perhaps the best preserved in northern Europe. The Stone Age dwellings, populated by four to eight family groups, were equipped with a prehistoric heating system. Diggings in the area have increased knowledge of the prehistory of northern Sweden. Visitors can see a full-size replica of the dwelling, and a cafe is surrounded by an exhibition of objects found during the excavations. A slide display offers a journey through thousands of years. A museum also includes other Stone Age exhibits.

Murjeksvägen 31. ⓒ 0976/101-65. www.vuollerim.se. Admission 50SEK ($10/£5). June–Sept daily 9am–6pm; Oct–May Tues–Wed 11am–5pm. Take Rte. 97 toward Boden and Luleå 45km (28 miles) southeast of Jokkmokk.

OUTDOOR & ADVENTURE

Exploring conditions are optimal from mid-June to mid-August; you (and, unfortunately, the mosquitoes) will find the area most accessible at this time. The best way to tackle the region is to first consult the tourist office (see above). They will help with maps and advice about how to see the surrounding wilderness, and they will advise you about local conditions.

You can hike to the mighty **Muddus Fall** ★★, in a deep ravine of the Muddus River. Trips are conducted from June 2 to August 24 daily 9am to 5pm; they last about 8 hours and cover a distance of some 13km (8 miles). The price, including food, guide, and transportation, is 750SEK ($150/£75) for adults, 325SEK ($65/£33) for ages 6 to 15. It's free for ages under 6. For more information, call ℭ **0971/122-20.**

At nearby **Lake Talvatissjön** you can catch Arctic char and rainbow trout (if you're lucky). Visit the tourist office for a *fiskekort* (fishing permit). At the lake is a cleaning table for the fish, and a fireplace or grill in case you'd like to cook your catch. We recently prepared our own grilled char luncheon, inviting some visiting Stockholmers to join us. They flattered us by telling us it was their best meal of the trip.

SHOPPING

At **Jokkmoks Tenn,** Järnvägsgatan 19 (ℭ **0971/554-20**), you will find the best collection of Sami traditional handicrafts. A workshop here is carried on as a family business. The best buys are in pewter objects and Lapp jewelry. If you'd like a selection of tough and durable clothing for winter, head for **Polstjärnan Atelje,** Hantverkargatan 9 (ℭ **0971/126-73**). At **Jokkmokks Stencenter,** Talvatis (ℭ **0971/122-35**), rocks and minerals from the surrounding region are turned into beautiful jewelry and other items. Some of the offerings include mylonite, which is warm and colorful in red-black shades; unakite, in pink and green with flower patterns; quartzite, with various patterns and colors; gabbro, which is black with golden flakes of pyrite; and hornfels, in a soft brown, almost beige, color. You can tour the workshop here Monday to Friday in July from 10am to 6pm, and at other times by appointment.

WHERE TO STAY & DINE

Hotel Jokkmokk ★ ⓕⓘⓝⓓⓢ   The largest and best-appointed hotel in town was built in the mid-1980s near the town center and close to Lake Talvatis and an adventure-laden northern wilderness. Designed in a modern format that includes simple, boxy lines and lots of varnished hardwoods, it offers well-maintained, well-organized, well-upholstered, and comfortable shelter against the sometimes-savage climate. The feeling that this really is a big-city hotel in a small town derives from the fact that some of its staff and managers are urban refugees from the Swedish capital, who moved here to get closer to the great outdoors. Guest rooms have big windows overlooking the lake, the forest, and, in some cases, the lakeside road. All have fresh colors inspired by a Scandinavian springtime, and shower-only bathrooms with plenty of very welcome hot water. Six of the units are designated as "ladies' rooms"—especially feminine bedrooms adorned with pastels and florals.

There's not a great variety of restaurant options in Jokkmokk, but you'll find the best evening dining in town in the Jokkmokk's well-managed **dining room.** Within a carpeted room with laminated ceiling beams and a sweeping row of windows overlooking the lake, you'll enjoy rich and flavorful specialties whose ingredients are found in the surrounding Lappish terrain. Specialties include a "Jokkmokk pan" that consists of a mixture of cubed reindeer filet, mushrooms, onions, and potatoes, bound together in an herb-flavored cream sauce and served in a copper chafing dish brought directly to the table. Other unusual choices include local freshwater char with saffron sauce, and filet of elk with forest mushroom sauce. Main courses are 195SEK to 315SEK ($39–$63/£20–£32).

Box 85, Solgatan 455-96231, S-262 23 Jokkmokk. ℭ **0971/777-00.** Fax 0971/777-90. www.hoteljokkmokk. se. 89 units. Mid-June to mid-Aug 975SEK ($195/£98) double; rest of year Mon–Thurs 1,575SEK ($315/£158) double, Fri–Sun 975SEK ($195/£98) double; year-round 1,850SEK ($370/£185) suites. Rates include buffet breakfast. AE, DC, MC, V. Free parking. **Amenities:** Restaurant; bar; gym; sauna; laundry service; dry cleaning; nonsmoking rooms; rooms for those w/limited mobility. *In room:* TV.

Hotell Gästis ★ You wouldn't know it from the rather bleak facade, but this hotel is a landmark, dating from 1915 when it was the only place to stay in the area. It lies in the exact center of town about 180m (591 ft.) from the rail station, so it has convenience going for it. Even though it has been considerably improved and upgraded, it still evokes the aura of a frontier country hotel. It offers well-maintained rooms with modern furnishings, and small bathrooms. Floors are either carpeted or covered in vinyl. The restaurant serves well-prepared meals, including continental dishes and *husmanskost* (good home cooking). Entertainment and dancing are presented once a week, and the sauna is free for all hotel guests.

Harrevägen 1, S-96 231 Jokkmokk. © **0971/100-12.** Fax 0971/100-44. www.hotell-gastis.com. 27 units. 1,095SEK ($219/£110) double; 1,200SEK ($240/£120) triple. Rates include breakfast. AE, DC, MC, V. Free parking. **Amenities:** Restaurant; bar; sauna. *In room:* TV, hair dryer.

6 KVIKKJOKK

1,109km (689 miles) N of Stockholm, 97km (60 miles) W of Gällivare, 172km (107 miles) W of Luleå, 119km (74 miles) NW of Jokkmokk

Unlike some of the dreary hamlets—mere refueling stops—we've passed through, Kvikkjokk is one of Lapland's most beautiful resorts. (It was once a silver ore mining center way back in the 1600s.) But the real reason visitors flock here is that it is the gateway to the Sarek National Park (see below), the largest wilderness area in Europe and the most evocative of the Swedish highlands.

This is the end of Route 805, which has taken us north to this remote wilderness. You'll have company at the end: Kvikkjokk is home to the Nordic bear, the lynx, the wolverine, and the Swedish golden eagle.

ESSENTIALS

GETTING THERE By Train & Bus Take the train to Jokkmokk (see above), from which you must change to a bus to Kvikkjokk. For rail information and schedules, call © **0771/75-75-75.** Two buses per day run between Jokkmokk and Kvikkjokk, a distance of 119km (74 miles). Unfortunately, the buses don't always connect with train arrivals from Stockholm. For schedules, call © **0200/21-82-18.**

By Car Take E4 north from Stockholm to Luleå, then head northwest along Route 97 through Boden to Jokkmokk. To get here from Jokkmokk, drive north on Route 45. After passing the town of Vaikijaur, turn west on a secondary road, following the signs to Klubbudden. Continue west on this road, passing through the towns of Tjåmotis, Njavve, and Arrenjarka until you reach Kvikkjokk.

VISITOR INFORMATION The tourist office at Jokkmokk (see above) can provide data about the area.

EXPLORING THE WILDERNESS

Talk about roughing it: We've hiked many parts of the world, and Sarek was one of our toughest challenges. Yet it is so fascinating and so filled with wonderful things that it's a grand adventure for those wanting to plunge into its vast miles of wilderness. The **Sarek National Park ★★★**, between the Stora and Lilla Luleälv, covers an area of 1,208 sq. km (466 sq. miles), with about 100 glaciers and 87 mountains rising more than 1,770m opens onto Lake Laidaure. In winter, sled dogs pull people through here.

In 1909, Sweden established this nature reserve in the wilderness so that it could be preserved for future generations. To take a mountain walk through the entire park would take at least a week; most visitors stay only a day or two. Although rugged and beautiful, Sarek is extremely difficult for even the most experienced of hikers. There is absolutely nothing here to aid visitors—no designated hiking trails, no tourist facilities, no cabins or mountain huts, and no bridges over rivers (whose undertows, incidentally, are very dangerous). Mosquitoes can be downright treacherous, covering your eyes, nose, and ears. You should explore the park only if you hire an experienced guide. Contact a local hotel such as **Kvikkjokk Fjällstation,** below, for a recommendation.

Kvikkjokk is the starting or finishing point for many hikers using the **Kungsleden Trail.** Call the **Svenska Turistforeningen** at ✆ **08/463-21-00** for information and also see "Abisko," later in this chapter. One- or 2-day outings can be made in various directions. Local guides also can lead you on a boat trip (inquire at the hotel listed below). The boat will take you to a fascinating delta where the Tarra and Karnajokk rivers meet. The area also is good for canoeing.

WHERE TO STAY & DINE

Kvikkjokk Fjällstation Originally established in 1907 by the Swedish Touring Club, and enlarged with an annex in the 1960s, this mountain chalet offers simple, no-frills accommodations for hikers and rock climbers. It's also the headquarters for a network of guides who operate canoe and hiking trips into the vast wilderness areas that fan out on all sides. Accommodations are functional, woodsy, and basic, and include eight double rooms, eight four-bed rooms, and two cabins with four beds each. There are a sauna, a plain **restaurant,** and access to canoe rentals and a variety of guided tours that depart at frequent intervals. The station is open only from February 4 to April 23 and June 17 to September 17. There is no laundry service, but there is a washing machine offered to guests. For information about the Kvikkjokk Fjällstation out of season, call the **tourist information office** in Jokkmokk (129km/80 miles away) at ✆ **0971/222-50.**

S-962 02 Kvikkjokk. ✆ **0971/210-22.** Fax 0971/210-39. 18 units, none with bathroom. 275SEK–415SEK ($55–$83/£28–£42) per person. AE, MC, V. Free parking. Closed Sept 19–Feb 15. **Amenities:** Restaurant; lounge; sauna. *In room:* No phone.

---

7 GÄLLIVARE

97km (60 miles) N of the Arctic Circle, 1,198km (744 miles) N of Stockholm

As one of the most important sources of iron ore in Europe, Gällivare has a grim, industrial look. Traditionally, it has been a rather dour mining town, despite its location at the center of some of the great unspoiled wonders of Europe. The town had no involvement with resort-style sports until the Dundret hotel (see "Where to Stay & Dine," below) began its high-energy marketing efforts.

This is a land of contrasts, from high mountain peaks to deep mines. We visit Gällivare only to explore the national parks, which range from primeval forests at Muddus to panoramic terrain at Stora Sjöfjället. If you come in winter, the northern lights are enthralling.

GETTING THERE **By Plane** There are two direct flights per day from Stockholm. There also are several commuter planes daily through Umeå to the Lapland Airport at Gällivare, which is 8km (5 miles) NE of the center of town. Instead, passengers can pay for a shared taxi, at 100SEK ($20/£10) per person each way. Call **Swedline** (✆ **0495/24-90-50**) for information and schedules.

By Train The night train from Stockholm leaves about midday, allowing you to wake up in the center of Gällivare in the morning in time for breakfast. For information and schedules, call ✆ **0771/75-75-75.**

By Bus The **Regional Express** has convenient daily runs that link the center of Gällivare with Luleå, Ostersund, and Narvik in Norway. For information and schedules, call ✆ **0200/21-82-18.**

By Car From Jokkmokk, continue northeast along Route 45.

VISITOR INFORMATION **Tourist Information,** Centralplan 3, SE-982 36 Gällivare (✆ **0970/166-60;** www.visit.gellivare.se), is normally open Monday to Friday 8am to 5pm. But from June 19 to August 13, it keeps daily hours 8am to 10pm when the sun is still shining.

FROM MOUNTAINS TO MINES

Many visitors, especially those from Stockholm, come for the winter skiing. Not us. We prefer the sunny alpine slopes of Switzerland or Austria—we don't like skiing in the dark. Often national ski teams from abroad come here for training, as the town itself lies only a 10-minute drive from the ski slopes and trails. Snow is virtually guaranteed here earlier than anywhere else in Sweden—from late October to late April. In fact, the ski season is Sweden's longest—200 days of the year.

The Dundret Hotel (see "Where to Stay & Dine," below) owns all the lifts and controls access to the slopes and other ski-related infrastructures in town. Lift tickets cost 300SEK ($60/£30) per day, or 700SEK ($140/£70) for 3 days. (**Note:** These prices are inexpensive when compared to those of the alpine resorts farther south.)

If you follow Route 45 8km (5 miles) south of Gällivare, you'll arrive at **Dundret,** or Thunder Mountain. We've found that this is the optimal spot to witness the spectacle of the midnight sun, best viewed from June 2 to July 12 from a table at the cafe on the summit, which is open daily in summer from 9pm to 1am. The **panoramic view** ★★ takes in the iron-ore mountain of Malmberget to the north and the peak of another mountain, Kebnekaise, to the northwest. You also can see the national parks of Sarek and Padjelanta to the west. Even the valley of the Lule River, with the mountains of Norway in the backdrop, can be viewed on a clear night.

Many visitors come here to take **mine tours,** which can be booked at the tourist office. Visitors can take two different tours, both offered only from June to August. One goes to an underground iron-ore mine daily at 9:30am and 1pm, and costs 250SEK ($50/£25); the other visits a copper mine Monday, Wednesday, and Friday at 2pm, and also costs 250SEK ($50/£25). The latter tour always takes in **Kåkstan,** which is the shanty town in Malmberget, dating from 1888 when jobs were plentiful and wages high—but housing was scarce.

The iron mine tour of **Gruvtur** takes 3 hours and also visits the Gruvmuseet (mining museum), which displays artifacts from 250 years of mining. You also can visit various production sites and go underground to the ore face. The copper mine tour lasts 3¹/₂ the largest copper mine still operating in Europe, and it's also Sweden's largest gold mine, producing 2 tons of gold annually. To our dismay, we discovered that no free samples are given away.

EXPLORING THE NATIONAL PARKS

Far more intriguing to us than the mines or winter skiing are the Gällivare parks—we consider them some of the greatest national forestlands in all of Sweden. Various little unmarked roads (open in summer only) west of Gällivare will take you through the parks, but the best way to visit them is to ask the tourist office to pinpoint a tour route for you—a wonderful service that takes your time and stamina into account. They also can give you up-to-date road conditions, supply maps, answer questions, and advise you on the best ways to experience the parks.

If you plan serious hiking, write (they don't accept calls) the **National Council on Mountain Safety,** Fjällsäkerhetsrådet at Naturvardsverket, S-171 85, Solna.

Muddus National Park ★★★

Muddus, south of Gällivare, is one of Sweden's most spectacular parks. Fortunately, it also is the park most often recommended to beginners or less experienced hikers. It's always best to check locally before starting out on any exploration deep into the wilderness, but some general guidelines are as follows: During May and early June, the ground at Muddus is most often boggy and wet because of rapid snowmelt. Conditions are best in July and early August, but keep in mind that summers are short and the weather conditions variable. It can be hot and sunny at Muddus one hour and raining the next. By mid-August snow could be falling.

Essentially, Muddus consists of marshland and forest (mostly pine) in the area between Gällivare and Jokkmokk. It's worth exploring some of its 48,000 hectares (118,611 acres), which house bears, moose, otters, wolverines, and many bird species. In summer, we've spotted grazing reindeer and even whooper swans. The Muddusjokk River flows through the park, providing a panoramic 42m (138-ft.) waterfall. Trails also cross the park; they're well marked and lead visitors to the most scenic spots.

If you have time only to sample the park's beauty and don't plan on an extensive in-depth penetration of the forest, you can explore the western edges of Muddus, which skirt Route 45 as it goes north from Gällivare. The best approach is to leave Route 45 at Liggadammen. Even if you don't have a car, several buses per day in summer run from Gällivare to Liggadammen. Once here, you'll see a trail leading to Skaite. You can follow this trail for a couple of hours, and once at Skaite, you can take an extensive hiking trail that stretches for 50km (31 miles). This well-marked trail has cabins along the way, plus a campsite by Muddus Falls, which is the most beautiful part of this national park.

Stora Sjöfället & Padjelanta ★★★

Stora Sjöfället, along with Padjelanta National Park, is Europe's largest national park. Padjelanta demands more mountain hiking experience than Stora Sjöfället. The forests here contain many of the same species as the alpine areas, but there also are blue hares, moose, foxes, ermines, squirrels, otters, martens, and lynx. The most common fish are trout, alpine char, grayling, burbot, and whitefish. Reindeer breeding is carried on throughout the year in both parks, with about 125 reindeer breeders owning a total of 25,000 animals. During spring, summer, and autumn, most Lapps live in these mountains at about seven settlements, which include Ritjem and Kutjaure. **Lake Virihaure ★★★** in Padjelanta National

A Winter Wonderland

At least a dozen well-maintained downhill slopes of varying degrees of difficulty are to be found at **Dundret ski resort** (see below). Six of these slopes are illuminated for use throughout the long, dark winter. On the mountain, there's also a small-scale ski jump; a health and fitness center with a limited array of spa facilities and a very attractive log-sided room that contains a heated indoor pool; facilities for snowboarding; and Snowland, a child-care and entertainment facility designed to interest and amuse young children, presumably while their parents take time out for themselves. (A regular sight here are snow bears, inspired by the characters at Disney, who ride with young children in motorized sleighs.) Kiosks and sports shops rent and sell ski equipment and accessories. The staff at the resort is adept at arranging snow-scooter safaris, ice fishing, dog-team trips, junkets on sleighs pulled by reindeer, overnight stays in Lapp tents, and outdoor barbecues, regardless of the season. They also can set up visits to remote mountain streams where you can catch graylings; the schools of graylings found in this part of Sweden are the most concentrated of this type of fish in all of Europe.

Park is often called Sweden's most beautiful lake. We're not quite sure about that, although it is truly lovely.

Both parks contain marked hiking trails, and overnight accommodations are available in cabins—mainly Lapp huts and cottages. Good hiking equipment, including a tent, is advisable if you're planning a long hike through either park. Huts are just basic cabins with a roof and four walls—you'll have to bring a sleeping bag. They generally have summer-only toilets. Cottages vary but may have beds (you provide your own sleeping bag) and cooking facilities. They also have toilets (but a shower is rare). Hikers usually just crash at huts, but cottages should be reserved. Call the **Swedish Touring Club** (© **08/463-21-00**) before you go. You can fish in Padjelanta with a permit (contact any tourist office), but not in Stora Sjöfället.

WHERE TO STAY & DINE

Dundret ★ (Kids)   Although Gällivare contains about a half-dozen other hotels and guesthouses, this is the only one that caters to ecology lovers, sports enthusiasts, and anyone interested in direct, firsthand exposure to Lapland's great outdoors. It dates from the 1920s, when nearby peaks hosted ski competitions for national athletic groups. The main building you'll see today was constructed in the 1950s, with frequent improvements and enlargements ever since. Known fondly by the staff as Björn Fälten (the Bear Trap), it's the longest log-built building in Europe, with all the idiosyncratic and rustic touches you'd expect.

The hotel resort has concentrated lately on the construction and maintenance of 90 cottages, each of them built of wood and outfitted in a rustic style appropriate to the far north. Each has a kitchen, holds up to four people, and receives a minimum of time and attention from the staff once the occupants have checked in. Preferable to us are the

conventional hotel rooms; each receives daily maid service and is outfitted in a cozy,
modern style that includes views over the surrounding wilderness, lots of heat and
warmth, and comfortable chairs, beds, and small sofas. Bathrooms (with showers in both
cottages and hotel rooms) are very compact, but they are well kept, with up-to-date
plumbing.

P.O. Box 82, S-982 21 Gällivare. © **0970/145-60.** Fax 0970/148-27. www.dundret.se. 35 units; plus 90
self-catering cottages with kitchen. 995SEK–1,390SEK ($200–$280/£100–£140) double; rate includes
breakfast. 895SEK–1,095SEK ($179–$219/£90–£110) 4-bed cottage, with linens; breakfast 70SEK ($14/£7)
extra per person. A 1-time final cleaning fee is 450SEK–680SEK ($90–$136/£45–£68), regardless of the
length of your stay in a cottage. AE, DC, MC, V. From Gällivare's center, drive 3.2km (2 miles) north, following the signs for Jokkmokk. **Amenities:** Restaurant; indoor heated pool; fitness center; sauna; children's
center; laundry service; nonsmoking rooms; winter sports; snowboarding; chairlift. *In room:* TV, Wi-Fi.

8 KIRUNA

193km (120 miles) N of Jokkmokk, 1,317km (818 miles) N of Stockholm

Covering more than 4,800 sq. km (1,853 sq. miles), Kiruna is the largest city in the world
in terms of geography. Its extensive boundaries incorporate both Kebnekaise Mountain and
Lake Torneträsk. This northernmost town in Sweden lies at about the same latitude as
Greenland. The midnight sun can be seen here from mid-May to mid-July.

Unless drastic changes are made, Kiruna as we know it may not exist a few years from
now. It's in danger of sliding down a hole left by the iron ore mines that put this Arctic
outpost on the map a century ago. Before the earth swallows it up, Kiruna is going to
have to be moved. Its railway station and new highway are being relocated first. At the
moment, the town's inhabitants face no immediate threat from the hole carved out by
mines more than a kilometer under their feet, but in the years ahead, many houses in the
affected area will be loaded onto large trailers and moved to new and safer locations.
Some of these buildings will be difficult to move—City Hall, for example, will have to
be cut into six pieces. A similar solution may have to be devised for the town's wooden
church, dating back to 1913.

During World War II, iron ore from the mines here was exported to Nazi Germany,
which did not earn "neutral" Sweden ever-lasting love from Norway, which suffered from
Nazi oppression.

ESSENTIALS

GETTING THERE   **SAS** (© **0770/72-77-27**) flies twice daily from Stockholm (flight
time: 95 min.). The airport is a 15-minute drive north of the town center; a Flygbuss
operates periodically, or a taxi is 350SEK ($70/£35) each way. Two or three trains per day
make the 16-hour trip to the center of Gällivare, a major rail junction. From here, you
can change trains to Kiruna, a trip of 1¹/₂ hours. For schedules and information, phone
© **0771/75-75-75.** There's also daily bus service between Gällivare and Kiruna. Contact
Länstrafiken at © **0926/756-80.** From Gällivare, continue northwest along E10.

VISITOR INFORMATION   Contact the **Kiruna Turistbyrå,** Lars Janssons Vagen 17
(© **0980/188-80;** www.lappland.se), open from June 15 to August 20 Monday to Friday
8:30am to 8pm, Saturday and Sunday 8:30am to 6pm; from August 21 to June 14
Monday to Friday 8:30am to 5pm, Saturday 8:30am to 2:30pm.

Kiruna, which emerged at the turn of the 20th century, owes its location to the nearby deposits of iron ore.

In summer, **InfoMine Tours** ★★ descends 540m (1,772 ft.) into the earth, where you can see the area where 20 million tons of iron ore are dug up every year. Tours leave every hour from 9am to 4pm, with groups forming outside the tourist office (see above). The cost is 250SEK ($50/£25) or 150SEK ($30/£15) for students and children. These tickets are available at the tourist office.

Southeast of the railroad station, the tower of the **Stadshus** (© 0980/704-96) dominates Kiruna. The cast-iron lookout, inaugurated in 1963, was designed by Arthur von Schmalensee and Bror Markland and features unusual door handles of reindeer horn and birch. A carillon of 23 bells rings out at noon and 6pm daily. The interior draws upon materials from around the world: a mosaic floor from Italy, walls of handmade brick from the Netherlands, and pine from the American Northwest. Note also the hand-knotted hanging titled *Magic Drum from Rautas,* a stunning work by artist Sven Xet Erixon. The upper part of the hanging depicts the midnight sun. Inside you'll find an art collection and some Sami handicraft exhibits. It's open June to August Monday to Friday 9am to 6pm, and Saturday and Sunday 10am to 6pm; September to May Monday to Friday 10am to 5pm.

A short walk up the road will take you to the **Kiruna Kyrka** ★★, Kyrkogatan 8 (© 0980/678-12), open Monday to Friday from 9am to 6pm, Saturday and Sunday 11am to 4:45pm. Gustaf Wickman designed the unusual 1912 church, which has a free-standing bell tower supported by 12 props, like a stylized Sami tent. Indeed, the dark timber interior evokes a Lapp hut, with an origami design of rafters and wood beams. Sweden's architects on several occasions have voted it as their country's most beautiful building. Christian Eriksson designed the gilt bronze statues standing sentinel around the roofline; they represent such states of mind as shyness, arrogance, trust, melancholy, and love. Above the main door of the church is a relief depicting groups of Lapps beneath the clouds of heaven, also Eriksson's creation. The altarpiece by Prince Eugen evokes Paradise as a Tuscan landscape, which strikes us as an incongruous image for this part of the world. Eriksson also created the cross that depicts Lapps praying and, at its base, a metal sculpture entitled *St. George and the Dragon.*

You also can visit **Hjalmar Lundbohmsgården** (© 0980/701-10; www.hjalmarsgard. se), the official museum of the city of Kiruna. It's situated in a manor house built in 1899 by the city's founder and owner of most of the region's iron mines, Hjalmar Lundbohm. Many of the museum's exhibits deal with the city's origins in the late 19th century, the economic conditions in Europe that made its growth possible, and the personality of the entrepreneur who persuaded thousands of Swedes to move north to work in the mines— no small accomplishment we'd say. It's open June through August Monday to Friday from 10am to 6pm; off season, you must phone ahead for opening hours, which could be any day of the week between the hours of 8am and 4pm. Admission is 35SEK ($7/£3.50) for adults, 20SEK ($4/£2) for children 7 to 15, free for children under 7.

VISITING SWEDEN'S HIGHEST MOUNTAIN

Eighty kilometers (50 miles) away from the commercial center of town, the highest mountain in Sweden, **Kebnekaise Mountain** ★★, rises 2,090m (6,857 ft.) above sea level. This is a trip best made from late June to September; otherwise, weather conditions can cause problems. To reach the mountain, take a bus to **Aroksjokk** village from the

Sweden's Doorway to the Universe

Unknown to much of the world, a few dozen kilometers from Kiruna in the middle of an Arctic forest lies **Esrange** ★★ (© **46/980-72-000;** www.ssc.se/esrange). This is Europe's only civilian rocket base and a major center of space and climate research on global warming. Rocket launches, the testing of unmanned aircraft, and balloon ascents are all conducted from this base.

Among other endeavors, Esrange is a center of research on the aurora borealis, or northern lights, and on the earth's shrinking atmospheric ozone layer. Visitors can see the local rocket launch area and the balloon launchpad where high-altitude balloons are sent into the atmosphere.

Esrange lies 40km (25 miles) east of Kiruna in the direction of Jukkasjärvi. Four-hour tours are conducted June to August at 9am, costing 390SEK ($78/£39) per person. Arrangements can be made at the tourist office (see above). Who would have thought that so much was going on in a cold, dark Arctic forest?

bus stop in Kiruna's center (no phone). Ask for schedules at the train station next door, where someone is usually on duty, or check with the Kiruna tourist office. From **Aroksjokk** village, a motorboat will take you to the Lapp village of **Nikkaluokta.** From here, it's a 21km (13-mile) hike (including another short boat trip) to the foot of the mountain. The trail is signposted at various points and runs along streams, and through meadows and pinewoods. Some of the Sami in the village of Nikkaluokta will offer you their services as guides on the hike; negotiate the fee depending on the time of the year and the number of your party. You do not have to seek them out; once you arrive at Nikkaluokta, they will come to you, eager to assist. The Samis can also arrange overnight stays and hikes or boating trips. The Swedish Touring Club has a mountain station at Kebnekaise, and the station guide here can arrange group hikes to the summit (requiring about 4 hr. for the ascent). It's a fairly easy climb for those in good physical shape; no mountaineering equipment is necessary. It also is possible to ski on Kebnekaise mountain in winter. Do so if you must, but you won't find us on this cold, dark mountain at that time.

SHOPPING

About 4km (2½ miles) north of Kiruna along highway E10 is a showcase of Lappish artifacts, **Mattarahkka** ★★ (© **0980/160-77**). Established in 1993, it's a log house capped proudly with the red, blue, yellow, and green Sami flag. The site includes workshops where visitors can watch traditional Sami products (knives, leather knapsacks, hats, gloves, and tunics) being made. Many of the items are for sale. The interior includes a simple cafe. The site is open from late June to August daily 10am to 6pm; off season Monday to Friday noon to 6pm.

WHERE TO STAY

In addition to the hotels listed below, **Jukkasjärvi Wärdshus och Hembygdsgård** ★ at Jukkasjärvi rents accommodations (see "Where to Dine," below).

Hotel Kebne och Kaisa This hotel doesn't pretend to be more than it is—in other words, it doesn't try to impress you with its facade or its public rooms. What it does

(Finds) The Ice Hotel ★★★

Since the late 1980s, the most unusual, and most impermanent, hotel in Sweden is re-created early every winter on the frozen steppes near the iron mines of Jukkasjärvi, 200km (124 miles) north of the Arctic Circle. Here, the architect Yngve Bergqvist, financed by a group of friends who (not surprisingly) developed the original concept over bottles of vodka in an overheated sauna, uses jackhammers, bulldozers, and chainsaws to fashion a 60-room hotel out of 4,000 tons of densely packed snow and ice. The basic design is that of an igloo, but with endless amounts of whimsical sculptural detail thrown in as part of the novelty. Like Hilton's worst nightmare, the resulting "hotel" will inevitably buckle, collapse, and then vanish during the spring thaws. Despite its temporary state, during the long and frigid northern midwinter, it attracts a steady stream of engineers, sociologists, and the merely curious, who avail themselves of timely activities in Sweden's far north: dog-sled and snowmobile rides, cross-country skiing, and shimmering views of the aurora borealis. On the premises are an enormous reception hall, a multimedia theater, two saunas, and an ice chapel appropriate for simple meditation, weddings, and baptisms.

Available for occupancy (temperatures permitting) between mid-December and sometime in March, the hotel resembles an Arctic cross between an Arabian casbah and a medieval cathedral. Minarets are formed by dribbling water for about a week onto what eventually becomes a slender and soaring pillar of ice. Domes are formed igloo-style out of ice blocks arranged in a curved-roof circle. Reception halls boast rambling vaults supported by futuristic-looking columns of translucent ice, and sometimes whimsical sculptures whose sense of the absurd heightens a venue that visitors describe as surreal. Some of these are angled in ways that amplify the weak midwinter daylight that filters through panes of (what else?) chain-sawed ice.

Purists quickly embrace the structure as the perfect marriage of architecture and environment; sensualists usually admire it hastily before heading off to warmer climes and other, more conventional hotels.

What's the most frequently asked question on the lips of virtually everyone who shows up? "Is it comfortable?" The answer is "not particularly," although a

promise are well-furnished bedrooms with comfortable beds and personalized service that only a small hotel can provide. Located next to the police station on the main road passing through Kiruna (airport buses stop at the door), it consists of two separate buildings, both constructed around 1911. The rooms are modern and comfortable, each decorated in a warm, cozy style. The hotel also operates one of the best **restaurants** in Kiruna.

Konduktogrsatan 7, S-981 34 Kiruna. (C) **0980/123-80.** Fax 0980/681-81. www.hotellkebne.com. 54 units. 790SEK ($158/£79) double. Rates include buffet breakfast. AE, DC, MC, V. Free parking. **Amenities:** Restaurant; bar; sauna; room service; laundry service; dry cleaning; nonsmoking rooms; solarium. *In room:* TV, safe.

stay probably will enhance your appreciation of the (warm and modern) comforts of conventional housing. Upon arrival, guests are issued thermal jumpsuits of "beaver nylon" whose air-lock cuffs are designed to help the wearer survive temperatures as low as –8°F (–22°C). Beds are fashioned from blocks of chiseled ice lavishly draped, Eskimo-style, with reindeer skins. Guests keep warm with insulated body bags that were developed for walks on the moon. Other than a temporary escape into the hotel's sauna, be prepared for big chills: Room temperatures remain cold enough to keep the walls from melting. Some claim that this exposure will bolster your immune system so that it can better fight infections when you return to your usual environment.

The interior decor is, as you'd expect, hyperglacial, and loaded with insights into what the world might look like if an atomic war drove civilization underground to confront its stark and frigid destiny. Most rooms resemble a setting from a scary 1950s sci-fi flick, sometimes with an icy version of a pair of skin-draped Adirondack chairs pulled up to the surreal glow of an electric fireplace that emits light but, rather distressingly, no heat. Throughout there's an endearing decorative reliance on whatever bas-reliefs and curios its artisans may have decided to chisel into the ice.

There's lots of standing up at the long countertop crafted from ice that doubles as a bar. What should you drink? Swedish vodka, of course, that's dyed a (frigid) shade of blue and served in cups crafted from ice. Vodka never gets any colder than this.

Interested in this holiday on ice? Contact the **Ice Hotel,** Marknadsvägen 63, S-981 91 Jukkasjärvi, Sweden (© **0980/668-00;** fax 0980/668-90; www.icehotel. com). Doubles cost from 3,800SEK to 4,900SEK ($760–$980/£380–£490) and suites from 5,800SEK to 7,000SEK ($1,160–$1,400/£580–£700) per day, including breakfast. Heated cabins, located near the ice palace, are available from 2,700SEK to 3,100SEK ($540–$620/£270–£310) per night for a double. Toilets are available in a heated building next door. From Kiruna, head east immediately along Route E10 until you come to a signpost marked JUKKASJÄRVI and follow this tiny road northeast for about 2.5km (1½ miles).

Scandic Hotel Ferrum ★ We were immediately won over by this hotel when we got rooms opening onto the mountains and the Kebnekaise massif in the distance. Run by the Scandic chain, it is named after the iron ore *(ferrum)* for which Kiruna is famous. The six-story building was built in 1967 and is one of the tallest in town. Functional and standardized in design, it's one of your best bets for lodging and food. It has two well-run restaurants, **Reenstierna** and **Matsalar.** Our favorite spot for socializing in Kiruna is the amusingly named and rustically decorated pub **Mommas.**

The staff arranges enough outdoor adventures to challenge an Olympic athlete: dog-sledge rides, snowmobiling, Arctic safaris, and river rafting, or mere skiing and fishing for those more faint of heart. Nothing is finer for us here than the sauna overlooking

Sweden's highest mountain. You can also wind down in the relaxation room, where on most days a roaring fire greets you. The rooms are modern and comfortably furnished with excellent beds and neatly kept bathrooms.

Lars Janssongatan 15, S-981 31 Kiruna. (C) **0980/39-86-00.** Fax 0980/39-86-11. www.scandichotels.com. 171 units. 750SEK–1,490SEK ($150–$298/£75–£149) double; 1,890SEK–2,490SEK ($378–$498/£189–£249) suite. Rates include buffet breakfast. AE, DC, MC, V. Parking 85SEK ($17/£8.50). Closed Dec 23–26. **Amenities:** 3 restaurants; bar; lounge; gym; sauna; laundry service; dry cleaning; nonsmoking rooms; rooms for those w/limited mobility; solarium; casino. *In room:* TV, hair dryer, trouser press, Wi-Fi.

Vinterpalatset (Winter Palace)   This privately owned hotel occupies what originally was built in 1904 as a private home for a prosperous entrepreneur in the iron-ore industry. Radically renovated and upgraded, it includes the much-improved main house, a 1950s-era annex containing 4 of the hotel's 20 individually designed rooms, a sauna/solarium complex, and a bar with an open fireplace. There's also a **dining room,** frequented mostly by other residents of the hotel, which serves rib-sticking Swedish food. Rooms are high-ceilinged, dignified-looking, and outfitted with hardwood floors and comfortable furniture. Bathrooms are quite small, each with a shower. While cold winds are blowing outside, our favorite place to settle in is at the on-site **King Bore's Bar,** with its open fireplace.

P.O. Box 18, Järnvägsgatan 18, S-981 21 Kiruna. (C) **0980/677-70.** Fax 0980/130-50. www.vinterpalatset. se. 20 units. Mid-June to mid-Aug and Fri–Sat year-round 930SEK ($186/£93) double; rest of year 1,530SEK ($306/£153) double. 4 annex rooms available mid-June to mid-Aug and Fri–Sat year-round 790SEK ($158/£79); rest of year 1,120SEK ($224/£112). Rates include buffet breakfast. AE, DC, MC, V. Free parking. **Amenities:** Restaurant; bar; Jacuzzi; sauna; room service; laundry service; dry cleaning; nonsmoking rooms; solarium. *In room:* TV, hair dryer, Wi-Fi.

WHERE TO DINE
Jukkasjärvi Wärdshus och Hembygdsgård ★ (Finds) SWEDISH   At the Ice Hotel, this is the best independent restaurant in the district, and the one that's frequently cited as a culinary beacon in the rest of Swedish Lapland. It contains room for 80 diners at a time, and is a venue that takes far-northern cuisine very, very seriously. Menu items are devoted to local ingredients and include filet of reindeer with Arctic shiitake mushrooms, fresh-caught Arctic salmon with lemon sauce, and a succulent filet of beef with garlic-flavored yogurt sauce. Expect wild berries (especially cloudberries), herring (many varieties), dried and smoked meats, reindeer in season, and mushrooms from the fields, along with salted fish.

Jukkasjärvi, Marknadsvägen 63. (C) **0980/668-00.** Reservations recommended. Fixed-price lunch 120SEK ($24/£12); main courses 195SEK–375SEK ($39–$75/£20–£38). AE, DC, MC, V.

9 ABISKO

86km (53 miles) NW of Kiruna, 1,467km (912 miles) N of Stockholm

Any resort north of the Arctic Circle is a curiosity; Abisko, on the southern shore of Lake Torneträsk, encompasses a scenic valley, a lake, and an island. An elevator takes passengers to Mount Nuolja (Njulla). Nearby is the protected Abisko National Park (see below), containing remarkable flora such as orchids.

(Moments) **Northernmost Golf in the World** ★★

Here's how to achieve one-upmanship on your golfing pals back home: Play at the northernmost golf course in the world. The **Björkliden Arctic Golf Course** has only 9 holes, occupying a terrain of mostly thin-soiled tundra with a scattering of birch forest. It is open from mid-June to mid-August. During that limited period, golfers can play 24 hours per day, as the course is lit by the midnight sun. For more information, contact Björkliden Arctic Golf Club, Kvarnbacksvägen 28, Bromma S-168 74 (℃ **08/56-48-88-30**). Bromma is a suburb of Stockholm.

ESSENTIALS

GETTING THERE **By Train & Bus** You can get a train to Kiruna (see earlier in this chapter). From here, there are both bus and rail links into the center of Abisko. For train information, call ℃ **0771/75-75-75.** For bus information, call **Länstrafiken** at ℃ **0926/756-80.**

By Car From Kiruna, continue northwest on E10 into Abisko.

VISITOR INFORMATION Contact the tourist office in Kiruna (see earlier in this chapter).

EXPLORING THE AREA

Abisko National Park ★★ (℃ **0980/402-00**), established in 1903, is situated around the Abiskojokk River, which flows into Lake Torneträsk. The name *Abisko* is a Lapp word meaning "ocean forest": There is a typical alpine valley here with a rich variety of flora and fauna, but the park's proximity to the Atlantic gives it a maritime character, with milder winters and cooler summers than the more continentally influenced areas east of the Scandes or Caledonian mountains. The highest mountain in the park is **Slåttatjåkka,** 1,170m (3,839 ft.) above sea level. Slightly shorter **Njulla,** which rises 1,140m (3,740 ft.), has a cable car.

Abisko is more easily accessible than **Vadvetjåkka National Park,** the other, smaller park in the area. Three sides of Vadvetjåkka Park are bounded by water that is difficult to wade through, and the fourth side is rough terrain with treacherously slippery bogs and steep precipices fraught with rock slides. Established in 1920, it lies northwest of Lake Torneträsk, with its northern limits at the Norwegian border. It's composed of mountain precipices and large tracts of bog and delta. It also has rich flora, along with impressive brook ravines. Its highest mountain is **Vadvetjåkka,** with a southern peak at 1,095m (3,593 ft.) above sea level.

Abisko is one of the best centers for watching the **midnight sun,** which can be seen from June 13 to July 4. It's also the start of the longest marked trail in the world, the **Kungsleden (Royal Trail)** ★★★, which may just prove to be the hike of a lifetime. This approximately 338km (210-mile) track runs through Abisko National Park to Riksgränsen on the Norwegian frontier, cutting through Sweden's highest mountain (Kebnekaise) on the way. If you're properly fortified and have adequate camping equipment, including a sleeping bag and food, you can walk these trails. They tend to be well maintained and clearly marked; all the streams en route are traversed by bridges; and in places where the ground is marshy, it has been overlaid with wooden planks. Cabins and rest stops (local guides refer to them as "fell stations") are spaced a day's hike (13–21km/8–13 miles) apart, so you'll have adequate areas to rest between bouts of trekking and hill climbing. Just be warned that these huts provide barely adequate shelter from the wind, rain, snow, and hail in case the weather turns turbulent, as it so often does in this part of the world. At most of the stops, you cook your own food and clean up before leaving. Most lack running water, although there are some summer-only toilets. At certain points, the trail crosses lakes and rivers; boats are provided to help you get across. The trail actually follows the old nomadic paths of the Lapps. Those with less time or energy will find the trail easily broken up into several smaller segments.

During the summer, the trail is not as isolated as you may think. It is, in fact, the busiest hiking trail in Sweden, and adventurers from all over the world traverse it. The trail is most crowded in July, when the weather is most reliable. Locals even operate boat services on some of the lakes you'll pass. Often they'll rent you a rowboat or canoe from a makeshift kiosk that's dismantled and hauled away after the first frost.

For maps and more information about this adventure, contact the local tourist office or the **Svenska Turistförening,** the Swedish Touring Club, P.O. Box 25, S101 20 Stockholm (© **08/463-21-00**).

WHERE TO STAY & DINE

Abisko Turiststation   Since 1902 this far northern inn has been welcoming guests in from the cold. It attracts visitors who want to trek through the great wilderness that envelops this place. Owned by the Swedish Touring Club since 1910, the big, modern complex about 450m (1,476 ft.) from the bus station offers accommodations in the main building, in the annex, and within 28 cabins. Each cabin is made up of two apartments suitable for up to six occupants, and each unit features a kitchen and a private bathroom. From the hotel you can see the lake and the mountains. The staff is helpful in providing information about excursions. The rooms are basic but reasonably comfortable, and some offer exceptional views. However, amenities such as TV don't exist. Swedish meals are served in the on-site **Restaurant Tjuonavagge** buffet-style. Also on the premises is the friendliest pub in town, **Storstugan.**

S-981 07 24 Abisko. © **0980/402-00.** Fax 0980/401-40. www.abisko.nu. 77 units, 43 with bathroom; plus 56 cabin apts. 680SEK ($136/£68) double without bathroom; 1,190SEK ($238/£119) double with bathroom. Rates include breakfast. Cabin apt. 1,150SEK ($230/£115) per night or 7,350SEK ($1,470/£735) per week up to 6 occupants. Breakfast not included. AE, MC, V. Free parking. Closed Sept 20–Feb 28. **Amenities:** Restaurant; bar; sauna; laundromat.

CROSSING THE BORDER TO NORWAY

Because Abisko is close to the Norwegian border, you may want to cross into Norway after your tour of Swedish Lapland. If so, just take E10 west across the border toward Narvik. From Kiruna, trains and buses go to the hamlet of Rigsgrånsen, the last settlement in Sweden, before continuing for the final, short leg to Narvik. Schedules depend entirely on the weather: For buses, call © **0200/21-82-18;** for trains, © **0771/75-75-75.** However, if you'd like to return to Stockholm, follow E10 east toward the coast, then head south on E4 to the capital city.

Appendix: Fast Facts, Toll-Free Numbers & Websites

1 FAST FACTS: SWEDEN

AMERICAN EXPRESS For local 24-hour customer service in Stockholm, call © **08/429-56-00.**

AREA CODE The international country code for Sweden is **46.** The local city (area) codes are given for all phone numbers in the Sweden chapters.

ATM NETWORKS/CASHPOINTS See "Money & Costs," p. 41.

BUSINESS HOURS Generally, **banks** are open Monday through Friday from 10am to 3pm. In some larger cities, banks extend their hours, usually on Thursday or Friday, until 5:30pm. Most **offices** are open Monday to Friday 8:30 or 9am to 5pm (sometimes to 3 or 4pm in the summer); on Saturday, offices and factories are closed, or open for only a half-day. Most **stores and shops** are open Monday to Friday 9:30am to 6pm, and Saturday from 9:30am to somewhere between 2 and 4pm. Once a week, usually on Monday or Friday, some of the larger stores are open from 9:30am to 7pm (July–Aug to 6pm).

CAR RENTALS See "Toll-Free Numbers & Websites," p. 391.

DRINKING LAWS Most restaurants, pubs, and bars in Sweden are licensed to serve liquor, wine, and beer. Some places are licensed only for wine and beer. Purchases of wine, liquor, and imported beer are available only through the government-controlled monopoly *Systembolaget.* Branch stores, spread throughout the country, are usually open Monday to Friday 9am to 6pm. The minimum age for buying alcoholic beverages in Sweden is 21.

DENTISTS For emergency dental services, ask your hotel or host for the location of the nearest dentist. Nearly all dentists in Sweden speak English.

DOCTORS Hotel desks usually can refer you to a local doctor, nearly all of whom speak English. If you need emergency treatment, your hotel also should be able to direct you to the nearest facility. In case of an accident or injury away from the hotel, call the nearest police station.

DRIVING RULES You drive on the right, and all passengers are required to wear seatbelts. It is mandatory to have low-beam headlights on at all times. Chances are your rental car will have automatic headlights that go on when the engine is turned on. Speed limits depend on the area you're driving through, of course, and are 30kmph (19 mph) in school districts or playground areas, rising to as high as 110kmph (68 mph) on open stretches of express highways.

DRUG LAWS Sweden imposes severe penalties for the possession, use, purchase, sale, or manufacture of illegal drugs. (*Illegal* is defined much like in the U.S.) Penalties are often (but not always) based on quantity. Possession of a small amount of drugs, either hard or soft, can lead to a heavy fine and deportation. Possession of a large amount of drugs can entail imprisonment from 3 months to 15 years, depending on the circumstances and the presiding judge.

DRUGSTORES Called *apotek* in Swedish, drugstores generally are open Monday through Friday from 9am to 6pm and Saturday from 9am to 1pm. In larger cities, one drugstore in every neighborhood stays open until 7pm. All drugstores post a list of the names and addresses of these stores (called *nattapotek*) in their windows.

ELECTRICITY In Sweden, the electricity is 220 volts AC (50 cycles). To operate North American hair dryers and other electrical appliances, you'll need an electrical transformer (sometimes erroneously called a converter) and plugs that fit the two-pin round continental electrical outlets that are standard in Sweden. Transformers can be bought at hardware stores. Before using any foreign-made appliance, always ask about it at your hotel desk.

EMBASSIES & CONSULATES All embassies are in Stockholm. The **United States** embassy is at Daj Hammarskjölds Väg 31, S-115 89 Stockholm (© **08/783-53-00;** http://stockholmusembassy.gov). The **United Kingdom** embassy is at Skarpoügatan 6–8, S-115 93 Stockholm (© **08/671-30-00;** www.britishembassy.se). The embassy for **Canada** is at Tegelbacken 4, S-103 23 Stockholm (© **08/453-30-00;** www.canadaemb.se). The embassy for **Australia** is at Sergels Torg 12, S-103 86 Stockholm (© **08/613-29-00;** www.sweden.embassy.gov.au). **New Zealand** has a consulate on the fourth floor at Stureplan 4C, 114 35 Stockholm (© **08/633 116).**

EMERGENCIES Call © **90-000** from anywhere in Sweden if you need an ambulance, the police, or the fire department (*brandlarm).*

HOLIDAYS Sweden celebrates the following public holidays: New Year's Day (Jan 1), Epiphany (Jan 6), Good Friday, Easter Sunday, Easter Monday, Labor Day (May 1), Ascension Day (mid-May), Whitsunday and Whitmonday (late May), Midsummer Day (June 21), All Saints' Day (Nov 1), and Christmas Eve, Christmas Day, and Boxing Day (Dec 24, 25, and 26, respectively). Inquire at a tourist bureau for the actual dates of the holidays that vary from year to year.

INSURANCE When traveling, any number of things could go wrong—lost luggage, trip cancellation, a medical emergency—so consider the following types of insurance.

Check your existing insurance policies and credit card coverage before you buy travel insurance. You may already be covered for lost luggage, canceled tickets, or medical expenses. The cost of travel insurance varies widely, depending on the cost and length of your trip, your age and health, and the type of trip you're taking, but expect to pay between 5% and 8% of the vacation itself. You can get estimates from various providers through **Insure MyTrip.com.** Enter your trip cost and dates, your age, and other information for prices from more than a dozen companies.

Medical Insurance For travel overseas, most health plans (including Medicare and Medicaid) do not provide coverage, and the ones that do often require you to pay for services upfront and reimburse you only after you return home. Even if your plan does cover overseas treatment, most out-of-country hospitals make you pay your bills upfront, and send you a refund only after you've returned home and filed the necessary paperwork with your insurance company. As a safety net, you may want to buy travel medical insurance, particularly if you're traveling to a remote or high-risk area where emergency evacuation is a possible scenario. If you require additional medical insurance, try **MEDEX Assistance** (© 410/453-6300; www.medexassist.com) or **Travel Assistance International** (© 800/821-2828; www.travelassistance.com). For general information on services, call the company's **Worldwide Assistance Services, Inc.** (© 800/777-8710; www.worldwideassistance.com).

Lost-Luggage Insurance On international flights, airline-provided baggage coverage may be limited. If you plan to check items more valuable than the standard liability, see if your valuables are covered by your homeowner's policy and get baggage insurance as part of your comprehensive travel-insurance package. Don't buy insurance at the airport, as it's usually overpriced. Be sure to take any valuables or irreplaceable items with you in your carry-on luggage, as many valuables (including books, money, and electronics) aren't covered by airline policies.

If your luggage is lost, immediately file a lost-luggage claim at the airport, detailing the luggage contents. For most airlines, you must report delayed, damaged, or lost baggage within 4 hours of arrival. The airlines are required to deliver luggage, once found, directly to your house or destination free.

Trip-Cancellation Insurance Trip-cancellation insurance helps you get your money back if you have to back out of a trip, if you have to go home early, or if your travel supplier goes bankrupt. Allowed reasons for cancellation can range from sickness to natural disasters to the State Department declaring your destination unsafe for travel. For information, contact one of the following recommended insurers: **Access America** (© 800/284-8300; www.accessamerica.com), **AIG Travel Guard International** (© 800/826-4919; www.travelguard.com), **Travel Insured International** (© 800/243-3174; www.travelinsured.com), and **Travelex Insurance Services** (© 800/228-9792; www.travelex-insurance.com).

to find a city that *doesn't* have a few cyber cafes. Although there's no definitive directory for cyber cafes—these are independent businesses, after all—two places to start looking are at **www.cybercaptive. com** and **wwws.cybercafe.com**.

LANGUAGE The national language is Swedish, a Germanic tongue, and many regional dialects exist. Some minority groups speak Norwegian and Finnish. English is a required course of study in school and is commonly spoken, even in the hinterlands, especially among young people.

LEGAL AID The American Services section of the U.S. Embassy (see above) will give you advice if you run into trouble abroad. They can advise you of your rights and will even provide a list of attorneys (for which you'll have to pay if services are used). But they cannot interfere on your behalf in the legal process of Sweden. For questions about American citizens who are arrested abroad, including ways of getting money to them, telephone the **Citizens Emergency Center** of the Office of Special Consulate Services in Washington, D.C. (© 202/647-5225). Citizens of other nations should go to their Stockholm-based consulate for advice.

LOST & FOUND Be sure to tell all of your credit card companies the minute you discover that your wallet has been lost or stolen. Your credit card company or insurer also may require you to file a police report and provide a report number or record of the loss. Most credit card companies have an emergency toll-free number to call if your card is lost or stolen; they may be able to wire you a cash advance immediately or deliver an emergency credit card in a day or two. **Visa**'s emergency number outside the U.S. is © 410/581-3836. **American Express** cardholders should call collect © 336/393-1111. **MasterCard** holders should call collect © 314/542-7111.

MAIL   Post offices in Sweden are usually open Monday through Friday from 9am to 6pm and Saturday from 9am to noon. Sending a postcard to North America costs 7.20SEK ($1.45/75p) by surface mail, 10.50SEK ($2.10/£1.05p) by airmail. Letters weighing not more than 20 grams cost the same. Mailboxes can easily be recognized—they carry a yellow post horn on a blue background. You can buy stamps in most tobacco shops and stationers.

NEWSPAPERS & MAGAZINES   In big cities such as Stockholm and Gothenburg, English-language newspapers, including the latest editions of the *International Herald Tribune, USA Today,* and the *London Times,* are usually available. At kiosks or newsstands in major cities, you also can purchase the European editions of *Time* and *Newsweek.*

PASSPORTS   Allow plenty of time before your trip to apply for a passport; processing normally takes 3 weeks but can take longer during busy periods (especially spring). And keep in mind that if you need a passport in a hurry, you'll pay a higher processing fee.

For residents of Australia: You can pick up an application from your local post office or any branch of Passports Australia, but you must schedule an interview at the passport office to present your application materials. Call the **Australian Passport Information Service** at © **131-232,** or visit the government website at **www.passports.gov.au**.

For residents of Canada: Passport applications are available at travel agencies throughout Canada or from the central **Passport Office,** Department of Foreign Affairs and International Trade, Ottawa, ON K1A 0G3 (© **800/567-6868;** www. ppt.gc.ca).

For residents of Ireland: You can apply for a 10-year passport at the **Passport Office,** Setanta Centre, Molesworth Street, Dublin 2 (© **01/671-1633;** www.irlgov. ie). Those under age 18 and over 65 must apply for a 12€ 3-year passport. You can also apply at 1A South Mall, Cork (© **021/494-4700**), or at most main post offices.

For residents of New Zealand: You can pick up a passport application at any New Zealand Passports Office or download it from the website. Contact the **Passports Office** (© **0800/225-050** in New Zealand or 04/474-8100; www.passports.govt.nz).

For residents of the United Kingdom: To pick up an application for a standard 10-year passport (5-year passport for children under 16), visit your nearest passport office, major post office, or travel agency, or contact the **United Kingdom Passport Service** (© **0870/521-0410;** www.ukpa. gov.uk).

For residents of the United States: Whether you're applying in person or by mail, you can download passport applications from the U.S. Department of State website at **http://travel.state.gov**. To find your regional passport office, either check the U.S. Department of State website or call the **National Passport Information Center** toll-free number (© **877/487-2778**) for automated information.

POLICE   In an emergency, dial © **90-000** anywhere in the country.

SHOE REPAIR   Shoe-repair shops rarely accommodate you while you wait. If all you need is a new heel, look for something called *klackbar* in the stores or shoe departments of department stores. They'll make repairs while you wait.

SMOKING   Smoking was banned in restaurants, cafes, bars, and nightclubs in 2005. Smoking rooms, however, are allowed in these institutions. The smoking rooms contain a few restrictions: No serving or consumption of food or beverages is allowed in the smoking rooms and it may not cover more than 25% of the institution's total area. Smoking is still allowed in hotel rooms and at airports that have designated smoking areas, including most major airports.

TAXES Sweden imposes a "value-added tax," called MOMS, on most goods and services. Visitors from North America can beat the tax, however, by shopping in one of the 15,000 stores with the yellow-and-blue tax-free shopping sign. To get a refund, your total purchase must cost a minimum of 200SEK ($40/£20). Tax refunds range from 12.5% to 17.5%, depending on the amount purchased. MOMS begins at 12% on food items but is 25% for most goods and services. The tax is part of the purchase price, but you can get a tax-refund voucher before you leave the store. When you leave Sweden, take the voucher to a tax-free Customs desk at the airport or train station you're leaving from. They will give you your MOMS refund (minus a small service charge) before you continue on to your next non-Swedish destination. Two requirements: You cannot use your purchase in Sweden, and it must be taken out of the country within 1 month after purchase. For more information, call **Global Refunds** at ✆ **08/545-28-440** in Sweden (www.globalrefund.com).

TELEPHONE Avoid placing long-distance calls from your hotel, where the charge may be doubled or tripled on your final bill. For information on telephoning in Sweden, refer to "Staying Connected," in chapter 3 (p. 54).

TIME Sweden is on central European time—Greenwich mean time plus 1 hour, or Eastern Standard Time plus 6 hours. The clocks are advanced 1 hour in summer.

TIPPING Hotels include a 15% service charge in your bill. Restaurants add 13% to 15% to your tab. Taxi drivers are entitled to 8% of the fare, and cloakroom attendants usually get 8SEK ($1.60/80p).

TOILETS The word for toilet in Swedish is *toalett,* and public facilities are found in department stores, rail and air terminals, and subway (T-bana) stations. DAMER means women and HERRAR means men. Sometimes the sign is abbreviated to D or H, and often the toilet is marked WC. Most toilets are free, although a few have attendants to offer towels and soap. In an emergency, you can use the toilets in most hotels and restaurants, although, in principle, they're reserved for guests.

WATER The water is safe to drink all over Sweden. However, don't drink water from lakes, rivers, or streams, regardless of how clean it appears.

2 TOLL-FREE NUMBERS & WEBSITES

MAJOR INTERNATIONAL AIRLINES

Air France
✆ 800/237-2747 (in U.S.)
✆ 800/375-8723 (in U.S. and Canada)
✆ 087/0142-4343 (in U.K.)
www.airfrance.com

Air India
✆ 212/407-1371 (in U.S.)
✆ 91/22-2279-6666 (in India)
✆ 020/8745-1000 (in U.K.)
www.airindia.com

Alitalia
✆ 800/223-5730 (in U.S.)
✆ 800/361-8336 (in Canada)
✆ 087/0608-6003 (in U.K.)
www.alitalia.com

American Airlines
✆ 800/433-7300 (in U.S. and Canada)
✆ 020/7365-0777 (in U.K.)
www.aa.com

British Airways
© 800/247-9297 (in U.S. and Canada)
© 087/0850-9850 (in U.K.)
www.british-airways.com

China Airlines
© 800/227-5118 (in U.S.)
© 022/715-1212 (in Taiwan)
www.china-airlines.com

Continental Airlines
© 800/523-3273 (in U.S. and Canada)
© 084/5607-6760 (in U.K.)
www.continental.com

Delta Air Lines
© 800/221-1212 (in U.S. and Canada)
© 084/5600-0950 (in U.K.)
www.delta.com

Finnair
© 800/950-5000 (in U.S. and Canada)
© 087/0241-4411 (in U.K.)
www.finnair.com

Iberia Airlines
© 800/722-4642 (in U.S. and Canada)
© 087/0609-0500 (in U.K.)
www.iberia.com

Japan Airlines
© 012/025-5931 (international)
www.jal.co.jp

Lan Airlines
© 866/435-9526 (in U.S.)
© 305/670-9999 (in other countries)
www.lanchile.com

Lufthansa
© 800/399-5838 (in U.S.)
© 800/563-5954 (in Canada)
© 087/0837-7747 (in U.K.)
www.lufthansa.com

Swiss Air
© 877/359-7947 (in U.S. and Canada)
© 084/5601-0956 (in U.K.)
www.swiss.com

Turkish Airlines
© 90 212 444 0 849
www.thy.com

United Airlines
© 800/864-8331 (in U.S. and Canada)
© 084/5844-4777 (in U.K.)
www.united.com

CAR-RENTAL AGENCIES

Auto Europe
© 888/223-5555 (in U.S. and Canada)
© 0800/2235-5555 (in U.K.)
www.autoeurope.com

Avis
© 800/331-1212 (in U.S. and Canada)
© 084/4581-8181 (in U.K.)
www.avis.com

Budget
© 800/527-0700 (in U.S.)
© 800/268-8900 (in Canada)
© 087/0156-5656 (in U.K.)
www.budget.com

Dollar
© 800/800-4000 (in U.S.)
© 800/848-8268 (in Canada)
© 080/8234-7524 (in U.K.)
www.dollar.com

Hertz
© 800/645-3131
© 800/654-3001 (international)
www.hertz.com

Kemwel (KHA)
© 877/820-0668
www.kemwel.com

National
© 800/CAR-RENT (227-7368)
www.nationalcar.com

MAJOR HOTEL & MOTEL CHAINS

Best Western International
✆ 800/780-7234 (in U.S. and Canada)
✆ 0800/393-130 (in U.K.)
www.bestwestern.com

Hilton Hotels
✆ 800/HILTONS (445-8667; in U.S. and Canada)
✆ 087/0590-9090 (in U.K.)
www.hilton.com

Holiday Inn
✆ 800/315-2621 (in U.S. and Canada)
✆ 0800/405-060 (in U.K.)
www.holidayinn.com

Hyatt
✆ 888/591-1234 (in U.S. and Canada)
✆ 084/5888-1234 (in U.K.)
www.hyatt.com

InterContinental Hotels & Resorts
✆ 800/424-6835 (in U.S. and Canada)
✆ 0800/1800-1800 (in U.K.)
www.ichotelsgroup.com

Marriott
✆ 877/236-2427 (in U.S. and Canada)
✆ 0800/221-222 (in U.K.)
www.marriott.com

Radisson Hotels & Resorts
✆ 888/201-1718 (in U.S. and Canada)
✆ 0800/374-411 (in U.K.)
www.radisson.com

Sheraton Hotels & Resorts
✆ 800/325-3535 (in U.S.)
✆ 800/543-4300 (in Canada)
✆ 0800/3253-5353 (in U.K.)
www.starwoodhotels.com/sheraton

(Tips) Common Swedish Phrases

When you're traveling, it helps to know the language, so we've included a list of certain simple phrases in Swedish for expressing basic needs.

English	Swedish	Pronunciation
Hello	*God dag*	Good dahg
How are you?	*Hur mår du?*	Hoor mor doo?
Fine, thank you	*Tack, jag mår bra*	Tak, yag moor brah
You're welcome	*Var så god*	Vahr sho good
Yes	*Ja*	Yah
No	*Nej*	Nay
Excuse me	*Ursäkta*	Oor-sehk-ta
I'm sorry	*Jag är ledsen*	Yaag ay les-sen
Goodbye	*Adjö*	A-juuh
Do you speak English?	*Talar du Engelska?*	Taah-lar doo En-gel-skah
Help!	*Hjälp!*	Yelp!
I don't understand	*Jag förstår inte*	Yag fur-stor een-ta
Where is the toilet?	*Var är toaletten?*	Vahr ay twa-lett-en
Can I use your phone?	*Får jag låna din telefon?*	Fohr yahg loh-na deen tel-le-fohn
What time is it?	*Vad är klockan?*	Vahd ahr clock-an
How do I get to . . .	*Hur kommer jag till . . .*	Hoor koo-mar yag teel . . .

INDEX

See also Accommodations and Restaurant indexes, below.

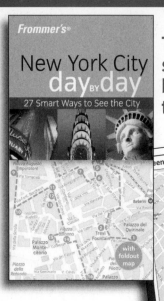
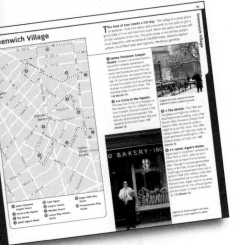